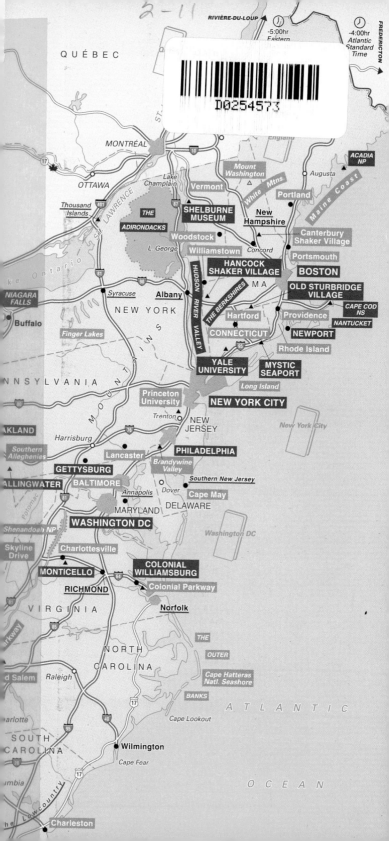

# USA EAST

© PhotoDisc, Inc

"A great revolution has happened—a revolution made, not by chopping and changing of power in any of the existing states, but by the appearance of a new state, of a new species, in a new part of the globe. It has made as great a change in all the relations and balances, and gravitations of power, as the appearance of a new planet would in the system of the solar world."

Edmund Burke, Note, *Detached Papers*, 1782, and *Works*, 1852

**Editorial Director**               Cynthia Clayton Ochterbeck

**THE GREEN GUIDE USA EAST**

**Editor**                          Jonathan P. Gilbert
**Contributing Writer**             Margaret Littman
**Production Coordinator**          Natasha G. George
**Cartography**                     GeoNova Publishing, Inc., Peter Wrenn
**Photo Editor**                    Lydia Strong
**Proofreader**                     Gwen Cannon
**Layout & Design**                 Isabelle Carbonel, John Higginbottom
**Cover Design**                    Laurent Muller and Ute Weber

**Contact Us:**                     The Green Guide
                                    Michelin Maps and Guides
                                    One Parkway South
                                    Greenville, SC 29615
                                    USA
                                    www.michelintravel.com
                                    michelin.guides@us.michelin.com

                                    Michelin Maps and Guides
                                    Hannay House
                                    39 Clarendon Road
                                    Watford, Herts WD17 1JA
                                    UK
                                    ☎ (01923) 205 240
                                    www.ViaMichelin.com
                                    travelpubsales@uk.michelin.com

**Special Sales:**                  For information regarding bulk sales,
                                    customized editions and premium sales,
                                    please contact our Customer Service
                                    Departments:
                                    USA      1-800-432-6277
                                    UK       (01923) 205 240
                                    Canada 1-800-361-8236

**Note to the Reader**
While every effort is made to ensure that all information printed in this guide is correct and up-to-date, Michelin Apa Publications Ltd. accepts no liability for any direct, indirect or consequential losses howsoever caused so far as such can be excluded by law.

# One Team …
# A Commitment to Quality

There's just one reason our team is dedicated to producing quality travel publications—you, our reader.

Throughout our guides we offer **practical information**, **touring tips** and **suggestions** for finding the best places for a break.

**Michelin driving tours** help you hit the highlights and quickly absorb the best of the region. Our descriptive **walking tours** make you your own guide, armed with directions, maps and expert information.

We scout out the attractions, classify them with **star ratings**, and describe in detail what you will find when you visit them.

**Michelin maps** featured throughout the guide offer vibrant, detailed and easy-to-follow outlines of everything from close-up museum plans to international maps.

Places to stay and eat are always a big part of travel, so we research **hotels and restaurants** that we think convey the essence of the destination, and arrange them by geographic area and price. We walk you through the best shopping districts and point you towards the host of entertainment and recreation possibilities available.

We **test, retest, check and recheck** to make sure that our guidebooks are truly just that: a personalized guide to help you make the most of your visit. And if you still want a speaking guide, we list local tour guides who will lead you on all the boat, bus, guided, historical, culinary, and other tours you shouldn't miss.

In short, we remove the guesswork involved with travel. After all, we want you to enjoy traveling with Michelin as much as we do.

**The Michelin Green Guide Team**

# PLANNING YOUR TRIP

# INTRODUCTION TO USA EAST

## SYMBOLS

| | |
|---|---|
| 🅸 | **Tourist Information** |
| 🕐 | **Hours of Operation** |
| 🕐 | **Periods of Closure** |
| 😊 | **A Bit of Advice** |
| 😊 | **Details to Consider** |
| 👓 | **Entry Fees** |
| Kids | **Especially for Children** |
| 🚶 | **Tours** |
| ♿ | **Wheelchair Accessible** |

# CONTENTS

## DISCOVERING USA EAST

# HOW TO USE THIS GUIDE

## Orientation

To help you grasp the "lay of the land" quickly and easily, so you'll feel confident and comfortable finding your way around the region, we offer the following tools in this guide:

- Detailed table of contents for an overview of what you'll find in the guide, and how the guide is organized.
- Map of USA East with the Principal Sights highlighted for easy reference.
- Detailed maps for major cities and villages, including driving tour maps and larger-scale maps for walking tours.
- Principal Sights organized alphabetically, by region, for quick reference.

## Practicalities

At the front of the guide, you'll see a section called "Planning Your Trip" that contains information about planning your trip, the best time to go, different ways of getting to the region and getting around, and basic facts and tips for making the most of your visit. You'll find driving and themed tours, and suggestions for outdoor fun. There's also a calendar of popular annual events, information on shopping, sightseeing, kids' activities and sports and recreational opportunities.

## WHERE TO STAY

We've made a selection of hotels and arranged them within the cities by price category to fit all budgets (♨️*see the Legend on the cover flap for an explanation of the price categories*). For the most part, we've selected accommodations based on their unique regional quality, their regional feel, as it were. So, unless the individual hotel embodies local ambience, it's rare that we include chain properties, which typically have their own imprint. If you want a comprehensive selection of accommodations in the Big Apple, see the red-cover **Michelin Guide New York**.

## WHERE TO EAT

We thought you'd like to know the popular eating spots, so we selected restaurants that capture the regional experience—those that have a unique regional flavor and local atmosphere. We're not rating the quality of the food per se: as we did with the hotels, we selected restaurants for many towns and villages, categorized by price, to appeal to all wallets (♨️*see the Legend on the cover flap for an explanation of the price categories*).If you want a comprehensive selection of dining recommendations in the Big Apple, see the red-cover **Michelin Guide New York**.

## Attractions

Principal Sights are arranged alphabetically. Within each Principal Sight, attractions for each town, village, or geographical area are divided into local Sights or Walking Tours, nearby Excursions to sights outside the town, or detailed Driving Tours—suggested itineraries for seeing several attractions around a major town. Contact information, admission charges and hours of operation are given for the majority of attractions. Unless otherwise noted, admission prices shown are for a single adult only. Discounts for children, seniors, students, teachers, etc. may be available; be sure to ask. If no admission charge is shown, entrance to the attraction is free.

If you're pressed for time, we recommend you visit the three and two-star sights first: the stars are your guide.

## STAR RATINGS

Michelin has used stars as a rating tool for more than 100 years:

|  |  |
|---|---|
| ★★★ | Highly recommended |
| ★★ | Recommended |
| ★ | Interesting |

## SYMBOLS IN THE TEXT

Besides the stars, other symbols in the text indicate sights that are closed to the public ⚬⟼; on-site eating facilities ✕; also see ⓖ; breakfast included in the nightly rate ☲; on-site parking 🅿; spa facilities Spa; camping facilities △; swimming pool ⟋; and beaches ⌂.

See the box appearing on the Contents page and the Legend on the cover flap for other symbols used in the text.

See the Maps explanation below for symbols appearing on the maps.

Throughout the guide you will find peach-coloured text boxes or sidebars containing anecdotal or background information. Green-coloured boxes contain information to help you save time or money.

## Maps

All maps in this guide are oriented north, unless otherwise indicated by a directional arrow. The term "Local Map" refers to a map within the chapter or Tourism Region. See the map Legend at the back of the guide for an explanation of other map symbols. A complete list of the maps found in the guide appears at the back of this book.

Addresses, phone numbers, opening hours and prices published in this guide are accurate at press time. We welcome corrections and suggestions that may assist us in preparing the next edition. Please send your comments to:

Michelin Maps and Guides
Hannay House
39 Clarendon Road
Watford, Herts WD17 1JA
UK
travelpubsales@uk.michelin.com
www.michelin.co.uk

Michelin Maps and Guides
Editorial Department
P.O. Box 19001
Greenville, SC 29602-9001
USA
michelin.guides@us.michelin.com
www.michelintravel.com

Forest Road, New England

©PhotoDisc, Inc

# PLANNING YOUR TRIP

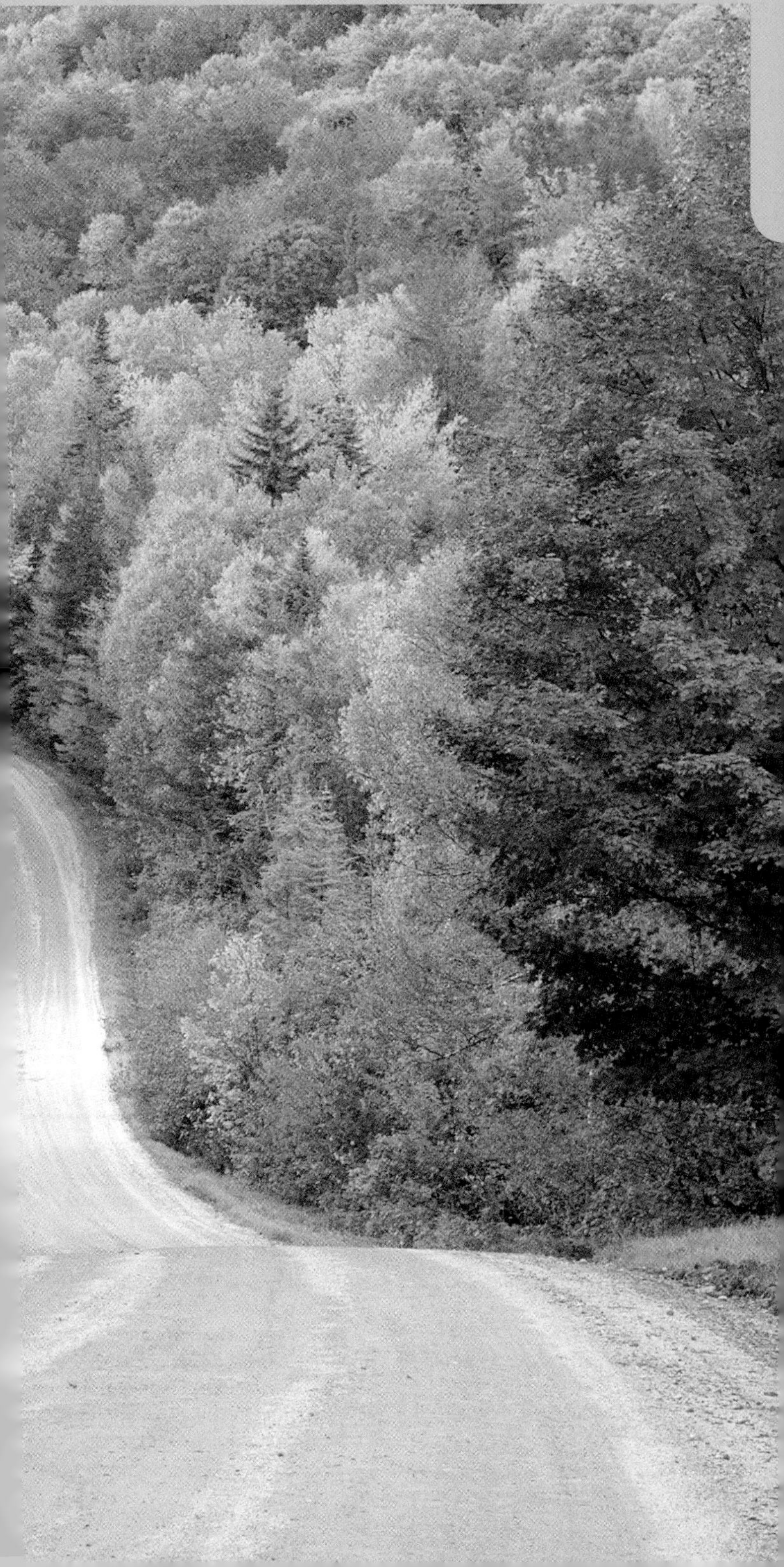

# MICHELIN DRIVING TOURS

You've got your car, you know the rules of the road, now get ready to go. We've outlined below several driving tours that will lead you to the highlights of the East's diverse regions, from the gleaming skyscrapers of New York City to the gracious plantations of the South. Bon voyage!

## DISCOVER NEW ENGLAND
*15 days*

Rich in both cultural and natural attractions, New England encompasses the states of Connecticut, Maine, Massachusetts, New Hampshire, Rhode Island and Vermont. Fall, when the leaves turn blazing shades of red, orange and gold, is the most popular time to visit.

Begin in **Boston** by exploring the city's colonial heritage along the **Freedom Trail** and visiting the **Museum of Fine Arts** and the **Isabella Stewart Gardner Museum**. If you're in Boston during baseball season, catch a Red Sox game at Fenway Park. Stroll the campus of venerable **Harvard University**, with its many museums, leaving time to peruse **Cambridge**'s myriad bookstores.

Then it's southeast via Route 3 and US-6 to **Cape Cod**, Massachusetts, where you can walk the beaches of **Cape Cod National Seashore**, poke around quaint villages like **Chatham**, or do the club circuit at **Provincetown** on the Cape's northern tip. From the Cape, you can take a ferry to the charming islands of **Nantucket** or **Martha's Vineyard**.

Drive southwest from Cape Cod to **Newport**, Rhode Island, via I-195, stopping to check out the **New Bedford Whaling Museum**. Touring Newport's fabulous mansions gives new meaning to "lifestyles of the rich and famous."

Spend a day in nearby **Mystic Seaport**, Connecticut and continue west through **New Haven**, home of **Yale University**, and go north on I-91. From **Hartford**, it's a short jaunt on I-84 northeast to the popular living-history museum **Old Sturbridge Village**.

Back in Massachusetts, head west on I-90 through **Stockbridge** to the undulating foothills of **The Berkshires**. North of Stockbridge on US-7, you'll come to bucolic **Hancock Shaker Village** and farther on, to the pristine colonial burg of **Williamstown**. Continue north on US-7 through southern Vermont to historic **Bennington**, and farther north to the stellar **Shelburne Museum**. Then swing east across Vermont and into New Hampshire for a scenic drive through the **White Mountains**; en route, leave time for a yummy tour of **Ben & Jerry's Ice Cream Factory** in Waterbury, Vermont.

Loop south via I-93 to **Canterbury Shaker Village** and cut east on Route 100 and north on I-95 to **Portsmouth**. From New Hampshire's only seaport, you can head back to Boston via I-95 South, or take a leisurely drive up US-1 along the **Maine coast**. If you choose the latter option, stop often to admire the spectacular views of rocky shores and lonely lighthouses, and to dine on lobster, fresh off the boat. End you coastal sojourn at **Acadia National Park** and return to Boston via I-95 South.

## FLORIDA SUNSHINE
*15 days*

Distinguished by its 1,197mi coastline, the Sunshine State's peninsula is edged by beautiful beaches. Warm winter temperatures make Florida a year-round playground, from Orlando's theme parks to the international flavor of Miami and the unique ecosystem of the Everglades.

Begin in **Orlando**, where a visit to **Walt Disney World** is de rigueur. The city's other theme parks, **Universal Studios** and **SeaWorld** will easily

*No tailgating required...*

occupy an additional couple of days of animal shows, thrill rides and family fun.

An hour's drive east of Orlando via the Beeline Expressway *(Rte. 528)*, science fiction comes alive at **Kennedy Space Center**, home to some of the world's most sophisticated technology. Plan a visit here to coincide with a **shuttle launch**. History buffs will enjoy a detour north via scenic Route A1A to **St. Augustine**, the oldest continuously occupied European settlement in the US.

For a leisurely coastal drive, head south on US-1 to **Palm Beach** and scout out the elite boutiques along Worth Avenue. Then it's on to **Miami**, to sample the Cuban cuisine in **Little Havana** and to soak up some rays and admire the Art Deco architecture in trendy **Miami Beach**. Be sure to try succulent stone crab claws if they're in season.

South of Miami, the vast "river of grass" protected by **Everglades National Park** harbors some 600 species of animals. To truly experience this rare subtropical wetland, spend time hiking its trails, canoeing its waters and taking park-sponsored wilderness cruises.

For a glimpse of Florida at its most bohemian, drive down to **Key West** along the dramatic Overseas Highway (US-1). A walking tour of Old Town, including bar-hopping along Duval Street and watching the sunset at Mallory Square Dock will make it clear

what has lured artists and writers—such as Ernest Hemingway—to this tiny isle.

Wind up your Florida tour with a drive up the Gulf Coast on Route 41. Along the way, savor the elegant little city of **Naples** and spend time shelling on the beaches of **Sanibel and Captiva Islands**. Heading north, the cities of **Sarasota**, **St. Petersburg** and **Tampa** draw culture mavens and sun seekers. From Tampa, return to Orlando via I-4.

## SOUTHERN SOJOURN
*14 days*

A tour through the southern states of **Georgia**, **Alabama**, **Tennessee**, **Mississippi** and **Louisiana** reveals antebellum plantations alongside international cities. As you go, you'll uncover the roots of America's classic music forms: jazz, blues and country. Begin in bustling **Atlanta**, where shopping in the tony **Buckhead** neighborhood vies with the city's many cultural attractions for visitors' time. For a soupçon of stately 19C architecture, detour east on I-16 to the lovely coastal city of **Savannah**.

Re-live the drama of the American civil rights movement in Alabama *(via I-20 West)* at the famed **Birmingham Civil Rights Institute**. Then it's north on I-65 toward Nashville, with a requisite stop at the **US Space and Rocket Center** in Huntsville, Alabama. Home of the Grand Ole Opry, **Nashville** is the US country-music capital.

From Nashville, take I-40 West to **Memphis**. Here you'll find **Graceland**, former residence of the city's most famous son, Elvis Presley, and the **Beale Street Historic District**, where the Memphis **blues** evolved in smoky backstreet clubs.

Head south on US-61 through Mississippi, leaving time for a stop at **Vicksburg National Military Park** and an overnight stay in one of the antebellum B&Bs a bit farther south in **Natchez**—including a paddlewheeler cruise on the Mississippi River. Continue south through **Baton Rouge** and follow the **River Road**, lined with a mix of elegant plantations and Creole cottages, to New Orleans, Louisiana. Lauded for its Cajun and Creole cuisine as well as for its **jazz** clubs, **New Orleans** kicks up its heels each Lenten season at the annual bacchanalian bash known as **Mardi Gras**. Head back toward Atlanta on I-10 East, first taking a respite on the white-sand beaches of the **Gulf Coast**. At **Mobile**, pick up I-65 North and swing through **Montgomery**, Alabama, and catch a performance at the **Alabama Shakespeare Festival**. From Montgomery, I-85 North will take you back to Atlanta.

## CULTURAL CAPITALS OF THE EASTERN SEABOARD
*13 days*

Within the I-95 corridor that runs from New York City south to Washington, DC *(roughly 230mi)*, you'll find some of the nation's greatest museums and its most revered monuments. Begin your tour in the bastion of culture that is **New York City**. Be sure to see a Broadway show, take the ferry out to the **Statue of Liberty**, and visit the **Metropolitan Museum of Art**. If you need a rest from the city's hustle and bustle, take US-9 North through the painterly landscapes of the **Hudson River Valley**.

Next head south on I-95 to **Philadelphia**, Pennsylvania, where the cradle of US independence is re-created at **Independence National Historical Park**. Feast your eyes on the many fine works in the **Philadelphia Institute**

**of Art**, then feast yourself on a Philly cheesesteak at the Italian Market in **South Philly**.

South of Philadelphia, you can detour east on the Atlantic City Expressway and try your luck in the casinos of **Atlantic City**, or take the Garden State Parkway south to the beaches of Victorian **Cape May**. Then on to **Baltimore**, Maryland, where you can shop, eat and tour the **National Aquarium** at the Inner Harbor; don't miss the **Baltimore Museum of Art** and the **Walters Gallery** nearby. Worthwhile excursions include historic **Annapolis** *(south on I-97)* and Maryland's **Eastern Shore** *(east on US-50)*, where you can sample the area's charming inns and enjoy the Chesapeake Bay's bountiful catch of **blue crabs**.

Make your way south on I-95 and end your tour at **Washington, DC**. Home to the **White House** and **The Capitol**, DC also boasts the many fabulous museums—including the **National Gallery of Art** and the ever-popular **National Air and Space Museum**—and monuments on **The Mall**. If you happen to wind up with an extra day in DC, head to **Colonial Williamsburg** *(via I-95 South & I-64 East)* in Virginia, where the early days of the nation come to life on a re-created 18C town site.

## GREAT LAKES ODYSSEY
*14 days*

Lining Lake Michigan and Lake Erie, the cities of Chicago, Milwaukee, Detroit and Cleveland have reigned as the Midwest's industrial and transportation centers since the early 19C. It's best to plan your visit here for warm weather; winter often brings snow and bone-chilling winds off the lakes. Begin your tour in **Chicago**, which prides itself as much on its ethnic neighborhoods as on its downtown architecture. America's third-largest city by population, Chicago contains the world-class **Art Institute of Chicago**, **Field Museum of Natural History**, and the **John G. Shedd Aquarium**. Be sure to do some upscale shopping on the **Magnificent**

# Distance Chart

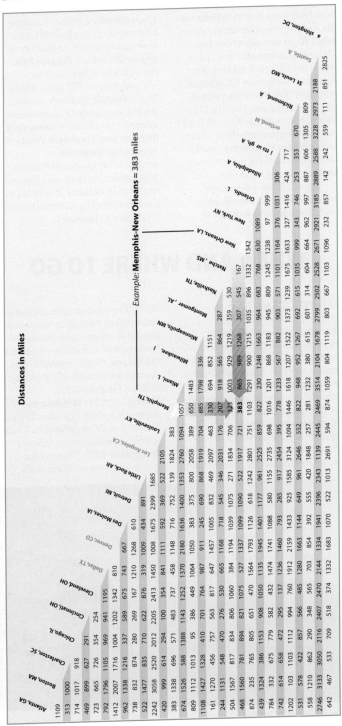

**Distances in Miles**

*Example: Memphis–New Orleans = 383 miles*

**Mile** and take in the city views from the top of the **Sears Tower**.

Then, head south on I-65 to **Indianapolis**, Indiana, site of the world-famous **Indy 500** car race. From here, take I-74 East to **Cincinnati**, Ohio. Spend time at the Cincinnati Art Museum; then head to adjoining Mt. Adams and explore its cozy shops, eateries and 19C Victorian houses. Over the Ohio River a short jaunt south on I-75 brings you to **Lexington** in the heart of Kentucky's **Bluegrass Country**. Nearby **Louisville** is home to the renowned **Kentucky Derby** horse race. Interstate 71 North will lead you through Ohio to **Cleveland**, which claims the **Rock and Roll Hall of Fame**. The city's former industrial heart, the Flats, has been revamped as a hip entertainment district. Several hours north of Cleveland via I-90 in New York lies one of the East's most popular attractions, **Niagara Falls**. From Cleveland, head west on I-90 and north on I-75 to the "Motor City"—**Detroit**, Michigan—where attractions highlight the automobile industry. Don't miss the **Henry Ford Museum and Greenfield Village** in neighboring **Dearborn**.

Return to Chicago via I-94 West. If time permits, continue past Chicago on I-94 to **Milwaukee**, Wisconsin, to experience the city's German heritage and to tour its breweries.

# WHEN AND WHERE TO GO

## When to Go

The eastern states have diverse climates (see INTRODUCTION) and weather patterns that are determined by geography, latitude, elevation, and proximity to the ocean and other bodies of water (chart opposite). Most attractions in major cities are open year-round.

The **Northeast** is a year-round vacation destination with four distinct seasons. Summer months are moderate and daytime temperatures (70-80°F) are comfortable without air conditioning. This region is especially popular in autumn, when hordes of "leaf peepers" come to see the brilliant **fall foliage**. Winter snowfall brings skiers to resorts in New England, New York and Pennsylvania.

Moving south, the **Mid-Atlantic** states—Maryland, Delaware, Virginia, Washington, DC, West Virginia—have warmer, humid summers (average temperature 80°F). Though snow is common in winter, warm spells

*Fall Colors in West Virginia*

often break up the cold winter weeks. Beginning in April, mild spring temperatures foster the bloom of dogwood and cherry trees, and countless crocuses, tulips and daffodils.

The **Southern** states, known for their torpid summer heat and humidity, are most affected by tropical storms, such as hurricanes. Fortunately, such tempests are infrequent and generally limited to the coastal areas. Summer temperatures average between 85°F and 90°F, with frequent afternoon thunderstorms. Sunny days are abundant in winter, when temperatures dip down to 50°F. Winter is high tourist

| City | January | | | June | | |
|---|---|---|---|---|---|---|
| | avg. high °F / °C | avg. low °F / °C | precip. in. / cen. | avg. hi °F / °C | avg. low °F / °C | precip. in. / cen. |
| Atlanta, GA | 33 / 1 | 17 / −8 | 2.2 / 5.5 | 79 / 26 | 57 / 14 | 3.2 / 8.1 |
| Atlantic City, NJ | 40 / 4 | 21 / −6 | 3.5 / 8.8 | 80 / 27 | 59 / 15 | 2.6 / 6.7 |
| Baltimore, MD | 40 / 4 | 23 / −5 | 3.1 / 7.7 | 83 / 28 | 62 / 17 | 3.7 / 9.3 |
| Baton Rouge, LA | 60 / 16 | 40 / 4 | 4.9 / 12.5 | 91 / 33 | 70 / 21 | 4.5 / 11.4 |
| Birmingham, AL | 55 / 13 | 37 / 3 | 5.5 / 13.7 | 88 / 31 | 68 / 20 | 3.7 / 9.5 |
| Boston, MA | 36 / 2 | 22 / −6 | 3.6 / 9.1 | 76 / 24 | 59 / 15 | 3.1 / 7.8 |
| Burlington, VT | 25 / −4 | 8 / −13 | 1.8 / 4.6 | 76 / 24 | 55 / 13 | 3.5 / 8.8 |
| Charleston, SC | 58 / 14 | 38 / 3 | 3.5 / 8.8 | 88 / 31 | 69 / 21 | 6.4 / 16.3 |
| Chicago, IL | 29 / −2 | 13 / −11 | 1.5 / 3.9 | 80 / 27 | 58 / 14 | 3.8 / 9.6 |
| Cincinnati, OH | 38 / 3 | 20 / −6.7 | 3.1 / 7.7 | 85 / 29 | 57 / 14 | 4.9 / 12.4 |
| Cleveland, OH | 32 / 0 | 18 / −8 | 2.0 / 5.2 | 78 / 26 | 57 / 14 | 3.7 / 9.4 |
| Des Moines, IA | 28 / −2 | 11 / −12 | 1.0 / 2.4 | 82 / 28 | 61 / 16 | 4.5 / 11.3 |
| Detroit, MI | 30 / −1 | 16 / −9 | 1.8 / 4.5 | 79 / 26 | 56 / 13 | 3.6 / 9.2 |
| Duluth, MN | 16 / −9 | −2 / −19 | 1.2 / 3.1 | 71 / 22 | 49 / 9 | 3.8 / 9.7 |
| Green Bay, WI | 23 / −5 | 6 / −14 | 1.2 / 2.9 | 76 / 24 | 54 / 12 | 3.4 / 8.6 |
| Indianapolis, IN | 34 / 1 | 17 / −8 | 2.3 / 5.9 | 83 / 28 | 61 / 16 | 3.5 / 8.9 |
| Jackson, MS | 56 / 13 | 33 / 1 | 5.2 / 13.3 | 91 / 33 | 67 / 19 | 3.2 / 8.1 |
| Kansas City, MO | 35 / 2 | 17 / −8 | 1.1 / 2.8 | 83 / 28 | 63 / 17 | 4.7 / 12.0 |
| Lexington, KY | 39 / 4 | 22 / −6 | 2.9 / 7.3 | 83 / 28 | 62 / 17 | 3.7 / 9.3 |
| Little Rock, AR | 49 / 9 | 29 / −2 | 3.9 / 9.9 | 89 / 32 | 67 / 19 | 7.8 / 19.9 |
| Louisville, KY | 40 / 4 | 23 / −5 | 2.9 / 7.3 | 84 / 29 | 63 / 17 | 3.5 / 8.8 |
| Madison, WI | 25 / −4 | 7 / −14 | 1.1 / 2.7 | 78 / 26 | 54 / 12 | 3.7 / 9.3 |
| Memphis, TN | 49 / 9 | 31 / −1 | 3.7 / 9.5 | 89 / 32 | 69 / 21 | 3.6 / 9.1 |
| Miami, FL | 75 / 24 | 59 / 15 | 2.0 / 5.1 | 88 / 31 | 45 / 7 | 9.3 / 23.7 |
| Milwaukee, WI | 26 / −3 | 12 / −11 | 1.6 / 4.1 | 75 / 24 | 55 / 13 | 3.2 / 8.2 |
| Minneapolis, MN | 21 / −6 | 7 / −14 | 1.0 / 2.5 | 79 / 26 | 57 / 14 | 4.5 / 11.2 |
| Mobile, AL | 60 / 16 | 40 / 4 | 4.8 / 12.1 | 90 / 32 | 71 / 22 | 5.0 / 12.8 |
| Nashville, TN | 46 / 8 | 27 / −3 | 3.6 / 9.1 | 87 / 31 | 65 / 18 | 3.6 / 9.1 |
| New Orleans, LA | 61 / 16 | 42 / 6 | 5.1 / 12.8 | 89 / 32 | 71 / 22 | 5.8 / 14.8 |
| New York, NY | 38 / 3 | 25 / −4 | 3.8 / 9.4 | 77 / 25 | 61 / 16 | 3.4 / 8.4 |
| Norfolk, VA | 47 / 8 | 31 / −1 | 3.8 / 9.6 | 83 / 28 | 65 / 18 | 3.8 / 9.7 |
| Orlando, FL | 71 / 22 | 49 / 9 | 2.3 / 5.8 | 91 / 33 | 72 / 22 | 7.3 / 18.6 |

| Philadelphia, PA | 38 / 3 | 23 / −5 | 3.2 / 8.2 | 82 / 28 | 62 / 17 | 3.7 / 9.5 |
|---|---|---|---|---|---|---|
| Pittsburgh, PA | 34 / 1 | 19 / −7 | 2.5 / 6.5 | 79 / 26 | 57 / 14 | 3.7 / 9.4 |
| Portland, ME | 30 / −1 | 11 / −12 | 3.5 / 9.0 | 73 / 23 | 52 / 11 | 3.4 / 8.7 |
| Providence, RI | 37 / 3 | 19 / −7 | 3.9 / 9.9 | 77 / 25 | 57 / 14 | 3.3 8.5 |
| Richmond, VA | 46 / 8 | 26 / −3 | 3.2 / 8.2 | 85 / 29 | 63 / 17 | 3.6 / 9.2 |
| Savannah, GA | 60 / 16 | 38 / 3 | 3.6 / 9.1 | 89 / 32 | 69 / 21 | 5.7 / 14.4 |
| St. Louis, MO | 38 / 3 | 25 / −4 | 2.3 / 5.8 | 85 / 29 | 66 / 19 | 4.6 / 11.4 |
| Syracuse, NY | 31 / −1 | 14 / −10 | 2.3 / 5.9 | 77 / 25 | 54 / 12 | 3.8 / 9.6 |
| Tampa, FL | 70 / 21 | 50 / 10 | 2.0 / 5.1 | 90 / 32 | 73 / 23 | 5.5 / 13.9 |
| Washington, DC | 42 / 6 | 27 / −3 | 2.7 / 6.9 | 85 / 29 | 67 / 19 | 3.3 / 8.4 |
| Williamsburg, VA | 49 / 9 | 31 / −4 | 3.7 / 9.4 | 85 / 29 | 62 / 17 | 3.5 / 8.8 |
| Winston–Salem, NC | 47 / 8 | 27 / −3 | 3.2 / 8.1 | 84 / 29 | 63 / 17 | 3.8 / 9.7 |

season in south Florida, which boasts average temperatures in the 70s.

The **Great Lakes** area experiences one of the most varied climates in the north. The influence of the large masses of water and resulting jet streams lead to variable weather year-round. Summers are warm and humid, with temperatures around 70°F. The duration of the seasons is also affected by the lakes, whose influence extends cool autumn weather and delays the arrival of summer. Winter makes its presence felt by strong winds blowing off the lakes and frequent snows. Harsh winters, consisting of strong wind chills and hearty snowstorms, usually keep winter temperatures in the **Midwest** around 32°F. Midwest summers don't begin until mid-June, with temperatures between 70°F and 80°F. In summer, fierce thunderstorms can spawn occasional tornadoes (☞WHAT TO SEE AND DO, Nature and Safety). ☞For weather conditions, try www. weather.com, or www.cnn.com/weather.

# KNOW BEFORE YOU GO

## Useful Websites

### www.flightstats.com
Flight departure/arrival boards.

### FlyerTalk.com
Looking for ways to make the most of your frequent flyer miles? Benefit from the experiences of others.

### SeatGuru.com
Tired of getting assigned cramped middle seats? Check out different plane seating charts here.

### Gridskipper.com
Those who are interested in seeing the gritty side of the US's urban destinations can find advice here.

### HotelChatter.com
Before you book the hotel—starred or otherwise—see what others who have slept there have to say.

### IgoUgo.com
Need inspiration for your travels? You'll find it here.

### Kayak.com
One of the best flight and hotel booking websites around, Kayak also lets you hire a car with ease; all through a simple search-engine style interface.

### www.vrbo.com
If traditional hotels aren't your thing, consider renting a privately-owned home from Vacation Rentals by Owner.

**Breezenet.com**
Find great deals on US car rentals at this user-friendly website.

**Concierge.com**
The inside track from Condé Nast Traveler—from hotel recommendations to travel advice—is compiled here.

**lastminute.com**
Looking for a last-minute getaway? This site compiles leads for trips that don't require months of planning.

## Tourism Offices

### US EMBASSIES AND CONSULATES

In addition to tourism offices, visitors from outside the US may obtain information from the nearest **US embassy or consulate** in their country of residence (⏺ *see details below*). For a complete list of American consulates and embassies abroad, access the US State Department Bureau of Consular Affairs listing on the Internet at: http://travel.state.gov/links.html.

### Australia
Moonah Place, Yaralumla ACT 2600
☎02 6214 5600

### Belgium
27, boul. du Régent,1000 Brussels
☎02 508 2111

### Canada
490 Sussex Street,
Ottawa Ontario K1N 168
☎613-688-5335 (US & Canada)

### China
3 Xiu Shui Bei Jie, Beijing 100600
☎86 10 6532 3831

### France
2, av. Gabriel, 75382 Paris
☎01 43 12 22 22 / 01 48 60 57 15
(Tourism information line)

### Germany
4-5 Neustadtische Kirchstrasse,
10117 Berlin. ☎30 238 5174

### Italy
Via Vittorio Veneto 121,
00187 Rome
☎06 4674 1

### Japan
1-10-5 Akasaka,
Minato-ku Tokyo 107-8420
☎0990-5-26160
(call from fax telephone
to make visa appointment)

### Mexico
Paseo de la Reforma 305, Col.
Cuauhtémoc, 06500 México, D.F.
☎01 5209-9100

### Netherlands
Lange Voorhout 102, 2514 EJ
The Hague, The Netherlands
☎70 310 2209

### Spain
Serrano 75, 28006 Madrid
☎91587 2200

### Switzerland
Jubiläumsstrasse 93,
CH-3005 Bern
☎31 357 7011

### United Kingdom
24 Grosvenor Square,
London W1A 1AE
☎0 20 7499-9000

### STATE TOURISM OFFICES

State tourism offices provide information and brochures on points of interest, seasonal events and accommodations, as well as road and city maps. Local tourist offices (⏺ *listed below*) provide additional information regarding accommodations, shopping, entertainment, festivals and recreation. Many countries maintain consular offices in major cities.

### Alabama
Alabama Bureau
of Tourism & Travel
401 Adams Ave., P.O. Box 4927,
Montgomery, AL 36103-4927
☎334-242-4169, 800-252-2262
www.touralabama.org

### Arkansas
Arkansas Department
of Parks & Tourism
One Capitol Mall,
Little Rock, AR 72201
☎501-682-7777
www.arkansas.com

### Connecticut
Commission on Culture
and Tourism
One Financial Plaza,
755 Main St.,
Hartford,CT 06106
☎860-288-4748
www.ctbound.org

### Delaware
Delaware Tourism Office
99 Kings Highway,
Dover, DE 19903
☎866-284-7483
www.visitdelaware.com

### District of Columbia
Washington, D.C.
Convention Tourism
901 7th St. Ave. N.W., 4th Floor,
Washington, DC 20001-3719
☎202-789-7000
www.washington.org

### Florida
VISIT FLORIDA,
P.O. Box 1100, Tallahassee, FL
32302-1100, ☎850-488-5607
www.visitflorida.com

### Georgia
Georgia Department
of Economic Development
75 Fifth St., NW, Suite 1200,
Atlanta, GA 30308
☎404-6962-4000,
www.georgia.org

### Illinois
Illinois Bureau of Tourism
100 Randolph St., Suite 3-400
Chicago, IL 60601
☎800-406-6418
www.enjoyillinois.com

### Indiana
Indiana Office of Tourism
Development, 1 N. Capitol Ave.,
Suite 100, Indianapolis,
IN 46204-2288
☎800-677-9800
www.enjoyindiana.com

### Iowa
Iowa Department of Economic
Development, 200 E. Grand Ave.,
Des Moines, IA 50309
☎515-242-4705
www.traveliowa.com

### Kentucky
Kentucky Department of Tourism
500 Mero St., 22nf Floor,
Frankfort, KY 40601-1968
☎502-564-4930
www.kentuckytourism.com

### Louisiana
Louisiana Office of Tourism
P.O. Box 94291, Baton Rouge,
LA 70804-9291
☎225-342-8119
www.louisianatravel.com

### Maine
Maine Tourism Association
327 Water St., Hallowell, ME 04347
☎207-623-0363
www.mainetourism.com

### Maryland
Maryland Office of Tourism
217 E. Redwood St
Baltimore, MD 21202
☎866-639-3526
www.mdisfun.org

### Massachusetts
Massachusetts Office
of Travel & Tourism
10 Park Plaza, Suite 4510,
Boston, MA 02116
☎617-973-8500
www.massvacation.com

### Michigan
Travel Michigan
300 N. Washington Sq.
Lansing, MI 48913
☎800-644-2489
www.michigan.org

### Minnesota
Explore Minnesota Tourism
100 Metro Square, 121 7th Pl. E.
St. Paul, MN 55101-2146
☎651-296-5029
www.exploreminnesota.com

### Mississippi
Mississippi Tourist
information Center
P.O. Box 1705,
Ocean Springs, MS 39566-1705
☎228-875-0933
www.mississippi.org

### Missouri
Missouri Division of Tourism,
Truman State Office Building,
P.O. Box 1055

☎573-526-5900
www.visitmo.org

**New Hampshire**
New Hampshire Office of Travel and Tourism Development, P.O. 172 Pembroke Rd., Concord, NH 03301-1856
☎603-271-2665
www.visitnh.gov

**New Jersey**
New Jersey Division of Travel and Tourism,
P.O. Box 820, Trenton, NJ 08625
☎609-777-0885
www.vistnj.org

**New York**
New York State Department of Economic Development Division of Tourism,
30 S. Pearl St., Albany, NY 12245
☎518-474-4116
iloveny.state.ny.us

**North Carolina**
North Carolina Travel and Tourism Division, Department of Commerce, 301 N. Wilmington St., Raleigh, NC 27601
☎919-733-4171
www.visitnc.com

**Ohio**
Ohio Department of Development Division of Travel and Tourism P.O. Box 1001, Columbus OH 43266-0101
☎800-BUCKEYE
www.ohiotourism.com

**Pennsylvania**
Pennsylvania Department of Community & Economic Development 400 North St., 4th Floor, Harrisburg, PA 17120-0225
866-466-3972
www.newpa.com

**Rhode Island**
Rhode Island Tourism Division, 315 Iron Horse Way, Suite 101., Providence, RI 02908
☎800-556-2484
www.visitrhodeisland.com

**South Carolina**
South Carolina Department of Parks, Recreation & Tourism 1205 Pendleton St., Columbia, SC 29201
☎803-734-1700
www.discoversouthcarolina.com

**Tennessee**
Tennessee's Department of Tourism Development 312 8th Ave., North, 25th Floor, Nashville, TN 37243
☎615-741-2159
www.tnvacation.com

**Vermont**
Vermont Department of Tourism and Marketing, National Life Building, 6th Floor, Drawer 20 Montpelier, VT 05620-0501
☎802-828-3237
www.travel-vermont.com

**Virginia**
Virginia TourismCorporation 901 E. Byrd St., Richmond, VA 23219
☎800-847-4882
www.virginia.org

**West Virginia**
West Virginia Division of Tourism 90 MacCorkle Ave., SW, South Charleston, WV 25303
☎304-558-2200
www.wvtourism.com

**Wisconsin**
Wisconsin Department of Tourism 201 W. Washington Ave., P.O. Box 8690, Madison, WI 53708-8690
☎608-266-2161
www.travelwisconsin.com

# International Visitors

## ENTRY REQUIREMENTS

Travelers entering the United States under the **Visa Waiver Program** (VWP) must present a machine-readable passport to enter the US without a visa; otherwise a US visa is required. Required entry documents must include biometric identifiers (fingerscans - full Visa Waiver Program requirements can be found on http://travel.state.gov). Citizens of countries participating in the VWP are permitted to enter the US for general business or tourism for up to 90 days without a visa. For a list of countries participating in the VWP, contact the US consulate in your country of residence. Citizens of nonparticipating countries must have a visa. Upon entry, nonresident foreign visitors must present a valid passport and round-trip ticket. As of December 31, 2006, travelers to and from Canada must present a passport or other secure, accepted document to enter or re-enter the US. Inoculations are generally not required, but check with the US embassy or consulate.

## CUSTOMS REGULATIONS

All articles brought into the US must be declared at the time of entry. **Exempt** from customs regulations: personal effects; one liter (33.8 fl oz) of alcoholic beverages (providing visitor is at least 21 years old); either 200 cigarettes, 50 cigars or 2 kilograms of smoking tobacco; and gifts (to persons in the US) that do not exceed $100 in value. **Prohibited items** include plant material; firearms and ammunition (if not intended for sporting purposes); meat or poultry products. For other prohibited items, exemptions and information, contact the US embassy or consulate before departing, or the US Customs Service (☎ 877-287-8667; www.customs.treas.gov).

## HEALTH

The United States does not have a national health program; doctors' visits and hospitalization costs may seem high to foreign visitors. Check with your insurance company to determine if your medical insurance covers doctors' visits, medication and hospitalization in the US. If not, it is wise to enroll in a travel insurance plan before departing. Prescription drugs should be properly identified and accompanied by a copy of the prescription.

# Accessibility

Many of the sights described in this guide are accessible to people with special needs. Sights marked with the ♿ symbol offer access for wheelchairs. However, it is advisable to check beforehand by telephone. Federal law requires that existing businesses (including hotels and restaurants)

increase accessibility and provide specially designed accommodations for the disabled. It also requires that wheelchair access, devices for the hearing impaired, and designated parking spaces be available at newly constructed hotels and restaurants. Many public buses are equipped with wheelchair lifts; most hotels have rooms designed for visitors with special needs. All national and most state **parks** have restrooms and other facilities for the disabled (such as wheelchair-accessible nature trails). Permanently disabled US citizens and permanent residents are eligible for a free **America the Beautiful-National Parks and Federal Recreational Lands Pass, Access Pass** (www.nps. gov/fees_passes.htm), which entitles the carrier to free admission to all national parks and a 50 percent discount on user fees (campsites, boat launches). For everyone else the pass is available at a single annual fee of $80, at any national park entrance. Contact:

> **National Park Service**,
> Office of Public Inquiries
> *1849 C Street NW, Room 1013*
> *Washington DC 20240*
> ☎*202-208-4747).*

Many attractions can make special arrangements for disabled visitors. For information about travel for individuals or groups, contact the **Society for Accessible Travel & Hospitality** (347 5th Ave., Suite 605, New York, NY 10016; ☎212-447-7284; www.sath.org).

## TRAVEL BY TRAIN

Train passengers who will need assistance should give 24hrs advance notice. Making reservations via phone is preferable to booking on-line since passenger's special needs can be noted on reservation by booking agent. The annual publication *Access Amtrak,* providing detailed information on Amtrak's services for disabled travelers, is available upon request (☎800-872-7245 and 800-523-6590 TDD) or may viewed on Amtrak's Web site, www.amtrak.com.

## TRAVEL BY BUS

Disabled travelers are encouraged to notify Greyhound 48hrs in advance. The annual publication *Greyhound Travel Policies* is available upon request: ☎800-752-4841 or 800-345-3109 (TDD), www.greyhound.com.

## RENTAL CARS

Reservations for hand-controlled cars should be made well in advance with the individual car rental agency.

## SENIOR CITIZENS

Many hotels, attractions and restaurants offer discounts to visitors age 62 or older (proof of age may be required). Discounts and additional information are available to members of the AARP *(601 E St. N.W. Washington, DC 20094; ☎888-687-2277, www.aarp. org)* or the National Council of Senior Citizens *(8403 Colesville Rd., Suite 1200, Silver Spring, MD 20910; ☎301-578-8800)*.

# GETTING THERE AND GETTING AROUND

## By Plane

### MAJOR AIRPORTS

 **Atlanta, GA**
Hartsfield-Jackson Atlanta International Airport (ATL); 10mi south of downtown
☎800-897-1910
www.atlanta-airport.com

 **Boston, MA**
Logan International Airport (BOS); 2mi northeast of downtown
☎800-235-6426
www.massport.com

 **Chicago, IL**
O'Hare International Airport (ORD); 14mi northwest of downtown
☎773-686-2200
Chicago Midway Airport (MDW); 10mi southwest of downtown
www.ohare.com
☎773-767-0500
www.flychicago.com

 **Charlotte, NC**
Charlotte-Douglas International Airport (CLT); 10mi west of downtown
☎704-359-4013
www.charlotteairport.com

 **Cincinnati, OH**
Cincinnati/Northern Kentucky International Airport (CVG); 13mi southwest of downtown
☎859-767-3151
www.cvgairport.com

 **Cleveland, OH**
Cleveland Hopkins International Airport (CLE); 11mi southwest of downtown
☎216-265-6000
www.clevelandairport.com

 **Detroit, MI**
Detroit Metropolitan Wayne County Airport (DTW); 20mi south of downtown
☎734-247-7678
www.metroairport.com

 **Memphis, TN**
Memphis International Airport (MEM); 11mi southeast of downtown, ☎901-922-8000
www.mscaa.com

**Miami, FL**
Miami International Airport (MIA); 7mi northwest of downtown

☎305-876-7000
www.miami-airport.com

### ✈ Milwaukee, WI
General Mitchell International
Airport (MKE); 11mi south of
downtown, ☎414-747-5300
www.mitchellairport.com

### ✈ Minneapolis-St. Paul, MN
Minneapolis-St. Paul
International Airport (MSP);
16mi south of Minneapolis
and St. Paul. ☎612-726-8100
www.mspairport.com

### ✈ Nashville, TN
Nashville International Airport
(BNA); 8mi east of downtown
☎615-275-1675,
www.nashintl.com

### ✈ New Orleans, LA
Louis Armstrong New Orleans
International Airport (MSY);
15mi west of downtown
☎504-464-0831
www.flymsy.com

### ✈ New York City, NY
- John F. Kennedy
  International Airport (JFK);
  15mi southeast of Midtown
  ☎718-244-4444
  www.kennedyairport.com

- LaGuardia Airport (LGA);
  8mi northeast of Midtown
  ☎718-533-3400
  www.laguardiaairport.com

- Newark Liberty
  *International Aiport (EWR)*;
  16mi southeast of Midtown
  ☎973-961-6000
  www.newarkairport.com

### ✈ Orlando, FL
Orlando International Airport
(MCO); 9mi southeast
of downtown,
22mi northeast of
Walt Disney World
☎407-825-2352
www.orlandoairports.net

### ✈ Philadelphia, PA
Philadelphia International
Airport (PHL); 8mi southwest
of Center City, ☎215-937-6800
www.phl.org

### ✈ St. Louis, MO
Lambert-St. Louis
International Airport (STL);
13mi northwest of downtown
☎314-426-8000
www.lambert-stlouis.com

### ✈ Washington, DC
- *Ronald Reagan Washington
  National Airport (DCA)*;
  4.5mi south of downtown
  ☎703-417-8000
  www.metwashairports.com

- *Washington Dulles
  International Airport (DIA)*;
  26mi west of downtown
  ☎703-572-2700
  www.metwashairports.com

- *Baltimore/Washington
  Thurgood Marshall
  International Airport (BWI)*
  28mi north of Washington;
  8mi south of Baltimore, MD
  ☎410-261-1000
  www.bwiairport.com

## By Train

The Amtrak rail network offers a relaxing alternative for the traveler with time to spare. Advance reservations are recommended to ensure reduced fares and availability of desired accommodations. On some trains, reservations are required; smoking is not allowed on any Amtrak train. Depending on the train and route, passengers can choose from first class, coach and cars with panoramic windows. In the East, service is provided along the following routes:

### ▭ Adirondack
New York City–Montreal
*Adirondacks, Lake Placid &
Saratoga Springs, Albany, NY*

#### Auto Train
Lorton, VA–Sanford, FL
*Alternative to driving I-95*

#### Capitol Limited
Chicago–Washington, DC
*Pittsburgh, PA. Cleveland, OH*

#### Cardinal/Hoosier State
Chicago–Washington, DC–
New York
*Virginia's Blue Ridge*
*West Virginia*
*Cincinnati, OH*

#### Carolinian/ Piedmont
New York City–Raleigh–Charlotte
*New York City, NY*
*Washington, DC*
*Richmond, VA*
*Raleigh, NC*

#### City of New Orleans
Chicago–Memphis–New Orleans
*Memphis, TN*

#### Crescent
New York City–New Orleans
*Washington, DC*
*Virginia's Blue Ridge*
*Atlanta, GA*
*Birmingham, AL*

#### Empire Service
New York City–Niagara Falls
*Hudson River Valley &*
*Finger Lakes, NY*

#### Keystone Service
Harrisburg–Philadelphia–
New York
*Lancaster County, PA*

#### Lake Shore Limited
Chicago–New York/Boston–
Albany
*Great Lakes*
*Cleveland, OH*
*Berkshires, MA*

#### Silver Services/Palmetto
New York–Jacksonville–Miami
*Richmond, VA. Charleston, SC*
*Savannah, GA. Orlando, FL*

#### Vermonter
Washington–New York–St. Albans
*Baltimore, MD*
*Philadelphia, PA*
*New York City*

**North America Rail Pass** links
Amtrak train routes with Canada's
VIARail system for 30 days with unlimited stops. **USA RailPass** (not available to US or Canadian citizens) offers
unlimited travel within Amtrak-designated regions at discounted rates;
15- and 30-day passes are available.
For schedules, prices and route information, call ☎800-872-7245 or www.
amtrak.com *(outside North America,
contact your travel agent)*.
The American Orient Express now has
just one train in the east: the Grand
Luxe Limited, which goes from Washington, D.C. to Miami and back.
It promises deluxe rail travel including
large cabins, a dining car where chefs
prepare gourmet meals and numerous
stops along the way for sightseeing. For schedules and fares contact
**American Orient Express**, 35715
US Hwy 40, Suite D302, Evergreen
CO 80439 ☎800-320-4206, www.
americanorientexpress.com.

## By Bus/Coach

**Greyhound** is the largest bus company
in the US with lower fares overall than
on other forms of transportation. Some
travelers may find long-distance bus
travel uncomfortable due to the lack
of sleeping accommodations. Advance
reservations are suggested.
Greyhound's **Discovery Pass** allow
unlimited travel for 7, 15, 30 or 60 days,
with stops along the way. Schedules,
prices and route information:

☎800-231-2222 *(US only)*
Greyhound Lines, Inc.
P.O. Box 660362, Dallas, TX 75266-0362

**Peter Pan** *(☎800-343-9999;
www.peterpanbus.com)* offers service
throughout the Northeast of the US.

# By Car

North-south **interstate highways** in the US have odd numbers (I-85, I-95) and east-west interstates have even numbers (I-20, I-80). Numbers increase from west to east (I-5 along the West Coast; I-95 along the East Coast) and from south to north (I-10 runs through the Sunbelt from Florida from Los Angeles, California; I-94 runs along the northern US from Milwaukee, Wisconsin to Billings, Montana).

Interstate **beltways** surround cities and have three digits: the first is an even number and the last two name the interstate off which they branch (I-290 around Chicago branches off I-90). There can be exceptions and duplication across states (there are I-495 beltways around Washington, DC, New York City and Boston).

Interstate **spurs** entering cities also have three digits: the first is an odd number and the last two represent the originating interstate as for beltways (I-395 into Washington DC and I-195 into Philadelphia).

Highways and roads that are not interstates are organized into US Routes, State Routes and County Routes. **US Routes** range from windy two-lane roads to major highways. North-south US Routes have odd numbers (US-23, US-1) and east-west routes have even numbers (US-6, US-50). All US Route numbers can have one, two or three digits. **State Routes** may also range from tiny two-lane roads to large highways; **County Routes** are usually smaller local or connector roads.

## RENTAL CARS

The national rental car companies (*listed on this page*) have offices at most airports and in the downtown areas of most major cities. Aside from these agencies, there are local companies that offer reasonable rental rates. *See Yellow Pages for listings.*

Renters must possess a major credit card (such as Visa/Carte Bleue, American Express or MasterCard/Eurocard) and a valid driver's license (international driver's license not required).

Minimum age for rental is 21 in most states. A variety of service packages offer unlimited mileage and discounted prices, often in conjunction with major airlines or hotel chains. Since prices vary from one company to another, be sure to research different companies before you reserve. All rentals are subject to a local tax not included in quoted prices. (To reserve a car from Europe, it is best to contact your local travel agent before you leave.) Liability **insurance** is not automatically included in the terms of the lease. Be sure to check for proper insurance coverage, offered at an extra charge. Most large rental companies provide assistance in case of breakdown.

Cars may be rented by the day, week or month, and mileage is usually unlimited. Only the person who signed the contract may drive the rental car; but for an additional fee, and upon presentation of the required papers, additional drivers may be approved. If a vehicle is returned at a different location from where it was rented, drop-off charges may be incurred. You must either fill the gasoline tank of the car before returning it or pre-pay for a tank of gasoline when you rent the car. Otherwise, the rental company will fill it for you at a higher price per gallon.

*Rental car **information and reservations** across the US may be accessed on the Internet (www.bnm.com) or by calling one of the companies listed below.*

| Rental Company | ☎Reservations |
|---|---|
| **Alamo** | 800-327-9633 |
| **Avis** | 800-331-1212 |
| **Budget** | 800-527-0700 |
| **Dollar** | 800-800-4000 |
| **Hertz** | 800-654-3131 |
| **National** | 800-227-7368 |
| **Thrifty** | 800-331-4200 |
| **Enterprise** | 800-325-8007 |

Jacque Stengel/SXC

## RECREATIONAL VEHICLE (RV) RENTALS

One-way rentals range from a basic camper to full-size motor homes that can accommodate up to seven people and offer a full range of amenities including bathroom, shower and kitchen with microwave oven. Reservations should be made several months in advance. There may be a minimum number of rental days required. A drop fee will be charged for one-way rentals. Cruise America RV ($800-327-7799, www.cruiseamerica. com$) features rentals with 24-hour customer assistance. The **Recreational Vehicle Rental Association** (RVRA) publishes a directory *($10; $15 via international mail)* of RV rental locations in the US: 3930 University Dr., Fairfax, VA 22030, ☎703-591-7130, www.rvra.org. **RV America** *(www. rvamerica.com)* offers an online database of RV rental companies as well as information on campgrounds and RV associations.

## ROAD REGULATIONS AND INSURANCE

The speed limit on most interstate highways in the contiguous US ranges from 55mph (88km/h) to 70mph (112km/h), depending on the state. On state highways outside of populated areas, the speed limit is 55mph (88km/h) unless otherwise posted. Within cities, speed limits are generally 35mph (56km/h), and average 25-30mph (40-48km/h) in residential areas. You must turn your headlights on when driving in fog and rain. Unless traveling on a divided road, motorists in both directions must bring their vehicle to a full stop when the warning signals on a **school bus** are activated.

Parking spaces identified with ♿ are reserved for persons with disabilities; anyone parking in these spaces without proper identification will be ticketed and/or their vehicle will be towed.

The use of **seat belts** is mandatory for all persons in the car. Children's safety seats are available at most rental car agencies; indicate need when making reservations. In some states, motorcyclists and their passengers are required to wear helmets. Hitchhiking along interstate highways is prohibited by law.

Unless otherwise posted, it is permissable to **turn right on a red light**, after coming to a complete stop.

## IN CASE OF AN ACCIDENT

If you are involved in an auto accident resulting in personal or property damage, you must notify the local police and remain at the scene until dismissed. If blocking traffic, vehicles should be moved as soon as possible. Automobile associations such as the **American Automobile Association (AAA)**, Mobil Auto Club *(☎800-621-5581)* and **Shell Motorist Club** *(☎800-355-7263)* provide their members with emergency road service. Members of AAA-affiliated automobile clubs overseas benefit from reciprocal services:

## Australia

Australian Automobile Association
(AAA) ☏02 6247 7311

## Belgium

Royal Automobile Club de
Belgique (RACB)
☏02 287 09 11
Touring Club de Belgique (TCB)
☏02 233 22 02

## Canada

Canadian Automobile Association
(CAA)
☏613 247 0117

## France

Automobile-Club de France (ACF)
☏01 43 12 43 12
Fédération Française du Sport
Automobile (FSA)
☏01 56 89 20 70

## Germany

Allgemeiner Deutscher
Automobil-Club E.V. (ADAC)
☏89 7676 0
Automobilclub von Deutschland
E.V. (AvD)
☏69 6606 610

## Great Britain

The Automobile Association (AA)
☏800 444 999
The Camping & Caravanning Club
(CCC)
☏203 694 995

The Caravan Club (CC)
☏01 342 326 944
The Royal Scottish Automobile
Club (RSAC)
☏141 946 5045

## Ireland

The Automobile Association
Ireland Ltd. (AA Ireland)
☏01 617 9999

## Italy

Automobile Club d'Italia (ACI)
☏06 49 98 1
Federazione Italiana del
Campeggio e del Caravanning
(Federcampeggio). ☏55 88 23 91
Touring Club Italiano (TCI)
☏02 85 26 1

## Netherlands

Koninklijke Nederlandsche
Automobiel Club (KNAC)
☏70 383 1612
Koninklijke Nederlandse
Toeristenbond (ANWB)
☏088 269 22 22

## Spain

Real Automóvil Club de España
(RACE)☏91 594 74 00

## Switzerland

Automobile Club de Suisse (ACS)
☏031 328 31 11
Touring Club Suisse (TCS)
☏022 417 27 27

# WHERE TO STAY AND EAT

*Hotels and Restaurants are described in the Address Books within the Discovering USA East section. For coin ranges, see the Legend on the cover flap.*

## Where to Stay

For a listing of recommended accommodations in the areas described in this guide, consult the **Address Book** sections included in each chapter. Luxury **hotels** generally are found in major cities, while **motels** normally are clustered on the outskirts of towns and off the interstates. **Bed-and-breakfast inns** (B&Bs) are found in residential areas of cities and towns, as well as in more secluded natural areas. Many properties offer special packages and weekend rates that may not be extended during peak summer months *(late May–late Aug)* and during winter holiday seasons, especially near ski resorts. Advance reservations are recommended for peak seasons. Many resort properties include outdoor recreational facilities such as golf courses, tennis courts, swimming pools and fitness centers. Activities—hiking, mountain biking and horseback riding—often can be arranged by contacting the hotel staff. Many cities and communities levy a hotel occupancy tax that is not reflected in hotel rates. Local tourist offices provide free brochures that give details about area accommodations *(telephone numbers and Web sites are listed under blue entry headings in each chapter)*.

### HOTELS & MOTELS

Rates for hotels and motels vary greatly depending on season and location. Expect to pay higher rates during holiday and peak seasons. For deluxe hotels, plan to pay at least $175/night per room, based on double occupancy. Moderate hotels will charge between $80 and $150/night while budget motels charge from $40 to $80/night. In most hotels, children under 18 stay free when sharing a room with their parents. When making a reservation, ask about packages including meals, passes to local attractions and weekend specials. Typical amenities at hotels and motels include television, alarm clock, smoking/non-smoking rooms, restaurants and swimming pools. In-room kitchenette are available at some hotels and motels. Always advise the reservations clerk of late arrival; unless confirmed with a credit card, rooms may not be held after 6pm.

### Major US Hotel Chains and Phone Numbers

| | |
|---|---|
| **Best Western** | 800-528-1234 |
| **Clarion, Comfort Inn, and Quality Inn** | 800-228-5150 |
| **Days Inn** | 800-325-2525 |
| **Four Seasons** | 800-332-3442 |
| **Hampton Inn** | 800-426-7866 |
| **Hilton** | 800-445-8667 |
| **Holiday Inn** | 800-465-4329 |
| **Howard Johnson** | 800-446-4656 |
| **Hyatt** | 800-233-1234 |
| **Marriott** | 800-228-9290 |
| **Nikko** | 800-645-5687 |
| **Omni** | 800-843-6664 |
| **Radisson** | 800-333-3333 |
| **Ramada** | 800-228-2828 |
| **Ritz-Carlton** | 800-241-3333 |
| **Sheraton** | 800-325-3535 |
| **Westin** | 800-228-3000 |

### Hotel Reservation Services

Hotel reservation services are abundant in the US, especially on the Internet. For a complete listing, search the Internet using the keyword "reservation services" or ask your travel

*The vast distances spanned by US highways popularized the humble motel.*

© iStockphoto.com/Mark Winfrey

agent. Following is a brief selection of reservation services.

**Accommodations Express**
☎800-444-7666
www.accommodationsexpress.com

**Central Reservation Service**
☎800-555-7555
www.crshotels.com

**Expedia**
☎800-397-3342
www.expediacom

**Hotel Discount.com**
☎800-715-7666
www.hoteldiscount.com

**Hotels.com**
☎800-246-8357
www.hotels.com

**Orbitz**
☎888-656-4546
www.orbitz.com

**Quikbook** (certain major cities only)
☎800-789-9887
www.quikbook.com

## BED & BREAKFASTS AND COUNTRY INNS

Most B&Bs are privately owned historic residences. Bed-and-breakfast inns are usually cozy homes with fewer than 10 guest rooms; breakfast is generally the only meal provided. Country inns are larger establishments; full-service dining is typically available. B&B amenities usually include complimentary breakfast and use of common areas such as garden spots and sitting rooms with fireplaces. Some guest rooms may not have private bathrooms. Reservations should be made well in advance, especially during holiday and peak tourist seasons. Minimum-stay, cancellation and refund policies may also be more stringent during these times. Most establishments will accept major credit cards. Rates vary seasonally but generally range from $125 to $200 for a double room per night. Rates will be higher for rooms with such amenities as hot tubs, private entrances and scenic views.

### Reservation Services

Numerous organizations offer reservation services for B&Bs and country inns. Many services tend to be regional. **Select Registry** (☎269-789-0393; www.innbook.com) publishes an annual register listing B&Bs and country inns by state. For a complete listing, search the Internet using the keyword "bed and breakfast," or ask your travel agent. The following is a selection of nationwide services;

**Reservation Services (TNN)**
www.go-lodging.com

**Professional Association of Innkeepers International**
☎800-468-7244
www.innplace.com

Maine Office of Tourism

*Blair Hill Inn, Greenville, Maine*

**Wakeman & Costine's North American Bed & Breakfast Directory**
www.bbdirectory.com

## HOSTELS

A simple, no-frills alternative to hotels and inns, hostels are inexpensive dormitory-style accommodations with separate quarters for males and females. Many have private family/couples rooms that may be reserved in advance. Amenities include fully equipped self-service kitchens, dining areas and common rooms. Rates average $14–$45 per night. Hostelling International members receive discounts on room rates and other travel-related expenses (airfare, railway and ferry tickets, car rentals, ski-lifts, passes, etc.). Hostels often organize special programs and activities for guests. When booking, ask for available discounts at area attractions, rental car companies and restaurants. For information and a free directory, contact **Hostelling International American Youth Hostels** (*8401 Colesville Rd., Suite 600, Silverspring, MD 20910;* ☎*301-495-1240; www.hiayh. org*). For more general information on hostels, try *www.hostels.com*. From outside the US, contact your local **Hostelling International** center.

**Australia**: Australian Youth Hostels Association, ☎2-9565-1699, www.yha.org.au.

**Belgium:** Les Auberges de Jeunesse, ☎02-219-56-76, www.laj.be.

**Canada:** Hostelling International-Canada, ☎613-237-7884, www.hostellingintl.ca.

**France:** Fédération Unie des Auberges de Jeunesse (FUAJ), ☎01-44-89-8727, www.fuaj.org.

**Ireland (Northern)**: Hostelling International-Northern Ireland, ☎028 9032 4733, www.hini.org.uk.

**Italy:** Associazione Italiana Alberghi per la Gioventù, ☎06-487-1152, www.ostellionline.org.

**Netherlands:** StayOkay, ☎20-5513155, www.stayokay.com.

**Spain:** Red Española de Albergues Juveniles, ☎91-347-7700, www.reaj.com.

**Switzerland:** Schweizer Jugendherbergen, ☎01-360-1414, www.youthhostel.ch.

**United Kingdom**: YHA (England & Wales) Ltd., ☎0870-870-8868, www.yha.org.uk.

## SPAS

Popular in large resort hotels, modern spas specialize in a variety of programs: fitness, beauty, wellness, stress relief, relaxation, and weight management. Guests are pampered with mud baths and daily massages and are given access to state-of-the-art fitness and exercise programs, cooking classes and nutritional counseling. Many spas offer luxurious facilities in settings that can include championship golf courses, equestrian centers and even formal gardens. Despite these surroundings, most spa facilities are casual.

Spa packages usually range from 2 to 10 nights; weekly rates *(per person, double occupancy)* vary from $800/week in summer to $3,500/week during the winter season, depending on choice of program *(age restrictions may apply)*. Spa packages generally include all meals, special diets, use of facilities, tax, gratuities and airport transportation. For more information, contact **Spa Finders**, 257 Park Ave., 10th Floor, New York, NY 10003, ☎212-924-6800, www.spafinders.com.

## CONDOMINIUMS

For families with children or larger groups traveling together, furnished apartments or houses are more cost-effective than hotels since they offer separate living quarters, fully equipped kitchens with dining areas, several bedrooms and bathrooms, and laundry facilities. Most condos provide televisions, basic linens and maid service. Depending on location, properties often include sports and recreational facilities. Most require a minimum stay of three nights or one week, especially during peak season. When making reservations, ask about cancellation penalties and refund policies. Chambers of commerce and convention and visitors bureaus keep listings of local property-management agencies that can assist with the selection.

## CAMPING & RECREATIONAL VEHICLE (RV) PARKS

Campsites are located in national parks, state parks, national forests, along beaches and in private campgrounds. Most offer full utility hookups, lodges or cabins, backcountry sites and recreational facilities. Advance reservations are recommended, especially during summer and holidays. In most parks and forests, campgrounds are available on a first-come, first-served basis.

**National park and state park** campgrounds are relatively inexpensive, but fill quickly, especially during school holidays. Facilities range from simple tent sites to full RV hookups *(reserve 60 days in advance)* or rustic cabins *(reserve one year in advance)*. Fees vary according to season and available facilities (picnic tables, water/electric hookups, used-water disposal, recreational equipment, showers, restrooms): camping & RV sites $8–$21/day; cabins $20–$110/day. For all US national park reservations, contact the park you are visiting or the **US National Park Reservation Service** *(☎877-444-6777; http://recreation.gov)*. For **state parks**, contact the state tourism office *(see KNOW BEFORE YOU GO)* for information.

**Private campgrounds** offering facilities from simple tent sites to full RV hookups are plentiful. They are slightly more expensive *($10–$60/day for tent sites, $20–$25/day for RVs)* but offer amenities such as hot showers, laundry facilities, convenience stores, children's playgrounds, pools, air-conditioned cabins and outdoor recreational facilities. Most accept daily, weekly or monthly occupancy. During the winter months *(Nov–Apr)*, campgrounds in northern regions may be closed. Reservations are recommended, especially for longer stays and in popular resort areas. Kampgrounds of America (KOA) operates campsites for tents, cabins/cottages and RV hookups throughout the US. For a directory *(include $6 for shipping)*, contact **KOA Kampgrounds**, P.O. Box 30558, Billings, MT 59114-0558, ☎406-248-7444, www.koakampgrounds. com. Listings of campgrounds throughout the US are easily found on the Internet. Search using keyword "campground directories."

The following is a selection of campground directories.

**Camping USA**
www.camping-usa.com

**CIS' RV-America Travel & Service Center** www.rv-america.com

**Go Camping America Directory**
www.gocampingamerica.com
*(official site of Nat'l Assn of RV Parks & Campgrounds)*

## Where to Eat

The eastern US serves up a bounty of culinary specialties, which vary from region to region. No matter what you crave, you'll find something to satisfy you. Just remember to pack your sense of adventure and your appetite: in America, portion sizes tend to be large. Most restaurants will accommodate special dietary concerns, such as food allergies and vegetarian diets. Kosher meals can be difficult to find outside of major metropolitan areas. When in doubt, it is advisable to call ahead and ask.

In the Northeast, you'll find yourself tempted by seafood of all sorts, from casual **clam** shacks to lobster dinners in white tablecloth restaurants. In New England lobster is a must. **Lobster rolls**, essentially lobster sandwiches, are a favorite summertime treat. Northern New York loves their **salt potatoes**, tiny new potatoes boiled in salt and slathered with butter. Don't stop in the state of Vermont without sampling the state's legendary cheddar cheese. The bottles of sweet maple syrup make great edible souvenirs for friends back home.

Further down the coast, seafood still reigns in Baltimore **crab cakes**. Also popular in the Mid-Atlantic is the salty **Smithfield ham**, and the hearty Amish dishes of the Pennsylvania Dutch country. Order **shoofly pie** for dessert, if you have a sweet tooth. It is made from molasses and brown sugar. In Philadelphia, order a **Philly Cheese Steak** sandwich.

Poet Carl Sandburg called Chicago "hot butcher for the world," and still today the Midwest likes its meat. While here you must try an **Italian beef** sandwich, a juicy delight of shaved roast beef topped with either hot or sweet peppers. All-beef **hot dogs** are another Chicago specialty, just don't put ketchup on yours if you are trying to look like a local. New York and Chicago bicker about whose **pizza** is better. In truth, they're just different. Chicago's thick, deep-dish variety is more like a pie. New York's thin slices can be eaten on the go.

The South is a culinary field trip, with **barbecue, key lime pie** and **Creole** and **Cajun** cooking. Even within the south, there are regional differences. Memphis barbecue is wetter (and more likely to be pork) than Texas' drier beef variety. When in New Orleans, don't miss the Creole specialties: crawfish etouffée, jambalaya or red beans and rice.

♿*For more restaurants information, see the Address Books within the Discovering USA East section. For restaurants in the Big Apple, see the red-cover* **Michelin Guide New York**.

# WHAT TO SEE AND DO

## Outdoor Fun

### ADVENTURE TRAVEL

The varying geography of the eastern US offers unlimited opportunities for outdoor adventure—from snorkeling off the coast of Florida to hiking in the mountains of Vermont. Contact state tourism offices (☙ see KNOW BEFORE YOU GO) for information on activities available in a specific geographic area, or consider taking an organized tour. The following is a sample of tour providers:

For exciting **all-inclusive vacations** involving activities such as bicycling, hiking and kayaking, contact **Backroads** (801 Cedar St., Berkeley, CA 94710-1800; ☎510-527-1555 or 800-462-2848; www.backroads.com). Programs include destinations in GA, LA, MA, ME, MS, NC, SC, VT and VA, as well as international trips.

🐎 For adventures on **horseback** in AR, GA, WV, FL, NY and VT—including riding tours, horse and cattle drives and visits to working ranches—contact **Hidden Trails**, 659A Moberly Rd., Vancouver, B.C. V5Z 4B3, ☎604-323-1141, www.bcranches.com.

🚴 **Cycling** enthusiasts can see the US on one of several tours offered by **America by Bicycle** (P.O. Box 805, Atkinson, NH 03811-0805; ☎603-382-1662 or 888-797-7057; www.abbike.com). Excursions range from 5-11 day mini-tours to 52-day coast-to-coast programs.

🧗 **Guides and Outfitters** – A list of accredited **mountaineering organizations** can be obtained from the **American Mountain Guides Association** (1209 Pearl St., Boulder, CO 80302; ☎303-271-0984; www.amga.com), a nonprofit organization and member of the International Federation of Mountain Guides Association. **America Outdoors** (P.O. Box 10847, Knoxville, TN 37939; ☎800-524-4814

www.americaoutdoors.org) offers an outfitter database on their Web site and publishes a list of US outfitters available (free) by mail.

**Wilderness Inquiry, Inc.** (808 14th Ave., SE, Minneapolis, MN 55414-1546; ☎612-676-9400 or 800-728-0719; www.wildernesinquiry.org) offers tours that include kayaking Maine's Moos River, **canoeing** in the Everglades and family adventures in Itasca State Park along the Mississippi River.

### SKIING THE EAST

Especially in the colder northern states of the eastern US, but also in the higher levels of the southern Appalachians, snow skiing is a popular winter sport. Ski areas are abundant, ranging from small local hills with a single chair lift and rope tow, to international resorts. Twenty-four eastern states—as far south as Alabama—boast at least one ski area; ski associations count over 267 in all, including 41 in New York and 39 in Michigan. The **Ski Town.com Mountain Resort Guide** (www.skitown.com) has full details on every North American ski resort and on many resorts overseas.
Major areas, those with at least six lifts and a 1,500ft vertical drop, include:

### Maine
Longfellow Mountains: Sugarloaf USA (☎207-237-2000). White Mountains: Sunday River (☎207-824-3000).

### New Hampshire
White Mountains: Attitash Bear Peak (☎603-374-2368); Bretton Woods (☎603-278-3300); Cannon Mountain (☎603-823-8800); Waterville Valley (☎603-236-8311); and Wildcat Mountain (☎603-466-3326). Lebanon area: Mount Sunapee (☎603-763-2356).

### New York
Adirondacks: Gore Mountain (☎518-251-2411) and Whiteface Mountain/

Lake Placid (☎518-946-2223). Catskills: Hunter Mountain (☎518-263-4223) and Windham Mountain (☎518-734-4300).

## Vermont

Green Mountains: Bolton Valley (☎802-434-3444); Killington (☎802-422-3333); Mount Snow (☎802-464-3333); Okemo (☎802-228-4041); Smugglers' Notch (☎802-644-1111); Stowe Stone Mountain (☎802-253-3000); Stratton Mountain (☎802-297-4000); and Sugarbush (☎802-583-2381). Cold Hollow Mountains: Jay Peak (☎802-988-2611).

## West Virginia

Allegheny Mountains: Snowshoe (☎304-572-1000).

# Nature and Safety

## WILDLIFE

In most parks, tampering with plants or wildlife is prohibited by law. When visiting any natural areas, remember that while the disturbance of a single person may be small, the cumulative impact of a large number of visitors may be disastrous. Avoid direct contact with any wildlife; an animal that does not shy away from humans may be sick. Some wildlife, bears in particular, may approach cars or campsites out of curiosity or if they smell food. **Food storage guidelines:** hang food 12ft off the ground and 10ft away from tree trunk, or store in a locking ice chest, car trunk or in lockers provided at some campgrounds. Improper storage of food is a violation of federal law and subject to fine. If a bear approaches, try to frighten it by yelling and throwing rocks in its direction (not *at* the bear). Never approach a mother with cubs, as she will attack to protect her young.

## HURRICANES

Beginning as tropical depressions, hurricanes can measure upward of 500mi in diameter and contain winds up to 200mph (a tropical depression

### ☺ Hurricane Precautions ☺

Check your car battery and fill up the gas tank.

Make sure you have a battery-operated radio and extra batteries.

Collect plenty of freshwater in containers and bathtubs.

When staying in coastal areas, familiarize yourself with evacuation routes.

Stay indoors during the hurricane.

Leave mobile homes and RVs for sturdier shelter.

Avoid low-lying areas that are subject to flooding.

Be aware of storm surges in coastal regions.

Most important, never take a hurricane lightly, and follow instructions issued by local authorities.

is classified as a hurricane once its winds reach 74mph). The East Coast of the US and the Gulf Coast region are vulnerable to these low-pressure storms from June to November, but the greatest activity occurs between August and October. The National Hurricane Center in Coral Gables and Miami, Florida, tracks all storms and issues advisories every six hours; a hurricane **watch** is announced if a storm may threaten an area within 36 hours; a hurricane **warning** is issued if landfall is expected within 24 hours.

## THUNDERSTORMS AND TORNADOES

Prevalent throughout the Deep South and Midwest during summer months, towering thunderheads can develop quickly. Some thunderstorms can be severe, producing hail and dangerous lightning. These severe storms can spawn **tornadoes**, or twisters, violently rotating columns of air reaching from the storm clouds to the ground. Winds generated by tornadoes can reach 300mph.

## BEACH AND WATER SAFETY

In the strong sun of coastal areas where white sand and water increase

## ☺ Safety Tips ☺

**Thunderstorm Safety Tips**

If outdoors, take cover and stay away from trees and metal objects.

If riding in a vehicle, remain inside until the storm has passed.

Avoid being in or near water.

If in a boat, head for the nearest shore.

Do not use electrical appliances, especially the telephone.

**Tornado Safety Tips**

If indoors, move to a predesignated shelter (usually a basement or stairwell); otherwise find an interior room without windows (such as a bathroom).

Stay away from windows.

Do not attempt to outrun the storm in a car; get out of the automobile and lie flat in a ditch or low-lying area.

the sun's intensity, visitors run the risk of sunburn, even in winter. Apply sunscreen even on overcast days, since ultraviolet rays penetrate the cloud cover. In the summer months when temperatures can be extreme, avoid strenuous exercise during midday and drink plenty of liquids.

Along public beaches warning flags are posted every mile: **blue flags** signify calm waters; **yellow flags** indicate choppy waters; **red flags** warn of dangerous swimming conditions such as riptides, strong underlying currents that pull swimmers seaward. Take precautions even when venturing into calm waters: never swim, snorkel or scuba dive alone, and supervise children at all times. Most public beaches employ lifeguards seasonally; swim at your own risk at unguarded beaches. Stinging creatures such as jellyfish, men-of-war and sea urchins can inhabit shallow waters. Although most jellyfish stings produce little more than an itchy skin rash, some can cause painful swelling; treating the affected area with papain-type meat tenderizer. Stingrays and men-of-war can inflict a more serious sting; seek medical treatment immediately.

Before beginning any water-sports activity check with local authorities for information on water and weather conditions. If you rent a canoe or charter a boat, familiarize yourself with the craft, obtain charts of the area and advise someone of your itinerary before setting out. **Life jackets** must be worn when boating. Many equipment-rental facilities also offer instruction; be sure to choose a reputable outfitter.

## MOUNTAIN AND HIKING SAFETY

When hiking in the backcountry, stay on marked trails; taking shortcuts is dangerous and causes erosion. It's best not to hike alone in the backcountry, but if you do, notify someone of your destination and planned return time.

Since mountain roads tend to be narrow, steep and twisting, exercise caution when driving. Observe cautionary road signs and posted speed limits. Always check weather conditions before driving or hiking in mountainous areas. Flooding due to heavy rains can cause roads and bridges to become impassable and make camping and hiking in low terrain hazardous. Be prepared for snowstorms if you are camping or traveling in the mountains during winter months.

*Copperhead Falls, Ozark Mountains*

© iStockphoto/Tomasz Szymanski

# National and State Lands

The US boasts an extensive network of federal and state lands, including national and state parks, that offer year-round recreational opportunities such as camping (*see WHERE TO STAY AND EAT*), fishing, horseback riding, snowmobiling and boating. US federal land-management agencies support a comprehensive online database (*www.recreation.gov*) with information on all federal recreation areas.

The National Park Service provides a listing of **National Wild and Scenic Rivers** on its Web site (*www.nps. gov/rivers/wildriverslist.html*).

Both national and state parks offer **season passes**. The America the Beautiful Annual Pass (*see KNOW BEFORE YOU GO*) is good for one year and includes admission to all national parks, sites and areas. The pass may be purchased at any park entrance or by mail: National Park Service, 1100 Ohio Dr. S.W., Room 138, Washington, DC 20242; Attention: Golden Eagle Passport. Most parks have information centers equipped with trail maps and literature on park facilities and activities. Contact the following agencies for further information:

◆ **National Forests**
US Department of Agriculture Forest Service National Headquarters
1400 independence Ave., SW
Washington, DC 20090-0003
☎202-205-8333 or www.fs.fed.us

◆ **National Parks**
The Department of the Interior
National Park Service
Office of Public Inquiries
1849 C St. N.W., Room 1013
Washington, DC 20240
☎202-208-4747 or www.nps.gov

◆ **State Parks**

**Alabama State Lands Division**
31115 Five Rivers Blvd.
Spanish Fort, AL 36507
☎334-242-3484
www.dcnr.state.al.us

**Arkansas Department of Parks & Tourism**
One Capitol Mall
Little Rock, AR 72201
☎501-682-7777
www.arkansas.com

**Connecticut State Parks Division**
79 Elm St., Hartford, CT 06106
☎860-424-3200
www.dep.state.ct.us

**Delaware Division of Parks & Recreation**
89 Kings Highway
Dover, DE 19901
☎302-739-9200
http://dpr.dc.gov

**District of Columbia Recreation & Parks Department**
3149 16th St. N.W.
Washington, DC 20010
☎202-673-7665
www.dcrecreation.com

**Florida Division of Recreation and Parks**
3900 Commonwealth Blvd.,
MS 49, Tallahassee, FL 32399
☎850-245-3029
www.dep.state.fl.us/parks

**Georgia State Parks & Historic Sites**
2 MLK Jr. Dr.
Suite 1352 East
Atlanta, GA 30334
☎404-656-2770
www.gastateparks.org

**Illinois Department of Natural Resources**
One Natural Resources Way
Springfield, IL 62702
☎217-782-6302
http://dnr.state.il.us/lands/landmgt

**Indiana State Parks Division**
402 W. Washington St.
Room W-298
Indianapolis, IN 46204
☎800-622-4931
in.gov/dnr

**Iowa Division of Parks, Recreation & Preserves**
Henry A. Wallace Building
502 E. 9th St.
Des Moines, IA 50319
☎515-281-5918
www.ioesdnr.com

## Hiking the "A.T."

The **Appalachian National Scenic Trail**, the longest continuous marked footpath in the US, stretches from Springer Mountain in north Georgia, traversing 14 states, 2 national parks, and 8 national forests in a high, well-maintained but often rugged path of more than 2,000mi to the rocky summit of Mt. Katahdin in Maine. The popular hiking trail, part of which overlays an ancient Native American route, is easy to reach from well-marked entry points at roughly 5mi to 10mi intervals all along its length.

Open all year except during serious blizzards, the "A.T." attracts thousands of day hikers, campers and backpackers from around the world, as well as a dedicated core of "through-hikers" who—after rigorous training—begin in Georgia in early spring and walk northward for three to four months, hoping to reach Maine before winter sets in. A series of rustic huts offer shelter for overnight camping along the trail.

A favorite of hikers for generations, the Appalachian Trail officially became a part of the National Park System in 1968.

The *Official Appalachian Trail Guides* are published by the **Appalachian Trail Conference** (ATC) and are available through retail bookstores worldwide (*a catalog of ATC publications is available from their national office;* ☙ *see National and State Lands, Hiking Trails*). The Ultimate Trail Store (☎304-535-6331 or 888-287-8673; *www.atctrailstore.org*) sells other Appalachian Trail-related items.

**Kentucky Department of Parks**
Capital Plaza Tower
500 Mero St., Suite 1100
Frankfort, KY 40601-1974
☎502-564-2172
www.state.ky.us

**Louisiana Office of State Parks**
P.O. Box 44426
Baton Rouge, LA 70804
☎225-342-8111
http://parks.kt.gov

**Maine Bureau of Parks & Lands**
22 State House Station
Augusta, ME 04333
☎207-287-3821
www.maine.gov/doc/parks

**Maryland State Park
& Forest Service**
Tawes State Office Building
580 Taylor Ave., Room E3
Annapolis, MD 21401
☎800-830-3974
www.dnr.state.md.us/publiclands

**Massachusetts
Division of State Parks
& Recreation**
251 Causeway St., Suite 600
Boston, MA 02114-2104
☎617-626-1250
www.mass.gov/dcr/forparks.htm

**Michigan Parks &
Recreation Division**
P.O. Box 30257
Lansing, MI 48909
☎517-335-4827
www.michigan.gov/dnr

**Minnesota Parks
& Recreation Division**
500 Lafayette Rd.
St. Paul, MN 55155
☎651-296-6157 or
www.dnr.state.mn.us/parks

**Mississippi Wildlife,
Fisheries & Parks**
P.O. Box 451
Jackson, MS 39205
☎601-432-2400
www.mdwfp.com/parks.asp

**Missouri Division of State Parks**
P.O. Box 176
Jefferson City, MO 65102
☎573-751-2479
www.mostateparks.com

**New Hampshire Division of Parks & Recreation**
P.O. Box 1856
Concord, NH 03302
☎603-271-3556
www.nhparks.state.nh.us

**New Jersey Division of Parks & Forestry**
P.O. Box 402
Trenton, NJ 08625
☎609-984-0370
www.state.nj.us/dep/forestry/divhome.htm

**New York Office of Parks, Recreation & Historic Preservation**
1 Empire State Plaza
Albany, NY 12238
☎18-474-0456
http://nysparks.state.ny.us

**North Carolina Division of Parks & Recreation**
1615 MSC
Raleigh, NC 27699
☎919-733-4181
http://ils.unc.edu/parkproject/ncparks.html

**Ohio State Parks**
2045 Morse Rd., Building 3
Columbus, OH 43229
614-265-6561
www.dnr.state.oh.us/odnr/parks

**Pennsylvania State Parks Bureau**
P.O. Box 8551, Harrisburg, PA 17105
☎717-787-6640
www.dcnr.state.pa.us

**Rhode Island Division of Parks & Recreation**
2321 Hartford Ave.
Johnston, RI 02919
☎401-222-2632
www.riparks.com

**South Carolina Parks, Recreation & Tourism Department**
1205 Pendleton St.
Columbia, SC 29201
☎803-734-1700
www.discoversouthcarolina.com

**Tennessee State Parks**
401 Church St.
L&C Tower, 7th Floor
Nashville, TN 37243
☎615-532-0001
www.state.tn.us/environment/parks

**Vermont Department of Forests, Parks & Recreation**
103 S. Main St., Building 10S
Waterbury, VT 05671
☎802-241-3655. www.vtfpr.org

**Virginia State Parks Division**
203 Governor St., Suite 214
Richmond, VA 23219
☎804-786-1712
www.dcr.virginia.gov/state_parks

**West Virginia State Parks & Forests**
State Capitol Complex
Building 3, Room 714

*Everglades National Park, Florida*

© iStockphoto/Tomasz Szymanski.

## Tips for Visiting Public Lands

Spray clothes with insect repellent (particularly around cuffs and waistline) and check for ticks every 3-4 hours when participating in outdoor activities.
Do not feed wild animals.
Do not litter; pack out everything you pack in.
Boil (5min) or chemically treat water from streams and lakes.
Cutting wood for fires is prohibited; only dead or fallen wood should be used. Campfires are limited to fire pits.
Hunting is prohibited in most parks; contact individual parks for hunting information.
All pets must be leashed and may be prohibited from certain park areas.
All plants and animals within parks are protected.
Taking natural objects (antlers/horns, historical objects, plants, rocks) is prohibited.

Charleston, WV 25305-0662
☎ 304-558-2764
www.wvparks.com
**Wisconsin State Park System**
P.O. Box 7921
Madison, WI 53707-7921
☎ 608-266-2181
www.wiparks.net

### ◆ Hiking Trails

The National Park Service, USDA Forest Service and Bureau of Land Management administer 17 national scenic and national historic trails in the US. For information on specific trail systems and recreational activities offered, download The *National Trails System Map and Guide* from the Federal Citizen Information Center *(Pueblo CO 81009; ☎ 888-878-3256; www.pueblo.gsa.gov/travel.htm)*.

**NATIONAL TRAILS SYSTEM BRANCH OF THE NATIONAL PARK SERVICE**
P.O. Box 37127, Washington, DC 20013, ☎ 202-343-3780

**APPALACHIAN NATIONAL SCENIC TRAIL**
Appalachian Trail Conservancy, P.O. Box 807, Harpers Ferry, WV 25425, ☎ 304-535-6331, www.atconf.org
National Park Service, Appalachian National Scenic Trail, P.O. Box 50, Harpers Ferry, WV 25425, ☎ 304-535-6278

**FLORIDA NATIONAL SCENIC TRAIL**
Florida Trail Association, 5415 S.W. 13th St., Gainesville, FL 32608, ☎ 352-378-8823 or 877-445-3352 (US), www.floridatrail.org
USDA Forest Service, Greenways & Trails, 1400 Independence Ave., SW., Washington, D.C. 20250-0003, ☎ 202-205-8333

**ICE AGE NATIONAL SCENIC TRAIL**
Ice Age Park and Trail Foundation, 306 E. Wilson St., Madison, WI 53703, ☎ 800-227-0046, www.iceagetrail.org
National Park Service, Ice Age National Scenic Trail, 700 Rayovac Dr., Suite 100, Madison, WI 53711, ☎ 608-264-5610, www.nps.gov/iatr

**NATCHEZ TRACE NATIONAL SCENIC TRAIL**
Natchez Trace Trail Conference, P.O. Box 6579, Jackson, MS 39282, ☎ 601-373-1447
National Park Service, 2680 Natchez Trace Parkway,Rural Route 1, NT-143, Tupelo, MS 38804, ☎ 601-842-1572

**NORTH COUNTRY NATIONAL SCENIC TRAIL**
North Country Trail Association, 229 E. Main St., Lowell, MI 49339, ☎ 866-HIKE-NCT
National Park Service, North Country National Scenic Trail, 700 Rayovac Dr., Suite 100, Madison, WI 53711, ☎ 608-264-5610

**POTOMAC HERITAGE NATIONAL SCENIC TRAIL**
Potomac Heritage Trail Association, 5529 Benson Ave., Baltimore, MD 21227
National Park Service, National Capital Region, Land Use Coordi-

### Hitting the Links

From multi-course complexes and resorts to municipal and daily-fee courses, US golfing facilities provide challenging play, beautiful natural scenery and gracious amenities for enthusiasts of all skill levels. Following is a list of some top-rated public-access courses in the eastern US:

| Course | Location | ☏ |
|---|---|---|
| Bay Hill | Orlando, FL | 407-876-2429 |
| Bethpage | Farmingdale, NY | 516-249-0700 |
| Cog Hill | Lemont, IL | 866-264-4445 |
| Doral | Miami, FL | 305-592-2030 |
| Grand National | Opelika, AL | 334-749-9011 |
| Sea Pines Harbour Town | Hilton Head Island, SC | 800-925-4653 |
| Kiawah Island | Kiawah Island, SC | 800-654-2924 |
| Pinehurst | Pinehurst, NC | 910-235-8507 |
| Sugarloaf | Carrabassett Valley, ME | 207-237-2000 |
| The Dunes | Myrtle Beach, SC | 843-449-5236 |
| The Greenbrier | White Sulphur Springs, WV | 800-453-4858 |
| The Homestead | Hot Springs, VA | 866-354-4653 |
| TPC at Sawgrass | Ponte Vedra Beach, FL | 904-273-3255 |
| Treetops Sylvan | Gaylord, MI | 989-732-6711 |

nation, 1100 Ohio Dr. S.W., Washington, DC 20242, ☏202-619-7027

**OVERMOUNTAIN VICTORY NATIONAL HISTORIC TRAIL**
Overmountain Victory Trail Association, c/o Sycamore Shoals State Historic Area, 1651 West Elk Ave., Elizabethton, TN 37643, ☏615-543-5808
National Park Service, Southeast Region, 75 Spring St., SW, Atlanta, GA 30303, ☏404-381-5465

**TRAIL OF TEARS NATIONAL HISTORIC TRAIL**
National Park Service, Branch of Long Distance Trails, P.O. Box 728, Santa Fe, NM 87504-0728, ☏505-988-6888

## Spectator Sports

### MAJOR LEAGUE BASEBALL (MLB)

**APR–OCT**
www.majorleaguebaseball.com

**Atlanta Braves**
Turner Field
☏404-249-6400

**Baltimore Orioles**
Oriele Park at Camden Yards
888-848-2473

**Boston Red Sox**
Fenway Park
☏617-267-1700

**Chicago Cubs**
Wrigley Field
☏312-831-2827

**Chicago White Sox**
US Cellular Field
☏312-674-1000

**Cincinnati Reds**
Great American Ball Park
513-4765-7400

**Cleveland Indians**
Jacobs Field
☏216-241-8888

**Detroit Tigers**
Comerica Park
☏866-668-4437

**Florida Marlins**
Dolphin Stadium, Miami, FL
☏305-623-6100

**Kansas City Royals**
Kauffman Stadium
☏816-504-4040

**Milwaukee Brewers**
Miller Park ☏414-902-4000

*United Center, home of the Chicago Bulls*

**Minnesota Twins**
Metrodome, Minneapolis, MN
☎800-338-9467

**New York Mets**
Shea Stadium, Flushing, NY
☎718-507-8499

**New York Yankees**
Yankee Stadium, Bronx, NY
☎718-293-6000

**Philadelphia Phillies**
Citizens Bank Park
☎215-463-1000

**Pittsburgh Pirates**
PNC Park,
☎412-323-5000

**St. Louis Cardinals**
Busch Stadium
☎314-345-9000

**Tampa Bay Devil Rays**
Tropicana Field
☎813-282-7297

## NATIONAL BASKETBALL ASSOCIATION (NBA)

**OCT–APR**
*www.nba.com*

**Atlanta Hawks**
Philips Arena
☎866-715-1500

**Boston Celtics**
TD Banknorth Garden
☎866-423-5849

**Charlotte Bobcats**
Charlotte Coliseum
☎704-688-9000

**Chicago Bulls**
United Center
☎312-455-4000

**Cleveland Cavaliers**
Quicken Loans Arena
☎216-420-2287

**Detroit Pistons**
The Palace
☎248-377-0100 or 248-645-6666

**Indiana Pacers**
Conseco Fieldhouse
☎317-917-2500

**Memphis Grizzlies**
FedEx Forum
☎901-205-2640

**Miami Heat**
AmericanAirlines Arena
☎786-777-1000

**Milwaukee Bucks**
Bradley Center
☎414-276-4545

**Minnesota Timberwolves**
Target Center, Minneapolis, MN
☎612-337-3865

**New Jersey Nets**
Continental Airlines Arena, Metrodome, NJ
☎800-765-6387

**New Orleans Hornets**
New Orleans Arena
☎504-525-4667

**New York Knicks**
Madison Square Garden
☎212-465-5867

**Orlando Magic**
Amway Arena
☎407-896-2442

**Philadelphia 76ers**
    Wachovia Center
    ☎ 215-339-7676
**Washington Wizards**
    Verizon Center
    ☎ 202-661-5050

## NATIONAL
## FOOTBALL LEAGUE (NFL)

**SEPT–DEC**
*www.nfl.com*

**Atlanta Falcons**
    Georgia Dome
    ☎ 404 223-8444
**Baltimore Ravens**
    M&T Bank Stadium
    ☎ 410-261-7283
**Buffalo Bills**
    Ralph Wilson Stadium, Buffalo, NY
    ☎ 716-649-0015
**Carolina Panthers**
    Bank of America Stadium, Charlotte, NC
    ☎ 704-358-7800
**Chicago Bears**
    Soldier Field
    ☎ 847-615-2327
**Cincinnati Bengals**
    Paul Brown Stadium
    ☎ 513-621-3550
**Cleveland Browns**
    Cleveland Browns Stadium
    ☎ 440-891-5050
**Detroit Lions**
    Ford Field
    ☎ 248-335-4151
**Green Bay Packers**
    Lambeau Field
    ☎ 920-496-5719
**Indianapolis Colts**
    RCA Dome
    ☎ 317-297-7000
**Jacksonville Jaguars**
    Jacksonville Municipal Stadium
    ☎ 904-633-6000
**Kansas City Chiefs**
    Arrowhead Stadium
    ☎ 816-920-9400
**Miami Dolphins**
    Dolphin Stadium
    ☎ 954-835-8326
**Minnesota Vikings**
    Hubert H. Humphrey Metrodome,

Minneapolis, MN
    ☎ 651-989-5151
**New England Patriots**
    Gillette Stadium, Foxboro, MA
    ☎ 508-543-1776
**New Orleans Saints**
    Louisiana Superdome
    ☎ 504-731-1700
**New York Giants**
    Giants Stadium, Meadowlands, NJ
    ☎ 201-935-8222
**New York Jets**
    Giants Stadium, Meadowlands, NJ
    ☎ 201-935-8111
**Philadelphia Eagles**
    Veterans Stadium
    ☎ 215-463-5500
**Pittsburgh Steelers**
    Heinz Field
    ☎ 412-323-1200
**Tampa Bay Buccaneers**
    Raymond James Stadium
    ☎ 813-879-2827
**Tennessee Titans**
    LP Field, Nashville, TN
    ☎ 615-565-4200
**Washington Redskins**
    FedEx Field. ☎ 301-276-6060

## NATIONAL
## HOCKEY LEAGUE (NHL)

**OCT–APR**
*www.nhl.com*

**Atlanta Thrashers**
    Philips Arena
    ☎ 404-584-7825
**Boston Bruins**
    TD Bank North Garden
    ☎ 617-931-2000
**Buffalo Sabres**
    Marine Midland Arena
    ☎ 716-855-4444
**Carolina Hurricanes**
    RBC Center
    ☎ 919-834-4000
**Chicago Blackhawks**
    United Center
    ☎ 312-455-7000
**Columbus Blue Jackets**
    Nationwide Arena
    ☎ 614-246-2000
**Detroit Red Wings**
    Joe Louis Arena
    ☎ 313-396-7575

**Florida Panthers**
 Bank Atlantic, Sunrise, FL
 ☎ 954-835-8000
**Minnesota Wild**
 Xcel Energy Center
 ☎ 651-726-8240
**Nashville Predators**
 Sommet Center
 ☎ 615-770-7825
**New Jersey Devils**
 Continental Airlines Arena
 Meadowlands, NJ
 ☎ 201-935-3900
**New York Islanders**
 Nassau Veterans Memorial
 Coliseum
 ☎ 631-888-9000
**New York Rangers**
 Madison Square Garden
 ☎ 212-465-6000
**Philadelphia Flyers**
 Wachovia Center
 ☎ 215-218-1825
**Pittsburgh Penguins**
 Mellon Arena
 ☎ 412-323-1919
**St. Louis Blues**
 Scottrade Center
 ☎ 314-421-4400
**Tampa Bay Lightning**
 St. Pete Times Forum
 ☎ 813-301-6600
**Washington Capitals**
 Verizon Center
 ☎ 202-266-2350

## Entertainment

**Atlanta Civic Center**
 ☎ 404-523-627,
 www.atlantaciviccenter.com

**Hi-Fi Buys Amphitheatre**,
 Atlanta, ☎ 404-443-5090,
 www.hob.com

**Boston Opera House**,
 www.bostonoperahouse.com

**Orpheum Theatre**,
 Boston, MA, ☎ 617-679-0810

**Civic Opera House**,
 Chicago, IL, ☎ 312-419-0033
 www.civicoperahouse.com

**Museum of Contemporary Art**,
 Chicago, IL, ☎ 312-280-2660,
 www.mcachicago.org

**Steppenwolf Theater Co**.,
 Chicago, IL, ☎ 312-335-1650,
 www.steppenwolf.org

**Riverbend Music Center**,
 Cincinnati, OH ☎ 513-232-6220,
 www.riverbend.org

**Max M. Fisher Music Center**,
 Detroit, MI, 313-576-5111,
 www.detroitsymphony.com

**Clowes Memorial Hall**,
 Indianapolis, IN, ☎ 317-940-9697,
 www.cloweshall.org

**Byron Carlyle Theater**,
 Miami, FL,
 ☎ 305-358-5885

**Milwaukee Theatre**,
 ☎ 414-908-6001,
 www.milwaukeetheatre.com

**Plymouth Playhouse**,
 Minneapolis, MN, ☎ 763-553-0404
 www.plymouthplayhouse.com

**Country Music Hall of Fame**,
 Nashville, TN, ☎ 615-416-2001,
 www.countrymusichalloffame.
 com

**Radio City Music Hall**,
 New York, NY, ☎ 212-307-7171,
 www.radiocity.com

**Pepsi-Cola Roadhouse**,
 Pittsburgh, PA, ☎ 724-947-7400

**National Air and Space Museum**,
 Washington, D.C.,
 www.nasm.si.edu

## Sightseeing

**National and City Tours** – Several
**national tour companies** provide
all-inclusive packages for motor-coach
tours of the US *(below)*. The scope of
tours may vary among tour operators,

but most offer packages of varying length, geographic coverage and cost. **TrekAmerica** *(P.O. Box 189, Rockaway, NJ 07866;* ☎*973-983-1144 or 800-221-0596; www.trekamerica.com)* caters to travelers who prefer small groups, varied sightseeing/sporting activities and flexible itineraries.

For those interested in more educational offerings, **Smithsonian Study Tours**, sponsored by the Smithsonian Institute in Washington, DC, offers a variety of single- and multi-day thematic programs covering topics such as architecture, performing arts, cuisine and Civil War history. Educators specializing in related fields lead these tours. For more information, call ☎877-338-8687 or www.si.edu.

Discover the rivers of the eastern US via **river barge** with RiverBarge Excursions, *(201 Opelousas Ave., New Orleans, LA 70114;* ☎*888-456-2743; www.riverbarge.com)*. Itineraries include routes on the Mississippi, Missouri and Ohio rivers as well as thematic excursions to Civil War military parks and scenic train rides.

Information on **city tours** can be obtained by contacting the convention and visitors bureaus in large US cities. **Gray Line Tours** provides half- and full-day sightseeing motorcoach tours for more than 70 US cities. For information, contact: **Gray Line Worldwide**, 1835 Gaylord St., Denver, CO 80206, ☎303-394-6920, www.grayline.com.

### National Tour Companies

**Brennan Vacations**
  Joseph Vance Bldg., 5301 South Federal Circle, Littleton, CO 80123
  ☎800-237-7249
  www.brennanvacations.com.

**Collette Vacations**
  162 Middle St., Pawtucket, RI 02860
  ☎800-340-5158,
  www.collettevacations.com.

**Globus and Cosmos**
  5301 S. Federal Circle, Littleton, CO 80123
  ☎888-218-8665
  www.globusandcosmos.com.

**Mayflower Tours**
  1225 Warren Ave., Downers Grove, IL 60515
  ☎800-323-7604
  www.mayflowertours.com.

**Trafalgar Tours**
  11 E. 26th St., Suite 1300, New York, NY 10010-1402
  ☎866-544-4434
  www.trafalgartours.com.

**Tauck Tours**
  10 Norden Pl., Norwalk, CT 06855
  ☎800-788-7885
  www.tauck.com.

## Activities for Children Kids

In this guide, sights of particular interest to children are indicated with a Kids symbol. Many of these attractions offer special children's programs. Some attractions offer discounted (if not free) admission to visitors under 12 years of age. In addition, many hotels and resorts offer family discount packages, and some restaurants provide a separate children's menu.

## Calendar of Events

### SPRING

EARLY MAR:
  ◆**Flower Show Week**, *Philadelphia, PA*
  ◆**Art Expo New York**, *New York City, NY*
  ◆**Carnaval Miami**, *Miami, FL*
  ◆**Sanibel Shell Fair**, *Sanibel Island, FL*
  ◆**Bike Week**, *Daytona Beach, FL*
  ◆**World Championship Sled Dog Derby**, *Laconia, NH*

MAR–EARLY APR:
  ◆**Natchez Spring Pilgrimage**, *Natchez, MS*

MID-MAR
  ◆**St. Patrick's Day Parades**, *Atlanta, GA, New Orleans, LA, Savannah, GA, New York City, NY*

*Head to Charleston in spring for the Festival of Houses & Gardens (Bay Street pictured)*

MID-MAR–MID-APR:
- **Festival of Houses & Gardens**, *Charleston, SC*

LATE MAR:
- **Annual Savannah Tour of Homes & Gardens**, *Savannah, GA*

MID-MAR–EARLY APR:
- **Vicksburg Spring Pilgrimage**, *Vicksburg, MS*

LATE MAR–MID-APR:
- **Festival of States**, *St. Petersburg, FL*

EASTER SUNDAY:
- **Easter Sunday Parade**, *New York City, NY*
- **National Cherry Blossom Festival**, *Washington, DC*
- **Easter Sunrise Service**, *Arlington National Cemetery, VA*

EASTER MON:
- **Easter Egg Roll and Egg Hunt**, *White House, Washington, DC*

APRIL:
- **Seven Mile Bridge Run**, *Marathon, FL*
- **Wildflower Pilgrimage**, *Great Smoky Mountains NP, TN*

APR–MAY:
- **Smoky Mountain Music Festival**, *Gatlinburg, TN*

2ND WEEKEND APR:
- **French Quarter Festival**, *New Orleans, LA*

APR–MID-MAY:
- **Chicago Park District Spring Flower Show**, *Chicago, IL*

APR–MAY:
- **Indianapolis 500 Festival**, *Indianapolis, IN*

EARLY APR:
- **Atlanta Dogwood Festival**, *Atlanta, GA*
- **Spring Festival**, *Cape May, NJ*

MID–LATE APR:
- **Tri-C Jazzfest**, *Cleveland,OH*

MID-APR–MAY:
- **Kentucky Derby Festival**, *Louisville, KY*

3RD WEEK APR:
- **Fayetteville Dogwood Festival**, *Fayetteville, NC*

3RD MON IN APR:
- **Boston Marathon**, *Boston, MA*

LAST WEEK APR:
- **Historic Garden Week**, *Virginia, statewide*

© iStockphoto/Daniel Cardiff

*Nags Head in North Carolina is home to a hang-gliding festival each summer.*

**LAST WEEKEND APR:**
- ◆**Annual Main Street Festival**, *Nashville, TN*

**4TH SUN APR:**
- ◆**Blessing of the Fleet,** *Charleston, SC*

**LATE APR–MAY:**
- ◆**New Orleans Jazz & Heritage Festival**, *New Orleans, LA*
- ◆**Philadelphia Open House**, *Philadelphia, PA*
- ◆**Hudson River White Water Derby,** *North Creek, NY*

**LATE APR–JUN:**
- ◆**Georgia Renaissance Festival**, *Atlanta, GA*
- ◆**Virginia Arts Festival,** *Norfolk, VA*

**MAY–JUN:**
- ◆**Cape May Music Festival,** *Cape May, NJ*

**1ST WEEKEND MAY:**
- ◆**Annual Tennessee Crafts Fair**, *Nashville, TN*

**EARLY MAY:**
- ◆**Schaeffer Eye Center/Beam's Crawfish Boil,** *Birmingham, AL*

**2ND WEEK MAY:**
- ◆**Tulip Time Festival,** *Holland, MI*

**2ND WEEKEND MAY:**
- ◆**International BBQ Festival**, *Owensboro, KY*
- ◆**Art Chicago**, *Chicago, IL*
- ◆**Annual Hang Gliding Spectacular,** *Nags Head, NC*

**3RD WEEKEND MAY:**
- ◆**Crawdad Days Music Festival**, *Harrison, AR*

**LATE MAY:**
- ◆**Indianapolis 500**, *Indianapolis, IN*

**MEMORIAL DAY WEEKEND:**
- ◆**Down Home Blues Festival**, *Huntsville, AL*
- ◆**Lobsterfest**, *Mystic, CT*

**LATE MAY–MID-JUN:**
- ◆**Spoleto Festival USA**, *Charleston, SC*

---

## SUMMER

**JUNE:**
- ◆**Sarasota Music Festival,** *Sarasota, FL*
- ◆**Spanish Night Watch**, *St. Augustine, FL*

**EARLY JUN:**
- ◆**Goombay Festival**, *Coconut Grove, Miami, FL*
- ◆**Yale-Harvard Regatta**, *New London, CT*
- ◆**Belmont Stakes**, *Belmont, NY*
- ◆**Syracuse Jazz Fest**, *Syracuse, NY*

◆**Festival of the Bluegrass**,
*Kentucky Horse Park, Lexington, KY*

2ND WEEKEND JUN:
◆**Chicago Gospel Festival**,
*Chicago, IL*

MID-JUN:
◆**Indy Jazz Fest**, *Indianapolis, IN*
◆**City Stages**, *Birmingham, AL*
◆**CMA Music Festival**, *Nashville, TN*
◆**Festival of Historic Houses,**
*Providence, RI*

MID-LATE JUN:
◆**JVC Jazz Festival New York**,
*New York City, NY*

JUN-JUL:
◆**Metropolitan Opera
Parks Concerts**, *New York City, NY*

JUN-AUG:
◆**'Unto These Hills'
Cherokee History drama**,
*Cherokee, NC*
◆**Shakespeare in the Park**,
*New York City, NY*

JUN-LATE AUG:
◆**Jacob's Pillow Dance Festival**,
*Becket, MA*

MID-JUN-EARLY JUL:
◆**International Freedom Fest**,
*Detroit, MI*

MID-JUN-LATE AUG:
◆**Grant Park Music Festival**,
*Chicago, IL*

MID-JUN-LABOUR DAY:
◆**Ravinia Festival,** *Chicago, IL*

LATE JUN-JUL:
◆**Summerfest,** *Milwaukee, WI*

LATE JUN-JUL 5:
◆**Taste of Chicago,** *Chicago, IL*

LATE JUN:
◆**Boston Harborfest,** *Boston, MA*

JULY:
◆**Minneapolis Aquatennial,**
*Minneapolis, MN*

◆**Hemingway Days**, *Key West, FL*
◆**NY Philharmonic
Parks Concerts in the Parks**,
*New York City, NY*

JUL 3:
◆**Independence Day
Concert & Fireworks**, *Chicago, IL*

JUL 4:
◆**Macy's 4th of July Fireworks**,
*New York City, NY*
◆**National Independence
Day Celebrations**,
*The Mall, Washington, DC*
◆**National Tom Sawyer Days,**
*Hannibal, MO*

EARLY JUL:
◆**Smithsonian Folklife Festival**,
*Washington, DC*

MID-JUL:
◆**Chicago Blues Festival**
*Chicago, IL*
◆**Newport Music Festival**,
*Newport, RI*

LATE JUL:
◆**Race to Mackinac**,
*Mackinac Island, MI*
◆**Pony Penning**, *Chincoteague, VA*

JUL-AUG:
◆**Mostly Mozart Festival,**
*Lincoln Center, New York City*
◆**Festival of Contemporary
Music**, *Lenox, MA*

LATE JUL-AUG:
◆**Racing Season,**
*Saratoga Springs, NY*

AUG:
◆**Uptown Art Fair**,
*Minneapolis, MN*

EARLY AUG:
◆**Birmingham Heritage Festival**
*Birmingham, AL*

MID-AUG:
◆**Iowa State Fair,** *Des Moines, IA*
◆**Bayfront Blues Festival**,
*Duluth, MN*
◆**Craftsmen's Fair**, *Newbury, NH*

AUG 18:
- ◆**Virginia Dare Birthday Celebration**, *Fort Raleigh NHS, Manteo, NC*

AUG 25:
- ◆**National Park Service Founder's Day**, *all National Parks*

LATE AUG:
- ◆**Virginia Wine Festival,** *Plains, VA*
- ◆**Chicago Air & Water Show,** *Chicago, IL*

LATE AUG–LABOR DAY:
- ◆**Michigan State Fair**, *Detroit, MI*

LAST WEEKEND AUG:
- ◆**Viva! Chicago Latin Music Festival**, *Chicago, IL*

LABOR DAY:
- ◆**Chicago Jazz Festival**, *Chicago, IL* weekend

## FALL

SEPT:
- ◆**Mountain Life Festival,** *Great Smoky Mountains NP, TN*
- ◆**Maryland State Fair**, *Timonium, MD*

1ST WEEKEND SEPT:
- ◆**Cleveland National Air Show**, *Cleveland, OH*

MID-SEPT:
- ◆**Kentucky Bourbon Festival**, *Bardstown, KY*
- ◆**Ozark Cultural Celebration**, *Harrison, AR*

LATE SEPT:
- ◆**Adirondack Balloon Festival**, *Glens Falls, NY*

LAST WEEKEND SEPT:
- ◆**Williamsburg Scottish Festival**, *Williamsburg, VA*
- ◆**IBMA Bluegrass Fan Fest**, *Louisville, KY*

LATE SEPT-OCT:
- ◆**Natchez Fall Pilgrimage**, *Natchez, MS*

- ◆**Northeast Kingdom Fall Foliage Festival**, *Northeast Kingdom, VT*

EARLY–LATE OCT:
- ◆**Chicago International Film Festival**, *Chicago, IL*

1ST WEEK OCT:
- ◆**Oktoberfest,** *Amana Colonies, IA*
- ◆**Grand Ole Opry Birthday Celebration**, *Nashville, TN*

3RD WEEKEND OCT:
- ◆**Great Mississippi River Balloon Race**, *Natchez, MS*

LATE OCT:
- ◆**Guavaween**, *Ybor City, FL*
- ◆**Penn's Colony Festival**, *Pittsburgh, PA*
- ◆**Victorian Week**, *Cape May, NJ*

MID-NOV:
- ◆**Veterans Day Ceremonies,** *Arlington National Cemetery, VA Vietnam Veterans Memorial and US Navy Memorial, Washington, DC*
- ◆**Magnificent Mile Festival of Lights,** *Chicago, IL*

THANKSGIVING DAY:
- ◆**Macy's Thanksgiving Day Parade**, *New York City, NY*
- ◆**Pilgrim Progress Procession**, *Plymouth, MA*

DAY AFTER THANKSGIVING DAY:
- ◆**City of Chicago Tree-Lighting Ceremony**, *Chicago, IL*
- ◆**Rockefeller Center Christmas Tree Lighting**, *New York City, NY*

## WINTER

EARLY DEC:
- ◆**National Christmas Tree Lighting,** *The Ellipse, Washington, DC*
- ◆**Williamsburg Grand Illumination**, *Williamsburg, VA*

LATE DEC:
- ◆**King Mango Strut**, *Coconut Grove, FL*

*Chinese Paper Dragon at the New Year Parade, New York*

◆**Indian Arts Festival,
Miccosukee Indian Village**,
*Everglades, FL*
◆**Christmas
Candlelight Tours**,
*White House, Washington, DC*

DEC 24–25:
◆**Christmas Celebration**,
*National Cathedral, Washington, DC*

DEC 31:
◆**New Year's Eve
Celebration**,
*New York City, NY*

JAN 1:
◆**Mummers Parade**,
*Philadelphia, PA*

JAN:
◆**Miss America Pageant**,
*Atlantic City, NJ*

JAN 6–EARLY MAR:
◆**Mardi Gras Season**,
*New Orleans, LA*

MID-JAN:
◆**Art Deco Weekend**,
*Miami Beach, FL*
◆**Stowe Winter Carnival**, *Stowe, VT*

3RD SUN JAN:
◆**Lowcountry Oyster Festival**,
*Charleston, SC*

LATE JAN–FEB:
◆**Chinese New Year Parade**,
*New York City, NY*

FEB:
◆**Gasparilla Pirate Festival**,
*Tampa, FL*
◆**Daytona 500**, *Daytona Beach, FL*

FEB–MAR:
◆**Chinese New Year Parade
& Festival**, *Washington, DC*

EARLY FEB:
◆**St. Paul Winter Carnival**,
*St. Paul, MN*

## Shopping

Shopping is considered a sport in many parts of the east, south and Midwest US. In some cities, discount and outlet malls are the main tourist attraction, drawing more visitors each year than local museums and other landmarks.

In general in the US people do not bargain in storefronts. The price marked is the price paid. Exceptions are flea markets and antique malls, where negotiating the price by 10 percent is expected.

Sales tax varies by state, city and county and is added to the purchase price. Occasionally, merchants will offer discounts for cash payments. Different regions of the country have different shopping specialties, just as they have different regional cuisines. Look for furniture in North Carolina, antiques in New England, handicrafts in the South and clothing in major metropolitan areas.

## Books

The eastern half of the USA is well represented in the country's literary offerings: Read some of these books before you go.

*The Adventures of Tom Sawyer.*
Mark Twain. (1876)
This classic tale recounts the childhood exploits of mischief-maker Tom Sawyer, set on the Mississippi River in the town of Petersburg, MO.

*Devil in the White City.*
Erik Larson. (2003).
Through the lives of two men during Chicago's landmark World's Fair—a renowned architect and infamous serial killer—this tale sheds light on Chicago's rich architectural history.

*Lost Man's River.*
Peter Matthiessen. (1997).
The second novel in this author's trilogy paints a rich landscape of the unconventional characters residing in the Florida Everglades.

*A Prayer for the City.*
Buzz Bissinger. (1998).
The factual story of Democratic Philadelphia mayor Ed Rendell's efforts to save this east-coast city from bankruptcy in the early '90s.

*A Streetcar Named Desire.*
Tennessee Williams. (1947).
New Orleans' dazzling French Quarter provides the backdrop for this renowned play, which tells the story of a wilting Southern belle who comes to stay with her sister and dominating brother-in-law.

*To Kill A Mockingbird.*
Harper Lee (1960).
This story of a widowed father and his two children provides a personal window into the judicial system and racism in Alabama during the Great Depression.

## Films

In America, most stories are about to become a movie, or are inspired by one. Catch one of these flicks to get a glimpse of USA East cities on screen.

*Chicago.* (2002).
This feature film version of the classic Broadway musical weaves a sultry web of crime, stardom and sensationalism in 1920s Chicago.

*Nashville.* (1975).
An ensemble cast of characters intertwined in Nashville's music business take center stage in this song-laden film directed by Robert Altman.

*The Thing Called Love.* (1993).
This is no "Nashville," but it is still an engaging story of aspiring singers and songwriters in the Music City.

*New York Stories.* (1989).
Three favorite directors, including Woody Allen, Francis Ford Coppola and MartinScorsese, tell their own stories about the Big Apple.

*Fever Pitch.* (2005).
Nick Hornby may be a Brit, but this movie, based on his book by the same name is as American as it gets. set in Boston, is about an obsession with the Boston Red Sox, one of the teams involved in America's pasttime: baseball.

*When The Levees Broke.* (2006)
Directed by Spike Lee, this documentary provides a close-up on the lives of New Orleans natives in the tragic aftermath of Hurricane Katrina. The film was originally

created for Home Box Office (HBO) cable television.

*The Color Purple.* (1985).
Based on the 1982 novel by Alice Walker, Stephen Spielberg's powerful film chronicles the life of a poor African-American girl growing up in rural Georgia.

*RENT.* (2005).
This movie version of Jonathan Larson's Tony-award winning musical (loosely based on the opera La Boheme) tells the story of eight friends struggling with their relationships, drug addictions and AIDS in the tenement-filled streets of New York City's gritty Alphabet City in the late '80s.

*All The President's Men.* (1975).
This iconic Washington, DC-set film follows investigative journalists Bob Woodward and Carl Bernstein as they break open the Nixon administration Watergate scandal, thanks to the help of an anonymous source named Deep Throat.

*Walk The Line.* (2005).
This Memphis-set film follows the tumultuous path of rising country music star Johnny Cash as he records his chart-topping tunes alongside legends such as Elvis Presley.

# BASIC INFORMATION

## Business Hours

In general, most businesses operate Mon–Fri 9am–5pm. Banking institutions are normally open Mon–Thu 9am–4:30pm, Fri until 5pm or 6pm. Some banks, especially in larger cities, may be open on Saturday morning. Most retail stores and specialty shops are open Mon–Sat 10am–6pm. Malls and shopping centers are usually open Mon–Sat 10am–9pm, Sun 10am–6pm.

## Electricity

Voltage in the US is 120 Volts AC, 60 Hz. Foreign-made appliances may need AC adapters (available at specialty travel and electronics stores) and North American flat-blade plugs.

## Emergencies

In the US (and Canada) there is one simple phone number (9-1-1) that cane used to call for emeregncy assistant anywhere in the country. Even cell phone that are not active

are programmed to still make 9-1-1 calls. However, operators cannot determine a caller's location instantly, as he or she can when calling from a traditional telephone line.
Like 9-9-9 in the United Kingdom, 9-1-1 is reserved for true emergencies, such as when you need medical attention, are in a threatening situation such as a fire, or are witnessing suspicious behavior. In many cities, dialing 3-1-1 will connect you to police or city operators who can assist in non-emergency situations.
If you need more assistance than the local authorities can provide, turn to the Travelers Aid (www.travelersaid. org) organization. The group is.staffed by volunteers at many airports, but also can provide referrals to other groups. they are experienced in dealing with emergency situations.

## Liquor Laws

The minimum age for purchase and consumption of alcoholic beverages is 21; proof of age may be required. Local municipalities may limit and restrict sales and laws differ among states. In

*US Postage Stamps*

© iStockphoto/Bill Fagan

many states, liquor stores sell beer, wine and liquor. Beer and wine may also be purchased in package-goods stores and grocery stores. In some states you can buy beer in gas-station convenience stores. However, in other states, wine and liquor are sold at state-operated shops and beer sold by licensed distributors. Certain states, especially in New England and the Southeast, do not permit alcohol sales on Sundays, even in restaurants (exceptions usually apply in large metropolitan and tourist areas).

## Major Holidays

Banks and government offices are closed on the legal holidays shown on the table on this page.

## Mail/Post

First-class postage rates within the US are: 41¢/letter (up to 1oz); 26¢/postcard. To Europe: 90¢/letter (under 1oz); 90¢/postcard. Most post offices are open Mon–Fri 9am–5pm, some may open Sat 9am–noon. Companies such as Mail Boxes Etc., Mail Express USA and Pak Mail *(consult the Yellow Pages under Mailing Services)* also provide

mail service for everything from postcards to large packages. These companies also sell boxes and other packaging material. For photocopying, fax service, Internet and computer access, FedEx/Kinko's has locations throughout the US *(☎800-254-6567; www.kinkos.com)* or consult the Yellow Pages under Copying Services for a listing of local companies.

| New Year's Day | January 1 |
|---|---|
| Martin Luther King Jr.'s Birthday* | 3rd Monday in January |
| President's Day* | 3rd Monday in February |
| Memorial Day* | May 30 or last Monday in May |
| Independence Day | July 4 |
| Labor Day* | 1st Monday in September |
| Columbus Day* | 2nd Monday in October |
| Veterans Day* | November 10 or 11 |
| Thanksgiving Day | 4th Thursday in November |
| Christmas Day | December 25 |
| *Many retail stores and restaurants remain open on these days | |

## Money

The American **dollar** is divided into 100 **cents**. A **penny** = 1 cent; a **nickel** = 5 cents; a **dime** = 10 cents; a **quarter** = 25 cents. Most national banks and Thomas Cook *(locations throughout the US; ☎800-287-7362; www.thomascook.com)* **exchange foreign currency** in local offices and charge a fee for the service.

## Smoking

The **Americans for Nonsmokers' Rights** *(www.no-smoke.org )* estimates that 50 percent of Americans live somewhere regulated by some sort of smoking ban. Many major cities, including New York and Chicago restrict smoking in public places, such as sports arenas, restaurants and bars, as well as workplaces and within 15ft of entrances to such places. Most venues clearly post their smoking rules and regulations, so it should be easy to assure that you do not violate them. Most hotels offer non-smoking rooms, which you may request when you make your reservations.

## Taxes and Tipping

In the US, with the occasional exception of certain food products and gasoline, **sales tax** is not included in the quoted price and is added at the time of payment. Sales taxes vary by state and range from 3 percent to 7 percent (except for Alaska, Delaware, New Hampshire and Oregon which charge no sales tax). Sales tax may often be higher in major cities due to local taxes. In some states, the **restaurant tax** appearing on your bill when you dine out may be higher than the state tax; also, expect additional **hotel taxes** and surcharges.

## Telephones

For **long-distance** calls in the US and Canada, dial 1 + area code (3 digits) + number (7 digits). To place a **local call**, dial the 7-digit number without 1 or the area code (unless the local calling area includes several area codes). To place an **international call**, dial 011 + country code + area code + number (country and city codes are listed at the beginning of local phone books). To obtain help from an **operator**, dial 0 for local and 00 for long-distance. For **information** on a number within your area code, dial 411. For long-distance information, dial 1 + area code + 555-1212. To place a **collect call**, dial 0 + area or country code + number; at the operator's prompt, give your name. For all **emergencies**, dial **911**. Since most **hotels** add a surcharge for local and long-distance calls charged to the room, it is less expensive to use your calling card or cellular telephone. Pre-paid calling cards are available at kiosks and stores all over the country. These can be the most frugal way to place a call. Many require dialing an toll-free number of access; some hotels charge for these calls. Local calls from public telephones vary, but most often cost 35¢ (25¢ in New York City). **Public telephones** accept quarters, dimes and nickels. You may also use your calling card or credit card (recommended for long-distance calls to avoid the inconvenience of depositing large amounts of change). Instruc-

---

### ☺ Tipping ☺

In restaurants, it is customary to leave the server a gratuity, or tip, of 15–20 percent of the total bill (unless the menu specifies that gratuity is included). Taxi drivers are generally tipped 15 percent of the fare. In hotels, bellmen are tipped $1 per suitcase and housekeeping $1 per night. Hairdressers may be tipped at the client's discretion.

---

### ☺ Toll Free Calls ☺

Unless otherwise indicated, telephone numbers that start with the area codes **800**, **888**. **866** and **877** are toll-free within the US.

# CONVERSION TABLES

## Weights and Measures

|  |  US flag | UK flag | |
|---|---|---|---|
| **1 kilogram (kg)**<br>6.35 kilograms<br>0.45 kilograms<br>**1 metric ton (tn)** | **2.2 pounds (lb)**<br>14 pounds<br>16 ounces (oz)<br>**1.1 tons** | **2.2 pounds**<br>1 stone (st)<br>16 ounces<br>**1.1 tons** | *To convert kilograms to pounds, multiply by 2.2* |
| **1 litre (l)**<br>3.79 litres<br>4.55 litres | **2.11 pints (pt)**<br>1 gallon (gal)<br>1.20 gallon | **1.76 pints**<br>0.83 gallon<br>1 gallon | *To convert litres to gallons, multiply by 0.26 (US) or 0.22 (UK)* |
| **1 hectare (ha)**<br>**1 sq. kilometre (km²)** | **2.47 acres**<br>0.38 sq. miles (sq.mi.) | **2.47 acres**<br>0.38 sq. miles | *To convert hectares to acres, multiply by 2.4* |
| **1 centimetre (cm)**<br>**1 metre (m)** | **0.39 inches (in)**<br>3.28 feet (ft) or 39.37 inches<br>or 1.09 yards (yd) | **0.39 inches** | *To convert metres to feet; multiply by 3.28; for kilometres to miles, multiply by 0.6* |
| **1 kilometre (km)** | **0.62 miles (mi)** | **0.62 miles** | |

## Clothing

| Women | EU | US | UK |
|---|---|---|---|
| | 35 | 4 | 2½ |
| | 36 | 5 | 3½ |
| | 37 | 6 | 4½ |
| **Shoes** | 38 | 7 | 5½ |
| | 39 | 8 | 6½ |
| | 40 | 9 | 7½ |
| | 41 | 10 | 8½ |
| | 36 | 6 | 8 |
| | 38 | 8 | 10 |
| **Dresses** | 40 | 10 | 12 |
| **& suits** | 42 | 12 | 14 |
| | 44 | 14 | 16 |
| | 46 | 16 | 18 |
| | 36 | 06 | 30 |
| | 38 | 08 | 32 |
| **Blouses &** | 40 | 10 | 34 |
| **sweaters** | 42 | 12 | 36 |
| | 44 | 14 | 38 |
| | 46 | 16 | 40 |

| Men | EU | US | UK |
|---|---|---|---|
| | 40 | 7½ | 7 |
| | 41 | 8½ | 8 |
| | 42 | 9½ | 9 |
| **Shoes** | 43 | 10½ | 10 |
| | 44 | 11½ | 11 |
| | 45 | 12½ | 12 |
| | 46 | 13½ | 13 |
| | 46 | 36 | 36 |
| | 48 | 38 | 38 |
| **Suits** | 50 | 40 | 40 |
| | 52 | 42 | 42 |
| | 54 | 44 | 44 |
| | 56 | 46 | 48 |
| | 37 | 14½ | 14½ |
| | 38 | 15 | 15 |
| **Shirts** | 39 | 15½ | 15½ |
| | 40 | 15¾ | 15¾ |
| | 41 | 16 | 16 |
| | 42 | 16½ | 16½ |

Sizes often vary depending on the designer. These equivalents are given for guidance only.

## Speed

| KPH | 10 | 30 | 50 | 70 | 80 | 90 | 100 | 110 | 120 | 130 |
|---|---|---|---|---|---|---|---|---|---|---|
| MPH | 6 | 19 | 31 | 43 | 50 | 56 | 62 | 68 | 75 | 81 |

## Temperature

| Celsius (°C) | 0° | 5° | 10° | 15° | 20° | 25° | 30° | 40° | 60° | 80° | 100° |
|---|---|---|---|---|---|---|---|---|---|---|---|
| Fahrenheit (°F) | 32° | 41° | 50° | 59° | 68° | 77° | 86° | 104° | 140° | 176° | 212° |

*To convert Celsius into Fahrenheit, multiply °C by 9, divide by 5, and add 32.*
*To convert Fahrenheit into Celsius, subtract 32 from °F, multiply by 5, and divide by 9.*
NB: Conversion factors on this page are approximate.

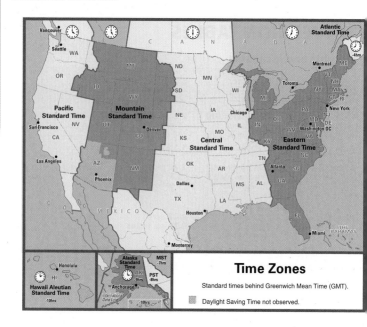

tions for using public telephones are listed on or near the phone.

## Time Zones

There are four different time zones in the contiguous United States: Eastern Standard Time (EST), Central Standard Time (CST), Mountain Standard Time (MST) and Pacific Standard Time (PST). Daylight Saving Time is observed in all states (except Arizona and Hawaii) from the second Sunday in March through the first Sunday in November. During this period, clocks are set forward one hour to Eastern Daylight Time (EDT), Central Daylight Time (CDT), Mountain Daylight Time (MDT) and Pacific Daylight Time (PDT). Eastern Standard Time is five hours behind Greenwich Mean Time (GMT), or Universal Time (UT).

# Little Red Riding Hood

**B**ut Little Red Riding Hood had her regional map with her, and so she did not fall into the trap. She did not take the path through the wood and she did not meet the big bad wolf. Instead, she chose the picturesque touring route straight to Grandmother's house, and arrived safely with her cake and her little pot of butter.

The End

With Michelin maps, go your own way.

**MICHELIN**
*A better way forward*

US Capitol, Washington, DC

PhotoDisc, Inc.

# INTRODUCTION TO USA EAST

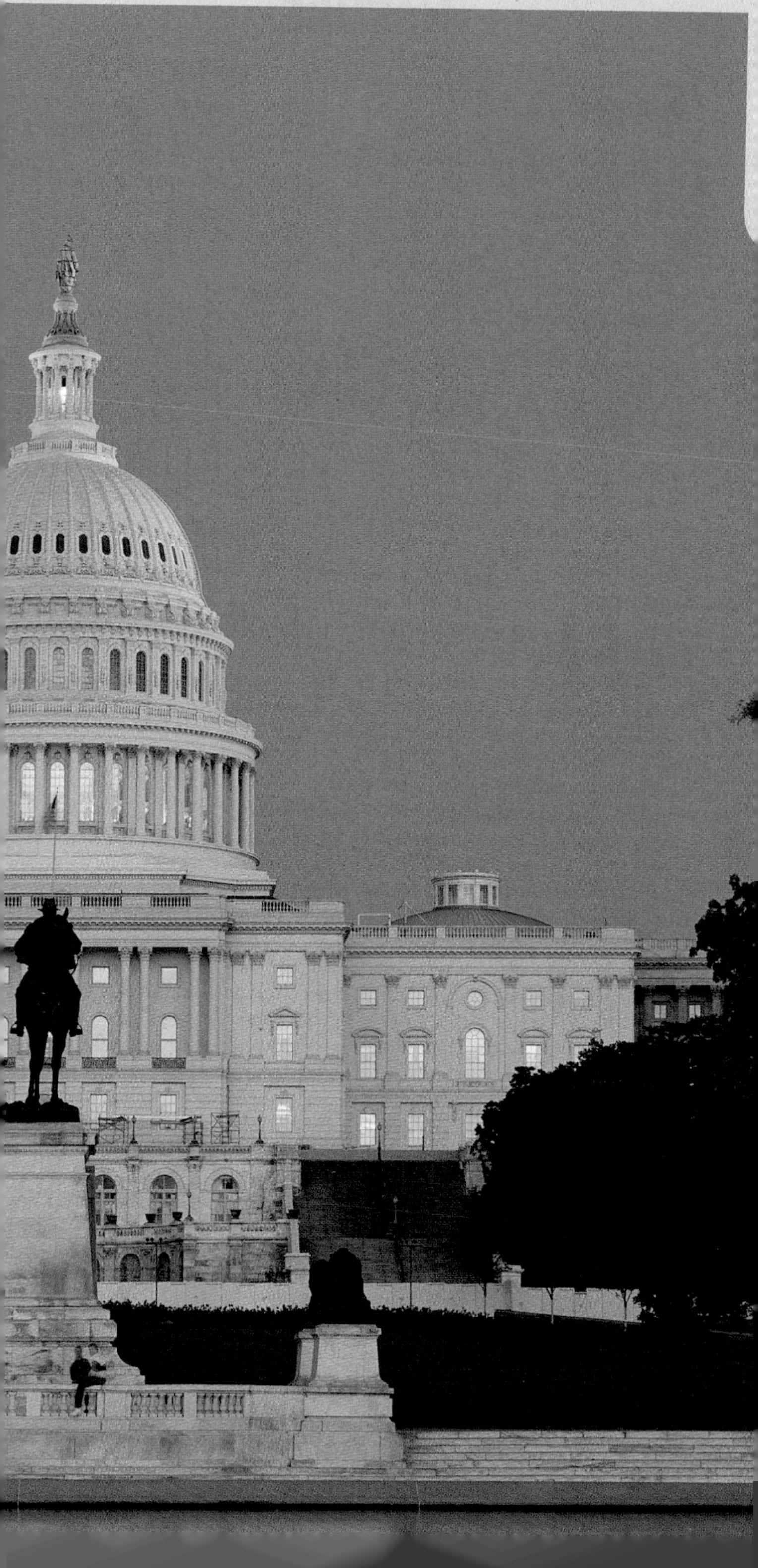

# NATURE

## Landscape

A sojourn in the eastern United States is a glimpse into the heart of what most travelers agree is on of the most diverse, overwhelming and contradictory nations on earth. This most populous part of the US offers visitors incomparable opportunities for scenic, recreational, historical and cultural excursions in an epic landscape of contrasts: rocky outcroppings on Maine's chilly shore and suffocating heat in the Mississippi delta, concrete canyons on Manhattan Island (New York City) and isolated "hollers" (small secluded valleys) in deepest Appalachia.

The sheer size of the country can be astonishing: the distance from New York City to Miami is 1,291mi; from New York City to Chicago is 831mi. Indeed, visitors seeking a glimpse of "how America lives" are often surprised at the distances ordinary citizens travel daily to work or school. For tourists, most of this travel occurs on the road. For better or worse, the US is a country best viewed by chartered tour bus or private automobile, along the nation's vast interstate highway system (45,000mi spanning the 48 contiguous states), which links every state, large metropolis and region.

The highways and byways of the eastern US lead through vistas of great beauty, both natural and man-made. A car trip through New England coasts past a rugged shoreline and bucolic farms. Farther south, the spires of New York City crown an elongated metropolis running southward to Washington, DC. Heading west, the urban centers of Chicago and St. Louis anchor a vast midwestern agricultural region rippling with 'amber waves of grain.' In Kentucky, thoroughbred horses graze on the "bluegrass," while in the Deep South, the broad Suwannee River joins a meandering network of streams winding their way through moss-draped live oak, cypress and palmetto trees to the sea.

In some respects the sheer size of the country and the American spirit of free enterprise has not always been kind to the land. Relentless commercialization plagues the landscape: farms have been replaced by mega-malls and parking lots; roads are lined with strips of shops, monotonous suburbs and the blinking neon signs of fast-food restaurants and gas stations.

Still, beneath the surface clutter lies a fascinating country with distinct regional differences, each offering unique environmental and ecological features. The eastern US has thousands of miles of coastline; a climate that ranges from bitter cold to tropical; an ancient, 1,500mi-long mountain range; five of the world's largest freshwater lakes and one of its longest rivers; and vegetation ranging from boreal forests to mangrove swamps. The observant traveler will find insights into the United States' immense variety with every new bend in the road, as the roots of the country's art, music, literature and history spring vividly to life.

## Geology

Scientists theorize that parts of the North American continent date back almost four billion years. The stable crust underlying the Canadian Shield, the continent's north central portion, was formed around 1.8 billion years ago; millions of years later, during the Paleozoic Era, this existing plate collided with other land masses to form the supercontinent of **Pangaea**. Geologic evidence indicates that the Appalachian Mountains resulted from folds in the earth's crust caused by repeated collisions during the formation of Pangaea. With a birth date of sometime between 435 million and 250 million years ago, these heavily forested, relatively low-lying eastern mountains (rising about 3,500ft above sea level) are the oldest mountains on the continent and among the oldest in the world.

Many of the eastern states' most pronounced geologic features, however

© iStockphoto/Matej Krajcovic

*Great Smoky Mountains National Park, North Carolina*

are the result of massive, slow-moving **glaciers** that began covering the continent during the Pleistocene Epoch about one million years ago and continued, with extraordinary effects on life forms, until approximately 10,000 years ago. The spectacular Great Lakes, thought to be 7,000 to 32,000 years old, owe their existence to these glaciers, as do countless other natural phenomena, ranging from the Finger Lakes of upstate New York to the thin soils of New England, the fossilized remains of ancient mastodons and saber-toothed tigers in coastal Florida, and the giant boulders strewn atop Lookout Mountain in Tennessee.

## REGIONAL LANDSCAPES

The eastern US rises out of the Atlantic and spans approximately half of North America in three distinct landforms: the Coastal Lowlands, the Appalachian Highlands and the Interior Plains.

### The Coastal Lowlands

The Coastal Lowlands are the above-sea-level portion of the great plain that forms the eastern perimeter of the North American continent. The submerged portion of this plain, known as the **Continental Shelf**, extends under shallow seawater off the Atlantic coastline for varying distances of up to 250mi.
In its northern stretches, much of the coastal plain was deeply depressed by

Pleistocene glaciers, leaving large portions of what is now New England with rocky cliffs instead of flat marshlands. In the northeast only a few low-lying regions—Long Island, Cape Cod and offshore islands such as Martha's Vineyard—are considered part of the Coastal Lowlands. Growing wider to the south, the lowlands embrace the famed Chesapeake Bay of Maryland, the aptly named Tidewater region of coastal Virginia, and wide swaths of the Carolinas. In Georgia, Alabama and Mississippi, the flat, gray-brown soil of the lowlands covers almost half of each state's land area and extends several hundred miles inland through the Mississippi delta, the vast alluvial plain that follows the Mississippi River until it empties into the Gulf of Mexico. The 59,988sq mi peninsula that forms Florida, the southernmost state, sits entirely on the coastal plain; its highest elevation lies only 345ft above sea level.

### The Appalachian Highlands

The Appalachians—a wide, complex system of mountains and uplands that runs almost the entire north-south length of North America—begin in northern Alabama and extend all the way to the Canadian border. An impenetrable natural boundary in the early years of US history, the Appalachians are now a popular tourist destination, as well as a haven for wildlife, Native American

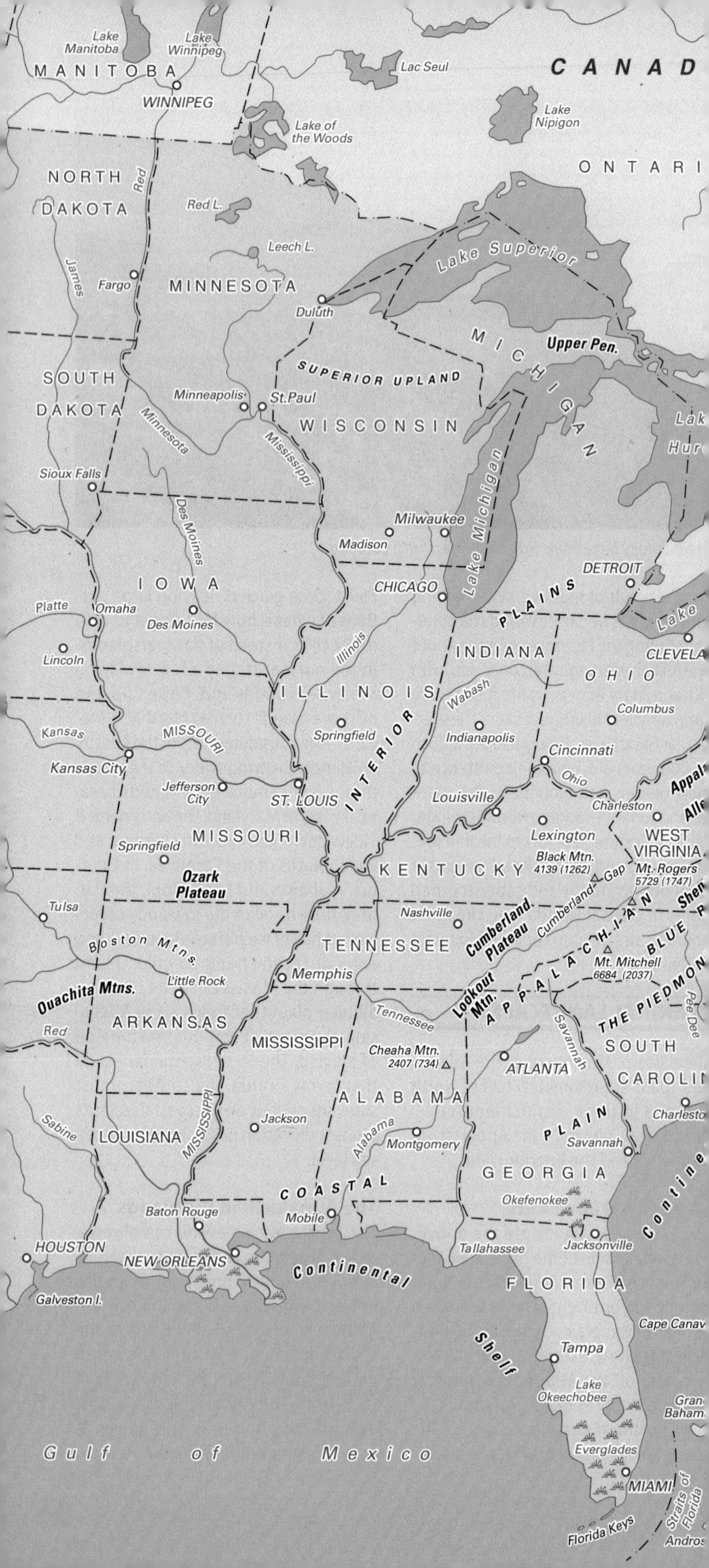

CANADA

MANITOBA

Lake Manitoba
Lake Winnipeg
WINNIPEG
Lac Seul

ONTARIO

Lake of the Woods
Lake Nipigon

NORTH DAKOTA
Red
Red L.
Leech L.
Fargo

MINNESOTA
Duluth

Lake Superior

MICHIGAN
Upper Pen.

James

SOUTH DAKOTA
Minneapolis
St. Paul
SUPERIOR UPLAND
WISCONSIN

Minnesota
Mississippi
Des Moines

Sioux Falls

Lake Michigan

Lake Huron

Milwaukee
Madison

IOWA
Platte
Omaha
Des Moines

CHICAGO

DETROIT

Lincoln

Illinois
INDIANA

OHIO
CLEVELAND
Lake

PLAINS

Kansas
MISSOURI
Springfield
ILLINOIS
INTERIOR
Wabash
Indianapolis

Columbus
Cincinnati

Kansas City
Jefferson City
ST. LOUIS
Louisville
Ohio
Charleston
Appal
Alle

Springfield
MISSOURI
KENTUCKY
Lexington
Black Mtn. 4139 (1262)
WEST VIRGINIA
Mt. Rogers 5729 (1747)
Cumberland Gap
Shen

Ozark Plateau
Nashville
Cumberland Plateau
Cumberland
APPALACHIAN
BLUE
THE PIEDMONT

Tulsa
Boston Mtns.
TENNESSEE
Mt. Mitchell 6684 (2037)
Pee Dee

Ouachita Mtns.
Little Rock
Memphis
Lookout Mtn.
Tennessee
Savannah

Red
ARKANSAS
MISSISSIPPI
Cheaha Mtn. 2407 (734)
SOUTH CAROLINA
Charleston

Sabine
LOUISIANA
Jackson
ALABAMA
Alabama
Montgomery
ATLANTA
PLAIN
GEORGIA
Savannah

COASTAL
Baton Rouge
Mobile
Okefenokee
Continental

HOUSTON
NEW ORLEANS
Continental
Tallahassee
Jacksonville
FLORIDA

Galveston I.
Shelf
Cape Canav

Tampa
Lake Okeechobee
Gran Baham

Gulf    of    Mexico
Everglades
MIAMI
Straits of Florida
Florida Keys
Andros

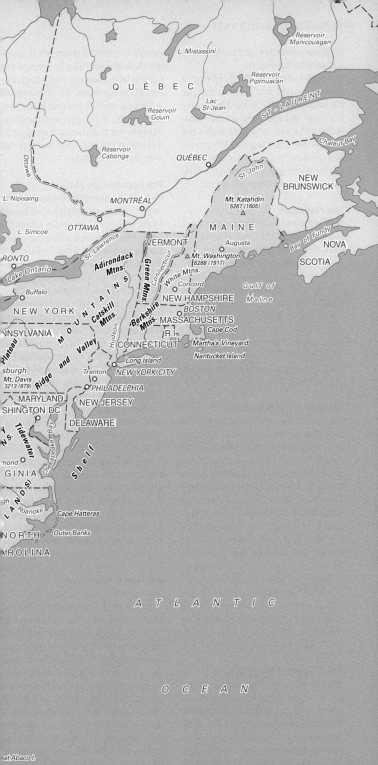

tribal communities, and professional and amateur naturalists.

The Appalachian Highlands consist of several regions and subregions: the Piedmont; the Blue Ridge Mountains; the Ridge and Valley region; the Appalachian Plateau, which includes the Cumberland and Allegheny Mountains; and the New England extension of the Appalachian system, including the Berkshire, Green, and White Mountains.

### The Piedmont

A rolling, transitional plateau, the Piedmont separates the Coastal Lowlands from the Blue Ridge Mountains, the easternmost range of the Appalachians. Stretching some 600mi from southern New York to Alabama, the Piedmont is characterized by fertile soil, numerous rivers, and long hills of modest height (300-1,800ft). Many of the Piedmont's waterways tumble abruptly into waterfalls along the "Fall Line," a rough demarcation where the Piedmont descends to the Coastal Plain.

### The Blue Ridge Mountains

Just north of the Piedmont begins the Blue Ridge, the first of several long mountain ranges that make up the Appalachian Mountain system. So named because its dense forests appear bluish from a distance, the Blue Ridge starts in northeast Georgia and includes Great Smoky Mountains National Park and the highest peak in the eastern US—**Mt. Mitchell**—which towers 6,684ft near Asheville, North Carolina. Although the southern Blue Ridge includes multiple rows of mountains, its northern end is easily identifiable as the long narrow ridge—traversed by the scenic Blue Ridge Parkway—forming the eastern border of Virginia's Shenandoah Valley.

### The Ridge and Valley Region

West of the Blue Ridge, the Ridge and Valley region divides the broad middle of the Appalachian Highlands into long northeast-southwest ridges and wide, fertile valleys. The Great Valley, a 20-80mi-wide limestone-based trench, runs almost the entire length of the Appalachians. It begins in the north as the valley of Vermont and extends through the Hudson River Valley to become the Cumberland, Lebanon, and Lehigh valleys of Pennsylvania, the Shenandoah in Virginia, the Valley of East Tennessee, Rome Valley in Georgia, and the Great Valley in north Alabama. The ridges in this region rise to 1,000ft and may run unbroken for 10-20mi.

### The Appalachian Plateau

Immediately west of the Ridge and Valley region is a high, ridged plateau ribboned by the Tennessee River and its tributaries and marked by several additional mountain ranges, notably the Cumberland Mountains of Tennessee and the Alleghenies, which run northeasterly through Virginia and Pennsylvania to southern New York State. On the southern edge of the plateau lies the famed **Cumberland Gap** (  see EAST TENNESSEE), a major east-west route for 18C pioneers. In its northern stretches, the Appalachian Plateau is a land of thin soil and rocky terrain and enormous deposits of bituminous coal. Known as Appalachia—once a synonym for impoverished, exploited mountain communities—these coal-mining regions of eastern Kentucky, southwest Virginia, West Virginia, and Pennsylvania fueled the early railroads and stoked the furnaces of steel mills, automobile manufacturers and other industries in cities such as Pittsburgh and Detroit for generations—often at great environmental and human cost. The region remains an important source of coal for industry and electricity generation.

### The New England Region

Although separated from the main expanse of the Appalachians by the Hudson River Valley, the numerous small mountain ranges of New England are generally considered part of the Appalachian Plateau. These landforms echo certain patterns of the southern Appalachians: the ridges and valleys around New England's Berkshire and **Green Mountains** look remarkably like the Ridge and Valley region of Virginia. The highest peak, **Mt. Washington** (6,288ft), in New Hampshire's White Mountains, strongly resembles the Blue Ridge range.

By contrast, the **Adirondacks** of northern New York State are younger, more rugged, and more closely related, geologically speaking, to the Superior Uplands of northern Wisconsin and Michigan.

## The Interior Plains

West of the Appalachian Mountain system lies the great heartland of America—the Interior Plains. The eastern portion of this enormous landlocked area is distinguished by three striking features: the Great Lakes, which connect the Interior Plains via the St. Lawrence River to the Atlantic Ocean; the upper Mississippi River system, which provides a transportation link, via the Chicago and the Illinois rivers, from the Great Lakes to the Gulf of Mexico; and an abundance of rich, dark soil, ideal for growing corn and grain and raising cattle.

## The Great Lakes

Taken together, the five Great Lakes have a combined area of 94,510sq mi and are the largest group of freshwater lakes in the world. In order of size, **Lake Superior** is largest, at some 32,000sq mi; next are **Lake Huron** and **Lake Michigan**, each around 23,000sq mi; then **Lake Erie**, markedly shallower than the others; and the smallest, **Lake Ontario**, about as large as the state of New Jersey.

Spanning the border between the US and the Canadian provinces of Ontario and Quebec, these five giant lakes form a vast inland water system that affects not only climate, flora and fauna, but human activity as well. Along with recreational and scenic benefits, the Great Lakes and their eastern outlet, the **St. Lawrence River**, have long served as a vital trade route for the region.

## The Mississippi River System

Nicknamed "the Big Muddy," the slow-moving Mississippi River is a mile wide in some places, usually looks opaque and murky brown, and is navigable by barge for almost 1,200mi—virtually the entire north-south length of the central US, from Minneapolis south to the Gulf of Mexico. The Mississippi and its tributaries, the Illinois, Wabash and Ohio rivers, drain the eastern portion of the Interior Plains and are largely responsible for the

rich alluvial soils that support the farm belts of Wisconsin, Indiana and Illinois.

## Climate

Situated between 25 and 50 degrees latitude, the eastern US is divided between the **humid subtropical** and **humid continental** climate zones. Although great differences exist between northern and southern states in terms of winter temperatures, length of summers and types of precipitation, the terrain east of the Rockies is subject to high humidity and summer temperatures of at least 75°F; the coastal plain as far north as New York City, frequently suffers temperatures well into the 90s. Southern states—Louisiana, Mississippi, Alabama, Georgia, Florida, and North and South Carolina—are legendary for oppressively hot and humid summers, which while ideal for mosquitoes, can cause heat stroke in the unwary. Only along the Great Lakes, in the Appalachians, and in New England are summer temperatures comfortable without air-conditioning. The southern half of the eastern US and the East Coast generally get between 40 and 80 inches of precipitation per year, while the drier northern portion receives between 20 and 40 inches.

In much of **New England**, winter temperatures routinely hover in the low to mid-teens (10-20°F) and snow may blanket the ground for weeks, making downhill skiing a popular pastime in the mountains of upstate New York, New Hampshire and Vermont. Although the Great Lakes temper the climate in the Midwest, Chicago is famous for its cold, windy winters, and the inland farming regions endure much snow.

In contrast, from the **Appalachian Plateau** southward to the Piedmont, winter temperatures often dip below freezing at night but rise to 35-40°F during the day. While the mountain peaks may be dusted with snow, the valleys get snow only intermittently. In the **Piedmont**, where snow is rare, freezing rain is a winter hazard.

Along the **Coastal Lowlands**, winters are rainy and mild (often 50-60°F), ena-

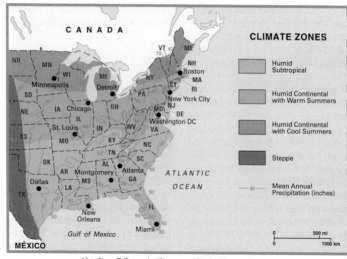

After Glenn T. Trewartha "Elements of Physical Geography," 1957.

bling farmers to grow abundant winter crops of vegetables. Off the southern tip of Florida, Key West ranks as the nation's hottest city with an average year-round temperature of 77.4°F.

The eastern states are also subject to violent storms. Intense tropical cyclones called **hurricanes** (see WHAT TO SEE AND DO, Nature and Safety), with winds ranging from 74 to 200mph, can pound the Gulf and Atlantic coasts between June and October. Powerful "**north-easters**" roar off the North Atlantic into New England in winter, dropping up to 10 inches of snow. And summer thunderstorms can spawn the vicious winds of funnel-shaped **tornadoes** that spiral at speeds of up to 300 mph—most commonly through the central and southern plains. The Mississippi River Valley, for example, endures more tornadoes than any other region on earth.

## Flora and Fauna

The eastern US enjoys a great diversity of vegetation and wildlife, as might be expected in so large a region. In fact, the Southern Appalachians are generally considered to hold greater biological diversity than any other region of the world, with the possible exception of certain tropical rain forests. On one three-hour Appalachian hike from the

lower to the uppermost elevations observant visitors will note that 98 per cent of the vegetation changes from bottom to top, representing nearly every kind of habitat common in eastern North America.

## FLORA

A small sliver of **boreal forest**—the northernmost, highest-altitude forest type on the continent—runs down the spine of the Appalachians from Canada to Georgia. Consisting primarily of tall conifers—pine, hemlock, spruce and fir—the dense, moist boreal forest also accommodates an undercover of flowering **rhododendrons**, wildflowers such as trilliums, and forest-floor mosses mushrooms and lichens.

Hiking at slightly lower elevations visitors will likely encounter a band of **transitional forest**, a combination of conifers (hemlocks, firs) and regionally distinct species of deciduous trees: yellow birch (Betula alleghaniensis) and sugar maple (Acer saccharum) in New England, or American basswood (Tilia americana) and quaking aspen (Populus tremuloides) along the Great Lakes. Speckled with patches of sunlight, the transitional-forest floor supports a lively undergrowth of ferns, smaller trees and shrubs. In broad outline, the transitional forest extends westward from Main

© iStockphoto/Greg Nicholas

*Moose and her Calf*

to Minnesota, surrounding the Great Lakes and covering much of New York and Pennsylvania. A narrow band runs southward along the Appalachians.

By far the largest proportion of existing forests in the eastern US, however, are of the **mixed deciduous** type: broadleaf hardwoods such as yellow poplar (*Liriodendron tulipifera*), sweetgum (*Liquidambar styraciflua*), and numerous species of oak and hickory mixed with evergreens, primarily pines (eastern white, loblolly, pitch, shortleaf, Virginia), magnolias, and smaller trees such as the American holly *(Ilex opaca)*. Interspersed with cleared fields and natural meadows, this variegated habitat extends south and west through the heartland, stretching from Massachusetts to Ohio, Indiana, Illinois, Wisconsin, and the eastern portions of Iowa, Missouri and Minnesota. In the Ozark Highlands of Arkansas, the distinctive **oak-hickory forest** represents the westernmost manifestation of deciduous forests in the US.

At higher elevations, especially in New England and the Appalachians, these forests attract millions of visitors every fall during "**leaf season**," when the hardwoods' leaves change from green to brilliant red, yellow, orange and gold.

The **Southern pinelands** describes the varied landscapes of the Piedmont and coastal plain. Extending for some ,000sq mi from New Jersey's Pine Barrens to Florida and westward along the Gulf of Mexico to Louisiana, the pinelands cover most of the Deep South. In northern areas, pines (longleaf, loblolly, shortleaf, slash, sand) commingle with deciduous trees; close to the coast, pinelands include live oaks draped with Spanish moss, hardwood hammocks, cypress swamps, maritime forests, bogs and bayous.

The Florida peninsula's dominant vegetation type is essentially **subtropical forest**, in a temperate zone. Boasting several hundred species of palm trees (only 15 of which are native), this vacation paradise encompasses not only beaches, but also slash-pine forests with saw-palmetto floors, air plants (or epiphytes—such as Spanish moss), sedge prairies and glades, and mangroves—the only trees known to survive in saltwater.

## FAUNA

Were it not for human intervention, the wonderfully rich and diverse environment of the eastern US would support an extraordinary wildlife population. 200 years ago, the land was well-stocked with large game (bear, moose, deer, mountain lion); the skies full of songbirds and soaring raptors (eagles, falcons, hawks); the waters full of beaver, otter, brown and speckled trout;

and the meadows sheltered myriad smaller animals such as foxes, wolves, bobcats, raccoons, opossums, rabbits and shrews.

However in 21C America, habitat destruction and an increasingly intrusive human presence, have pushed larger animals into ever-smaller, more isolated high-country regions. Only a few large mammals—notably, black bears (Ursus americanus) and white-tailed deer (Odocoileus virginianus)—have adapted to human co-habitation. Meanwhile, the reduction of natural predators has boosted stocks of grazing animals; deer bounding along roadsides are a common hazard to rural drivers. In state and national forests, park rangers repeatedly warn hikers to protect their foodstuffs and refrain from feeding the bears.

Orchestrated breeding and restoration efforts have reestablished viable populations of bald eagles (Haliaeetus leucocephalus), golden eagles (Aquila chrysaetos) and peregrine falcons (Falco peregrinus); the banning of chemical substances such as DDT has helped improve songbird and fish populations; and coastal areas strictly prohibit interference with endangered sea turtles' nests or human interaction with wild dolphins. On the other hand, an attempt by federal wildlife experts to reintroduce the gray wolf (Canis lupus) to its original

eastern habitats has met with opposition from farmers and hunters.

In populated areas, casual visitors are unlikely to glimpse any but the most common birds and small mammals— blue jays, robins, mourning doves, rabbits, chipmunks and squirrels. For the more watchful, sightings of hummingbirds, pileated woodpeckers (Dryocopus pileatus), red-tailed hawks (Buteo jamaicensis) and raccoons (Procyon lotor) are quite possible. The coast and mountainous areas offer variety and accessibility for viewing greater numbers of wildlife, especially in protected areas such as Great Smoky Mountains National Park and designated national forest preserves. Florida's 1.5 million-acre Everglades National Park, supports more than 350 species of birds, both year-round and migratory, and 600 species of fish, alligators, snakes, mammals and sea turtles. Ranging from the large black and easily recognized anhinga (Anhinga anhinga) to little blue herons (Egretta caerulea), elusive American bitterns (Botaurus lentiginosus), and endangered wood storks (Mycteria americana), the Everglades' winged wildlife draws bird-watchers from around the globe. In addition to birds, the world's last remaining Florida panthers (Felis concolor coryi) prowl the Everglades, and the endangered American crocodile (Crocodylus acutus) thrives here—as does its cousin the American alligator (Alligator mississippiensis), now plentiful in swamps throughout the South.

Like native species in many highly developed areas of the world, the indigenous flora and fauna of the eastern US fight a constant battle against not only human encroachment, but importation of nonindigenous species. For example, the glorious American chestnut tree (Castanea dentata) that once reigned throughout the Appalachians were decimated by a blight caused by an accidentally imported fungus first identified in New York City in 1904. By 1945 the species was all but wiped out, though sprouts continue to grow from old roots. Kudzu (Pueraria thunbergiana), a hardy vine introduced from Japan in 1911 to help control erosion, now twines its way over millions of acres in the Southeast.

Bald Eagle

© iStockphoto/Darcy Stuart

uffocating native pines and shrubs in ...s greedy grip. In the animal kingdom, mports like the European wild boar (Sus crofa) have had a profound impact on native plants and animals. Rooting voraciously, boars damage tree roots and seedlings and compete with black bears and other native animals for food.

# HISTORY

## The First Americans

he first people to inhabit what is now he Eastern US, were Asians who arrived round 28,000 years ago. Traveling over he Bering Strait on the land bridge, nen connecting Siberia with Alaska, hey made their way south, eventually eaching the Americas. Evolving into umerous linguistically and culturally eparate tribes, these early inhabitants re thought to have numbered between .5 and 2 million in the continental US y the time Christopher Columbus discovered the New World.

roups such as the **Adena** and **Hopewell** cultures established sizable opulations in the Ohio Valley as early s 1000 BC. Known collectively as the **mound builders**, these advanced cultures were characterized by the conical r dome-shaped burial mounds they uilt—some even in the form of totemic nimals. The rich soil of southeastern verbeds fostered the master farmers nd skilled artisans of the **Mississippian** ulture, who settled into villages where hey raised corn, beans, squash and ther crops. Remains of a number of Mississippian sites (AD 800-1600)—which eature huge temple mounds—are scatered throughout the east, from Ocmulee and Etowah in Georgia to Cahokia n Illinois. Although the North American tribes never achieved the degree of ivilization reached by their Mayan and ztec predecessors, artifacts unearthed t their sites suggest complex societies, vith well-developed economic, governmental and religious systems.

t the time of European settlement f the US, various groups of **Eastern Woodland Indians** occupied the vast and stretching the length of the Atlantic eaboard south to the Gulf of Mexico, vest across the Appalachians to the Mississippi Valley and north to the Great Lakes. These hunter-gatherers were also fishermen and farmers who found food as well as material for shelter, tools and fuel in the dense forests that blanketed the east. Within two basic language groups—the Algonquian speakers who lived in communal wooden longhouses, and the Iroquoian speakers who lived in wigwams (conical huts overlaid with bark or animal hides)—the Woodland Indians comprised many smaller tribes. Settlers in the northeast met such tribes as the Massachuset, Pequot, Mohawk, Oneida and Delaware; in the Midwest and Great Lakes regions, Europeans encountered the Shawnee, Illinois, Sauk, Ottawa, Fox and Potawatomi. The Powhatan, Secotan, Cherokee, Chickasaw, Creek, Seminole and Natchez tribes, among others, held sway in the south. Unfortunately, the Europeans brought with them a host of diseases—smallpox, influenza, measles—that took their toll

St. Augustine Hisorical Society

Osceola (c.1837),
Portrait by John Rogers Vinton

on Native American populations, who had no immunity to such previously unknown plagues.

# Colonial Period

Some historians believe the Vikings explored North America as early as AD 1000, but the evidence is murky. What is known is that beginning in 1492, when Columbus discovered the Caribbean, numerous Spanish, Dutch, French and English adventurers explored the Americas, laying claim to various areas. The Spanish, then the dominant European military power, concentrated on Florida, the Gulf Coast and California, while the English emphasized the eastern seaboard and the French gained a foothold in Canada and along the Mississippi River after unsuccessful attempts at colonization on the southeast coast. In 1565, the Spanish established the first permanent US settlement at St. Augustine, Florida, and soon after established a garrison across the state at Pensacola. The English followed 22 years later with an unsuccessful attempt at **Roanoke Colony** (see THE OUTER BANKS) in present-day North Carolina. Undaunted, the English founded **Jamestown** a bit farther north in 1607. By 1624 Jamestown was a thriving settlement, with flourishing crops of a plant called tobacco and even a fledgling legislature. Meanwhile, some 600mi up the coast, an English religious sect called the Puritans had established the **Plymouth Colony** in 1620. Others followed in 1629, settling the area around present-day Boston. The 1660 restoration of Charles II to the English throne launched a frenzy of new colonization. The colony of **Connecticut** was chartered in 1662, Carolina in 1663, and New York—colonized by the Dutch as New Amsterdam in 1624—was claimed for England in 1664. **Pennsylvania** and **Delaware** followed. The 13th and last colony, **Georgia**, was chartered in 1732 as a refuge for English debtors.

## LIFE IN THE COLONIES

From 1700 to 1775, the colonial population increased almost tenfold, aided by massive immigration of German, Dutch Irish and Scotch-Irish farmers and laborers seeking a better life. In 1700 approximately 250,000 colonists inhabited the mainland; by 1800 that number had reached 5.3 million.

Vibrant cities emerged, among them New York, Boston, Philadelphia and Charleston. Although not as populous as their European counterparts (mid-18C Philadelphia, for example, had a population around 25,000, compared to more than a half-million in London), these burgeoning cities were not only lively centers of business and trade, but also seats of learning and culture.

At the beginning of the 18C, the colonists looked to England to set the tone in fashion, architecture, religion and the arts; but by mid-century, cultural patterns were assuming a distinctly "American" flavor. Before the Revolutionary War, seven colleges were founded, including the northern Ivy League institutions of Harvard, Yale, Princeton and Brown, and William and Mary in Virginia. Most notably, an independent spirit was beginning to blossom among the colonists—many of whom were beginning to chafe under English rule.

## REVOLUTIONARY WAR

Tensions between the colonists and the Crown escalated during the 1760s. Britain's decision to maintain troops in the colonies after the end of the French and Indian War (1754-63) infuriated many settlers. A further alienating factor was the British Parliament's decision in 1763 to forbid settlement beyond the Appalachian Mountains. The final straw was the passage of a series of taxes—including a tax on tea—levied on the colonists, who lacked representation in Parliament. In late 1773 a group of Patriots boarded cargo ships in Boston Harbor and tossed cases of tea overboard. The incident today known as the **Boston Tea Party** prompted the English to clamp down even harder on the rebellious citizens. Sixteen months later, in April 1775, colonists clashed with English soldiers at Lexington, Massachusetts in the first battle of the American Revolution.

During the first months of the war, the English held the advantage, winning most of the battles and laying siege to Boston. Still, the colonists persevered, meeting in Philadelphia in July 1776 to adopt the **Declaration of Independence**, formally severing ties with England. Written by **Thomas Jefferson**, the declaration relied on the Enlightenment-era idea of government as a social contract.

In December of 1776, the war's tide turned when Gen. George Washington repelled British general William Howe at Trenton, New Jersey. Although Howe returned to take Philadelphia the following summer, Washington's triumph galvanized the colonists. Their cause was further bolstered in 1778 when Britain's old enemy, France, came to the aid of the Colonial army.

In 1781 Revolutionary and French forces managed to trap Gen. Charles Cornwallis on the narrow peninsula at Yorktown, Virginia. Cut off from the British navy, Cornwallis surrendered. The 1783 **Peace of Paris** granted the young nation independence from Britain and established its western boundary at the Mississippi River. Only parts of Florida remained under Spanish rule.

## THE NEW NATION

In 1781 colonial delegates had met in Philadelphia, adopting the formal name of the **United States of America** and issuing the **Articles of Confederation**. That document set up a Congress charged with carrying out the country's foreign relations. But after the war, it soon became clear the Articles were much too weak to govern the infant country. The confederation had no control over the states, no taxing power and no ability to stabilize currency. These limitations led to the Constitutional Convention of 1787 in Philadelphia, where the **US Constitution** was drafted, establishing a centralized, democratic government with executive, legislative and judicial branches. In gratitude for his war service, convention delegates elected **George Washington** 1732-99) as the first president of the young Republic.

# Federal Period (1800-1850)

From 1800 to 1850 three major themes dominated the American experience: westward expansion, the coming of industry and massive strides in transportation. By 1800 the new union boasted 16 states; Vermont was added in 1791, Kentucky in 1792 and Tennessee in 1796. The republic's 5.2 million citizens were almost evenly divided between North and South, most inhabiting a narrow coastal strip stretching along the Atlantic from New England to the Florida border.

As the population increased in the East, these coastal residents came to view the West as the land of opportunity. In 1775 frontiersman **Daniel Boone** (*see WESTERN KENTUCKY*) blazed a trail through the Cumberland Gap, a natural passage in the Appalachians leading from Virginia into Kentucky and the fertile lands beyond. Twenty years later, the **Wilderness Road**, which traced Boone's trail, was opened to covered-wagon and stagecoach traffic. Between 1775 and 1810, more than 300,000 Americans crossed the Cumberland Gap to begin new lives in the West.

Westward expansion got a further boost in 1803 with the **Louisiana Purchase**, orchestrated by President Thomas Jefferson. In this $15 million deal that doubled the country's size, Congress purchased the French-owned territory—bounded by the Mississippi River, the Rocky Mountains, Canada and the Gulf of Mexico—from Napoleon. Jefferson's sponsorship of the scientific expedition of **Meriwether Lewis** and **William Clark** a year later underscored the importance of the historic purchase.

However, as the settlers moved west they usurped more and more of the Indians' land. This led to mounting tensions and, eventually, to armed conflict. Looking for a permanent solution to the "Indian problem," President **Andrew Jackson** engineered the **Indian Removal Act** in 1830. By the terms of this law, eastern tribes were to be relocated to a designated area west of the Mississippi River; they would be paid for their land

*Abraham Lincoln, Lincoln Memorial, Washington, D.C.*

in the east and would hold perpetual title to their new territories in the west. The Cherokees were the last group to leave on the infamous "**Trail of Tears**," ushered westward on a cruel trek by US soldiers.

## TRADE AND TRANSPORTATION

The nation's economy expanded along with its geographical horizons. **Eli Whitney**'s 1793 invention of the **cotton gin** pushed the South's production and export of cotton from 10,000 pounds to 8 million pounds annually between 1790 and 1800. As the nation pushed westward, the Midwest became the leading producer of pork, corn and wheat.

This outburst of industrial activity was facilitated by enormous strides in transportation. Begun in 1811, the first **National Road** covered the distance from Cumberland, Maryland, to Vandalia, Illinois, by 1838. The success of the first commercial **steamboat**, launched by Robert Fulton and Robert Livingston in 1807, opened the way for increased trade on the Mississippi River and spurred the growth of great port cities such as New Orleans. Back east, the 363mi-long **Erie Canal**, completed in 1825, made New York State the conduit of trade and migration between the eastern seaboard and the Great Lakes. The first steam-powered **railroad** began operations in England the same year the

Erie Canal opened. By 1854 more tha 17,000mi of rail lines crisscrossed th eastern US, and an additional 12,000n of track were under construction. Thes advances drastically reduced the tim and money needed to move raw mate rials to factories and finished good to market.

By 1850 Americans could justifiably fe smug about their country. The popula tion stood at an all-time high of 23 mi lion, the country had expanded to 3 states (California became the 31st o September 9, 1850), industrial produc tion was at its peak, and literacy rate were higher than those in Europe. Bu looming over all this optimism wa the dark cloud of slavery. Of all th issues dividing North and South, th institution of slavery provoked th strongest emotion.

## THE SLAVERY QUESTION

Slaves were first imported by the Bri ish from Africa around 1619, primarily t work plantations in the South (Norther ers used slaves as well, although to a fa lesser extent). As the South's fertile sc and mild climate fostered its lucrativ plantation economy, the practice of slav ery steadily increased. The Constitutio banned the importation of slaves afte 1808, but illegal importation continue until the Civil War. By 1860 there wer four million slaves in the US, the majorit of them in the South.

Numerous moves to ban this "peculia institution" were introduced in both th Congress and state legislatures as earl as the 1780s, supported by those wh felt slavery was tyrannical and immora But after cotton gained ascendancy, tha support withered. Southern delegate knew that abolishing slavery woul mean the end of their economic main stay and affluent lifestyle.

With westward expansion the contro versy grew increasingly rancorous an an active **Abolitionist movemen** emerged. The Abolitionists, who wante slavery abolished by law, operated a **Underground Railroad** system b means of which they helped slaves fle the South. In Congress, Northerner argued that slavery should be banne

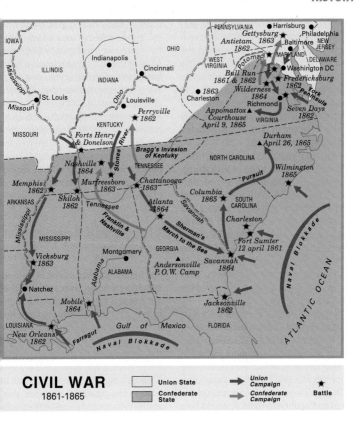

**CIVIL WAR**
1861-1865

| | | |
|---|---|---|
| ☐ Union State | → **Union Campaign** | |
| ▨ Confederate State | → **Confederate Campaign** | ★ Battle |

from the western territories, and a series of compromises narrowly averted armed conflict. John Brown's failed raid on the US arsenal at Harpers Ferry, Virginia, in 1859 crystallized Southern paranoia. With the election of Republican president Abraham Lincoln in 1860, conflict seemed inevitable.

## Civil War

On the eve of the Civil War, the North and South, roughly equal in population, were two separate and radically different societies. The North was dominated by trade and manufacturing, the South by agriculture. Since large-scale cultivation of crops such as cotton, rice, indigo and tobacco depended on slavery for its huge profits, most Southerners supported the practice, while most Northerners abhorred it. Northerners also favored a strong, centralized gov-

ernment; Southerners preferred leaving governing to the states.

No longer able to compromise by 1861, the separate regions became separate nations. South Carolina was the first state to secede from the Union in December 1860. In February 1861, the **Confederate States of America** was formed, with **Jefferson Davis** as its president and Montgomery, Alabama, as its capital (the Confederate capital was moved four months later to Richmond, Virginia). By March six more southern states had seceded. On April 12, the Civil War began when Confederates fired on Fort Sumter, in Charleston, South Carolina's harbor.

In the beginning, the South won decisive victories at **Bull Run**, Virginia—in both 1861 and 1862—and in the **York Peninsula Campaign** of 1862. Pushing north into Maryland that September, Confederate general Robert E. Lee's forces held fast at the **Battle of Antietam**—with

23,000 men killed or wounded, it was the bloodiest one-day battle in American history. Although Lee retreated, the fact that his army survived the battle emboldened him to push farther north. But when Confederate forces under Lee made their way toward the Pennsylvania capital of Harrisburg in July 1863, they were trounced by Gen. George Meade's troops at **Gettysburg**.

That same year, on the western front, Ulysses S. Grant's siege of **Vicksburg**, Mississippi, ended with a Confederate capitulation. With the Mississippi River now firmly in Union control and a blockade against southern Atlantic ports, the South began to suffer from a lack of food and supplies. In 1864 Union general William Tecumseh Sherman's conquest and burning of Atlanta on his "March to the Sea" campaign sealed the secessionists' fate.

In April 1865 Lee surrendered at **Appomattox Courthouse**, Virginia. An estimated 600,000 men had been killed and several thousand more injured in what remains the highest casualty rate for any war ever fought by Americans. The war's legacy left the South in physical and economic ruins. It would be a long time before relations between North and South were cordial again.

### RECONSTRUCTION

To add insult to injury, certain political voices emerged urging strict punishment of the South. Although Lincoln's plan was to welcome the former Confederacy back into the Union without imposing harsh penalties, his plan died along with him when he was assassinated by actor John Wilkes Booth five days after Lee's surrender.

Instead, the vindictive voices of the Radical Republicans won out. The 1867 **Reconstruction Act** placed the southern states under martial law. Federal troops patrolled the streets and the Radical Republicans ran corrupt state legislatures. By the time Reconstruction was over in 1876, white Southerners were even more alienated than they had been at war's end.

The situation was not a whole lot better for blacks. Lacking education or skilled training, many had no jobs: those who did, often worked as tenant farmers for the masters who had once owned them. Although Lincoln's **Emancipation Proclamation** had technically granted slaves in the Confederate states their freedom in 1863, the passage of the 13th and 14th Amendments furthered their cause by banning slavery (1865) and guaranteeing civil rights (1868). All men—not women—were granted the right to vote per the 15th Amendment (1870), regardless of "race, color or previous condition of servitude."

## The Gilded Age: 1870-1912

The Gilded Age was a time of unprecedented invention and capitalism that did not see its equal until the high tech revolution of a century later. Not unlike the unfettered individualism of the 1990s, the Gilded Age glorified the entrepreneur and the worship of materialism. It was during this era that America's captains of industry came to power—the great railroad barons, steel and oil tycoons and shipping magnate (Cornelius "Commodore" Vanderbilt, John D. Rockefeller, Andrew Carnegie). Achieving enormous wealth (there was as yet no federal income tax), they built lavish homes in places like Newport, Rhode Island, New York City and Palm Beach, Florida.

In 1870 the US population stood at 38.6 million, up 15 million from 20 years earlier. Many of the additions were immigrants, lured to eastern US cities by the prospect of industrial jobs. As their ranks swelled, so did the cities. By 1900 almost 40 percent of the country's population were urban dwellers.

After the Civil War, industrialization spread rapidly and oil, coal, copper and steel production soared. While this upsurge began in the Northeast, within a decade it was spreading westward. After 1880, the discovery of iron in northern Minnesota and Alabama expanded the steel industry westward into Minneapolis and south to Birmingham. Meatpacking became a major US enterprise after 1875, centered in Chicago and St. Louis.

*Ellis Island Immigration Museum, New York City*

Flour milling, brewing and the manufacture of farm equipment also found bases in the Heartland.

Factories operating at full speed spelled employment for the thousands of immigrants an others streaming into the cities east of the Mississippi River. But vast discrepancies in income and lifestyle separated the ultra-rich industry titans from those who toiled for them. Cities became crowded and dirty as workers poured in and factories filled the air with smoke and noxious fumes. Low factory wages meant workers could not afford decent housing, and slums appeared. Finally, these inequalities erupted into full-blown labor hostilities as workers fought for their rights against an unsympathetic political establishment.

Things began to change with the dawn of the **Progressive Era** (1890 to 1920). Prompted in part by the writings of authors such as Upton Sinclair (*The Jungle*, 1906), who brought the horrors of Chicago's meatpacking industry to the fore, several states passed laws regulating wages, hours and workplace safety.

In 1901 **Theodore Roosevelt** became president, following the assassination of President William McKinley. Although born to wealth, Roosevelt believed the monopolistic practices of industrial tycoons were counter to the public good. After breaking up a railway monopoly in 1903, he established the Department of Commerce and Labor as a federal regulatory agency to oversee business and industry. Concerned that industrialization was squandering the nation's natural resources, he set aside large tracts of land as forest preserves and national parks. He also pushed through legislation regulating the drug and meatpacking industries.

The end of the Gilded Age was marked by the passage of the **16th Amendment** in 1913. This amendment, which established a federal income tax, put an end to the era's outrageous excess.

## World War I and The Roaring Twenties

The sinking of another luxury liner a few years later precipitated US entry into World War I, which had been raging in Europe since 1914. When German U-boats attacked the British passenger ship *Lusitania*, killing 124 Americans, German-American relations deteriorated, leading to President **Woodrow Wilson**'s decision to enter the war in 1917. Fighting against the **Central Powers** (Germany, Austria, Turkey) on behalf of the **Allies** (Britain, France, Belgium, Russia, Italy) were 4.7 million Americans. In March 1918 the first Americans served in battle in France. Six months later, the war was over, 116,000 American lives had been lost, and the US teetered on the brink of the greatest era of prosperity in its history.

By 1920 the country's transformation from an agricultural economy into an industrial power was complete. The population stood at over 100 million and for the first time ever, more people lived in cities of 2,500 or more than in rural areas. Efficiencies of production and economies of scale had made items formerly reserved for the elite—such as automobiles, refrigerators and telephones—affordable for the masses.

New inventions proliferated—radio, motion pictures, the airplane—bringing the outside world to formerly isolated areas. The first commercial passenger flights began in 1925 when Congress authorized the US Post Office to contract private carriers for airmail routes. By mid-decade, unemployment stood at 2 percent, and the average American enjoyed a higher quality of life than ever before.

The decade soon earned the name "Roaring Twenties," not only because of its prosperous economy, but also owing to the sudden, massive societal changes that transformed the culture. The **19th Amendment** finally granted women the right to vote in 1920, unleashing other new freedoms. Bobbing her hair and donning shocking knee-length dresses, the "flapper" became the icon for feminism.

Even though the US had legally banned liquor with the adoption of the **Prohibition Amendment** in 1919, alcohol flowed freely in clubs known as speakeasies—to the tune of a sultry new sound called jazz. Since distillers were outlawed from manufacturing spirits—except for a few who gained exemption for "medicinal manufacturing"—a new, illegal liquor industry arose. Called "bootlegging," the business soon came under the auspice of powerful gangsters, such as Al Capone and Charles "Bugs" Moran, who controlled its manufacture and distribution.

One of the wildest parties of all, though, was on Wall Street. During the 1920s, for the first time, average Americans began buying common stocks, entering what had once been the sole province of the wealthy. As the good times continued, investors grew giddier, bidding stocks up to dizzying heights. Even though construction and factory production began to decline in 1927, few heeded the warning. Finally, on October 29, 1929, the bubble burst and the market collapsed, wiping out fortunes overnight and erasing $75 billion in market value.

## The Great Depression

The 1929 crash was followed by a surge of bank failures the next year, ushering in the greatest period of economic peril the country has ever known. By 1932, nearly a quarter of Americans were unemployed, industrial production was at 40 percent of capacity and the median national income had been cut in half. Compounding the misery, a drought across the Great Plains decimated crops and turned the area into a dust bowl. It was a disaster of epic proportions.

A young New Yorker named **Franklin D. Roosevelt** was elected president in 1932 (he would serve an unprecedented three terms in office) and immediately launched a massive program to turn the country around. Roosevelt's **New Deal** expanded the federal government's ability to shore up the economy by setting the price at which the government would buy gold, increasing the money supply, and instituting price controls and farm price supports. It also put into place agencies to regulate the stock exchange and insure individual bank deposits.

The other part of the New Deal aimed to create jobs and prevent exploitation of the workforce. Its most important elements were a system to provide pension payments to aged and disabled Americans (the Social Security Administration); a public works program to provide government jobs for the unemployed; and enactment of minimum-wage, collective bargaining and child-labor laws.

## World War II

During the late 1930s, a series of totalitarian governments had come to power around the globe: now they were threatening Europe and Asia. Americans became increasingly alarmed as Adolf Hitler's armies marched through Europe.

the isolationism spawned by World War I was crumbling.

On December 7, 1941, the Japanese bombed the American naval base at **Pearl Harbor**, Hawaii. The following day, Congress declared war on Japan. That same week, the two other **Axis Powers** (Germany and Italy) declared war on the US.

Within the space of one mind-boggling week, the US had committed to defensive war on two fronts. In the European theater, the Americans and their allies (Great Britain, France, and the Soviet Union) invaded North Africa, defeating the German army at El Alamein. Meanwhile, the Japanese were making steady headway in the Pacific. They were finally stopped at the **Battle of Midway**, a three-day contest between the Allies and the Japanese fought almost entirely by air over 2sq mi Midway Island in the Pacific Ocean.

Back in Europe, the invasion of Normandy on the west coast of France began on June 6, 1944. On what became known as **D-Day**, Allied soldiers stormed the beaches, and by the following April, the Allies had breached German lines and were fast closing in on Hitler. As Allied troops approached Berlin later that month, Hitler committed suicide and Germany surrendered.

A few months later, Japan finally capitulated, following President **Harry S Truman**'s decision to drop atomic bombs on Hiroshima and Nagasaki, Japan. By mid-August 1945 the war was over; more than 400,000 American lives had been lost.

## THE POSTWAR YEARS

The years immediately following World War II were marked by domestic prosperity. Returning war veterans began promising corporate careers or went into business for themselves. Housing developments sprang up overnight and the birthrate increased so dramatically that the generation born during these years earned its own moniker—the "Baby Boomers."

While the Soviet Union had been an ally to the US in World War II, conflicting political ideologies—Western free-market democracy versus the controls of Communism in the Soviet Union—culminated in a 40-year standoff known as the **Cold War**. This era was marked by constant tension, exacerbated by military buildups, covert operations, nuclear-weapons testing and propaganda campaigns on the part of both countries.

Although **Dwight D. Eisenhower**, elected president in 1952, was not politically progressive, his tenure was highlighted by an activist Supreme Court. Presided over by Chief Justice Earl Warren, the court outlawed racial segregation, spelled out the rights of criminal defendants, and laid down the "one man, one vote" rule, stipulating that all citizens must be represented equally in their state legislatures.

## A Decade of Revolution

The 1960s were a tumultuous time, distinguished by violence and profound social change. It began on a hopeful note with the election of **John F. Kennedy** (1917-63) who, at 44, was the youngest president ever to occupy the White House. It continued with the movement for full racial equality. Then, in quick succession, President Kennedy, his brother Attorney General Robert Kennedy, and civil rights leader **Dr. Martin Luther King, Jr.** were all assassinated by gunfire. The assassinations, coupled with an unpopular war in Vietnam, angered and alienated America's youth. There was growing discontent with the country's big government, big business and materialistic culture.

By the mid-60s, a youth revolt was in full swing. Groups such as Students for a Democratic Society (SDS), formed by two University of Michigan students, were spawning antiwar demonstrations on college campuses across the US. Gradually, violence replaced passive civil disobedience as draft resisters and Black Power activists became more militant—and the "establishment" became less tolerant. Driven away from radical politics by the violence of the late 60s, members of the youth "counterculture" heeded

# The Civil Rights Movement

*"I have a dream that one day on the red hills of Georgia the sons of former slaves and the sons of former slaveowners will be able to sit down together at the table of brotherhood."*

*Martin Luther King, Jr., from his speech at the Civil Rights March on Washington, DC, August 28, 1963*

As every American child learns in school, President Abraham Lincoln signed the Emancipation Proclamation abolishing slavery in 1863, in the middle of a terrible Civil War. Why, then, did Americans of African descent need a "civil rights movement" 100 years later?

Martin Luther King, Jr. in Birmingham, Alabama, 09 May 1963

The answer, complex and painful, can be summed up in a few phrases: a white Southern terrorist group known as the Ku Klux Klan, state-by-state "Jim Crow" laws enforcing racial segregation in all aspects of everyday life, and an 1896 Supreme Court case, *Plessy v. Ferguson*, declaring segregation legal as long as blacks and whites had schools and other public facilities that were "separate but equal." In reality, the public facilities and protections for black citizens—from public water fountains to voter registration to tax distributions for black schools—were never equal to those for whites.

By the 1930s and 40s, black citizens were moving north in search of factory jobs and fewer racial restrictions. After World War II, organizations such as the **Congress for Racial Equality** (CORE) and the **National Association for the Advancement of Colored People** (NAACP) began calling on President Harry Truman to eliminate segregation as the law of the land.

On May 17, 1954, voting on a Kansas case *(Brown v. Board of Education)* brought by the NAACP, the US Supreme Court ruled unanimously that racially segregated schools were "inherently unequal." This landmark case—and the Southern states' deliberate slowness in following its requirements—is generally viewed as the beginning of the modern civil rights movement.

Over the next 15 years, "the movement" involved thousands of activists, both black and white, and took many forms: boycotts, sit-ins, street marches and giant rallies. Beginning in December 1955, black citizens boycotted segregated buses in Montgomery, Alabama, for more than a year, until the Supreme Court outlawed the practice of making blacks give up their seats for whites. The **Southern Christian Leadership Conference** (SCLC), organized by the **Reverend Dr. Martin Luther King, Jr.** (*see ATLANTA*), a Baptist minister, helped black churches and communities all over the South organize nonviolent protests (based on the example of India's Mahatma Gandhi) and raise funds for a widespread, continuing fight against segregation. In 1957 nine black teenagers successfully integrated a Little Rock, Arkansas, high school, but they had to be accompanied by federal troops.

Soon hundreds of young black people were staging sit-ins and protests against segregated restaurants, parks, swimming pools, libraries and theaters in more than 100 Southern cities. Many of these activities, conducted in the face of escalating violence from whites, were organized by a new group, the **Student Nonviolent Coordinating Committee** (SNCC). Within a year, some 70,000 people had participated in such protests, and at least 3,600 had been arrested.

Still the movement continued to gain momentum. "Freedom Riders" tested interstate bus integration in Alabama and Mississippi; schoolchildren faced down police dogs and fire hoses in Birmingham, Alabama, and 250,000 people marched on Washington, DC, inspired to further action by Dr. King's famous words: "I have a dream." When four young black girls were killed by a terrorist bomb in a Birmingham church in 1963, the public outcry led Congress to pass the comprehensive **Civil Rights Act** of 1964, outlawing racial discrimination in any form.

By 1965 movement leaders had begun concentrating on another egregious legacy: "poll taxes," literacy tests, and other roadblocks to prevent blacks from registering to vote. After violent clashes in Selma and Montgomery, Alabama, the US Congress passed the 1965 **Voting Rights Act**. With the "Black Power" movement of the mid-1960s, civil rights protests took a more militant tone. A series of destructive, violent riots, primarily in impoverished black urban neighborhoods, led Dr. King to begin planning a "Poor People's March" on Washington for the summer of 1968.

But Dr. King's dream of uniting poor blacks and whites in peaceful civil protest never materialized. On a trip to Memphis, Tennessee, to speak on behalf of striking garbage workers, the nation's foremost civil rights leader was assassinated. To millions of mourners, much of the optimism and the promise of the civil rights movement died with him on April 4, 1968.

The movement never again had a leader of the stature and influence of Dr. Martin Luther King, Jr. But the cause he and thousands of others worked for—with extraordinary and heroic success—continues to be a profound and far-reaching theme in American political, social and economic life.

Harvard professor Timothy Leary's invitation to "tune in, turn on, and drop out." Known as "hippies," these disaffected young people grew their hair long, wore blue jeans and tie-dyed shirts, listened to rock music, and experimented with mind-altering drugs and communal living arrangements. "Free sex" was rampant, with the introduction of the birth-control pill allowing women control over their reproductive lives for the first time.

Punctuated by the long and costly Vietnam War and the Watergate scandal, which led to the resignation of President **Richard Nixon** in 1974, the decade from 1965 to 1975 generated widespread distrust of political officials. **Watergate**, which took its name from the Washington, DC apartment building where its most famous offense occurred, included a number of administration officials involved in instances of burglary, illegal cover-ups, use of government agencies to harass political opponents, and illegal use of campaign contributions. Several officials were tried and convicted of criminal activities.

Not surprisingly, the 1980s (sometimes called the "me decade") were marked by a number of movements aimed at achieving personal and spiritual fulfillment.

## The End of a Millennium

Two major trends underscored the 1990s—an increasingly diverse population mix and the technological revolution. By 1990 ever-faster computers and fax machines made global communication instantaneous and, in some cases, rendered offices obsolete, as increasing numbers of workers began to "telecommute" from home. Portable devices such as cellular phones, pagers and laptop computers enabled workers to perform their duties anywhere. By the mid-90s, widespread use of the Internet was revolutionizing traditional ways of doing business.

The other trend with wide-ranging cultural ramifications involved the sudden rise in ethnic diversity as Hispanic and

*John F. Kennedy Campaigning (1960)*

Asian immigrants added to the existing mix of European and African stock. In the decade from 1980 to 1990, Asians increased their presence in the population by an astounding 107 percent; Hispanics increased by 53 percent. By 2010 the Hispanic population is expected to displace blacks as the country's largest minority group.

## A New Millennium

The new century started with less of a bang than was expected. Fears about Y2K, a glitch that may have made computers not recognize the new date and there was concern that everything electronic would stand still. Instead, the transition from 1999 to 2000 went off without a hitch.

The smooth sailing of the new century quickly ended. A close election between presidential candidates George W. Bush and former vice president Al Gore necessitated recounts, the first formal contest in the history of a presidential election and a trip to the US Supreme Court. In January 2001 Bush is sworn in as the 43rd president of the United States.

On September 11, 2001 (known as *9-11*), two airplanes piloted by Islamic extremists terrorists hit New York's World Trade Center, causing the towers to fall and killing nearly 3,000 civilians. Another plane hit the Pentagon in Washington, D.C., while a fourth crashed in a Pennsylvania field. As a result of the attacks, security at airports, high-rises, public facilities and government buildings changed, in some cases dramatically.

Despite the difficult foreign relations that 911 begat, the eastern US continued to thrive. Faster, more efficient technology further increased incidence of telecommuting, as well as distance learning.

At the turn of the second millennium, the eastern US remains America's core, with the majority (9 out of 15) of the country's most populous urban complexes lying east of the Mississippi River. New York City still ranks as the country's financial and commercial nerve center and remains its undisputed leader in the arts. Similarly, Washington, DC is America's political leader—the city that world leaders uniformly look to in time of crisis. And Chicago, center of the Midwest, reigns as a major transportation hub, with 19 rail lines linking it to every major American and Canadian city, as well as O'Hare International Airport, the nation's second-busiest.

## Time Line

**1565—** Pedro Menéndez de Avilés founds St. Augustine, Florida, the first permanent European settlement in North America.

**1607—** Captain John Smith founds **Jamestown** on the coast of

Virginia, the first permanent English settlement in the New World.

1619— First African slaves arrive in the colonies.

1620— English Puritans establish **Plymouth Colony** in Massachusetts.

1626— Peter Minuit purchases Manhattan Island from Indians.

1718— Jean Baptiste Le Moyne, sieur de Bienville founds New Orleans.

1754— **French and Indian War** begins.

1763— **Treaty of Paris** ends the French and Indian War. England gains Canada and Louisiana east of the Mississippi River from France, and Florida from Spain.

1764-67— Britain imposes a series of taxes on colonists.

1770— British soldiers kill three colonists in the Boston Massacre.

1773— Irate Bostonians stage the **Boston Tea Party**, throwing cargoes of tea into Boston Harbor to protest British taxation.

1775— **Revolutionary War** begins as Minutemen clash with British troops at Lexington and Concord, Massachusetts. Daniel Boone blazes a trail across the Cumberland Gap, opening the way for settlement of the west.

1776— Colonists declare their independence from England when they adopt the **Declaration of Independence** in Philadelphia on July 4.

1781— British troops surrender to colonists at Yorktown, Virginia.

1783— **Peace of Paris** formally ends the Revolutionary War, declaring American victory and setting the western US boundary at the Mississippi River.

1793— Eli Whitney invents the cotton gin.

1803— Congress completes the **Louisiana Purchase**, thus securing a vast stretch of more than 800,000sq mi lying between the Mississippi River and the Rocky Mountains.

1804— President Thomas Jefferson sends Meriwether Lewis and William Clark out to explore the Louisiana Purchase lands.

1807— Robert Fulton invents the steamboat.

1812— The **War of 1812** begins with Britain.

1825— The **Erie Canal** is completed, linking the Great Lakes with New York City.

1827— The first US railroad, the Baltimore and Ohio (B&O), is chartered.

1838-39— Cherokee Indians are removed from their southeastern lands and forced by the US government to march west to reservations in Oklahoma.

1844— First telegraph message is sent from Washington, DC, to Baltimore, Maryland, by inventor Samuel Morse.

1848— The first **Women's Rights Convention** is held at Seneca Falls, New York. Their Declaration of Sentiments calls for educational and professional opportunities equal to those of men, and the right to vote.

1861— **Confederate States of America** are organized; opening shots of the Civil War are fired at Fort Sumter, South Carolina.

1863— Union forces win the Battle of Gettysburg. President Lincoln issues his **Emancipation Proclamation**, declaring all slaves in the Confederate states to be free as of January 1, 1863.

1865— Civil War ends. Congress passes the 13th Amendment to the Constitution, outlawing slavery. Abraham Lincoln is assassinated at Ford's Theatre in Washington, DC.

**1869—** The **New York Stock Exchange** is established. Rail service spans the continent as the Union and Central Pacific lines are joined by a golden spike at Promontory, Utah.

**1870—** The **15th Amendment** passes, granting "all men" the right to vote.

**1879—** Thomas Edison invents the lightbulb.

**1883—** The Brooklyn Bridge opens.

**1913—** The **16th Amendment** passes, establishing a federal income tax.

**1917—** The US enters World War I on the side of the Allied Powers.

**1919—** The 18th, or **Prohibition Amendment** is adopted, banning the sale of alcoholic beverages.

**1920—** The **19th Amendment** grants women the right to vote.

**1927—** Charles Lindbergh completes the first solo transatlantic flight from New York to Paris.

**1929—** US stock market crashes, precipitating the Great Depression.

**1931—** The Empire State Building, tallest in the world, opens in New York City.

**1933—** President Franklin D. Roosevelt's initiates his **New Deal** policy.

**1941—** Japanese attack Pearl Harbor in Hawaii; US enters World War II.

**1944—** Allies land on Normandy beaches in France.

**1945—** World War II ends. President Roosevelt dies in office.

**1947—** Jackie Robinson becomes the first black player in major-league baseball when he joins the Brooklyn Dodgers.

**1954—** Supreme Court outlaws school segregation in *Brown vs. Board of Education*.

**1960—** Black students stage the first sit-in of the civil rights movement at a lunch counter in Greensboro, North Carolina.

**1961—** Astronauat Alan Sheard makes the first American space flight aboard *Freedom 7* on May 5.

**1962—** President John F. **Kennedy** begins sending military advisers to **Vietnam** in an effort to contain Communism.

**1963—** President Kennedy is assassinated in Dallas, Texas. Civil-rights demonstrations in Montgomery, Alabama, are broken up by local police.

**1964—** Congress passes the landmark **Civil Rights Act** of 1964. US air strikes begin against North Vietnam.

**1965—** Congress passes the Voting Rights Act of 1965. President Lyndon Johnson commits combat troops to Vietnam.

**1968—** Martin Luther King, Jr. is assassinated in Memphis, Tennessee.

**1969—** Astronaut **Neil Armstrong** takes man's first steps on the moon.

**1972—** Richard **Nixon** becomes first American president to visit China.

**1973—** Last US troops leave Vietnam, thus ending the nation's longest war; American death toll 57,685.

**1974—** President Nixon resigns for the illegal cover-up of a break-in at Democratic headquarters—a scandal known as Watergate.

**1976—** Supreme Court upholds death penalty in *Gregg vs. Georgia*.

**1979—** The first major nuclear power plant accident occurs at Three Mile Island in Pennsylvania.

**1986—** Space shuttle *Challenger* explodes in Florida, killing seven passengers, including first US civilian selected for space travel.

**1989—** Hurricane Hugo strikes the coast of the Carolinas, inflicting more than $7 million in damages.

**1990—** US troops engage Iraqi forces in the Gulf War called Operation Desert Storm.

**1992—** Hurricane Andrew devastates Miami and the Florida Keys.

**1996—** The **Centennial Olympic Games**, in Atlanta, Georgia.

©iStockphoto.com/Bryan Reese

*Aerial View of the World Trade Center Site, March 2007*

**1999—** President Bill Clinton becomes the first elected president in US history to be impeached by the House of Representatives for lying in a federal proceeding and obstructing justice. He was acquitted by the Senate.

**2000—** Former vice president Al Gore receives more popular votes, but Texas governor George W. Bush received more electoral votes in the US presidential election. The US Supreme Court halts recounts and declares Bush the winner of the election.

**2001—** George W. Bush is sworn in as the 43rd president of the United States. Bush is the son of George H.W. Bush, the 41st president.

**2001—** Terrorists fly hijacked jumbo jets into New York's **World Trade Center**, felling the two skyscrapers and killing 2,979 people.

President Bush sends US troops to **Afghanistan**, with international support, to destroy Al-Qaeda terrorist camps and depose the Taliban government.

**2002—** The **XIX Winter Olympic Games** are held in Salt Lake City, Utah.

**2003—** US troops engage in a coalition military operation in **Iraq**, code-named *Operation Iraqi Freedom*.

The space shuttle Columbia disintegrates over Texas during re-entry.

**2004—** George W. Bush is re-elected to a second term as president.

**2005—** Hurricane Katrina, the third-strongest hurricane to make landfall in the US, hits the Gulf Coast. The city of New Orleans was one of the hardest hit cities.

**2006—** The US population passes the 300 million person mark.

**2007—** Gerald Ford: 38th president's state funeral in Washington, DC.

# ART AND CULTURE

## Art

With New York City as the visual-art capital, important art museums in major urban centers, thriving galleries in cities both large and small, and many fine collections maintained at colleges and universities, the eastern US affords abundant opportunities to absorb the grand scope of American visual art from colonial times to the present.

## PAINTING, SCULPTURE AND PHOTOGRAPHY

### 18th Century
Sometimes called the father of American painting, New Englander **Benjamin West** spent the latter part of his career in London after touring Europe to absorb the works of the Old Masters. Artists who trained in his London studio included **Charles Willson Peale**, the first American resident history painter; and **Gilbert Stuart**, known for his oil sketch of George Washington. Bostonian **John Singleton Copley** became famous for his portraits of political and social leaders.

### 19th Century
America's first landscapist, **Thomas Cole** arrived in Philadelphia from England in 1818 and set out to record the unspoiled reaches of the Hudson River Valley and the Catskill Mountains. He and other artists of the **Hudson River school** such as **Frederic Edwin Church** (who rendered the period's definitive portrait of Niagara Falls) presented a romanticized view of nature imbued with moral overtones. Other important artists of this period include **John James Audubon**, whose studies in art and ornithology produced *The Birds of America* (1827-38); American marine painter **Fitz Hugh Lane**; **Martin Johnson Heade**, a Pennsylvania landscape artist; and Missourian **George Caleb Bingham**, the first significant American painter from the Midwest. The works of Lane, Heade and Bingham all display characteristics of **Luminism**, an aspect of mid-19C painting concerned with the study and depiction of light. Sculptors **Augustus Saint-Gaudens** and **Daniel Chester French** broke from the Neoclassical tradition of American sculpture to create bold, naturalistic memorials and monuments throughout the eastern US.

Massachusetts-born **James Abbott McNeill Whistler**, who settled in Paris in 1855, inspired a sea change in American art with his philosophy that art should exist for its own sake and not to convey a moral or narrative. **John Singer Sargent**, also active in Europe, is best known for his exquisitely rendered portraits of the wealthy. America's finest Impressionist painter was Philadelphian **Mary Cassatt**, who lived most of her life in Paris. **William Merritt Chase**, who founded his own art school in New York in 1896, became one of that city's preeminent society portraitists. In Boston, **Winslow Homer** produced genre scenes of American life that focused on the sea. **Henry Tanner**, the first black American painter to achieve renown outside the US, eschewed the stylistic traditions of his day, expressing his experiences as an African-American through his deeply spiritual works.

Postimpressionist painters **Maurice Prendergast** and **Thomas Eakins** favored a return to realism over academic theory. Eakins' work influenced **Robert Henri**, who, with followers **George Luks**, **John Sloan** and **George Bellows**, turned to the harsh realities of everyday life in New York as subject matter; their gritty style was dubbed the **Ash Can school**.

### 20th Century
Photographer **Alfred Stieglitz** likewise rebelled against academism. His 291 Gallery in New York City, which he cofounded in 1909, mounted works by new American artists such as **Marsden Hartley** and **Arthur Dove** (America's first abstract painter), and became a center for the city's artistic avant-garde. The 1913 International Exhibition of

Modern Art, known as the Armory Show, presented new works by European Post-impressionists, Fauvists, Pointillists and Cubists to a shocked American public. The show also established New York City as the art capital of the nation.

The environment and life of the nation fueled the Depression-era works of American scene painters **Stuart Davis** and **Edward Hopper**. Black life in 1930s Harlem inspired African-American painter **Jacob Lawrence**, who fused bold forms and primary colors to create eloquent social statements—exemplified by his famed 60-panel narrative of the black migration from the rural South to the industrial North. Also during this period, **American scene painting** flowered in the Midwest, where artists such as Missouri native **Thomas Hart Benton** and Iowan **Grant Wood** sought to depict rural America in the face of encroaching industrialization. Wood is perhaps best known for *American Gothic* (1930), a hard-edged portrait of a Midwestern farmer/preacher and his daughter.

The onset of World War II brought a wave of European artists such as Max Ernst, Ynes Tanguy and Salvador Dalí to New York City. Along with Armenian émigré Arshile Gorky and German-born Hans Hofmann, they inspired a new avant-garde that gave rise in the 1940s to **Abstract Expressionism** (*see NEW YORK CITY infobox*). Practitioners of this radical American art movement include "Action" painters **Willem de Kooning**, **Jackson Pollock** and **Franz Kline**; "Color Field" painters **Mark Rothko** and **Barnett Newman**; as well as **Clyfford Still**, **Helen Frankenthaler** and **Robert Motherwell**. Meanwhile, artists **Andrew Wyeth** and magazine illustrator **Norman Rockwell** reacted to the effect of modernization on regional culture through their nostalgic depictions of American folkways.

Mass commercialism enabled by new advances in media and communications gave rise in the 1960s to **Pop Art**. **Andy Warhol**, **Roy Lichtenstein**, **Jim Dine**, **James Rosenquist** and sculptor **Claes Oldenburg** embraced the commonplace with works based on commercial products, comic strips and billboards.

American iconography also proved integral to works by collagist **Robert Rauschenberg** and painter/printmaker **Jasper Johns**. The 1960s also saw the rise of **Conceptualism**, a movement based on the notion that ideas take precedence over form. Raised in Harlem, **Romare Bearden** was a political cartoonist before beginning to paint in the 1950s; his innovative use of collage gained him renown by the 1970s.

## FOLK ART

Throughout the history of the eastern US, artists and craftspeople have created paintings, textiles, sculptures, furniture, pottery, glasswork and aesthetically pleasing objects for everyday use that fall under the broad category of folk art. Like a local accent, folk art is region-based, the product of non-academically trained artists working within provincial traditions to produce objects for their communities.

Native American cultures in the east produced objects for artistic, ritual and utilitarian purposes, including intricately woven and painted baskets, pottery vessels and effigy jars; cornhusk and leather dolls and masks; and carved wooden ware and figures. Tribes of the eastern woodlands were particularly known for their fine beadwork and body ornaments of metal and mica.

Folk art traditions in the eastern US include **Fraktur** (from the German *Frakturschrift*, or "fractured writing"), a type of illuminated calligraphy used by German immigrants in Pennsylvania to illustrate formal documents; **quilting**, a practical art that peaked in eastern Amish communities in the late 19C; and **furniture making**, typified by the simple designs crafted in the Shaker communities of New York, Kentucky and New England.

Well-known folk painters include itinerant portraitist **Ammi Phillips** (1788-1865); **Joshua Johnson** (1764-1824), the first African-American painter to create a recognized body of work; and **Grandma Moses** (1860-1961), who at the age of seventy-six began painting realistic scenes of her early rural life in New York.

# Architecture

Punctuated by the skyscraper, America's great contribution to architecture, the built environment of the eastern US reveals influences from the nation's many immigrant groups as well as technological and aesthetic innovations that originated here; resulting in some of the world's foremost examples of building artistry.

There were no trained architects among the European colonists who arrived in America in the 16C-17C; survival was initially more important than aesthetics. Settlers raised their own simple structures according to building traditions from their homelands, using locally available materials such as hardwood timber in New England, fieldstone in the mid-Atlantic states and cypress planks in Florida. In the southern colonies and along the Gulf Coast, raised cottages utilized opposing windows, wide porches and detached kitchens to combat heat and humidity, while on some New England farms, houses were linked to barns, sheds and other dependencies to eliminate the need for going outside in cold weather. Similar considerations of material, climate and culture gave rise to the saltbox house in New England; the Creole cottage in New Orleans; the shotgun house of the Gulf Coast, the coquina structures of St. Augustine, Florida, and other forms of vernacular residential architecture throughout the fledgling eastern US.

## 18TH CENTURY

As settlement increased and cities took shape, colonists began to create structures that were visually pleasing as well as functional. Amateur architects and skilled builders armed with English pattern books spread the **Georgian** style throughout the colonies. The symmetrical façades, Classical ornamentation, ample scale and geometric proportion of Georgian buildings at the new capital of Williamsburg reflected colonial determination.

After the American Revolution, the **Adam** style—a British Neoclassical tradition based on Roman villas and houses—was adopted by a growing merchant class in seaport towns along the coast. Called the **Federal** style in the US, it displayed clarity and simplicity of form, and restraint, delicacy and refinement. Garlands, urns and festoons decorated wall surfaces, fireplace mantels and entryways, and circular or oval shaped rooms were common.

Builders of public structures turned to Roman Classical orders for inspiration. Thomas Jefferson's Virginia State Capitol (1798) in Richmond was based on the Maison Carrée, a Roman temple in Nîmes, France, giving rise to the Classical Revival, or **Jeffersonian**, style.

One of the first trained professional architects to work in the US was **Benjamin Henry Latrobe**, who arrived from England in 1796. An admirer of architectural forms of ancient Greece, Latrobe patterned the Bank of Pennsylvania (1800) in Philadelphia after an Athenian temple, pioneering the **Greek Revival** style for public buildings in America. The Greek temple front with Classical orders became so prevalent for banks, government buildings, churches and eventually residences—particularly plantation houses in the antebellum South—that the style was dubbed the "National style." **Charles Bullfinch**'s design of the Massachusetts State House, with its central dome and columned frontispiece, served as the model for state houses across the country.

Victorian House, Cape May, New Jersey

Anne Culberson/MICHELIN

# 19TH CENTURY

The commercial availability of good-quality nails and lumber in uniform sizes brought about the invention in the 1830s of the light, inexpensive and speedily constructed "balloon frame." Other mass-produced components included pressed brick, cut stone, plate glass, cast iron and jigsawed wood. Houses were built rapidly, and, as the country entered the Victorian age in the latter half of the 19C, were designed and embellished in a plethora of eclectic substyles that quickly rose and fell in popularity. **Gothic Revival**-style structures sported pointed-arch windows, steep cross-gables and dormers decorated with intricately cut-out bargeboards. The architecture of Italy inspired the more formal **Italianate** style, characterized by square towers, shallow roofs, wide eaves with imposing cornices supported by brackets, and rounded windows and doors with hooded moldings. More elaborate still, **Second Empire**-style buildings sported Italianate features, with the addition of an imposing mansard roof and Classical ornamentation. Some clapboard or board-and-batten homes displayed post-and-beam structural members or diagonal braces as part of the exterior ornamentation in a variant known as the **Stick** style. The immensely influential New York architectural firm of **McKim, Mead & White** initially rose to popularity with their **Shingle**-style homes, in which a continuous flow of variously patterned shingles covered walls, dormers and trim. The most eclectic and picturesque of the Victorian substyles, however, is the **Queen Anne**. Homes in this fanciful style were laid in irregular plans of projecting wings, bays, towers, turrets and cross axes, lavishly ornamented with latticework, shingles, scrollwork, spindles and balusters, and painted in eye-catching colors.

Toward the end of the 19C, Boston-born, Paris-trained architect **Henry Hobson Richardson** adapted Romanesque forms from France and Spain in a distinctly American style known as **Richardsonian Romanesque**. Characterized by heavy, rounded arches, rusticated stone surfaces and deeply inset doors and windows, the style was popular for public structures including churches and railroad terminals.

Commercial architecture underwent a revolution following the Civil War as iron mills previously devoted to the war effort turned to production of cast-iron building components. By the 1870s structures framed entirely in iron, hung with prefabricated cast-iron façade panels and equipped with improved passenger elevators rose to heights not possible with masonry construction. Cast-iron façades were especially popular in New York, St. Louis, Charleston and New Orleans.

In 1893 a team of architects including **Daniel Burnham** and **Frederick Law Olmsted**, America's most influential landscape architect, created a "White City" of classically ornamented buildings for the **World's Columbian Exposition** in Chicago, stimulating a national taste for the illustrious past in public architecture and city planning. Domes, pedimented porticoes and sweeping staircases characterized **Neoclassical** federal buildings in Washington, while **Richard Morris Hunt** and other practitioners of the more ornate **Beaux-Arts** style adorned courthouses, libraries, museums and mansions with paired columns, wreaths, swags, festoons, cartouches and statuary.

Turning away from the past, Chicago architect **Louis Henri Sullivan** espoused instead the notion that architectural design should be of its time. Sullivan and colleagues William Le Baron Jenney, Dankmar Adler, William Holabird and Martin Roche formed the **Chicago school** in the 1880s, and set about utilizing new advances in construction technology to create ever-taller commercial buildings in which non-load-bearing "curtain" walls were draped on a steel framework. The skeleton was visible on the façade in the horizontal spandrels and vertical piers separating windows of unprecedented size, and the shaft, rising from a defined base at entry level, was capped by an emphatically decorated cornice. Chicago school buildings achieved heights of up to 20 stories, prefiguring the modern **skyscraper** (⊚see CHICAGO infobox).

*Robie House, Chicago, Illinois*

## 20TH CENTURY

In the boom decade following World War I, developers in Manhattan latched onto the concept of the vertical city as a means of multiplying the profits of small building sites by creating rentable space out of the air. New technologies pushed buildings higher, necessitating a 1916 city ordinance requiring architects to create setbacks at the upper levels to allow sunlight to reach the street.

By the 1930s, a number of European architects working in America, including

*Sears Tower, Chicago, Illinois*

© Chicago Architecture Foundation/Anne Evans

**Ludwig Mies van der Rohe**, and **Walter Gropius**—founder of the Bauhaus design school in Germany—introduced Bauhaus principles of minimalism and functionalism in what became known as the **International** style.

Influenced by the simple forms and austere surfaces of the International style, coupled with the ideas displayed at the 1925 Paris Exposition des Arts Décoratifs et Industriels Modernes, **Art Deco** adopted the sleek lines, cubic massing and new materials of the technology-oriented modernist aesthetic. Deco's geometric, abstracted motifs such as chevrons, sunbursts and lightning bolts worked in sleek, reflective materials were wildly popular throughout America for corporate headquarters, theaters and hotels—the latter particularly in Miami Beach, Florida. Pyramidal Art Deco skyscrapers such as New York City's Chrysler Building and the Empire State Building came to symbolize American power and ingenuity.

In the Midwest, **Frank Lloyd Wright** (*see CHICAGO infobox*) led a group of architects known as the **Prairie school** in development of a new style incorporating the natural environment into planning and design. Remaking the concept of horizontality, Wright's Prairie-style houses—typified by his **Robie House** in Chicago—hugged the flat Midwestern landscape; movable room partitions created flexible interior spaces and flat or shallow roofs surmounted long bands of windows.

*Art Deco Buildings, Miami Beach, Florida*

©iStockphoto.com/Nick Tzolov

In the mid-20C, the **Seagram Building** (1958, Ludwig Mies van der Rohe) in New York City, a rectangular skyscraper sheathed in glass and set amid a large plaza, strongly influenced the "glass box" look of office buildings in urban centers such as Boston, Detroit, Atlanta and Miami. The advent of rigid-tube construction in the 1970s allowed the soaring height of Chicago's 110-story **Sears Tower** by the prolific architectural firm of **Skidmore, Owings & Merrill**. Contemporary architects such as **Philip Johnson**, **I.M. Pei**, **Michael Graves** and **Robert Venturi** have since broken from the strict functionalism of International school design, altering the urban landscape with **Postmodern** structures that honor the past through free interpretations of historical motifs while utilizing new technologies and materials.

## Literature

With its beginnings in the writings of early Virginia and New England settlers, the development of American literature has reflected the development of the US through nationhood, expansion, industrialization, war and urbanization. In colonial times, publishing was confined mostly to sermons, journals, religious writings, political treatises and almanacs. In 1732 **Benjamin Franklin** began writing his *Poor Richard's Almanack*, a compendium of calendars, proverbs, practical information, popular science and humor. Various newspapers, broadsheets and political tracts disseminated opinion during the years leading up to the American Revolution. Englishman **Thomas Paine** turned the tide of colonial opinion toward a break from Great Britain with his pro-independence pamphlet *Common Sense* (1776).

## 19TH CENTURY

Popular literature in the early 19C found its way to readers via newspapers and chapbooks and inexpensive digests of moral musings. **James Fenimore Cooper** charted the disappearing wilderness of the American frontier with his *Leatherstocking Tales*, which included the novel *The Last of the Mohicans* (1826). The first American author to achieve international fame was **Washington Irving**, author of *Rip Van Winkle* (1820) and *The Legend of Sleepy Hollow* (1820). The poems and short stories of romantic Gothicist **Edgar Allan Poe** ("The Fall of the House of Usher," 1839) chilled readers with their themes of horror.

By the 1840s the **transcendentalist movement** ( *see BOSTON) leaders*, **Ralph Waldo Emerson** and **Henry David Thoreau**, settled in the Boston area, establishing New England at the forefront of American thought and literary expression. In Boston, James Russell Lowell helped found the *Atlantic Monthly*, a literary periodical whose contributors

*A Greenwich Village Brownstone*

©iStockphoto.com/David Meaders

included **Henry Wadsworth Longfellow**, the most widely read poet of his day. **Nathaniel Hawthorne** explored Puritan ethics with novels such as *The Scarlet Letter* (1850). In Amherst, Massachusetts, reclusive poet **Emily Dickinson** penned more than a thousand short lyric verses, most of them undiscovered during her lifetime. Elsewhere in the northeast, **Herman Melville** wrote *Moby Dick* (1851), his epic novel of the sea, after spending 18 months on a whaler; and **Harriet Beecher Stowe** fanned the flames of abolitionist sentiment with *Uncle Tom's Cabin* (1852). Poet **Walt Whitman** published the first edition of *Leaves of Grass* in 1855.

As the nation expanded in the last half of the 19C, a literary movement known as **regionalism** sought to preserve awareness of regional differences in scenery and speech. Humorist **Mark Twain** (né Samuel Clemens) captured the era of his boyhood in a Mississippi River town in *The Adventures of Tom Sawyer* (1876). In the South, **Joel Chandler Harris**' Uncle Remus stories rank among the greatest in black folk literature; **Richard M. Johnston** penned humorous sketches of life in rural Georgia; and **George Washington Cable** described the Creole society of New Orleans.

## 20TH CENTURY

A preponderance of writers, artists and thespians made New York City's **Greenwich Village** the bohemian capital of the US in the first decades of the 20C. The cultural ferment there produced a number of literary magazines whose contributors included experimental poet **e.e. cummings** and novelist **Floyd Dell**. The Greenwich Village production of the plays of **Eugene O'Neill** (*Desire Under the Elms*, 1924) brought him recognition as the period's preeminent American playwright. And **F. Scott Fitzgerald** (*The Great Gatsby*, 1925) established himself as the foremost chronicler of the jazz age.

In Chicago, the aftermath of the 1893 World's Columbian Exposition spawned a literary renaissance in that city, which served as the backdrop for social realists **Henry Blake Fuller** (*The Cliff Dwellers*, 1893), **Theodore Dreiser** (*Sister Carrie*, 1900), **Frank Norris** (*The Pit*, 1903) and **Upton Sinclair** (*The Jungle*, 1906). The life and character of rural New England formed the subject for the poems of **Robert Frost**, who lived most of his life in the region, while works by **Sherwood Anderson** (*Winesburg, Ohio*, 1919), **Sinclair Lewis** (*Main Street*, 1920) and playwright **Thornton Wilder** (*Our Town*, 1938) explored the nature of small-town America.

A number of writers fled the political upheaval of America in the aftermath of World War I for Paris. There, the literary salon of Gertrude Stein nurtured dozens of young American writers, among them **Henry Miller**, **William Carlos Williams** and **Ernest Hemingway**, who later described the brilliant intellectual atmosphere of Paris in the 1920s in *A Moveable Feast* (1964).

In the 1930s, Mississippi native **William Faulkner** fictionalized the setting of his boyhood in a series of tales that explored societal, racial and moral tensions in the South. Faulkner's work began a revival of Southern literature by **Marjorie Kinnan Rawlings** (*The Yearling*, 1938), **Carson McCullers** (*The Heart Is a Lonely Hunter*, 1940), **Robert Penn Warren** (*All the King's Men*, 1946) and **Eudora Welty** (*Delta Wedding*, 1946).

Flannery O'Connor (*Wise Blood*, 1952) and playwright **Tennessee Williams** (*Cat on a Hot Tin Roof*, 1955).

The celebration of black culture, the struggle for integration and civil rights, and the experiences of African Americans in both the South and the North have provided the themes of African-American writing in the 20C. The ] of arts beginning in the 1920s drew black writers from around the eastern US, including poet **Langston Hughes** (*Shakespeare in Harlem*, 1942), **Ralph Ellison** (*Invisible Man*, 1952) and **Zora Neale Hurston** (*Their Eyes Were Watching God*, 1937). Chicago's slums formed the backdrop for works by **Richard Wright** (*Native Son*, 1940) and poet **Gwendolyn Brooks** (*The Bean Eaters*, 1960). Contemporary African-American writers include **Maya Angelou** (*I Know Why the Caged Bird Sings*, 1969), who wrote and delivered a poem at President Clinton's 1993 inauguration; poet **Rita Dove** (*Thomas and Beulah*, 1986) and authors **Toni Morrison** (*Beloved*, 1987) and **Alice Walker** (*The Color Purple*, 1982).

Although New York City is considered the nation's literary capital, contemporary writers flourish all over the eastern US. Recognized figures include novelists **Tom Wolfe** (*The Bonfire of the Vanities*, 1987) and **John Updike** (the *Rabbit* series, ending with *Rabbit at Rest*, 1990); and playwrights **Wendy Wasserstein** (*The Heidi Chronicles*, 1988) and **Edward Albee** (*Three Tall Women*, 1994).

# Music and Dance

## MUSIC

Musicians of the eastern US have created and refashioned an astonishing variety of musical styles. Cutting-edge and traditional forms can be heard live in concert halls, nightclubs and outdoor music festivals. Most cities of even modest size support a symphony or chamber orchestra as well as a club scene that nurtures local pop artists. Although New York City has traditionally been the home of music production facilities in the East, today one of the largest segments of the US recording industry is based in Nashville, Tennessee.

Classical composers in Europe and the US have been inspired by American hymns and folk songs. New England businessman and part-time composer **Charles Ives** (1874-1954), for example, borrowed dance tunes, church music and the raw sounds of bells and parades, mixing them into complex scores using 20C innovations of dissonance and contrasting rhythms. Pennsylvania native **Samuel Barber** (1910-81), best known for his serenely beautiful "Adagio for Strings," chose a more melodic approach. No composer embodied the American frontier spirit more than Brooklynite **Aaron Copland** (1900-90), who based his "Appalachian Spring" on a Shaker song. **George Gershwin** (1898-1937), also from Brooklyn, captured an urban electricity with "Rhapsody in Blue" and "Piano Concerto in F," both strongly influenced by jazz techniques.

## Singin' The Blues

Along the Mississippi delta from the late 1890s, a style of music called **"the blues"** (*see MEMPHIS*) evolved primarily among African Americans playing guitars, harmonicas and other simple instruments. Sung by performers such as **Muddy Waters**, **B.B. King** and **Etta James**, the blues have become one of America's most enduring music genres, inspiring countless musicians including Eric Clapton, Bob Dylan and other rock-and-roll greats. The music flourishes in Memphis, New Orleans, Chicago and Kansas City, where blues artists have thrived since the days of speakeasies—bars where alcohol was sold illegally during Prohibition.

## All That Jazz

The amalgam of styles known as **jazz** has many roots, including blues. "**Ragtime**," the earliest form of jazz to have a wide appeal, began its long period of popularity in the 1890s. A piano style, ragtime emphasized syncopation and polyrhythm, best interpreted by composer **Scott Joplin**.

New Orleans is widely accepted as the birthplace of jazz. Its earliest influences might have been slave dances held in

*Louis Armstrong*

Congo Square, but the style grew up in the Storyville prostitution houses, riverboats and social clubs in the early 20C. Small ensembles of cornets, clarinets, trombones and, later, saxophones played standard and improvised melodies backed by lively, mixed rhythms. As the style evolved, colorful **Dixieland** music added banjo beats and a wild mix of instrumental solos played at once in a magical blend.

New Orleans pianist **Jelly Roll Morton** and clarinet player **Sidney Bichet** were two of the greatest influences of early jazz. The most famous jazzman of all, trumpet player **Louis Armstrong**, grew up in New Orleans but left in 1922 to join his mentor, King Oliver, in Chicago. The second great city of jazz, Chicago harbored many musicians who, like Armstrong, sought to escape the South's racial restrictions.

Closely following the development of jazz was the **Big Band** movement, large ensembles of horns that, with the help of radio, flourished from the 1920s to World War II. **Glenn Miller**, **Benny Goodman** and **Artie Shaw** were among its greatest proponents. Swing bands brought a more jazzy big-band sound that introduced energetic swing dancing, popular from 1930 to 1945 and recently revived. **Duke Ellington** was a giant on the music scene for years as a band leader, composer and performer from the time he worked at New York's famous Cotton Club (1927-32) until his later years writing religious music (he died in 1974). Crooners like New Jersey-born **Frank Sinatra** got their start singing with big bands.

Around the mid-1950s, **rock and roll** exploded on the American popular music scene as several artists, including **Fats Domino**, **Little Richard**, and especially Memphis-based **Elvis Presley**, began combining jazz and blues influences with electrically amplified guitars, intricate bass lines and hopped-up rhythms. Wildly popular with teenagers, the pounding beat of rock came to represent a culture of sex, drugs and youthful rejection of societal norms. Guitarist **Chuck Berry**, vocalist **Buddy Holly** and pianist **Jerry Lee Lewis** all claimed huge followings, and Elvis Presley's theatrical sex appeal catapulted him to international fame.

## The American Musical

With roots in burlesque, comic opera and vaudeville, the musical rose to popularity early in the 20C and thrives today in theaters across the country. In the 1920s and early 30s, the bright productions, comedic plots and frivolous song-and-dance numbers by composers Jerome Kern, Irving Berlin, Cole Porter and George and Ira Gershwin provided a welcome escape from the cares of daily life. Richard Rodgers and Oscar Hammerstein II's *Oklahoma!* changed the direction of the genre in 1943 by integrating musical numbers with the plot line and featuring serious ballet. Jule Styne, Frank Loesser, Leonard Bernstein and Alan Jay Lerner and Frederick Loewe all followed this trend. The complex lyrics and innovative plots of shows such as Stephen Sondheim's *A Little Night Music* broke new ground in the 1970s. This decade also saw the rise of inventive new work by director/choreographers Jerome Robbins, Bob Fosse, Tommy Tune and Michael Bennet, whose musical, *A Chorus Line*, enjoyed the longest Broadway run to date (1975-90). The six-year run of The Producers (2001-07) reinvigorated the genre.

### Pickin' and Grinnin'

By far the most popular music in America is **country & western**, or simply Country (see *NASHVILLE*). The music's performance and recording capital is still Nashville, where the Grand Ole Opry was once the undisputed hall of fame for country music artists. Taking its roots in pioneer folk music, country is epitomized in the singing style of **Hank Williams**. A variant of country music, **bluegrass music** grew up in the Appalachian region, highlighted by the virtuoso guitarist **Doc Watson** and bluegrass legend **Earl Scruggs**.

### Traditions and Trends

Regions in the eastern US lay claim to several musical traditions. Detroit, known as Motown (short for Motor Town) for its auto-making industry, is famous for its **Motown Sound**, a mix of gospel, pop, and rhythm and blues. **Smokey Robinson**, the **Temptations**, **Gladys Knight** and **Diana Ross and the Supremes** were some of Motown's greatest stars. The lyrics of American folksingers **Woody Guthrie**, **Pete Seeger** and **Bob Dylan** were inspired by civil rights and societal protest from the 1930s through the 60s.

Popular American music today reflects myriad styles and influences. **Alternative rock** bands have for the most part succeeded the heavy-metal and acid-rock groups that formed during the 1970s and 80s. The sound of urban protest, **rap** features hard-driving rhythms, booming bass and raging lyrics often laced with profanity. And the bouncing beats of Latin music, much of it based in South Florida, are leaving a growing mark on the American music scene.

## DANCE

The rise of dance as a performance art came relatively late to the US. Since the turn of the 20C, the American dance environment has nurtured preeminent classical ballet companies such as New York's **American Ballet Theater** (ABT) and the distinguished **New York City Ballet**, which flourished for years under the guidance of artistic director **George Balanchine**. Choreographers **Agnes de Mille** and **Jerome Robbins**, both associated with ABT, transferred their talents to Broadway; de Mille's use of traditional folk themes in musicals such as *Oklahoma!* inspired distinctively American ballet forms.

The intriguing history of **modern dance** in America began with **Isadora Duncan**, who in the 1890s introduced her revolutionary belief that the body should be free to improvise and express personal feelings. **Ruth St. Denis** and her husband **Ted Shawn** laid the foundations for modern dance in America with their influential Denishawn School, founded in 1915. But it was innovator **Martha Graham** who made America the center of modern dance in the middle of the century. Her studies of physical structure and movement, coupled with the belief that energy originates in the center of the body and not in its extremities, made for a stark, percussive style that was at first derided by critics and audiences. Graham's work influenced nearly every important modern choreographer, including **Merce Cunningham**, **Paul Taylor** and **Twyla Tharp**, all of whom founded their own companies in New York.

Scottish, English and Irish jigs and reels inspired distinctly American folk-dance forms, including the **square dances** and **contra dances** that grew to popularity as a means of group recreation in rural areas. Irish clog dances were combined with elements of African step dances and the rhythms of jazz music to form the basis of complex **tap dances** that have enlivened many a Broadway musical and Hollywood film. Adapted by music-hall performers, tap was performed on vaudeville stages by greats such as Bill "Bojangles" Robinson and John Bubbles, and has enjoyed a recent revival.

## Theater and Film

### THEATER

Theatrical fare in the eastern US indulges virtually every taste. Companies throughout the US stage timeless explorations of the human condition by mid-century dramatists **Eugene O'Neill**, **Arthur Miller**, **Tennessee Williams**, **Thornton Wilder** and **William Inge** as well as the sparkling comedies of prolific playwright Neil Simon. Avant-garde works by **Edward Albee**, **Lanford Wilson** and South African **Athol Fugard** are taking their place in the modern repertoire, as are contemporary works by New Yorker **Wendy Wasserstein**, Chicago-born **David Mamet** and Iowan **David Rabe**. Inspired by the groundbreaking work of **Laurie Anderson**, performance artists create genre-bending works combining music, dance, poetry and visual art.

Currently claiming some 240 theaters, New York City has always been the theater capital of the US. Mainstream professional theater here is synonymous with **Broadway**, the renowned entertainment district in Manhattan. The first theaters were established here around the turn of the 20C, and the rise of the musical comedy in the 1920s catapulted the area to worldwide prominence. Today Broadway boasts some 40 legitimate theaters, most of them presenting big-budget musicals that can run for many years. Smaller **Off Broadway** theaters mounting lower-budget productions also flourish in the city. And nonprofit **Off-Off Broadway** theaters favor experimental works by emerging playwrights.

Elsewhere in the East, performance halls frequently host traveling companies of major Broadway productions, and many large cities support their own professional theaters and repertory troupes. Minneapolis, for example, boasts more theaters per capita than any American city besides New York, and Chicago's Steppenwolf Theatre Company and Second City Theatre are famous for spawning the careers of numerous actors and comedians. Stars of stage, screen and television frequently can be seen performing in summer festivals and regional theater companies such as Maine's Ogunquit Playhouse, Flat Rock Playhouse in North Carolina, and the Red Barn Playhouse in Saugatuck, Michigan.

### FILM

Although California has long been the filmmaking capital of the world, the American film industry got its start in New Jersey, where **Thomas Edison** perfected the mechanisms for making and projecting 35mm movies in 1893. As cinema progressed from novelty to industry during the first decade of the 20C, American movie studios set up shop in New Jersey, Connecticut and Philadelphia, with the most important companies headquartered in Chicago (Selig and Essanay) and New York (Edison, Vitagraph and Biograph). Rural New Jersey even served as the exterior location for Edison's *The Great Train Robbery* (1903), and other early Westerns. Several

© The United Centre

*Chicago Bulls Game at their Home The United Center, Chicago*

studios also established facilities in Jacksonville, Florida, to take advantage of year-round filming opportunities as well as lush tropical backdrops.

The early movie-going public paid a nickel for admission to films screened in small theaters known as **nickelodeons**. In 1913 New York entrepreneurs erected the first "movie palaces"—large, fantastically decorated theaters where live vaudeville shows preceded movie screenings.

Even after the film industry headed west in the 1920s, "underground" films by Shirley Clarke, John Cassavetes and Andy Warhol in the 1960s and 70s signaled the presence of an avant-garde film movement in New York. Today, Orlando, Florida, brings Hollywood back east with its theme parks/production facilities—established by both Universal and Disney-MGM studios in the 1980s.

## Sports and Recreation

For exercise, for entertainment, for drama and for fellowship, Americans love to play and watch sports. Almost no event inspires more patriotic spirit than the quadrennial **Olympic Games**, and a year-round slate of professional, collegiate and amateur competition keeps the fever pitch high. Collegiate sports, particularly football and bas-

ketball, attract the excited attention of fans and alumni nationwide, especially during the annual college football "bowl games" in January and the "Final Four" basketball tournament in March.

### Take Me Out to the Ball Games

Sometimes called the "national pastime," **baseball** originated in 1845 in New York City, when the New York Knickerbockers Base Ball Club set down the rules that eventually developed into the modern game. Played on a diamond-shaped field, the corners of which are marked by three bases and a home plate, baseball inspires legions of devoted fans who follow teams with religious intensity. Although it may appear slow-paced, the game can be fraught with suspense, the outcome often resting on a final confrontation between pitcher and batter—when victory can vanish with a ball thrown just off-center or a bat swung seconds too late. Following **spring training**, which many teams spend at practice facilities in Florida, the professional season runs from April to October, culminating in the **World Series**, a best-of-seven-games match between the American and National League champs.

Fast-paced **basketball** draws participants and spectators from every walk of life. Players in this sport score goals by successfully throwing a ball through

*Kentucky Derby at Churchill Downs*

Greater Louisville Convention & Visitors Bureau/www.gotolouisville.com

hoops suspended at either end of an indoor court. The National Basketball Association (NBA) organizes some 29 professional teams throughout the US, all competing for a berth in the **NBA Finals** held in June. Founded in 1997, the 12-team Women's National Basketball Association (WNBA) brought women's basketball to the professional level.

Appealing for its potent combination of brute force and skilled maneuvering, American **football** demands strength, speed and agility from its players in their quest to carry, pass and kick the football down a 300ft-long field to the goal. The National Football League (NFL) oversees some 32 teams in two conferences: the American and the National Football Conference. Football season begins in late summer and culminates in late January with the annual **Super Bowl** contest between the conference champions; the game draws more viewers each year than any other televised event.

## Other Professional Sports

Though **ice hockey** was born in Canada, it was in the US that the sport rose to the professional level. In this break-neck sport, skated players use sticks to maneuver a hard rubber puck into a goal at either end of an ice arena. The 29-team National Hockey League (NHL) pits Canadian and American teams in an annual race for the coveted **Stanley Cup**, with finals held in June.

**Golf** originated in Scotland; however the US now ranks as the preeminent golf nation. Public and private courses abound, especially in the Southeast, where the climate allows play nearly year-round—Florida alone claims more than 1,000 golf courses. Audiences flock to important international tournaments, such as the annual **Masters** in Augusta, Georgia. America also hosts the **US Open**; held in Flushing Meadow, New York, this tournament ranks among the top four in the world. The world's largest single-day sporting event, the annual **Indianapolis 500** (see INDIANAPOLIS) pits 33 top international contenders against each other, while Florida's **Daytona 500** attracts diehard stock-car fans. An aura of romance surrounds the annual **Kentucky Derby** (see LOUISVILLE) at Churchill Downs in Louisville; the race marks the first contest in the famed **Triple Crown** series of Thoroughbred horseracing. The prestigious **Boston Marathon** footrace, which celebrated its hundredth anniversary in 1996, numbers among the world's important marathons.

## A Recreational Paradise

From skiing in New England's White Mountains to surfing off the coast of Florida, from white-water rafting on Pennsylvania's Youghiogheny River to hiking the 2,050mi **Appalachian Trail** (see PLANNING YOUR TRIP), the eastern US offers countless opportunities for recreation. Seekers of physical fitness and natural beauty take full advantage of the East's wealth of mountains, forests, rivers and oceanfront, as well as urban parks and bike and running paths. In-line skating, snowboarding and mountain biking are all relatively recent additions to the panoply of popular recreational sports. In recent years thrill-seekers ever in search of a new challenge have popularized **extreme sports**, riskier versions of already established pursuits with names like big-air snowboarding, skysurfing, and downhill skating.

# THE REGION TODAY

## Government and Politics

When the delegates gathered in Philadelphia in 1787 to organize the government of their young country, there were varying ideas as to how it should be set up. Influenced by the theories of 18C philosophers, they believed that government should exist to protect the rights of the people, and that the will of the people—rather than that of a monarch—should prevail. Delegates also distrusted placing too much power in popular hands, worrying that it could lead to mob rule. Similarly, they saw the need for a strong leader, but not one so powerful as to become a tyrant. What they came up with was a federal structure with divided powers and a system of checks and balances whereby no one branch of government could wield total power.

Three levels of government operate in the US: federal, state and local. The structure of most **state governments** closely resembles that of the federal government, with a governor as chief executive, a two-house legislature (except for Nebraska, which has only one house) and a system of trial and appellate courts. Local governments also function along the lines of a three-pronged system, but with more variations. All states in the eastern US have **county government** units, with the exception of Rhode Island and Connecticut. Counties levy and collect taxes, provide services, enact ordinances applicable to county residents and enforce state and local laws under some form of commission/executive government—whereby an elected three-to-five-member commission sets policy and an elected or appointed executive administers those policies.

Further down the line are the **municipal governments**, which perform many of the same functions as county governments. Traditionally, municipal governments in large cities have operated with an elected mayor as executive and an elected council as the legislative arm.

### FEDERAL GOVERNMENT

The US Constitution divides the government into three separate branches with varying responsibilities. Although the Constitution leaves all powers not specifically delegated to the federal government to the states and municipalities, there is overlap in certain areas.

### Executive Branch

The executive branch consists of a president and vice president—both elected together to a maximum of two four-year terms of office. In addition, 14 **cabinet departments**, whose heads are appointed by the president, and 80 separate agencies help carry out executive-branch functions and advise the president frequently on issues of state. Cabinet departments include: State, Treasury, Defense, Justice, Interior, Agriculture, Commerce, Labor, Health and Human Services, Education, Transportation, Housing and Urban Development, Energy, and Veterans Affairs. The Executive Office also includes a number of independent agencies, such as the Central Intelligence Agency, the National Security Agency, and the National Aeronautics and Space Administration.

The main function of the executive branch is to carry out and enforce laws and regulations. Both the president and vice president must be at least 35 years old, be native US citizens, and have lived in the US for at least 14 years prior to taking office. Although their candidacies are submitted to popular vote, both the president and vice president are actually elected by an elaborate system called the **electoral college**. Under this system, voters casting their ballots for a certain candidate actually vote for a slate of electors committed to that candidate. Electors cast their pro forma votes several weeks after the popular election at the electoral college meeting.

The Constitution designates the president as head of state, chief treaty maker, and commander-in-chief of the armed forces. He has wide-ranging appointive powers, including that of ambassadors, Supreme Court justices and lower court judges, and heads of federal departments "with the advice and consent of the Senate."

As a check on the Congress, the president has the power to veto legislation; but that veto can be overridden by a two-thirds vote of both houses of Congress.

Although not specifically granted him by the Constitution, the president's responsibilities have expanded over the years to include drafting domestic legislation and devising and implementing foreign policy.

The vice president presides over the Senate; otherwise, that office has no specific duties except to step into the breach if the president dies or becomes so disabled that his is unable to perform his duties.

Most of the administrative work of the various executive departments and agencies is performed by nonpartisan civilian employees. Numbering approximately 2.5 million, this civilian cadre works primarily in Washington, DC, and other major US cities. A significant majority (70 percent) are employed by just four federal agencies: the departments of Defense, Veterans Affairs, Treasury and Justice.

## Legislative Branch

The legislative, or lawmaking, branch is made up of two sections—a **House of Representatives** and a smaller **Senate**, collectively known as the Congress. The House, where states are represented according to population, at present numbers 435 members. The Senate, in contrast, contains two members from each of the 50 states no matter how large or small the state.

Senate candidates run for six-year terms in staggered years—thus about one-third of the Senate faces re-election every two years. To run for office, Senate candidates must be at least 30 years old. Representatives, who run for office every two years, must be at least 25 years old.

Unlike the presidency or vice presidency neither senators nor representatives are required to be native-born. Senators must have lived in the US for nine years representatives for seven.

By far the largest part of contemporary congressional business is taken up with drafting and passing laws. Other powers granted to the Congress include declaring war, levying taxes, regulating interstate commerce, and impeaching and trying other government officials including presidents and judges. As a check on the president, the Senate must confirm all presidential appointees and ratify all treaties made with other governments by the executive branch Responsibility for originating tax and appropriations bills rests with the House of Representatives.

## Judicial Branch

Smallest of the three branches of government, the judiciary interprets the law of the land. It consists of the **US Supreme Court** (the country's highest tribunal), some 94 courts of original federal jurisdiction called **district courts** and 13 **appellate courts**. There are also a number of special courts, among them US Claims Court, US Tax Court and the US Court of Military Appeals.

The Supreme Court considers constitutional questions arising from both the lower federal courts and the state court system. This power gives it a check on the Congress by allowing review of laws passed by that body.

Its nine justices—one chief justice and eight associates—are appointed by the president, confirmed by the Senate, and have lifetime tenure. The last provision gives judges a large measure of independence, helping to ensure that political pressures do not unduly influence judicial opinions. District and appeals-court judges are likewise appointed to lifetime terms. Beginning its term the first Monday in October and lasting through June, the court usually hears about 150 cases per year.

## Revenue

Approximately $1 trillion is collected each year to operate the US government, the lion's share from personal ncome taxes. Other revenue sources nclude corporate income taxes; excise taxes on items such as gasoline, cigarettes and liquor; energy and timber sales; Social Security taxes; customs duties; and estate taxes.

## Armed Forces

The US maintains military bases around the world and forces numbering some 1.4 million in the form of a full-time army, navy, marine corps and air force. Additional forces are available from reserves, which may be called upon in times of war. Military service has been voluntary since 1973, when conscription ended.

## STATE GOVERNMENTS

As in the federal system, the chief executive and legislators in each state are elected. While most state judges previously were elected, that practice has begun to change, with many now being appointed by the governor.

The US Constitution stipulates that each state operates under its own constitution. Thus, state governments have a number of responsibilities, including maintaining state roads and facilities, regulating businesses and professions, regulating driver and motor-vehicle licensing, setting standards for educational institutions, regulating the sale of liquor and tobacco products, and passing and enforcing laws.

State laws and regulations can vary widely. Some allow civilians to carry a concealed firearm as long as they have a valid permit; in other states, this practice is strictly forbidden. Liquor laws and motor-vehicle speed limits also vary considerably from state to state. Frequently, state and local responsibilities overlap with federal regulations. The operation of public schools, for example, is the responsibility of local school boards, even though public schools must also meet various federal requirements.

## POLITICAL PARTIES

Since the presidency of Abraham Lincoln (1861-65), two major political parties—

the generally liberal **Democrats** and the relatively conservative **Republicans**—have dominated US politics. While third parties, such as the Reform and Libertarian parties, often field candidates, it's difficult for them to gain enough followers to win an election because most voters choose to remain within the mainstream rather than vote for a candidate who has little chance of winning. Although most Americans over the age of 18 are eligible to vote, only about 50 percent of registered voters participate in national elections.

## Economy

More than 200 years after its founding, the democratic and economic mythology of the United States remains immensely appealing. According to the American ideal, any enterprising person, regardless of race, creed or social class, should have equal opportunity to work hard, earn money by any legal means, and improve his or her lot. As the rags-to-riches lives of countless immigrants, celebrities and CEOs attest, the "American Dream" has come true for millions. On average, US citizens enjoy a higher per capita income and a higher standard of living than any other people on earth.

The US economy thrives on its unique historical system of free enterprise—a laissez-faire capitalism whereby individuals can create, own and control the production of virtually any marketable good or commodity they can conceive, without undue government interference, except in matters of consumer protection.

A **federal income tax** on earnings helps support state and federal government activities, including national defense, space exploration, the public school system, and major public works projects such as airports and interstate highways. In addition, most Americans contribute a small percentage of their annual income to the federal Social Security system, which provides retirement benefits and medical care for older citizens.

Like other industrialized nations, the US has transformed itself over the last few generations from an agriculturally based economy to one based on service industries and manufacturing. Today the nation's $8 trillion **gross national product** (**GNP**)—the combined value of all goods and services—is the largest in the world.

Rich farming areas, manufacturing and trade centers, and large metropolitan areas of the eastern US account for almost 70 percent of this output. However, the economies of individual states vary widely according to their natural resources, labor pools, transportation networks and geography.

For example, many residents in the urban Northeast (Connecticut, Massachusetts, New York, Pennsylvania) work in high-end professional services such as banking, finance and law, earning per capita personal incomes among the highest in the nation. In the New York City financial district, dubbed "Wall Street," investors buy and sell millions of shares of corporate stock through the three major US stock exchanges—the **New York Stock Exchange** (NYSE), the **American Stock Exchange** (AMEX) and **NASDAQ** (an electronic network regulated by the National Association of Securities Dealers).

To the west, by contrast, the five **Great Lakes** anchor a region characterized by its fertile farmland, abundant natural resources and navigable inland waterways, which support prosperous agribusinesses, heavy industry and the shipping trade.

## NATURAL RESOURCES

Few economies are as abundantly supplied with natural resources as the eastern US. In addition to fertile soils, a favorable climate and adequate water supplies for agriculture and hydroelectric power, this varied terrain contains a wealth of fossil fuels, minerals, stone, timber and freshwater and ocean fish. Throughout the East, extractive industries harvest coal, natural gas, kaolin, crushed stone and sand, marble and granite, iron ore, gems and even gold. Altogether, mining accounts for some $120 billion of the US GNP.

In general, the most flagrant and careless examples of environmental damage from strip mining and agricultural practices have been regulated out of existence in the eastern US in recent decades. However, as the nation burns an ever-growing tonnage of fossil fuels (oil, coal and natural gas) for electricity, manufacturing and transportation, air and water quality have suffered. Many eastern cities from Atlanta to Boston suffer visibly high levels of air pollution (haze and smog).

## AGRICULTURE

In the 21C, US agriculture coexists uneasily with global markets and expanding urbanization. Today California and Texas lead the nation in overall agricultural production, but picturesque vistas of American farm life still dominate large swaths of the Midwest and the South. Iowa, the nation's third most productive agricultural state, is a cornerstone of the **Corn Belt**, a broad warm-summer region nestled between the Ohio and the lower Missouri rivers. To the north cooler summers yield crops of clover hay and small grains, supporting an elongated **Dairy Belt** from Wisconsin (famous for its cheeses) eastward along the Great Lakes into New England. With its upstate agricultural areas, New York ranks second to Vermont in the production of maple syrup.

Among the southern states, North Carolina, the top tobacco-grower, ranks highest—seventh nationally—in cash receipts from total agricultural production. Florida, the nation's leading grower of oranges and other citrus fruits, ranks ninth agriculturally; and Georgia, the largest state east of the Mississippi, ranks tenth in total agricultural output and leads the nation in the production of peanuts.

## SERVICE INDUSTRIES

Even in states where agriculture and manufacturing are major parts of local economies, service industries are a prominent and fast-growing segment—23 percent of earnings in Ala-

*Corn Field in the Corn Belt*

© PhotoDisc, Inc

ama, 33 percent in Florida, 28 percent n Illinois, 27 percent in New Hampshire. A broad collective category, service industries vary from low-paying retail or food-service businesses to high-level executive consulting. The largest non-government, private-sector service industry in the US is **health services**, which accounted for $460 billion of the total US GNP in 1997.

Tourism and travel-related services (lodging, transportation, meals, entertainment) also account for an increasing proportion of US employment, goods and services, and tax revenues—as much as $515 billion per year. With five million international visitors each year, New York City ranks as a top US city. But Florida, home to sunny beaches, Walt Disney World and multicultural Miami, is an even more popular destination, attracting 25 percent of the 46 million international visitors to the US each year.

## MANUFACTURING

While many US businesses desire a national or global focus for their marketing and product lines, production for specific industries continues to decentralize. Leading telecommunications or pharmaceutical companies may have signature buildings in New York and other cities, while production and research facilities are scattered from West Virginia to Florida. The high-tech industry, birthed in upstate New York in the 1950s by International Business Machines (IBM), now occupies a prominent role not only in California's Silicon Valley, but also in the Washington, DC area; the Research Triangle in Raleigh-Durham, North Carolina; Atlanta, Georgia, and many points in between.

The US space industry, officially based in Washington, DC (home to the National Aeronautics and Space Administration), also concentrates thousands of high-tech employees in Huntsville, Alabama, and Cape Canaveral, Florida. Similarly, the big three US automobile manufacturers (General Motors, Ford and DaimlerChrysler) are headquartered in Michigan but have large plants in other states.

The US continues to lead world production in many categories of manufacturing, including the making of aluminum, numerous chemicals and plastics, forest products, and paper and paperboard.

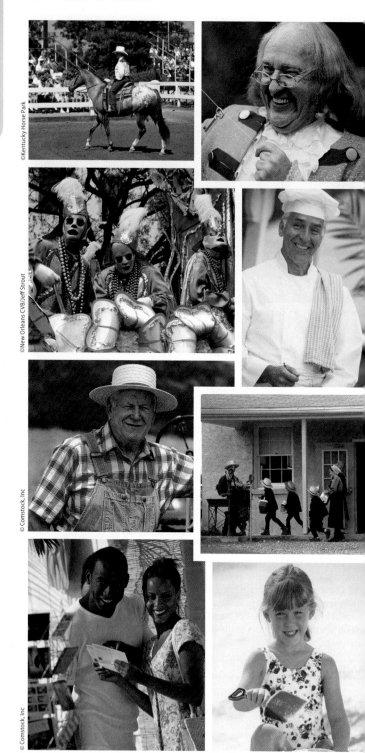

©Kentucky Horse Park

©New Orleans CVB/Jeff Strout

© Comstock, Inc

© Comstock, Inc

# People and Society

From the time the Puritans established their colonies here in the 17C, America has had a reputation as a land of hope, a place to wipe the slate clean and start new. Its population today is largely made up of immigrants and descendants of immigrants, people who fled economic hardship, religious intolerance or political persecution in their homelands in the hopes of living the "American Dream" of equal opportunity for all. This steady influx has resulted in a heady mix of cultural traditions, influences and customs that is commonly described as a "melting pot." Multiculturalism pervades American society, and diversity is perhaps its chief characteristic—in the 1990 census, just 5 percent of the country's residents claimed to be of "American" ancestry.

New York City, the major port of entry into the New World, nurtures an exceptional number of strong, closely-knit immigrant communities, as do Chicago, Miami, Milwaukee and Washington, DC. The state of New York claims more Polish-Americans and Italian-Americans than any other state, and the Northeast boasts the highest concentrations of immigrants from the Dominican Republic, Puerto Rico, Ecuador, Syria, Jamaica and Haiti. More than half of the nation's persons of Scandinavian and Slavic origin are clustered in the Midwest—Minnesota has more Norwegian-descended residents than any other state. Close to half of Americans claiming Scotch-Irish ancestry live in the South, and large numbers of immigrants from the Caribbean and Central America have settled in Florida, giving that state one of the largest Hispanic populations in the nation.

Most African Americans in the US are descended from slaves who were brought here in the 18C-19C to work on massive plantations south of the Mason-Dixon Line, the boundary between Pennsylvania and Maryland that served as a symbolic border between slave and free states. After the Civil War, industry boomed in Chicago, Detroit, Cleveland, Philadelphia and other cities in the North and Midwest, attracting newly freed slaves and contributing to a black diaspora that carried the African-American culture to those regions. Today some 3.2 million African Americans live in New York State, the highest concentration in the nation.

## REGIONAL IDENTITY

Descended from hard-working, frugal Puritans, **New Englanders** are characterized by their manner of self-reliance and reserve. The region's academic tinge comes from the presence of many of the nation's top-ranked colleges and universities—some of them referred to as the "Ivy League" in reference to their long histories. With low crime levels and high home-ownership rates, the New England states rank among the nation's top places to raise children.

The **Mid-Atlantic** region is the nation's most populous, and an urban lifestyle prevails in cities such as New York City, Philadelphia, Baltimore and Washington, DC. Seat of the nation's government, Washington is characterized by its political power brokers. Sharing a reputation for brusqueness, residents of the financial and cultural capital of New York City include high-rolling Wall Street types as well as many of the movers and shakers of the performing- and visual-arts scene.

Known for its conservative traditional values and friendly people, the **Midwest** contrasts the brawny industrialized cities of Chicago, Detroit and Minneapolis with pastoral farm communities. Every four years, presidential hopefuls, looking to confirm their viability as candidates, hold a "straw poll" in Iowa—indicating a belief that the pulse of mainstream America beats in the Heartland.

In a country in which everything seems to be on the move, **Southerners** tend to live life at a slower pace. They are known for their open manner toward strangers—thus the term "Southern hospitality." With the rise to prominence of dynamic cities such as Atlanta, New Orleans and Miami, the region has lately shrugged off its undeserved reputation as a cultural backwater, and a new influx of foreign investment in the Carolinas

*Lobster Dinner*

© Comstock, Inc

and Georgia makes for a distinctly cosmopolitan atmosphere in some areas. Regardless of where they live, Americans are known to be ardent defenders of the individual rights and freedoms defined in their Constitution—to exercise free speech, to assemble, to keep and bear arms, and to enjoy privacy and freedom of religion, among others. Such liberties come at a price, however, as recent debates over gun control and abortion attest.

The people of the United States—a country still in the process of defining itself—defy most attempts at classification. Social scientists, demographers and the media are quick to tag segments of society with labels such as "Baby Boomers" (the generation born after World War II) and "Gen-Xers" (persons born in the late 1960s-70s). Yet exceptions contradict every rule, keeping alive the challenge to create a definitive description of mainstream America

## Food and Drink

Blessed with an impressive variety of locally produced ingredients and myriad foodways imported by immigrant populations, the eastern US serves up a bounty of culinary specialties, which differ from region to region.

### NORTHEASTERN TRADITIONS

Casual clam shacks and rural dinner halls invite seafood lovers to sample the abundance of fish and shellfish draw from the cold Atlantic waters off Ne England. Crab, clams, blue mussel oysters and bay scallops are serve steamed, boiled, fried or simmered i thick, milk-based chowders. **Maine lobster** wins the day here—whether yo order it boiled whole with butter in a elegant restaurant presentation, or ea the succulent meat lightly tossed wit mayonnaise and stuffed into bread o a **lobster roll** at a waterside fish join Regional menus also feature swordfish striped bass, Atlantic salmon, bluefisl tuna, cod and haddock. Held on th beach, a traditional **New Englan clambake** includes lobsters, shellfisl onions, new potatoes and ears of cor packed in wet seaweed and steame atop charcoal-heated stones in a p dug into the sand.

Orchards and bogs yield ingredient for apple cider, Concord grape jam, an cranberry juice. In Vermont, sap fro sugar-maple trees is boiled down int thick **maple syrup** and eaten on par cakes, drizzled over ice cream and bake into pies, cookies and puddings. Don miss a chance to try tart Maine **blue berries** (in pies, pancakes or muffins **Vermont Cheddar** cheese, or **Bosto baked beans** and **brown bread**.

### MID-ATLANTIC MELTING POT

A mustard-laced hotdog from a stree vendor; lox and bagels or a slice o creamy cheesecake in a Jewish deli; dir sum in a family-owned Chinatown eat ery; trendsetting cuisine in a world-class restaurant—all qualify as a typical culinary experience in New York City. Travel to the wine-growing region around the upstate Finger Lakes to taste fine vintages from European varietals.

**Crab** ( *see BALTIMORE*) is king along the eastern shore of Maryland and Virginia, where mouth-watering crabcakes are a signature dish. Salty slices of **Smithfield ham** tucked inside velvety homemade biscuits is another Virginia treat.

In the Pennsylvania Dutch region of Lancaster County, Pennsylvania, German culinary traditions inspire hearty dishes, served family-style in many area restaurants: **snitz and knepp** (boiled cured ham with dried apples and dumplings), sauerkraut served with pork and mashed potatoes, **chowchow** (a pickled relish made with beans, peppers and corn) and sweet **shoofly pie**, a crumb-topped confection made with molasses and brown sugar.

## HEARTLAND FARE

Midwestern cooking takes advantage of the abundant products of lake, garden, field and forest—wild rice from Minnesota, pecans and walnuts from Missouri, sour cherries from Michigan, fish from the Great Lakes, and beef, pork and lamb from the farms of Illinois. The northwest corner of Wisconsin ranks as the most productive dairy land in the nation, annually churning out two billion pounds of cheese.

In larger cities, search out steakhouses for thick cuts of corn-fed, aged **Midwestern beef**. Small towns often hold all-you-can-eat Friday-night fish fries, proffering piles of sizzling whitefish with tartar sauce on the side. Immigrants who settled here in the late 19C originated such regional fare as Scandinavian fruit soups, Polish pierogi, German bratwurst, and the famed **deep-dish pizza** of Chicago. Distinctive **Cincinnati chili** (served over spaghetti and topped with cheese) was created in Greek-owned chili parlors, and many of Milwaukee's famed **breweries** were founded by German immigrant families.

*Key Lime Pie*

©iStockphoto.com/Stephen Walls

## DOWN-HOME COOKIN'

**Barbecue** is a high art in the South: experts rub pork with a mix of dry spices, smoke the meat slowly over a hickory fire, and dress it with tangy vinegar and red pepper or a tomato-based sauce (sauce preferences vary regionally). Traditional barbecue is served with a side of "slaw"—a creamy salad of shredded cabbage, carrots, mayonnaise and vinegar. For a typical southern lunch, collard greens, black-eyed peas or green beans are seasoned with bacon or fatback, simmered for hours and served alongside crispy fried chicken, catfish or ham. In Georgia, look for sweet **Vidalia onions** and fried green tomatoes. The South Carolina Lowcountry is the place to order **shrimp**; try shrimp and grits or Frogmore stew, a heady boil of shrimp, sausage and corn. Fresh Gulf of Mexico seafood—Apalachicola Bay oysters, amberjack, grouper, pompano, red snapper and stone crab—headline menus in Florida and along the southern Gulf Coast. End a meal here with a slice of tart **Key lime pie**. International influences are evident in Miami in the paring of grilled fish with tropical-fruit salsa, and Cuban fare including black beans with rice, and *arroz con pollo* (chicken with yellow rice). Visitors go to New Orleans expressly to indulge in spicy **Cajun and Creole** ( *see NEW ORLEANS*) specialties such as crawfish etouffée, jambalaya, seafood gumbo and red beans and rice.

New Hampshire village

# ATLANTA AREA

Framed by the foothills of the Blue Ridge Mountains, and blessed with a temperate climate, Atlanta is also Georgia's largest city. The Atlanta metropolitan area today encompasses a sprawling 6,126sq mi in 20 surrounding counties, and harbors more than four million people. Within an hour-and-a-half drive south of the city, near Macon, you'll find historic memorials to those who shaped Georgia's past, from its prehistoric mound-builders to its Civil War prisoners. Stretching along Georgia's 105mi section of Atlantic coastline, the gracious city of Savannah and the nearby Golden Isles offer a respite from Atlanta's frenetic pace.

The state now known as Georgia began as a vast tract of land between the 31st and the 36th parallels that King Charles II granted as the Carolina colony to eight Lords Proprietor. In 1732 George II gave the land between the Savannah and Altamaha rivers to 21 trustees, including English soldier and philanthropist **James Edward Oglethorpe**. European settlers established plantations in this new land, and an agrarian economy grew up around the cultivation of rice and indigo. The invention of the cotton gin (*'cotton engine'*) by Eli Whitney in 1793, made cotton cultivation highly profitable, by accomplishing the formerly arduous task of separating the fiber from the seed. Accordingly, textile mills and railroads were established, and Atlanta was founded in 1836 as a rail center.

*Atlanta Skyline*

At the dawn of the 21C, Atlanta ranked as the country's twelfth-largest metropolitan area: transportation, along with finance and retail, contributed the lion's share of the city's revenue. Today, Atalanta has 20 colleges and universities, a symphony orchestra, a ballet company, myriad museums, and an international airport (Atlanta Hartsfield), which recently surpassed Chicago's O'Hare as the country's busiest. **Lenox Square** and **Phipps Plaza** malls create consumer heaven in Buckhead, while the 2.2-million-sq ft **Mall of Georgia**, which opened in August 1999 *(north of Altanta off I-85)*, is the largest in the state. A plethora of fine restaurants rounds out Atlanta's menu of offerings, serving up simple Southern dishes and sophisticated continental cuisine.

## Area Address Book

### WHERE TO STAY

🪙 *For coin ranges, see the Legend on the cover flap.*

**$$$ The Ritz-Carlton, Buckhead** – *3434 Peachtree Rd., Atlanta, GA.* ✗ & 🅿 ☎*404-237-2700. www.ritzcarlton.com. 553 rooms.* Buckhead seems a logical setting for one of the city's most opulent hotels. The mahogany-paneled lobby is brimming with 18C and 19C English antiques and artwork. Guest rooms are a spacious 365sq ft, and **The Dining Room ($$)** receives constant praise.

**$$$ The Gastonian** – *220 E. Gaston, Savannah, GA.* 🅿 ☎*912-232-2869. www.gastonian.com. 17 rooms.* Two adjoining Regency-style mansions house this luxurious historic-district inn. All guest quarters have working fireplaces and are individually decorated with antique four-poster beds and Oriental rugs. Some come with whirpools. Attentive service defines Southern hospitality.

**$$ The Jekyll Island Club Hotel** – *371 Riverview Dr., Jekyll Island, GA.* ✗ & 🅿 ⛴ ☎*912-635-2600. www.jekyllclub.com. 157 rooms.* Victorian architecture and period reproductions give the restored historic landmark a palatial feel. With three 18-hole golf courses, 9 tennis courts, and a nearby beach club, you may never want to leave the family-friendly complex.

**$ The Eliza Thompson House** – *5 W. Jones St., Savannah, GA.* & ☎*912-236-3620. elizathompsonhouse.com. 25 rooms.* Named for the society widow who built the stately historic-district house back in 1847, this B&B features antique furnishings. Spend a few hours in the pretty courtyard listening to the fountain's quiet hum. Room rate includes free downtown parking pass.

### WHERE TO EAT

**$$$ Au Pied de Cochon** – *3315 Peachtree Rd., Atlanta, GA* ☎*404-946-9000.* **French.** What could be more Parisian than somewhere you can order pigs feet, escargot or pommes frites 24 hours a day? This brasserie is lavish and indulgent, not or those on a diet or on a budget. Singles appreciate the brisk bar scene.

**$$$ Elizabeth on 37th** – *105 E. 37th St., Savannah, GA.* ☎*912-236-5547.* **New Southern.** Chef Elizabeth Terry prepares traditional 18C and 19C dishes, with a nod to health-conscious fare, in this Greek Revival-style mansion. Black-eyed-pea patty with curry cream and sesame-almond crusted grouper are among the winning choices. *Reservations required.*

**$$ Canoe** – *4199 Paces Ferry Rd. N.W., Atlanta, GA.* ☎*770-432-2663.* **American.** A rustic dining room that looks like the interior of a spruced-up cabin (soaring cherry-wood ceilings, shiny limestone walls) is the setting for this beloved restaurant in the Vinings area. Duck with sweet potato and green onion hash, and herb-crusted grouper get raves. The landscaped patio overlooks the Chattahoochee River.

**$$ South City Kitchen** – *1144 Crescent Ave., Atlanta, GA.* ☎*404-873-7358.* **New Southern.** Determined to dispel the image that Southern cuisine is heavy, the chef fuses regional ingredients with a light touch. Stellar results include rock shrimp and green onion beignets, and sweet potato ravioli with shredded chicken. This contemporary Midtown bungalow enjoys a high-energy buzz.

**$ The Crab Shack** – *40 Estill Hammock, Tybee Island, GA.* ☎*912-786-9857.* **Seafood.** This bare-bones eatery, 17mi east of Savannah, offers the freshest shellfish around. Huge portions of boiled or steamed crabs, shrimp and oysters come with corn on the cob and potatoes, and are served on wooden tables.

**$ Gladys Knight and Ron Winans Chicken & Waffles** – *529 Peachtree St NE, Atlanta, GA* ☎*404-874-9393.* **Southern.** A classic southern experience, this late-night eatery serves soul food to groups, couples, families and those leaving the clubs after a night of dancing. Don't miss the peach cobbler or the grits.

# ATLANTA★★

Atlanta pulses with activity, as the commercial center of the Southeast, while retaining its signature Southern hospitality. The city sprawls atop a high granite ridge against a leafy backdrop of wooded hills. From its gleaming downtown skyscrapers to the pricey boutiques of Buckhead, contemporary Atlanta offers visitors a smorgasbord of cultural, entertainment, shopping and dining opportunities.

🛈 **Information:** Atlanta Convention & Visitors Bureau, 233 Peachtree St., NE. ☎404-521-6688 or www.atlanta.net.

🅿 **Parking:** Driving in Atlanta is more civilized than in other major metropolitan areas. If you decide to drive, ask those at your destination if they validate parking. Validation rates are often substantially discounted.

👁 **Don't Miss:** The insider look at broadcast news at the CNN Studio.

**Kids:** A tour of New World of Coca-Cola.

👤 **Also See:** *BIRMINGHAM, MONTGOMERY*

## A Bit of History

Incorporated in 1845, Atlanta became an important Confederate transportation hub. As such it was the prime target of Union general William T. Sherman during the Civil War. On Kennesaw Mountain north of Atlanta on July 2, 1864, Sherman drove Gen. Joseph E. Johnston and his 65,000 men from the Kennesaw line. Today **Kennesaw Mountain National Battlefield Park** (*off I-75 near Marietta at Old Hwy. 41 & Stilesboro Rd.;* ☎*770-427-4686*) preserves more than 2,800 acres, including 11mi of original earthworks from the battle. Sherman pushed on, his advance culminating in the bloody **Battle of Atlanta** on July 22. In September 1864 Sherman occupied the city; two months later he burned Atlanta to the ground.

Like its symbol, the phoenix, Atlanta rose from the ashes of the Civil War and re-established itself as the South's transportation and distribution center. In the early 20C, the practice of racial segregation blocked Atlanta's efforts to become a major US city, but the civil rights movement (👁*see INTRODUCTION*) in the early 1960s, led by **Dr. Martin Luther King, Jr.**, ultimately resulted in the end of legal segregation.

The city gained international status in 1996 as host of the Centennial Olympic Games. Two lasting legacies from that event are the 21-acre **Olympic Centennial Park** (*Marietta St. & International Blvd., 404-223-4412*) and **Turner Field** (*755 Hank Aaron Dr.;* ☎*404-522-7630*) The park, with its centerpiece Olympic Rings fountain, hosts special events downtown; Turner Field is now home to the **Atlanta Braves** baseball team.

# Midtown/Downtown

tlanta's attractions range along its main rtery, **Peachtree Street**, which runs orth to south from **Buckhead**★★ — te of the city's trendiest restaurants nd shopping areas—through the arts istrict of **Midtown**★★ to the office owers of **Downtown**★★. Midtown is where you'll find the city's best-known erforming-arts centers—the **Fox heatre**★ *(660 Peachtree St.;* &*404-81-2100)*, a grand restored 1920s movie alace that now stages live productions; nd the **Woodruff Arts Center**★ com-lex *(Peachtree at 16th St.;* ✗&*)*, which ncludes Atlanta Symphony Hall *(*&*404-33-4900)*, the Alliance Theatre *(*&*404-33-4650)*, the High Museum and the tlanta College of Art.

▸ *Sights below are organized from south to north, beginning with Downtown.*

## NN Studio Tour★★

*NN Center, Techwood Dr. & Marietta St., owntown.* ◷ *Open daily 9am–5pm.* ◉*$12* &*404-827-2300 (ticket office). http:// nn.com/studiotour.*

n 1980 Atlanta entrepreneur Ted Turner aunched the Cable News Network CNN), the first 24-hour cable news sta-ion, which broadcasts from 14-story **NN Center**. The 50min studio tour hows visitors the inner workings of the etwork and allows access to a glassed-n gallery where visitors can watch CNN eporters and newscasters at work.

## nderground Atlanta★★

*0 Upper Alabama St., Downtown.* ✗&*404-523-2311. www.underground-tlanta.com.*

his thriving mix of street vendors, retail utlets, entertainment and dining facili-es occupies the site of the city's birth. s Atlanta grew as a railroad center, the round level became congested with racks. To accommodate street traffic, iaducts were built over the tracks, and ommerce shifted to the upper levels. In 990 developers revitalized the under-round, re-creating six blocks of early aloons, shops and restaurants. **Upper**

## A Street Named Peachtree

One of Atlanta's most puzzling para-doxes is represented by the city's main artery, Peachtree Street.

More than 37 streets in Atlanta bear the name Peachtree, yet, surprisingly, you would be hard-pressed to find a single peach tree in the city.

Although the name dates back to 1825, no one truly knows its origin. Some believe that it derives from a Cherokee word for pine tree.

**Alabama Street Plaza** is used for spe-cial events, such as the dropping of a giant peach from the plaza's light tower to mark the New Year. Anchoring the south end of the complex is the 1869 **Georgia Railroad Freight Depot**.

## New World of Coca-Cola★★

Kids *121 Baker St., Downtown.* ◷*Open daily 9am–5pm.* ◉*$14* &*404-676-5151, www. woccatlanta.com.*
Located just outside the Kenney's Alley entrance to Underground Atlanta, this brand new facility is a tribute to the world's best-selling soft drink, born in Atlanta in 1886. Displays here trace the Coca-Cola story from its humble begin-nings at a downtown Atlanta drug store to its multinational presence today. The new World of Coca-Cola opened in May, 2007. No more soda jerks; today it includes a 4-D theater and fully-functional bottling line. At the exhibit's end, enjoy Coca-Cola products from around the globe in the tasting experience exhibits.

## Georgia State Capitol★★

*Washington & Courtland Sts., Downtown.* &*404-656-2844. www.sos.state.ga.us.*
Situated on five acres of one of Down-town's highest ridges, Georgia's Classical Renaissance 1889 limestone capitol, with its four-story portico, is a scaled-down ver-sion of the US Capitol in Washington, DC. Here in the state's political nerve center, are the offices of Georgia's governor, the state Senate and House of Representatives.

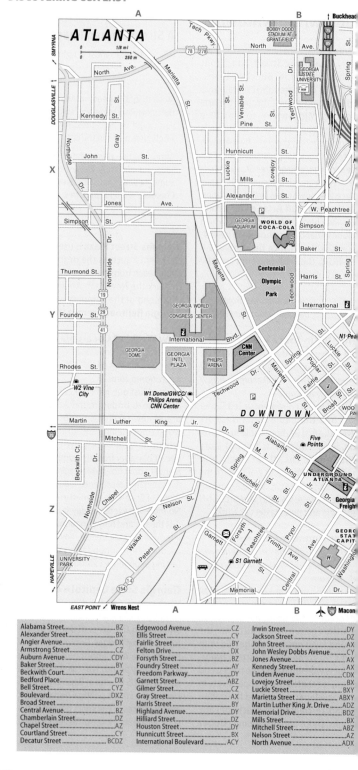

ATLANTA

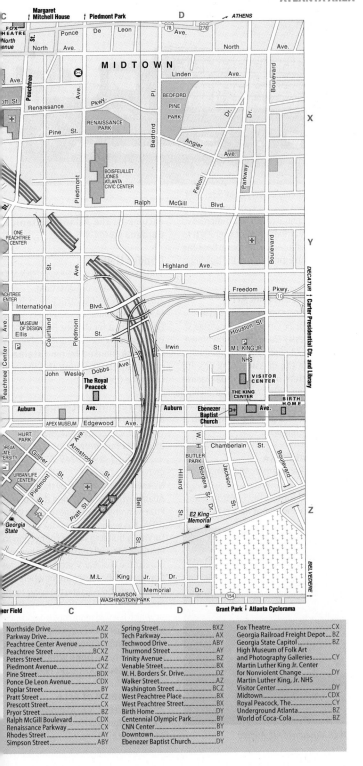

*The Coca-Cola delivery truck from 1934*

Inside the central **rotunda**, an impressive three-story atrium rises just over 237ft to the dome. Housed on the fourth floor, the **Capitol Museum** recounts the building's history.

### High Museum Folk Art and Photography Galleries★

*Georgia-Pacific Center, 133 Peachtree St. at John Wesley Dobbs Ave., Downtown.* ♿☎404-577-6940.

Located in the massive, pink granite headquarters of the Georgia-Pacific Corporation, this branch of the High Museum focuses on all manifestations of folk art and photography, with a Southern emphasis.

### Piedmont Park★

*Piedmont Ave. & 12th St., Midtown.* ☎404-875-7275.

Developed for the 1895 Cotton States Exposition, Piedmont Park's 185 acres

*High Museum of Art, Atlanta*

encompass the **Atlanta Botanical Gardena** (☎404-876-5859).

### Rhodes Hall ★

*1516 Peachtree St. N.W., Midtown.* P ☎404-885-7800. www.georgiatrust.org.

This 1904 castle-like structure of Stone Mountain granite, headquarters of the Georgia Trust for Historic Preservation, is noteworthy for its grand mahogany **staircase**, flanked by nine **stained-glass panels** depicting the rise and fall of the Confederacy.

### Margaret Mitchell House and Museum★★

*10th & Peachtree Sts., Midtown.* Visit by guided tour only, daily 12 pm–5pm. $12. ♿ P ☎ 404-249-7015. www.gwtw.org.

Nicknamed "the dump" by the sprightly Atlanta writer who penned the Pulitzer Prize-winning novel *Gone with the Wind* (1936), this restored house is the city's only surviving building with a connection to Margaret Mitchell (1900-49) and her epic novel of the Civil War. Visitors can view the tiny, ground-floor apartment where the author lived (1925-32) and the living-room nook where she wrote the renowned classic, which has sold more copies worldwide than any other book except the Bible. Filled with memorabilia, props and footage from the 1939 film, the **Gone With The Wind Movie Museum** opened in 1999.

### High Museum of Art★

*280 Peachtree St. N.E., Midtown.* Closed Mon. $15. ♿☎404-733-4444. www.high.org.

The star in the Woodruff Arts Center's crown is this striking contemporary **structure**a (1983, Richard Meier) covered with white porcelain-enameled steel panels. Rodin's sculpture *The Shade*, a gift from the French government, presides over the front lawn. The musuem was expanded in 2005; inside, highlights from the permanent collection—some 11,000 works—include American decorative arts, 19C American landscapes and contemporary American art.

## Atlanta History Center★★

Kids *130 W. Paces Ferry Rd., Buckhead.*
✕ ♿ P ☎ *404-814-4000.*
*www.atlhist.org.*
This complex comprises a history museum, a research library and archives, two historic houses, a series of gardens and a restaurant. Four excellent permanent exhibits in the **Atlanta History Museum**★★ bring the city's defining experiences to life.
Be sure to visit the elegant 1928 **Swan House**a (*☛visit by guided tour only*), designed by Philip Shutze. In contrast, the simple frame buildings of **Tullie Smith Farm** (1845) provide a glimpse into the lifestyle of an early Georgia farm family.

## Georgia Governor's Mansion★★

*391 W. Paces Ferry Rd. N.E., Buckhead.*
*☛Visit by guided tour only.* ☎ *404-261-1776.*
Its Doric-columned façade facing one of Buckhead's main thoroughfares, the 24,000sq ft Greek Revival-style brick structure contains a museum-quality collection of **Federal antiques**. Upstairs rooms are reserved for the use of the current governor and his family.

## Additional Sights

## Grant Park

*Entrance at the intersection of Boulevard & Cherokee Ave. S.E.*
Grant Park is the name given to both the city's second-largest park and the adjacent neighborhood. Its rolling terrain is home to two popular attractions: the Cyclorama and the 40-acre **Zoo Atlanta**

(*800 Cherokee Ave.;* Kids ✕ ♿ P ☎ *404-624-5600*).

## Atlanta Cyclorama★★

*800 Cherokee Ave. S.E.* ◷*Open daily 9am–4:30pm.* ◷*Closed Mon.* ♿ P ☎*404-624-1071. www.bcaatlanta.com.*
One of three existing cycloramas in the country (the other two are in Gettysburg, PA (♿*see GETTYSBURG*); and at New York City's Metropolitan Museum of Art), this 42ft-tall painting-in-the-round weighs more than 9,000 pounds and measures 358ft in circumference. Its scenes—which took a group of German, Austrian and Polish artists 22 months to complete—depict the Battle of Atlanta, the Civil War standoff that broke the back of the Confederacy. Visitors sit on a viewing platform surrounded by the painting and watch the events of July 22, 1864 unfold as the stage revolves.

## Carter Presidential Center and Library★★

*441 Freedom Pkwy.* ◷*Open Mon-Sat 9am–4:45pm, Sun 12pm-4:45pm.* ◷*$8.* ✕ ♿ P ☎ *404-865-7100. www.jimmycarterlibrary.org.*
The official library/museum of **Jimmy Carter**, the 39th president of the US (1977-81), was built in 1986. Its **Carter Library Museum**★ features a pictorial biography of Carter's rise from a Georgia peanut farmer to president, exhibits describing his major political accomplishments, and a replica of the Oval Office. Next door, the nonprofit Carter Center *(not open to the public)* was established by the former president to promote worldwide democracy and to fight disease and poverty.

## Wren's Nest

*1050 Ralph David Abernathy Blvd.*
*☛Visit by guided tour only.* ☎*404-753-7735. www.accessatlanta.com/community/groups/wrensnest.*
The sprawling c.1867 Wren's Nest is the Victorian home of **Joel Chandler Harris** (1848-1908), journalist and author of the Uncle Remus tales for children. The man who brought to life Brer Fox and Brer Rabbit wrote the tales in the dialect of coastal Georgia slaves. Especially

## Sweet Auburn

Known as "Sweet Auburn," Atlanta's **Auburn Avenue** saw its heyday as the commercial and social hub of Atlanta's black community from 1890 to the 1960s. Community leader John Wesley Dobbs coined the nickname based on the "sweet" success the district enjoyed in the 1930s, despite the economic downturn of the Great Depression. The street blended a rich mixture of African-American businesses, retail outlets, nightclubs and churches. In the 1960s, it became a gathering spot for leaders of the burgeoning Civil Rights Movement. Auburn Avenue also claims the birthplace and pulpit of the movement's leading voice, **Dr. Martin Luther King, Jr.** (1929-68), who won the Nobel Peace Prize in 1964 and was assassinated four years later in Memphis, Tennessee.

During the 1980s, a revitalization of the historic street began when the blocks where Dr. King had lived and worked were designated a National Historic District. Begin a tour at **The Martin Luther King, Jr., National Historic Site Visitor Center★★** (450 Auburn Ave.; ☎404-331-5190), where the history of black America, including the civil rights movement and the pivotal role played by Dr. King, is told through a series of modules, each one chronicling a different aspect of the story.

Across the street is the **Martin Luther King, Jr. Center for Nonviolent Social Change★** (449 Auburn Ave.; ☎404-526-8900), where a number of King's pastoral accoutrements are displayed. King is buried outside in a simple marble tomb.

Other King-related sights on Auburn Avenue include the Queen Anne-style **Birthhome**a (no. 501), and **Ebenezar Baptist Church** (no. 407). Dr. King, his father and maternal grandfather all served as pastors of this 1922 brick church.

Several blocks west stands **The Royal Peacock** nightclub (186 Auburn Ave.). Founded during the 1930s as a performance venue for black entertainers, The Peacock hosted the likes of Ray Charles, James Brown and Aretha Franklin.

popular here are the lively storytelling sessions Kids.

# Excursions

## Stone Mountain Park★★

Kids *16mi east of Atlanta via US-78. Take Ponce de Leon Ave. to Stone Mountain Freeway; follow signs to park. ☎ $24 △ ✗ ♿ ☎ 770-498-5690. www.stonemountainpark.com.*
Recreational opportunities abound in this 3,200-acre park, built around 825ft-high **Stone Mountain**, the world's largest granite outcropping. The park's focal point is the giant **Confederate Memorial** carving of Jefferson Davis and generals Robert E. Lee and Stonewall Jackson on the face of the mountain. Stone carver Gutzon Borglum, known for the presidential profiles on Mt. Rushmore, began work here in 1923; the carving was completed in 1972. In the **Discovering Stone Mountain Museum**, you'll learn how the on-again, off-again project was finally realized.

## Georgia Music Hall of Fame★

*75mi south of Atlanta in Macon via I-75 south to I-16. Turn right on Martin Luther King, Jr. Blvd. and continue to Hall of Fame at no. 200. ☎478-751-3334. www.georgiamusic.org.*
One of the state's premier attractions, the Hall of Fame (1996) honors Georgia's myriad native musicians. Configured like a small town, the "**Tune Town**" exhibit hall commemorates musical artists as diverse as blues singer Ray Charles, the Allman Brothers Band, and classical conductor Robert Shaw. In **The Music Factory** Kids, children can experiment with music and dance.

## Ocmulgee National Monument★

*90mi south of Atlanta in Macon. Take I-75 South to Macon and go east on I-16 to Exit 4; go east on US-80 and follow signs to Ocmulgee at 1207 Emery Hwy. ♿ ☎478-752-8257. www.nps.gov/ocmu.*
Humans have inhabited this fertile Ocmulgee River bottomland for more than 12,000 years, but it wasn't until 1934 that archaeo-

logical digs unearthed artifacts here dating to the last Ice Age. Several mounds remain on the property as relics of the advanced Mississippian culture, a farming people who inhabited the site between 900 and 1100 AD. The best-preserved structure is the **earthlodge**, thought to have been used as a council chamber; the highest earthen mound is the 55ft-high **Great Temple Mound**.

### Andersonville National Historic Site★
*160mi south of Atlanta in Andersonville. Take I-75 South to Exit 41. Take Rte. 26 West to Montezuma; pick up Rte. 49 and follow it south 7mi.* ○*Open daily 8am–5pm.*

○*Closed major holidays.* ⟟ 🅿 ☏*229-924-0343. www.nps.gov/ande.*

This peaceful meadow contained one of the most horrific Civil War prison camps. The thousands of Union soldiers interred here succumbed to the effects of disease, poor sanitation and malnutrition. Today the 26.5-acre prison site houses the National Prisoner of War Museum, replicas of portions of the stockade that once enclosed the grounds, and memorials erected by Union survivors. Adjacent to the prison is Andersonville National Cemetery, burial site for 13,000 Union soldiers and other US war veterans

# SAVANNAH AND THE GOLDEN ISLES★

MICHELIN MAP 584 R 12   EASTERN STANDARD TIME

POPULATION 128,453 (SAVANNAH); 71,874 (GLYNN COUNTY, GA)

Set on a bluff between the Savannah and Altamaha rivers, Savannah survives as a testimony to visionary 18C city planning and modern historic preservation. The city, with its stately mansions, landscaped plazas, Spanish moss-draped live oaks and friendly populace, is a quintessentially Southern city. An hour's drive south of Savannah via Interstate 95 brings you to St. Simons and Jekyll islands, and to the wild shores of Cumberland Island, all beads on a string of Atlantic Coast resorts known as the Golden Isles. Despite its humid summers, the coast of Georgia entices visitors with its beautiful beaches, abundant seafood and rich history.

- 🅸 **Information:** ☏ 877-728-2662. www.savannahvisit.com
- 🅐 **Don't Miss:** The remarkable historic district and one of the country's oldest synagogues, as well as one of the oldest black churches.
- 🅺🅸🅳🅢 **Kids:** Girl Scouts will want to see Andrew Low house, while older kids get to hear ghost stories about the haunted city.
- 🅒 **Also See:** *ATLANTA*

## Savannah★

The city of Savannah was born in 1733 when English army officer and philanthropist **James Oglethorpe** and a group of more than 100 settlers landed at Yamacraw Bluff above the Savannah River. One of 21 trustees to whom King George II had granted the tract of land between the Savannah and Altamaha rivers, Oglethorpe envisioned the

colony of Georgia as an environment where the British working poor and "societal misfits," could carve out a living cultivating agricultural products desired by the Crown.

In its early years, the region's agrarian economy, based on rice and tobacco and later cotton, fueled Savannah's growth as a port and a center for commodities trading. By 1817 Savannah's City Exchange, which occupied the site now taken by City Hall, was setting the market price for the world's cotton: all that ended with the Civil War. When General Sherman finally reached Savannah in December 1864, city leaders surrendered without a fight. Sherman, acknowledging the city's beauty, presented Savannah to President Abraham Lincoln as a Christmas gift.

Revitalization efforts begun in the 1940s have led to a growing economy based on industry, manufacturing, port commerce and tourism. Today, Savannah's landmark historic district attracts more than one million visitors a year, and its year-round host of festivities culminates in Savannah's famed **St. Patrick's Day** celebration, when the riverfront becomes one big festival ground.

# Historic District★★

Oglethorpe's revered original city plan incorporates a series of 21 grassy squares connected by broad thoroughfares and edged with stately 19C examples of Greek Revival, Federal, Regency and Georgian architecture. Today these plazas are preserved in downtown's 2.5mi historic district (bounded by Gaston St., E. Broad St., Martin Luther King Jr. Blvd. and the river). Twenty-acre **Forsyth Park**, with its graceful fountain, anchors the south end of Bull Street.

Begin your visit at the **Savannah Visitor Information Center** (301 Martin Luther King Jr. Blvd.; ☎912-944-0455), where you can catch one of the popular trolley tours. Adjoining the center is the **Savannah History Museum** (☎912-238-1779; www.chsgeorgia.org). When you're ready for a break, sample the outdoor cafes and myriad shops of **City Market** (Jefferson St. at West St. Julian St.; ☎912-232-4903; www.savannahcitymarket.com).

## Scarbrough House★
41 Martin Luther King Jr. Blvd. 🅿 ☎912-232-1511.
A block west of City Market, a charming garden invites visitors into this 1819 Regency villa designed by English architect William Jay. Today the villa houses the **Ships of the Sea Maritime Museum**★ (www.shipsofthesea.org) which presents nautical history and

seafaring culture through a fine selection of paintings and model ships.

## First African Baptist Church★
23 Montgomery St. ☎ 912-233-6597., www.oldestblackchurch.org. ⏳Visit by appointment only
Established in 1773 by freed slave George Leile, this church is considered the oldest black Baptist church in North America. By 1826 church members had established the first African-American Sunday School in the US. The current structure was built in 1859 by members of the congregation.

## Congregation Mickve Israel
Gordon St. ⏰Open daily 10am–1pm, 2pm–4pm ⏰Closed Jewish holidays ☎912-233-1547, . www.mickveisrael.org
The only Gothic-style synagogue building in the country, Congregation Mickve Israel is also of interest for being the third-oldest Jewish congregation in American. The synagogue faces Monterey Square and is open for architectural tours as well as worship.

## Factors Walk★★
Shops and restaurants now occupy the riverfront warehouses along Bay Street (between Bay & Rivers Sts.), surrounding Factors Walk, a 19C center of cotton commerce. Here cotton traders would buy and sell from the bridgeways that connect the offices on the upper portion of the bluff with the warehouses below. The 1887 **Old Cotton Exchange** (100 E. Bay St., at Drayton St.; now a Masonic Lodge) was the center of Savannah's post-Civil War cotton trade. Separating East and West Factors Walk, 1905 **City Hall** (corner of Bay & Bull Sts.), with its golden dome, reigns as a vibrant local landmark.

## Telfair Academy of Arts and Sciences★
121 Barnard St. ⏰Open Mon 12pm–5pm, Tues-Sat 10am–5pm, Sun 1pm-5pm. 💲$10 ♿☎912-790-8800,
www.telfair.org. Another creation of William Jay, the Regency-style mansion was initially built in 1818 as the home of Alexander Telfair. The expanded structure now houses a noteworthy

*Historic District architecture, Savannah*

collection of works by members of the Ash Can school—Robert Henri, George Luks and George Bellows—as well as American portraiture, and collections of early-19C furniture and silver.

### Owens-Thomas House★★

*124 Abercorn St. ⟿Visit by guided tour only. ☎912-233-9743. www.telfair.org.* Belle of Oglethorpe Square, the Owens-Thomas House is considered one of architect William Jay's finest works—and the only unaltered example of his surviving designs. Now administered by the Telfair Academy of Arts and Sciences, this house was completed in 1819 when the architect was only 25. The stately structure typifies Jay's English Regency style; its tabby and coadestone exterior as well as the elegant interior detailing have been carefully restored. Also on the grounds, the mansion's carriage house includes one of the earliest intact urban slave quarters in the South.

### Davenport House

*324 E. State St. ⟿Visit by guided tour only. ☎912-236-8097.* When threatened by demolition, this fine two-story Federal structure became a rallying point for citizens interested in preserving Savannah's stately homes. The community effort resulted in saving the home and establishing the **Historic Savannah Foundation**, a grassroots organization that has played a key role in the rejuvenation of the historic district.

### Andrew Low House★

*329 Abercorn St. ⟿Visit by guided tour only ◷Closed Thu. ⌦$8. ☎912-233-6854. www.andrew lowhouse.com.* In 1848 wealthy cotton merchant Andrew Low commissioned John Norris to create this Classical house with its elaborate cast-iron balconies. Low's daughter-in-law, Savannah-born **Juliette Gordon Low** (1860-1927), founded the Girl Scouts USA—the world's largest voluntary organization for girls—here on March 12, 1912.

## The Golden Isles★

Forming part of Georgia's Atlantic Coast barrier islands, the Golden Isles of St. Simons, Little St. Simons (*accessible only by boat from St. Simons Island*), Sea and Jekyll islands are located 70mi south of Savannah. These popular tourist destinations boast wide, sandy beaches, award-winning golf courses, plentiful wildlife refuges and historic resorts. One such hotel, **The Cloister** on **Sea Island** (*entrance off Sea Island Dr.; ☎912-638-5159; www.cloister.com*) was designed by renowned Florida architect Addison

*Sunrise at Fishing Pier, Jekyll Island*

Mizner. Just south of Jekyll Island as the crow flies, Cumberland Island claims a pristine national seashore.

By 1586 the Spanish had established missions along the coast and maintained a stronghold here until 1742, when James Oglethorpe routed the Spanish on St. Simons Island during the **Battle of Bloody Marsh** (*a monument on Demere Rd preserves the site*). By the time he set sail for England in 1743, Oglethorpe had left behind the seeds of civilization that would blossom into manufacturing centers and playgrounds for the wealthy.

To access the Georgia coast, trave south on I-95 from Savannah to US-17 A detour to **Sapelo Island** (*accessible by ferry from Meridian Ferry Dock, Rte. 99, ☎912-437-3224*) will take you to one ot the existing Gullah (*see CHARLESTON* communities.

## St. Simon's Island★

*77mi south of Savannah. From I-95, take Exit 9 and follow US-17 South to St. Simons Causeway.*

Known for its beautiful beaches, St Simon's heralds its past in the 1872 working **lighthouse** and the adjacent

---

## Midnight in the Garden of Good and Evil

A stately Italianate manor overlooking Savannah's Monterey Square, the c.1860s **Mercer House**–designed by New York architect John Norris–became famous as a crime scene. It was in this house in 1981 that resident antiques dealer Jim Williams was accused of fatally shooting 21-year-old Danny Hansford.

Jim Williams' murder trial set staid Savannah on its ear, and was later immortalized in John Berendt's best-selling 1994 book, *Midnight in the Garden of Good and Evil*. Both the book and the movie that followed in 1997 painted a vivid picture of Savannah's eccentric populace, from Jim Williams–the alleged shooter, whose favorite game, Psycho Dice, was his own invention–to Lady Chablis, an oversexed transvestite. The most recognized icon from both the book and the movie is perhaps the *Bird Girl* statue (1938), which appears on the books cover. The work of artists Sylvia Shaw Judson, the statue once stood in Savannah's **Bonaventure Cemetery**. *Visitors can now find Bird Girl in the Telfair Academy of Arts and Sciences.*

**Museum of Coastal History** (*101 Twelfth St.;* ☎*912-638-4666; www.saintsimonslighthouse.org*), and in the ruins of **Fort Frederica National Monument**★ (*at the end of Frederica Rd.;* ☎*912-638-3639; www.nps.gov/fofr*) built by James Oglethorpe in 1736.

## Jekyll Island★★

*From I-95, take Exit 6 and follow US-17 South to Jekyll Island Welcome Center on Jekyll Island Causeway.* △ ※ ⑤ 🅿. ☎*912-653-5955. www.jekyllisland.com.*
Purchased for $125,000 in 1886 by a consortium of East Coast millionaires—with names such as Gould, Goodyear, Pulitzer and Rockefeller—Jekyll Island served as a winter playground for the nation's captains of industry until World War II intervened. Here in 1887, consortium members—calling themselves the Jekyll Island Club—hired architect Charles Alexander to build a 60-room clubhouse. Members soon supplemented the clubhouse with "cottages" up to 8,000sq ft in size. Today the **Jekyll Island Club Historic District**★ preserves several of the remaining structures and is in the process of restoring others. The Victorian clubhouse is now restored as the **Jekyll Island Club Hotel** (*371 Riverview Dr.;* ☎*912-635-2818; www.jekyllclub.com*). A guided tram tour of the historic district begins at the **Museum Visitor Center** in the old club stables (*Stable Rd.;* 🅿 ☎*912-635-4036*).

## Cumberland Island National Seashore ★★

*Take Exit 2 off I-95 South; turn left on Rte. 40 and follow it 9mi east to St. Marys, GA. Accessible by ferry only from downtown St. Marys; reservations required.* △ ⑤ 🅿 ☎*912-882-4335 www.nps.gov/cuis.*

No supplies available on the island. Saltwater marshes, maritime forests and 18mi of lonely beaches compose the complex ecosystem that is Cumberland Island. The largest and least developed of Georgia's Golden Isles, the island lies across Cumberland Sound from the town of St. Marys, Georgia. Stately 1898 **Plum Orchard** (*visit by guided tour only;* ☎*912-882-4335*) and the 1884 **Dungeness**—of which only eerie ruins remain—were both once occupied by members of Pittsburgh's monied Carnegie family. Another former Carnegie mansion now operates as the upscale **Greyfield Inn**. Begin your visit on the mainland at **Cumberland Island National Seashore Visitor Center** (*107 St. Marys St.;* ☎*912-882-4336*).

## Okefenokee Swamp Park★★

*64mi southwest of Brunswick, GA. Take US-82 West to Hwy. 177; take Hwy. 177 11mi south to park.* ⊚*$12.* ※ 🅿 ☎*912-283-0583. www.okeswamp.com.*
Serving as the northern entrance to **Okefenokee National Wildlife Refuge**, the nonprofit park provides an excellent introduction to the swamp's 700sq mi of canals, moss-draped cypress trees and lily-pad prairies. The Seminoles named this area, formed by the headwaters of the Suwannee and St. Mary's rivers, Okefenokee—"Land of Trembling Earth." This is the only entrance to the swamp where you can take a guided boat tour and enjoy daily "Eye on Nature" shows featuring live denizens of the swamp. Park admission fee includes a ride on the new 1.5mi railroad. To penetrate the swamp's deeper reaches, rent a canoe and paddle through the tea-colored waters along the refuge's 120mi of canoe trails.

# BIRMINGHAM AREA

Alabama's largest city lies roughly in the middle of a state whose vigorous economy is based on agriculture, manufacturing, service industries and technology. Birmingham has a thriving mix of well-preserved 19C architecture, interspersed with skyscrapers named for their Fortune 500 owners, yet its most important history is found in the Civil Rights District.

Native Americans occupied Alabama's mountain forests and verdant river valleys for at least 9,000 years. Evidence of these native cultures, both early and late, lives on in scores of historic sites and mellifluous place names—including Alabama, derived from the Chickasaw word *Alibamu*, meaning "thicket clearers." One such site, **Moundville Archaeological Park**★★ *(72mi southwest of Birmingham off Rte. 69 at Moundville; ☎205-371-2234)*, was once home to the largest Native American settlement in the southeast during the Mississippian Period (AD 800-1600). Today, more than two dozen flat-topped earthen mounds remain, built as platforms for temples, council houses and homes of tribal leaders.

As settlers expanded steadily westward in the early 1800s, a series of bloody battles with the Indians culminated in Gen. Andrew Jackson's crushing defeat in 1814 of the last remaining Creek Indians at Horseshoe Bend northeast of Montgomery. **Horseshoe Bend National Military Park**★ *(on Rte. 49 near the Georgia border, 12mi north of Dadeville; ☎256-234-7111)* preserves the battle site where the decimated Creek signed the Treaty of Fort Jackson on August 9, 1814, ceding some 20 million acres of land to the US—land that in 1819 became the state of Alabama.

The struggles of Alabama's African-American citizens made headlines around the world in 1955, as civil rights advocates boycotted the bus system in Montgomery for 381 days and emerged victorious with a 1956 order from the US Supreme Court outlawing bus segregation in Montgomery.

Today the cruel reminders of Alabama's segregationist past are largely confined to historic markers and museums such as the Birmingham Civil Rights Institute. Visits to three of the state's four largest cities—Birmingham, Montgomery and Huntsville (Mobile is second-largest, and growing rapidly)—offer thought-provoking and sometimes surprising juxtapositions of past and present in the "Heart of Dixie," as the state is nicknamed.

*Pathfinder Shuttle Exhibit*

## Area Address Book

ⓒ *For coin ranges, see the Legend on the cover flap.*

### WHERE TO STAY

**$$ The Tutwiler** – *2021 Park Pl. N., Birmingham, AL.* ✗&🅿 ☎205-322-2100. *www.wyndham.com. 147 rooms.* Housed in a 1913 red-brick landmark, this downtown hotel has hosted everyone from Henry Kissinger to Stevie Wonder. Note the lobby's restored coffered ceilings. European paintings, on loan from the nearby Birmingham Museum of Art, line the first-floor hallways.

**$ Red Bluff Cottage** – *551 Clay St., Montgomery, AL.* 🅿 ☎334-264-0056. *www.redbluffcottage.com 4 rooms.* This raised-cottage-style B&B overlooks the city and river plain in the historic Cottage Hill district. Antique pencil-post beds, handmade quilts and family photos make you feel right at home. Walk to the Civil Rights Memorial and Riverfront Park.

### WHERE TO EAT

**$$$ Highlands Bar & Grill** – *2011 11th Ave. S., Birmingham, AL.* ☎205-939-1400. **Regional American.** A national stand-out thanks to chef Frank Stitt's creative take on Southern cuisine. Vintage French food ads decorate the romantic southside dining room. Baked grits, grilled pork tenderloin in Jack Daniel's-spiked sauce, and "Alabama cream pie" highlight the daily menu.

**$$ Jubilee** – *1057 Woodley Rd., Montgomery, AL. Closed Sun.* ☎334-242-6224. **$$ Seafood.** Just-caught fish from the Gulf of Mexico keeps folks waiting in line for a table at this casual Old Cloverdale eatery. Cobia, trigger fish and yellowfin grouper turn up on the changing menu. Blackened red snapper, oysters on the half-shell, and barbecued bacon-wrapped shrimp are top sellers.

**$ Irondale Cafe** – *1906 1st Ave. N., Irondale, AL. Closed Sun -Mon.* ☎205-956-5258. **Southern.** Seven miles from downtown Birmingham, the railway diner that inspired the novel *Fried Green Tomatoes at the WhistleStop Café* is a lunchtime favorite. Freight trains rumble by while you eat fried chicken, boiled squash, and of course, fried green tomatoes. Save room for peach cobbler.

# BIRMINGHAM★

MICHELIN MAP 584 P 12
CENTRAL STANDARD TIME
POPULATION 242,820

...resided over by the 56ft-tall, cast-iron Guiseppe Moretti sculpture of **Vulcan★★** *(US-31 & Valley Ave.;* ☎205-933-1409), Birmingham is laid out in an orderly grid of ...umbered streets that crisscross the city's three interstate highways and climb ...p and down hills. Many of the star attractions in Alabama's largest city lie within ...valking distance of each other downtown. Streets in **Five Points South**a *(20th St.* ...*. at Eleventh Ave. S.),* the city's revitalized 1890s shopping, strolling and entertain-...nent district near the University of Alabama campus, are lined with restaurants, ...ars and cafes. Adjoining the district is pedestrians-only **Cobb Lane**, a short ...rick-paved block with restaurants, art galleries and bars wedged charmingly ...nto vintage Craftsman-style apartments at Thirteenth Avenue South.

**Information:** 2200 Ninth Ave., North. ☎205-458-8000; ☎800-458-8085. www.birminghamal.org.
**Don't Miss:** The sites detailing America's Civil Rights Movement.

The Alabama Bureau of Tourism & Travel/Dan Brothers

*Rosa Parks exhibit at Civil Rights Institute*

# A Bit of History

Unlike most of its southern sisters, Birmingham boasts no Civil War survival stories—because it dates back to only 1871, six years after the war ended. During those turbulent years of Reconstruction, industrialists mined Red Mountain and the adjacent hills to make fortunes from the land's rich deposits of coal, limestone and iron ore. The key role that iron played in the city's history is evident today at **Sloss Furnaces National Historic Landmark**★★ *(32nd St. & First Ave. N.; ☎205-324-1911)*, constructed in the early 20C, and at **Tannehill Ironworks Historical State Park**★★ *(31.7mi southwest of Birmingham in McCalla; ☎205-477-5711)* where Confederate soldiers produced up to 20 tons of pig iron a day for Rebel cannons and bullets.

Named after England's then-thriving industrial hub, the new Alabama town of Birmingham grew rapidly around two rail lines, the Alabama & Chattanooga and the South & North. Heralded as the "Pittsburgh of the South," By the 1960s, the US iron-and-steel industry was rusting, and Birmingham became known as "Bombingham," owing to the murderous bombings and beatings endured by the city's civil rights activists.

Today the city's racial strife has largely healed, and its economy depends far more on medicine and academics than on metal-working.

# Sights

### Civil Rights District ★

Bounded by 15th to 17th Streets and 3rd to 7th Avenues, Birmingham's Civil Rights District commemorates sites where civil rights activists banded together and changed the face of America with their protests during the 1960s. Here you'll find several soul-food restaurants as well as the **Sixteenth Street Baptist Church**★ *(1530 Sixth Ave. N. at corner of 16th St.; ☎205-251-9402)*. Designed by African-American architect Wallace Rayfield, this twin-towered church (1911) was bombed by white racists in 1963.

### The Birmingham Civil Rights Institute★★★

*520 16th St. N. Sun 1pm-5pm. ◷ Open year-round Tue-Sun 10am-5pm. ◷ Closed major holidays. ◉$10. ☎205-328-9696. www.bcri.org.*

Anchoring the Civil Rights District, this self-directed museum and memorial (1992, J. Max Bond, Jr.) guides visitors through a series of engrossing multimedia and three-dimensional exhibits that bring the drama and tumult of the American civil rights movement to vivid, sometimes frightening, life. In chronological order, room-sized exhibits detail the major confrontations, achievements and tragedies of the struggle, highlighting such pivotal events as Dr. Martin Luther King, Jr.'s "I Have a Dream" speech during the 1963 march on Washington, DC.

Beginning with the late-19C years of harsh segregation, the exhibit weaves first-person reminiscences with media accounts that immerse visitors in the sights and sounds of "the movement"— film footage of snarling police dogs turned on black children, and eerie footage of a nighttime cross-burning by hooded members of the Ku Klux Klan. Visitors can view the burned-out shell of a bus ridden by the Freedom Riders, and the door of the cell where Dr. King wrote his "Letter from Birmingham Jail."

Across from the Civil Rights Institute lies quiet **Kelly Ingram Park**★ *(Fifth Ave. & 16th St.)*, where sculptures by James Drake evoke some of the more horrific events that took place here.

## Birmingham Museum of Art ★★★

*2000 8th Ave. N. Open year-round Tue-Sun 12pm-5pm. Closed major holidays. ☎205-254-2566. www.artsbma.org.*

A modern building near the convention district, the museum houses an outstanding collection of **Wedgwood**

**pottery**★, as well as 18C French paintings and decorative arts donated in 1991 by coal heiress and Birmingham native Eugenia Woodward Hitt. On the second floor, the **American Galleries** showcase 19C landscapes and portraits.

# MONTGOMERY★

MICHELIN MAP 584 P 12
CENTRAL STANDARD TIME
POPULATION 201,568

A pleasant, well-kept city on the banks of the Alabama River, this shiny modern day capital bears little trace of its early history—a claim staked by Hernando De Soto for Spain in 1540; by French explorers as they established nearby Fort Toulouse in 1717; by the British at the end of the French and Indian War in 1763; and by the half-Scottish, half-Indian Alexander McGillivray for the Creek Indian Nation from 1783 to 1793. Montgomery was already a busy regional marketplace and transportation center when it became Alabama's capital in 1846.

**Information:** 300 Water St. ☎334-262-0013. www.montgomerychamber.com; www.visitingmontgomery.org.

**Organizing Your Time:** Most of the Montgomery sites require throughtful contemplation... these are not amusement parks. Plan accordingly.

## A Bit of History

Named as the temporary capital of the Confederate States of America in 1861, Montgomery survived the war years virtually unscathed. After Reconstruction, the city prospered again as a transportation center, shipping cotton to markets in the northeast and Europe. In the early years of the 20C, lumber and textile mills were established. Bolstered by the arrival of the **Alabama Shakespeare Festival**★★ in 1985, the city now hosts a lively community of theatrical and performing arts.

From fanciful **Court Street Fountain** *(corner of Court St. & Dexter Ave.)* downtown, the **view** due east up Dexter Avenue is imbued with historical significance. On the right is the Italianate **Winter Building** *(2 Dexter Ave.)*, from which the War Department of the Confederacy telegraphed orders to fire on Fort Sumter in April 1861, thus beginning the Civil War. Straight ahead is an impressive view of the Alabama State Capitol—the same view seen

by black seamstress **Rosa Parks** when she boarded a bus here on December 1, 1955, and was promptly arrested for refusing to yield her seat to a white passenger. Parks' arrest, which inspired the year-long Montgomery bus boycott, is considered the beginning of the civil rights movement. In 1999 Parks, then age 86, received the Congressional Gold Medal, the highest civilian accolade awarded by Congress. Today the round, table-like **Civil Rights Memorial**★ *(400 Washington Ave.)*, designed by Maya Lin, pays homage to 40 civil rights martyrs, including Dr. Martin Luther King, Jr.

## Sights

### Alabama State Capitol★★

*600 Dexter Ave. ☎334-242-3935.*

A stunning Greek Revival building, Alabama's National Historic Landmark capitol was rebuilt in 1850-51 after a previous capitol on the site burned in 1849. Interior highlights include the restored c.1880s trompe l'œil **paneling** in the

*First White House of the Confederacy*

The Alabama Bureau of Tourism & Travel/Dan Brothers

original suites belonging to the governor and the secretary of state. The **Old Senate Chamber** appears as it did in February 1861, when delegates from the seceding southern states met to form the Confederate States of America .

### Alabama Department of Archives and History★★

*624 Washington Ave.* ○*Open Mon-Sat 8:30am-4:30pm* ⚓ 🅿 ☎*334-242-4435. www.archives.state.al.us.*
Three floors of research and exhibit space here hold an eclectic collection

of Alabama artifacts, ranging from pre historic pottery shards to cheap glass beads manufactured in Venice for trade with 19C American Indians to Civil Wa paraphernalia. Tours must be booked in advance.

### First White House of the Confederacy★★

*644 Washington Ave.* ○*Open Mon-Fr 8am-4:30pm* ⚓ ☎*334-242-1861.*
**Jefferson Davis** (1808-89), President of the Confederate States of America used this 1835 wood-frame, Italianate house as his executive mansion during Montgomery's three-month reign (February–May 1861) as the CSA's capital With well-preserved period furnishing and many Davis family belongings, the home feels as though Mrs. Davis may return momentarily to play the Chicker ing square piano.

### Dexter Avenue King Memorial Baptist Church★

*454 Dexter Ave. Visiting hours vary* ○*Open Tues-Fri 10am-4pm, Sun 10am 2pm .* ☎*34-263-3970, www.dexterking memorial.org.*
The Reverend Dr. Martin Luther King, Jr. was pastor here in 1955, when he and other civil rights leaders launched the 381-day Montgomery bus boycott in support of Rosa Parks' heroic refusal to yield her seat to a white man.

## Alabama Shakespeare Festival

Originally located in Anniston, this 200-person professional repertory theater relocated to Montgomery in 1985 after Montgomery-based industrialist Wynton M. Blount and his wife, Carolyn, pledged funds to build a new, $21.5 million performing-arts complex. The fifth-largest Shakespeare festival in the US, the Alabama troupe is the only American group invited by Britain's Royal Shakespeare Company to fly the Royal Shakespeare flag. The **Carolyn Blount Theatre**, housing the 750-seat Festival Stage and the 255-seat Octagon, occupies a lakefront English-garden setting on this 250-acre site. Shakespearean and contemporary dramas, including musical revues and Broadway-bound tryouts, are performed year-round. A new facility, **Shakespeare's Gardens and Amphitheatre**, offers outdoor seating for 325 and an Elizabethan garden sown with plants mentioned in Shakespeare's plays. *1 Festival Dr.* ⚓ 🅿 ☎*334-271-5353 or 800-841-4ASF, www.asf.net.*

The site is also home to the **Montgomery Museum of Fine Arts** *(1 Museum Dr.;* ○*Open Tues-Sat 10am-5pm;* ☎*334-240-4333; www.fineartsmuseum.com)*, which houses the Blount Collection of American Paintings.

### Fitzgerald Museum★

919 Felder Ave. ☎334-264-4222 or 334-262-1911. www.fitzgeraldmuseum.com. Fans of The Great Gatsby find memorabilia and an informative videotape in the former home of F. Scott and Zelda Fitzgerald. The couple shared this house—where Fitzgerald penned Tender Is the Night—from 1931 to 1932.

## Excursion

### Tuskegee Institute National Historic Site★★

49mi east of Montgomery in Tuskegee. Take I-85 North to Rte. 29 South; then right on US-80 to Tuskegee University campus. 1212 Old Montgomery Rd. Visitor center is located in the Carver Museum. ♿☎334-727-3200. www.nps.gov/tuin.

**Booker T. Washington** (1856-1915) founded Tuskegee Normal School (now Tuskegee University) in 1881 to train African Americans as teachers, skilled laborers and farmers in the impoverished, segregated Reconstruction-era South. By 1899 Tuskegee was financially secure and internationally known, and Washington commissioned a Queen Anne-style home, **The Oaks** (Old Montgomery Rd.; guided tours depart from visitor center), for his family.

# U.S. SPACE AND ROCKET CENTER★★★

MICHELIN MAP 584 P 11

CENTRAL STANDARD TIME

Located 99mi north of Birmingham in Huntsville, the U.S. Space and Rocket Center harbors the world's largest collection of spacecraft. The most heavily visited tourist destination in Alabama, the center lies on the perimeter of the US Army's legendary **Redstone Arsenal**, a 37,910-acre military post just southwest of the city center.

🕐 **Organizing Your Time:** If you are in town for long periods of time, check out the more intensive space camps for both kids and grown-ups.

## A Bit of History

The former mill town of Huntsville changed abruptly during World War II when the US Army created Redstone Arsenal to make chemical weapons. Then, in 1950, the Army hired Dr. Werner von Braun and 117 other German rocket scientists to propel the US into the forefront of space exploration. With the creation of the National Aeronautics and Space Administration (NASA) in 1958, the team of scientists became civilian rather than military employees, and the large NASA research site at Redstone was converted to **Marshall Space Flight Center**. The Space Flight Center ranks as the major research and testing arm for US space exploration.

Since Redstone Arsenal and the Marshall Space Flight Center are restricted, the state of Alabama opened "the world's largest space-travel attraction" nearby in 1970. Home to the popular children's **U.S. Space Camp®**, the Space Center is filled with hands-on and interactive gadgetry, as well as complex exhibits.

## Visit

📷 1 Tranquility Base, off I-565 in Huntsville. 🕐 Open daily 9am-5pm. ☜$20.95, $15.95 children. ⚠♿♿📶☎256-837-3400. www.ussrc.com.

Visitors to this surprisingly small, jam-packed dome have several options: a guided tour, a self-guided tour, or several simulated space-shuttle rides (to Mars, Jupiter, and points beyond). Displays in the main exhibit area include the actual 1972 **Apollo 16 command module** and a walk-in module of the tiny quarters of the **Russian Mir Space Station**. A Skylab mock-up used for astronaut training offers a fascinating glimpse into the human realities of long-term space travel—such as how to take a shower when the soap and water float.

Just outside the main exhibit area, a giant curved-screen **Spacedome IMAX Theater** shows films hourly; one favorite is *Destiny in Space*, a dizzying 45min simulated rocket trip with actual footage taken by astronauts in flight.

The exhibit continues outdoors, where brave hearts may enjoy amusement-style rides such as **Centrifuge** ("feel the gravitational forces of lift-off!") and **Space Shot**, which blasts riders 140ft into the air and induces the sensation of weightlessness during the descent. Less daring visitors can stroll the **Rocket and Shuttle Park** to see the gigantic Saturn V rocket and a full-scale model of the *Pathfinder* space shuttle, complete with external tank and rocket boosters.

A 1.5hr narrated bus tour leaving from the Space Center provides visitors' only access to the **Marshall Space Flight Center**. Tour stops vary according to activities within the NASA compound.

# Excursions

### Helen Keller Birthplace★

*3000 W. Commons, 75mi west of Huntsville in Tuscumbia. Take US-72 to N. Main St. in Tuscumbia; go north 2mi to Keller Lane. Open Mon-Sat 8:30am-4pm, Sun 1pm-4pm. $6, $5 children. 256-383-4066. www.helenkellerbirthplace.org.*

The charming Virginia-style cottage called Ivy Green was the birthplace of Helen Keller (1880-1968). Stricken blind and deaf as a child, Keller learned to sign, talk and write with help from her teacher, Annie Sullivan. The house showcases a custom-made Braille watch, writing tools and other mementos of Keller's extraordinary life.

### Russell Cave National Monument★★

*90mi north of Huntsville. Take US-72 North to Bridgeport Exit and follow Rtes. 98 & 75 northwest 8mi. Open daily 8am-4:30pm. 256-495-2672. www.nps.gov/ruca.*

In the early 1950s, a team of archaeologists from the National Geographic Society and the Smithsonian Institution excavated human remains and tools in Russell Cave dating back at least 9,000 years. One of the oldest verified sites of human habitation in the southeastern US, the cave held tools of stone and bone, pottery and shell jewelry indicating occupation in the Paleo (10,000 BC), Archaic (7000 to 500 BC) and Woodland (500 BC to AD 1000) periods. Visitors can follow a short path with self-guiding markers into the cave's shallow upper mouth and overhang (*guided tour available*).

# BLUE RIDGE PARKWAY

One of America's great roads, the Blue Ridge Parkway, skirts several of the tallest peaks east of the Mississippi River, offering breathtaking vistas as it cuts through Virginia and heads southwest to North Carolina and Tennessee. The 469mi-long highway dips into the fragrant woodlands that encompass six national forests, anchored on the north by Virginia's Shenandoah National Park and on the south by Great Smoky Mountains National Park in North Carolina.

Stretching from southern Pennsylvania to northern Georgia, the Blue Ridge gets its name from a filmy haze that bathes its slopes in shades of velvety blue. This atmospheric *trompe l'œil* results from a combination of water vapor and organic compounds emitted by the forests. The range is part of the Appalachian chain, a 2,000mi-long spine that runs from Newfoundland, Canada, south to Alabama. For more than 10,000 years, Cherokee Indians and their ancestors occupied the mountainous area; but they began to lose their hold early in the 18C as Europeans pushed farther into the colonial frontier. Relations with the Indians grew increasingly tenuous as the white man encroached farther and farther onto Indian land and unsuccessfully tried to impose their idea of civilization on

Blue Ridge Parkway

© Comstock, Inc

*Great Smoky Mountains National Park*

the Native Americans. By the middle of the 19C, the new US government under President Andrew Jackson had forcibly relocated nearly all the Indians to grim reservations in the Midwest, in a series of marches known as the "Trail of Tears." Even so, a handful of Cherokees remained hidden in remote corners of the mountains, where their descendants still live today.

After the Civil War the hillsides were stripped of timber and the mountains bellies for copper, coal and manganese. Opening Shenandoah and Great Smoky Mountains national parks and the Blue Ridge Parkway in the early part of the 20C saved the land. Experience the natural grandeur of this region by hiking its wooded trails or rafting down its many waterways.

## Area Address Book

*For coin ranges, see the Legend on the cover flap.*

### WHERE TO STAY

**$$$ The Inn at Little Washington** – *Corner of Middle & Main Sts., Little Washington, VA. Closed Tue, except May & Oct.* ✗ ☎540-675-3800. *14 rooms.* Described as "sumptuous and extraordinary," this plush inn and restaurant, 67mi west of the nation's capital, has become a destination in itself. Theatrical guest rooms are designed with reproduction William Morris wallcoverings and period antiques. Food lovers book months ahead to savor chef Patrick O'Connell's artful seven-course meals *($98 prix-fixe).*

**$$$ Boar's Head Inn** – *Rte. 250 West, Charlottesville, VA.* ✗ ☐ ☎804-296-2181. www.boarsheadinn.com. *173 rooms.* Three miles from town, the main building resembles an English manor house in the Blue Ridge foothills. Seventeenth-century antiques create an informal, pub-like feel in the common areas, and guest rooms are done in neutral tones with four-poster beds and damask duvets. Golf and tennis are also available at this 573-acre estate.

**$$$ Richmond Hill Inn** – *87 Richmond Hill Dr., Asheville, NC.* ✗ ☐ ☎828-252-7313. www.richmondhillinn.com. *36 rooms.* Statesman Richmond Pearson built his mountaintop mansion 3mi from downtown back in 1889. Portraits of Pearson and his wife oversee the house's cozy, oak-paneled living room. The lived-in feeling continues to the bedrooms, furnished with Queen Anne antiques. Rooms in the adjacent croquet cottages and the Garden Pavilion are larger, and some come equipped with gas fireplaces.

**$$ The Grove Park Inn Resort** – *290 Macon Ave., Asheville, NC.* ✗ ☐ ☎828-252-2711. www.groveparkinn.com. *510 rooms.* Set on 140 acres in the Blue Ridge Mountains, the historic hotel has been a haven for celebrities—including F. Scott Fitzgerald and Franklin D. Roosevelt—since its 1913 opening. Arts and Crafts antiques decorate rooms in the original wing. An 18-hole golf course and several tennis courts are also on site.

### WHERE TO EAT

**$$$ The Market Place** – *20 Wall St., Asheville, NC. Closed Sun.* ☎828-252-4162. **Contemporary.** Organic produce and local ingredients (including Biltmore Estate berries) are staples at this downtown restaurant. Inventive dishes—crispy potato cake with goat cheese; spinach, caper and polenta-stuffed trout; white chocolate mousse—are served in the contemporary dining room. In good weather, eat on the patio, which opens onto brick-paved Wall Street.

**$ Salsas** – *6 Patton Ave., Asheville, NC. Closed Sun.* ☎828-252-9805. **Mexican/Caribbean.** Locals don't mind waiting for tables at the hottest place downtown, which fuses Latin and island flavors. Roasted banana stuffed with spinach and goat cheese is rolled in a flour tortilla.

# SHENANDOAH NATIONAL PARK★★

MAP P133
EASTERN STANDARD TIME

he best-known feature within the more than 196,030 acres of Shenandoah ational Park, **Skyline Drive** follows former Indian trails along the backbone of he Blue Ridge as it runs through western Virginia from Front Royal to Rockfish ap. Meticulously landscaped and punctuated by 75 overlooks girdled with ow stone walls, the 105mi drive offers one dazzling view after another. To the ast, the Piedmont's gentle, rounded hills slope down into the coastal plain. he western peaks give way to the Shenandoah Valley, named for the river that vinds lazily past fields, woods and picturesque farms. More than 500mi of trails hread through Shenandoah, including 101mi of the 2,175mi-long **Appalachian rail** (ⓒsee PLANNING YOUR TRIP), which runs from Maine to Georgia.

- **Information:** ☎540-999-3500. www.nps.gov/shen
- **Orient Yourself:** The park is just 75mi from the nation's capital in the Blue Ridge Mountains. Four highways bisect the park. Sights on the 'Skyline Drive,' below, are organized from north to south.
- **Organizing Your Time:** Allow two days (Skyline Drive - 105mi).
- **Don't Miss:** Reflections of stalactites in Mirror Lake.

# A Bit of History

etween 1928 and 1935, the state of Virinia purchased almost 280sq mi of priate mountain land in more than 3,000 eparate parcels, which it in turn ceded to the federal government. President Franklin D. Roosevelt dedicated Shenandoah National Park in 1936. To compensate for years of lumbering and grazing, Roosevelt's newly created Civilian Conservation Corps descended on the

## Visiting Shenandoah National Park

### VISITOR INFORMATION

Two park **visitor centers**, Dickey Ridge (mile 4.6) and Harry F. Byrd (mile 51) are open May–Oct. Maps, free backcountry permits, and information on accommodations, facilities and recreational activities are available at visitor centers and at **Park Headquarters** (3655 US-211 East, Luray, VA 22835-9036; ⚠✗♿🅿☎540-999-3500).

The park is open year-round, though portions of **Skyline Drive** may be temporarily closed in winter due to weather conditions. Many facilities are closed during the winter (late Nov–Mar). Entrance to the park (valid for 7 consecutive days) is $10/vehicle, $8/pedestrian or cyclist.

The speed limit in the park is 35mph. Expect roads to be crowded during peak foliage season (Oct). Concrete mile markers located on the west side of the road are numbered in increasing order from north to south. Mountain temperatures range from mid-70s in summer to the teens in winter. Temperatures vary with elevation, so it's best to wear layers of clothing.

### WHERE TO STAY

Overnight **accommodations** are available at Skyland (mile 41.7) and at Big Meadows Lodge (mile 51.2). Advance reservations for park lodging are a must at the height of fall foliage season in October. For food and lodging information and reservations, contact ARAMARK (P.O. Box 727, Luray VA 22835; ☎800-999-4714). Shenandoah's four campsites are open on a first-come, first-served basis, except for Big Meadows (reservations required; ☎1-800-365-2267).

region in 1933 to plant trees, clear trails, grade the hillsides along Skyline Drive and control erosion. Weathered log cabins and rambling stone walls are all that remains of the mountaineers' world, as nature slowly reclaims its own.

## Skyline Drive★★

▶ Allow 2 days (105 mi).

### Skyline Caverns
*1mi south of park entrance on US-340, Front Royal, VA.* 🚶Visit by guided tour only. 🅿☎540-635-4545.
Highlights in this 60-million-year-old limestone cave include a rare calcite formation known as Anthodites, or cave flowers; **Fairyland Lake**a, whose glassy surface shimmers in the glow of multicolored lights; and **Capitol Dome**, a massive column formed 12,000 years ago when a stalagmite on the cave floor fused with a stalactite on the ceiling.

### Front Royal to Thornton Gap
*31.5mi.*
Skyline Drive begins at US-340 at the south edge of Front Royal and climbs to **Shenandoah Valley Overlook** *(mile 2.8)*, where the sweeping **view**★★ west takes in Massanutten Mountain. Skyline Drive then ascends to 2,085ft at **Signal Knob Overlook** *(mile 5.7)*, named for the point at the right end of Massanutten that served as a Confederate signal station. **Hogwallow Flats Overlook** *(mile 13.8)* looks east over lumpy peaks called monadnocks, lone remnants of a range that predates the Blue Ridge.

### Luray Caverns★
▥*9mi west of Thornton Gap Entrance on US-211, Luray, VA.* 🍴 🅿 ☎540-743-6551, *www.luraycaverns.com.*
Lying 160ft underground, popular Luray Caverns is a wonderland of shimmering stalactites and flowstone that drips from the ceiling like wet fabric. Razor-sharp subterranean mounds rising up from the depths of **Mirror Lake** are only reflections of stalactites hanging above (the water is only 18 inches deep). In the Cathedral Room, you can hear

the haunting notes made by the cave' unique **Stalacpipe Organ**.

### New Market Battlefield State Historical Park
*1mi west of Thornton Gap entrance o US-211, New Market, VA.* ♿🅿☎540 740-3101.
On these bucolic pastures west of th Blue Ridge, 257 cadets from the Virgini Military Institute in Lexington prevaile over Union forces in May 1864. Today th military institute oversees the histori cal park, which comprises the 287-acr battlefield; the **Hall of Valor**, com memorating the cadets' courage; an 19C **Bushong Farm**, which served as hospital during the battle.

### Marys Rock Tunnel to Rockfish Entrance Station★★
*73mi.*
The short length of **Marys Rock Tunnel** *(mile 32.4)* belies its arduous crea tion: For three months, workers drille through more than 600ft of rock befor cars began driving through in 1932 From **Stony Man Overlook** *(mile 38.6* you can see Old Rag, crowned in one-bil lion-year-old granite—the oldest roc in the park.
At mile 42, **Skyland** resort dates fron the late 1880s. Flat fields at **Big Mead ows**a *(mile 51)* differ dramatically fron other parts of the park. West of Bi Meadows, **Byrd Visitor Center** house changing exhibits.
Skyline Drive ends at **Rockfish Ga** *(mile 105.4)*, where two major east west highways, US-250 and I-64, cros the mountains.

### Staunton★
*13mi west of Rockfish Gap Entrance vi US-250, I-64 West and I-81 North.*
In this small hilly city (pronounced STAN ton), you'll find the birthplace *(18-24 N Coalter St.;* 🚶*visit by guided tour only* ♿🅿☎540-885-0897) of the nation' 28th president, **Woodrow Wilso** (1856-1924), and an attractive down town full of shops, bistros and restore homes. Maps of historic downtown ar available at the **Staunton-August Visitor Center** *(1250 Richmond Ave.* ☎540-332-3971).

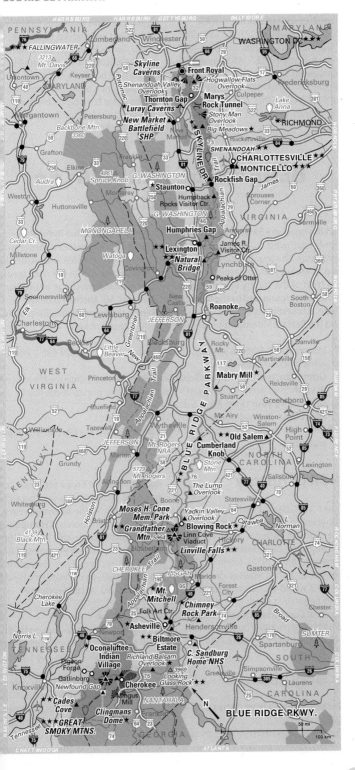

### Frontier Culture Museum★★

*0.5mi west of I-81 Exit 222 off US-250 West. Visit by guided tour only Jan–mid-Mar.*   ☎540-332-7850. www.fron-tiermuseum.org.

Nestled in the farmlands of the Shenandoah Valley, this 78-acre outdoor living-history complex synthesizes the region's European heritage through a series of farm buildings that wer dismantled and moved to this site: c.1700 German peasant farmhouse; mid-1700s Scotch-Irish farm; late-160C English farm buildings; and a mid-1800 Virginia farm. Costumed interpreter demonstrate farming techniques an such skills as blacksmithing, weavin and sheep shearing.

# BLUE RIDGE PARKWAY★★

MAP P133
EASTERN STANDARD TIME

Picking up where Skyline Drive leaves off, the magnificent Blue Ridge Parkwa winds southwest from Rockfish Gap, Virginia, to North Carolina's border wit Tennessee. The countryside becomes wilder and more remote between Ashevill and Cherokee, North Carolina. At Ridge Junction *(mile 355.3)*, the road leave the crest of the stately Blue Ridge and enters the southern fringe of the Blac Mountains, dominated by the tallest peak in the east, Mt. Mitchell (6,684ft). Fron there, it courses through the Great Craggy Range, the French Broad River Valle and the Balsam Mountains before meeting the Great Smokies.

- ▣ **Information:** America's Byway: The Blue Ridge Parkway. ☎828-298-0398. www.blueridgeparkway.org.
- ▶ **Orient Yourself:** Sights on the '*Scenic Drive*' listed below are organized from nort to south. The Parkway is designed for leisurely driving: plan to take it slowly.
- ◷ **Organizing your time:** Allow 5 days (469mi).
- ◉ **Don't Miss:** The majestic Vanderbilt Biltmore Estate.
- Kids **Kids:** Watching hawk migration from Humphries Gap is a once-in-a-lifetime experience.

## A Bit of History

When the idea of building a road between Great Smoky Mountains and Shenandoah national parks came to the attention of President Franklin D. Roosevelt in the 1930s, North Carolina and Tennessee had different ideas about where it would go. Construction of the road began just south of the Virginia border at **Cumberland Knob** *(mile 217.3)* in 1935. The parkway, built in noncontiguous sections, opened in 1939.

## Scenic Drive

### Rockfish Gap to Humphries Gap★

*45.6mi.*

Views along this stretch of the parkway, beginning at its northern terminus at Rockfish Gap, are broad and beautiful sprinkled with buildings weathered tc a silvery gray. At the **Mountain Farm Museum** on the grounds of **Humpbac Rocks Visitor Center** *(mile 5.8)* you'll ge a close-up look at five examples of 19C highland structures. From **Humphries Gap** *(mile 45.6)* you can watch the hawk migrate in mid- to late September.

### Lexington★★

*11mi west of Humphries Gap on US-60 Maps and information are available a the Lexington Visitor Center, 106 E. Washington St.* ☎540-463-3777.

The presence of two renowned Confederate generals, **Robert E. Lee** (1807-70) and **Stonewall Jackson** (1824-63) pervades this charming college town, home to the Virginia Military Institute (1839) and Washington and Lee University

## Visiting the Blue Ridge Parkway

### VISITOR INFORMATION

The park's eleven **visitor centers** are open May–Oct (The Folk Art Center is open year-round). Maps and information on area activities and accommodations are available at visitor centers or from **Parkway Headquarters** (199 Hemphill Knob Rd., Asheville, NC, 28802; ⚠✕🅿 ☎828-298-0398).

The parkway is open year-round, though sections may be closed due to severe weather during the winter months. Traveling the parkway is free. The speed limit on the parkway is 45mph (35mph in developed areas). Expect roads to be crowded during peak foliage season (Oct). Concrete mile markers along the road are numbered in increasing order north-to-south starting at mile 0 (the north entrance to the parkway at Rockfish Gap, VA) and ending at mile 469 (the south entrance to the parkway off US-441 in Cherokee, NC). Mountain temperatures range from mid-70s in summer to the teens in winter. Temperatures vary with elevation; wear layers of clothing.

### WHERE TO STAY

The nine campgrounds are open May–Oct. Most lodges and facilities along the parkway are closed during the winter (except Peaks of Otter Lodge, open year-round, ☎540-586-1081). Reservations are recommended during the peak tourist season in fall.

---

(1749). Lee, whom both the North and South asked to lead its armies during the Civil War, served as the president of the university that now bears his name. Today he is honored by a small museum in the 1868 brick **Lee Chapel** (on Washington and Lee campus; &🅿☎540-458-8768), where he is interred.

General Thomas J. Jackson's home for the last four years of his life was at 8 E. Washington Street (☎540-463-2552). He is buried at the **Stonewall Jackson Memorial Cemetery** (S. Main & McDowell Sts.).

### Natural Bridge★★

16mi west of Terrapin Hill Overlook (mile 61.4) on Rte. 130, Natural Bridge, VA. ✕🅿 ☎540-291-2121. www.natural bridgeva.com.

Called "one of the sublimest curiousities in nature" by Thomas Jefferson, Natural Bridge soars 215ft above Cedar Creek. Designated a National Historic Landmark in 1998, this limestone span began forming about 100 million years ago. Geologists believe the water level was once much higher. As the level dropped over time, the arch grew taller and wider, worn away by the rushing waters.

The moderate mile-long hike beyond the bridge to **Lace Falls** is more than worth the short trek.

### Terrapin Hill Overlook to Roanoke★

58.6mi.

The parkway drops to its lowest point—649ft—at a verdant spot near Virginia's James River. A short trail from the **James River Visitor Center** (mile 63.6) leads to a restored lock from the Kanawha Canal (1851), which once linked tidewater Virginia to the frontier. South of the visitor center, you'll find a lodge and restaurant at the **Peaks of Otter** (mile 85.6).

At **Roanoke**, the largest urban center along the parkway, the landscape flattens to rolling hills as the parkway crosses the Roanoke River.

### Mabry Mill★

Mile 176.2.

One of the most charming spots on the parkway—and a popular photo opportunity—this rustic mill was built in 1910 by Ed and Lizzie Mabry. The massive wheel of the wooden gristmill still churns through a small pond.

### Cumberland Knob to Moses H. Cone Memorial Park

76mi.

You'll cross the border from Virginia into North Carolina at **Cumberland Knob** (mile 217.5), the location of another visitor center. Continuing south, you will pass through **The Lump Overlook**

# Old Salem

In the mid-18C, the area around present-day Winston-Salem, North Carolina was owned by Earl Granville, heir to one of the eight "Lords Proprietor" charged with governing England's holdings in the colony of Carolina. Hoping to populate his domain with law-abiding citizens, Granville approached members of the Moravian sect, a Protestant group who had escaped religious persecution in their native Germany. The Moravians purchased 100,000 acres from Granville and in 1753 they established the settlement of **Bethabara** (Hebrew for "house of passage"). Nineteen years later, the group moved 6mi southeast to the permanent site of Salem.

Saved from demolition after World War II, **Old Salem**★★ (70mi east of the parkway, via US-421 East through Wilkesboro to Winston-Salem. Exit on Business 40, take Main St. Exit and go south 1mi; ✕ 🅿 ☎336-721-7300) is a charming mixture of 18C and 19C houses, shops and taverns set along brick streets (centered on Main St. between Race & Cemetery Sts.).

Begin your visit at the **Old Salem Visitor Center** (Old Salem Rd. at Academy St.), where you can purchase tickets and obtain self-guided tour maps to the 13 buildings open to the public. Costumed docents inside these structures provide information about life in the early Moravian community. Across from Salem Square, the **Single Brothers House**★★ provided living space for unmarried men from the age of 14 until they either married or died. The original part of this three-story structure, with its distinctive half-timbered façade, dates to 1769. Salem Square is bordered on the east by **Home Moravian Church** (1800), a brick edifice with English accents that continues to serve a Moravian congregation. A short distance up Church Street, the imposing 1802 **Vierling House** (at Bank St.) overlooks the Moravian cemetery, **God's Acre**. Rows of identical white headstones here illustrate the sect's belief that all are equal in death, as well as in life. Stop in the 1818 **Winkler Bakery** (on Main St. between Academy & Bank Sts.), where you can sample traditional goodies such as Moravian sugar cake and thin, crisp ginger cookies.

(mile 264.4), where an exhibit remembers local criminal Tom Dula, whose hanging in 1868 provided inspiration for the folk ballad "Hang Down Your Head Tom Dooley." **Yadkin Valley Overlook** (mile 289.8) surveys the valley where famed explorer **Daniel Boone** (☾ see WESTERN KENTUCKY) honed his hunting skills.

## Blowing Rock★

*3.8mi east of Moses H. Cone Memorial Park (mile 293.5) on US-321, Blowing Rock, NC. ♿ 🅿 ☎828-295-4636.*
Jutting out over the Johns River Gorge, this 4,000ft-high cliff is named for a phenomenon caused by the walls of the gorge 3,000ft below. Narrow rock walls form a flume through which winds often gust with enough force to return light objects tossed off the cliff.

## Grandfather Mountain★★

*1mi south of milepost 305 on US-22, 2mi north of Linville, NC. ✕ 🅿 ☎828-733-2013. www.grandfather.com.*

The world's only privately owned international biosphere reserve, Grandfather Mountain (5,964ft) lies within a 4,000-acre park. Here you'll find the **Mile High Swinging Bridge**, strung between two peaks; a nature museum; and a network of beautiful, but rigorous, hiking trails. Be sure to traverse Grandfather's perimeter via the elevated roadway of **Linn Cove Viaduct** (mile 304), from which you'll enjoy panoramic views of the valleys below. Building the viaduct in 1987 marked the completion of the Blue Ridge Parkway, more than 50 years after it was begun.

## Linville Falls★★

*0.5mi off the parkway from milepost 316.4, Linville, NC. 🅿 ☎828-765-1045.*
The Linville River once flowed over the top of the 2,000ft-deep gorge here, until a flood in 1916 cracked the rock, creating the falls that exist today. You can hike to the foamy chutes via two different trails (ranging from .6mi to 1mi) hacked though rhododendron thickets.

## Mount Mitchell State Park★

*4.8mi northwest of parkway via Rte. 128 from milepost 355, Burnsville, NC.* ⌂✕⛟🅿 ☎828-675-4611.

Driving to the top of the tallest mountain east of the Mississippi is an ear-popping ride around hairpin turns with amazing views of the landscape below. From atop the 6,684ft peak unfolds a haunting scene of wind-stunted trees, ravaged by air pollution, acid rain and an insect called the Balsam Woolly Adelgid.

Just north of Asheville at the **Folk Art Center** *(mile 382)*, you'll find an assortment of pottery, basketry, quilts and other handmade items from members of the Southern Highland Craft Guild.

## Biltmore Estate★★

*Take US-25 North Exit off the parkway and continue 4mi north on US-25 to Biltmore entrance.* ✕⛟🅿 ☎800-624-1575. www.biltmore.com.

Asheville's most popular tourist attraction, George Vanderbilt's 250-room mansion (1895) embodies architect Richard Morris Hunt's interpretation of a Loire Valley château. Allow at least a half-day to see the estate, including the winery and Frederick Law Olmsted's 75 acres of formal **gardens**★★.

Commissioned by George Vanderbilt (grandson of New York railroad tycoon Cornelius Vanderbilt), this extravagant castle was a technological marvel in its day, boasting central heating, electric-

*Front Door, Biltmore Estate*

ity and two elevators. Highlights of the self-guided tour include the vast **Banquet Hall**, hung with richly hued 16C Flemish tapestries; the **Salon**, which displays chess pieces used by Napoleon Bonaparte; and the two-story **Library**, lined with some 10,000 leather-bound volumes. The tour continues upstairs with the family and guest bedrooms, and ends downstairs with the kitchens, pool, bowling alley and servants' quarters.

Across from Biltmore's entrance, **Biltmore Village** was laid out in 1889 by Frederick Law Olmsted as a commercial complement to Vanderbilt's estate. Now the village houses boutiques, restaurants

*Mile High Swinging Bridge*

## Grove Park Inn

Presiding over **Asheville** from atop Sunset Mountain as it has since 1913, the venerable Grove Park Inn began as a six-story, 150-room hotel. Built of local granite boulders and topped with a red clay-tile roof, the original structure boasts one of the nation's largest collections of antique **Arts and Crafts furnishings**, as well as hand-hammered copper light fixtures fashioned by artisans at the Roycroft Campus in upstate New York. On either end of the lobby sit 15ft-wide **fireplaces**, which once heated the entire building. Be sure to stroll out on the verandah that flanks the back of the lobby for a sweeping **view** of the hazy Blue Ridge Mountains. Although the Grove Park Inn has now mushroomed into a modern resort comprising 512 rooms, four restaurants, an 18-hole golf course and a full-service spa *(opening in 2000)*, its spirit remains, in the words of its original owner, Edwin Grove: "an old-time inn with a home-like and wholesome simplicity."*290 Macon Ave.* ✗ ♿ 🅿 ☎*828-252-2711. www.groveparkinn.com.*

and galleries, including a noteworthy selection of high-quality crafts at **New Morning Gallery** *(7 Boston Way)*.

## Asheville★

*From the parkway, go 3mi west on US-74; take I-240 West to downtown exits.* ⚠✗♿🅿☎*828-258-6101. www.exploreasheville.com.*

This artsy town boasts an impressive collection of Art Deco buildings downtown, where art galleries, antique shops, bookstores and an eclectic group of restaurants line Haywood Street and Patton and Lexington Avenues.

Nearby, at 48 Spruce Street, is the white frame Queen Anne-style home on which author **Thomas Wolfe** (1900-38) based the boarding house in his most famous work, *Look Homeward, Angel* (1929). Adjacent to the house, the **Wolfe Memorial Visitor Center** *(52 N. Market St.; ☎828-253-8304)* maintains an exhibit detailing Wolfe's life and work.

## Chimney Rock Park★★

*25mi south of Asheville on US-74; entrance on right in the village of Chimney Rock.* ☎*800-277-9611.*

Ascending the summit of this 2,280ft-high granite monolith can be a rigorous hike or a short elevator trip up the equivalent of 26 stories. At the top, sweeping **views**★★ overlook the terrain that provided the backdrop for the film *The Last of the Mohicans* (1992). Millions of years ago, rock and mountain were one. Over the eons, water filled fractures

within the mountain, eventually isolating Chimney Rock.

## Carl Sandburg Home National Historic Site

*24mi south of Asheville in Flat Rock, NC. Take I-26 to Exit 22 (US-25) and follow signs to 81 Carl Sandburg Ln.* ➡ *Visit by guided tour only.* 🅿☎*828-693-4178.*

Named Connemara by a previous owner, this secluded farmhouse (c.1838) reflects the unpretentious comfort favored by American poet Carl Sandburg (1878-1967). The writer, who won a Pulitzer Prize for history (1940) for his six-volume biography of Abraham Lincoln, spent the last 22 years of his life here.

## French Broad River to Cherokee

*75.6mi.*

Some of the parkway's most dramatic scenery adorns its southernmost leg. Beginning at the French Broad River *(mile 393.5)*, this rugged stretch passes through 17 tunnels as it courses through Pisgah and Nantahala national forests. At mile 417, the smooth granite face of 3,969ft **Looking Glass Rock**★★ is breathtaking. The road then curves west and climbs to its highest point (6,053ft) at **Richland Balsam Overlook**★ *(mile 431.4)*. From here, the parkway continues to its southern terminus at US-441 just north of Cherokee.

## Cherokee

*Cherokee Center, 498 Tsali Blvd.* ♿🅿☎*800-438-1601. www.cherokee-nc.com.*

Gateway to Great Smoky Mountains National Park (*see GREAT SMOKY MOUNTAINS*), this small burg lies within the 56,000-acre Qualla Boundary Indian Reservation, home to some 9,000 members of the Eastern Band of Cherokees, who have occupied these mountains for centuries. Amid the sprawl of souvenir shops, motels and the popular Harrah's Cherokee Casino, this reservation town preserves sites that detail the history of the Cherokee tribe.

## Museum of the Cherokee Indian★

*From US-441 North, turn left on Drama Rd.* & P ☎828-497-3481.
This well-interpreted museum walks visitors chronologically through Cherokee history from the Paleo-Indian period to the present. The journey begins with a 5min film introducing the Cherokee version of creation. Afterward, visitors are free to walk through the exhibits, which include a fine collection of Indian artifacts enhanced by lively dioramas and poignant recorded narratives. Don't miss the Cherokee language **Bible**, translated in the mid-19C by Cherokee intellect Sequoyah (*see EAST TENNESSEE*).

## Oconaluftee Indian Village★

*.5mi off US-441 North at the end of Drama Rd.* Visit by guided tour only. & P ☎828-497-2315.
A living re-creation of the Cherokee's past, the village contains structures ranging from a 16C thatched-roof cottage to an 18C sweathouse, similar to those that were used by Cherokee ancestors.

# CHARLOTTESVILLE★★

MAP P133
EASTERN STANDARD TIME
POPULATION 38,223

Set amid the eastern foothills of the Blue Ridge Mountains and surrounded by the lush horse farms of Albemarle County, this university town takes pride in its natural beauty, rich history and cultural attractions. Founded as the county seat in 1762, Charlottesville became the heart of a network of tobacco plantations, and wheat and corn-growing farms. Well removed from Virginia's established aristocracy, the area fostered a tough self-reliance that would produce many leaders, including three of the country's first five presidents—**Thomas Jefferson** (1743-1826), **James Madison** (1751-1836) and **James Monroe** (1758-1831). In addition to Jefferson's Monticello, **Ash Lawn-Highland★** (*Rte. 53 east of Rte. 20; visit by guided tour only;* ☎434-293-9539) preserves the remains of Monroe's tobacco plantation, and **Montpelier★★** (*24mi northeast of Charlottesville via Rte. 20;* ☎540-672-2728) affords visitors a look at Madison's former estate.

**Information:** Charlottesville Albemarie Convention and Visitors Bureau. ☎804-293-6789. www.charlottesvilletourism.org

**Parking:** A free trolley will take you from downtown to campus and back, no car necessary.

**Orient Yourself:** Charlottesville is located 25mi east of the Blue Ridge Parkway from the Rockfish Gap Entrance via I-64.

**Don't Miss:** Two of the country's most significant architectural sites.

# A Bit of History

In recent years Charlottesville has been consistently ranked high for quality of living. One of the town's most popular locales for strolling, the seven-block pedestrians-only **downtown mall** (*Main St. between 2nd St. N.W. & 6th St. N.E.*) is graced by fountains, plantings and benches, as well as boutiques, restaurants and bars that occupy brick commercial buildings from the early 20C.

*Monticello*

# Sights

### Monticello★★★

*On Rte. 53, east of Rte. 20, following signs.* 🕒*Open daily 8am–5pm.* 💲*$15.* ♿📍☎*434-984-9822. www.monticello.org.*
Included on the UNESCO World Heritage List of international treasures, Thomas Jefferson's remarkable "essay in architecture" stands as an enduring monument to the guiding spirit of the birth of America. Best known as the author of the Declaration of Independence, Thomas Jefferson held positions including governor of Virginia, minister to France, secretary of State, vice president and third US President (1801-09).

An accomplished statesman, musician, draftsman and naturalist, Jefferson began building his home in 1768 on the little mountain ("Monticello") that commands views of the countryside.

A **visitor center** at the base of the mountain *(Rte. 20, just south of I-64, Exit 121; ☎434-977-1783)* offers exhibits and a film. Tours of the house begin in the **entrance hall**, which Jefferson used as a museum. Thoughtful innovations are evident at every turn, from heat-conserving double doors to skylights and a dumbwaiter. On the way up the mountain, stop at **Historic Michie Tavern**a *(683 Thomas Jefferson Pkwy.;* 🍴♿📍☎*434-977-1234)*. Established in 1784, this rambling white structure is popular today for its set midday fare of fried chicken, stewed tomatoes, black-eyed peas and cornbread.

### University of Virginia★★

*US-29 & US-250 Business (Emmet St. & University Ave.). Campus maps available at University Police Department (US-29 & Ivy Rd.).* ☎*434-924-0311. www.virginia.edu.*
One of only four works of architecture in the country to rate inclusion on the UNESCO World Heritage List, the university began in 1817 as Thomas Jefferson's retirement project, a carefully planned "academical village" that embodies the limitless freedom of the human mind. Today the university enrolls some 20,000 students and ranks as one of the top universities in the East.

The heart of Jefferson's village, the graceful **Rotunda**★★ *(University Ave & Rugby Rd.)*, completed in 1826, was patterned on the Pantheon in Rome, its shape more or less a perfect sphere seated within a cube. From the south Rotunda steps you can take in a sweeping view of the **Lawn**, flanked by colonnades that link student rooms with ten pavilions, each modeled after a different Greek or Roman temple.

# GREAT SMOKY MOUNTAINS NATIONAL PARK★★★

MAP P133
EASTERN STANDARD TIME

Straddling the North Carolina-Tennessee border, the lofty mountains that form the nation's most visited park are named for the ever-present shroud of blue-gray mist that inspired Cherokee Indians to call them *Shaconage*, or "place of blue smoke." Water and hydrocarbons released by the leafy woods and by more than 1,600 kinds of blooming plants that grow on the slopes, produce the vaporous 'smoke' (pollution has added to the mix, cutting visibility by about 60 percent since 1940 and damaging the red spruces). Today Great Smoky is a UNESCO World Heritage site and an International Biosphere Reserve; it preserves the best examples of eastern deciduous forest and is the habitat for more than 60 mammals, including the black bear, and more than 200 species of birds.

**Information:** National Park Service. ☎865-436-1200. www.nps.gov/grsm

**Organizing Your Time:** Allow a day. Park sights listed below are organized beginning at the south entrance in North Carolina.

**Don't Miss:** Great views and sunsets at Clingmans Dome.

**Kids:** Find plenty of amusement park fun at Dollywood.

## A Bit of History

In 1920, 75 percent of the 521,621 acres that would become Great Smoky Mountains National Park was owned by lumber companies. These lands were saved from being clear-cut through the support of national auto clubs, anxious

## Address Book

### ADMISSION
The park is open year-round, though roads may close due to severe winter weather. Entrance to the park is free. Facilities and roads within the park may be closed due to severe weather during the winter *(Nov-Mar)*. Expect roads to be crowded in summer *(Jul–Aug)* and during the peak foliage season *(Oct)*.

### VISITOR CENTERS
The park's visitor centers, Oconaluftee *(2mi north of Cherokee, NC on US-441; ☎865-436-1200)*, Sugarlands *(2mi south of Gatlinburg, TN on US-441; ☎865-436-1200)*, and Cades Cover Visitor Center *(on Cades Cover Loop Rd.; access via Little River Rd. off the northern end of US-441; ☎865-436-1200)* are open year-round. Newfound Gap Road *(33mi)* connects the park's north and south entrances (at Oconaluftee and Sugarlands visitor centers). Maps and information, including accommodations, weather conditions and recreational activities, may be obtained at visitor centers or from **Park Headquarters** *(107 Park Headquarters Rd., Gatlinburg, TN 37738; ☎865-436-1200)*.

### WHERE TO STAY
The park maintains more than 800mi of trails, ten developed campgrounds *($10-$14-$23/night; reservation information ☎877-444-6777 or http://reservations.nps.gov)* and five horse camps. Permits *(free; available at visitor centers or ranger stations)* are required for all backcountry camping *(Backcountry Reservations ☎865-436-1231)*. The only lodging in the park is LeConte Lodge, accessible only by trail *(advance reservations required; ☎865-429-5704)*.

### SAFETY
Mountain temperatures range from mid-70s in summer to the teens in winter. Temperatures vary with elevation, so be sure to wear layers of clothing.

*Gregg-Cable House in Cades Cove, built 1879*

to provide their members with scenic drives, and the combined efforts of the legislatures of North Carolina and Tennessee. To defray the costs of acquiring thousands of parcels of property, oil magnate John D. Rockefeller pitched in $5 million in 1928; the park opened in 1934.

Near the park's northern entrance lie the regional commercial centers of **Gatlinburg** and **Pigeon Forge**, Tennessee. As US-441 enters Gatlinburg, it becomes a vast strip of hotels, fast-food restaurants and outlet malls that provide a jarring contrast to the peaceful parkland. Seven miles farther west on US-441, Pigeon Forge attracts visitors to its 118-acre theme park, **Dollywood** *(☎865-428-9488)*, owned by country music diva Dolly Parton, who grew up nearby.

## Sights

### Oconaluftee Visitor Center
*At the park's south entrance on US-441 in Cherokee, NC.* 🅿 ☎828-497-1900.
After driving south down the Blue Ridge Parkway, begin here, at the southern entrance to the Great Smokies, where wall panels chronicle area logging in the 19C. **Mountain Farm Museum** showcases a restored early-19C mountain homestead.

### Newfound Gap Road★
Leading northwest from Oconaluftee Visitor Center, this scenic route *(closed to commercial vehicles)* winds up the crest of the Great Smokies and provides numerous pullouts from which to enjoy breathtaking vistas. Just up the road *(.5mi north of visitor center)* is **Mingus Mill**, with an 1886 water-powered gristmill. Stop for **views**★★ from the crest of **Newfound Gap** *(15.5mi north of visitor center)*, where the Appalachian Trail crosses the road.

### Clingmans Dome★
From Newfound Gap, pick up the winding 7mi spur to the park's tallest mountain (6,643ft). Take the steep, paved .5mi trail from the parking lot to the **observation tower** for a dizzying panorama that extends across the Carolinas, Georgia and Tennessee. This lookout is also the perfect place to watch the sunset on a clear evening.

### Cades Cove★★
*From the north end of US-441 at Sugarlands Visitor Center, take Little River Rd. 24mi west.*
Nestled in a stunning secluded valley surrounded by the forested peaks of the Great Smoky Mountains, Cades Cove was settled in the early 19C by pioneers from Virginia, North Carolina and East Tennessee who came here in search of affordable farmland. At the beginning of the 11mi one-way loop road is an orientation shelter, where you can purchase a booklet that details the cabins, mills and churches you'll discover along the way—vestiges of a community that thrived until the park's creation in the 1920s.

# BOSTON AND SOUTHERN NEW ENGLAND

he three states that make up Southern New England—Massachusetts, Con-ecticut and Rhode Island—offer some of the most diverse attractions in the S. The area's greatest asset is its strong sense of history, which is preserved n its museums, tiny villages and architecturally significant neighborhoods. oston, Massachusetts' historic capital is southern New England's largest and nost dynamic urban center. Although only about 500,000 people live within the 6sq mi city proper, roughly 5 million occupy the metropolitan area. It was here hat the American Revolution got its start, and the city has done an admirable ob of protecting much of its legacy in centuries-old cemeteries, twisting brick treets, and the chain of historic downtown sights along a downtown brick path alled the Freedom Trail. The Boston area is also a cultural mecca, claiming several najor universities—Harvard, Massachusetts Institute of Technology, University f Massachusetts and Boston University—along with a host of world-class art nd history museums.

listory buffs will get their fill in the Bos-on area, from the Revolutionary War attlefields of Lexington and Concord o **Plymouth**★★, *(40mi south of Bos-on)*, where 102 Pilgrims came ashore n 1620. Their settlement is re-created t **Plimoth Plantation**★★ Kids *(2.5mi outh of downtown Plymouth via Rte. 3A; 508-746-1622.* Open March 24-Nov 5 *daily 9am–5pm. Rest of the year Mon–Fri 9am–5pm, Sat-Sun 9am–8pm. Adults $25, children $15, seniors $22).*

oston Waterfront

For beach lovers, southern New England boasts 400mi of coastline, including ever-popular Cape Cod. Visitors pack the Cape and the offshore islands of Martha's Vineyard and Nantucket in summer, but it is in the autumn that New England really shows its color. Blazing fall foliage transforms the inland countryside into a palette of vivid gold, oranges and scarlets.

## Area Address Book

*For coin ranges, see the Legend on the cover flap.*

### GETTING THERE

**Logan International Airport (BOS):** ☎800-235-6426 *(ground transport information)*, www.massport.com; 2mi northeast of downtown. Taxis *($18-$20)*, water taxis *($10)* and commercial shuttles *($14)* provide transportation to downtown. Major rental car agencies are located near the airport. **Massachusetts Bay Transportation Authority** (MBTA) Blue Line services the airport and it's Silver Line rapid transit bus service connects to South station. Airport Water Shuttle *(☎330-8680 or 800-235-6426)* runs between the airport and Rowes Wharf.

**North Station** *(135 Causeway St. at Canal St.)* and **South Station** *(700 Atlantic Ave.)* link national and regional rail service. **Greyhound** *(☎800-231-2222; www.greyhound.com)* and **Peter Pan** *(☎800-343-9999; www.peterpanbus.com)* **bus lines** both depart from South Station, as do Amtrak **trains** *(☎800-872-7245, www.amtrak.com)*. MBTA suburban commuter trains *(☎722-3200; www.mbta.com)* depart from both North and South stations.

### GETTING AROUND

For information on road closures and Boston-area traffic, call ☎228-4636. **Boston Harbor Cruises** *(☎227-4321)* provides commuter **ferry** service between Long Wharf and Charlestown Navy Yard. The **MBTA** operates underground and surface transportation in the greater Boston area. Stations are indicated by the 'T' symbol at street level. Most lines operate Mon–Sat 5:15am–12:30am, Sun 6am–12:30am. **Subway** fare is $1.70; **bus** fare is $1.25 *with a Carlie Card, available at station vending machines.* MBTA **LinkPass** *(available at some stations and hotels)* are good for one *($9)* or seven *($15)* days of unlimited travel on all MBTA subway and local bus lines. Subway maps are available at main stations; MBTA system maps *can b e downloaded at www.mbta.com.* **Taxi:** Checker Taxi, ☎536-7000; Green Cab, ☎628-0600; Red Cab, ☎734-5000; Town Taxi, ☎536-5000.

**Visitor Information** – For free maps and information on accommodations, shopping, entertainment, festivals and recreation, contact: **Greater Boston Convention and Visitors Bureau**, 2 Copley Place, Suite 105, Boston MA 02116, ☎617-536-4100 or 800-888-5515, www.bostonusa.com; **Boston Common Visitor Center**, Tremont & West Sts., ☎800-888-5515.

**Accommodations** – **Hotel reservation services**: Citywide Reservation Services, 839 Beacon St., Boston MA 02115, ☎617-267-7424 or 800-468-3593; Host Homes of Boston, P.O. Box 117, Waban Branch, Boston MA 02468, ☎244-1308 or 800-600-1308. **Bed & Breakfast reservations**: Bed and Breakfast Cambridge & Greater Boston, P.O. Box 1344, Cambridge MA 02238, ☎720-1492 or 800-888-0178.

### WHERE TO STAY

**$$$ Fairmont Copley Plaza** – *138 St. James Ave., Boston, MA.* ⚹♿🅿 ☎617-267-5300. www.fairmont.com/copleyplaza. *383 rooms.*Back Bay's palatial property has been home base for visiting US presidents and foreign dignitaries since 1912. A look at the lobby's gilded coffered ceilings, crystal chandeliers and ornate French Renaissance-style furnishings may explain why Elizabeth Taylor and Richard Burton spent their second honeymoon here. A recent $34 Million guestroom renovation has mixed in decidedly modern amenities with classic fabrics and Louis XIV reproductions.

**$$$ XV Beacon** – *15 Beacon St., Boston, MA.* ⚹♿🅿 ☎617-670-1500. www.xvbeacon.com. *60 rooms.* Beacon Hill's most stylish hotel offers unsurpassed luxury. Past the intimate lobby's "living room" alcove, the Beaux-Arts building's original cage elevator (1903) takes guests up to oversized studios and suites, all of which are outfitted with canopy beds, gas fireplaces and mahogany paneling.

Amenities include personalized business cards and heated towel racks.

**$$ Steamboat Inn** – *73 Steamboat Wharf, Mystic, CT.* ♿🅿 ☎860-536-8300. *www.steamboatinnmystic.com. 11 rooms.* An eclectic mix of antiques and contemporary furnishings give the spacious guest rooms, individually decorated in colors ranging from neutrals to jewel tones, a luxurious look. Most have Mystic River views. Since the hotel is set behind the town's main street, you won't hear the traffic en route to the seaport, a short walk away.

**$$ The Pineapple Inn** – *10 Hussey St., Nantucket, MA.* ♿🅿 *Closed mid-Dec–mid-Apr.* ☎508-228-9992. *www.pineappleinn.com. 12 rooms.* Four blocks from the ferry landing, the 1838 Greek Revival house has been carefully restored with Federal antiques. Guest rooms, named for local whaling captains, come with handmade four-poster canopy beds, goose-down comforters and cable TV. For breakfast, it's fresh-squeezed juice, cappuccino and fresh-baked pastries.

**$$ Wequassett Resort and Golf Club** – *Pleasant Bay, Chatham, MA.* 🍴♿🅿⊛ *Open year-round.* ☎508-432-5400. *www.wequassett.com. 104 rooms.* Welcoming guests for more than 50 years, the resort's spring colors, patchwork quilts and flower-filled wicker baskets create a cozy setting. The main dining room is in a 19C house transported from nearby Brewster, and the reception building dates back to c.1740. You'll find a beach and tennis courts on the beautiful grounds.

**$ A Cambridge House** – *2218 Massachusetts Ave., Cambridge, MA.* ♿🅿 ☎617-491-6300. *www.acambridgehouse.com. 16 rooms.* You'll never go hungry at this 1892 Greek Revival inn. Bowls of M&Ms and homemade cookies are set on antique side tables and credenzas all day. Pastel floral wall coverings, plush canopied beds, and jewel-tone chaise lounges create a cheerful Victorian ambience. Continental breakfast is included in the rate.

**$ The Red Lion Inn** – *30 Main St., Stockbridge, MA.* ☎413-298-5545. *www.redlioninn.com. 110 rooms.* It's no wonder notables such as Theodore Roosevelt, John Wayne and Bob Dylan have stayed here. The lavish property, which has operated continuously since the late 1700s, is filled with Staffordshire china,

18C furnishings and colonial pewter pieces collected over time by the original owners and their descendants.

## WHERE TO EAT

**$$$ Harvest** – *44 Brattle St., Cambridge, MA.* ☎617-868-2255. **American.** Pepper-colored banquettes punctuate the corn-yellow walls in this elegant setting. The seasonal menu reflects Northeastern bounty; you might find dishes like New England clam chowder, char-grilled ribeye with cheddar and scallion mashed potatoes, and olive-crusted halibut with parsnip and yukon gold gratin. Milk chocolate banana charlotte is a great ending to any meal.

**$$$ Olives** – *10 City Square, Charlestown, MA.* ☎617-242-1333. **Mediterranean.** Bostonians still pack this favorite, which opened in 1989 as a small eatery just down the street from its current location. A communal farmhouse table forms the centerpiece of the rustic dining room where chef Todd English prepares memorable meals in the open kitchen. Classic picks: wood-grilled chunks of squid and octopus in a chickpea, tomato and toasted-garlic vinaigrette; sweet-and-savory butternut squash tortelli; and vanilla-bean soufflé.

**$$ Front Street** – *230 Commercial St., Provincetown, MA. Closed Jan–Apr & Tue in season.* ☎508-487-9715 **Mediterranean.** Brick walls, antique wooden booths, and lacquered handmade tables give this dining room a romantic appeal. The menu—American food with Mediterranean accents—changes every Friday. Specials may include filet mignon stuffed with crab, but herb-crusted rack of lamb and smoked duck are always available.

**$$$ C'Espalier** – *30 Gloucester St., Boston, MA.* ☎617-266-4600. **French.** Chef and ownder Frank McClelland was warded the (2007) James Beard Award for Best Northeast Chef for his sophisticated melding of New England and French cuisine. His talents are showcased in tasting menus feeeaturing dishes like smoked organic chicken with white truffle macaroni and cheese and sweared striped bass with pommes puree and braised oxtail. The restaurant sits in an 1889 Back Bay townhouse painted in sophisticated creams and browns with stunning woodwork and fireplaces.

# BOSTON★★★

MAP P148
EASTERN STANDARD TIME
POPULATION 581,616

A bright, chaotic melding of old and new, modern Boston bears little resemblance to the spindly peninsula the Indians called Shawmut prior to the 17C. The first colonists, about 1,000 **Puritans** led to the area by **John Winthrop**, initially named the region Trimountain because of the three hills that defined its topography. Soon thereafter, the town's name was changed to Boston, after the town in Lincolnshire, England, from which many of the Puritans hailed. The colony quickly became the New World's largest, its ports bustling day and night with ships from Europe and Asia.

- 🛈 **Information:** ☎617-536-4100. www.bostonusa.com
- 🅿 **Parking:** Driving in Boston is a wild ride, and not always for the better. Leave the car and hail a cab or take public transportation instead.
- 🕐 **Organizing Your Time:** Leave time to hike the 2.5mi Freedom Trail.
- 🄺🄸🄳 **Kids:** Kids get to ride the subway at the Children's Museum.
- ⚲ **Also See:** NEW YORK.

## A Bit of History

Though many Bostonians remained loyal to the Crown, tensions mounted when the Crown began enforcing previously uncollected taxes on imported goods after the costly French and Indian War. Colonists opposed "taxation without representation," because although they were British citizens, they had no voice in parliament. England made some concessions, but in general bore down harder on the colonists. The 1770 **Boston Massacre**, during which Redcoats shot into a crowd of demonstrating colonists, killing five, marked the first act of overt British aggression. Patriots used this event to rile Bostonians toward revolution. To protest a tax on tea in 1773, colonists dumped the cargo of tea-laden British ships into Boston Harbor—in what would become known as the **Boston Tea Party**. By 1775 the War of Independence was under way.

The famous **Battle of Bunker Hill** took place in Charlestown, north of Boston, in June 1775. Although the British succeeded in taking the fort that colonists had built during the night, the Redcoats were seriously weakened. In early 1776, Patriots used supplies captured at Fort Ticonderoga in New York to drive the British out of Boston.

Over the course of the 19C, Boston's population skyrocketed from 18,000 in 1790 to more than half a million at the turn of the 20C; its landmass also quadrupled with the a series of ambitious landfill projects. Near the end of the 19C, Frederick Law Olmsted designed the swath of greenery—now known as the "**Emerald Necklace**"—around the city. Beginning at **Boston Common**★ (bounded by Charles, Beacon, Park, Tremont & Boylston Sts.), a 50-acre park that dates back to the 1630s, the necklace stretches west along tree-shaded walkways from Commonwealth Avenue to Franklin Park.

Today the city is a product of the twin poles of the Boston psyche: Puritan preservationism and Patriot progressivism. While pockets like the North End and Beacon Hill retain a distinguished Old World ambience, Boston politicos and architects are relentlessly trying to update what they consider "blighted" districts. In the 1950s interstate highways scored the city into difficult-to-access fragments—a problem the "Big Dig" sought to remedy. Officially called the **Central Artery and Tunnel Project**, the largest highway construction project in American history finally put Interstate 93 underneath the city after incurring problems with its budget, poor execution, and even death following part of the tunnel's collapse. Visitors may still find the city, with its European-style tangle of narrow streets intersecting with gargantuan (and often traffic-clogged) highways, a bit of a nightmare to navigate. But a good map, sturdy shoes and a pocketful of subway tokens for the "T" will help uncover Boston's seemingly untouched Colonial landmarks, gleaming Postmodern skyscrapers, sylvan parks and world-class museums.

## Freedom Trail★★★

*Greater Boston Convention and Tourist Bureau information center: Tremont & West Sts., ☎617-536-4100. National Park Service visitor center: 15 State St., ☎617-242-5642, www.nps.gov/bost. Sights listed below are arranged roughly from south to north, in order of their appearance on the trail.*

The popular 2.5-mi walk, beginning at **Boston Common★** and ending at Bunker Hill Monument in Charlestown, includes 16 sites related to Boston's 18C and 19C history, particularly those that played major roles in the Revolution. Marked by a painted red line or red bricks embedded in the sidewalk, the trail wends through several distinct neighborhoods: the "Old Boston" of Beacon Hill, the dense and bustling **Financial District**, the Faneuil Hall shopping complex, the twisting streets of Italian **North End★**, and **Charlestown★**, an Irish residential enclave.

### Old South Meeting House★★

*310 Washington St. ♿ Open April-Oct. Daily 9:30am-5pm. Nov-March weekdays 10am-4pm, weekends 10am-5pm. ☎617-482-6439.*

Built in 1729, plain brick "Old South" remains a cherished Boston landmark. It was from the pulpit here that noted orators Samuel Adams and James Otis inspired the colonists to take arms against the British. Sparse decoration, compass windows, box pews and a balcony (for the poor) characterize this 18C New England meetinghouse.

### Old State House★★

*Washington & State Sts. ♿ ☎617-720-3290. www.boston-history.org. Open daily 9:30am-5pm.*

Boston's oldest public building (1713), this stately brick edifice headquartered British officials until the Revolution. The **Boston Massacre** took place outside the building in 1770, and on July 18, 1776, the Declaration of Independence was read from its balcony. Inside, two floors accessed by a spiral staircase feature excellent historical **exhibits**.

### Faneuil Hall★★★

*Dock Square. ♿ ☎617-242-5675. www.thefreedomtrail.org.*

Second floor meeting hall and market level information desk open daily 9am-5pm. National Park Service rangers present historical talks every thirty minutes, 9:30am-4:30pm, except when Hall is in use for special events.

Built and donated to the city of Boston in 1742 by the merchant Peter Faneuil (pronounced FAN-yul), this revered landmark was enlarged by preeminent Boston architect Charles Bulfinch in 1806. It was called "the cradle of liberty" because of the protests against British policy voiced in its second-floor **Great Hall** *(accessible via the grand staircase facing Quincy Market)*. The third floor holds the museum and armory of the **Ancient and Honorable Artillery Company** *(♿ ☎617-227-1638)* of Massachusetts; the first floor has always been a market. Atop the roof, the 1742 **grasshopper weather vane** symbolizes the port of Boston.

Behind Faneuil Hall stands a trio of long, two-story buildings. Officially called Faneuil Hall Marketplace, it is often referred to as **Quincy Market★★**, the name of its 1826 Greek Revival centerpiece. This complex of restaurants, outdoor cafes and shops now ranks among the city's most popular attractions.

▸ *Freedom Trail continues in the North End.*

### Paul Revere House★

*19 North Square. Open April 15-Oct 31, daily 9:30am-5:15pm; Nov 1-April 14, daily 9:30am-4:15pm. Closed Thanksgiving,*

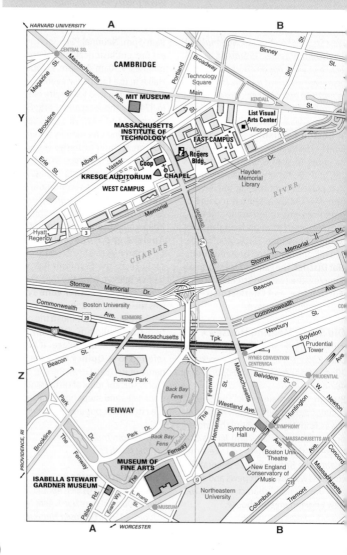

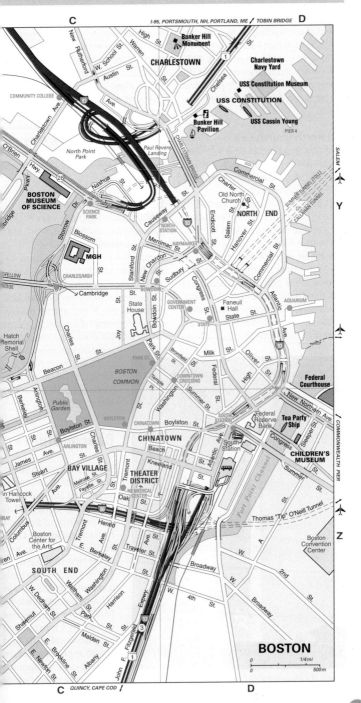

*Dec 25 and Jan 1, and Mondays, January through March.* *Adults $2.50; Seniors age 62+ and college students with ID $2; Children 5-17 $1; Under age 5, free.* *617-523-2338. www.paulrevere-house.org.*

This small clapboard house (1680) is famed as the starting point of the historic ride of Patriot Paul Revere (1735-1818) to Lexington on April 18, 1775 to warn Revolutionary troops that the British were coming. Inside you'll find Revere family furniture and personal effects.

### Old North Church★★★

*193 Salem St.* *Open daily 9am-5pm, Sunday services 9am and 4pm.* *Voluntary donations are welcome.* *617-523-6676. www.oldnorth.com.*

Built in 1723, "Old North" earned its place in history during the Revolution. Here, on the evening of April 18, 1775, the sexton displayed two lanterns in the steeple to signal the departure of the British from Boston to Lexington by boat, thus prompting the ride of Paul Revere and igniting the American Revolution. The original bronze name plaques, dating from the 1720s, remain on each of the box pews.

▶ *Freedom Trail crosses the mouth of the Charles River and continues in Charlestown. The following sights are located within .5mi of the North End.*

### Bunker Hill Monument

*Monument Square, Charlestown.* *617-242-5641. www.thefreedomtrail.org Visitor lodge and exhibits* *Open daily 9am-5am; monument is open to climb until 4:30am.*

The 221ft granite obelisk (1842), which actually stands on Breed's Hill where the 1775 battle was fought, is Charlestown's most prominent landmark. A 294-step staircase leads to the top of the monument, where the **view**★ includes Boston and the harbor.

### USS Constitution★★

*Kids Constitution Rd., Charlestown.* *Visit by guided tour only.* *617-242-5641 www.ussconstitution.navy.mil.*

Completed in 1797, this beloved 44-gun frigate is the oldest commissioned warship afloat. Undefeated in 33 battles, she earned her nickname "Old Ironsides" during the War of 1812 against the British, when enemy fire seemed to bounce off her wooden planking without causing damage. Entertaining tours, led by US Navy personnel, detail the intricate workings of the massive ship.

## Beacon Hill★★

Bounded by Beacon Street, Bowdoin Street, Cambridge Street, and Storrow Drive, Beacon Hill started off as the province of Boston's high society, known as the Boston Brahmins, as well as the first community of African Americans. Virtually undisturbed by the passage of nearly two centuries, the "Hill" today remains one of the city's most prized neighborhoods. The best way to appreciate Beacon Hill is to stroll its charming cobblestone streets, where

*Bunker Hill Monument*

© PhotoDisc, Inc

block after block of 19C town houses recalls Federal-era Boston. Be sure to take in lovely **Mt. Vernon Street**★★; **Louisburg Square**★★, a private park surrounded by Greek Revival bowfront houses; and **Charles Street**★, the main shopping thoroughfare.

## Massachusetts State House★★

*Corner of Park & Beacon Sts.* ⚒🕐*Open Mon-Fri 10am to 4pm.* ☞*Free tours available.* ☎617-727-3676

Two centuries ago, the golden dome of Massachusetts' capitol building took the place of the original beacon that lit up this historic hill. The monumental brick structure (1798, Charles Bulfinch) endures as a sparkling Boston landmark. The **interior** is embellished with murals, stained glass, columns, mosaic floors and carved Honduran mahogany paneling. Note the Hall of Flags and the oval House of Representatives chamber, where you'll find the wooden **Sacred Cod**, a symbol of Boston's fishing prosperity.

## Museum of Science★★

Kids *Just north of Beacon Hill off O'Brien Hwy. between Charles St. & Commercial Ave.* 🕐*Summer hours: Sat-Thurs 9am-7pm, Fri 9am-5pm; regular hours: Sat-Thurs 9am-5pm, Fri 9am-9pm.* ✗⚒🅿☎617-723-2500. www.mos.org.

A kaleidoscopic array of exhibits in this mammoth structure overlooking the Charles River range from 1950s-era taxidermed animals to cutting-edge, hands-on displays that encourage kids and adults to think through thorny scientific problems. Exhibits include a solar race track, 90ft **wave tank**, "visible-music" machine, and **mathematics lab** that melds classical thought with modern-day applications. The **Charles Hayden Planetarium** and **Mugar Omni IMAX Theater** present larger-than-life shows.

# Waterfront★

▸ *Sights listed are arranged S to N.*

The locus of Boston's long period of maritime prosperity, the waterfront fell on hard times in the first half of the 20C with the decline of the shipping business and the construction of a highway overpass that severed the waterfront from the rest of the city. Since the 1960s the area has rebounded with a flurry of hotel construction and adaptive re-use projects, as well as the establishment of the popular New England Aquarium.

## Children's Museum★★

Kids *300 Congress St. at Museum Wharf.* ✗⚒🕐*Open Mon-Thurs 10am-5pm, Fri 10am-9pm.* ☞*Adults $10, seniors $8, children $8, toddlers $2, infants free.* ☎617-426-8855. www.bostonkids.org.

## There She Blows!

Spotting whales, the largest mammals on earth, has been a New England pre-occupation since the heyday of the whaling industry, immortalized in Herman Melville's 1851 novel *Moby Dick*. Today humpback, finback and minke whales can be seen on their plankton-filled migration route from the Caribbean to Greenland and Newfoundland from early spring to mid-October, primarily along the **Stellwagen Bank** *(27mi east of Boston)* in the Gulf of Maine. About a dozen companies offer narrated whale-watching excursions from major New England harbors. Most companies guarantee sightings and recommend advance reservations. The popular three- to four-hour trip sponsored by the New England Aquarium *(☎617-973-5281; www.neaq.org)* departs from Boston on a high-tech boat staffed by naturalists and aquarium educators. **Hyannis Whale Watcher Cruises** *(☎508-362-6088; www.whales.net)* runs their state-of-the-art vessel from Barnstable Harbor on Cape Cod to the bank and back in 3-1/2 hours. From Gloucester, **Yankee Whale Watch** *(☎978-283-0313)* sponsors 4-hour excursions. For a list of whale-watching tours, contact the visitor bureau in Boston, Gloucester or Cape Cod.

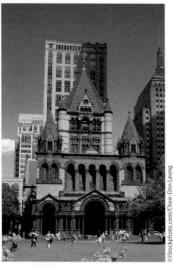

*Trinity Church*

Housed in a brick warehouse with timbered ceilings, Boston's popular children's museum features four levels of fun interactive displays, many with a multicultural twist (in **Teen Tokyo** visitors can ride a Japanese subway car). On the second-floor **Science Playground**, kids can experiment with physics.

### New England Aquarium★★

Kids *Central Wharf.* ⓒ*Summer hours: open Mon-Thurs 9am-6pm, Fri-Sun 9am-7pm; regular hours: Mon-Fri 9am-5pm, Sat-Sun 9am-6pm.* ⓐ*Adults $18.95, children $10.95. Whale watch: adults $36.70, children $30.40. IMAX: adults $9.95, children $7.95.* ☎*617-973-5200. www.neaq.org.*

In this colossal aquarium, interpretive panels, demonstrations and special exhibits foster understanding of some 600 species of fish, invertebrates, mammals, birds, reptiles and amphibians. Fronted by a shimmering stainless-steel entry, the original 1969 structure centers on the spectacular four-story, cylindrical **Giant Ocean Tank**. Encircled by a graded ramp, the 200,000-gallon tank offers sensational views of a wide array of sea creatures. The penguin exhibit contains more than 150,000 gallons of filtered Boston Harbor seawater and is home to three colonies of penguins. **Sea-lion shows** are offered daily aboard the floating pavilion *Discovery*.

# Back Bay and the Fenway★★

Built entirely on landfill, the Back Bay neighborhood occupies a massive trapezoid defined by Massachusetts Avenue, the Charles River, Arlington Street and Columbus Avenue. Within these boundaries visitors will find everything from the chic thoroughfare of **Commonwealth Avenue★★** to the sprawling indoor shopping malls of **Prudential Center** *(access from Boylston St.)* and **Copley Place**. At the northeast end of Commonwealth Avenue, the stunning 24-acre **Public Garden★★**, with a pond plied by beloved **swan boats**, continues to be Boston's prettiest public space. Eight-block-long **Newbury Street★**, lined with open-air cafes and high-end boutiques, is *the* place for Boston's fashion elite.

Bordering Back Bay to the west, the swampy greensward known as the Fens (part of the city's Emerald Necklace of parks) is home to students, the **Boston Symphony**, two world-class museums, and venerated **Fenway Park**★ *(4 Yawkey Way at Brookline Ave.;* ☎*617-267-1700)* home field of the Boston Red Sox baseball team.

### Trinity Church★★

*206 Clarendon St. (Copley Square).* ⸜⸜*Guided tours vary daily.* ☎*617-536-0944. www.trinitychurchboston.org.*

Recognized as the masterpiece of architect **Henry Hobson Richardson** (1838-86), this imposing granite and sandstone pile (1877) initiated the popular style known as Richardsonian Romanesque. A massive central tower dominates the church, but it is the **west porch** that catches the eye with its carved statues and biblical friezes. The church's cool, dark **interior** is brightened by lavish stained glass and murals by John La Farge.

### Boston Public Library★★

*700 Boylston St.* ♿ⓒ*OpenMon-Thurs 9am-9pm, Fri-Sat 9am-5pm.* ⓒ*Closed Sun.* ☎*617-536-5400. www.bpl.org*

Widely cosidered the epitome of the Renaissance Revival style, this handsome edifice (1895, McKim, Mead and White), influenced the design of countless public

©iStockphoto.com/Chee-Onn Leong

uildings in the US. The granite façade is adorned with **wrought-iron lanterns**, and relief panels by Augustus Saint-Gaudens. Inside, the vaulted **grand entry** is faced with yellow Siena marble, and barrel-vaulted **Bates Hall** (2nd floor) is a paean to learning.

## ohn Hancock Tower★★

00 Clarendon St. www.galinsky.com/ uildings/hancockboston.

More a sculpture than a building, this gleaming blue 60-story edifice, sheathed in 10,344 units of half-inch-thick mirrored glass, was designed by I.M. Pei. Since its completion in 1976, the tower has reigned as New England's tallest skyscraper. The 60th floor observatory was closed after the September 11th terrorist attacks and remain so at press time.

## Museum of Fine Arts★★★

65 Huntington Ave. ♿🍴🅿🕐OpenMonues, Sat - Sun 10am-4:45pm, Wed-Fri 0am-9:45pm. ◉Adults $17, seniors and tudents $15, youth $6.50, children and members free. ☎617-267-9300. www. nfa.org.

One of the country's leading museums, he massive Museum of Fine Arts (MFA) houses an encyclopedic collection of treasures from prehistoric times through the present representing nearly all cultures of the world. Private collections, together with works from the Boston Athenaeum and Harvard University, formed the core of the museum's holdings in the years following its founding in 1870. A need for more exhibition space prompted construction of the present Neoclassical structure in 1909. The modern West Wing (I.M. Pei) was added in 1981, containing a small permanent collection of 20C art and traveling exhibits. Today the MFA's labyrinthine interior covers some 540,000sq ft of gallery space, and the collection comprises 00,000 objects.

The stellar collection of **Asian art**★★★, which includes rare works from China, India, Southeast Asia, the Himalayas and Japan, is widely considered to be one of the most comprehensive in the US. **Ancient .gyptian, Nubian and Near Eastern rt**★★ comprises sculpture, tombs and jewelry. The museum's holdings of **Ameri-**can art★★ include more than 60 portraits by John Singleton Copley and 50 by Gilbert Stuart. A massive renovation project, due to be completed in 2010, includes a new American wing, a new visitor center, and a glass-enclosed courtyard.

## Isabella Stewart Gardner Museum★★★

280 The Fenway. 🕐OpenTues-Sun 11am-5pm. ◉Adults $12, seniors $10, college students $5, children free.☎617-566-1401. www.gardnermuseum.org.

Daring and vivacious, Isabella Stewart was born in New York City in 1840, and became part of Boston's high society when she married financier Jack Lowell Gardner in 1860. After her husband's sudden death in 1898, she poured her energy into the construction of **Fenway Court**, the current museum building, to house her formidable collection of art and artifacts. Completed in 1903, the museum—which resembles a 15C Venetian palazzo—and the arrangement of the 2,500 objects within have remained unchanged since her death in 1924.

Arranged as Gardner wished, in a setting that would "fire the imagination," the works are not chronological and many are unlabeled. Among the priceless paintings here are works by John Singer Sargent (El Jaleo, 1882) and Manet (Mme Auguste Manet, 1870); Raphael (Pietà, c.1504) and Rembrandt (Self-Portrait, 1629); Titian (Europa, 1562) and Botticelli (Madonna of the Eucharist, 1475). The second and third floors are illuminated by light from the stunning central **courtyard**, which brims with seasonal blooms.

# Cambridge★★

Chosen as the Bay Colony's capital in 1630, Cambridge is now thought of as one of the most literate municipalities in the US. Named after the English university town, Boston's brainy little sibling is home to both Harvard University and **Massachusetts Institute of Technology**★ (☎617-253-4795; www. mit.edu), one of the nation's premier science and research universities (1861), which straddles Massachusetts Avenue

## Cambridge Bookstores

Cambridge allegedly has more bookstores per capita than any other American city. Fueled by the 200,000 college students in the area, many of these shops stay open late (by Boston's Puritan standards), sponsor lectures and readings, and encourage browsing. In the Harvard Square area, the **Harvard Book Store** *(1265 Massachusetts Ave.)* is considered the best of the big independent bookstores. Founded in 1927, **Grolier Poetry Book Shop** *(6 Plympton St.)* is one of only two stores in the US devoted to poetry. **Schoenhof's Foreign Books** *(76-A Mt. Auburn St.)*—a linguist's mainstay since 1856—has titles representing more than 700 languages and dialects, while the **Globe Corner Bookstore** *(90 Mt. Aburn St.)* specializes in travel.

along the Charles River. The campus, host to roughly 10,000 students from 100 countries, includes the **MIT Museum**★ Kids *(265 Massachusetts Ave.; ☎617-253-4444; ◷open Mon-Sun 10am-5pm; ⌕adults $7.50, youth, students, seniors $3, MIT ID and children free, Sun 10am-noon free)*, which displays stop-motion photographs, kinetic sculptures and holograms.

### Harvard University★★★

*Harvard Information Center located in Holyoke Center 1539 Massachusetts Ave. (off Auburn St.). ☎617-495-1573. www. harvard.edu.*

The first college established in America, Harvard has been one of the nation's most prominent educational institutions since it was founded in 1636. Its enrollment has grown from 12 men to 20,000 male and female degree candidates in its undergraduate college and 10 graduate schools. Boasting a $29 billion endowment, it is the richest university in the world. Today the campus sprawls along Massachusetts Avenue from Harvard Square to the Charles River. The oldest part of the university, **Harvard Yard**★★ forms the core of the campus.

In addition to its renowned academic programs, Harvard claims several fine museums. The **Fogg Art Museum**★ *(32 Quincy St.; ⌖☎617-495-9400)* showcases Western art from the Middle Ages to the present; the contiguous **Busch-Reisinger Museum**★ *(accessible from the Fogg's 2nd floor)* specializes in the art of 20C German-speaking Europe. Collections in the Postmodern **Arthur M. Sackler Museum**★ *(485 Broadway; ⌖☎617-495-9400)* focus on Ancient,

Near Eastern and Far Eastern art. (A museums: ◷open Mon-Sat 10am-5p, Sun 1pm-5pm; ⌕$9.) Children enj exploring natural wonders of the wor collected by Harvard researchers in th **Harvard Museum of Natural Histo ry**★★ Kids *(26 Oxford St.; ☎617-495-304 ◷open Mon-Sun 9am-5pm; ⌕adul $9, non-Harvard students $7, seniors $ children $6).*

## Excursions

### Salem★★

*16mi north of Boston via Rte. 1A. Visito center at 2 New Liberty St. ☎978-74 1650. www.salemweb.com.*

Founded in 1626, the port of Saler derives its name from the Hebrew wor *shalom* ("peace"). Ironically, intoleranc and violence dominated the early day of this Puritan village, culminating i the notorious **witch trials** in the 1690 Salem captures this gruesome chapte in its history with such attractions a the **Salem Witch Museum** *(19 1/ Washington Square; ⌖☎978-744-169. ◷open Mon-Sun 10am-5pm; July-Au 10am-7pm; ⌕adults $7.50, seniors $6.5 children $5)* and the 1642 **Witch Hous** *(310 1/2 Essex St.; ⌕visit by guided tou only; ☎978-744-0180; ⌕adults $10, ser iors $8, children $6, under 6 yrs free).*

Salem's rise and fall as a seaport i detailed at the **Salem Maritim National Historic Site**★ *(174 Derby S ☎978-740-1650; ◷open Mon-Sun 9an 5pm; ⌕adults $5, children and senio $3, under 6 years old free).* And fans writer **Nathaniel Hawthorne** *(1804-6 won't want to miss the 1678 **House o he Seven Gables★ *(54 Turner St.; visit y guided tour only;* ✗ *☎978-744-0991;* ⏲*open July-Oct 10am-7pm, Oct week-nds 10am-11pm, Nov-Dec 10am-5pm;* ⏱*$12)*, which Hawthorne immortalized n his 1851 novel of the same name.

## Peabody-Essex Museum★★★

*ast India Square.* ✗ ♿⏲*Open Mon-Sun 0am-5pm.* ⏱*$13.* ☎*978-745-1876.* www. *em.org.*

Salem's premier museum's collections nclude more than 2.4 million works of rt and culture with an emphasis on eafaring and international trade. The argest department is **Maritime Art and History**, which includes a fasci-ating collection of 19C carved ships' **igureheads** and an expansive exhibit on Yankee **whaling**. The **Asian Export Art** collection is the world's biggest col-ection of decorative art made in Asia for xport to the West. Across the street, he Phillips Library contains "**The Real Witchcraft Papers**," a selection of tes-imonies from the 1690s that show, in rabbed Puritan script, the true perver-ity of the infamous trials. The Peabody lso sponsors guided tours of **historic houses** *(reservations required)* that trace he evolution of architecture, values nd life in Salem. In 2003, the museum noved into a massive, new building hat includes a suite of new gallenes nd made it one of the 25 largest art nuseums in the country.

## New Bedford Whaling Museum★★

🏛*18 Johnny Cake Hill.* ♿⏲*Open Mon-un 9am-5pm, summer Thurs 9am-9pm.*

⏱*Adults $10, seniors and students $9, children $6.* ☎*508-997-0046.* www.whal ingmuseum.org.

A fascinating array of artifacts, pho-tographs, paintings and displays out-line the history of whaling here, from harpooning, lancing and flensing a whale, to the cultural works the indus-try inspired—most notably Herman Melville's *Moby Dick* (1851). Exhibits revolve around the half-scale model of the 1826 whaling bark **Lagoda** and include **scrimshaw** (carved whalebone), harpoons, log books, whale oil and riches brought back from the Orient on whaling expeditions.

## Concord and Lexington★★

*20mi northwest of Boston. Take Massa-chusetts Tpk. (I-90) to I-95/Rte. 128 North; exit at Rte. 2A West and follow signs to Lexington. Concord is 5mi west of Lexing-ton via Rte. 2A.*

On April 18 and 19, 1775, these two towns became the crucible for the Amer-ican Revolution. Setting out from Bos-ton for Concord to confiscate a cache of colonists' weapons, British troops were intercepted on **Lexington Green**★★ by colonial **minutemen** thanks to the warning brought by **Paul Revere** and **William Dawes**. It's not certain which side first fired the "shot heard round the world," but at the end of the skirmish five revolutionaries lay dead.

Spread over Lexington, Lincoln and Concord, the 750-acre **Minute Man National Historical Park**★ *(visitor center 3mi west of Lexington Green on Rte. 2A;* ♿*☎978-369-6993; www.minute-man.areaparks.com)* commemorates the

## Transcendentalism

Concord found its way into history again in the 19C thanks to **Ralph Waldo Emerson** (1803–82), a Concord native who spearheaded his transcendentalism movement—a philosophy built on the belief that God exists in both man and nature—here. Another follower of the movement, **Henry David Thoreau** (1817–62) spent two years in a primitive cabin he built in the woods at **Walden Pond**, now a nature preserve *(1.5mi south of Concord on Rte. 126)*; he recorded his experi-ences in his 1854 book *Walden*. Philosopher **Amos Bronson Alcott** (1799-1888) and his daughter, *Little Women* author **Louisa May Alcott** (1832-88), also lived in town. Many of these literary figures are buried on Author's Ridge in tranquil **Sleepy Hollow Cemetery** *(Rte. 62, Concord)*, and several of their homes can be toured *(contact the Concord visitor center for information:* ☎*978-369-3120)*.

events that took place April 19, 1775, and includes a replica of the **Old North Bridge**★ where colonists advanced on the British. Centered on Lexington Green, **Historic Lexington**★★ preserves several buildings that played important roles in the battle. In the **Concord Museum**★ *(200 Lexington Rd., Concord;* ♿🕐*openJan-March: Mon-Sat 11am-4pm, Sun 1pm-4pm. April-Dec, Mon-Sat 9am-5pm, Sun 12pm-5pm; June-Aug: Sun 9am-5pm.* ▧*$10.* ☎*978-369-9609; www.concordmuseum.org)* artifacts and documents survey the city's rich history.

## Lowell National Historical Park★★

📷*67 Kirk St., Lowell.* ✗♿☎*978-970-5000. www.nps.gov/lowe.*
The history of Lowell, as told through the excellent exhibits housed in this complex of 19C mill buildings, illustrates the successes and failures of industrialization. In the early 19C, a group of investors affiliated with the late New England merchant **Frances Cabot Lowell** chose this spot on the Merrimack River for a large textile mill. By the mid-19C, Lowell ranked as the nation's largest cotton textile producer.
At the visitor center in Market Mills you can view the multi-image program **Lowell: The Industrial Revelation**, as well

as a riveting labor-oriented film strip **Wheels of Change: The First Centur of American Industry**. Built in 1873, th imposing brick factory complex **Boot Cotton Mills** *(French & John Sts.)* is th park's main attraction.

## Cape Cod★★★

*55mi southeast of Boston via Rte. 3 an US-6. Visitor information at the junc tion of US-6 & Rte. 132 and on Rte. 25 i Wareham.* ☎*508-362-3225. www.cape codchamber.org.*
Shaped like a muscular arm curled i a flex, celebrated Cape Cod, the area beloved summer and fall getawa spot, is fringed with 300mi of sand beaches, whitewashed fishing village towering sand dunes and salt marshes It was named in 1602 by explorer Bar tholomew Gosnold, who was impresse by its cod-filled waters. The first colonia settlement on Cape Cod, **Sandwich**★ founded in 1637, became known in th 19C for its colored-glass production Today the quaint downtown, arraye around the village green, include the **Sandwich Glass Museum**★ *(12 Main St./Rte. 130;* ♿☎*508-888-025* 🕐*open April-Dec: Mon-Sun 9:30am 5pm; Feb-March: Wed-Sun 9:30am-4pm Closed January;* ▧*adults $4.75, childre $1, under 6 free).* The active port o

*Cape Cod*

## Nantucket and Martha's Vineyard

Five miles south of Cape Cod, the island of **Martha's Vineyard**★★ *(accessible via ferry from Falmouth, Hyannis, Woods Hole, Nantucket & New Bedford and by airplane; b508-693-0085 or www.mvy.com)* comprises rolling heaths that give way to maritime forests, seaside cliffs and broad beaches. Ferries arrive either at upscale **Vineyard Haven** or at **Oak Bluffs**★, whose core of Victorian gingerbread **cottages**★ dates back to the 1850s. Tony **Edgartown**★, the oldest settlement on the island, is dominated by handsome dwellings built by ships' captains in the 1820s and 30s. Located at the western tip of the Vineyard, **Gay Head Cliffs**★★ expose striated layers of clay that date back 100 million years.

Lying 30mi south of Cape Cod, **Nantucket**★★★ *(accessible via ferry or airplane; for information: b508-228-1700 or www.nantucketchamber.org)* is a flat, triangular patch of land 14mi long and 3.5mi wide, whose population swells from 10,000 to 50,000 people each summer. It served as the world capital of the **whaling industry** between 1740 and the 1830s.

**Chatham**★ on the south shore successfully blends commercialism with historical preservation on its charming main street. Occupying the northern tip of Cape Cod, **Provincetown**★★ attracts throngs of summer visitors—many gay and lesbian—to its white-sand beaches, galleries and clubs.

Despite its popularity, the Cape nonetheless retains vast stretches of unspoiled beach along the **Cape Cod National Seashore**★★★, which stretches from Chatham north to Provincetown along the Atlantic Ocean *(visitor centers located on US-6 in Eastham, ☎508-255-3421; and on Race Point Rd., near Provincetown, ☎508-487-1256)*.

With its Colonial architecture, wharfside shopping and cobblestone streets, **Nantucket Village**★★★ reigns as one of the most charming, well-preserved towns on the East Coast. Shaded by venerable elms, **Main Street**★★★ has preserved its colonial atmosphere despite the upscale boutiques and galleries that fill its storefronts. Explore the island's whaling heritage at the **Whaling Museum**★ Kids *(Broad & S. Beach Sts.; ☎508-228-1894)*; or bike the 7mi from Nantucket Village to the 17C fishing village of **Siasconset**★ on the southeast side of the island.

# CONNECTICUT★★

MICHELIN MAP 583 T, U 6, 7
EASTERN STANDARD TIME
POPULATION 3,504,809

This rectangle bears the name of the river that divides it almost in half. Called Connecticut, after an Indian word meaning "beside the long tidal river," the state's first settlers were staunch Puritans who arrived in 1633, after finding Boston too liberal. By 1639 they had adopted the **Fundamental Orders of Connecticut**—the first formal statutes of government in the New World—thus earning the official designation, the **Constitution State**.

- **Information:** ☎860-270-8080. www.ctbound.org
- **Orient Yourself:** This is a small state, just 90mi from east to west and 55mi from north to south.
- **Don't Miss:** Yale University's impressive art gallery.
- **Also See:** BOSTON.

# A Bit of History

Throughout the 18C and 19C, Connecticut thrived by virtue of its "Yankee ingenuity," manufacturing everything from clocks to firearms and then selling them across the colonies. Among the best-known Connecticut inventions are the **Colt .45 revolver**, the **Winchester rifle**, and Eli Whitney's **cotton gin**, though items such as hats, brass and silverware were more common. Hit hard by English raids, Connecticut was nonetheless an important provider of munitions to the Patriots during the Revolutionary War. While continuing to manufacture such military supplies as jet engines and nuclear submarines, today the state is a study in diversity. Connecticut's major industrial cities—Hartford, Stamford, Bridgeport, Stratford and New Haven—all have suffered economically in the 20C, but its southwestern suburbs (suburbs of New York City, that is) rank among the wealthiest in the nation. That said, Connecticut remains predominantly rural, with attractive colonial villages scattered throughout the hilly woodlands of the interior and along the picturesque southeastern coast.

# Mystic

The village of Mystic, on the Mystic River in southeastern Connecticut, has been a shipbuilding center since the 17C. Today it is known for Mystic Seaport, a museum-village that occupies the former site of shipyards along the waterfront, and for its excellent aquarium.

## Mystic Seaport★★★

Kids *From I-95, take Exit 90 and follow Rte 27 1mi south. 75 Greenmanville Ave. ☎860-572-5315. www.mysticseaport.org.*
Located at the mouth of the Mystic River, this 17-acre complex pays homage to America's 19C maritime past. More than 60 buildings in the **village** house shops and businesses typically found in a 19C seaport, containing workshops where visitors can watch demonstrations of the lost art of wooden shipbuilding. Three vessels are moored at the waterfront, including the 1841 **Charles W. Morgan** ★★, the last surviving wooden whaling ship from America's 19C whaling fleet. The **Children's Museum** (*Open Nov-March: Mon-Sun 10am-4pm; April-Oct: Mon-Sun 9am-5pm; ☞adults $17.50, seniors and students $15.50, children $12, under 6 free*) allows youngsters to participate in games and shipboard activities that were popular during the sailing era (try to ge them to swab the deck), the three-story **Stillman Building** contains outstanding collections of **ship models** and **scrimshaw** (intricately carved whale bone and teeth), and the **Wendell Building** houses an array of painted wooden **ship's figureheads**

*Mystic Seaport*

orgeous folk-art talismans used for ood fortune at sea.

## Mystic Aquarium & Institute or Exploration★★

55 Coogan Blvd. (Exit 90 from I-95). Open March-Nov: Sun-Sat 9am-6pm; Dec-Feb: Mon-Fri 10am-5pm, Sat-Sun and holidays 9am-6pm. $22. 860-572-955. www.mysticaquarium.org.

More than 6,000 sea creatures make their home in one of the nation's largest aquariums. The "Alaskan Coast" exhibit a one-acre outdoor beluga whale display, while "Sunlit Seas" features species that thrive in estuaries and coral reefs. Watch stellar sea lions frolic in the "Lions of the Sea" exhibit.

## Excursion

### Mashantucket Pequot Museum and Research Center★★

mi northeast of Mystic. From I-95, take Exit 2, then Rte. 2 West and follow signs. Open Mon-Sun 10am-4pm. $15. 860-396-800. www.pequotmuseum.org.

This tribally owned and operated museum is devoted to the history and culture of the Mashantucket Pequot Indians, a southeastern Connecticut tribe who has lived continuously on the 3,000-acre reservation granted to them by the Connecticut Colony in 666. Inside the museum, dioramas, videos and recorded bird songs create a multisensory experience that details the Pequot's day-to-day life from prehistoric times to the present. A highlight is Pequot Village, a re-creation of a 16C native dwelling site.

## New Haven★★

Home of illustrious Yale University, New Haven was founded by Puritans in 638. New Haven's downtown centers on the 1638 New Haven green, a 16-acre public park. Visitors can stroll the serene residential streets—including Whitney Avenue, Hillhouse Avenue and Prospect Street—and the quaint commercial district along College and Chapel Streets.

## Yale University★★★

Visitor center at 149 Elm St. 203-432-2302. www.yale.edu.visitor.

One of the eight prestigious "Ivy League" schools, Yale was founded as the Collegiate School in Saybrook, Connecticut in 1701 by a group of Puritan clergymen. It was moved to New Haven in 1716 and renamed for the school's benefactor, wealthy merchant **Elihu Yale**. Today Yale enrolls more than 11,000 students.

Designed in the Gothic tradition after England's Oxford University, Yale was given a Postmodern facelift beginning in the 1950s thanks to architects Louis Kahn, Eero Saarinen and Philip Johnson.

**Yale University Art Gallery**★★ (1111 Chapel St.; Open Sept-June: Tues-Sat 10am-5pm, Thurs 10am-8pm, Sun 1pm-6pm; closed Mondays and major holidays; free; 203-432-0600; www. artgallery.yale.edu) was founded in 1832 with a gift of about 100 works of art from American artist **John Trumbull** (1756-1843). Today the gallery comprises two interconnected units—a 1928 building in the Gothic style and a 1953 addition by Louis Kahn. The museum's 80,000-piece collection emphasizes American decorative arts, and 19C and 20C European painting and sculpture.

Across the street, the **Yale Center for British Art**★★ (1080 Chapel St.; 203-432-2800; www.yale.edu/ycba; open Tues-Sat 10am-5pm, Sun 12-5pm; closed Mondays and holidays; free) is housed in a concrete, steel and glass building (1977, Louis Kahn) that allows natural light to filter down three- and four-story open courts to display areas. The holdings—the most comprehensive collection of British art outside the United Kingdom—revolve around Paul Mellon's bequest to the university in 1966.

## Hartford★★

Visitor information booth: 1 Civic Center Plaza on Trumbull St. between Asylum & Church Sts., 860-728-6789 or 800-793-4480, www.enjoyhartford.com.

Nicknamed "the Insurance Capital of the Nation," Connecticut's capital city hosts the headquarters of myriad insurance companies. The city's downtown long suffered from urban blight, but more than $2 billion in public and private funds have been invested in revitalizing the city's core. A new convention center, upscale hotels, retail shops, restaurants, and housing are breathing life into the historic city once again. Lively bars and cafes have line the streets around the award-winning **Hartford Stage Company** (50 Church St.; ☎860-527-5151), as do several landmarks by noted architects. Designed in 1792 by Charles Bulfinch, the Federal-style **Old State House**★ (800 Main St.; ☎860-522-6766) contains graceful touches inside and out; while the completely unrestrained 1879 **Connecticut State Capitol**★ (210 Capitol Ave.; ☎860-240-0222), a whimsical pile of turrets, finials, gables and towers by Richard Upjohn, was the talk of the town when it was built.

### Wadsworth Athenaeum★★

600 Main St. ◷Open Wed-Fri 11am-5pm, Sat-Sun 10am-5pm, first Thurs 11am-8pm. ◷Closed Mon, Tues, holidays. ◉Adults $10, seniors $8, students $5, members and children free. ☎860-278-2670. www.wadsworthatheneum.com.
Founded in 1842, this formidable art museum and oldest public art museum in the US has grown to include 50,00 works of art spanning more than 5,00 years. The structure is made up of fiv connected buildings of varying architectural styles; recent renovations includ an extensive overhaul of the sculptur garden. Highlights include a spectacular collection of **Hudson River schoo landscapes**; the distinguished **Wallac Nutting collection** of early America Colonial furniture; **19C Europea paintings**; and **American portraitur** (Copley, Eakins, Peale).

### Mark Twain House★★

351 Farmington Ave. ◷Visit by guide tour only Mon-Sat 9:30am-5:30pm, Su 12pm-5:30pm. ◷Closed Tues Jan-Marc ◉Adults $13, seniors $11, children $ under 6 free.☎860-247-0988.
This memorial to the well-known auth was commissioned by Twain in 187 Its exterior sports a profusion of ope porches, balconies, towers, bracket and steeply pitched roofs. Inside, th splendid 1881 decor has been restore A high-spirited individualist, **Samue Clemens** (1835-1910), under the pe name Mark Twain, wrote seven of h most famous works here, including Th Adventures of Huckleberry Finn (1884).

# RHODE ISLAND★★

MICHELIN MAP 583 U, V 6
EASTERN STANDARD TIME
POPULATION 1,067,610

The smallest state in the nation is not an island at all, but a largely flat, most rural trapezoid whose defining feature is **Narragansett Bay**. The first Europea to navigate the bay was Giovanni da Verrazano in 1524, but Rhode Island was no formally colonized until the 1630s, when the liberal-minded **Reverend Willia Blackstone** and **Roger Williams** came here seeking religious freedom from th Puritans in Boston and Salem. Other religious exiles followed, including Jew and Quakers, earning the state the disdain of the Puritans, who called it "Rogue Island." Throughout the 17C and 18C Newport and Providence prospered as cent ers for maritime trade. Fortunes were made from the unsavory Triangle Trade (i which rum was exchanged for slaves, who were in turn exchanged for molasse in the West Indies to make more rum), as well as from trade with China.

🛈 **Information:** ☎800-556-2484. www.visitrhodeisland.com
▶ **Orient Yourself:** Rhode Island measures only 48mi long and 37mi wide.
☺ **Don't Miss:** The creative inspiration you can find at the **Rhode Island Schoo of Design Museum**.
⌚ **Also See:** BOSTON.

# A Bit of History

Today Rhode Island retains intriguing glimpses of all eras of its past, from its main cities, Providence and Newport, to the quaint colonial villages of **Jamestown** and **Wickford** on Narragansett Bay, to pristine **Bristol★** and **Warren** (both accessible via Rte. 114), which are great for antiquing. The white-sand **beaches** of South County, which stretch 3mi between the resort town of **Narragansett** to Point Judith, are some of the finest in New England, attracting a mix of families, sun worshipers and surfers.

# Newport★★★

*Visitor information: 23 America's Cup Ave., 401-849-8048, www.gonewport.com.*
A resort once devoted exclusively to the wealthy, Newport is today a major sailing center and home to three renowned music festivals: the 17-day **Newport Music Festival** in July, during which classical concerts are given in the sumptuous mansions, and the **Newport Folk Festival** and the **Newport Jazz Festival**, both held in August at Fort Adams State Park.

Centered on Thames Street, the structures of **Colonial Newport★★** constitute one of the nation's great architectural treasures. Handsome **Colonial mansions**, including the elegant, fully furnished **Hunter House★★** (54 Washington St.; visit by guided tour only; 401-847-1000), a 1754 Georgian home partially crafted by famed 18C cabinetmakers Townsend and Goddard, crowd Newport's side streets. .

# Mansions

World-famous for their mammoth size, decor and ostentation, Newport's "cottages" were built in the late-1800s and early 1900s by some of America's richest families. Several designs were based on the castles of Europe, while others were idiosyncratic monuments to personal whims and hubris. Taken together (nine remain open to the public) they provide a fascinating picture of the excesses of the gilded age.

A number of the mansions may be seen by driving along **Bellevue Avenue**aaa and **Ocean Drive★★**. The 3mi pedestrian **Cliff Walk★★** *(Memorial Dr. to Bailey's Beach),* kept open to the public thanks to the protests of 19C fishermen, runs along the rocky shoreline, offering stunning **views** of the ocean and of the back sides of several estates. The mansions may also be visited by guided tour *(combination tickets available for up to five houses; 401-847-1000; www.newportmansions.org).* Below is a selection of the most popular homes.

## The Breakers★★★

*44 Ochre Point Ave. Adults $16, youth $4.*
Newport's grandest and most visited mansion, The Breakers is an opulent 70-room Italian Renaissance-style palace (1895), designed by Richard Morris Hunt. Outfitted with French and Italian stone, marble and bronze, red alabaster and gilded plaster, it was used as a summer retreat for the family of shipping magnate **Cornelius Vanderbilt II**. The two-story-high **Great Hall** displays a spectacular array of creamy French Caen stone pilasters. In the airy **Morning Room**, four corner panels representing the Muses are painted in oil on silver leaf. The Breakers' most richly embellished room is the formal **Dining Room**, which boasts rose alabaster columns; a vaulted ceiling ornamented with carving, oil paintings and gilt; and two 12ft-high Baccarat-crystal chandeliers.

## Marble House★★★

*596 Bellevue Ave. Open Sat-Sun, holidays, and Feb 19-23 for the Newport Winter Festival. Adults $11, youth $4.*
Renowned architect Richard Morris Hunt used 500,000 cubic feet of American, African and Italian marble in the lavish 1892 "cottage" that he designed for millionaire yachtsman **William K. Vanderbilt**. The classical portico is supported by four marble Corinthian columns. Inside, two 17C Gobelins tapestries greet visitors in the two-story Siena marble entrance hall. The **Gold Ballroom**—Newport's most ornate—decked with gilt chandeliers, panels and mirrors, is modeled after the Hall of Mirrors at Versailles. Don't miss the **Chinese Tea-**

*Rhode Island State House*

**house** at the rear of the property, where the Vanderbilts hosted small receptions and tea parties.

### Rosecliff★★
*548 Bellevue Ave. Open Sat-Sun, holidays, and Feb 19-23 for the Newport Winter Festival. Adults $11, youth $4.*
Designed by Stanford White to resemble the Grand Trianon at Versailles, this H-shaped manse faced with white-glazed terra cotta was completed in 1902 for one of Newport's most celebrated hostesses, **Theresa Fair Oelrichs**. Its grand 80ft-by-40ft **ballroom** was the scene for some of Newport's most spectacular events.

### The Elms★★
*367 Bellevue Ave.*
Inspired by the Château d'Asnières near Paris, architect Horace Trumbauer designed this dignified country estate (1901) for coal "king" **Edward J. Berwind**. Decked out in the French classical style, the entrance hall and dining room are hung with monumental 18C Venetian paintings. Take time to stroll around the 12 acres of lovely landscaped **grounds**.

## Providence★★

*Visitor information: 30 Exchange Terrace, ☎401-751-1177, www.providencecvb.com.*

Small as it is, Providence is nonetheless a cultural hub and architectural showcase. Downtown features the landmark Art Deco **Fleet Building** (1 Westminster St. at Fulton St.) as well as the 1828 **Providence Arcade**, a sort of ancestor to the modern shopping mall whose skylit interior is lined with shops between Weybosset and Westminster Streets. Theaters, music clubs and bars are following the lead of the venerable **Trinity Repertory Theater Company** (201 Washington St.; ☎401-351-4242). Rhode Island's largest art's organization and one of the most respected regional theaters in the country. Once paved over, the Providence River now flanks the downtown core, crossed by bridges and lined with footpaths.

Directly west of downtown lies the lively Italian district **Federal Hill**, centered on Atwells Avenue, where the city's best European-style eateries are located. To the north, the 1901 McKim, Mead and White neoclassical **Rhode Island State House**★ (82 Smith St.; ☎401-222-2357, tours daily) looms above the city from its hilltop perch. Its freestanding **dome** is the world's second largest. Weekday morning tours are available.

### Rhode Island School of Design Museum★★
*224 Benefit St. Open Tues-Sun 10am-5pm. Adults $8, senior citizens $ youths $2; college students $3. Free Su 10am-1pm, third Thurs of every mon 5pm-9pm, Fri 12pm-1:30pm, and the la Saturday of the month. ☎401-454-650 www.risd.edu.*
Collections of art from various period and civilizations are presented her Adjoining the museum is **Pendleto House**, built in 1906 for the **Charle Pendleton collection** of 18C America furnishing and decorative arts.

### John Brown House Museum★★
*52 Power St. at Benefit St. Visit guided tour only, Tues-Sat 10am-5pm, S noon-4pm. Closed Jan-Feb. Adu*

7, seniors and students $5.50, children 4. ☎401-273-7507.

his three-story brick mansion (1788) was designed for financier John Brown by his brother Joseph. From the outside it is a model in Georgian restraint.

Within, the carved doorways, columns, fireplaces, cornices, wood trim and plasterwork provide an appropriate setting for the treasured collection of Rhode Island **furnishings**

# WESTERN MASSACHUSETTS★★

MICHELIN MAP T, U 6
EASTERN STANDARD TIME

Western Massachusetts presents different faces: here you'll find several industrial owns (**Springfield, Worcester, Pittsfield**); seven liberal-arts colleges (**Amherst, Mt. Holyoke, Smith**) situated around hip, countercultural **Northhampton**; and miles of rolling farmland, woodland and meadows, cut with rivers and rising, s one travels west, into mountains. It is this westernmost portion of the state, ust south of green Vermont and north of urban New York, that most visitors seek. Pristine colonial villages abut thick woods and mountains provide ample opportunities for recreation year-round.

**Information:** ☎617-973-8500. www.massvacation.com.
**Don't Miss:** The romantic nights at the Tanglewood Music Festival.
**Organizing Your Time:** Plan your days so you have time to enjoy the living history attractions that dot the maps in Western Massachusetts.

## A Bit of History

Running from Millers Falls (east) to the New York border (west), the scenic 63mi stretch of Route 2 through northwestern Massachusetts known as the **Mohawk Trail**★★ meanders along the banks of the Deerfield and Cold rivers through tiny mountaintop hamlets, sheer gorges and dense forests. Hikers and outdoor enthusiasts enjoy spectacular **views** of the region from the highest point in the state—3,491ft **Mount Greylock**★★ 5mi south of North Adams).

## Old Sturbridge Village★★★

59mi west of Boston via I-90 (Massachusetts Tpk.). Take Exit 9 (I-84) and follow signs to village in Sturbridge, MA. ☎508-347-3362. www.osv.org.
One of New England's best-known attractions, Old Sturbridge Village is a living-history museum that authentically re-creates life c.1790-1840 in a rural New England community. Interpreters

wearing 19C dress farm the land, cook, make tools, sew and celebrate according to traditional customs. The result, enhanced by the beauty of the village's woodsy site, is a glimpse into the everyday lives of early New Englanders.
Architecture ranges from the modest clapboard **Friends Meetinghouse** (1796) to the generously proportioned, Federal-style **Towne House** (also 1796), its attic rooms adorned with Masonic symbols. Several exhibition halls display period antiques, such as glass, firearms and clocks. However, the fascinating **demonstrations** of trades such as blacksmithing, bookbinding, printing, coopering, weaving, and working an 1820 **water-powered sawmill** are the real draw here.

## The Berkshires★★★

Tourist information: ☎413-443-9186; www.berkshires.org.
Blessed with a pastoral landscape virtually unrivaled in New England, the Berkshires have long been a haven for

*Hancock Shaker Village*

cityfolk and naturalists, artists and writers. These undulating foothills, arrayed along the fertile **Housatonic River Valley** on the western edge of Massachusetts, are set against the dramatic backdrop of the **Taconic** and **Hoosac** ranges, creating scenery that is idyllic, especially in the fall.

The **Mohegan** tribe lived peacefully in the area until the arrival of explorers and colonists. Bent on Christianizing the few Native Americans who remained after centuries of disease and warfare, the English established a mission at Stockbridge in the early 18C. Farming dominated the region through the early 19C, when milling gained prominence. The advent of the railroad brought on a golden age of estate building ended by tax reform and the Great Depression.

Today the Berkshires harbor a large number of luxurious second homes along with such charming villages as **Great Barrington**, **Tyringham** and **Lenox**★. In summer, culture mavens flock to the world-renowned summerlong **Tanglewood Music Festival** (☎ 617-266-1492; www.tanglewood. org), the **Berkshire Theatre Festival** (☎413-298-5536; www.berkshiretheatre. org), and the international **Jacob's Pillow Dance Festival** (☎413-243-0745; www.jacobspillow.org; June-Aug).

### Norman Rockwell Museum★★

Kids 2.5mi from Stockbridge center 9 Glendale Rd., Rte. 183. ◷ OpenNov-Apr Mon-Sun 10am-4pm, May-Oct: Mon Sun 10am-5pm; weekends and holiday 10am-5pm. ⬤Adults $12.50, college st dents $7, under 18 free. ☎413-298-410 www.nrm.org.

Occupying a 36-acre estate overlookin the Housatonic River Valley, the museu is the repository of the largest collectio of original works by America's premie 20C illustrator. A Stockbridge reside from 1953 until his death, Norman Roc well (1894-1978) is best known for th hundreds of homespun covers he illu trated for the **Saturday Evening Pos** The museum's nine galleries displa Rockwell works culled from a collectio of more than 500 paintings and draw ings. Also on the grounds is Rockwell simple **studio**.

### Massachusetts Museum of Contemporary Art★★

87 Marshall St., North Adams, MA; o Rte. 8, .25mi north of Rte. 2. ◷Open Mon Sun 10am-6pm. ◷Closed Tues. ⬤$12.5 ☎413-664-4481. www.massmoca.org. This new modern art museum (1999) us the vast wood-floored interiors of ren vated brick factory buildings to displa gigantic contemporary works that hav

one largely unseen because their size nd weight had heretofore made exhibi- on impossible. Works by such artists as bert Rauschenberg, Mario Merz and seph Bueys come from studios and useums around the world and change a regular basis. The 27-building com- ex also features sound-art installations nd theatrical performances.

## Hancock Shaker Village★★★

*In Pittsfield, at junction of US-20 & Rte. , 9mi north of I-90 (Exit 1).* ☎413-443- 88; www.hancockshakervillage.org. ade up of 20 Shaker structures and 200 acres of farm, meadow and wood- nd, Hancock Shaker Village is a living- story museum that commemorates and scribes the active Shaker community cated here from 1790 to 1960. An off- oot of a group of Quakers in Manchester, ngland, the Shakers got their name from e whirling and shaking that affected em in heightened spiritual states. They oved to America to avoid religious per- ecution and established 19 communities etween Kentucky and Maine from 1778 1836. Although the Shakers are consid- red the most successful of the communi- rian groups established in the late 18C, eir emphasis on celibacy limited their ngevity.

oday the complex interprets their fe through some 10,000 objects, and emonstrations of such daily tasks as ilking cows, spinning yarn and cook- g. That the Shakers put their "hands work and hearts to God" is evident the simplicity and functionalism of eir **furniture** and architecture. The 826 **Round Stone Barn** is a classic haker design, and the **Brick Dwelling** 830) contains living quarters for nearly 00 members.

# Williamstown★★

This beautiful colonial village *(at the junction of US-7 & Rte. 2; www.william-stown.net)* nestles in the northwest cor-ner of the state, where the Mohawk Trail enters the Berkshires. Verdant rolling hills provide a lovely setting for pres-tigious liberal arts **Williams College**, chartered in 1793, and for the renowned **Williamstown Theatre Festival** (☎413-597-3400; www.wtfestival.org).

## Sterling and Francine Clark Art Institute★★★
*225 South St.* ☎413-458-2303. *www.clarkart.edu.*
The works of art amassed by Robert Ster-ling Clark and his wife, Francine, between World War I and 1956 are worthy of being compared to some of the world's finest collections. Though the couple lived in New York City, they chose Williamstown for their museum. Surrounded by hills and meadows, the original white marble building (1956) suggests a private resi-dence in scale, natural light and architec-tural detail. A red granite annex houses additional galleries.

At the heart of the collection are paint-ings, prints and drawings by the **Old Masters** and **19C French and American artists**. More than 30 canvases by Renoir are presented along with works by Euro-peans Corot, Millet, Degas, Monet and Toulouse-Lautrec, and Americans Rem-ington, Homer and Sargent. Rich holdings of **17C and 18C silver** are another high-light. Acquisitions of **early photography** (1839 to 1910) invite the viewer to ponder the varied currents of 19C art.

# CHICAGO AREA

Located in Illinois, less than an hour's drive from Indiana to the southeast ar
Wisconsin to the north, Chicago occupies a strategic position on the southe
end of Lake Michigan. Stretching north and east over 22,300sq mi, this majes
lake is the fifth-largest body of freshwater in the world and the only one of th
five Great Lakes whose borders lie entirely within the US. Its temperate breez
can turn a winter's day lovely; while an angry northerly can just as easily blo
through a summer's afternoon. The Chicago River flows west from the lak
bisecting downtown and then forking north and south just over a mile inlan

From its perch at water's edge, the city
proper spills north, west and south to
cover 228sq mi. Outranked in population
size only by New York City and Los Angeles, this polyglot city of nearly three million prides itself on its neighborhoods,
some 175 in all. While some are the
stuff of developers' dreams, many trace
their outlines around the historic ethnic
enclaves from which the city was built.
Beyond its borders, suburbs, exurbs
and collar counties encircle the city like
growth rings on a tree, adding another
4,400sq mi to "Chicagoland." Recent
years have seen an explosion of suburban growth, as downtown employers
opt for less expensive locations outside
the city, creating thriving commercial
and residential corridors in surrounding communities.

For now, the city and its far-flung sate
lites seem to have struck a happy ba
ance. Revitalization of urban space
inside and out, has reawakened a
interest in city living and working. An
while thousands of suburbanites mal
the daily commute to work downtow

*Chicago Skyline along Wacker Drive*

growing number "reverse-commute" to work outside the city limits.

hough many of Chicago's cultural gems luster in the downtown neighborhoods, here is much to be seen slightly farther field. To the west, **Oak Park**★★★ is trove of architectural treasures by rank Lloyd Wright. The windswept dunes, marshes and forests of the Lake Michigan shore are best enjoyed at ndiana Dunes National Lakeshore★

(☎219-926-7561), which spreads along Highway 12 in Indiana less than an hour's drive from Chicago. For those who wish to venture farther still, Indianapolis, 177mi to the southeast, hosts the famed Indianapolis 500 auto race each May. And several sights related to the life of the nation's 16th president, Abraham Lincoln, are located in the Illinois state capital of **Springfield**, approximately 200mi southwest of Chicago.

## Area Address Book

### GETTING THERE

**O'Hare International Airport (ORD)**: ☎773-686-2200, www.ohare.com; 14mi northwest of the Loop. Information booths located on the lower level of terminals 1, 2 and 3, and on the upper and lower levels of terminal 5. **Chicago Midway Airport (MDW)**: ☎773-767-0500, www.flychicago.com; 10mi southwest of the Loop. Information booths located on the lower level of the main terminal near baggage claim. Airport Express (☎312-454-7800) operates shuttles from both airports to downtown. CTA (below) Blue and Orange line trains run from O'Hare and Midway, respectively, to downtown. Rental car agencies are located at the airport.
**Union Station** (225 S. Canal St.) links national and regional rail service by **Amtrak**, (☎800-872-7245; www.amtrak. com) with **Metra** commuter trains (below). **Greyhound bus** station: 630 W. Harrison St., ☎312-408-5800 or 800-231-2222, www.greyhound.com.

### GETTING AROUND

**Bus** and **rapid-transit** maps and the Downtown Transit Sightseeing Guide available (free) at train stations, hotels, and visitor centers and downloadable on www.transitchicago.com. Timetables available from the Regional Transportation Authority Information Center (175 W. Jackson Blvd., suite 250; ☎312-913-3110). CTA fares are $1.75 for bus and $2 for the El one-way, exact change required. All fares are $1.75 with a Chicago Card (available through www. transitchicago.com). **Taxi**: Checker Taxi Co., ☎312-243-2537; and Yellow Cab Co., ☎312-829-4222.

### VISITOR INFORMATION

For a free visit planner, maps and information on accommodations, shopping, entertainment, festivals and recreations, contact: **Chicago Office of Tourism**, Chicago Cultural Center, 78 E. Washington St., Chicago IL 60602, ☎312-744-2400, www.choosechicago. com; **Chicago Convention and Tourism Bureau**, 2301 S. Lake Shore Dr., Chicago IL 60616, ☎312-567-8500. **Chicago Office of Tourism Visitor Centers**: Chicago Cultural Center (above); Chicago Water Works, 163 E. Pearson St. at Michigan Ave.; Millenium Park Welcome Center, 201 E. Randolph St.

### WHERE TO STAY

**Hotel reservation services**: Accommodations Express, www.accommodationsexpress.com; Hotel Discount!.com, ☎800-364-0801, www.180096hotel. com. **Bed & Breakfast reservations**: Bed and Breakfast Association, www. chicago-bed-breakfast.com. **Hostels**: Chicago International Hostel, ☎773-262-1011; Hostelling International Chicago Summer Hostel, ☎312-360-0300, www. hichicago.org.

*For coin ranges, see the Legend on the cover flap.*

**$$$ The Drake Hotel** – 140 E. Walton Pl., Chicago, IL. ☎312-787-2200. www.thedrakehotel.com. 535 rooms. Since 1920, the Italian Renaissance-style limestone building at the top of the Magnificent Mile has long been *the* address for visiting celebrities. Lobby highlights include antique solid-brass candelabras and the original mahogany ceiling inset with hand-painted tiles. Rooms, some of which overlook Lake

Michigan, combine floral fabrics with dark woods.

**$$$ Canterbury Hotel** – *123 S. Illinois St., Indianapolis, IN.* 🍴♿🅿 ☎*317-634-3000. www.canterburyhotel.com. 99 rooms.* Downtown's finest boutique property offers personalized service in an Old World setting. Queen Anne- and Chippendale-style pieces, dark wood paneling and gold-plated fixtures deocrate this 1928 landmark. There's a private lobby entrance to Circle Center mall. The award-winning **Danielli Restaurant & Gallery** is a favorite romantic dining spot.

**$$$ Omni Severin Hotel** – *40 W. Jackson Pl., Indianapolis, IN.* 🍴♿☎*317-634-6664. www.omnihotels.com. 424 rooms.* Located across from Union Station downtown, this 1913 high rise was *the* place to stay until the late 1930s. The main entrance has been updated, but the back lobby's original chandelier, Palladian windows and marble staircase remain intact. Guest rooms blend contemporary furnishings with traditional jewel tones.

**$$ Hotel Allegro Chicago** – *171 W. Randolph St., Chicago, IL.* 🍴♿🅿☎*312-236-0123. www.allegrochicago.com. 483 rooms.* Bold colors and prints have transformed the North Loop theater district's 1926 Bismarck Hotel into a stylish Hollywood set. The lobby's fluted-glass and oak-paneled walls are the backdrop for cobalt-blue velvet chaise lounges and red velour sofas. Guest rooms feature eye-opening pink wallcoverings, melon-and-magenta bedspreads and oval desks.

**$$ Hotel Monaco** – *225 N. Wabash St., Chicago, IL.* 🍴♿🅿 ☎*312-960-8500. www.monaco-chicago.com. 192 rooms.* Two blocks from the Magnificent Mile, this boutique property was designed as the world-traveler's 1930s Art Deco-style living room. In the oversized lobby, the registration desk is modeled after a classic steamer trunk. Whimsical amenities: an in-room pet goldfish on request, and your choice of lottery tickets or candy at turndown.

## WHERE TO EAT

**$$$ Charlie Trotter's** – *816 W. Armitage St., Chicago, IL. Closed Sun & Mon.* ☎*773-248-6228.* **Contemporary.** Tables at this culinary wunderkind's Lincoln Park restaurant get booked 4 to 12 weeks

in advance. The draw? One-of-a-kind dishes prepared with only naturally raised meats, organic produce and vegetable-based sauces. Housed in a late-19C brownstone, the dining room's understated Biedermeier-style decor complements the food. Choose from several daily prix-fixe tasting menus.

**$$$ Blackbird** – *619 W. Randolph St., Chicago, IL. Closed Sun.* ☎*312-715-0708.* **Contemporary.** In contrast to its minimalist decor, the food at this Market District hot spot is a feast for the eyes. Dig into seared Alaskan halibut with spring unions or venison with black mission figs.

**$$$ Dunaway's Palazzo Ossigeno** – *351 S. East St., Indianapolis, IN.* ☎*317-638-7663. Closed Sunday.* **American.** On the edge of the Fletcher Place Historic District, the restaurant is in a 1930 Art Deco gem that originally housed an oxygen manufacturing plant. Its restored interior was transformed into five elegant dining rooms where locals sup on Mediterranean-inspired comfort food such as veal chops stuffed with sage and prosciutto, and hazelnut-crusted chicken.

**$$$ one sixtyblue** – *1400 W. Randolph St., Chicago, IL.* ☎*312-850-0303.* **Contemporary.** Michael Jordan is a silent partner of this trendy Market District restaurant, but celebs and locals come for chef Martial Noguier's original creations. Sleek and sexy, the loft-like dining room sets the mood for inventive dishes like peekytoe crab salad, red snapper with smoked sturgeon, and rack of lam with morel mushrooms.

**$ The Original Gino's East** – *162 E. Superior St., Chicago, IL.* ☎*312-266-3337.* **Pizza.** Natives swear that this 1966 landmark off the Magnificent Mile is *the* place to go for the city's classic deep-dish pie. The gooey two-inch-thick slices, with its signature cornmeal crust, are layered with mozzarella, tomato sauce, parmesan, romano and your choice of extras. Bring a marker to sign the graffiti walls—it's a tradition.

**$$ Hot Chocolate** – *1747 N. Damen Ave., Chicago, IL.* ☎*773-489-1747 www.hotchocolatechicago.com.* **American.** Chef/owner Mindy Segal's desserts are legendary. And for good reason.

# CHICAGO ★★★

MAP P172
CENTRAL STANDARD TIME
POPULATION 2,896,016

Fulcrum of modern American commerce, Chicago takes its name from the Potawatomi word *She-caw-gu*, meaning "stinking onion"—a reference to the garlic that grew wild in the area. The city, which today covers 228sq mi, began as a trading outpost on the swampy banks of the river in 1779. Its first permanent inhabitant, Jean-Baptiste Point du Sable, was a trader of African-Caribbean descent.

**Information:** ☎312-744-2400. www.ci.chi.il.us/tourism
**Also See:** MILWAUKEE.

## A Bit of History

When incorporated as a city in 1837, Chicago had a population of a mere 4,000; it would top 300,000 by 1871 and 1.5 million by the turn of the century. During that time, its central location straddling East and West, between the Mississippi River and the Great Lakes, became increasingly strategic as the hub of transportation and shipping, commerce and industry in an expanding America. Lumber, grain and livestock funneled through Chicago in monumental quantities. City fathers frantically constructed tunnels, bridges and sewers to accommodate the busy metropolis, and Irish and German laborers arrived in droves to do the work.

In October 1871, the **Great Chicago Fire** broke out, burning for three days and destroying the central city. Rebuilding began immediately and growth continued unabated; the population tripled in the decade following the fire. In spite of crowding, poor sanitation and grueling working conditions, Chicago rose above the miasma of its stockyards and steel mills. After 1880 the central city grew tall on the talents of a coterie of architects who pioneered the **Chicago School of Architecture** (☞ *see INTRODUCTION, Architecture*).

By the 1890s, elite residents had leisure time and money enough to establish cultural institutions. The crowning achievement would be the staging of the **World's Columbian Exposition** in 1893 on the South Side lakefront. A showcase of Neoclassical architecture and modern technology, the fair established Chicago as a world-class city.

In the 20C, the Roaring Twenties left a permanent scar as bootlegging gangsters, **Al Capone** foremost among them, committed hundreds of murders in their attempts to control the illegal liquor business. Together with the fire and the fair, this gangster heritage still plays a leading role in defining the city's diverse urban personality. Reinforcing that diversity, Chicago's population today is 40 percent African American, nearly 20 percent Hispanic and close to 4 percent Asian. Another 80 additional ethnic strains enrich the mix. Contemporary Chicago will continue to navigate its urban hazards to ensure the city's diversity, vitality and livability in the new millennium.

## The Loop ★★★

Looming large along the lakefront, Chicago's busy Loop and its environs have been fertile grounds for architectural innovation since the fire in 1871. Named for the elevated tracks that girdle them, these blocks bustle with workday energy as Chicagoans transact daily business in an array of office towers that catalogs the city's growth skyward since the 19C. The **James R. Thompson Center** ★★ (*bounded by Clark, LaSalle, Randolph & Lake Sts.;* ✗ ⅙), designed by Helmut Jahn in 1985, may be the Loop's quirkiest structure, its pastel panels enclosing a soaring **atrium**★. Representing the apex of the International style is

*Sears Tower and Buckingham Fountain*

Ludwig Mies van der Rohe's **Federal Center★★** *(Dearborn St. between Adams St. & Jackson Blvd.)*, completed in 1974, and the 1965 **Richard J. Daley Center** *(bounded by Washington, Randolph, Clark & Dearborn Sts.)*, by C.F. Murphy Associates. Both these buildings feature stunning plaza sculptures: Alexander Calder's 1973 **Flamingo** adds a burst of red outside the Federal Center. From Daley Plaza rises an untitled work by **Pablo Picasso**.

Stretching between the river and Congress Parkway, State Street was once the city's grand retail concourse. Today, two late-19C landmark stores endure: **Marshall Field & Company★** *(between Randolph & Washington Sts.)*, designed by D.H. Burnham & Co., is famous for its richly embellished exterior clocks and its Frango mint chocolates (in 2006, Marshall Fields was bought by Macy's).

### Sears Tower★★★

*233 S. Wacker Dr. ◷Open April-Sept daily 10am-10pm. Oct-march 10am-8pm. Open all holidays. ⟨Adults $12.95, youth $9.50, under 3 free. www.thesearstower.com.*

This 110-story feat of engineering cuts an unmistakable profile on the city's skyline. At the time of its construction (1968-74), the city did not require a zoning variance for the tower, allowing it to rise to an unsurpassed height of 1,450ft. In 1996 architect Cesar Pelli's Petronas

Towers in Kuala Lumpur, Malaysia topped the Sears in height, although th latter still claims the highest roof an the highest occupied floor. Designed b architect Bruce Graham and chief eng neer Fazlur Khan for Skidmore, Owing & Merrill, the tower is solidly anchore into the bedrock hundreds of feet belov ground; its structural skeleton require 76,000 tons of steel. Enter on Jackso Street for the **Skydeck** [Kids] (&.☏312 875-9696) and soar 103 stories up t enjoy spectacular **views**★★★ of th city and the lake.

### Chicago Cultural Center★★

*78 E. Washington St. ☏312-744-6636 egov.cityofchicago.org.*

This marvelous Neoclassical palazz served as the city's first library whe completed in 1897 after designs b Shepley, Rutan & Coolidge. Admir the inlaid-marble grand stairway tha ascends from the Washington Stree entrance to **Preston Bradley Hall**★ with its Tiffany stained-glass dome *(fre concerts are offered here every Wednesdd at 12:15).* The **Chicago Office of Tourisr Visitor Information Center** *(☏312-74 2400)* on the north side of the buildir makes a good place to start a Loop tou The **Museum of Broadcast Commu nications** *(☏312-245-8200; openin at its new location at Kinzie and State* which features exhibits, video and audi

## Scraping the Sky

It took a talented and energetic cohort of architects to rebuild Chicago after the 1871 fire. Within a year of the blaze, 10,000 new buildings rose up at a cost of $45 million. By 1890, the booming population increased the pressure on the downtown district to accommodate more people, more services and more offices. With no place to go but up, Chicago architects and engineers created the skyscraper. In traditional masonry construction, thick walls support the weight of the building. Architect **William Le Baron Jenney** reversed the formula by developing a skeletal steel frame on which to hang "curtain" walls, allowing buildings to grow taller. Based on this steel-frame construction, Jenney's 1884 nine-story Home Insurance Building, now demolished, is considered the first modern "skyscraper." At the same time, engineers mastered ways to anchor tall buildings in Chicago's swampy soil and to reduce the effects of high winds. Improvements to the elevator and telephone made vertical height practical. These innovations gave birth to the **Chicago School of Architecture**, recognized as the first significant new movement in architecture since the Italian High Renaissance. With it came a new aesthetic, and by 1894 most Chicago School architects had rejected historical ornament in favor of vertical sculptures made of piers, spandrels and windows. Their work would change the texture of city architecture around the world.

Visitors on foot can still glimpse the scale of 19C Chicago. The **Monadnock Building★★** *(53 W. Jackson Blvd.)* combines both the old load-bearing masonry style in its northern half (1891, Burnham & Root) and the revolutionary steel-frame construction in its southern portion (1893, Holabird & Roche). The **Reliance Building★★** *(32 N. State St.)*, designed and completed by Charles Atwood and David Burnham in 1895, anticipated the glass skyscrapers of the 1980s. Built in 1891, 1895, and 1905 respectively, **Pontiac★** *(542 S. Dearborn St.)* the **Marquette★★** *(140 S. Dearborn St.)*, and the **Chicago** *(7 W. Madison St.)* buildings by Holabird & Roche are masterpieces of Chicago school skyscraper design. At the southeast corner of LaSalle and Adams Streets, the **Rookery★★** (1888, Burnham & Root) houses a rare commercial interior by Frank Lloyd Wright (1905).

amplings of historic programming, and which archives the history of radio and TV.

## Chicago Board of Trade Building★

*1 W. Jackson Blvd.* ☎312-435-3590. *www. bot.com/cbot/building*

One of the city's finest Art Deco skyscrapers, this building, designed by Holabird & Root (1930), and its two annexes house the world's oldest and largest futures exchange (1848).

## Grant Park★

The city's 319-acre "front yard," located between Randolph Street on the north and **Soldier Field** (1929, Holabird & Roche) on the south, Lake Michigan on the east and Michigan Avenue on the west, marks roughly the midpoint in the swath of parks that trims Chicago's 28mi lakeshore. The park has been shaped by landfill, accretion, erosion and the human hand since 1835 when state commissioners set aside a thin strip of land along the shoreline to "remain forever open, clear and free." Sixty years later, mail-order magnate A. Montgomery Ward conducted a lengthy and successful battle with the city to clear the stables, railroad tracks and other eyesores that had rooted there in spite of the old edict. In 1909 Daniel Burnham's Plan of Chicago called for "a formal focal point," and the elegant landscaping of the park began to emerge as construction started in 1915. Though the automobile age sliced the green space with busy streets, the park still offers peaceful gardens, picnic spots and lovely vistas of the city and lake. Centerpiece of the park, 1927 **Buckingham Fountain★★** was modeled on the Latona Basin at Ver-

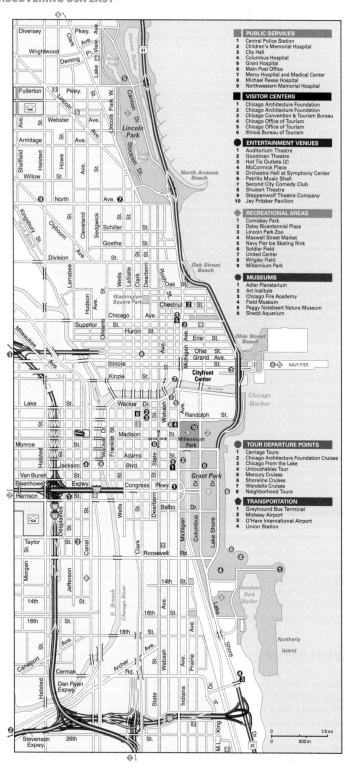

**PUBLIC SERVICES**
1 Central Police Station
2 Children's Memorial Hospital
3 City Hall
5 Columbus Hospital
4 Grant Hospital
6 Main Post Office
7 Mercy Hospital and Medical Center
8 Michael Reese Hospital
9 Northwestern Memorial Hospital

**VISITOR CENTERS**
1 Chicago Architecture Foundation
2 Chicago Architecture Foundation
3 Chicago Convention & Tourism Bureau
4 Chicago Office of Tourism
5 Chicago Office of Tourism
6 Illinois Bureau of Tourism

**ENTERTAINMENT VENUES**
1 Auditorium Theatre
2 Goodman Theatre
3 Hot Tix Outlets (2)
4 McCormick Place
5 Orchestra Hall at Symphony Center
6 Petrillo Music Shell
7 Second City Comedy Club
8 Shubert Theatre
9 Steppenwolf Theatre Company
10 Jay Pritzker Pavilion

**RECREATIONAL AREAS**
1 Comiskey Park
2 Daley Bicentennial Plaza
3 Lincoln Park Zoo
4 Maxwell Street Market
5 Navy Pier Ice Skating Rink
6 Soldier Field
7 United Center
8 Wrigley Field
9 Millennium Park

**MUSEUMS**
1 Adler Planetarium
2 Art Institute
3 Chicago Fire Academy
4 Field Museum
5 Peggy Notebaert Nature Museum
6 Shedd Aquarium

**TOUR DEPARTURE POINTS**
1 Carriage Tours
2 Chicago Architecture Foundation Cruises
3 Chicago From the Lake
4 Untouchables Tour
5 Mercury Cruises
6 Shoreline Cruises
7 Wendella Cruises
8 Neighborhood Tours

**TRANSPORTATION**
1 Greyhound Bus Terminal
2 Midway Airport
3 O'Hare International Airport
4 Union Station

sailles. On summer evenings its waters are illuminated to spectacular effect. At the south end of the park, the 10-acre **Museum Campus** unites in spirit and space Chicago's great triad of natural science museums: the Field Museum, the Shedd Aquarium and the Adler Planetarium. And each July, the grounds come alive with the city's largest outdoor festival, the **Taste of Chicago**.

## Millennium Park

*201 E. Randolph St. ◷Open daily 6am—11pm. ☎312-742-1168. www.millenniumpark.org.*

Opened in 2005, this 24.5-acre park is quickly becoming Chicago's best-loved tourist attraction... even for locals. Year-round Millennium Park offers something for adults and kids alike, be it public art (and water-spouting) **Crown Fountain** to wade in for free ice skating. You could spend days here looking at all the different attractions and enjoying the different entertainment options. You'll be able to see the steel elements of the Frank Gehry-designed **Jay Pritzker Pavilion** from a few blocks away.

In warm months you can sit here and enjoy an outdoor concert. Gehry also designed BP Bridge, a 925-feet span that is the architect's first bridge. Anish Kapoor's sculpture is called **Cloud Gate**, but everyone refers to it as "the bean." Get up close and person with the giant sculpture. Unlike so much public art, feel free to touch. The **Lurie Garden** features native plants. Go to the park's Web site for information on downloadable audio tours for use on mp3 players.

## Art Institute of Chicago★★★

*111 S. Michigan Ave. at E. Adams St. ✗♿◷Open Mon-Weds 10:30am-5pm, Thurs-Fri 10:30am-9pm, sat-Sun 10am-5pm. ✑Adults, $12, children, students, and seniors $7, under 12 free. Thurs-Fri evenings after 5pm are free May 31-Aug 31. ☎312-443-3600. www.artic.edu.*

One of the first art schools in the US, the Art Institute was founded in 1866 as the Chicago Academy of Design. This museum is among the greatest in the world and is preeminent in the Midwest. It has been housed in this monumental limestone building designed by Shep-

*Grant Park Music Festival*

© Brook Cllins

## The Perfect Town

George M. Pullman was the founder of the Pullman Palace Car Company railcar company. But he is better known for being credited for causing the country's first labor strike when he lowered Pullman's worker's wages in 1894. But as he decreased wages he didn't lower rents for the homes in which he required them to live.

What Pullman lacked in social policy know-how he had in urban planning acumen. The worker's town he created is now a landmark and oft-referred to as the "most perfect town." Expect to see blocks of preserved brick rowhouses and parks, and remnants of a shopping arcade and other public buildings. A fire ravaged the original 1880 Pullman Factory and Clock Tower in the 1990s, but preservationists have worked to keep the self-contained community vibrant.

Your first stop should be the **Historic Pullman Visitor Center** *(11141 S. Cottage Grove Ave.,* ◷*Open Tues-Sun 11am–2pm.* ☎*773-785-8901.* *)* where you can see a very small, but worthwhile exhibit. You'll get a map and the lay of the land. Then you can stroll the manicured streets, looking at Arcade Park and the historic home exteriors.

ley, Rutan & Coolidge since 1893; several wings have been added over the years, bringing its size to 400,000sq ft. In 2009, construction will end on the newest wing adding 264,000sq ft.

Spanning five millennia, its collections cover a multitude of cultures, though its reputation is based largely on its cache of **Impressionist and Postimpressionist paintings**★★★, one of the largest and most important outside France. This assemblage of painterly genius encompasses important works by Courbet, Manet, Monet, Cézanne, Renoir, Degas and Seurat. Besides these treasures,

the institute has a strong collection o **American fine and decorative arts**★★ ranging from Colonial furniture and silver to molded 20C chairs by Eerc Saarinen and Charles Eames; as well a a fine group of **Modernist painting and sculpture**. Covering 5,000 year from the Neolithic Age to the 20C, the institute's **Chinese, Japanese and Korean**★★★ holdings rank among the finest in the US. A significant collec tion of 15,000 **Japanese woodbloc prints**★, and a fine group of **archai Chinese jades**★ constitute some o the highlights. Delicately crafted and

*The Field Museum*

istorically precise period rooms, the 68 **Thorne Miniature Rooms**★★ Kids are a perennial favorite. Of local interest is the architectural collection, which includes fragments of demolished buildings and a re-installation of the **Trading Room of the Chicago Stock Exchange**★★ (1894, Adler & Sullivan).

### Field Museum of Natural History★★★

Kids *1400 S. Lake Shore Dr. on the Museum Campus.* ✗ ♿ 🅿 ⏰ *Open Mon-Sun 9am-5pm.* ⊗ *$12.* ☎ *312-922-9410. www.fieldmuseum.org.*

More than nine acres of exhibit halls and 20 million artifacts inhabit the vast Neoclassical edifice (1921, Daniel Burnham) that houses this world-class natural history museum. Amassed for the World's Columbian Exposition in 1893, the collections finally acquired their permanent home in 1921. Dinosaur bones are a specialty here, represented by **Sue**, the most complete *Tyrannosaurus rex* skeleton found to date, and the extensive exhibit **Evolving Planet**★, which covers life on earth from the days before the dinosaurs to the Ice Age. The new 5,000sq ft **Underground Adventure** takes visitors through the subterranean world. Other colorful, interactive exhibits explore **Africa**★★ and **Ancient Egypt**, while a number of quieter gal-

leries present finely crafted animal taxidermy and wildlife dioramas. Superb ethnographic holdings thoroughly cover the cultures of the Americas and Oceania, and the hall of **Gems**★ highlights the earth science collection.

### Shedd Aquarium★★★

Kids *1200 S. Lake Shore Dr. on the Museum Campus.* ✗ ♿ ⏰ *Open daily May-Sept Mon-Sun 9am-6pm; Sept-May Mon-Fri*

### City of the Big Pizzas

Chicago ranks as one of the country's greatest spots for pizza. Aficionados rave about the city's deep-dish variety, sometimes called thick-crust or pan pizza. This savory concoction of tomatoes, cheese, sausage and vegetables ladled over a thick, doughy crust was developed in the 1940s by restaurateur Ike Sewell, whose restaurants **Pizzeria Uno** *(Ohio St. & Wabash Ave.)* and **Pizzeria Due** *(on Wabash at Ontario)* still serve the genuine article to crowds of eager eaters. More than 2,000 restaurants in Chicago offer some permutation of this mouth-watering dish, with toppings ranging from mushrooms to clams and artichokes

*Hard Rock Café*

© The Magnificent Mile®

*The Magnificent Mile*

*9am-5pm, Sat-Sun 9am-6pm.* ☎312-939-2438. www.sheddaquarium.org.
The world's largest indoor aquarium, the Shedd includes some 250,000 aquatic animals comprising nearly 2,000 species. One of the last Beaux-Arts buildings (Graham, Anderson, Probst & White) in Chicago, it opened in 1930. Today it houses fish from around the world, including those in the **Caribbean Reef**★. Added in 1991, the **Oceanarium**★★, with its sweeping views of Lake Michigan, houses marine mammals in a naturalistic Northwest coast setting. Formal 20min demonstrations of natural behaviors are presented throughout the day *(check presentation times at entrance)*. One level down, you can view the animals underwater and visit the denizens of **Penguin Shore**.

### Adler Planetarium & Astronomy Museum★★
Kids *1300 S. Lake Shore Dr. on the Museum Campus.* ✗&🅿◐*Open Mon-Sun 9:30am-4:30pm, open in summer until 6pm. First Fri monthly 9:30am-10pm.* ✆*Adults $10, children $6, seniors $8.* ☎312-922-7827. www.adlerplanetarium.org.
Occupying a beautiful vantage point, the planetarium offers commanding **views**★★ up and down the lakefront. The oldest planetarium in the Western Hemisphere (1930, Ernest A. Grunsfeld, Jr.), the Adler is renowned for its

fine collection of historic astronomical instruments and its splendid sky shows. The 60,000sq ft Sky Pavilion, opened in 1999, houses a series of colorful hands-on exhibits that explore the universe. The state-of-the-art **StarRider Theater** offers interactive virtual-reality sky shows. Traditional sky shows take place under the planetarium's original 68ft dome.

## Magnificent Mile★★★

The Champs Elysées of Chicago, this promenade along North Michigan Avenue is the city's most prestigious thoroughfare. Lined with exclusive boutiques and large retail stores, luxury hotels and premier residential and office high rises, the "Boul Mich" has come a long way from its beginnings as an ordinary city street. Its most distinctive relics survived the Great Fire in 1871: the castellated 1889 **Water Tower**★ still stands toward the north end at Chicago Avenue. Across the street, the old pumping station (1866) houses a **visitor information center** (☎312-744-2400). The opening of the **Michigan Avenue Bridge**★ *(Wacker Dr. & N. Michigan Ave.)* joined the north and south sides of the city in 1920, catalyzing an incredible building boom that spawned most of the landmarks on the avenue. Among them, the French Renaissance **Wrigley Building**★★ at nos. 400-410 (1920, 1924, Graham, Anderson, Probst & White) may be most familiar, especially by night when floodlights illuminate its terra-cotta cladding. The John Hancock Center and **Water Tower Place**★ *(no. 835)* ushered in a new era of skyscrapers and retailing in the early 1970s, when Michigan Avenue displaced State Street as the city's shopping corridor.
Two busy neighborhoods flank the "Mag Mile." Between the lake and Michigan Avenue, **Streeterville** is the home of Northwestern University's Chicago campus and the residential towers at **860-880 N. Lake Shore Drive**★★, which established the high-rise influence of Ludwig Mies van der Rohe in the early 1950s. Nestled in the crook between the Chicago River east of Wabash Avenue

River North★, an eclectic district of **art galleries**, celebrity-owned restaurants and trendy clubs.

## John Hancock Center★★★

*875 N. Michigan Ave.* ✗♿🅿🕐*Open daily 9am–11pm.* 📷*$10.25.* ☎*888-875-8439. www.hancock-observatory.com.* Muscular and monumental, the profile of "Big John" is a Chicago icon. Completed in 1970 by Skidmore, Owings & Merrill, the 100-story tower is a city unto itself, its 2.8 million square feet housing retail, restaurant, office and residential space. Its efficient obelisk-shaped design, distinguished by brawny cross-braces, includes 46,000 tons of steel that easily carry gravity and wind loads. Soar to the 94th-floor **observatory** *(☎312-751-3680)* for spectacular **views**★★★ of lake and landscape some 1,127ft below.

## Museum of Contemporary Art★

*220 E. Chicago Ave.* ✗♿🅿🕐*Open Wed-Sun 10am–5pm, Tues 10am-8pm.*☎*312-280-2660. www.mcachicago.org.*

Founded in 1967, the museum presents a wide range of contemporary visual and performing arts by both well-established artists and those on the leading edge, and has been housed in this nicely sited building by Berlin architect Josef Paul Kleihues since 1996. The MCA presents works on loan and traveling exhibits along with installations from its 7,000-piece permanent collection, which includes post-1945 works by Marcel Duchamp, Alexander Calder, Joan Miró and Andy Warhol.

## Navy Pier★★

🧒*600 E. Grand Ave. at Lake Michigan.* ✗♿🅿 ☎*312-595-7437. www.navypier. com.* Encompassing 50 acres of shops, eateries and entertainment, the pier is a bustling and festive place that draws throngs of visitors. Built in 1916 as a passenger and freight terminal, the pier also served as a naval training base and a university campus. The pier's most prominent feature is the 150ft Ferris wheel that is illuminated

## Frank Lloyd Wright

From the fertile ground that nourished the creativity of Chicago's innovative sky-scraper architects rose another master, whose best-known works revolutionized residential building design. Born in Wisconsin in 1867, Frank Lloyd Wright came early under the influence of Louis Sullivan, apprenticing in his studio until striking out on his own at age 25. Living and working in suburban Oak Park, he developed his distinctive Prairie style, its strong horizontal lines and overhanging eaves inspired by the flat Midwestern landscape. Inside, Wright allowed rooms to flow into one another and designed furniture to complement his organic designs.

The quintessential Prairie school **Robie House**★★ *(5757 S. Woodlawn Ave.; visit by guided tour only; ☎708-848-1976)*, on the University of Chicago campus, made Frank Lloyd Wright world famous in 1910 and helped "break the box" of traditional architecture. Today a large enclave of Wright-designed homes comprises the **Frank Lloyd Wright and Prairie School of Architecture Historic District** *(bordered by Division, Lake, Ridgeland & Marion Sts.).* At its heart, his studio (1889-1909) is open to visitors and makes an excellent place to begin a walking tour *(951 W. Chicago Ave.; visit by guided tour only; ☎708-848-1976).* Wright executed commissions elsewhere during this time as well, notably the c.1904 Prairie-style **Dana-Thomas House**★★★ *(301 E. Lawrence Ave., Springfield, IL; ☎217-782-6776)*, renowned for its size, complexity and 250 art-glass windows and doors.

In 1909, Wright left his wife and six children in a scandal that effectively ended his practice in socially conservative Oak Park. His architecture became more expressionistic in the 1910s and 20s, and in 1931 he established Taliesin (🍂see MADISON) in his home state to train architects. Following construction of the stunning 1936 house called Fallingwater (🍂see SOUTHERN ALLEGHENIES) in Pennsylvania, Wright opened Taliesin West in Arizona and remained in the limelight until his death in 1959 at age 91.

## Abraham Lincoln in Illinois

A revered figure in America, **Abraham Lincoln** (1809-65) began life in a Kentucky log cabin, attending less than a year of school, but reading avidly between hours of manual labor. A year after his family moved to Illinois in 1830, Lincoln—then 22—settled in the village of New Salem and held a variety of jobs including storekeeper, postmaster and surveyor. **Lincoln's New Salem State Historic Site★** *(2mi south of Petersburg, IL on Rte. 97; ☎217-632-4000)* re-creates many of the buildings where Lincoln worked.

In 1837, Lincoln, now a lawyer, moved to Springfield—the Illinois state capital—where he set up his law practice. There Lincoln met and married Kentucky socialite Mary Todd and purchased a house. Today you can tour this two-story brown clapboard Greek Revival structure (the only home Lincoln ever owned) at **Lincoln Home National Historic Site★★** *(426 S. 8th St., Springfield, IL; visit by guided tour only; tours depart from visitor center on-site; ☎17-492-4241; Mon-Sun 8:30am-5pm. Tours free.).*

Lincoln rose quickly as an attorney in Springfield, and in 1858 he ran for Senate, debating Illinois' leading politician, Stephen A. Douglas, on the issue of slavery. Although Lincoln lost the election, he won a national following that garnered him the Republican nomination for US president in 1860. Within weeks of President Lincoln's inauguration, the Southern states seceded from the Union, foreshadowing the beginning of the Civil War in April 1861.

Author of the 1863 Emancipation Proclamation freeing Southern slaves, and the eloquent Gettysburg Address ( see GETTYSBURG), Lincoln was elected to a second term in 1864. Although Lincoln promised «malice toward none" and "charity for all» in his inaugural speech, the president was assassinated by John Wilkes Booth on April 14, 1865, while attending a performance at Ford's Theatre in Washington, DC. General Robert E. Lee's surrender to Ulysses S. Grant at Appomattox, Virginia, had taken place just five days earlier. Back in the city, Lincoln once called home, 75,000 mourners filed past the president's coffin as he lay in state in the **Old State Capitol** *(6th & Adams Sts., Springfield, IL).* Today the man who became a myth is buried at **Lincoln's Tomb State Historic Site★** *(Oak Ridge Cemetery, 1500 Monument Ave., Springfield, IL; 212-782-2717; March-Oct: Mon-Sun 9am-5pm; Nov-Feb: 9am-4pm.).*

*Springfield is located 210mi south of Chicago via I-55.*

at night. Another attraction is the **Chicago Children's Museum★** *(☎312-527-1000; ○ open Sun-Wed and Fri 10am-5pm, Thurs and Sat 10am-8pm; free first Mondays monthly; ∞adults $8, children $8, seniors $7, under 1 free),* where interactive exhibits invite children to have supervised fun. Local cruise and sightseeing vessels dock on the south side of the pier.

## Additional Sights

### Gold Coast★★
*Between Oak St. & North Ave., Lake Michigan & LaSalle St.*

This slice of Chicago's lakefront has been home to the city's elite for over a century. While all but a few of the mansions that once lined Lake Shore Drive have been demolished, a strong late-19C ambience is well preserved along landmark **Astor Street★★**, where quaint Victorian town houses and graystones occupy tiny beautifully cultivated lots. Frank Lloyd Wright designed the **Charnley-Persky House**a *(1365 N. Astor St.; visit by guided tour only; ☎312-915-0105)* in 1892. Chic **Oak Street Beach** lies at the doorstep of the Gold Coast *(Lake Shore Dr. at Michigan Ave.).*

## Lincoln Park★★

*Along the lakefront, between North Ave. & Fullerton Pkwy.*

This sweeping expanse is today one of Chicago's most compelling landscapes. Stretching 6mi and 1,200 acres along the shoreline, Lincoln Park trims the city's watery edge with a peaceful greenbelt, beaches, playing fields and picnic spots. Its most striking feature is **Lincoln Park Zoo**★★ 🛝 *(2001 N. Clark St.;* ✗ ♿ 🅿 ☎*312-742-2000),* a wonderfully accessible zoo that houses more than 1,200 animals in recently renovated historic habitats and new exhibits. Just north of Fullerton Parkway stands the park's newest addition, the **Peggy Notebaert Nature Museum**, an indoor-outdoor facility featuring a 4,000sq ft butterfly haven and exhibits that challenge visitors to connect with the natural world.

## Graceland Cemetery★★

*4001 N. Clark St. Site plan available at entrance.* 🅿 ⏲*OpenMon-Sun 8am-4:30pm.*☎*773-525-1105.*

One of Chicago's most evocative sites, this 119-acre cemetery (1860) contains Louis Sullivan's masterful **Getty Tomb**★ (1890) as well as the Egyptian-style mastaba (1887) he designed for Martin Ryerson. Sullivan himself is buried here, as are Potter Palmers, Marshall Field, Daniel Burnham and Ludwig Mies van der Rohe.

## Glessner House Museum★★

*1800 S. Prairie Ave.* ⬅*Visit by guided tour only Wed-Sun tours at 1pm, 2pm, and 3pm.* ☜*Adults $10, students and seniors $9, children $5.* ☎*312-326-1480. www. glessnerhouse.org*

Cornerstone of the **Prairie Avenue Historic District**★, Glessner House was designed for a wealthy farm-implement manufacturer by Henry Hobson Richardson in 1886. The house revolutionized domestic American architecture with its open floor plan and unadorned Romanesque façade. The **interior**a contains an abundance of Arts and Crafts detail, including William Morris wall and tile patterns.

## Museum of Science and Industry★★★

🛝*57th St. at Lake Shore Dr.* ✗ ♿ 🅿 *Park underground; floor plans and tickets for applicable exhibits are available at the information desk, located in the new entryway.* ⏲*Open Mon-Sat 9:30am-5:30pm, Sun 11am-5:30pm.* ☜*Adults $11, children $7, seniors $9.50, members free.* ☎*773-684-1414. www.msichicago.org.*

This cacophonous hall of wonders is one of Chicago's most popular attractions. Since 1933, the "MSI" has occupied the only building left after the World's Columbian Exposition of 1893, designed in the grand Beaux-Arts style by Charles B. Atwood. Over the years, the museum has amassed an amazing array of artifacts. To make sense of these huge and diverse collections, the museum is organized into thematic "zones" covering the human body, transportation, communication, energy and the environment, space and defense, and manufacturing. Among its huge vehicular treasures are the 197ft **Pioneer Zephyr** train *(underground entryway),* the World War II German **U-505 Submarine**a *(ground floor),* and a cutaway **Boeing 727**a suspended from the second-story balcony. On the first floor, lines form early for the **Coal Mine**aa tour and for rides in authentic flight simulators in the **Navy: Technology at Sea**a gallery. East of the main building, the **Henry Crown Space Center** houses the OMNIMAX theater and exhibits on space exploration.**ntuit: The Center for Intuitive and Outside Art**

*756 N. Milwaukee Ave.* ⏲*Open daily Wed-Sat 12pm-5pm.*☎*312-243-9088. outsider. art.org.*

This was one of the country's first art institutions devoted to the works of outsider artists such as Henry Darger and Sister Gertrude Morgan. Stop here to see the works of those who developed their talent independent of classic art influences.

## National Museum of Mexican Art

*1852 W. 19th St.* ⏲*Open 10am-5pm Tues-Sat.* ☎*312-738-1503. www.national museumofmexicanart.org.*

In the heart of Chicago's Pilsen neighborhood is the National Museum of

Mexican Art, the nation's largest Latino arts institution and the only Latino museum accredited by the American Association of Museums. An interesting cross-section of temporary and perma- nent exhibitions gives insight into th tradition of art. Highlights include work by Diego Rivera and an open-air plaz Don't miss the gift shop.

# INDIANAPOLIS★

MICHELIN MAP 583 P 8
EASTERN STANDARD TIME
POPULATION 781,870

The busy government and commercial center of Indianapolis had inauspiciou beginnings. Named the state capital in 1825, its unnavigable location on th White River and failed Wabash and Erie Canal drew sparse settlement, even afte the **National Road** was built, connecting Indianapolis with the East Coast befor the railroads arrived in the 1830s. Railroads and the city's role as a staging poin for the Civil War finally produced rapid growth after 1860. Meat packing and agri cultural trade lined the city's coffers, and in 1876 Civil War colonel **Eli Lilly** (1838 98) established a pharmaceutical company that remains a dominant economi and cultural force in the area. Lilly's company led the world in the production o penicillin, insulin and the polio vaccine, and the family helped create a major ar museum and the nation's leading state historic preservation organization, th Historic Landmarks Foundation of Indiana. In the early 20C, automobiles sucl as the Stutz, Cole, and Duesenberg were made in Indianapolis.

- **Information:** ☎317-639-4282. www.indy.org
- **Orient Yourself:** The city is located in the center of Indiana 185mi southeast of Chicago.
- **Kids:** Even big-city kids are impressed by the Children's Museum of Indianapolis.
- **Also See:** CHICAGO.

## A Bit of History

Beginning in 1911, the famed **Indianap-olis 500**★★★ (*see opposite*) auto race has attracted hordes of fans to the city each year. In addition to state and fed- eral government, the city's institutional base includes the combined campus of Indiana University/Purdue University Indianapolis. Long satirized as a boring backwater, the city today is vibrant and rich in cultural attractions.
Conceived by Alexander Ralston, the city's original plan called for a series of streets radiating out from a central cir- cle. Although the radial plan was never realized, **Monument Circle** still forms the focal point of downtown. Anchor- ing the west end of Market Street from Monument Circle, the 1888 Renaissance Revival **Indiana State House** (*200 W. Washington St.;* ☎*317-233-0589*) was

designed by Adolf Sherrer and Edwi May. Its restored interior features rotunda with a **stained-glass dome** South of the circle, new retailers hid behind the historic façade of **Circl Centre** (*49 W. Maryland St.*). This two block, four-story mall links via elevate walkways the **Indiana Conventio Center** (*100 S. Capitol Ave.*) and th adjoining **RCA Dome** sports stadiun with neighboring hotels and with th **Indianapolis City Center** (*201 S. Capito Ave.;* ☎*317-237-5206*), which provides wealth of information for visitors.

## Sights

### Monument Circle★
*At the intersection of Meridian & Market Sts.*

# The Indy 500

The largest single-day sporting event in the world, the Indianapolis 500 auto race was first run at the **Indianapolis Motor Speedway**★★ *(4790 W. 16th St.;* 🍴⚙️🅿️ ☎️*317-481-8500; www.indy500.com)* in 1911. Local automobile magnate Carl Fisher financed the construction of the track in 1909, and the initial race held on this 2.5mi oval (then paved with brick) consisted of two laps (5mi). A 24-hour competition was scheduled for 1910, but the following year Fisher and his partners agreed that 500mi was the ideal distance for a race. The winner of that first Indy 500 was Ray Harroun, who averaged a speed of 74.6mph.

His six-cylinder Marmon Wasp along with more than 75 other racing cars are on display at the **Hall of Fame Museum**★★ *(☎️317-492-6784)* located on the speedway infield. Classics here include the 1965 Lotus, the 1969 STP Oil Treatment Special driven by Mario Andretti, and the 1977 Texaco Star driven by Janet Guthrie, the first woman Indy 500 racer.

Having celebrated its 90th birthday in 1999, the speedway today attracts more than 400,000 avid fans every Memorial Day *(last weekend in May)* to watch 33 open-wheel racecars roar off at the sound of those famous words: "Gentlemen, start your engines." 🚗*Tours of the speedway are available when the track is not in use.*

*Adrenalin, petrol fumes and burning rubber at the Indy 500*

IMS Photo by John Cote

Dedicated in 1902, the 284ft-high obelisk of the Indiana **Soldiers' and Sailors' Monument**★★ forms the center of the circle. The limestone shaft, commemorating veterans of the Civil War, is surrounded by terraces and fountains and capped by a 38ft-high statue of Victory. Surrounding buildings curve in deference to the memorial, whose observation tower offers a **view** 231ft above the city.

The monument's neighbors on the circle include the 1857 Gothic Revival **Christ Church Cathedral** *(no. 125)*; the tiered wedding-cake roof of **Circle Tower**; and the temple façade of the 1916 **Hilbert Circle Theater** *(no. 45;* ☎️*317-262-1100),* home to the Indianapolis Symphony Orchestra.

## Indiana War Memorials★★

From Monument Circle, a series of war memorials occupy five public plazas as you head north on Meridian Street to St. Clair Street. Beginning the procession, the square at **University Park**★ *(between New York & Vermont Sts.)* was once a Civil War drilling ground. Just north, the **Indiana World War Memorial Plaza**★★ *(between Vermont & Michigan Sts.; ☎317-232-7615)* centers on the Classical **Memorial Building**, its south steps graced by the 25ft-high bronze *Pro Patria* (1929, Henry Hering). Inside the building is the awe-inspiring **Shrine Room**★ ; the lower concourse houses a military museum.

Just north, a black and gold obelisk marks **Veterans Memorial Plaza** *(between Michigan & North Sts.).* The last memorial on Meridian Street is the two-block-long **American Legion Mall**★ *(between North & St. Clair Sts.),* which features a black granite cenotaph honoring Indiana's war dead. On the west side of Meridian, the massive, 1929 Gothic-style **Scottish Rite Cathedral**★ *(no. 650)* is crowned with a 212ft tower.

### James Whitcomb Riley Museum Home★★

*528 Lockerbie St. Guided tour only.☎317-631-5885. Tues-Sat 11am-4pm, Sun 12-4pm.*
Set in the historic **Lockerbie Square** neighborhood with its trim mid-19C Victorians, this never-restored 1872 home presents the actual finishes and furnishings of Magdalene and Charles Holstein. Indiana-born poet James Whitcomb Riley (1849-1916) was a houseguest here for the last 23 years of his life. The drawing room contains Riley's guitar and player piano; the library across the hall was Riley's favorite room. Upstairs, framed examples of Riley's poetry decorate the walls.

### Canal Walk★

West of downtown, a residential and museum complex edged with a water-side promenade follows 1.2mi of the never-completed Wabash and Erie Canal. The canal's L shape follows West Street from St. Clair Street to Ohio Street, then angles west through **White River State Park**. The canal turns toward the White River at **Military Park** *(bounded by Blackford, New York & West Sts.)* and crosses a footbridge over the river to the **Indianapolis Zoo** Kids *(1200 W. Washington St.; ☎317-630-2001).*

### Eiteljorg Museum of American Indians and Western Art★★

*500 W. Washington St. ♿🅿🕐Open Mon, Wed-Sat 10am-5pm, Tues 10am-8pm, Sunday 12-5pm. ⸜Public tours 1pm.⊜Adults $8, seniors $7, children and students $5, under 4 free. ☎317-636-9378. www.eiteljorg.org.*
Rising above the canal like a cubic desert mesa, the contemporary 73,000sq ft museum is known for its collections of Native American and Western art. On the first floor, **The American Western Gallery** contrasts the work of early-19C artist-historians George Catlin and Albert Bierstadt with the more romantic views of Frederick Remington and Charles Russell. A highlight here is the large group of works by **Taos Society Artists** amassed by businessman and collector Harrison Eiteljorg. Second-floor galleries trace the **Art of Native America**, with strengths in Plains and Southwest Indian artifacts.

### Benjamin Harrison Home★

*1230 N. Delaware St. 🅿🕐Open Mon-Sat 10am-3:30pm, Sun 12:30pm-3:30pm. ⸜Tours on the hour and half-hour. ⊜Adults $6, seniors $5, students $3, under 4 free.☎ 317-631-1888. www.presidentbenjaminharrison.org.*
The nation's 23rd president, Benjamin Harrison (1833-1901) built this 1874 Italianate home during his legal career, campaigned from its front porch in 1888, returned to it in 1893, and died here eight years later. Harrison's office is reconstructed on the second floor. The third-floor ballroom holds changing exhibits relating to Harrison's life.

### Indianapolis Museum of Art★★

*4000 Michigan Rd. 🍴♿🅿🕐Open Tues, Weds, and Sat 11am-5pm. Thurs-Fri 11am-9pm, Sun 12pm-5pm. Free.☎317-923-1331. www.ima-art.org.*
Founded in 1883, this fine institution shares its concrete building with the Indianapolis Civic Theatre in 52 acres of woods and sculpture gardens that incorporate the 1914 French Provincial **Oldfields Lilly House & Gardens**. Inside the museum, three levels of galleries in three adjoining pavilions contain an impressive array of more

than 50,000 works of European, American, Asian and African art dating from 500 BC to the present. The museum's main entrance brings you into the Kranhert Pavilion, which displays **American art** and changing exhibits. Upper floors hold Pre-Columbian art and Asian art, 20C European art, decorative arts and Contemporary works. Highlights of the Hulman Pavilion include a splendid collection of **Postimpressionist art**★, featuring works by Georges Seurat, and an impressive group of 1,400-plus **African art**★ objects. Last, but not least, the Clowes Pavilion holds **Old Masters** and Renaissance art on its first floor. On the second floor, 19C English drawings and watercolors include a fine group of works by **J.M.W. Turner**.

## Children's Museum of Indianapolis★

Kids *3000 N. Meridian St.* ✗ ♿ 🅿 ☎*317-334-3322. www.childrensmuseum.org.* Exhibits in this massive, five-story structure explore myriad topics from construction to cultural diversity in an interactive format. A highlight is "**What If**," where kids can discover an ancient Egyptian tomb.

# Excursion

## Conner Prairie Living History Museum★★

*6mi northeast of Indianapolis in Fishers, IN. From I-465, take Exit 35N (Allisonville Rd.). 13400 Allisonville Rd.* ✗ ♿ 🅿 ☎*317-776-6000.* ☞*Adults $11, seniors $10, youth $7, under 4 and members free.*

A premier living-history museum, Conner Prairie comprises four distinct sections. Interpretation of the sites varies from the costumed character actors at **Prairietown**, a composite 1836 Midwestern village, to the hands-on **1886 Liberty Corner**, where visitors learn about Quaker life. Begin at the **Museum Center**, which displays dioramas, photos and artifacts that track 19C cultural, economic and environmental changes brought to the area by European settlers. A guided tour of the Federal-style 1823 **Conner Homestead** focuses on Ohio fur trader William Conner, who lived among the local Delaware Indians for 17 years.

# CINCINNATI AREA

Cradled by the Ohio River, which borders the state from the east and south befor
feeding into the Mississippi, south-central Ohio is a mostly rural enclave, wit
livestock, soybeans and corn gracing its gently rolling hills and fertile valleys
Prehistoric earthworks, including burial plots, enclosures and effigy mounds
attest to the presence of nomadic tribes in the region between 1000 BC an
500 AD. Two of its three main cities, Cincinnati and Dayton, grew up as trade cent
ers, ferrying agricultural products via a network of rivers and canals. Columbu
is the state capital and home to the massive Ohio State University.

First explored around 1670 by French-man René Robert Cavelier de La Salle, Ohio remained the province of Native Americans well into the 18C. However, an increasing demand for furs, land and control of river trade, made the region a bone of contention during the French and Indian War (1754-63). The loss of that war marked the end of French hopes to connect Canadian territories with the port in New Orleans. English victory brought about westward expansion and the settlement of the area through a series of broken treaties with—and ultimately the massacre of—local Indian tribes.

In 1803 Ohio became the first state to be chipped out of the Northwest Territory. Called the Gateway to the West, it was soon scored with roads, canals and finally railroads. River and canal traffic sparked the growth of Cincinnati and Dayton. Columbus was named state capital in 1816. Today these three cities remain the focal points of history an culture in the region. All boast excellen museums for cities of their size: art an science museums are especially stron in Columbus and Cincinnati, while Day ton's Air Force Museum showcases the largest collection of military airplane in the world. Set in clusters around th countryside, ancient earthworks now preserved as historic sites provide a rar window into the world of prehistori North America.

*Cincinnati Skyline*

## Area Address Book

*For coin ranges, see the Legend on the cover flap.*

### WHERE TO STAY

**$$$ The Cincinnatian Hotel** – *601 Vine St., Cincinnati, OH.* ⚓*513-381-3000. www.cincinnatianhotel.com. 147 rooms.* This Second French Empire-style property in the heart of downtown has been accommodating visitors since 1882. Beyond its limestone exterior and the lobby's grand staircase, you'll find a luxury boutique hotel with modern decor and a skylit atrium. The original number of rooms was reduced by half to create larger, contemporary living quarters, but Old-World service remains a trademark.

**$$ Hilton Cincinnati Netherland Plaza** – *35 W. 5th St., Cincinnati, OH.* ⚓*513-421-9100. www.hilton.com. 516 rooms.* A downtown Art Deco jewel that's dazzled guests—from Elvis Presley to Winston Churchill—since 1931. The lobby looks like a Hollywood movie palace, with rosewood paneling and climbing-vine wall sconces in silver. A Baroque mural of Apollo decorates the 20ft-tall ceiling above the bar. Neutral-toned guest rooms are much less ornate. Don't miss the filigree work in the Hall of Mirrors. The Omni Netherland's signature restaurant, **Orchids**, *(closed Sun & Mon)* is just as opulent as the rest of the hotel and its inspired American dishes get raves.

**Amos Shinkle Townhouse** – *215 Garrard St., Covington, KY.* ⚓*859-431-2118. www.amosshinkle.net. 6 rooms.* **$** About two blocks from the suspension bridge, the 1854 Greco-Italianate house is an antebellum throwback. Original trompe l'œil and ornate crown moldings adorn common areas. Guest rooms are decorated with four-poster beds, floral bedding and massive armoires.

### WHERE TO EAT

**$$ Porkopolis Tavern and Grill** – *1077 Celestial St., Cincinnati, OH.* ⚓*513-721-5456.* **American.** This 1892 building in trendy Mount Adams is where one of the country's most renowned ceramic collectibles was produced until the late 1960s. Today the original red-brick, circular kilns are dining rooms that serve some of the best ribs and pork chops in town.

**$$ Mike Fink Restaurant** – *At the foot of Greenup St., Covington, KY.* ⚓*859-261-4212.* **American.** Moored across downtown Cincinnati's suspension bridge on the banks of the Ohio River, this sternwheeler towboat-cum-eatery has been serving generous portions of steak and seafood for more than 30 years. Raw-bar specialties and the majestic view of the "Queen City" skyline are highlights.

# CINCINNATI★

MICHELIN MAP 583 P 9
EASTERN STANDARD TIME
POPULATION 308,728

The downtown district is laid out on a grid and flanked by steep hills that harbor the **University of Cincinnati, Eden Park★** and the quaint **Mount Adams★** district, a warren of Victorian dwellings, shops and pubs along St. Gregory Street.

**Information:** Cincinnati Convention and Visitors Bureau. ⚓513-21-2142. www.cincyusa.com

**Orient Yourself:** Cincinnati lies just across the Ohio River from picturesque Covington, Kentucky.

**Don't Miss:** The National Underground Railroad Freedom Center, a legacy to efforts to abolish human enslavement.

**Also See:** *COLUMBUS, LOUISVILLE*

## A Bit of History

Named after the Roman soldier and statesman Cincinnatus, the city was founded in 1788 and thrived as a center of river commerce—the "Queen City" of the Ohio Valley, it was called—until the 1850s, when the railroad diverted traffic through Chicago. Cincinnati continued to prosper, however, as a manufacturing and, more recently, white-collar business center. The first bridge to link Ohio with Kentucky, the 1867 **Roebling Bridge**★ *(Walnut St. & Mehring Way)* is one of the city's most vigorous structures. It was a prototype for John A. Roebling's 1883 masterpiece, the Brooklyn Bridge in New York City.

Today the city is witnessing a spurt of architectural renovation and new development. Downtown, the **Aronoff Center for the Arts** *(650 Walnut St.; ☎513-621-2787)*, designed by Cesar Pelli and completed in 1995, comprises three theaters and an art gallery. On the banks of the river, two massive stadiums sate fans of the **Cincinnati Bengals** (football) and the Cincinnati **Reds**, the nation's first professional baseball team. Meanwhile, the **Over-the-Rhine** district *(Main St. between 12th & 14th Sts.)* is home to the 3,500-seat Gothic-style **Music Hall** *(1241-43 Elm St.)*, which dates from 1878.

## Sights

### Cincinnati Art Museum★★

*953 Eden Park Dr. Open Tue-Sun 11am–5pm, Wed 11am–9pm.* ◑*Closed Mo.* ☒ ♿ 🅿 ☎513-639-2995. www.cincinna artmuseum.org.

Opened in 1886, the hilltop museum scenic Eden Park is the first art museu west of the Alleghenies to have its ow building. Over the years the collectic has grown from a single Native Americ jar to more than 60,000 works coverir 6,000 years of art making, and the orig nal Richardsonian Romanesque museu structure has expanded accordingl Today an eclectic melding of architectur styles (Beaux-Arts, International, Dor temple) echoes the impressive diversi of its collection, which is especially stror in European **Old Masters**★★, Nativ American Art, non-Western art (inclu ing the only collection of **Nabataean a** outside Jordan) and American paintir from the 19C and 20C.

### Museum Center at Union Terminal★★

🄺🄸🄳🅂*1301 Western Ave.* ◑*Open Mon-S 10am–5pm, Sun 11am–6pm.* ☒*$6.2* ☒ ♿ ☎ 513-287-7000. www.cinc museum.org.

Formerly a train station capable accommodating 17,000 passengers ar

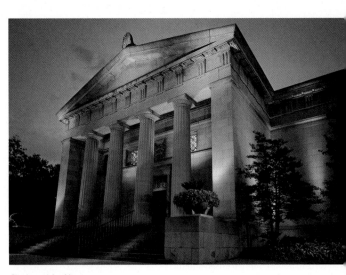

*Cincinnati Art Museum*

16 trains a day, the **structure**★★ is a 1933 Art Deco masterpiece of awesome proportions. Designed by Alfred Fellheimer-Steward Wagner, it boasts the largest half-dome in the western hemisphere (180ft wide and 106ft high), as well as gigantic, brightly colored mosaic murals depicting work, progress and history. Three full-size museums and a large-format theater fit easily within the multilevel building. Using multimedia walk-through exhibits, the **Cincinnati History Museum**★★ brilliantly re-creates the city's history through the 1940s and includes a working model of the city. Both the **Museum of Natural History and Science** and the **Children's Museum** are geared to kids, full of hands-on exhibits and play areas.

## National Underground Railroad Freedom Center

50 E. Freedom Way. ○Open Tue-Sun 11am–5pm. ✆$12. ♿🅿☎513-333-7500. www.freedomcenter.org.

A sobering yet inspirational experience, this $110-million facility uses the Underground Railroad, which traveled through this site on the banks of the Ohio River, as the backdrop against which visitors can explore past and present freedom issues from around the world. Opened in 2004, it features three pavillions full of interactive exhibits. Visitors can get a get a chilling feel for the stark reality of slave life in The Slave Pen, an authentic structure used to store as many as 75 slaves at a time, or join a moderated discussion about freedom issues in the Dialogue Zone.

## William Howard Taft National Historic Site★★

2038 Auburn Ave. ○Open daily 8am–4pm. ○Closed major holidays. ♿🅿 ☎513-684-3262. www.nps.gov/wiho.

The nation's 27th president, William Taft (1857-1930), lived in this handsome Greek Revival dwelling (1841) from his birth until he embarked on his political career 20 years later. The house today is split evenly between the Tafts' downstairs living spaces and upstairs **exhibition rooms**★★ that trace the trajectory of Taft's life and times with personal mementos, photographs and even

music. Happy to give up the cutthroat politics of the presidency, Taft became the 10th chief justice of the Supreme Court. He remains the only American to have held both positions.

## Taft Museum of Art★

316 Pike St. ○Open Tue-Sun 11am–5pm. ○Closed Mon. ✆$8. ♿🅿☎513-241-0343. www.taftmuseum.org.

This Federal-style house (1820) was the Tafts' home from 1873 until 1930. In 1931 the house opened as a museum to display the 600 works of art collected by Charles Phelps Taft (the president's half-brother) and his wife, Anna Sinton Taft. Rembrandt, Gainsborough, Millet, Corot, Turner and Whistler are all represented in the collection.

## Cincinnati Zoo and Botanical Garden★

3400 Vine St. ○Open daily 9am–5pm. ✆$7.25. ✗♿🅿☎513-281-4700. www.cincyzoo.org.

You'll find more than 740 species of animals and 3,000 types of plants in this garden setting. Don't miss the chimpanzees and orangutans in **Jungle Trails**, or the zoo's popular inhabitants at **Manatee Springs**.

## Excursion

### Dayton

52mi north of Cincinnati via I-75.
Ohio's sixth-largest city sits on the Miami River floodplain, which fueled its industry in the late 19C. Dayton's most famous native sons are **Wilbur and Orville Wright**, whose experiments at their bicycle-repair shop (22 S. Williams St.) led to the first successful airplane flight in 1903 (♦see THE OUTER BANKS). The **Dayton Aviation Heritage National Historical Park** (☎937-225-7705) tracks the Wrights' discoveries throughout the city.

### Dayton Art Institute★★

456 Belmonte Park N. ✗♿🅿 ☎937-223-5277. www.daytonartinstitute.org.
A 1997 expansion added 35,000sq ft of gallery space to the existing structure, a 1930 Italian Renaissance-style landmark building. Arranged chronologically

on an octagonal floor plan, more than 10,000 works on two levels of galleries trace the development of both Western and non-Western art. Strengths include 17C-19C **European paintings**★, 20C **American paintings**, and the fine collection of **Asian art**★.

### National Museum of the US Air Force★★
*4mi east of Dayton at Wright Patterson Air Force Base. Take 3rd St. 2mi east to Springfield St.* ⓒ*Open daily 9am–5pm.*

✕ ♿ 🅿 ☎ *937-255-3286. www.nationc museum.af.mil.*

Dayton's most popular attraction, thi gargantuan institution sprawls over 1 acres and features more than 400 aero space vehicles, some of which visitor can climb aboard. In the **Early Year Gallery** you'll learn the history of fligh and the principles of aeronautics. Th **Modern Flight Gallery** is layered wit Korean and Vietman War aircraft of ever shape and kind; a flight simulator her takes visitors for a virtual ride.

# COLUMBUS

MICHELIN MAP 583 Q 8
EASTERN STANDARD TIME
POPULATION 730,657

Ohio's capital city, Columbus marks the approximate center of the state. Situate on the banks of the Scioto and Olentangy rivers 109mi northeast of Cincinnat Columbus takes its name from explorer Christopher Columbus; a replica of hi flagship, the *Santa Maria*, is docked downtown.

🛈 **Information:** ☎614-221-6623. www.experiencecolumbus.com
**Kids** **Kids:** The exhibits at Center of Science and Industry are made for curious kids
⚑ **Also See:** *CINCINNATI, CLEVELAND*

## A Bit of History

Columbus is a lively place, combining a strong preservationist ethic with forward-thinking development. Completed in 1861, the Greek Revival **Ohio Statehouse**★ *(Broad & High Sts.)* is one of the few state houses without a dome. Bordering the **Brewery District**, where old brick warehouses have been converted into clubs and brewpubs, German Village comprises 233 acres of mid-19C residences centered around Third Street. The **Short North** boasts hip galleries, cafes, restaurants and bars along High Street *(from Goodale St. to 5th Ave.)*. A few blocks farther north sprawls **The Ohio State University**; with 59,000 students, it boasts one of the largest enrollments in the nation. Its celebrated **Wexner Center for the Arts**★★ *(1871 N. High St.; ☎614-292-0330)* is the place in Columbus to see world-famous performers, contemporary art exhibitions and film.

## Sights

### Columbus Museum of Art★★
*480 E. Broad St.* ⓒ*Open Tue-Wed, Fr Sun 10am–5:30pm, Thu 10am–8:30pm* ⓒ*Closed Mon.* ⬤*$6* ✕ ♿ 🅿 *. ☎614 221-6801.*

Founded in 1878, the museum ha amassed an impressive collection tha seeks not to give the usual broad ove view of Western art, but to highlight spe cific schools and movements. America Precisionism, European Cubism, Germa Expressionism and the Ash Can scho all merit their own galleries, as does **20 American art**★.

Two blocks south of the museum *(corn of Washington Ave. & E. Town St.)*, a fa cinating **Topiary Garden**★ re-create with carefully pruned life-size shrub Georges Seurat's famous 1884 pain ing *Sunday Afternoon on the Island of L Grande Jatte*.

*Columbus Museum of Art*

Photo courtesy of Randall L. Schieber

## Center of Science and Industry (COSI)★★

Kids *333 W. Broad St.* ◯ *Open Tue-Sat 10am–5pm, Sun 12pm–5pm.* ◯ *Closed Mon.* ✗ ♿ ☎*614-228-2674. www.cosi.org.* Ohio's premier science and industry museum moved into these spacious digs on the Scioto River in November 1999. Designed by the Japanese-born architect Arata Isozaki, the structure cleverly incorporates a 1924 Beaux-Arts high school and encompasses 320,000sq ft of space. Nestled within are a giant "Extreme Screen" theater, a Dome Theater, and seven state-of-the-art "Learning Worlds." These are among the most advanced science exhibits you'll find.

## Ohio's Mound Builders

Southern Ohio has its share of rolling hills, but some of them are not what they seem. Under the surface of the fertile soil lie troves of prehistoric artifacts, mastodon bones and human remains. Before development, farming and erosion took their toll, some 6,000 conical mounds, enclosures and effigies dotted the countryside here—more than anywhere else in North America. Though not much is known about the mounds or the people who built them, ongoing archaeological research has revealed that three distinct groups once occupied the region: the **Adena** group (1000 BC to AD 100); the **Hopewell** group (200 BC to AD 500); and the **Fort Ancient** group (AD 900 to 1500).

Two hilltop enclosures, **Fort Ancient** *(30mi northeast of Cincinnati on Rte. 350, Oregonia;* ☎*513-932-4421)* and **Fort Hill** *(off Rte. 41, 3mi south of Cynthiana;* ☎*614-297-2630)* are among the largest and most scenic of Ohio's prehistoric monuments. Both feature sloping earthen walls enclosing open spaces once used for ceremonies, as well as new visitor centers and networks of hiking trails. One of the best interpreted sights, **Hopewell Culture Historical Park**★ *(Rte. 104, Chillicothe;* ☎*740-774-112)* is a "Mound City" consisting of an earthwork wall enclosing 13 acres and 23 substantial mounds. The best-known—and least understood—earthworks in Ohio can be found at **Serpent Mound State Memorial**★★ *(Rte. 73, 4mi north of Locust Grove;* ☎*937-587-2796).* Here visitors will find a .25mi-long, 5ft-high earthen snake with a rippling body, a coiled tail and a hyperextended jaw ready to chomp down on an oval that could be an egg or a frog. The mound is thought to have been created around AD 1070 by the Fort Ancient people. ◱For more information about mound builders in Ohio, contact the *Ohio Historical Society, 1982 Velma Ave., Columbus, OH,* ☎*614-297-2300, www.ohiohistory.org.*

**189**

# CLEVELAND AND THE WESTERN RESERVE

When Ohio was opened for settlement after the Revolutionary War, the State of Connecticut reserved three-and-a-half-million acres of land in northeastern Ohio, which became known as the Western Reserve. The reserve is bounded by Pennsylvania on the east, the Cuyahoga River on the west, Lake Erie on the north and Akron on the south: it was first surveyed in 1796 by Connecticut Land Company representative Moses Cleaveland. It was Cleaveland's job to establish townships east of the Cuyahoga River (lands to the west were under Indian control). He chose a plain on the east bank of the river, where it meets Lake Erie, for his settlement of Cleveland (the "a" was later dropped).

For two decades after its creation, this disease-ridden northern outpost floundered, settlers flocking instead to the fertile farmlands in the southern part of the reserve. Cleveland finally began to attract interest in 1827, when the city became the terminus for the Ohio and Erie Canal. In the 1850s, the railroad linked Cleveland to raw materials in the east and west, giving birth to the steel and oil-refining industries along the flats lining the river. Inspired by the city's economic growth during Cleveland's industrial heyday, Jeptha H. Wade consolidated a number of Midwest telegraph lines into the **Western Union Telegraph Company** in 1856, and industrialist **John**

**D. Rockefeller** (1839-1937) founded the Standard Oil Company in 1870.

European immigrants, the majority of them from Eastern Europe, swelled Cleveland's population in the late 19C and early 20C, drawn by the promise of jobs in the city's burgeoning industries. By 1920, Cleveland ranked as the nation's fifth-largest city; the Cleveland metropolitan area is now home to nearly three million people.

Outside the city, amid acres of peaceful farmland, several historical sites commemorate the region's cultural diversity. About 85mi south of Cleveland, the town of Berlin in Holmes County, Ohio harbors the nation's largest population of Amish. The first Christian mission in Ohio, started by a group of Moravians in 1772, is preserved at **Schoenbrunn**

*Cleveland Skyline*

©Jeffrey Greenberg@aol.com/Courtesy of www.travelcleveland.com

*90mi south of Cleveland, on Rte. 259 in New Philadelphia, OH; ☎330-339-3636).* At **Zoar** *(75mi south of Cleveland in Zoar, OH; ☎330-874-3011)* you can learn the ways of a group of German Separa-

tists who sought religious freedom in a quiet Ohio valley in 1817. Northwest of Cleveland, near Sandusky, a cluster of Lake Erie islands makes a delightful day's excursion.

## Area Address Book

♿*For coin ranges, see the Legend on the cover flap.*

### WHERE TO STAY

**$$  Glidden House** – *1901 Ford Dr., Cleveland, OH.* ✗♿🅿 ☎216-231-8900. *www.gliddenhouse.com. 60 rooms.* Located in University Circle, the 1910 French Gothic-style mansion retains its residential feel. Individually decorated rooms combine an inviting decor with modern amenities. Breakfast is served in the plant-filled sunroom on bistro tables. The restaurant is next door in the carriage house.

**$$  Renaissance Cleveland Hotel** – *24 Public Square, Cleveland, OH.* ✗♿🅿⬚ ☎216-696-5600. *www. renaissancehotels.com. 491 rooms.* Downtown's grande dame opened as the Hotel Cleveland in 1918. The regal lobby recalls the past with vaulted ceilings, soaring columns accented with gold-leaf-painted moldings, and crystal chandeliers centered around the City of Culture marble fountain. Guest rooms are large and traditionally decorated.

**$$  The Baricelli Inn** – *2203 Cornell Rd., Cleveland, OH.* ✗ 🅿 ☎216-791-6500.

*7 rooms.* Behind the serious façade of this University Circle brownstone, you'll find the ambience of a country inn. Guest rooms are decorated with matching pastel floral bedspreads and curtains, handmade four-poster beds and antique French armoires. The inn's restaurant is one of the city's best.

### WHERE TO EAT

**$$$  Blue Point Grille** – *700 W. St. Clair Ave., Cleveland, OH.* ☎216-875-7827. **Seafood.** There are no barriers at this Warehouse District eatery. From the main dining room, you'll catch the action at the huge mahogany bar through arches cut out in the dividing brick wall. Crabcakes come with honey mustard, and sautéed grouper is served with lobster mashed potatoes and spinach.

**$  Flat Iron** – *1114 Center St., Cleveland, OH.* ☎216-696-6968. **Irish**. Since 1910 this has been the go-to authentic Irish pub in Cleveland. Dine on shepherd's pie, Irish bangers and mash and fish-and-chips. The restaurant, near Browns Stadium, is closed on Sundays when there aren't any games scheduled.

# CLEVELAND★

MICHELIN MAP 583 Q 7
EASTERN STANDARD TIME
POPULATION 452,208

Beneath a modern skyline, Cleveland bills itself as the "New American City;" its conservative, hard-working citizens live up to the image. The city remains closely linked to the lake with a busy port and a dynamic set of lakefront attractions that have been tied together with a new rapid-transit line.

▌ **Information:** ☎216-621-4110. www.travelcleveland.com
▸ **Orient Yourself:** Cleveland's epicenter is at the mouth of the Cuyahoga River.
⊘ **Don't Miss:** America's signature sound and celebrity royalty at the Rock and Roll Hall of Fame and Museum.
▦ **Kids:** The Great Lakes Science Center has an OMNIMAX theater.

# A Bit of History

Once the city's industrial heart, the **Flats** *(accessible via W. 25th St. on the west, and Old River Rd. on the east)*, located on both banks of the river, have been revamped as a hot nightspot. In ethnically diverse **Ohio City** *(west bank of the river adjacent to downtown)*, the **West Side Market** *(1995 W. 25th St.)*, the largest indoor/outdoor market in the country, continues to to trade produce as it has since 1912.

Seat of Cleveland's cultural institutions, University Circle is flanked by Case Western Reserve University and the Cleveland Clinic, renowned for its work in cardiology. Encircling the city, 14 generous parkland reserves offer 60mi of paved trails and activities including golfing, fishing and sunbathing.

Modern Cleveland is well on its way to recovering from the economic nosedive the city took in the 1960s and 70s, as industries began to leave the city. No longer derided as "the mistake on the lake," Cleveland has achieved its early potential as the cultural and economic center of the Western Reserve. Service industries, especially in the areas of health care and business, have filled the vacuum left by heavy industry. Today, after 200 years of growth and change, Cleveland sparkles anew with its towering office buildings and redeveloped lakefront.

# Downtown

Wedged between the Cuyahoga River and Lake Erie, Cleveland's downtown was originally laid out around a 10-acre village green now called Public Square. Today, revitalized historic districts flank the downtown core. To the west, Cleveland's oldest neighborhood, the **Warehouse District** *(bounded by Superior Ave., W. 3rd St., Lakeside Ave. and W. 10th St.)*, bustles with trendy restaurants, jazz clubs and upscale condominiums. The **Gateway District** *(south of Superior Ave. and east of E. 9th St.)* boasts **Jacobs Field** *(2401 Ontario St.)*, home of the Cleveland Indians baseball team, and **Quicken Loans Arena** *(1 Center Ct.)*, which hosts basketball and hockey. To the east, the **Theater District** *(east of*

E. 9th St. & south of Superior Ave.)* center on **Playhouse Square**★ *(1501 Euclid Ave.* the largest performing-arts center outsid New York City. Its five restored early-20 theaters—the Allen, State, Ohio, Palac and Hannah—stage ballet, opera an Broadway productions.

## Public Square★★

*Intersection of Ontario & Superior Aves.*
Focal point of downtown, Public Square four landscaped quadrants contain som of the city's finest architecture. Loomin over the square from the southwest co ner, the **Tower City Center** originall contained the Union Railroad Station Now a three-level shopping mall fill the former concourse below the 52 story Beaux-Arts **Terminal Tower** (1927, Oris and Mantis Van Sweringen which connects to office buildings an hotels on either side. Dominating th southeastern quadrant is the 125ft high granite shaft of the **Soldiers an Sailors Monument**, erected in 1894 a a monument to Civil War veterans. O the square's southeast corner, the eigh story atrium of **BP America Buildin** (1985) showcases an elaborate wate cascade. Next door, the splendid 189 stone-and-brick **Cleveland Arcade**★ *(401 Euclid Ave.)* reflects the exuberan optimism of the city's heyday. Its tw nine-story structures are connected b a five-story, glass-roofed arcade. On th northern edge of Public Square stands familiar Cleveland landmark, 1858 **Ol Stone Church** *(91 Public Square)*. Eas across Ontario Street rises the city's tall est building, 888ft **Key Tower**.

## Cleveland Mall

*Bounded by Lakeside Ave., E. 9th St., Rockwell Ave. & W. 3rd St.*
Inspired by the 1893 Chicago Columbia Exposition, Cleveland's leaders con ceived a plan in 1903 to erect a monu mental grouping of public buildings. Th plan was carried out by architects Danie Burnham, John Carrère and Arnold Brun ner. Their work, set on a T-shaped serie of grassy malls, yielded some of the city Beaux Arts and Renaissance Revival jew els. These include the 1912 **Cuyahog County Courthouse** *(1 Lakeside Ave.* the Neoclassical **City Hall** *(601 Lakesid*

Courtesy of www.travelcleveland.com

ock and Roll Hall of Fame and Museum

ve.); the 1922 **Public Auditorium** *(1220
6th St.),* now part of the city's conven-
on center; and the 1911 Old **Federal
uilding** *(201 Superior Ave.).*

## North Coast Harbor

te of the Port of Cleveland, the North
oast district borders the Lake Erie shore
orth of downtown at Erieside Avenue
nd East Ninth Street. Beginning at
he western edge of the harbor is the
**leveland Browns Stadium** *(1085 W.
rd St.).* Clustered around the harbor to
he east are the Rock and Roll Hall of
ame, a science museum and a lakefront
ark. Two historic ships are docked on
he eastern side of the pier; farther east
till lies Burke Lakefront Airport, which
ontains the **International Women's
ir & Space Museum, Inc.** *(1501 Mar-
inal Rd.; ☎216-623-1111).*

## ock and Roll Hall of Fame
nd Museum★★★
ne Key Plaza. ◷Open daily 10am–
30pm. ☜$20. ✕ & ☎ 216-515-8444.
ww.rockhall.com.

ike the music it represents, this muse-
m's geometric design (1995, I.M. Pei)
bold and energetic. Focal point of
leveland's renewed waterfront since
s opening in 1995, the Hall of Fame
ncompasses six levels of exhibits
anging from the roots of rock and roll
regional music scenes and the careers

of individual artists. Begin with the slick,
two-part video presentation in adjacent
ground-floor theaters. Then proceed to
the circular exhibit hall where the permanent installment **Legends of Rock
and Roll**★ displays an impressive array
of costumes and artifacts, surrounded
by interactive stations featuring the
music of more than 500 performers.
In a drum-shaped wing that opened in
1998, the **Hall of Fame**★★ *(level 3)* honors over 220 rock legends with a multimedia production that incorporates music,
film excerpts and taped interviews.

### Great Lakes Science Center
🄺 *601 Erieside Ave.* ◷*Open daily
9:30am–5:30pm.* ☜*$9.50.* ✕& 🄿 ☎*216-
694-2000.* www.glsc.org.
Next door to the Rock and Roll Hall of
Fame, the center boasts an awesome
main entrance comprising a concrete-
metal-and-glass, nine-story atrium with
views of Lake Erie. More than 400 hands-
on exhibits occupy the west wing and
are organized into three major themes:
science, environment and technology.

### Steamship William G.
Mather Museum★
*305 Mather Way. Open daily 9:30am–
5:30pm.* ☜*$6.* ☎*216-574-6262.* www.
wgmathernhlink.net.
Referred to as "the ship that built Cleveland," the *Mather* carried iron ore and
coal to Great Lakes factories and mills for
nearly 55 years beginning in 1925. Visitors

Courtesy of www.travelcleveland.com

*Western Reserve Historical Society Exhibit*

can walk through the restored freighter, with its oak-paneled **pilot house** and four-story **engine room**. The forward cargo hold contains displays that recount the history of Great Lakes shipping.

### USS Cod

*East of the pier off N. Marginal Rd. Open daily 10am–5pm.* ⊚$6. 🄿 ☎216-566-8770. www.usscod.org.

The last completely authentic World War II American submarine in existence today, the *Cod* completed her final patrol in 1945. Inside the sub's cramped quarters, the smell of diesel fuel and machine oil still lingers.

## University Circle

Cleveland's cultural center, University Circle is located 4mi east of downtown near Case Western University. One square mile in size, it was laid out in 1895 to improve access to the "heights," a series of plateaus around the city that sheltered Cleveland's affluent residents. Most famed of these, **Shaker Heights**, was laid out in the 1920s as a planned residential community. Edged by East Boulevard and Martin Luther King, Jr. Drive, **Wade Park** forms the hub of the circle. Here you'll find Cleveland's major cultural institutions and the **Cleveland Botanical Gardens** *(11030 East Blvd.; ☎216-721-1600. www.cbgarden.org)*, all within easy walking distance.

### Cleveland Museum of Natural History★

Kids *1 Wade Oval Dr.* ⊙*Open Mon-S... 10am–5pm. Wed 10am–10pm. Su... 12pm–5pm.* ⊚$9. 🍴 🕭 ☎216-231-460... www.cmnh.org.

Designed as a quadrangle, the lobby ... the museum is brightened by shafts ... sunlight pouring in from the invitin... Environmental Courtyard. In the Kir... land Hall of Prehistoric Life, you'll find ... cast of the three-million-year-old ske... eton named **Lucy**★, the most famou... fossil of a human ancestor. Or soar acro... the terrain of any planet in the solar sy... tem via an interactive computer static... in multisensory "**Planet e.**" More tha... 1,500 precious gemstones, jewelry ar... lapidary artworks sparkle in the **Wad... Gallery of Gems & Jewels**.

### Western Reserve Historical Society★★

*10825 East Blvd. Entrance on Magnol... Dr.* ⊙*Open Mon-Sat 10am–5pm. Su... 12pm–5pm.* ⊚$8.50. 🕭 🄿 ☎216-72... 5722. www.wrhs.org.

This sprawling institution consists ... two museums, a historic home and a... adjoining research library. Founded ... 1867, the Western Reserve's collection... housed in two adjoining Italian Rena... sance mansions. The Bingham-Hann... mansion (1919) holds exhibits relatin... to Cleveland's development and sho... cases portions of the society's collecti... of more than 30,000 pieces of 18C-20... clothing in the **Chisholm Halle Co...**

ume Wing★. The 1911 **Hay-McKinney Mansion** (👁️visit by guided tour only), designed by Abram Garfield (son of President Garfield), reflects the lifestyles of Cleveland's elite and showcases a fine collection of decorative arts. In a separate wing, the **Crawford Auto-Aviation Museum**★ displays historic aircraft and some 200 vintage automobiles.

## Additional Sights

### Cleveland Metroparks Zoo★★

3900 Wildlife Way. Open daily 10am–5pm. ☎216-661-6500. www.clemetzoo.com.

Located 5mi south of downtown Cleveland, this 165-acre wooded zoo re-creates ecosystems for more than 600 animal species. Here you can see a sleek pack of gray wolves close-up in **Wolf Wilderness**, or visit the steamy **Rainforest**, which brings together more than 6,000 plants and 600 animals from the jungles of Africa, Asia and the Americas beneath a glass biosphere.

### NASA-Glenn Research Center

21000 Brookpark Rd. (Rte. 17). Open Mon-Fri 9am–4pm, Sat 10am–3pm, Sun 1pm–5pm. ☎216-433-2000. www. grc.nasa.gov.

Near Cleveland-Hopkins International Airport, this National Aeronautic and Space Administration's research and development center for aerospace propulsion, power and satellite communication welcomes the public. Exhibits highlight historical and current NASA projects, and include an **Apollo Command Module** used on Skylab 3.

## Excursions

### Hale Farm and Village★★

21mi south of Cleveland in Bath, OH. Take I-77 South to Exit 143 and turn right onto Wheatley Rd. At first stoplight turn left on Brecksville Rd., then left again on Ira Rd. to 2686 Oak Hill Rd. ☎330-666-3711. www.wrhs.org.

Located in a quiet meadow, Hale Homestead was settled in 1810 by Connecticut farmer Jonathan Hale. An early-19C West-

ern Reserve village has been re-created on the original site of his farm. On one side of Oak Hill Road, which bisects the site, artisans demonstrate crafts in the buildings around **Hale House** (1826).

### South Bass Island★★

75mi west of Cleveland on Lake Erie. Take I-90 West (Ohio Tpk.) to Hwy. 2 West and follow Rte. 53 North to Catawba Point; or stay on Hwy. 2 to Port Clinton. Access via ferry from Catawba Point and Port Clinton: Miller Boat Line ☎419-285-2421; Jet Express ☎419-732-2800. Information: ☎419-285-2832 or www.putinbay.com.

Cool breezes blowing across the lake and sunlight glittering off the water make the journey to this unpretentious little island a delight. Part of a cluster of Lake Erie islands that played a part in the War of 1812, South Bass is located northwest of Sandusky, Ohio.

The island's most prominent natural feature is its 30 **caves**, a result of the island's rock layers being eroded by water over millions of years. Two are open to the public: **Perry's Cave** (979 Catawba Ave.; ☎419-285-2405), a 50ft-deep limestone cave that Admiral Perry is credited with discovering in 1813; and **Crystal Cave** (across from Perry's Cave at Catawba Ave. & Thompson Rd.; ☎419-285-2811), where blue-green crystals line the walls.

### Perry's Victory and International Peace Memorial★★

93 Delaware Ave., Put-in-Bay. ☎419-285-2184. www.nps.gov/pevi.

This 352ft-high pink granite column (1915) commemorates the victory of Commodore **Oliver Hazard Perry** (1785-1819) over the British during the War of 1812. Commander of the American fleet, Perry forced the surrender of six British vessels in September 1813 in the Battle of Lake Erie. With this victory, the Americans took control of Lake Erie and most of the Northwest. Perry's battle report to Gen. William Henry Harrison contained the now-famous words: "We have met the enemy and they are ours."

The **view**★ from the observation platform on a clear day reaches 10mi northwest to the battle site.

# COASTAL CAROLINAS

Countless barrier islands, sounds, inlets and bays define the jagged Atlantic edg■ of the Carolinas' coastal plain. The area ranges from the high, windswept dunes ■ the Outer Banks of North Carolina to the golf courses of Hilton Head, South Carolin■. National seashores, wildlife refuges and state parks offer ample outdoor activiti■ for naturalists, while well-developed resorts such as **Nags Head**, North Carolin■ and **Myrtle Beach** and **Hilton Head**, South Carolina, pack in sunseekers who desir■ the more urban pursuits of golf, tennis and family amusement parks.

European settlement began in the late 16C with Sir Walter Raleigh's ill-fated colony on Roanoke Island and Huguenot Jean Ribault's short-lived settlement on Parris Island in Port Royal Sound. In 1633 King Charles II deeded the land south of Virginia between the 31st and 36th parallels to eight True and Absolute Lords Proprietor to show his gratitude for their political support. The new colony was named Carolina. Carolina's split into North and South in 1712 reflected an economic schism; Charleston was a thriving South Carolina port, while North Carolina claimed only three small towns: Bath, Edenton and New Bern.

In the ensuing years, this region witnessed great moments in the country's history, such as the opening volleys of

the Civil War fired at Fort Sumter in Cha■ leston Harbor, and the first powere■ airplane flight by the Wright brothe■ at Big Kill Devil Hill on North Carolina■ Outer Banks.

*Charleston, South Carolina*

oday vacationers flock to the wide, andy beaches of the resorts that line he coast, while Charleston, the area's argest city, extends its mannerly charms o more than three million visitors each ear. The surrounding **Lowcountry** oasts its own unique cuisine and folk- vays, and descendants of early Creole slaves still speak their distinctive **Gullah** (ⓒ *see CHARLESTON*) dialect in isolated pockets here. Farther north, North Carolina's chief port of **Wilm- ington** *(169mi north of Charleston on US-17)*, on the Cape Fear River, celebrates its history in a number of colonial and Civil War sites.

## Area Address Book

ⓒ*For coin ranges, see the Legend on the cover flap.*

### WHERE TO STAY

**$$$ Charleston Place Hotel** – *130 Market St. (entrance on Hassell St.), Char- leston, SC.* ✕⬥🅿🛏🏊 ☎*843-722-4900. www.charlestonplacehotel.com. 440 rooms.* A curving central staircase gra- ces the lobby of this recently renovated Charleston institution, now operated by Orient Express Hotels, Inc. Guest rooms are elegantly appointed with 19C period furnishings. Amenities include a new spa and fitness facility, and the adjoining Charleston Place shopping mall. Don't miss chef Bob Waggoner's innovative Southern cuisine at the hotel's **Charleston Grill**.

**$$$ John Rutledge House Inn** – *116 Broad St., Charleston, SC.* 🅿 ☎*843-723- 7999. www.johnrutledgehouseinn.com. 19 rooms.* A rough draft of the Constitu- tion was written in this 1763 house, and John Rutledge was one of the 55 men who signed it. Inlaid parquet floors, canopied rice beds and carved plaster moldings are indicative of the National Historic Landmark's restoration to its mid-18C appearance. Smaller carriage- house rooms reflect true Colonial style.

**$$$ Planters Inn** – *112 N. Market St., Charleston, SC.* ✕⬥🅿 ☎*843-722-2345. www.plantersinn.com. 62 rooms.* Most accommodations in the original 1844 building of this historic-district Relais & Châteaux property are elegantly designed in subtle colors with four- poster canopy beds. The new building in back carries over the vintage feel, with 21 rooms overlooking the court- yard's palm trees and fountains. The inn's **Peninsula Grill** gets raves.

**$$ Harbour View Inn** – *2 Vendue Range, Charleston, SC.* 🅿 ☎*843-853-* *8439. www.harbourviewcharleston. com. 52 rooms.* This historic district property overlooks Charleston Harbor. Lowcountry-style guest rooms feature four-poster beds, wicker chests and sea- grass rugs. Rates include a continental breakfast delivered to your room, after- noon wine and cheese, all-day snacks and iced tea, evening cookies and milk, and turn-down service.

**$$ The Beaufort Inn** – *809 Port Repub- lic St., Beaufort, SC.* ✕⬥🅿 ☎*843-379- 4667. www.beaufortinn.com. 29 rooms.* An 1897 mansion in historic downtown where Lowcountry hospitality shines. Each guest room is so uniquely deco- rated, you could stay in a different one every night and never get bored. Styles range from rich Victorian to cotton-can- dy pastels with hand-painted furniture. A full American breakfast and afternoon cheese and lemonade reception are part of the package.

**$$ The White Doe Inn** – *319 Sir Walter Raleigh St., Manteo, NC.* ⬥🅿 ☎*252-473- 9851. www.whitedoeinn.com. 8 rooms.* The aromas of early-morning coffee and French toast will make you feel right at home here. Yet this elegant B&B, two blocks from the historic waterfront, doesn't skimp on creature comforts such as silky Egyptian-cotton linens. All of the guest rooms have bedside fireplaces and 19C antiques befitting the Queen Anne-style house.

### WHERE TO EAT

**$$$ 82 Queen** – *82 Queen St., Char- leston, SC.* ☎*843-723-7591.* **South- ern.** Charleston's special-occasion restaurant has been a beloved favorite for nearly 20 years. Located in the heart of the historic district, 82 Queen's two connecting 19C row houses contain 11 romantic dining rooms. Ask for a table in the courtyard, shaded by a Magnolia tree. Award-winning she-crab soup and Southern Comfort BBQ shrimp and grits highlight the Lowcountry cuisine.

**$$ Carolina's** – *10 Exchange St., Charleston, SC.* ☎843-724-3800. **Lowcountry.** Regional seafood stars in this casual-chic eatery. Dishes such as sautéed Charleston shrimp with andouille sausage and cheese grits, and local grouper crusted with almonds and sesame seeds are guaranteed to please.

**$$ Louis's** – *200 Meeting St., Charleston, SC.* ☎843-853-2550. **Lowcountry**. Chef Louis Osteen refines Lowcountry mainstays here amid a warm atmosphere of buttery walls and organic light fixtures—billowing scrims and

large fabric boxes that veil magnolia branches within. Start with McClellanville lump crabmeat and lobster cakes with grained-mustard sauce. Entrées range from Blue Ridge rainbow trout stuffed with lump crabmeat and bacon to grilled free-range veal chop with wild-mushroom bread pudding.

**$ Kaminsky's** – *78 N. Market St., Charleston, SC. Open until 2am.* ☎843-853-8270. **Desserts.** Just across from City Market, Kaminsky's is the locals' pick for late-night dessert and coffee—or cordials and single-malt scotch. A wide array of cakes and confections crowd the display case as you walk in. The wait for a table allows time to narrow down your choices.

# THE OUTER BANKS★★

MAP P200-201
EASTERN STANDARD TIME

One of the major beach destinations in the southeastern US, the Outer Bank comprise a 125mi-long system of narrow Atlantic barrier islands wedged betwee inland sounds and ocean. These fragile dunes and marshlands, constantly pounde by wind and surf, are notorious for their offshore shoals where more than 60 shipwrecks have occurred, earning the coastline the dubious sobriquet, "Graveyar of the Atlantic." First occupied by the Secotan Indians, this area (Roanoke Island was the site of the first English colony in the Americas in 1585.

- **Information:** ☎252-473-2138. www.outerbanks.org
- ▶ **Orient Yourself:** The Banks extend from North Carolina's northern border sout to its midsection.
- ☺ **Don't Miss:** History in flight at the Wrights Brothers National Memorial.
- ☽ **Also See:** WASHINGTON, DC.

## A Bit of History

A popular resort spot for more than a century now, the northern end of the Outer Banks is packed with vacation homes, hotels, shops and restaurants. But south of the town of **Nags Head**, commercialism subsides, as Route 12, the only road threading the length of the contiguous northern Banks, passes occasional villages and the Pea Island National Wildlife Refuge on its way to **Cape Hatteras**.

Just beyond the town of Hatteras, where the road ends, state ferries (☎877-368-

4968) carry passengers and cars acros Hatteras Inlet to **Ocracoke Island**★ Here wide beaches and tiny Ocracok Village attract travelers looking for quiet vacation.

At the southern tip of the Outer Banks **Cape Lookout National Seashore** preserves a 55mi-long paradise of unin habited sand beaches *(accessible via ferr from Harkers Island, Davis, Atlantic, Beau fort & Morehead City; for ferry schedule and general information, contact* **Hark ers Island Visitor Center,** *off Rte. 70 o Harkers Island Rd.;* ☎252-728-2250*).*

ust west of the Outer Banks, lining the sounds and rivers that chisel the mainland, lie some of North Carolina's earliest settlements. Established in 1712, the colonial seaport of **Edenton**★ *(northwest of Nags Head on Rte. 32)* graces the banks of Albemarle Sound. On the Neuse River, **New Bern**—settled in 1710 by Germans and Swiss who named it after Bern, Switzerland—became the seat of the colonial government from 1766 to 1776 and the state capital from 1776 to 1794. And west of Cape Lookout, the fishing village of **Beaufort** (pronounced BOW-furt) on US-70 preserves its early-18C heritage in the restored buildings at **Beaufort Historic Site**★ *(130 Turner St.; ⟍visit by guided tour only; ☎252-728-5225)*, and at the **North Carolina Maritime Museum** *(315 Front St.; ☎252-728-7317)*.

## Sights

### Cape Hatteras National Seashore★★

*Information about the seashore is available at the Bodie Island Visitor Center, near* the Bodie Island Lighthouse on Rte. 12. P ☎252-473-2111. www.nps.gov/caha. Protecting several discontinuous units of beaches, dunes and marshlands on the sound, the seashore encompasses 45sq mi of land. Aside from its natural attractions, the seashore is famous for its historic lighthouses. Tallest lighthouse in the US, the 208ft, 1870 **Cape Hatteras Lighthouse**★ *(off Rte. 12 near Buxton; ☎ 919-995-4474)* was moved inland

---

### The Single House

The city's distinctive contribution to American architecture is based on a typical West Indian design (many of Charleston's early settlers were planters from Barbados). One room wide and two rooms deep, the classic Single House includes a long piazza—or porch—lying behind a "false" front door on the narrow side of the house that opens onto the street (the real entrance to the house is off the piazza). A variation on this theme, the Double House is a near square with a room in each corner, divided by a central hall.

---

### The Lost Colony

In 1585 **Sir Walter Raleigh** sent forth seven English ships bearing 108 colonists with instructions to establish a settlement in the "most fertile and pleasant ground" of Virginia. Landing on the shores of **Roanoke Island** *(southeast of Nags Head via US-158 South & US-64 West)* in Roanoke Sound, the colonists built a fort and made a tentative peace with the local Indians, but by the spring of 1586, the group feared for their survival and returned to England. In the spring of 1587, Raleigh sent another group forth, and by August the colony could boast the first English child born in the New World—**Virginia Dare**, granddaughter of the settlers' leader, John White. Soon after her birth, White sailed for England to re-supply the colony, but his return to the colony was delayed by several years. When at last he sailed up to the fort, he found it deserted, with no clue to the colonists' fate save the Indian word "CROATAN" carved into a post. Were the colonists killed by Indians? Did they move to another location? To this day, no one knows for certain—the fate of these colonists remains one of American history's most compelling mysteries.

The colonists' Elizabethan-style encampment and a replica of the *Elizabeth II*—one of seven vessels that brought the 16C English settlers to Roanoke Island—are re-created at **Roanoke Island Festival Park**★ *(Dare St. near downtown Manteo; ☎252-475-1500)*, where the docudrama, "**The Legend of Two Path**," dramatizes the life of local Indians before and after European contact. The actual location of the first colony is preserved at **Fort Raleigh National Historic Site**★ *(off US-64 in north Manteo; ☎252-473-5772)* on Roanoke Sound. Outdoor productions of the stage play, **The Lost Colony**★, have been staged at the Waterside Theater here each summer since 1937 *(for information, call ☎252-473-3414)*.

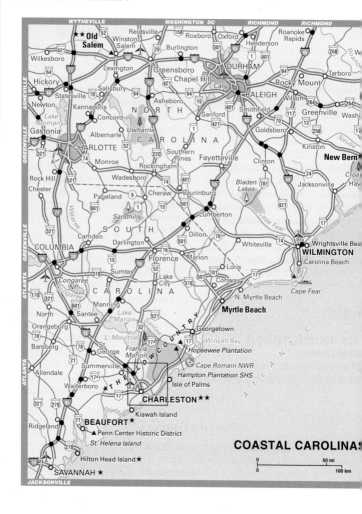

COASTAL CAROLINA

2,900ft to the southwest in summer 1999 to protect it from the advancing ocean. During the summer visitors can climb its tower for panoramic **views**★★ of the sweeping arc of the Outer Banks. The 1823 **Ocracoke Island Lighthouse** *(on the southern end of the island in Ocracoke Village)* is the oldest in the state.

## Wright Brothers National Memorial★

*Milepost 8 off US-158, in Kill Devil Hills, NC.* ♿ 🅿 ☎️ *252-473-2111. www.nps.gov/wrbr.*

On this site on December 17, 1903, brothers **Wilbur and Orville Wright**, owners of a bicycle shop in Dayton, Ohio, made the first successful control-

led, powered airplane flights. The cur rent 431-acre memorial houses a **visito center** with exhibits on the brothers' lif and achievements and reproductions o their 1902 glider and 1903 *Flyer*. Hourl lectures explain the Wrights' struggle and final victory here on the high dun of Big Kill Devil Hill, where soft sand and consistent winds allowed them t experiment with aerodynamic princi ples. In December 1903, after severa seasons of failed experimentation, the made four successful powered flights the longest measuring 852ft and last ing 59 seconds. On the grounds of th memorial stand reconstructions of th Wrights' simple 1903 **camp buildings** and the **Wright Brothers Monument**,

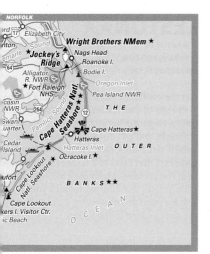

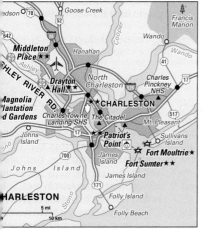

sweep off its top also make it one of the East's most popular hang-gliding sites. Stop in the **visitor center** to learn about dune formation, then climb to the top of the dune or take the 1.5mi interpretive **Tracks in the Sand Trail** that leads to Roanoke Sound.

## Additional Sights

### Tryon Palace Historic Sites and Gardens★★

*On US-17 in New Bern, NC. Corner of George & Pollock Sts.* ⚑Visit of interiors by guided tour only. ♿🅿☎252-514-4900. www.tryonpalace.org.

Set amid the shaded residential streets of **New Bern**, the multi-building complex features restored and re-created buildings from the 18C and early 19C. Centerpiece of the complex, stately Georgian **Tryon Palace**★★ is a reconstruction of the structure built in the late 1760s as the official colonial assembly meeting place and residence of Royal Governor William Tryon. After the American Revolution, the building served as the North Carolina capitol until 1798, when it burned to the ground. Inside, 18C furnishings and ornate paneling depict the opulence of a royal governor's life. Attached to the palace by curved colonnades are two brick dependencies: the **Kitchen Office** (east side), where costumed interpreters demonstrate 18C cooking; and the **Stable Office** (west side), the only palace building to survive into the 20C. Surrounding the palace, flower-and-boxwood parterred gardens are reminiscent of colonial landscaping.

...0ft-high pylon of gray granite topping ...ig Kill Devil Hill.

### ...ockey's Ridge State Park★

*...Milepost 12 on US-158 bypass.* ♿🅿 ☎252-441-7132.

...he 420-acre park protects the high-...st natural sand dune on the East ...oast, 80-100ft (its height varies due ...o shifts in the sand) Jockey's Ridge. Its ...oft, forgiving sides and the winds that

# CHARLESTON★★

MAP P203
EASTERN STANDARD TIME
POPULATION 541,159

Set on a narrow peninsula of land at the confluence of the Ashley and Coope
rivers on the South Carolina coast, the city of Charleston fancies itself a gran
Southern dame, venerable in her history, elegant in her architecture, and gente
in her manner. On this 5.2sq mi peninsula, you will discover some of the city
most legendary sights and its loveliest structures, along with a multitude c
boutiques, antique shops and restaurants that cater to a wide range of taste
and wallets. The area boasts some of the prettiest and most-challenging go
courses in the country. If you like the greens, don't forget to pack your club
Dolphins, alligators and other wildlife are yours for the viewing during naturalis
tours. Sea kayaking is a good way to get up-close to the action.

- 🚹 **Information:** ☎843-853-8000. www.charlestoncvb.com
- 🏞 **Don't Miss:** The regional pleasures of the Magnolia Plantation and Gardens.
- 🕐 **Organizing Your Time:** Plan to spend time to stroll at a leisurely pace throug
  the Historic District.
- 🧒 **Kids:** Kids won't get bored at the Charleston Museum thanks to hands-on histo
  exhibits.

## A Bit of History

In 1670 a group of English colonists landed on the western bank of the Ashley River, just south of a Kiawah Indian village. The archaeological ruins of the settlement they named Charles Towne, after King Charles II, remain at the living-history park at **Charles Towne Landing** (northwest of Charleston on Rte. 171; ☎843-852-4200). Plagued by disease and mosquitoes on their swampy site, the colonists relocated their town to the peninsula across the river in 1680. Charles Towne grew to be the fifth-largest city in colonial America by 1690, with a wealthy merchant class supporting its bustling port. Rice, indigo and cotton thrived in the Lowcountry's temperate, humid climate, and soon hundreds of plantations—largely dependent on slave labor for their prosperity.

Charles Towne witnessed the first great victory of the Revolutionary War in 1776, when the colonists trounced the British in the **Battle of Fort Moultrie**. After the war, Charleston was incorporated as South Carolina's first city in 1783.

The Civil War, which began in Charleston Harbor in the early morning hours of April 12, 1861, changed the city forever. By war's end, the once-thriving port had

been shelled and burned into a virtu
ghost town. With the abolition of sla
ery, the region's plantation econom
gradually disintegrated.

Plagued by natural disasters over th
years, plucky Charleston has rebui
itself after repeated fires, hurricane
and earthquakes (the city sits on th
second most active fault in the US).
order to protect its historic structure
Charleston became the first America
city to enact a historic zoning ordinanc
in 1931, thus becoming a model for th
preservation movement in other U
cities. Today Charleston's stunning **18
and 19C architecture**★★★ alone me
its a visit.

One of the Carolina coast's top touri
destinations, Charleston boasts th
fourth-largest container port in th
US—handling more than 10 million to
of cargo a year—The city also clain
two venerable academic institution
the **College of Charleston** (66 Georg
St. between St. Philip & Coming Sts.) w
founded in 1770; and **The Citadel Mil
tary College of South Carolina** (1.
Moultrie St.) enrolled its first cadets
1842.

In recent decades, the city has aga
revived its downtown, first with th
annual **Spoleto** performing-arts fest

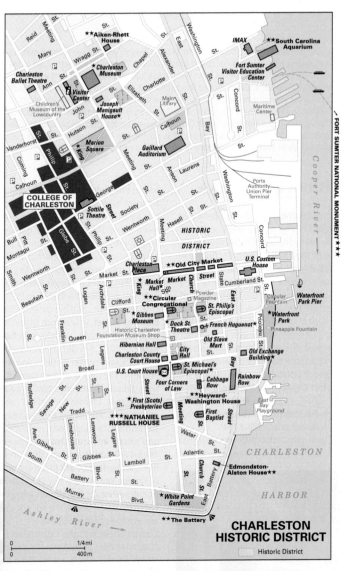

**CHARLESTON HISTORIC DISTRICT**

al *(late May)*, started in 1977 by Maestro ian Carlo Menotti as the counterpart o his Festival of Two Worlds in Spo-to, Italy; then in the late 1980s with e opening of the luxury hotel com-

plex now known as **Charleston Place** *(130 Market St.)*. The **South Carolina Aquarium**★★, opened in 2000, extends over the Harbor and has a stunning 300,000-gallon Great Ocean Exhibit.

## Sweetgrass Baskets

In the Old Market and along the streets in Charleston, you will see women making and selling a wide variety of coiled grass baskets. The coiled basketry craft came to South Carolina with slaves from West Africa 300 years ago. During the pre-Civil War plantation era, slaves stored foodstuffs and winnowed rice in baskets made by coiling marsh grass with strips of palmetto leaves. In the early 20C women began producing and selling "show baskets" made of sweetgrass, a now-scarce dune grass found along the South Carolina coast. This art form, passed down from generation to generation, is now prized as a dying folk art. Labor-intensive sweetgrass baskets take anywhere from 12 hours to 3 months to make.

# Historic District★★★

Occupying the lower tip of the peninsula formed by the Ashley and Cooper rivers—named for Anthony Ashley Cooper, one of the English Lords Proprietor—Charleston's historic district encompasses the area specified in the original 17C city plan, called the **Grand Modell**. A stroll along the brick, palmetto-fringed streets here hearkens back to the days when Charleston was London in miniature—a prosperous aristocratic city peopled by landed gentry. Walking-tour booklets are available at the **Visitor Center** (375 Meeting St.; ☎843-853-8000) and at the **Historic Charleston Foundation Museum Shop** (108 Meeting St.; ☎843-724-8484).

As you stroll the district, note the wrought- and cast-**ironwork** that adorns the garden gates. This decorative art form evolved from 19C plantation blacksmiths who made and repaired tools. Inside the gates nestle gardens bright with oleander, jessamine and hibiscus. Many private homes in the district are open for tours during the annual **Festival of Houses & Gardens** (late Mar–late Apr; ☎843-723-1623).

Fine restaurants and art galleries line **East Bay Street**, which leads to the Battery. Along the way, colorful **Rainbow Row** (79-107 E. Bay St.) showcases the largest intact cluster of Georgian row houses in the US; the earliest dwellings here date to 1680. A few blocks away, **King Street**, Charleston's major commercial thoroughfare since colonial days, still brims with shops, inns, restaurants and pricey **antique shops** (between Market & Broad Sts.). Along the Cooper River, **Waterfront Park** (main entrance at Vendue Range, off E. Bay St.), with its signature Pineapple Fountain, occupies the space once filled by the warehouses and wharves of the old port.

Church Street was the inspiration for "Catfish Row" in dubose Heyward's story "Porgy." This later became the jumping off point for Gershwin's opera "Porgy and Bess," which was based on real Charleston residents.

## The Battery★★

*Bordered by East & South Battery at the point of the peninsula.*

The high seawall that lines the Cooper River side of Charleston Harbor replaced the masonry wall built in 1700 to fortify the city. Strengthened over the years to ward off hurricanes, this wall became known as the High Battery for the gun emplacement stationed here during the

*Historic District Architecture*

©Charleston Area CVB/www.charlestoncvb.com

## "Constitution Charlie"

Oft-forgotten founding father and son of a wealthy planter, **Charles Pinckney** (1757-1824) is one of four Charlestonians who went to Philadelphia in May 1787 to help draft the new Constitution of the United States. Prior to leaving, Pinckney and John Rutledge conceived a version of the Constitution, which they later presented to the convention. More than 30 provisions cited in "the Pinckney Draught" were incorporated into the final Constitution; these included eliminating religious testing as a qualification for holding public office, assigning impeachment power to the House of Representatives, and establishing a single chief executive. Disliked by James Madison—whose journals provide the best source of information about the convention—the pompous Pinckney never received the credit he deserved for his contributions. As his personal papers were later destroyed by fire, Pinckney left no records himself.

Vestiges of his country estate, Snee Farm, are now preserved at the **Charles Pinckney National Historic Site** (*11mi northeast of Charleston in Mt. Pleasant, off US-17 North on Long Point Rd.; ☎843-881-5516; www.nps.gov/chpi*). The visitor center here contains exhibits detailing the plantation's history and Pinckney's political career, which included three terms as South Carolina governor, one term in the US Senate, and a four-year stint as ambassador to Spain under President Thomas Jefferson.

War of 1812. Today this popular promenade attracts strollers, joggers and bikers, who enjoy **views**★ of the river and of the graceful homes that line East and South Battery. These elegant pastel structures, positioned so that their airy piazzas catch the prevailing breezes, provide stellar examples of Charleston's noted **antebellum residential architecture**★★★. At the tip of the point, **White Point Gardens**★—named for the mounds of oyster shells that once accumulated here—were laid out by John Charles Olmsted in 1906.

### Edmondston-Alston House★★

*21 East Battery. Visit by guided tour only. ☎843-722-7171. www.middletonplace.org.*
Scotsman and cotton trader Charles Edmondston built this home in 1825. When the cotton market turned sour 3 years later, Edmondston sold the house to monied Charleston rice planter Charles Alston, who added the third-floor piazza and other Greek Revival details. A tour of the manse, with its triple-storied piazza supported by Doric and Corinthian columns, depicts the life of Charleston's 19C elite. The second-floor **library** contains more than 1,000 rare volumes.

### Calhoun Mansion★

*16 Meeting St. Visit by guided tour only. ☎843-722-8205.*
With 24,000sq ft of living space, Calhoun Mansion ranks as Charleston's largest single residence. Built in 1876 for wealthy banker George Williams, the home passed to William's daughter Sally and her husband, Patrick Calhoun (grandson of statesman John C. Calhoun). The mansion encompasses 35 rooms, fitted with lavish Victorian-era furnishings. The airy second-floor **music room** rises 45ft high to a glass skylight.

### Nathaniel Russell House★★

*51 Meeting St. Visit by guided tour only. ☎843-723-1623. www.historiccharleston.org.*
Called an "urban plantation" when it was completed in 1808, Nathaniel Russell's Federal-style residence is still flanked by a formal English garden. Inside, the reception room opens onto a hall containing a **"flying" staircase**—a freestanding spiral that circles up to the third floor. Restored to its 1808 glory, the home exemplifies the Adamesque style in the ornate carved **woodwork** and **moldings** that adorn the rooms.

*Drayton Hall Plantation*

### Heyward-Washington House★★

*87 Church St. Visit by guided tour only, daily 10am–5pm. $15. ☎843-722-0354. www.charlestonmuseum.org.*

Lawyer and patriot Thomas Heyward was the original owner of this red-brick double house. The site on which the home stands is within the boundaries of the old walled city. Inside, the rooms are decorated with a remarkable collection of 18C Charleston-made **furniture**★, including pieces attributed to **Thomas Elfe**, one of the early city's most prominent cabinetmakers.

### Four Corners of Law

Originally intended to be a grand public square, the intersection of Broad and Meeting Streets is now graced with public buildings that represent state, federal and municipal law: the 1788 **Charleston County Court House** (*northwest corner*); the 1896 Renaissance Revival **U.S. Court House and Post Office** (*southwest corner*); and the 1801 Palladian-style **City Hall** (*northeast corner*). Georgian-style **St. Michael's Episcopal Church** (*southeast corner*) represents God's law.

### Old Exchange Building★

*122 E. Bay St. Open daily 9am-5pm. $7. ☎843-727-2165. www.oldexchange.com.*

Built by the British in 1771 as an Exchange and Customs House, this Palladian-style building was where South Carolina Patriots ratified the US Constitution in 1788. Some of the very men who signed the document had been imprisoned downstairs in the gloomy **Provost Dungeon** (*visit by guided tour only*) during the British occupation of the city. Visitors to the dungeon today can see part of the original wall built in 1690 to fortify the city.

### Old City Market★★

*Stretching from Meeting St. to the harbor along Market St. 6am-11:30pm.*

Consisting of a three-block row of vendors' sheds, the market is fronted by 1840 Greek Revival **Market Hall** (*Market St. at Meeting St.*), designed by Edward Brickell White to resemble the Temple of Fortuna Virilis in Rome. Today the long sheds offer a virtual flea market of foodstuffs, T-shirts jewelry and sweet grass baskets.

### Charleston Museum★

*360 Meeting St. ☎843-722-2996. www.charlestonmuseum.org.*

Across the street from the visitor center, America's first museum was founded in 1773. Now housed in a contemporary structure, the collections cover Charleston and the Lowcountry's social and natural history from pre-settlement days to the present. A fine exhibit of **Charleston silver** reflects the changing tastes of Charleston society. Kidstory (*Open daily 10am-5pm; $1* features hands-on natural history.

## oseph Manigault House★

50 Meeting St., across from Charleston
useum. Visit by guided tour only,
aily 10am-5pm. $10. ☎843-723-2926.
ww.charlestonmuseum.com.

esigned by gentleman-architect
abriel Manigault for his brother Joseph,
is stately brick manse (1803) captures
e lifestyle of prosperous early-19C
uguenot planters. Typical of the Adam
tyle of architecture, the house incorpo-
ates a variety of shapes and delicately
arved woodwork in addition to its fine
eriod furnishings.

## iken-Rhett House★★

8 Elizabeth St. Visit by guided tour
nly, daily 10am-5pm. $10. ☎843-723-
159. www.historiccharleston.org.

nlike other Charleston historic homes
at have been restored to their former
lamour, the Regency-style Aiken-
hett House has been preserved as it
ppeared c.1860. Built as a brick single
ouse in 1817, the home was purchased
y the Aiken family who remodeled
nd expanded it during their residence
1833-87). The ravages of time are evi-
ent here, especially in the occasional
ieces of original furniture, but that is
art of the property's charm. Out back,
e original 1817 outbuildings include
e slaves' quarters.

## very Research Center for
frican-American History
nd Culture

25 Bull St. Open Mon-Fri 10am-5pm.
843-953-7609. www.cofc.edu/avery.

his mission of this facility is to collect
nd preserve the history of the African
mericans in the South Carolina Low-
ountry. Stop here, on the campus of the
ollege of Charleston, to learn about the
ave trade. At the height of the Atlantic
ave trade, 40 percent of Africans who
vere forcibly shipped to North America
nded in South Carolina.

## oone Hall Plantation

235 Long Point Rd. Open Mon-Sat
am-5pm, Sun 1pm-4pm. $14.50.
843-884-4371. www.boonehallplan-
ationcom.

outhern history comes to life from the
econd you see the rows of oak trees lin-

ing up to the entrance of this still working plantation. See 300 years of heritage
through gardens, slave cabins and more
as well as the oak-lined avenue.

## Old Slave Mart Museum

6 Chambers St. ☎843-958-6467.
www.charlestoncity.info.

This museum depicting the history
of the city's role iin the salev trade is
underconstruction. Check the Web site
for updates.

# Ashley River Road★★

In colonial times, the river served as
the main route to the stately plantations that faced the Ashley River. By
land, an arduous back road followed
part of an ancient Cherokee Indian trail.
Today, tree-lined Highway 61 (Ashley
River Road) provides easy access to the
plantations, a 20min drive southwest
of Charleston.

## Drayton Hall★★

3380 Ashley River Rd. ♿ 🅿 Hours vary
by season. $14. ☎843-769-2600.
www.draytonhall.org.

The only plantation house on the Ashley River to survive the Revolutionary
and Civil Wars intact, Drayton Hall was
occupied by seven generations of the
Drayton family, wealthy English planters who came to the Lowcountry from
Barbados in the late 17C. Built c.1742
for John Drayton, who was born next
door at Magnolia plantation, this stunning brick edifice (whose architect is
unknown) with its striking two-story
portico embodies the Georgian Pallad-
ian architectural style. Symmetry and
classical detail distinguish the unfurnished **interior**, which showcases
ornate hand-carved and cast-plaster
ceilings and hand-carved decorative
moldings. The last finished coat of paint
on the walls dates to 1885.

## Magnolia Plantation
and Gardens★

3550 Ashley River Rd. Open daily
9am. $15. 🍴 🅿 ☎843-571-1266.
www.magnoliaplantation.com.

*Middleton Place, Garden*

This popular tourist attraction comprises a 500-acre informal **garden**★ known for its spring-blooming azaleas, and a **plantation house** (👁‍🗨*visit by guided tour only*) that once formed part of the 17C estate owned by Englishman Thomas Drayton. More recent additions to the site include nature train and boat tours, and the adjoining **Audubon Swamp Garden**, where boardwalks traverse 60 acres of blackwater cypress and tupelo swamp.

### Middleton Place★★

*4300 Ashley River Rd.* ⏰*Open daily 9am.* 🎟*$25.* 🍴♿🅿☎*843-556-6020. www. middletonplace.org.*
Sweeping down to the Ashley River, 110 acres of terraced lawns and formal 18C English **gardens** burst into their fullest glory in early spring. Laid out in 1741 b Henry Middleton—who was electe president of the First Continental Cor gress in 1774—the gardens once forme part of the Middleton rice plantatio The original plantation house wa burned during the Civil War; the bric structure that remains, **Middleton Plac House** (👁‍🗨*visit by guided tour only* was built as a gentlemen's guest win After strolling through the gardens, vis the **stableyards** near the house, wher plantation life is re-created.

## Excursions

### Patriot's Point★★

Kids *3mi north of Charleston in Mt. Plea ant. Take US-17 North, turn right o*

*Ruins of Fort Sumter Officers' Quarters*

Rte. 703 and follow signs to Patriot's Point Rd. ⏱Open daily 9am-6:30pm. 💲$15. 🍴♿🅿 ☎843-884-2727. www.patriotpoint.org.

Built to honor the men and women who have served the US Navy in the 20C, Patriot's Point features four historic ships, the National Congressional Medal of Honor Museum, and a mock-up of a Vietnam naval support base. The site's centerpiece is the World War II aircraft carrier **Yorktown**★★, known as the "Fighting Lady." Visitors are free to explore this vast, 888ft-long floating museum from engine room to bridge, following any of eight self-guided tours. In all you'll find 25 naval aircraft on board, some exhibited in the **hangar bay**, others up on the **flight deck**.

Additional World War II ships berthed at Patriot's Point include the submarine *Clamagore*, the destroyer *Laffey*, and the Coast Guard cutter *Ingham*.

### Fort Sumter★★

*In Charleston Harbor; accessible only by boat from Patriot's Point or City Marina on Lockwood Dr. (for boat schedules, call ☎843-722-2628). www.nps.gov/fosu.*

This man-made island at the entrance to Charleston Harbor saw the first shots of the Civil War in 1861. Named for Revolutionary War hero Thomas Sumter, the

© National Park Service

*Union Officers, Fort Sumter, 12-13 April, 1861*

five-sided brick fort was 90 percent complete in December 1860 when South Carolina seceded from the Union. Six days later, Union major Robert Anderson occupied Fort Sumter, and over the ensuing months the battlement became the focal point of tensions between the North and South. At 3:30am on April 12, 1861, Rebels opened fire on Sumter. The cannonade continued for 34 hours, until Major Anderson surrendered the fort

## Gullah, The Language That Time Forgot

The Sea Islands of South Carolina and Georgia are home to a small community of African Americans who speak Gullah, remnants of a language and way of life passed on from early slaves who worked the mainland plantations. Kidnapped from their homelands and unable to communicate with whites or with each other, the slaves created a unique language based on their disparate West African tongues. Also referred to as Geechee, this creole dialect incorporates the vocabulary and grammar from the West African languages of Vai, Mende, Twi and Ewe, peppered with words from English, Spanish and Dutch, among others. The solitude experienced by slaves who were relatively isolated on the coastal islands facilitated the preservation of many African customs, from storytelling and medicine to folk arts.

Gullah strongholds remain on **St. Helena**, Daufuskie and Sapelo (🔗 see SAVANNAH) islands. On St. Helena, the 17 buildings of the **Penn Center Historic District** (6.3mi south of Beaufort on US-21; turn right at Martin Luther King, Jr. Dr.; ☎843-838-2432; www.penncenter.com) focus on the school established in 1862 by Philadelphia Quakers Laura Towne and Ellen Murray to educate African Americans. Photographs, African artifacts and oral history recordings at the **York W. Bailey Museum** (☎843-838-2474) interpret the impact that the center had on the coastal community. Plan a visit in mid-November to celebrate the **Penn Center Heritage Days**, or in May for the **Gullah Festival** held in Beaufort. The best local enclave for Gullah folk art is **The Red Piano Too Art Gallery** (853 Sea Island Pkwy./US-21; ☎843-838-2241).

on April 13. "A thrill went through the whole city," wrote Stephen Lee, General Beauregard's Aide-de-Camp. "It was felt that the Rubicon was passed…."

Visitors can inspect the garrison and its casemates on the self-guided walking tour. A **museum** in Battery Huger, added in 1898, tells the story of the fort and its role in the Civil War through informative panels, armaments and artifacts.

### Fort Moultrie★

*9mi northeast of Charleston via US-17 North & Rte. 703. 1214 Middle St., on Sullivan's Island.* ⏱*Open daily 9am-5pm.* ☎*843-883-3123. www.nps.gov/fomo.*

Built with wood from abundant local palmetto trees, Fort Moultrie gained fame as the crude rampart that held off the British during the Revolutionary War battle for Sullivan's Island in 1776. The soft palmetto logs that formed the walls of the early fort helped thwart the Redcoats' attack by absorbing the British shells. After the battle, the palmetto tree was adopted as the South Carolina state symbol—today South Carolina is known as the Palmetto State. The present brick fort dates to 1809 and was an active military installation until 1947.

## The Lowcountry★

Named for the marshy coastal prairies that line the low-lying South Carolina coast north and south of Charleston, the Lowcountry is remarkable for its culture as well as its cuisine. From the banks of the Santee River to Beaufort, quaint towns and water-laced lowlands harbor a range of attractions, from historic plantations to wildlife refuges frequented by alligators and myriad species of birds. Two popular family-friendly resorts anchor each end of the South Carolina coast: **Myrtle Beach** *(98mi north of Charleston on US-17)* and the golf resort of **Hilton Head Island**★ *(135mi south of Charleston via I-95 South & US-278 East)*. Closer to Charleston lie the residential **Isle of Palms** *(north)* and **Kiawah Island** *(south)*, a lovely private resort.

The area's history was defined in the 18C by wealthy rice, indigo and cotton planters, who developed the region's agricultural economy with the help of slaves forcibly imported from West Africa. After these so-called "rice lords" lost their free labor at the end of the Civil War, Lowcountry plantation owners saw their fortunes fall. Vestiges of the area's plantation heyday remain at **Hopsewee Plantation** *(53mi north of Charleston via US-17 at 494 Hopsewee Rd.; ☎843-546-7891)* and at **Hampton Plantation** *(50mi north of Charleston via US-17 at 1950 Rutledge Rd.; ☎843-546-9361).*

Another highlight is the **Frampton House** *(*⏱*Open daily 9am-5:30pm.* ☎ *843-717-3090. www.southcarolinalowcountry.com)*, which was rebuilt after General Sherman's tropps burnt it in 1865. Today it houses a recreation of a 1900 plantation parlor, museum artifacts and a gift shop.

While you're in the area, be sure to sample the unpretentious **Lowcountry cooking**. Flavored by rice and okra from Africa, spices and fruits from the West Indies, and plentiful shrimp, crab and oysters caught off the coast, this traditional cuisine adds a dollop of Southern accents—grits, black-eyed peas, fried green tomatoes—just for good measure.

### Beaufort★

*70mi south of Charleston on US-21. Various tours of the city depart from the Greater Beaufort Chamber of Commerce Visitors Center, 1106 Carteret St.* ☎*843-986-5400.*

The walkable 304-acre historic district comprises the entire original town of Beaufort (pronounced BEW-furt), chartered as part of the colony of Carolina in 1711. A day spent here offers an intimate look at the wealth generated by South Carolina's 18C planter class. Leave your car at **Waterfront Park** *(Bay & Newcastle Sts.)*, where restaurants, a covered market and a marina line the river. Bordering the park, **Bay Street** is lined with bookstores, shops and restaurants as well as some of the city's most venerated private homes. The 18C Federal-style **John Verdier House Museum** *(801 Bay St.;* ⏱*visit by guided tour only;* ☎*803-524-6334)* illustrates the "Beaufort style"—with its raised first floor, double piazza, T-shaped floor plan, and shallow, hipped roof—designed to take full advantage of prevailing river breezes.

# DES MOINES AREA

Lying just south of the state's geographical center, Des Moines ranks as Iowa's capital and largest city. This Heartland hub boasts many of the state's finest cultural attractions, as well as the summertime **State Fair★★★**, a must for anyone wanting a hands-on experience of America's agricultural Midwest.

The rugged Driftless Area in the northeast corner of Iowa was the only landform in the state unaffected by glaciers: elsewhere, the landscape is characterised by uneven heaps of glacial drift, now covered with tallgrass prairie. Long before the arrival of French and British fur traders in the 18C, the region was home to the Sauk and Mesquakie Indians, who called this area Moingonia, or "river of the mounds." French explorers later translated the name as "La Rivière des Moines."

Des Moines

Permanent settlers began to arrive in the 1830s. In 1842, a sham treaty saw the Native Americans cede 10 million acres of land to the federal government, along with the removal of the resident tribespeople to a Kansas reservation. The Iowa Territory—which included present-day Iowa, part of Minnesota and the Dakotas—was created in 1838, with Iowa City named as its capital. Iowa entered the Union as the 29th state in 1846. Responding to pressure for a more central location for the capital, the state government relocated to Des Moines in 1857.

In the late 19C, agriculture thrived as steamboat and rail travel helped bring crops to mills and markets. Iowa still depends on agriculture for the major portion of its revenues. The state has been the nation's largest corn producer since 1890, and is covered by a verdant patchwork blanket of corn and soybean crops.

Despite the sophisticated big-city attractions of Des Moines, rolling farmland takes up 93 percent of the state's area. Here small towns still thrive in and among the fields, nurturing regional folk art and hearty stick-to-your-ribs cuisine, influenced by the area's German heritage.

*Des Moines Skyline*

Greater Des Moines Convention & Visitors Bureau

# DES MOINES★

MICHELIN MAP 583 M 7
CENTRAL STANDARD TIME
POPULATION 198,682

Straddling the V of the Des Moines and Raccoon rivers, Iowa's capital city is also its economic and political seat. While the city's late-20C downtown skyline is bland, the excellent art museum and glittering capitol are anything but.

- **Information:** Greater Des Moines Convention and Visitors Bureau. ☎515-242 4705 or 800-451-2625. www.seedesmoines.com.
- **Don't Miss:** A day trip back in time at the Amana Colonies.
- **Also See:** Palace of the Prairie and other examples of US Second Empire-style architecture as well as modern architectural feats.

## A Bit of History

Through the late 19C, Des Moines' economy grew up around business and agriculture. Insurance became particularly important around 1867, when Connecticut native Frederick Hubbell helped found the Equitable Life Insurance Company here. Today the city ranks third in the world—after London and Hartford, Connecticut—in the insurance industry.

Today most of Des Moines' downtown activity happens in the **Court Avenue District** (Court Ave. from 5th Ave. to S.W. 1st St.), where 19C Italianate brick storefronts house nightclubs and cafes; on Saturday mornings from May to October, a terrific **farmers' market**★—ranked among the top 10 in the US by Bon Appétit magazine—fills the street with fresh produce, baked goods, music and crafts. The west side of town, including the **Sherman Hill Historic District**, contains beautiful Victorian residences and most of the city's best restaurants.

## Sights

### Des Moines Art Center★★

4700 Grand Ave. Open Tue-Wed, Fri 11am–4pm, Thu 11am–9pm, Sat 10am–4pm, Sun 12pm–4pm. Closed Mon. ☎515-277-4405. www.desmoine sartcenter.org.

The Des Moines Art Center meanders through galleries designed by three great architects of the 20C. **Eliel**

**Saarinen**'s original museum building (1948), a one-story U-shaped structure made of pale Lannon stone, hugs a hilltop perch and encircles a reflecting pool. Its galleries house the center's collection of late-19C and early-20C art, with works by Americans Grant Wood and Edward Hopper, and Europeans Joan Miró, Paul Klee, Marc Chagall and Henri Matisse. The first addition (1968), by **I.M. Pei**, was designed specially for large works of sculpture. Dark and echoey, it holds mammoth works by Claes Oldenberg, George Siegal and Frank Stella. **Richard Meier** designed the most recent wing (1986), a curvaceous four-level pile of porcelain, glass and metal.

### State Capitol Building★★

E. 9th St. and Grand Ave. ☎515-281-5591.

Completed in 1886—the second capitol on this site—the Beaux-Arts Iowa State Capitol sparkles on its perch overlooking downtown. While its most recognizable feature is its glittering, 23-carat-gold-covered dome (modeled after Les Invalides in Paris), the structure's interior, which incorporates 29 types of marble, is a truly phenomenal public space. The **Grand Staircase**★★ is surmounted by stained glass and a gigantic mural depicting pioneers' arrival in Iowa. The stunning **law library**★★ occupies the entire west wing of the second floor. Full-length windows let in copious light, illuminating the colorful ceiling fresco.

## Address Book

*For coin ranges, see the Legend on the cover flap.*

### WHERE TO STAY

**$ Savery Hotel and Spa** – *401 Locust St., Des Moines, IA.* ✗♿🅿🛗 ☎515-244-2151. *www.savery.com. 224 rooms.* A $9-million renovation has revived downtown's 1919 Greek Revival gem, which is directly linked to the 4.5mi Skywalk. Peach-hued florals take the edge off traditional dark cherry wood armoires and leather armchairs. The fully equipped health spa, complete with two saunas and three Jacuzzis, is one of the best in town.

### WHERE TO EAT

**$$ Raccoon River Brewing Company** – *10th & Mulberry Sts., Des Moines, IA.* ☎515-283-1941 or 800-532-1466. *www. raccoonbrew.com.* **American.** Soaring ceilings, dark wood booths, and a pool hall overlooking the main dining room give this downtown pub a welcoming feel. But the food is a notch above your average beer hall. Maple-glazed Iowa pork chops and a 10-ounce sirloin with portabello mushroom stuffing set the standard. Tallgrass Prairie Gold is the best-seller of five house brews.

## State of Iowa Historical Building★

*600 E. Locust St.* ⏱*Open Mon-Sat 9am–4pm, Sun 12pm–4:30pm*✗ 🅿 ☎515-281-5111. *www.state.ia.us/government/dca.* One block away from the State Capitol, the red granite and glass ziggurat contains eye-catching exhibits about various periods of Iowa history. On the west side of the building, three levels of exhibits—which don't shy away from thorny topics such as the wresting of land from Native Americans, racism, and industry's deleterious effects on the environment—surround a bright, oak-floored atrium.

## Terrace Hill★

*2300 Grand Ave., 2mi west of downtown.* ⏱*Open Tue-Sat 10am–1:30pm.* ☎515-281-3604. *www.terracehill.org.* Dubbed "Palace of the Prairie" upon its completion in 1869, 21-room Terrace Hill is considered one of the best-preserved examples of the Second Empire style in the US, designed by Chicago architect W.W. Boyington (also credited with Chicago's Water Tower, *see CHICAGO*). Restored to its 1880s appearance, the elegant red-brick manse now serves as the governor's residence. Highlights include 15ft stenciled ceilings, said to have taken 6,000 hours to paint.

*State Capitol Building*

Greater Des Moines Convention & Visitors Bureau

# Iowa State Fair

**KLM** *Grounds entrance at E. 30th & University Aves. For information, contact Iowa State Fair, State House, 400 E. 14th St., Des Moines, IA 50319-0198,* ⓒ *Open daily 8am–midnight.* ☎515-262-3111 or www.iowastatefair.org.

Known as America's Classic State Fair, the **Iowa State Fair**★ epitomizes the rural Midwest: massive, friendly, wholesome, fattening and fun. A visual and culinary feast running for 11 days each August, it boasts everything from prize pigs and beauty pageants to fried dough, corn dogs and apple-rhubarb pie.

The first Iowa State Fair was held in 1854; it moved to these 400-acre grounds in 1886 and has thrived here ever since as one of the oldest and largest fairs in the country. Lined with trees and old-fashioned lamp posts, as well as turn-of-the-20C structures for four-legged summer guests, the fairgrounds' **Main Street**★ is a testament to the permanence of the event. Around it sprawl acres of rolling terrain used for arts and crafts displays, carnival rides, food tents and campgrounds. The 1909 **Grandstand**, a massive coliseum that forms the centerpiece of the fair, hosts concerts by top-billing country-music performers as well as tractor pulls, the prize-animal parade and a rodeo. But the main draw here instead is the quirky slices of American life that you won't find anywhere else—monster arm-wrestling contests, a bust of Elvis carved entirely out of butter, cutthroat baking competitions, and nearly every food you can imagine (pickles, ice cream, hot dogs, pretzels, dough) perforated with a stick for maximum portability.

## Salisbury House★

*4025 Tonawanda Dr. From downtown, take I-235 West to 42nd St., and turn left on Tonawanda Dr.* ✒*Visit by guided tour only, Tue-Fri 1pm and 2:30pm, Sun 1pm and 2:30pm.* ⓒ*$7* ☎515-274-1777. www.salisburyhouse.org.

Nestled on 11 wooded acres stands what may seem an anachronism: a Medieval manor in a state that wasn't settled until the Victorian era. But cosmetics tycoon Carl Weeks was bent on re-creating the King's House, a royal-family retreat in Salisbury, England, in his native Iowa. The 42-room mansion, completed in 1928, incorporates three architectural styles—Gothic, Tudor and Carolean.

## Excursion

### Amana Colonies★

*88mi east of Des Moines. Take I-80 East to Exit 225 (Rte. 151 North). A visitor center for the colonies is located at the junction of US-151 and Rte. 220 in Amana.* ☎319-622-7622 or 800-579-2294. www.amanacolonies.org.

This cluster of seven now-touristy villages marks the site where, in 1855, one of the largest communal enclaves in America was founded. Due to ideological conflicts, the group voted to end the commune in 1932, forming a profit-sharing corporation instead.

Today about one-third of the 1,800 residents of the villages belong to the Church of the True Inspiration (a splinter group of the Lutherans). Architecture ranges from simple 19C brick, stone and frame structures to modern split-levels. More than 70 shops, 12 restaurants and bed-and-breakfasts fuel a brisk tourist trade. In the largest and oldest village, **Amana**, the **Museum of Amana History**★ *(4310 220 Trail;* ☎319-622-3567*)* describes the religious beliefs and daily life of the Amanans through artifacts and a slide show.

# DETROIT AREA

If the lower peninsula of Michigan is shaped like a mitten, defined by lakes Erie, Huron, Michigan and St. Clair, then the Detroit metropolitan area lies at the base of the thumb, in the southeastern sector of the state. Detroit, whose name is derived from the French *d'étroit*, meaning "of the strait," spreads out in a flat semicircle from the Detroit River, which joins Lake Erie to picturesque Lake St. Clair. Across the river lies Windsor, Ontario, its huge neon casino signs reflected in the water.

Long known by the moniker "Motor City," Detroit is the birthplace of the automobile in America. **Henry Ford** (*see DEARBORN*) implemented assembly-line production here, and suburban factories still crank out more cars than any other place in the US. In the early 1920s, the founding families of automobile history—among them, the **Fords**, the **Dodges** and the **Fishers**—built (or moved) their enormous mansions and factories outside city limits. In 2003 General Motors moved its corporate headquarters to the glittering Renaissance Center downtown. Today the suburbs—such as **Dearborn**, home to Ford's estate and production plants—thrive as mostly residential enclaves, while the city itself continues its efforts at revitalization, including an elevated light-rail loop (the People Mover) and impressive new stadiums for the Detroit Tigers baseball team and the Detroit Lions football team.

Today the Detroit vicinity extends north to Rochester, west to **Ann Arbor**★, home to the more than 30,000-student **University of Michigan** (founded in 1817), and east to the posh suburb of **Grosse Pointe**. Detroit proper forms the geographical center of the area: cultural attractions, ranging from the sumptuous auto-baron mansions to Henry Ford's Smithsonian-like museum to the sylvan Detroit zoo, may be up to 30mi away, and are best reached by car.

*Ford F-150 trucks being built. Ford Rouge Factory tours.*

## Area Address Book

*For coin ranges, see the Legend on the cover flap.*

### WHERE TO STAY

**$$$ Grand Hotel** – *Mackinac Island, MI.* Closed Nov–Mar. ☏*906-847-3331. www.grandhotel.com. 385 rooms.* The world's largest summer resort has been welcoming guests at the dock by horse-drawn carriage *(no cars are permitted on the island)* since 1887. Everything here is larger than life. Accommodations resemble summer cottages, with period antiques and cheery chintz fabrics. Tennis and golf facilities are on site; horseback riding is available nearby.

**$$ The Atheneum Suite Hotel** – *1000 Brush Ave., Detroit, MI.* ☏*313-962-2323. www.atheneumsuites.com. 174 rooms.* A two-story lobby mural of Trojan War figures sets the scene for trendy Greektown's popular all-suite property. Contemporary armchairs, cherry side tables, and white ceramic urn lamps decorate the bilevel living quarters. Attentive service makes this the first choice for visiting celebs. Downstairs, **Fishbone's Kitchen Cafe** is a local hot spot for Cajun and Creole seafood.

### WHERE TO EAT

**$$$ Tribute** – *31425 W. Twelve Mile Rd., Farmington Hills, MI.* Closed Sun. ☏*248-848-9393. www.tributerestaurant.com.* **Contemporary.** Notables such as Monaco's Princess Caroline have made the 35mi trek from downtown Detroit to this posh barrel-vaulted restaurant with swag curtains and Hollywood-style booths. Chef Don Yamauchi's innovative dishes include pheasant roulade with hedgehog mushrooms, veal sweetbreads, and rack of lamb in saffron-curry sauce. *Reservations required.*

**$$$ Duet** – *3663 Woodward Ave., Detroit, MI.* Closed Sun. ☏*313-831-3838.* **Regional American.** A musical setting next to downtown's Orchestra Hall. There's a brass "trumpet" hood above the open kitchen that overlooks the dining room's circular red-velvet booths, which are elevated opera-style. Local ingredients are kitchen staples. Try the mixed grill: beef tenderloin bordelaise, tuna with Mission figs, duck confit with huckleberries. Live jazz is part of the local draw.

**$$ Harmonie Pointe Grill** – *1407 Randolph St., Detroit, MI.* Closed Sun except during opera season. ☏*313-963-6244.* **$$ American.** This trendy bistro in the Harmonie Park theater district features dark wood booths offset with modern tear-drop-shaped light fixtures and a black and purple color scheme. Entrees, from the 12-ounce ribeye to the Lake Superior whitefish, are prepared on the open grill. Theater-goers come after the show for key lime pie.

# DETROIT ★

MAP P218
EASTERN STANDARD TIME
POPULATION 951,270

Encompassing 143sq mi on the banks of Lake St. Clair, Detroit is home to a metropolitan population of four million spread over more than 6,000sq mi. Key to that growth is the **automobile**, Detroit's most revered product. Thanks to inventor entrepreneurs like Henry Ford, Ransom E. Olds, and John and Horace Dodge, the car has become the symbol of the Motor City, but Detroiters are quick to point out that despite their contributions, these men didn't build the place from scratch.

- **Information:** ☏800-338-7648. www.visitdetroit.com
- **Don't Miss:** The remarkable public art and dramatic historic architecture; the historic Pewabic Pottery Tudor building and museum.
- **Kids:** Singing tour guides at the Motown Historical Museum.
- **Also See:** *DEARBORN*

# A Bit of History

here were about nine American Indian ribes in the northern Great Lakes area rior to European settlement. Detroit got its start in 1701 when **Antoine de a Mothe Cadillac** and a cadre of French oldiers, concerned about English incursions into the fur-trading industry, built fort on the Detroit River. Indians laid iege to the fort in 1763, as part of an nsuccessful wave of attacks led by Ottawa chief **Pontiac** to regain control f North American lands. Placed under ritish rule by the Treaty of Paris until mericans claimed it at the end of the evolutionary War in 1783.

n the early 19C, Detroit was a center f abolitionist activity, the last U.S. top (before Canada) on some of the **nderground Railroad** routes that onveyed escaped slaves from the South o freedom in Canada. After the Civil War nded in 1865, manufacturing became he city's chief activity. Trees, iron ore, lentiful water power and cheap trade outes made the area a choice industrial enter. Beginning in 1896, Henry Ford ut those resources to work building ars, and introduced assembly-line roduction in 1913.

he prosperity of the Roaring Twenties ielded several Art Deco masterpieces, ncluding the 1929 **Guardian Build-ng** *(500 Griswold Ave.)*, decorated with ocally made Pewabic tiles, and the 1928 **isher Building**★ *(2nd Ave. & W. Grand lvd.)* by Detroiter Albert Kahn, featuring ramatic setbacks and an exquisite inte-or **arcade**★. Also from this era are two f the city's most prized theaters—the assive Byzantine **Fox Theatre**★ *(2111 Woodward Ave.; ☎313-596-3200)* and he Spanish Revival **Gem Theater** *(333 Madison Ave.; ☎313-963-9800)*—as well s Cass Gilbert's Renaissance Revival **etroit Public Library** *(5201 Woodward ve.; ☎313-833-1000)*.

uring World War II, a huge influx f African Americans emigrated to etroit from the South to work in fac-ories converted to make war supplies. acial tensions led to the first of the ity's race riots in 1943. In July 1967, nother riot resulted in 43 deaths and fire that razed 1,300 buildings. Over

Detroit Marriott Renaissance Center

©iStockphoto.com/Alexey Stiop

the past 40 years the city has lost half its population, nearly a million people, to the suburbs. New urban renaissance projects—including major-league ball-parks, gorgeously restored theaters and riverfront casinos—flank downtown on all sides, with the hope that the enthu-siasm and wealth will spread to the city center in coming years.

For good views of the city, visit the top-floor observation deck of the 73-story **Detroit Marriott Renaissance Center** *(Jefferson Ave. between Brush & Beaubien Sts.)* or drive out to **Belle Isle** *(accessible via the MacArthur Bridge at E. Jefferson Ave. & E. Grand Blvd.)*. The latter is a 983-acre island park in the Detroit River that includes a zoo, nature center, aquarium, conservatory and the Dossin Great Lakes Museum. Art admirers art will find wor-thy works downtown: Isamu Noguchi's doughnut-shaped *Matilda Dodge Memo-rial Fountain*; Marshall Frederick's *Spirit of Detroit*; and Robert Graham's *Joe Louis Fist*—at the intersection of Woodward and Jefferson Avenues.

Housed in a 1907 Arts and Crafts structure, **Pewabic Pottery** *(10125 E. Jefferson Ave.; ☎313-822-0954, www. pewabic.com)* was built for ceramicist Mary Chase Perry Stratton, whose sig-nature iridescent-glazed architectural tiles still decorate many 1920s-era build-ings. Crammed with 750,000 titles, **John K. King Used and Rare Books** *(901 W. Lafayette Blvd.; ☎313-961-0622)* is Michi-gan's largest bookstore and a real treat for bibliophiles. The **Eastern Market** *(Gratiot Ave. & Russell St.; ☎313-833-9300)*, with its brightly painted Victorian

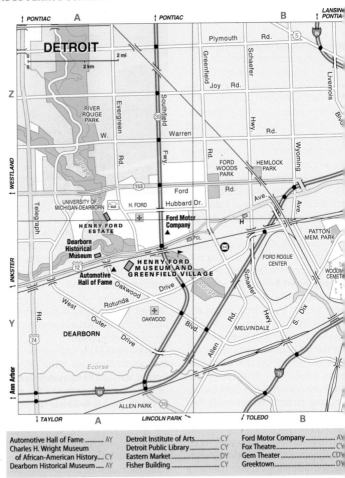

sheds, draws greengrocers, craftspeople and musicians on Saturdays year-round. For nightlife, try **Greektown**★ *(Monroe St. between Randolph St. & I-375)* with its profusion of festive cafes, restaurants and casinos. Adjacent **Harmony Park** hosts a cluster of trendy restaurants.

## Sights

### Detroit Institute of Arts★★
*5200 Woodward Ave.* ✕ ♿ 🅿 ☎313-833-7900. www.dia.org.
Boasting a strong and meticulously displayed collection of works spanning the centuries from ancient times to the present, the Detroit Institute of Arts is the one of the largest fine-arts museum in the country. The central Renaissance Revival-style building opened in 1927;

two wings were added in the 196( and 70s, and again in late 2007. Tod; the collection exceeds 55,000 objec spread over more than 100 gallerie Strengths of the permanent collectic include nine **18C French gallerie** which feature 200 paintings, pieces sculpture, decorative art objects and t prized **Firestone silver** collection, wi 40 items dating between 1729 and 179 In the third-floor European art galleri hang several large works by Rubens a Bruegel; the newly refurbished **moder and contemporary art galleries** co tain excellent examples of nearly all th major 20C schools.
Diego Rivera's fresco cycle **Detro Industry**★★ remains the institute pièce de résistance. Commissioned 1932 to paint murals on two walls

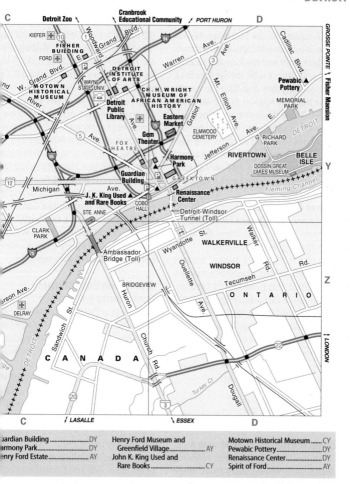

hat is now Rivera Court, the Mexican
tist was so captivated by the grit and
ace of Detroit's assembly plants that
ended up painting all four walls with
mesmerizing visual narrative explor-
g the relationship between humanity
d technology, life and death, workers
d bosses.

## arles H. Wright Museum of
## rican-American History★

315 E. Warren Ave. ◷Open Tue-Wed
m–5pm, Thu 9am–8pm, Fri-Sat 9
n–5pm, Sun 1pm–5pm✕&🅿 ☏313-
4-5800. www.maah-detroit.org.
e world's largest institution of Afri-
n-American history deals with the life
d culture of African Americans from
ve-trade days to the present. Wright,
ocal doctor, started the museum in

three row houses in 1965; the present
glass-domed structure was completed
in 1997. The moving, mutimedia exhibit
**"Of The People: The African-Ameri-
can Experience"** interprets 600 years
of American history from an Afrocentric
perspective. An art gallery and temporary exhibits occupy other galleries.

## Motown Historical Museum★

2648 W. Grand Blvd. ◷Open Tue-Sat 10am–
6pm. ◷Closed Sun-Mon. ☜$8. &☏313-
875-2264. www.motownmuseum,com.
In 1959 **Berry Gordy. Jr.**, a local African-American songwriter, purchased
this brick house and named it "Hitsville
USA" in hopes that his record company,
the **Motown Record Corp.**, would make
a dent in the charts. By 1966 Motown's
offices occupied eight dwellings on the

block and boasted performers such as the Temptations, the Supremes, Marvin Gaye, Stevie Wonder, Smokey Robinson, Gladys Knight and the Pips, the Jackson Five and others who merged gospel, pop, and rhythm-and-blues to create what became known as the Motown sound. Today the house contains a gallery charting Motown's success, and the actual tiny recording studio where dozens of hits were made. Visitors get to test their vocal chords in that very studio, and tour guides often break into song.

### Fisher Mansion

*383 Lenox Ave.* Open Fri-Sat 12pm–8:30pm, Sun 12pm–6:30pm. Closed Mon-Thu ☒ ☎313-331-6740.
One of the few "auto baron" estates not to imitate the gray stone manors of England, this extravagant Mediterranean-style villa was designed in 1928 by C. Howard Crane for **Lawrence P. Fisher**, founder of the Fisher Body Co. and general manager of Cadillac Motors. The mansion, now owned by the International Society for Krishna Consciousness, is filled with Vedic art.

## Excursions

### Edsel & Eleanor Ford House★

*8mi east of Detroit in Grosse Pointe Shores. Take E. Jefferson Rd./Lake Shore Rd. to 1100 Lake Shore Rd.* ☒ ☐ ☎313-884-4222. www.fordhouse.org.
The only child of Henry Ford and Clara Bryant, Edsel Ford was an avid art collector and built this house for his family as well as their growing collection of fine artworks, most of which they later donated to the Detroit Institute of Arts. Completed in 1929, the dwelling was designed by Detroit architect Albert Kahn to resemble an English country manor. Its 60 richly appointed rooms feature dark wood paneling, decorative plaster ceilings and leaded glass. The **Modern Rooms**, however, were streamlined in the 1930s by Walter Dorwin Teague to include polished wood veneers and Art Deco furniture. Acclaimed landscape architect **Jens Jensen** designed the beautiful grounds fringing the shoreline of Lake St. Clair.

### Detroit Zoo★

Kids *10mi north of Detroit in Royal Oa. Take I-75 and I-696 to Exit 16 (Woodwa Ave.) and follow signs to 8450 W. 10 M Rd.* Open daily 10am–5pm. $11 ☒ ☎248-398-0900. www.detroitzoo.org.
This zoo was one of the first in th country to feature open, natural env ronments for its animals. Loop trai and a miniature train wind amid its 12 park-like acres, home to 1,500 mammal birds and reptiles. Habitats include th four-acre **Arctic Ring of Life** (the large polar-bear exhibit in the world) and th new **National Amphibian Conserva tion Center**. Inside a renovated 192 glass-domed bird house, the **Wildlif Interpretive Gallery** incorporates butterfly garden and an aquarium.

### Cranbrook Educational Community★★

*17mi north of Detroit in Bloomfield Hil Take I-75 North to I-696 West. Exit Woo ward Ave. North to 39221 N. Woodwa Ave.* ☒ ☐ ☎877-462-7262. www.cr brook.edu.
Longtime art collectors and philanthr pists, George Gough Booth and Elle Scripps Booth used the fortune the earned in the newspaper business found this 315-acre multipurpose a community in the 1920s. The stunnin campus was conceived as a "total wo of art" by Booth and Finnish-America architect **Eliel Saarinen** (1873-195 who presided over the Cranbrook Aca emy of Art. Saarinen's bold **peristy** (1942), flanked by fountains containir works by Swedish sculptor **Carl Mille** forms the focal point of the campus a is breathtaking even to the most jade visitor. It joins the library with the a **museum**★, which contains works generations of Cranbrook faculty a students. The **Saarinen House**★ ( visit by guided tour only May-Oc designed in 1927 by the architect for h family, has been meticulously renovate to appear as it did during the architect tenure here. Also on campus is the **Cra brook Institute of Science**★ Kids, a sc ence and natural history museum.

# Advent of the Automobile

"I think that cars today are almost the exact equivalent of the great Gothic cathedrals: I mean the supreme creation of an era, conceived with passion by unknown artists, and consumed in image if not in usage by a whole population which appropriates them as a purely magical object." *Roland Barthes, Mythologies, 1957.*

Long a symbol of freedom, style, sex appeal and wealth, the car is synonymous with the American identity. Americans own 30 percent of the world's passenger vehicles, while constituting only about 4 percent of its population. More than 90 percent of US households have at least one car; most have two. Traffic worsens and smog thickens, yet Americans persist in their love affair with the automobile.

The "horseless carriage" was initially the dream of European inventors who saw the possibility of the steam engine for personal conveyance. In the early 1800s, steam cars were introduced in England but essentially banned in 1865 for being too dangerous, too smoky and too loud. Electric cars later showed promise, but batteries limited their speed and usefulness. Ultimately **Gottlieb Daimler** and **Karl Benz**, two Germans working separately, jump-started the automobile industry with the invention of the four-stroke gasoline engine in 1885, opening the way for the creation of French production companies **Peugeot** and **Renault**, and the Italian firm **Fiat**. Europe led the world in production numbers until 1900, when the US—Detroit in particular—overtook.

Detroit's resources were both industrial (proximity to trade routes, plentiful water power, lumber and steel) and intellectual. **Ransom E. Olds**, **Henry Ford** and the **Dodge brothers** were all tinkerers and salesmen, looking for ever new ways to improve and market the car. While European cars remained handmade, American car makers began building cars using interchangeable parts, a method used for years to build firearms and farm equipment. When Henry Ford combined that concept with the **moving assembly line** in 1913, output tripled and costs dropped. The beloved **Tin Lizzie**, as Ford's Model T was known, cost only $260 in 1924, while comparable European cars cost $2,000. During the 1920s, the number of US automakers also dropped sharply, from 108 in 1923 to 44 by 1927. By the end of the 1930s, only the "Big Three"—**Ford**, **Chrysler** (now DaimlerChrysler) and **GM**—remained, spinning out shiny new models each year.

Those three companies, all headquartered in and around Detroit, still dominate US automobile production, but their grip has weakened since the 1960s. In the late 1980s, Japan outstripped the US in car production, and American companies began moving assembly plants to countries with cheaper labor costs. As a result, Detroit's industry has suffered, even as American car consumption continues to outpace that of the rest of the world.

## ranbrook House nd Gardens★

*80 Lone Pine Rd., adjacent to campus. 248-645-3147.  Visit by guided tour nly May–Sept.*

esigned for the Booths by Albert Kahn  1908, this pristine English manor features excellent examples of decorative rts from the Arts and Crafts movement. on't miss the forty-acre **gardens★★**, vith their formal terraces sweeping own toward the forested rim of the ranbrook campus.

## Meadow Brook Hall

*25mi north of Detroit on the east campus of Oakland University in Rochester, MI. Take I-75 to Exit 79 East (University Dr.) to the university's main entrance; turn left at Squirrel Rd. Turn left on Walton Blvd., right on Adams Rd., then right at east campus entrance and follow signs.  2701 Troy Center Dr., 248-269-7672. www.mbhconcours.org, or www.meadowbrookhall.org.*

This 110-room, 80,000sq ft Tudor Revival-style monolith was completed in 1929 for **Matilda Dodge**, widow of automotive giant **John Dodge**, and her second husband, Alfred G. Wilson. Inspired by English country manors, it boasts 24 fireplaces, exquisite archi-

tectural detailing and original famil furnishings. On the grounds stand **Knole Cottage**, a playhouse for Mat ilda's daughter.

# DEARBORN ★

MAP P218
EASTERN STANDARD TIME
POPULATION 91,691

A southwestern suburb of Detroit, Dearborn is best known as the former hom of industrialist Henry Ford and for the headquarters and main assembly plant of the **Ford Motor Company**, which provide the city's economic base.

**Information:** Detroit Metro Convention and Visitors Bureau.
☎313-202-1800 or 800-338-7648. www.visitdetroit.com
**Parking:** This is Motor City USA! There is plenty of parking wherever you go.
**Also See:** *DETROIT*

## A Bit of History

The area was inhabited by Wyandot Indians when European colonists settled here in 1701. Dearborn was the site of the United States Arsenal from 1833 to 1875; two of the original buildings—the Commandant's Quarters and the McFadden-Ross House are now preserved as the **Dearborn Historical Museum** *(21950 Michigan Ave. & 915 Brady St.; ☎313-565-3000)*. Incorporated in 1927, the city is home to many Ford workers and executives, and students who attend the University of Michigan at Dearborn.

## Henry Ford Estate (Fair Lane) ★

*4901 Evergreen Rd., on University of Michigan-Dearborn campus.* Visit by guided tour only. *Closed Mon* ☎313-593-5590. www.henryfordestate.org.
This 56-room, English-style mansion, made of rough-hewn Ohio limestone with a crenellated roofline and turret, set the opulent standard for "auto baron" dwellings. Built for automobile magnate Henry Ford and his wife, Clara, in 1915, the house is decorated with roseleaf mahogany paneling, silver chandeliers and hand-carved **woodwork** ★. A tunnel

containing some 35mi of pipes connect the house to a six-story **powerhouse** contrived by Ford and his friend **Thoma Edison** (1847-1931) to make Fair Lan self-sufficient for electricity and hea The 72-acre estate grounds, designe by renowned architect **Jens Jense** (1861-1953), contain some of the fines examples of landscape art in America

## Henry Ford Museum and Greenfield Village ★★★

20900 Oakwood Blvd. *Open dai 10am–5pm.* ☎313-271-1620. www hfmgv.org.
Sprawled over nearly 100 acres, thi constitutes the world's largest indoo outdoor museum. Ford founded th museum and village in 1929 to "sho how far and fast we have come" in term of technological advancement. Toda holdings include more than a millio objects and 25 million historic pape spanning three centuries.

### Henry Ford Museum ★★★
Fronted by a replica of Philadelphia Independence Hall, the museum resem bles a colossal (12-acre) automobi factory within and presents a veritab

## Henry Ford

The man who revolutionized factory production was born one of eight children to an Irish immigrant farmer in Greenfield, Michigan, in 1863. At age 16, Ford dropped out of school and took a job as a machinist's apprentice in Detroit. Three years later, he returned to his family's farm and tinkered with building his own engines when not working part time for the Westinghouse Engine Company. Ford married Clara Bryant in 1888 and moved back to the city, where he secured a position as chief engineer at the Detroit Edison Company plant. Having completed his first "horseless carriage" by 1896, Ford and his backers started the Detroit Automobile Company in 1898. In 1903 he formed the Ford Motor Company, whose **Model T**—"a motor car for the great multitude," as Ford called it—was an instant success when it was launched in 1908.

In 1913 Ford incorporated an assembly-line method of production in his new plant that turned out a complete chassis every 93 minutes—a significant improvement over the 840 minutes previously required. Improvements in mass-production techniques eventually enabled Ford's plant to produce a Model T every 24 seconds. The societal revolution brought about by mass production of the automobile was buoyed by the fact that Ford offered his workers wages that were nearly double the industry standard, enabling his employees to purchase the very products they made. After Ford died at home in April 1947, his only child, Edsel Bryant Ford assumed presidency of the company. Edsel's son, Henry Ford II, took over as company president in 1945 (he died in 1987). Today Henry Ford's great-grandsons Edsel B. Ford II and William Clay Ford, Jr. serve on the company's board of directors.

*The Henry Ford Estate*

treasure trove of Americana. The museum's most popular exhibit, "**100 Years of the Automobile in American Life**"★★, tells the story of the car's evolution and how it has changed the world. More than 50 cars and trucks are displayed, from the last remaining 1896 Duryea (American's first production car) to the classic 1959 Cadillac Eldorado convertible. The museum's other large exhibit, "**Made in America**"★★, puts the automobile in the context of the Industrial Revolution by showing the development of technology from a **1760 steam engine** to the computer-dependent factories of today. Around these exhibits lie row upon row of fascinating objects, from the historic (the theater seat in which President Abraham Lincoln was assassinated) to the hilarious (the Oscar Mayer Wienermobile).

## Mackinac Island: Fudge and Gingerbread

From Detroit, a day's drive north along the shore of Lake Huron via Route 25 and US-23 brings you to tiny **Mackinac Island★**, which lies between Michigan's Upper and Lower Peninsulas where lakes Huron and Michigan meet.

Only 8mi around, Mackinac (pronounced MAK-i-naw) has a remarkably rich history and flourishes today as a carefree retreat. Its location at the intersection of lakes and land made the Island a gathering place for Native Americans who called it *Michilimackinack*, or "Great Turtle," for its shape. When the British built **Fort Mackinac** atop its bluff in 1779, the island eclipsed other nearby settlements as a center of fur trading and military importance.

A host of historic sites, including the fort and several museums, recall the island's early days, but it was the rush of tourism in the mid-1800s that really made it famous. Indeed, its lavish Victorian architecture, horse-drawn vehicles, and quiet ways still echo a bygone era. Venerable hostelries, the regal 1887 **Grand Hotel** *(West Bluff Rd. at Cadotte Ave.; ☎906-847-3331)* topping the list, and abundant bed and breakfasts occupy lovely gingerbread gems. The absence of cars on the island ensures a leisurely pace, and the north woods air is clear and clean. If at times the crush of summer day visitors—called "fudgies" after the island's scrumptious specialty—grows thick around the harbor, a bicycle ride to the island's breezy north shore or wooded interior makes an easy escape.

You can reach Mackinac Island by passenger ferry from Mackinac City or St. Ignace *(Arnold Transit Co., ☎906-847-3351; Shepler's Mackinac Island Ferry, ☎231-436-5023 or 800-828-6157 or Star Line, ☎906-643-7635 or 800-638-9892).* ☐*For more information, contact the Mackinac Island Chamber of Commerce, ☎906-847-3783 or www.mackinacisland.org.*

Adjacent to the museum, an IMAX Theatre shows two- and three-dimensional films on its 62ft-by-80ft flat screen.

### Greenfield Village★★

Henry Ford uprooted more than 75 historic structures from all over the country and plopped them down in his idealized village in an effort to preserve the way of life that, ironically, disappeared with the birth of Ford's Model T. Among the buildings designed to illustrate the work of famous people are Ford's own humble **birthplace**; the **Wright Brothers'** home and one of their four bicycle shops from Dayton, Ohio, in which they performed experiments leading to the first successful airplane flight; **Thomas Edi-**son's **Menlo Park laboratory**★, where nearly 400 inventions originated in New Jersey; and the 1823 house where **Noah Webster** wrote the *American Dictionary of the English Language*. Don't miss the daily **demonstrations**★ by tinsmiths, glassblowers, printers and weavers.

Two relative newcomers, the **Spirit of Ford** Kids *(1151 Village Rd.; ☎313-317-7474)* and the **Automotive Hall of Fame** Kids *(21400 Oakwood Blvd.; ☎313-240-4000)* share a more commercial focus. Spirit of Ford showcases futuristic cars, hands-on computer exhibits and motion simulator, while interactive Hall of Fame exhibits include crank-starting a Model T Ford.

# KENTUCKY

Kentucky is largely rural, claiming only two cities with populations exceeding 100,000—Lexington and Louisville. Bordered by Tennessee, Missouri, Illinois, Indiana, Ohio, West Virginia and Virginia, the state's geography varies from the rugged Appalachian Mountains of the eastern coal country, to the gentle terrain of the Bluegrass, to the flatlands of the Mississippi River on its extreme western edge. Temperate climate and high annual rainfall render the central and western regions of the state ideal for agriculture.

As long as 12,000 years ago, Mississippian Indians roamed what is now Western Kentucky. Evidence of their presence can be found at **Wickliffe Mounds** (5mi northwest of Wickliffe, KY, on US-51/60/62; ☎502-335-3681) and just over the Kentucky border at **Angel Mounds State Historic Site** (8215 Pollack Ave., off I-64 at Covert Ave. Exit; ☎812-853-3956) in Evansville, Indiana.

Kentucky

Indian attacks were a constant threat when the first settlers arrived in the late 1700s, via the Wilderness Trail that explorer and folk hero **Daniel Boone** (👆see WESTERN KENTUCKY) had blazed through the Cumberland Gap. In 1775 only one settlement—Harrodsburg—existed in Kentucky. By the time Kentucky was granted statehood in 1792, settlers were raising hemp and tobacco, and breeding horses—giving rise to the state's modern Thoroughbred industry. Kentucky's fertile soil also nourished an abundance of corn, which ultimately sprouted the manufacture of bourbon whiskey (👆see BLUEGRASS COUNTRY).

Churchill Downs, Louisville

When war was declared between the states in 1861, Kentucky was a slave state, but it nonetheless had strong economic ties to the North. Although the state never seceded from the Union, a number of its young men fought for the Confederacy. Union victories at **Columbus-Belmont**, on the western fringe, and at **Perryville**, south of Harrodsburg, dashed Confederate hopes of winning control of Kentucky.

Coal mining began in the 1890s, and Kentucky soon led the nation in coal production. Today it ranks third (behind Wyoming and West Virginia) but the state's $4.1 billion coal industry still produces nearly 119 million tons of "black gold" annually. Another significant part of Kentucky's revenue derives from distilleries, tobacco and horseracing. Recent years have seen an expansion of the economic base with the introduction of auto manufacturers and corporate headquarters. Even so, the Bluegrass state remains timeless—a mélange of meadowlands and scenic winding roads threading through pastoral towns.

## Area Address Book

⚭*For coin ranges, see the Legend on the cover flap.*

### WHERE TO STAY

**$$$ The Brown** Hotel– *335 W. Broadway, Louisville, KY.* ✗⚒♿🅿☎ *502-583-1234. www.brownhotel.com. 292 rooms.* Equestrian paintings and sculptures pay tribute to horse country in this downtown thoroughbred's English Renaissance-style lobby. Coffered ceilings and gilded screens are remnants of its grand opening in 1923. Guest rooms, at 400sq ft, are exceptionally large and classically designed with rich florals and walnut armoires.

**$$ The Seelbach Hilton** – *500 Fourth Ave., Louisville, KY.* ✗⚒♿☎ *502-585-3200. www.hiltons.com. 321 rooms.* Frequent visitor F. Scott Fitzgerald set parts of *The Great Gatsby* in this Gilded Age downtown landmark. Guests are still swept away by the palatial lobby's hand-painted murals and imposing bronze staircase. Bedrooms vary in size and shape, but all have rice-carved four-poster beds and mahogany armoires. In **The Oak Room**, chef Todd Richardsuses the best local ingredients to whip up delicious regional specialties.

**$ Bed & Breakfast at Silver Springs Farm** – *3710 Leestown Pike, Lexington, KY.* 🅿 ☎ *859-255-1784. www.bbsilver-springsfarm.com. 3 rooms.* This Federal-style house sits on a 21-acre property that operated as a bourbon distillery from 1867 until Prohibition. Complete with stables and paddock, the farm now boards horses year-round. The two large bedrooms in the main house have brass beds and a mix of antiques. The two-bedroom cottage is great for families.

### WHERE TO EAT

**$$ a la lucie** – *159 North Limestone St., Lexington, KY.* ☎ *606-252-5277.* **Contemporary.** Downtown's "bohemian" dining room is accented with Gaudí-style chandeliers and leopard-print booths. Locals come for the chef's updated comfort food: buttermilk-fried quail with cream gravy and bourbon-tabasco pork chops with corn pudding.

**$$ Club Grotto** – *2116 Bardstown Rd., Louisville, KY.* ☎ *502-459-5275.* **Contemporary.** Residents keep coming back for revised Southern favorites served in this vibrant bistro. Start with fried green tomatoes with white balsamic slaw. Bourbon-brined pork tenderloin with garlic-cream cheese grits and blackened tuna with spicy soy-mustard are best-selling entrées. Save room for the chocolate soufflé.

**$$ Merrick Inn** – *1074 Merrick Dr., Lexington, KY.* ☎ *606-269-5417. http://murrays-merrick.com.* **Southern.** Located in residential Lansdowne, the city's most popular eatery was the manor house of a pre-Civil War horse farm. Early-20C antiques and fireplaces give the four dining areas a homey feel. Prime rib and fried walleyed pike come with salad and fluffy homemade biscuits. Ask about the butterscotch pie.

# BLUEGRASS COUNTRY ★★

**MAP P227**

**EASTERN STANDARD TIME**

Named for the finely bladed native grass that takes on a faint bluish cast each spring, the Bluegrass roughly encompasses a seven-county area radiating outward from Lexington. It was the first region settled because it was easier to farm than the eastern mountains. Distinguished as the center of the Thoroughbred industry, the Bluegrass is marked by rolling meadows dotted with horse farms outlined by white plank fences.

**Information:** ☎ 606-233-7299. www.kentuckytourism.com

**Don't Miss:** The Old State Capitol that made Gideon Shryock famous.

**Kids:** Get up close and personal with the animal that made the region famous at Kentucky Horse Park.

## A Bit of History

Many of the Bluegrass towns—such as Harrodsburg, Danville and Bardstown—date from the late 1700s and, except for Lexington—the second-largest city—have remained small and somewhat isolated. Even the capital of Frankfort is small. Consequently, a large number of the early buildings survive, including many imposing Federal and Georgian homes.

In addition to its repository of antebellum structures, the Bluegrass is distinguished as the center of the equine industry, which brings $5.4 billion into the state annually and accounts for a significant part of its tourism. In recent years, the Bluegrass economy has become more diverse with the migration of new industry to the area, including Toyota Motor Manufacturing and Lexmark International.

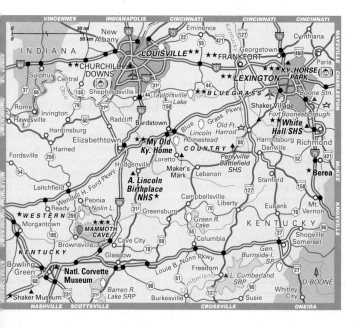

## Bourbon

Whiskey-making was a favorite Kentucky pastime before Kentucky was a state. Many early settlers distilled their own, and soon discovered that the region's limestone-rich water gave their corn liquor a coveted flavor. But the invention of bourbon whiskey came about quite by accident in the late 18C when a fire accidentally charred the oak barrels in which Baptist minister and whiskey-maker Elijah Craig aged his stock. Craig used them anyway and the end result was a darker, mellower beverage. Folks called it bourbon after Bourbon County. By 1891 Kentucky boasted 172 distilleries and bourbon manufacturing was one of the state's largest industries. A century later, that number had dwindled to nine, the result of Prohibition, economic downturns and changing tastes. Today, 98 percent of all bourbon whiskey sold in the US comes from Kentucky's distilleries.

Almost all of Kentucky's bourbon whiskey is made within a 50mi radius of **Bardstown**, home to Jim Beam, Heaven Hill and Barton, with Maker's Mark located in nearby Loretto. Most of the distilleries offer free tours. **Maker's Mark** *(3mi east of Loretto on Rte. 52;* ☎ *502-865-2099)*, conducts one of the best.

# Frankfort★★

Tucked into the Kentucky River Valley, between Lexington and Louisville, Frankfort was established as Kentucky's capital in 1792. This small (population 27,210) city concerns itself primarily with governing the state. Best known for its grand 1909 Beaux-Arts **State Capitol**★ *(Capital Ave.;* ♿ 🅿 ☎ *502-564-3449)*, Frankfort also contains the **Kentucky Military History Museum**, *(E. Main St. at Capital Ave.;* 🕐 *open Tue-Sat 10am–5pm;* 💰*$4;* ☎ *502-564-1792)*, which features firearms, artillery and uniforms dating from the Revolutionary War.

## Old State Capitol★★

*300 Broadway (corner of Broadway & Lewis Sts.).* ☎ *502-564-1792. www.historyky.org.*
This small gem of a building was designed by Kentucky's foremost antebellum architect, **Gideon Shryock**. Then relatively unknown, Shryock soon became famous for his flawless Greek Revival creation in Frankfort. Constructed in 1830, the building mimics the Greek Temple of Minerva with the addition of a cupola. Inside, the rotunda features rust-colored floors crafted from Kentucky river-bottom marble. A free-standing spiral **staircase** leads from the rotunda to the second-floor legislative chambers, preserved as they were in the 1850s with several original desks.

## Thomas D. Clark Center for Kentucky History Center★★

🄺🄸🄳🅂 *100 W. Broadway.* ♿ 🅿 ☎ *502-564-1792. www.historyky.org.*
This $29 million museum celebrates the state with a plethora of lifelike exhibits and state-of-the-art technology. The block-long, red-brick structure in the city's oldest district seeks to blend Palladian and Greek Revival details amid its blocky, contemporary styling. Inside, the atrium's focal point is a sweeping spiral stairway, patterned after the one in Frankfort's Old Capitol. As you walk through the main exhibit, "**A Kentucky Journey**," you'll feel the sway of the keelboat and hear the water lapping at an early river settlement. In addition to the permanent exhibit, the museum includes a research library.

# Lexington★★

The heart of the Bluegrass, Lexington was founded in 1779 and soon became a center of learning, wealth and culture. Transylvania University *(300 N. Broadway)*, the oldest college west of the Alleghenies, was chartered in 1780, followed by the state's first lending library in 1795 and the University of Kentucky *(500 S. Limestone St.)* in 1865. A group of the city's early-18C Federal and Georgian mansions are clustered in the 12-block **Gratz Park Historic District** *(bounded by N. Broadway, Upper, 2nd & 3rd Sts.).*

Today, the combined Lexington-Fayette County area has a population of 268,080, and contains a vibrant mix of educational, cultural and business interests. Despite economic diversification in recent years, the horse industry remains the backbone of the local economy. With 450 horse farms, two racetracks and two Thoroughbred auction facilities, the Lexington area still reigns as the "Horse Capital of the World."

Kentucky Horse Park Entrance

© Kentucky Horse Park

## Mary Todd Lincoln House★

*578 W. Main St.* 🗫*Visit by guided tour only Mon-Sat 10am–4pm.* ◑*Closed Sun.* ♿🅿︎☎859-233-9999.

This rambling 14-room brick house, just west of downtown, was the girlhood home of Mary Todd Lincoln (1818-82), later the wife of Abraham Lincoln, 16th president of the US. Surviving family furnishings include a mahogany table where Lincoln is believed to have played cards. Note the rare collection of coin-silver **mint-julep cups** crafted by 22 Kentucky silversmiths.

## Ashland★★

*120 Sycamore Rd.* 🗫*Visit by guided tour only.* 🍴🅿︎☎859-266-8581.

Known as "the great compromiser," **Henry Clay** (1777-1852) was Kentucky's pre-eminent 19C statesman. The US Senator, Speaker of the House of Representatives and three-time candidate for president made his home on a 600-acre estate he named Ashland. When the original 1806 structure was torn down in 1852, Clay's son rebuilt a brick Italianate villa on its foundation, using the same Federal floor plan. Later remodeling by a granddaughter reflects Victorian tastes. An octagonal entryway and dining room, beautiful inlaid wood floors, Sheffield silver doorknobs and marble mantels highlight the interior.

## Kentucky Horse Park★★★

Kids *4089 Iron Works Pike.* ◑*Open daily 10am–5pm.* 👓$15 🍴♿☎859-233-4303. *www.kyhorsepark.com.*

A Mare with her Foal at Kentucky Horse Park

© Kentucky Horse Park

Set on the rolling pastureland of a former working horse farm, this facility is a paean to the state's best-loved domestic animal. Everywhere the horse is celebrated, whether it is in the excellent introductory movie, **Thou Shalt Fly Without Wings**; amid the displays in the **International Museum of the Horse**, chronicling the animal's history and evolution; or at the twice-daily **Parade of Breeds**, where horses of every size, shape and pedigree strut their stuff. Envisioned as a facility to showcase part of Kentucky's heritage, the park became a reality in the 1970s when the state purchased the farm and turned it into a tourist attraction. It is also a premier exhibition center, staging numerous equestrian events annually. A statue of **Man O' War**, considered the greatest racehorse of all time, presides over the entrance. The acclaimed horse's remains were moved to the park in 1978 from nearby Faraway Farm where he died in 1947 at age 30.

The adjacent **American Saddle Horse Museum** (4093 Iron Works Pkwy.; ☎859-259-2746) commemorates the only breed native to Kentucky.

## Excursions

### White Hall State Historic Site★★
*19mi south of Lexington via I-75 at 500 White Hall Shrine Rd., Richmond.* ☞Visit by guided tour only, daily 10am–5:30pm. ☞$5. ☎606-623-9178. www.kystateparks.com.

This brooding, Italianate-style house guarded by concrete lions was home to the "Lion of White Hall," the flamboyant abolitionist **Cassius Marcellus Clay** (1810-1903). Scion of a wealthy family, Clay never realized his ambition to serve in Congress, but he was elected to the Kentucky General Assembly and was later appointed ambassador to Russia by President Abraham Lincoln.

His grand home consists of a house within a house: the simple 1798 Georgian residence built by his father and the elaborate overlay added after 1861. A notable feature is the indoor bathroom, which utilized rainwater collected from the rooftop.

### Shaker Village at Pleasant Hill★★
*25mi southwest of Lexington on US-68.* ⏱Open daily 10am–4:30pm. ☎859-734-5411. www.shakervillageky.org.

The United Society of Believers in Christ's Second Appearing, also known as "Shakers" for their odd movements during worship, had two colonies in Kentucky—this one and a smaller group at South Union (☞see WESTERN KENTUCKY). Simplicity, fine craftsmanship and celibacy were hallmarks of their way of life. On 4,000 acres high above the Kentucky River, the Pleasant Hill community flourished from 1805 until 1910. Its 500 members farmed

---

## Horse Industry

Early settlers in the Bluegrass discovered that the limestone strata underlying the region's rich soil fortified the water building strong bones, a requisite for winning racehorses. Horse farms sprang up around Lexington, and by 1789 the city claimed more horses than people. Today 450 horse farms dot the area. Although development has steadily encroached upon the farms as the area's population has soared, breeding champion racehorses remains a staple here. Here they can see their favorite steeds cavorting in a Bluegrass meadow, hard at work at the racetrack, or bought and sold.

A number of companies offer tours of the farms encircling Lexington: **Horse Farm Tours** (☎606-268-2906); **Blue Grass Tours** (☎606-252-5744); and **Edelstein Tours** (☎606-266-5465), to name a few. Or you can set out on your own driving tour with a special map provided by the **Lexington Convention and Visitors Bureau** (301 E. Vine St.; ☎606-233-7299; www.visitlex.com). If the bugle and the cry "they're off," get your blood pumping, you'll probably want to visit **Keeneland** (racemeets Apr & Sept; 4201 Versailles Rd., Lexington, KY; ☎606-254-3412) or **Louisville's Churchill Downs** (☞see LOUISVILLE).

and sold the products of their cottage industries (brooms, wooden boxes, garden seeds) as far afield as New Orleans. Today costumed interpreters demonstrate typical Shaker activities in 14 of the 33 restored buildings that are open to visitors. Don't miss the daily performance of Shaker songs and dances.

## Berea ★

*39mi S of Lexington (I-75). www.berea.com.*
The small city of Berea is known primarily as a craft center. **Berea College** *(101 Chestnut St.),* established in 1855 by wealthy landowner Cassius Clay, was founded to serve Appalachian youth. All students work for their tuition-free education. To sample the students' excellent crafts, visit the **Log House Craft Gallery** on Chestnut Street *(☎859-985-3226).* You can watch weavers at work at **Churchill Weavers** *(100 Churchill Dr.; ☎606-986-3127),* Berea's first non-college manufacturer.

# LOUISVILLE★★

MAP P227
EASTERN STANDARD TIME
POPULATION 256,231

Kentucky's largest city was founded in 1778 by George Rogers Clark, the military hero whose campaigns secured the west. Situated at the falls of the Ohio River, it was an ideal stopping point for westward travelers and soon became an important port and trading center. After the steamboat's demise, Louisville's central location made it an important rail hub. Iron foundries sprang up to serve the railroad industry, and by the turn of the century Louisville produced much of the country's decorative ironwork.

**Information:** Louisville Convention and Visitors Bureau. ☎502-584-2121. www.gotolouisville.com

**Don't Miss:** Churchill Downs, home of the world-famous Kentucky Derby.

**Kids:** Little ones like to swing at bat at the Louisville Slugger Museum.

## A Bit of History

Louisville's downtown is a bustling blend of commerce, government, and entertainment. Along the major thoroughfare, West Main Street, you'll find the Louisville Slugger Museum, **Louisville Science Center** *(727 W. Main St.; ☎502-561-6100),* and the lofty headquarters of healthcare giant Humana (1985, Peter Graves), its pink granite entrance flanked by two 50ft waterfalls. Across the street, steps lead to the *Belle of Louisville*—one of the few steamboats still plying the Ohio—is docked *(4th St. & River Rd.; ☎502-574-2992).*
Also downtown is the restored 1928 **Palace Theater** *(625 4th St.),* still used today for concerts, and Gideon Shryock's Greek Revival-style **Jefferson County Courthouse** *(531 W. Jefferson St.),* completed in 1860.

Long a cultural center, Louisville boasts the acclaimed Actor's Theatre, a respected symphony and ballet, and the Speed Art Museum. Well-known local pottery maker, **Louisville Stoneware** *(731 Brent St.; ☎502-582-1900)* offers tours of its facility.

## Sights

### Speed Art Museum★

*2035 S. 3rd St. ☎502-634-2700. www.speedmuseum.com.*
Numerous artists are represented in this delightful classically inspired building adjoining the University of Louisville campus. Although the museum, which opened in 1927, contains the work of numerous masters (Monet, Rembrandt, Rubens), two particular collections stand out: the **European Galleries** and the

**Kentucky Room**. The former features tapestries and Medieval decorative arts; the latter showcases paintings, sculpture and decorative arts with a Kentucky connection.

## Louisville Slugger Museum★

*800 W. Main St. ⏰Open Mon-Sat 10am–5pm, Sun 12pm–5pm. ∞$9. ♿☎502-588-7228. www.sluggermuseum.com.*

It would be hard to miss this downtown attraction with the 120ft-high baseball bat marking its threshold. Hillerich and Bradsby, manufacturers of the world-famous bats, have been a Louisville mainstay since 1884, when they became the first company to mass-produce this baseball essential.

The tour begins with an excellent movie introducing the sport of baseball. Visitors then walk through a baseball dugout to a full-size replica of Baltimore's Camden Yards stadium. Next, it's on to the exhibit area, where in one interactive highlight you can select your favorite pitcher to hurl a baseball your way at 90mph (as you watch behind Plexiglass). The tour ends with a walk through the factory that turns out 2,000 white-ash and maple bats a day.

## Farmington★

*3033 Bardstown Rd. ⏱Visit by guided tour only. ☐ ☎502-452-9920. www.historicfarmington.org.*

*Belle of Louisville on the Ohio River*

Greater Louisville CVB/www.gotolouisville.com

It's easy to see the Jeffersonian influence in this restored 1816 Federal home, with its secret stairway, wide central hallway and many-sided rooms. The spacious 14-room home was the centerpiece of a 550-acre hemp plantation operated from 1808 to 1865 by members of the Speed family. It was here that John and Lucy Speed raised their 11 children to appreciate a cultured lifestyle. Today Farmington reflects pieces of that lifestyle in its furnishings and objets d'art.

## Locust Grove★★

*561 Blankenbaker Lane. ⏰Open Mon-Sat 10am–4:30pm, Sun 1pm-4:30pm. ⏱Visit of house by guided tour only. ∞$6. ☐ ☎502-897-9845. www.locustgrove.org.*

Historically important as the last home of Louisville founder George Rogers Clark, this sweeping 1790s homestead was owned by his sister Lucy and her husband, William Croghan. Elderly and ill, Clark was cared for here by Lucy from 1809 until his death in 1818. It was here that William Clark, George's brother, and his partner Meriwether Lewis returned in 1806 after their historic expedition. One of the first brick houses in the region, Locust Grove is distinguished by its paneled walls, unusual built-in cabinets and its **ballroom**, which boasts extravagant 18C French wallpaper. Although few of the furnishings are original to the house, almost all are Kentucky-made, including the pair of andirons owned by the state's first governor, Isaac Shelby.

## Falls of the Ohio State Park and Interpretive Center★

Kids *201 W. Riverside Dr., Clarksville, IN. ⏰Open Mon-Sat 9am–5pm, Sun 1pm-5pm. ∞$4. ♿☐ ☎812-280-9970. www.fallsoftheohio.org; www.cismall.com/fallsoftheohio.*

The adjacent banks and bottom area of this peaceful park, just across the Ohio River from downtown Louisville, contain some of the richest Devonian **fossil deposits** in the world. The park's striking contemporary **Interpretive Center** is constructed of tiers of limestone and multicolored bricks, mirroring the fossil beds it interprets. Inside, a documentary traces the evolution of he fossil beds, formed more than 350 million years ago.

## hurchill Downs★★

*700 Central Ave. Visit by guided tour nly. Racemeets May, June & Nov.* 🍴♿️🅿️ *xcept during racemeets* ☎502-636-400. www.churchilldowns.com.

erhaps no Kentucky landmark is more amiliar than the twin spires of Churchill owns, home of the famed **Kentucky erby**★★★, the first contest in the Triple Crown series (the other two are the elmont in New York and the Preakess in Maryland). First run in 1875, he Derby is America's oldest continual ports event.

isitors to Churchill Downs can view the risp green and white barns and grandtand of the historic track as well as the **entucky Derby Museum**★★ *(704 entral Ave. www.derbymuseum.com),* whose pièce de résistance is its opening **video presentation**. Projected on a anoramic 360-degree screen, the presntation captures the full flavor of Derby ay as Thoroughbred hooves thunder o the finish line amid background trains of "My Old Kentucky Home." The useum also possesses tapes of every erby since 1918 and offers interactive xhibits where guests can test their agering abilities. Isaac Murphy and ther black Derby-winning jockeys are eatured in an exhibit celebrating Afrian Americans in racing.

## Excursions

### My Old Kentucky Home State Park★★

*40mi south of Louisville via US-31 East in Bardstown. 501 E. Stephen Foster Ave. (US-150).* �*Visit by guided tour only.* ⚠️♿️🅿️ ☎502-348-3502. http://kystate parks.com/stateparks/mk.

The "Old Kentucky Home" immortalized in a ballad by composer **Stephen Foster** (1826-64) is actually Federal Hill, a Federal-style brick home built in 1818 by Foster's cousin, Judge John Rowan. It was on a visit to his cousin's house in 1852 that Foster, already a well-known songwriter, composed what is now Kentucky's state song. In 1923 the home was officially renamed "My Old Kentucky Home" when it was bequeathed to the state by Rowan heirs.

### Abraham Lincoln Birthplace National Historic Site★

*58mi south of Louisville on US-31 East, 3mi south of Hodgenville.* ♿️🅿️ ☎270-358-3137. www.nps.gov/abli.

Abraham Lincoln (👆*see CHICAGO infobox*) spent the first two years of his life on this rocky land, known locally as the Sinking Spring farm. Go outside to climb the 56 steps—one for each year of Lincoln's life—to the granite and marble **memorial** (1909, John Russell Pope) that encloses a replica of the cabin where Lincoln was born.

# WESTERN KENTUCKY★

MAP P227

CENTRAL STANDARD TIME

rom the edge of the Bluegrass westward to the Mississippi River lies the more ecently settled region of western Kentucky, an area of fertile farms, burley obacco and barbecue. What visitors will find in western Kentucky is the world's ost extensive known cave system and the site of a Civil War battle at the stragic Mississippi River town of Columbus. Here **Columbus-Belmont State Park** *te. 58, in Columbus;* ☎270-677-2327) commemorates the February 1862 battle in hich Union forces beat back the Rebels and gained control of the river.

**Information:** Kentucky's Western Waterland.
☎270-928-4411. www.kentuckylakebarkley.org
**Orient Yourself:** Once the unknown West, the area was a magnet for experimental communities such as the Shakers and Harmonists.
**Don't Miss:** Mother Nature's majesty at Mammoth Cave.

## Daniel Boone

In the annals of Kentucky history, Daniel Boone (born in Pennsylvania in 1734) has achieved almost mythic status. Every Kentucky schoolchild knows how he carved his name and the words "killed a bar [bear]" into a Kentucky tree in 1760. But Boone's lasting legacy is his creation of a major transportation link to the west.

In 1775 Boone blazed the first trail through the natural pass in the Appalachians known as the Cumberland Gap (*psee EAST TENNESSEE*) to the Bluegrass, opening the land route westward. That same year, he established Boonesborough, an outpost on the Kentucky River near present-day Richmond, Kentucky. Beset by Indian attacks and frequent flooding, the fort did not survive. Reconstructed in 1974, **Fort Boonesborough** (*in Fort Boonesborough State Park on Rte. 627, 4375 Boonesborough Rd., Richmond, KY; ☎859-527-3131*) is now a living-history museum.

Boone spent his final years exploring, venturing as far west as present-day Yellowstone National Park. He died in Missouri; his remains and those of his wife, Rebecca, were moved to the **Frankfort Cemetery** (*215 E. Main St., Frankfort, KY*).

# Sights

## Mammoth Cave National Park★★★

IIIII *8mi west of Cave City via Rte. 70 (or 9mi northwest of I-65 from Exit 48 at Park City).* •Visit of cave by guided tour only (park open daily year-round); reservations recommended in summer, ☎301-722-1257. ⚠☒♿📇Park information; ☎270-758-2180. www.nps.gov/maca.

The world's longest cave (more than 350mi of the five-level labyrinth have been mapped), Mammoth underlies three Kentucky counties.

Several tours are offered into Mammoth's depths, taking visitors as far as 360ft below ground. Among the sights are the ruins of an 1810-12 saltpeter mining operation; a decorative stone formation called **Frozen Niagara**; and the underground **River Styx**, home of eyeless fish. Designated a UNESCO World Heritage site and an International Biosphere Reserve, the cave is home to the world's most diverse cave ecosystem, including some life forms that cannot survive outside its walls. *Cave temperatures average 54°F year-round; bring a sweater or light jacket.*

## National Corvette Museum

*350 Corvette Dr. (off I-65 Exit 28), Bowling Green.* ◷Open daily 8am–5pm. ♿📇 ☎270-781-7973. www.corvett museum.com.

This unique museum was inspired by its neighbor across the road, the only plant in America where Corvettes are assembled. The low-slung building with brightly colored modules harbors 68,000sq ft of exhibits tracing the evolution of the first American sports car.

## Shaker Museum at South Union★

*Near the junction of US-68/80 & Rte. 144 in South Union.* 📇 ☎270-542-4167. www lshakermuseum.com.

This community, though smaller than the Pleasant Hill group, was wealthier in land and property. Its 349 members owned 6,000 acres and more than 20 buildings—only a fraction of which remain. Like their Pleasant Hill counterparts, they sold a variety of products. The colony lasted from 1807 until 1921 when the Industrial Age and declining membership sealed its fate.

# MEMPHIS AREA

Like the ancient Egyptian city for which it is named, Memphis, Tennessee, grew beside a great river to become a hub of trade, culture and population for the surrounding delta and beyond. The major urban presence on the Mississippi River between St. Louis and New Orleans, Memphis began as a 19C cotton exporting town and evolved into a distinctive business, transportation and tourism center with a wide-reaching regional identity—unusual for US cities. For those who wonder where "the South," "the Midwest," and "the West" merge (or collide) in the American imagination, the answer is "somewhere around here."

Memphis, home of Elvis Presley and the blues, sits just across the river from Arkansas, home of the quintessential "New South" Democrat, US President Bill Clinton (whose Southern accent sounds remarkably like Elvis'). Yet in Memphis, Civil War and Old South sights are far less prominent than the city's African-American musical and civil rights legacies. Although Little Rock, the Arkansas capital, is definitely Southern, the state is overrun with mountains and imbued with a pioneer sensibility that leans more westward than toward the Deep South. A few hours' drive north lies historic Eureka Springs, a popular resort in the heart of the Ozark Mountains. Like Hot Springs National Park near Little Rock, Eureka Springs has been a tourist attraction offering "healing" waters for generations. From Eureka Springs, it's only 60mi to **Branson**, Missouri, an incongruously pioneer setting for big-production-style musical theater. In Branson, top country and Las Vegas performers offer mainstream middle-American entertainment (no edgy, experimental productions here) and draw crowds of thousands.

From a vantage point high on the Memphis bluffs overlooking the Mississippi, it is easy to understand why westbound explorers, hardscrabble pioneers, cotton merchants, riverboat gamblers, and innumerable hopefuls toting harmonicas and guitars all began—or ended—their journeys in Memphis. For the modern traveler, an intriguing cultural question is where and how—somewhere between Memphis and Branson, a distance of 300mi—the South has irretrievably ended and the Midwest has begun.

## Area Address Book

For coin ranges, see the Legend on the cover flap.

### WHERE TO STAY

**$$$ The Peabody** – *149 Union Ave., Memphis, TN.* ☎901-529-4000. *www.memphis.com. 464 rooms.* The city's largest and oldest hotel (1925) remains the hub of downtown's social scene. Guests gather in the two-story lobby at 11am and 5pm to watch the resident ducks march down a red carpet to take their rightful place in the famous marble fountain. New classic-style furnishings and pale pastel fabrics have polished the aging dowager's appearance.

**$$ Talbot Heirs Guesthouse** – *99 S. 2nd St., Memphis, TN.* ▣ ☎*901-527-9772. www.talbothouse.com. 8 rooms.* Celebrities call this intimate property across the street from the Peabody home away from home. Accommodations are mini-apartments ranging in style from retro 1960s to simple Shaker design. All come with separate living areas and full kitchens—stocked on request. Breakfast muffins, scones and fresh fruit are already in the pantry when you arrive.

**$$ The Capital Hotel** – *111 W. Markham St., Little Rock, AR (for Ozarks).* ⚹⚹▣ ☎*501-374-7474. www.thecapitalhotel. com. 123 rooms.* Since Bill Clinton's first presidential campaign, this landmark has been the headquarters of politicians and international media. The cast-iron façade was pre-assembled and bolted onto the original building back in the 1870s. A stained-glass skylight caps the two-story lobby. Four-poster and canopy beds provide Old World glamour.

### WHERE TO EAT

**$$ Benne Vita** – *3710 Cantrell Rd., Little Rock, AR (for Ozarks).* **Northern Italian.** This fine Italian eatery proffers such rich entrees such as lobster ravioli with alfredo lemon butter sauce and lasagna madde with veal, beef, prok, Italian sausage and portabellas. There also a fairly priced wine list and alfresco dining on the covered deck.

**$ Blues City Cafe** – *138 Beale St., Memphis, TN.* ☎*901-526-3637.* **Southern.** The top jukebox joint on the downtown club strip. Aluminum chairs and worn Formica tables create the right atmosphere to down hefty portions of porterhouse steak, meaty pork ribs and fried catfish. The kitchen serves until 3am on weekdays and until 5am on weekends, so you can eat before or after enjoying the live blues band in the next room.

**$ The Rendezvous** – *52 S. 2nd St., Memphis, TN.* 🕐*Closed Sun & Mon.* ☎*901-523-2746.* **Barbecue.** Residents swear this basement restaurant off a downtown alley makes the best pit-barbecued pork ribs in town. The dry rub is a secret family recipe, so don't ask. Ample portions come with requisite baked beans and "slaw."

# MEMPHIS★★

MAP P238
CENTRAL TIME
POPULATION 650,100

Known as "the home of the blues and the birthplace of rock and roll," this bustling Mississippi River port is a lively place with an appealing blend of Southern manners, cosmopolitan riches, and rough-and-tumble river blues; its most internationally famous resident, the late Elvis Presley, personified all these characteristics. Today, visitors to Memphis' legendary Beale Street find that the spirit of Presley's music—as well as that of bluesmen W.C. Handy, B.B. King and countless others—is alive and thriving in dozens of small clubs. On a more somber note, Memphis was also the site of the 1968 assassination of civil rights leader Dr. Martin Luther King, Jr.

▯ **Information:** ☎901-543-5300. www.memphistravel.com
▶ **Orient Yourself:** Memphis lives on the Mississippi, across the river from Arkansas
◔ **Don't Miss:** The American icon of Graceland.
🄺🄸🄳🅂 **Kids:** No one of any age can resist watching ducks walking the red carpet at the Peabody Hotel.

## A Bit of History

Although French explorer René-Robert Cavelier, Sieur de La Salle claimed the area for France in 1682, this desirable property high on a bluff above the river delta was sought after by indigenous Chickasaw tribes, as well as by Great Bri in and Spain. After the Revolutionary War the area came under control of the newly formed United States, and by 1819 military hero **Andrew Jackson** and others had organized and named the new settlement Memphis. The town became a center for merchants and slave traders who bought and sold cotton, slaves and supplies for plantations throughout the vast fertile delta, from Kentucky south to the port of New Orleans. A strategic target during the Civil War, Memphis was held by Union forces from 1862 until the war's end.

Three virulent yellow fever epidemics decimated the city between 1867 and 1878, with thousands dying (primarily the more susceptible white population) and thousands more fleeing the mosquito-infested terrain. In 1879 the city went bankrupt, had its charter revoked by the state legislature and officially ceased to exist for 12 years.

Steamboat trade revitalized the river port in the 1890s, and by the early 20C, Beale Street, the African-American commercial and entertainment district, was home to the nation's leading black-owned businesses. For a new generation of free Americans of color—former slaves, aspiring merchants and ambitious entertainers—Memphis became one of the most attractive destinations in the country.

Following a difficult period in the mid-20C—marked by the Great Depression, Jim Crow laws, and a decline in the US cotton market—the city has rebounded with the revival of Beale Street and the preservation of the surviving Adams Avenue mansions in the **Victorian Village Historic District**. The latter includes the nearby Second Empire-style **Woodruff-Fontaine House Museum** (680 Adams Ave.; ☎901-526-1469), built in 1871. Today the **Pyramid Arena** (1 Auction Ave.; ☎901-521-9675), a silver-and-glass sports arena, gleams on the river, and the historic **Peabody Hotel** (149 Union Ave.; ☎901-529-4000) parades its main attraction—a group of mallard ducks—on a red carpet across the lobby twice each day.

To the casual observer, the giant river that flows past Memphis seems oddly ignored, except by the **Memphis Queen Line** sightseeing riverboats (45 Riverside Dr.; ☎901-527-5694) and the occasional barge. Appearances aside, the Port of Memphis continues to rank as one of the country's busiest inland ports, with cotton again a major export.

## Sights

### Graceland★★★

*3764 Elvis Presley Blvd. Tours originate at the visitor center at Graceland Plaza. ◉Open Mon-Sat 9am–5pm, Sun 10am–4pm. ☞$25. ✗ ♿ 🅿 ☎ 901-332-3322. www.elvis-presley.com.*

Even for those inured to the Elvis myth, a visit to Graceland is by far the best way to begin to understand the exuberant cross-cultural heritage of country, blues, gospel, soul and rock that put Memphis and its favorite son on the world's musical map. Graceland, the estate of the late **Elvis Presley** (1935-77), the "King of Rock 'n' Roll," sits on 13 acres in suburban Memphis and vividly illustrates the rags-to-riches life of a young man who, by the age of 22, had become one of the most famous people in the world. Born poor in a tiny two-room

Courtesy Memphis Convention & Visitors Bureau

*Beale Street*

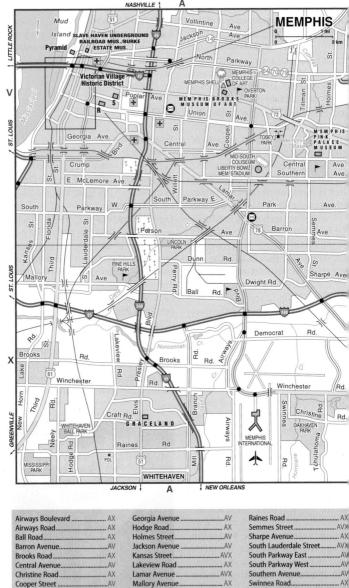

house about 90mi south of Memphis in Tupelo, Mississippi, Presley moved to a poor Memphis neighborhood near Beale Street when he was a teenager. In 1957 the singer purchased Graceland, a Southern Colonial-style mansion built in 1939 for a wealthy Memphis doctor.

Stepping through the doorway of Graceland—one of the few places where Presley could escape the incessant attention of media and fans—visitors immediately sense how much the singer became a prisoner of his own fame. Furnished in 1950s to 1970s style—white plush carpeting, a themed den called "the jungle room," avocado and harvest-gold kitchen appliances—the house was equipped above all for music, with Elvis' sound system carrying music to every room. In addition to touring the mansion, visitors are steered through **Elvis' Trophy Building**—which contains the singer's gold records, awards, costumes, jewelry and guitars—and the meditation garden where Elvis is buried.

Tours begin and end across the street from the house at Graceland Plaza, a complex of gift shops, restaurants and a US Post Office (for an official Graceland postmark). Three additional attractions can be found here: the **Lisa Marie** and **Hound Dog II JetStar** custom jet airplanes; the **Sincerely Elvis Museum**; and the **Elvis Presley Automobile Museum**, which displays Elvis' pink 1955 Cadillac, among other vehicles.

After touring Graceland, fans can take a free shuttle to **Sun Studio** (706 Union Ave.; visit by guided tour only; ☎901-521-0664), where Elvis got his start, along with some of the biggest names in American music (Jerry Lee Lewis, Johnny Cash). A half-hour studio tour consists of standing inside the recording room and listening to session outtakes.

*Sun Studio*

## The National Civil Rights Museum★★

450 Mulberry St. ○Open Mon-Sat 9am–pm, Sun 1pm–5pm. ≈$12. &🅿☎901-21-9699. www.civilrightsmuseum.org.

From the outside, this unusual museum looks exactly like what it once was—the 1950s-era Lorraine Motel, the finest lodging available for generations of Jim Crow-era African Americans traveling through Memphis. The hotel hosted such luminaries as Cab Calloway, Aretha Franklin, B.B. King, and civil rights leader **Dr. Martin Luther King, Jr.**, who was assassinated on the balcony outside his room here on April 4, 1968.

Today the former hotel is a 22,800sq ft memorial depicting key events of the US civil rights movement in the 1950s and 60s. Visitors will be moved by the spectacle of life-size mannequins—Memphis' striking garbage workers—who bravely carried picket signs declaring "I AM A MAN" in front of police armed with bayonets.

By far the most emotionally wrenching space in the museum, however, is the **upstairs balcony** and **hotel rooms 306 and 307**, left as they were on April 4, 1968, as Dr. King's aides tried frantically to save him after the sniper's attack. In silent testimony to enduring grief, memorial wreaths adorn the balcony railing, and the two vintage Cadillacs used by the King entourage are still parked below.

## Beale Street Historic District★★

*Beale St. between Main & 4th Sts.* ✗ & www.bealestreet.com.

A four-block-long, neon-lit midway of clubs, restaurants, record stores and souvenir shops (where automobiles are off-limits after dark on weekends), Beale Street is a living museum that nurtures new talent for America's most distinctive musical genre—the **Mississippi blues**.

## Singin' The Blues

As Archibald MacLeish once versified, "a poem should not mean, but be," and so it is with the blues, as difficult to define as poetry.

While certainly descriptive of a state of mind, the term *blues* derives from what musicologists call a "blue note"—a technique of deliberately flatting (lowering) the third, fifth or seventh note of a major chord from time to time to give a minor or "bent" sound on certain phrases in a song.

In its most basic form, blues is a powerfully rhythmic, repetitive, guitar-based folk music with simple, often wry lyrics that mourn or mock the players' lives of hard labor, love and loss. With three-line stanzas of recurring phrases and chord progressions that are easy to follow, blues music is accessible to listeners and amateur musicians alike. In the hands of highly skilled blues artists such as the legendary **Robert Johnson** (1911-38), **Muddy Waters** (1915-83) or **B.B. "Blues Boy" King** (b.1925), the blues can be a spellbinding evocation of universal human emotions.

An amalgam of African slave chants, work songs and spirituals, this unique American musical form was born in the dusty cotton fields of the Mississippi River delta and traveled north on the "blues highway"—US-61—that ran alongside the river from Vicksburg to Memphis. By the early 1900s, the music was known as the Delta, Mississippi, or Memphis blues (as distinguished from the Chicago blues, a northern descendant with a more urban, amplified and less acoustic sound). In Memphis, this indigenous music was adapted and expanded upon—and published in precise musical scores—by classically trained African-American composer and bandleader **W.C. Handy** (1873-1958). Known as "the Father of the Blues," Handy composed hundreds of songs—the "Memphis Blues," the "St. Louis Blues," the "Beale Street Blues"—and popularized them among black and white musicians and listeners nationwide. His sophisticated tunes had a major impact on the development of American jazz and cabaret music as well as, of course, rock and roll.

Today, devoted blues fans from around the world can find first-rate live blues, both old and new, in dozens of clubs and outdoor venues in Memphis and smaller towns across the region. Memphis' **Beale Street** district draws thousands to blues festivals each year, including the annual **W.C. Handy Blues Awards** weekend *(late May)*, the **Memphis Music Festival** *(summer)* and the **Labor Day Weekend Blues Bash** *(Sept)*.

A stroll down Beale on a spring evening is a trip through a musical wonderland, with impossibly sweet guitar licks and bluesy voices emanating from every door. The **Center for Southern Folklore** (☎901-525-3655), a combination of blues club, soda fountain, folk-art and rare-records gallery, museum and archive, is a blues fanatic's paradise; it's the sort of place where bluesman Gatemouth Moore or harmonica great Charlie Musselwhite may simply drop in to play. Another required stop is the small white-frame **W.C. Handy House** (no. 352; P ☎901-527-3427), relocated from north Alabama in honor of the bandleader and composer of "Beale Street Blues" and countless other tunes.

### Hunt-Phelan Home★★
*533 Beale St.* 🍴♿P ☎901-525-822⁙
*www.huntphelan.com.*
Owned by the same family for 160 year⁙ this elegant Georgian mansion designe⁙ by Robert Mills still boasts most of it⁙ original **furniture**—much of which wa⁙ hidden from the Yankees in an elabo⁙ rately fitted railroad boxcar, Mrs. Hunt⁙ refuge during the Civil War.

### Mud Island River Park★
*Accessible via monorail; station at 12⁙ S. Front St.* 🍴♿P ☎901-576-7241 (He⁙ ritage Tours). www.mudisland.com.
A man-made island just offshore fro⁙ downtown Memphis, this 52-acre ente⁙ tainment complex includes a 5,000-sea⁙

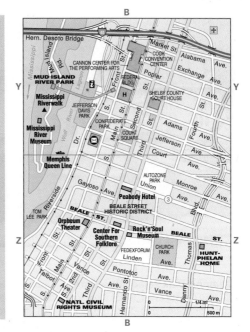

amphitheater, a museum of river history, a topographically accurate scale model of the Mississippi River, and the **Memphis Belle Pavilion**, featuring one of the most famous B-17 bombers of World War II. At the **Mississippi River Museum** visitors can tour life-size replicas of a Mississippi riverboat and an ironclad Civil War gunboat. Outside, wade in the half-mile-long **Mississippi Riverwalk**, which replicates in miniature the river's 1,000mi journey from Cairo, Illinois, to the Gulf of Mexico.

## Slavehaven/
### Burkle Estate Museum★

*826 N. 2nd St.* ♿ 🅿 ☎*901-527-3427.*
This c.1850 bungalow on the edge of "the Pinch" district of Memphis—so named because of the poverty of its early immigrant settlers—is thought to have been a stop on the **Underground Railroad**, the secretive network of abolitionists and sympathizers who helped slaves escape

the Deep South. Built by German immigrant Jacob Burkle, the house has a trap-door and a **cellar** where runaway slaves could hide on their route north.

## Memphis Brooks
## Museum of Art★

*1934 Poplar Ave., in Overton Park.* 🕐*Open Tue-Wed, Fri 10am–4pm, Thu 10am–8pm, Sun 11:30am–5pm.* 🕐*Closed Mon.* ✺*$7.* ✗♿🅿 ☎*901-544-6200. www.brooks museum.org.*
Tennessee's oldest fine-arts museum, the Brooks houses works by Italian Renaissance and Baroque masters (Van Dyck, Manfredi); French Impressionists (Corot, Pissarro, Renoir, Sisley); 18C and 19C English and American artists (Gainsborough, Stuart, Homer); and 20C and contemporary works (O'Keeffe, Wesley). Exhibits in the original 1916 Beaux-Arts building range from Greek and Roman antiquities to the Renaissance

Courtesy Memphis Convention & Visitors Bureau

*Pink Palace*

### Memphis Pink Palace Museum★

Kids *3050 Central Ave.* ◎*Open Mon-Sat 9am–5pm, Sun 12pm–5pm.* ⊜*$8.75.* ☎*901-320-6320.*

Opened in 1930 as the Memphis Museum of Natural History and Industrial Arts, the pink marble mansion houses an unusual mix of human history, anthropology and biological wonders that range from the scientific to the bizarre. The original structure was begun in 1922 as the home of Memphis entrepreneur Clarence Saunders, whose Piggly Wiggly stores became the first modern, serve-yourself grocery chain. Exhibits in the expanded 170,000sq ft facility—which contains an IMAX theater and planetarium—include a replica of the first Piggly Wiggly store and other features of Memphis history.

### Dixon Gallery and Gardens ★

*4339 Park Ave.* ⚹ P ☎*901-761-5250. www.dixon.org.*

Opened to the public in 1976, this first-rate art gallery is set among 17 acres of formal English gardens. Here works of art by the likes of Braque, Utrillo, Cézanne, Chagall, Monet and Renoir are displayed in two distinctly different settings: hung in the elegant living and dining rooms of the original Georgian-style **Dixon Residence** (built in 1941 for British-born cotton merchant Hugo Dixon and his Memphis-born wife); and arrayed gallery-style in a modern addition. The Dixon's decorative arts include the 300 plus-item **Adler Pewter Collection**, which spans three centuries, and the stunning nearly 600-piece Stout Collection of **18C German porcelai**n.

## Excursion

### Shiloh National Military Park★

*110mi east of Memphis. Take Hwy 72 East to Hwy 22 North to the park.* ⚹ P ☎*901-689-5696. www.nps.gov/shna.*

Nearly 24,000 soldiers were killed, wounded or missing after the two-day Civil War battle that raged here in 1862. Beginning with a Confederate surprise attack on Gen. Ulysses S. Grant's Army of Tennessee, the prolonged battle employed 62 cannon on a site called "the Hornet's Nest," and included gunboat fire from ironclads on the Tennessee River. At battle's end, the Confederates retreated.

Take the self-guided, 9.5mi **driving tour** of the 4,000-acre battlefield that leads from the National Cemetery and Pittsburg Landing on the river past mass burial trenches, numerous state markers, "Bloody Pond" and the site of the Shiloh Meeting House—from which the battle took its name.

# THE OZARKS ★

MICHELIN MAP 584
CENTRAL STANDARD TIME

Strictly speaking, the Ozark Mountains define the region north of the Arkansas River including northern Arkansas, southern Missouri, northeast Oklahoma and part of southern Illinois. The mountains are actually an eroded sandstone and limestone plateau that uplifted out of the ocean some 285 million years ago, rather than a true mountain range. Rugged valleys, heavily forested hills, fast-flowing rivers, spectacular limestone caverns, and abundant springs (including Hot Springs National Park) characterize this region, providing enough outdoor activities to keep even the most energetic visitor busy.

- **Information:** ☎501-682-7777. www.arkansas.com
- **Don't Miss:** The William J. Clinton Presidential Library.
- **Organizing Your Time:** Save time for the healing waters of the Hot Springs.

## A Bit of History

Traces of the region's earliest inhabitants can be found in the form of pictographs and petroglyphs etched into the walls of limestone caves. In 1686 Frenchman Henri de Tonti established the first permanent white settlement near the confluence of the Arkansas and Mississippi rivers. In 1819 de Tonti's post became the capital of Arkansas Territory. Two years later the territorial capital was moved upriver to centrally located **Little Rock**, which today remains the state capital as well as the jumping-off point for sojourns to the Ozarks (*Little Rock Convention & Visitors Bureau, 7 Statehouse Plaza, 400 W. Markham St.; ☎501-376-4781; www.littlerock.com*). **President Bill Clinton** made his election-night victory speeches in both 1992 and 1996 at the 1842 Greek Revival **Old State House Museum**★ (*300 W. Markham St.; ◷Open Mon-Sat 9am–6pm, Sun 1pm-5pm. ☎501-324-9685*). In 2004 The **William J. Clinton Presidential Library** (*1200 President Clinton Ave.; ☎501-374-4242*) opened its doors. The little town of **Mountain View** (*104mi north of Little Rock at the intersection of Rtes. 9, 5 & 14*) prides itself on its folk-music tradition, which draws country and folk musicians from far and wide to events such as the annual **Arkansas Folk Festival** in April. At the **Ozark Folk Center**★ (*1.5mi north of Mountain View off Rte. 9; ☎870-269-3851*), you can watch artisans woodworking, weaving and playing folk music.

Fans of a wider variety of music flock to **Branson**, just over the Arkansas state line in Missouri (*168mi north of Little Rock; tourist information ☎417-334-4136*), where a dazzling array of Las Vegas-style shows star performers such as the Osmonds and comedian Yakov Smirnoff. With more theater seats than Broadway, "America's live-entertainment capital" attracts millions of visitors each year to its strip of theaters along congested Route 76.

## Hot Springs National Park ★★

*58mi southwest of Little Rock (take I-30 South to US-270 West to Rte. 7/Central Ave.). Visitor center located in the Fordyce Bathhouse on Central Ave. in Hot Springs, AR. ⚠ ☎501-624-3383. www.nps.gov/hosp.*

Hot Springs' therapeutic waters have been attracting visitors for hundreds, perhaps thousands, of years, beginning with the early Indians who bathed here. Extraordinarily pure water from the springs is heated thousands of feet below the earth's surface, and bubbles up through faults in the underlying sandstone at a constant 143°F. The warm water flows from 47 springs at

*Bathhouse Row, Hot Springs National Park*

© National Park Service/Gail Sears

the average total rate of 850,000 gallons per day.

Famous 20C visitors have included presidents Franklin Delano Roosevelt and Harry Truman, and gangster Al Capone.

Begin your tour at the visitor center on magnolia-lined Central Avenue, also known as **Bathhouse Row**★. The 1915 **Fordyce**★ is the grandest of the eight remaining early-20C bathhouse structures, most of which went out of business when bathing declined in the 1970s. It has been completely restored and offers visitors a vivid look at what "taking the waters" once meant. Guided tours of teh Fordyce Bathhouse are given by volunteers; special group tours are available by reservation.

Today visitors can enjoy a traditional bathing experience at the **Buckstaff Bath House** (509 Central Ave.; ☎501-623-2308), the only one of the original bathhouses currently open to the public. Most of the springs have been capped, with the waters diverted to a central distribution center, but the spring at the corner of Central Avenue and Fountain Street is easily accessible. It tumbles down the hillside like most springs originally did.

A short drive from town, the 216ft **Hot Springs Mountain Tower** (take Central Ave. to Fountain St. to Hot Springs Mountain Dr.; ☎501-623-6035) offers sweeping **views**★ of the town and surrounding countryside.

# Northern Arkansas

Nestled among the mountains and deep valleys here are a host of historic sites, charming small towns, and the popular resort of Eureka Springs. For a lovely drive, take **Scenic Highway 7**★ from Russellville (77mi northwest of Little Rock via I-40) and drive north to Harrison. This 88mi stretch traverses the **Ozark National Forest** and snakes through the mountains, past towns with names such as Marble Falls and Booger Hollow—"Population 7, Countin' One Coon Dog," reads the sign.

## Blanchard Springs Caverns★

*15mi northwest of Mountain View on Rte. 14.* ☞*Visit by guided tour only, daily 8am–5pm.* △ ☺ ℗ ☎ 479-964-7200. www.fs.fed.us/oonf/ozark/recreation/caverns.html.

Part of Ozark National Forest, this cave, filled with flowstones, rimstone terraces and underground rivers, is among the most beautiful of America's cave systems. A guided tour (1hr; offered all year) of the .4mi **Dripstone Trail** covers the older part of the caverns (240ft deep) and takes in the 1,150ft-long **Cathedral Room**. The more challenging 1.2mi **Discovery Trail** tour (1 1/2hrs; offered only in summer) passes through a younger, deeper system (366ft deep) and requires visitors to navigate 700 steps.

## Eureka Springs★

*42mi west of Harrison on US-62.* ℹ*Visitor Information Center is located at 137 W. Van Buren St.* ☎501-253-8737. www.eurekasprings.org.

Located just south of the Missouri border, Eureka Springs was long revered by native Indians for the rejuvenating waters that flow from its 42 springs. A famed health resort in the 1890s, Eureka Springs now offers antique shops and crafts galleries (along Spring St.) as well as the splendidly preserved turn-of-the-century buildings that line the steep, winding streets of the downtown **Eureka Springs Historic District**. The 1901 Palace Hotel and Bath House (135 Spring St.; ☎501-253-7474) is one of several places in town that carry on the 19C bathing tradition.

# MIAMI AREA

Called the Gold Coast in part because of its proliferation of valuable real estate, Florida's most heavily developed strip extends along the Atlantic in a 70mi-long megalopolis from Miami to Palm Beach, and encompasses one-third of the state's population. In sharp contrast, just to the west lie the nearly unpopulated expanses of the Everglades, linked to Miami by the Tamiami Trail (US-41).

Before the arrival of the first European explorers, such as Spaniards Pedro Menéndez de Avilés and Ponce de León, Tequesta and Calusa Indians inhabited South Florida. With the exception of the swampy Everglades, the interior of the region—still predominantly agrarian—was conducive to the hunting and gathering methods of these early inhabitants, who supplemented their diet with fish and mollusks.

Synonymous with warm sunshine and fresh oranges, the Miami area became an established tourist mecca in the 1890s after the Florida East Coast Railway (FEC), bankrolled by railroad tycoon Henry Flagler, finally reached Palm Beach and Miami. Between 1945 and 1954, more new hotels were established in the Greater Miami area than in all other US states combined. Today southeast Florida still attracts hordes of visitors to its year-round warm weather, clear blue waters and white-sand beaches.

Miami

A cultural melting pot of peoples, foods, festivals and languages, the Miami area offers a diverse range of entertainment; snorkeling on offshore coral reefs; dancing to Latino rhythms in Miami nightclubs; admiring the Art Deco architecture of Miami Beach; and alligator-watching in the grassy expanses of the Everglades.

© Greater Miami CVB

*Collins Avenue, Miami Beach*

# Area Address Book

## GETTING THERE

**Miami International Airport (MIA):**
☎305-876-7000 or www.miami-airport.com; 7mi northwest of downtown. Multilingual Information Service in Concourses B, D, G & E. Transportation to downtown via SuperShuttle (*$15;* ☎871-8210), taxi (*$20–$25*), Metrobus and hotel courtesy shuttles. Rental car agencies are located near the airport.
**Amtrak train** station: 8303 N.W. 37th Ave., ☎305-835-1221 or 800-872-7245, www.amtrak.com. **Greyhound/Trailways bus** stations: Miami International Airport; 4111 N.W. 27th St.; 700 Biscayne Blvd.; and 7101 Harding Ave., Miami Beach; ☎800-231-2222, www.greyhound.com.

## GETTING AROUND

Miami-Dade Transit Agency connects Greater Miami and the beaches via Metrorail, Metromover and Metrobus. **Metrorail** trains connect downtown Miami to surrounding areas (*$1.50, exact change required*). **Metromover** elevated rail system links the Brickell Ave. and Omni areas, and loops around downtown (*free*). **Metrobus** operates countywide (*$1.50, exact change required*). Schedules and route information: ☎305-770-3131. Disabled visitors: ☎800-874-7245. Tri-Rail provides **commuter rail** service between West Palm Beach and greater Miami and connects to Metrorail (*$3.50–$9.25 round-trip*). Schedules and route information: ☎728-8445, www.tri-rail.com. **Taxi:** Metro Taxi (*☎305-888-8888*); Flamingo Taxi (*☎305-885-7000*); Yellow Cab (*☎305-444-4444*). **Water Taxi** shuttle (*☎954-467-6677*) operates 7 days a week throughout Ft. Lauderdale (*$11, all day pass*).

## VISITOR INFORMATION

For a free visit planner, maps and information on accommodations, shopping, entertainment, festivals and recreational activities, contact the **Greater Miami Convention and Visitors Bureau**, 701 Brickell Ave., Suite 2700, Miami FL 33131, ☎305-539-3000, www.miamiandbeaches.com; or **Miami Beach Visitor Center**, 1920 Meridian Ave., Miami Beach FL 33139, ☎305-674-1300, www.miamibeachchamber.com.

## WHERE TO STAY

**Hotel reservation services**: Greater Miami Hotel & the Beaches Association, ☎305-531-3553; Accommodations Express, www.accommodationsexpress.com; Central Reservation Service, ☎407-740-6442, www.reservation-services.com. **Bed & Breakfast reservations**: Florida Bed and Breakfast Inns, ☎281-499-1374, www.florida-inns.com. **Hostels**: **Hostelling International**: Miami Beach, ☎305-534-2988, www.ClayHotel.com; and Key West, ☎305-296-5719.

## WHERE TO STAY

*For coin ranges, see the Legend on the cover flap.*

**$$$ The Biltmore Hotel** – *1200 Anastasia Ave., Coral Gables, FL.* ☎05-445-1926. *www.biltmorehotel.com. 279 rooms.* Coral Gables' National Historic Landmark looks like a misplaced Spanish palace. Vaulted hand-painted ceilings, palm-filled courtyards and balustraded balconies are just some of the features that have attracted royalty and movie stars here since 1926. Then there's the 1.25-million-gallon pool and personalized service.

**$$$ Delano** – *1685 Collins Ave., Miami Beach, FL.* ☎305-672-2000. *www.delano-hotel.com. 238 rooms.* South Beach's minimalist trend started with Philippe Starcke's redo of this 1947 beachside oasis. Billowing white curtains—no doors—give access to the lobby, where more curtains separate lounge areas sparsely clad with antiques, bric-a-brac and Modern art. Contemporary white-on-white guest quarters boast top amenities.

**$$$ Naples Grand Resort & Club** – *475 Seagate Dr., Naples, FL.* ☎239-597-3232. *www.naplesgrandresort.com. 474 rooms.* Clam Pass Park wildlife preserve forms the backyard of this resort. A contemporary decor dighlighted by greens, golds, and oranges set a sophisticated tropical mood. Amenities include an 18-hole golf course and 15 tennis courts.

**$$ The Hotel** – *801 Collins Ave., Miami Beach, FL.* ☎305-531-2222. *www.thehotelofsouthbeach.com. 52 rooms.* Todd Oldham designed nearly everything in this renovated Art Deco gem (1936) off Ocean Drive. A huge tile mosaic and velveteen couches, in rose, green and gold, pick up colors from the lobby's original terrazzo floor. Blue and green cottons and pale wood furniture brighten up bedrooms. The hotel restaurant, **Wish**, serves up terrific fish dishes.

**$$ The Marquesa Hotel** – *600 Fleming St., Key West, FL.* ✗🄿🛏 ☎305-292-1919. *www.marquesa.com. 27 rooms.* Three 1884 Conch houses—a cross between Federal and Bahamian—make up the historic-district favorite. A palm-filled garden with trellised orchids surrounds two pools nestled behind the houses. Breezy guest rooms mix soft tropical colors with Chippendale pieces and West Indies wicker. The hotel's **Cafe Marquesa** specializes in Caribbean-inspired dishes with Asian and Central American influences.

## WHERE TO EAT

**$$$ Joe's Stone Crab** – *11 Washington Ae., Miami Beach, FL. Closed late-July–mid-Oct.* ☎305-673-0365. **Seafood.** Located at the southern end of Miami Beach, this high-energy eatery has been a local institution since 1913. Stone-crab claws are conveniently cracked open and served chilled with the house mustard sauce. Sides—coleslaw and creamed spinach—are big enough for two. To avoid long lines, order from the take-away counter and have a surfside picnic.

**$$ Versailles Restaurant** – *3555 S.W. 8th St., Miami, FL.* ☎305-445-7614. **Cuban.** Local transplants get their fix of home cooking at this Little Havana mainstay. Most rib-sticking dishes, such as roast pork and grilled *palomilla* steak with garlic and onions, come with generous portions of black beans and white rice. Finish your meal with a shot of potent, ultra-sweet *café cubano*.

**$ News Cafe** – *800 Ocean Dr., Miami Beach, FL.* ☎305-538-6397. **$ American.** People-watching is a 24-hour activity at this sidewalk cafe that opened in the 1980s to give production crews and models a casual place for a quick bite. Everything from French toast to salads is listed on the extensive menu.

# MIAMI★★★

MAP P249
EASTERN STANDARD TIME
POPULATION 386,417

One of the most popular resort destinations in the US, Miami draws some nine million visitors from around the world yearly with promises of golf, water sports, deep-sea fishing, lively nightlife and a seemingly inexhaustible supply of sunshine. With a population of over two million, Miami-Dade County is ethnically diverse; close to 50 percent of the county's inhabitants are Latino. The proximity of Miami to Cuba *(180mi)* and its similar climate make this American city a logical destination for Cuban exiles.

🄸 **Information:** Greater Miami Convention and Visitors Bureau. ☎305-539-3000 or www.miamiandbeaches.com

🕐 **Organizing Your Time:** Leave time to eat at one of the city's many excellent Cuban eateries.

Kids **Kids:** Today's kids may not remember Flipper, the TV show that was filmed at Miami Seaquarium, but they will still enjoy a stop here.

👁 **Also See:** MIAMI BEACH, PALM BEACH.

## A Bit of History

Since the first permanent settlement founded by Spaniard **Pedro Menén-dez de Avilés** in 1567, early inhabitants found life in the Miami area to be challenging; peace had to be negotiated with local Indian tribes, and pirates scavenged the coast. By the mid-1830s only a handful of pioneers had settled in the area. **Julia Tuttle**—who came to be known as the "Mother of Miami"—was largely responsible for putting Miami on the map. Tuttle convinced railroad magnate **Henry Flagler** to bring his **Florida East Coast Railway** (FEC) south, trading half of her land for Flagler's work as city developer and planner. The first train rolled into Miami in 1896; the fledgling city was incorporated three months later.

While Miami's growth corresponded directly to the development of the railroad and the federal highway system, a handful of visionaries, including Miami Beach developer **Carl Fisher** and Coral Gables planner **George Merrick**, earned the real credit for creating the pastel boomtowns that turned Miami into a winter resort for wealthy Northerners, the "Sunshine of America."

The tide, however, started turning in the mid-1920s. In 1925 a cargo embargo laid the city low. Then a one-two punch—delivered by a deadly hurricane that damaged nearly every building downtown in 1926, and the stock market crash of 1929—knocked the city to its knees. After such a beating, Miami stumbled slowly to its feet, bolstered by liquor supplied by rumrunners during Prohibition and the legalization of pari-mutuel betting in 1931.

Today's metropolis benefits from an amalgamation of ethnic groups and enterprises. Its international population is evident in the distinct ethnic communities of Little Havana and Little Haiti. Composed of architecturally innovative office towers, downtown Miami houses some 250 multinational businesses. The **Port of Miami**, the world's busiest cruise harbor, serves a total of eight cruise lines and boasts an annual passenger count nearing three million. Despite the income generated by the port and other commerce, tourism still reigns as king of industry in Miami.

## Downtown

Defined by the Miami River on the south and by **Bayfront Park** on Biscayne Bay, the vibrant 1.5sq mi quarter known as Miami's downtown exudes the bustling atmosphere of a Latin city. In recent years a large cluster of contemporary high-rise hotels and office buildings, including the tiered tower of **International Place** (100 S.E. 1st St.) and Wachovia **Financial Center** (200 S. Biscayne Blvd.) have created a dramatic skyline—illuminated at night in neon outlines. The spread

### Little Havana

Immediately west of downtown, Little Havana is one of the city's most lively and exotic neighborhoods. **Calle Ocho**, or Eighth Street—the heart of activity in Little Havana—vibrates with a spirited street life where pungent tobacco and heady *café Cubano* scent the air, and English is rarely spoken. Each year on the second Sunday in March, over one million revelers flock to this thoroughfare for the gala street party **Calle Ocho Open House**, a culmination of the week-long Lenten festival known as Carnaval Miami. Stretching along Calle Ocho (between S.W. 17th & S.W. 12th Aves.), the **Latin Quarter** invites tourists to walk its brick sidewalks set with stars bearing the names of an international array of prominent Hispanic entertainers, including Julio Iglesias and Gloria Estefan.

Since the influx of Cubans escaping the Cuban revolution in 1959, Little Havana has remained a magnet for refugees from a variety of Spanish-speaking nations as well as the political nerve center of the influential Cuban exile colony. Cuban history is remembered in places such as **José Martí Park** (351 S.W. 4th St.), named for the apostle of Cuban independence who was killed in Cuba in 1895.

Commemorating the chief of the Cuban Liberating Army, **Máximo Gómez Park** (southeast corner of S.W. 15th Ave.)—also known as Domino Park—is where locals assemble daily for games of dominoes, chess and checkers. Before you leave, be sure to sample Little Havana's profusion of authentic Cuban restaurants.

GREATER MIAMI

of downtown south of the Miami River along **Brickell Avenue** has resulted in the emergence of that area—once lined with the homes of Miami's richest citizens—as an international financial district.

### Miami-Dade Cultural Center★
*101 W. Flagler St.* ♿ 🅿 ☎*305-375-1896.*
*www.miamiartmuseum.org.*
A complex of three Mediterranean Revival buildings—the **Miami Art Museum** (☎*305-375-3000*), the Historical Museum of Southern Florida and the Miami-Dade Public Library—the center rests atop a tiled plaza, illustrating architect Philip Johnson's design for a cultural oasis above the busy downtown streets.

### The Historical Museum of Southern Florida★★
♿ 🅿 ☎*305-375-1492. www.hmsf.org.*
Housed on the museum's second floor, the permanent exhibit **"Tropical Dreams: A People's History of South Florida"** recounts the area's colorful past via a wealth of artifacts and mixed-media presentations, including an early Tequesta Indian settlement and treasures from sunken Spanish galleons. The first floor holds temporary exhibits focusing on Miami history and folklife.

### Bayside Marketplace★
*401 Biscayne Blvd.* 🍴 ♿ 🅿 ☎*305-577-3344. www.baysidemarketplace.com.*
Composed of several buildings connected by plazas and open-air walkways, Bayside and its profusion of boutiques, chain stores and eateries overlooks Biscayne Bay on downtown's northeastern edge.

## Additional Sights
### Museum of Contemporary Art (MoCA)★
*Joan Lehman Building, 770 N.E. 125th St., in North Miami.* ♿ 🅿 ☎*305-893-6211.*
*www.mocanomi.org.*
Designed by architect Charles Gwathmey, the simple but elegant building on palm-studded grounds within the North Miami civic complex features a permanent collection of works by nota-

bles such as Dennis Oppenheim, Julia Schnabel, John Baldessari and Jo. Bedia. Among the artists highlighted the changing exhibits are French sculptor Annette Messager and American p artist Keith Haring.

### Ancient Spanish Monastery★★
*6711 W. Dixie Hwy., in North Miami.* ♿
☎*305-945-1461.*
A superb example of early Gothic architecture, the Cloister of St. Bernard of Cla vaux was completed in 1141 in Segov Spain. Wealthy newspaperman **Willia Randolph Hearst** purchased the mo astery in 1925, intending to reconstru it on the grounds of his California estat San Simeon. But Hearst never finishe his estate, and after his death in 1951 t cloister was sold to two South Flori developers who planned to open it a tourist attraction. Reconstructing t cloister, however, was tantamount to giant jigsaw puzzle; the shipping box had been dismantled and re-crated yea earlier in New York due to a quarantir The resulting 10,751 jumbled packag that arrived in Florida took 19 months assemble.
Inside the 200-pound wrought-ir entrance gate lies a lush subtropical ga den. On the garden's southern perimet stands the entrance to a long cloiste Once serving as the monks' refector the **Chapel of St. Bernard of Clairva** occupies the first corridor. Two circul stained-glass **telescopic windows** (named for the three rings of recedir frames that encase them) are as old the monastery.

## Coral Gables★★

The grandest and most successful South Florida's boomtown develo ments, Coral Gables covers a 12.5sq area just southwest of downtow Miami, which encompasses a thrivir international commercial center ar the **University of Miami** campus. T area's fine **Mediterranean Reviv architecture**, featuring clay roof tile breezy courtyards and loggias, as well mature tropical landscaping, helps ma

oral Gables one of the most desirable
sidential enclaves in Greater Miami.
Miami's Master Suburb" was the brainchild
developer **George Merrick** (1886-1942)
ho began laying out Coral Gables in 1925.
e incorporated broad boulevards—like
e main east-west artery, **Coral Way**—
d park-like landscaping associated with
uropean cities. Designed to set Coral
ables apart, grand drive-through portals
e the **Douglas Entrance** (Tamiami Trail &
ouglas Rd.) border the eastern and north-
n perimeters.

## he Biltmore Hotel★★

00 Anastasia Ave. ✗ ♿ **P** ☎305-445-
926. www.biltmorehotel.com.
augurated in 1926 as South Florida's
emier winter resort, this 275-room
editerranean Revival "wedding cake"
corporates a 300ft-high tower with
ple cupola that is visible from miles
ound. In its heyday, the Biltmore
tracted Hollywood stars such as Bing
osby, Judy Garland and Ginger Rog-
s. Now restored to its former glory,
e hotel boasts an ornate **lobby**★, an
egant **ballroom** with a vaulted ceiling,
d a 1.25-million-gallon **pool**.

## enetian Pool★★

01 DeSoto Blvd. ✗ ♿ **P** ☎305-460-
306. www.venetianpool.com.
limestone quarry that supplied build-
g materials for the area's early homes
rms the base of this whimsical munici-
al pool. Footbridges and striped light
les reminiscent of those lining Ven-
e's Grand Canal adorn the free-form
vimming area. Today the renovated
ol, ornamented with waterfalls and
cked with rock caves, provides a
ique recreational venue.

## airchild Tropical
otanic Garden★★

901 Old Cutler Rd. ✗ ♿ **P** ☎305-667-
51. www.fairchildgarden.org.
amed for plant explorer David Fair-
ild, the largest botanical garden in
e continental US is set on 83 well-
nded acres studded with a series of
man-made lakes. The garden boasts
ore than 2,500 species of plants and
ees from around the world, arranged
spaces that vary dramatically from

narrow allées to open beds; a tram tour
(45min) takes visitors past a sampling of
the garden's flora.

## Parrot Jungle and Gardens★

**Kids** 1111 Parrot Jungle Trail. ✗ ♿ **P** ☎305-
400-7000. www.parrotjungle.com.
A rainbow of vivid-colored macaws
perched inside the entrance greets visitors who come to view more than 1,100
exotic birds, including some 80 pink flamingos that frequent **Flamingo Lake**.
Winding through lush tropical gardens,
a pathway leads to a walk-through aviary; trained macaws and cockatoos perform in the amphitheater.

# Coconut Grove★★

Stretching 4mi south of Rickenbacker
Causeway along Biscayne Bay, Miami's
oldest community owes its name to
Horace Porter, a Connecticut doctor who
dreamed of starting a coconut plantation here in 1873. By the early 20C, bayfront estates here were a prime winter
address for affluent industrialists such as
James Deering. The Grove's intellectual
and artistic community flourished in the
1920s and 30s, drawing notables such as
poet Robert Frost.
Annexed by the city of Miami in 1925,
this area has managed to retain a strong
sense of history in its quiet residential
neighborhoods. Catering to the under-
40 crowd, **Coconut Grove Village**★
(Grand Ave. & Main Hwy.) provides a

Biltmore Hotel

© The Biltmore Hotel

haven of sidewalk cafes and tony boutiques, including the **Streets of Mayfair** mall *(Grand Ave. between Virginia & Mary Sts.)* and **CocoWalk** *(3015 Grand Ave.)*, an ensemble of bars, chain stores and movie theaters. Inaugurated in 1963, the annual, three-day **Coconut Grove Arts Festival** celebrates the Grove's long-standing interest in the arts.

### Vizcaya★★★

*3251 S. Miami Ave.* ✗ ♿ ℗ ☎ *305-250-9133. www.vizcayamuseum.com.*

Overlooking the calm blue waters of Biscayne Bay, this ornate Italian Renaissance-style villa and its formal gardens embody the fantasy winter retreat of their builder, Illinois entrepreneur **James Deering** (whose family developed the International Harvester Company). Under the supervision of decorator **Paul Chalfin**, New York architect **F. Burrall Hoffman, Jr.** designed a villa to hold all of Deering's European treasures. Vizcaya (a Basque word meaning "elevated place") took 1,000 workers more than two years to complete.

The 34 rooms that are open to the public incorporate elements of four major styles: Renaissance, Baroque, Rococo and Neoclassical. Two floors of rooms surround a central courtyard (now roofed to protect the priceless art within). Looking out over the gardens, the **Tea Room**★ is actually an enclosed loggia with a stained-glass wall displaying Vizcaya's emblematic sea horse and caravel. The **East Loggia**, with its striking colored-marble floor, opens out onto the terrace that fronts Biscayne Bay. Just off the terrace sits the **Stone Barge**★, an ornamental Venetian-style breakwater.

More than 10 acres of formal **gardens**★★★, planned by Colombian architect Diego Suarez, flank the mansion's south side. The fan-shaped Italian hill garden, with its curvilinear parterres, centers on a two-room Baroque **Casino**, or garden house, set on an artificial hill.

### The Barnacle State Historic Site★★

*3485 Main Hwy. ☎305-442-6866.*

This five-acre bayfront site preserves one of the last patches of tropical hard-wood hammock in Coconut Grove, along with the 1891 home of yacht designer **Ralph Middleton Munroe**. Munroe first came to the Grove in 1877. In 188_ he purchased a 40-acre tract of property and, using lumber salvaged from shipwreck, built a five-room home. The Bahamian-style, hip-roofed structure was nicknamed "The Barnacle" for it octagonal roof that tapers to a small open-air vent. In 1908 Munroe enlarged the single-story house by adding a new ground floor in concrete. A replica of the 28ft sailboat *Egret,* which Munroe designed, is moored on the waterfront behind the house.

### Miami Seaquarium★

Kids *4400 Rickenbacker Causeway just east of Coconut Grove on Key Biscayne.* ✗ ℗ ☎ *305-361-5705. www. miamiseaquarium.com.*

In the late 1950s, this 37-acre marine park served as the set for the TV series *Flipper* and as home to its star. Today the **killer whale show** and shark feeding in the reef tank focus on entertainment with an educational subtext. The main building provides two viewing levels for a peek at some 10,000 varieties of aquatic animals, while **Lost Island Wildlife Habitat** features endangered reptiles, mammals and birds.

## Excursions

### Miami Metrozoo★★

Kids *18mi southwest of Miami. Take the Florida Turnpike south to Exit 16. Go west on S.W. 152nd St. and follow signs to zoo at 12400 S.W. 152nd St.* ✗ ♿ ℗ ☎ *305-25_-0400. www.miamimetrozoo.com.*

The best way to see the more than 1,30_ reptiles, birds and mammals in the popular cageless zoo is to wander along the 3mi loop trail that winds through the 300-acre park; an elevated monorail also makes regular runs around the ground offering its riders a bird's-eye view of the animal habitats. Among the highlights are an affectionate band of **lowland gorillas** (a walk-in viewing cave permits a close-up look) and a group of **Bengal tigers**.

### iscayne National Park★

*8mi south of Miami in Homestead. Take
the Florida Turnpike south to N. Canal Dr.
Convoy Point Visitor Center is at the end
of S.W. 328th St.* △ & P ☎305-230-7275.
www.nps.gov/bisc.

Located in the Atlantic Ocean and
Biscayne Bay, the largest marine park
in the US was established in 1980 to
help protect a 270sq mi area of coastal
wetlands, mangrove shorelines, coral
reefs and a string of barrier islands. The
**reefs★★★** are located about 10mi offshore, where warm Gulf Stream currents
nurture some 50 species of living coral.
For those wishing to explore the reefs,
the park sponsors boat tours *(reservations: ☎305-230-1100)* and rents scuba
and snorkeling gear.

*Tiger at Miami Metrozoo*

# MIAMI BEACH★★★

MAP P249
EASTERN STANDARD TIME
POPULATION 87,925

Touted as one of the country's great tropical paradises, Miami Beach is justifiably famed for its fabulous palm-studded shoreline, eccentric architecture and
colorful locals. The city of Miami Beach was built on the dreams and speculation
of northern developers and entrepreneurs such as Pennsylvania nurseryman
**Henry Lum**, New Jersey horticulturalist **John C. Collins** and Indiana automobile
magnate **Carl Fisher**. The city occupies a narrow barrier island (7mi long and
.25mi wide) located 2.5mi off the mainland. After World War I, Collins and Fisher
pooled their resources, promoting Miami Beach to monied northerners. By 1921
the former mangrove swamp was alive with sprawling Mediterranean Revival
estates, luxury hotels, polo grounds and tennis courts.

Today, the famous **South Beach** area *(below 23rd St.)* and rejuvenated **Art Deco
Historic District**, with its fashionable clubs and boutiques, are reached directly
by the MacArthur Causeway. People-watching is a prime pastime in SoBe (local
slang for South Beach), now a magnet for fashion models, designers and assorted
litterati. The real stars, however, are the buildings themselves.

**Information:** ☎305-672-1270. www.miamiandbeaches.com
**Parking:** You'll need a car to cruise down the legendary Ocean Drive.
**Don't Miss:** The Art Deco architecture on Collins Avenue.
**Also See:** PALM BEACH.

## Art Deco
## Historic District★★★

Listed on the National Register of
Historic Places in 1979, this enclave

of small-scale Art Deco hotels and
apartment houses dating from the late
1920s to the early 40s amounts to the
largest concentration of architecture
of its kind in the world. Derived from

*Life Guard Station, Miami Beach*

© Greater Miami CVB

the European minimalist **International Style**, Art Deco used decorative stylized elements to embellish simple massive forms. Reveling in its sun-washed locale, Miami Deco went a step further, outlining structures in neon lights at night, and incorporating flamingos, palm trees and other tropical motifs into exuberant door grills, bas-relief plaques, murals and etched windows.

The official district measures about 1sq mi and is roughly bounded by the Atlantic Ocean on the east, Lenox Avenue on the west, Sixth Street on the south and Dade Boulevard to the north. A commercial thoroughfare encompassing chic restaurants, hip dance clubs and

---

### Stone Crabs

Harvested off Florida's Gulf Coast between October and May, stone crabs are sought after for their succulent claw meat, which rivals lobster for sweetness. The rust-colored crustaceans possess the ability to generate new claws within 12 to 18 months (fishermen take only the claws, since they contain the crab's only edible meat). Miami Beach's legendary restaurant **Joe's Stone Crab** *(227 Biscayne St.; closed Aug–mid-Oct;* ☎*305-673-0365)* serves its namesake delicacy to droves of diners who are willing to brave the long lines (Joe's doesn't take reservations).

---

Cuban coffee shops, **Washington Avenue** is enlivened by the colorful Mediterranean Revival architecture of **Espanola Way**★ *(between Washington & Drexel Aves.)*. Located along the oldest commercial street on the island, **Lincoln Road Mall** is a pedestrians-only enclave featuring shops, galleries, restaurants and a central mall adorned with quirky tiled fountains. Cultural offerings here range from New World Symphony concerts at the **Lincoln Theatre** *(nos. 541-555)* to working artisans' studios at **Artcenter South Florida** *(nos. 924)*.

The Miami Design Preservation League (MDPL) offers a variety of tours of the Art Deco district *(☞walking tours depart from Art Deco Welcome Center in Oceanfront Auditorium, 1001 Ocean Dr.; bike tours depart from Miami Beach Bicycle Center, 601 5th St.; reservations required for both tours, ☎ 305-672-2014)*.

### Ocean Drive★★

Along this lively north-south boulevard bordering the Atlantic Ocean beats the heart of the SoBe scene. Locals and tourists lunch at shaded sidewalk cafes while scantily clad youths streak by on in-line skates; nightfall brings revelers to some of Miami's hottest bars and dance clubs. Across the street lies lovely **Ocean Beach**★★, which offers a great **view** of Ocean Drive and its pastel parade of Art Deco hotels: the seven-story blue tinted **Park Central** *(no. 640)*; the **Leslie** *(no. 1244)*; and the eleven-story **The Tides** *(no. 1220)*, the largest on the drive. Located in **Lummus Park**, fronting the beach, is the Oceanfront Auditorium, which houses the **Art Deco Welcome Center** *(☎305-531-3484)*.

### The Wolfsonian★★

*1001 Washington Ave.*
♿☎*305-531-1001.*

The former Washington Storage Company building (1927, Robertson and Patterson) is distinguished by an elaborate gold-colored Moorish relief façade of cast concrete. Owned and operated by Florida International University, the building now houses a museum and research center that oversees the

*ean Drive illumination at night*

itchell Wolfson Collection of over ,000 pieces of American and Euro-an art and design dating from 1885 1945. The museum devotes its fifth oor to a permanent collection of some 0 works that illustrate how design has en used to help people adjust to the odern world.

### ass Museum of Art★
*21 Park Ave.* ♿☎*305-673-7530.*
is landmark 1930 Art Deco structure ins its name from New York entrepre-ur and philanthropist John Bass, who nated his art collection to the city of ami Beach. The permanent collection cludes European paintings from the 15C 20C, with an emphasis on the **Dutch d Flemish Masters**; an outstanding splay of 16C-19C **textiles**; as well as dec-orative arts spanning the 14C to 20C. The 2002 completion of the first phase of the museum's ongoing expansion—designed by Japanese architect Arata Isozaki—more than doubled the museum's size.

### Collins Avenue★
One of the main traffic arteries in Miami Beach, Collins Avenue boasts such lauded 1940s Art Deco hotels as the **National** *(no. 1677)*, the **Delano** *(no. 1685)* and the **Ritz Plaza** *(no. 1701)*, with their squared, stepped-back façades and quirky central towers. At 44th Street, a 13,000sq ft **mural** by Rich-ard Haas bears the trompe l'œil image of a triumphal arch framing Morris Lapidus' extravaganza, the **Fontainebleau**. The real Fontainebleau Hilton Resort and Towers lies just around the corner.

# EVERGLADES NATIONAL PARK★★★

MICHELIN MAP 584 S 15
EASTERN STANDARD TIME

Renowned throughout the world, the vast "river of grass" known as the Everglades covers the southern end of the Florida peninsula. One of only a few American parks that enjoy status as a UNESCO World Heritage site and as an International Biosphere Reserve, Everglades National Park is a subtropical wetland that gives rise to such diverse ecosystems as hardwood hammocks and mangrove swamps harboring hundreds of species of birds, mammals and reptiles.

- **Information:** ☎305-242-7700. www.nps.gov/ever
- ▶ **Orient Yourself:** The Everglades on at the southern tip of Florida, about as far south as you can go in the state.
- **Don't Miss:** The different eco systems of this landscape.
- **Kids:** Will love nature in action, as seen from a tour of Shark Valley.
- **Also See:** MIAMI, PALM BEACH.

## A Bit of History

The Everglades is actually a slow-moving river—formed during the last Ice Age—which starts at Lake Okeechobee in south-central Florida and slopes south, where it drains into the Gulf of Mexico. Although this sheet of moving water is 50mi wide, it averages only 6in in depth. The fragile ecosystem of the Everglades was seriously compromised in the early 20C when Florida governor Napoleon Broward implemented a plan to divert water from the Glades to irrigate farmland and provide suburban drinking water.

In 1916 the tide of development was stemmed as the first Everglades preserve, **Royal Palm State Park**, was set aside. When 107,600 acres were added to its boundaries with the 1989 **East Everglades Expansion Act**, the 1.5-million-acre park became the third-largest national park in the continental US.

Preserving the Everglades' ecosystem and managing its water flow has long

*Whitewater Bay, Southern Everglades*

## Address Book

### ADMISSION

Everglades National Park is open daily year-round. Admission is $10/car for a seven-day pass. The southern entrance to the park is on Route 9336 *(45mi south of Miami International Airport)*; the northern entrance is at Shark Valley *(30mi west of Miami via US-41)*.

### SEASONS

**Winter** is the best time to visit; daytime temperatures range from 60° to 80°F, mosquitoes are tolerable, and wildlife is easier to spot. In **summer** *(the rainy season, May–Oct)* temperatures often soar to 95°F, and high humidity attracts clouds of biting insects *(bring insect repellent)*. Parts of the park may close in summer due to flooding. If you're planning a visit in the winter high season, make lodging and tour reservations several months in advance.

### WHERE TO STAY

Campsites are located at Long Pine Key and Flamingo. For maps and information facilities and recreational acitivities, contact **Park Headquarters**, 40001 State Road 9336, Homestead, FL 33034, ☎305-242-7700.

---

been a critical issue, as human needs continue to encroach on conservation efforts. Championed by activists such as Florida journalist **Marjory Stoneman Douglas** (1890-1998), the Everglades have benefited from legislation such as the Everglades Forever Act (1994) and the Everglades and South Florida Ecosystem Restoration Act (1996), which are attempting to re-establish water flow and exterminate exotic rivals (human-introduced natural enemies such as the water-consuming Australian Melaleuca tree) that threaten the Everglades' native vegetation.

## Southern Everglades

While you can see the park highlights in a day, the best way to experience the Everglades and its wildlife is to spend some time hiking its trails and boating in its waters. The southern entrance *(on Rte. 9336)* leads past designated stops along its 38mi course to Flamingo, the southern terminus of the park.

### Pa-hay-okee Overlook ★★

This elevated platform provides a sweeping **view**★★ of a seemingly endless prairie of saw grass, the Everglades' most dominant flora.

### Flamingo

This small outpost overlooking Florida Bay provides the only source of food in the southern part of the park. Here nature lovers can take **wilderness cruises**★★ that tour the backcountry canals and the open waters of Florida Bay *(depart from park visitor center at Flamingo; ☎39-695-2945)*.

## Northern Everglades

Cutting across the Everglades, the Tamiami Trail (US-41) links Miami with Naples on the west coast. The main entrance into the national park along this route is at Shark Valley. Coursing through the Everglades' western coastal region, the navigable **Wilderness Waterway** winds for 99mi from Flamingo to Everglades City. The park offers **cruises of the Ten Thousand Islands**★★ *(☎239-695-2591)* affording visitors a look at the marine world of Chokoloskee Bay.

Also within the scope of the northern Everglades are **Big Cypress National Preserve** *(52mi west of Miami; accessible from US-41 & I-75)*, habitat of the endangered Florida panther, and **Faka-hatchee Strand State Preserve**★ *(north of Everglades City; accessible from US-41 and Rte. 29)*.

### Shark Valley★★

*30mi west of Miami, entrance on south side of US-41. ☎305-221-8776.*

Actually a basin lying a few feet lower than the rest of the Everglades, Shark Valley is named for the shallow, slow-flowing slough that empties into the brackish—and shark-infested—Shark

## Everglades Wildlife

One of the major wetlands left on this continent, the Everglades supports some 600 species of animals—including 350 types of birds, 60 species of mosquitoes and 26 kinds of snakes. The southern Everglades is the only place in the world where you'll find both crocodiles and alligators. Only a few hundred **American crocodiles** inhabit the Glades' brackish mangrove inlets. Once a species with a poor prognosis for survival, the **alligator** has made a strong comeback in the park. Often seen swimming in canals or basking on the banks, these sluggish-looking reptiles can sprint at speeds nearing 15mph for distances of 50 yards.

Birds provide the greatest spectacle in the park, with herons, egrets, ibis, cranes and **anhingas** almost always within sight. Bald eagles, ospreys and the small, endangered **snail kite** also make their home here.

Florida's designated state animal, rare **Florida panthers** roam the Everglades' wetlands, the only habitat left for them in the eastern US. These big tawny cats avoid humans, and their nocturnal hunting habits make them difficult to spot.

*American Alligator*

River. The park's naturalist-led **tram tours**★ (☎305-221-8455) provide the best glimpse of the expansive landscape.

### Miccosukee Indian Village

*5mi west of Shark Valley entrance, on south side of US-41.* ✕ ♿ 🅿 ☎305-552-8365. www.miccosukee.com.

The Miccosukee people have inhabited the Everglades since the mid-19C, when they sought refuge in these wetlands from the Seminole Wars and the federal government's mandatory internment on reservations. In an attempt to preserve their native culture, the Miccosukee Indians, now numbering some 500 people, have re-created a traditional settlement complete with chickees (palm-thatched, open-sided shelters), a tribal art and culture **museum** and an **alligator arena** where modern Miccosukee "hunters" demonstrate bare-handed alligator wrestling techniques.

# THE FLORIDA KEYS★★

**MICHELIN MAP 584 R, S 16**
**EASTERN STANDARD TIME**

n 1904 railroad magnate Henry Flagler launched plans to extend his Florida
ast Coast Railway from Miami to Key West. Known as the **Overseas Railroad**,
he train first pulled into Key West in 1912. Though destroyed in 1935 by a killer
urricane that claimed the lives of some 400 people, the railroad literally paved
he way for the **Overseas Highway**, completed in 1938 along the former railroad
ed. Fifty miles south of Miami, the Keys are known for their laid-back atmos-
here, enhanced by the diverse characteristics of the individual islands. Along
S-1 (the Overseas Highway), small green mile-marker (MM) posts delineate the
ocations of sites, giving distances from Key West (MM 0).

> **Information:** ☎305-451-1414 (Key Largo); ☎305-664-4503 (Middle Keys);
> ☎305-872-2411 (Lower Keys). http://fla-k eys.com
> **Orient Yourself:** Curving southwest 220mi from Biscayne Bay to the Dry Tor-
> tugas, these islands scribe a narrow archipelago separating the waters of the
> Atlantic from Florida Bay and the Gulf of Mexico.
> **Also See:** MIAMI, PALM BEACH.

## A Bit of History

he **Upper and Middle Keys** serve as
umping-off points for anglers, divers,
norkelers and wildlife enthusiasts inter-
sted in the wealth of marine life that
hrives on the offshore **Florida Reef
ract**★★★, the largest living coral-
eef system in North American waters.
tretching 26mi in length, but only 1mi
t its widest point, **Key Largo**★ *(MM 110)*
s the largest and northernmost in this
hain of coral-rock isles. Below Key
argo *(MM 85-MM 45)*, the **Middle
eys**—notably **Islamorada**—offer
ishermen such deep-sea trophies as
ailfish, tarpon and marlin.
panning the distance from **Mara-
hon** to the **Lower Keys**, **Seven-Mile
ridge**★★ *(MM 47-40)*, with its 288 135ft
ections, ranks as the world's longest
egmental bridge. Driving its length
ffords expansive **views**★★ of blue-
reen waters.

## Key West★★★

*ourist information is available at the
ey West Chamber of Commerce, Mallory
quare, ☎305-294-2587.*

irates, wreckers, writers, US presi-
ents and Cuban freedom fighters

have at one time all found a haven on
this small island at the southernmost
tip of the continent. Closer to Havana
than to Miami, Key West cultivates an
atmosphere of sublime laissez-faire that
appeals to artists, the gay community
and droves of tourists who flock to the
eateries, boutiques and bars on 14-
block-long **Duval Street**, hub of the
200-square-block historic area known
as Old Town.

Named *Cayo Hueso* ("Island of Bones") by
Spanish explorer Ponce de León in 1513,

*Seven-Mile Bridge*

Andy Newman/Florida Keys News Bureau

**259**

Key West became the 19C headquarters for the lucrative enterprises of wrecking and, later, cigar-making. When Henry Flagler's Overseas Railroad reached its terminus at Key West in 1912, the town began its incarnation as a tourist resort. Writers Ernest Hemingway, Tennessee Williams and John Dos Passos, Cuban liberator José Martí, and President Harry Truman number among the notables drawn to Key West over the years.

# Old Town★★

One of the largest National Historic Districts on the National Register, Old Town boasts diverse architecture, from simple wood-frame vernacular Conch houses and gingerbread-trimmed Victorians to imported Bahama houses and gracious Classical Revival mansions built by transplanted New England seafarers in the 19C. Among the indigenous features added to the latter style, the "**eyebrow**" is unique. This West Indian element designed to block the tropical sun consists of eaves that partly overhang second-story windows, resembling a brow over squinting eyes.

Though Old Town is easily navigated on foot, the narrated **Old Town Trolley tours** (☎05-296-6688) provide a good introduction to the area. At dusk, locals and visitors alike gather at **Mallory Square Dock** (behind Mallory Square) for the time-honored Key West ritual of watching the island's spectacular **sunsets**★★.

## Shipwreck Historeum★

*1 Whitehead St. in Mallory Square.* ☞Visit by guided tour only. ✗ ☎305-292-8990 www.shipwreckhistoreum.com.

The feel of a 19C dockside warehouse is re-created here as actors recount the thrills and hazards of the wrecking business. Exhibits fill two floors with items salvaged from an 1856 shipwreck.

Facing the Historeum, the **Key West Aquarium** (Wall St.; ☎305-296-2051) allows visitors a look at some of the sea life found in the waters off the Keys.

## Mel Fisher Maritime Heritage Society★

*200 Greene St.* ☎305-294-2633 Exhibits here recount the story of treasure-hunter Mel Fisher's 16-year search for the 1622 wreck of the Spanish galleon *Nuestra Señora de Atocha*. A video details the 1985 discovery of the *Atocha* and its mother lode—valued at more than $400 million—while displays on the first floor highlight the fabulous gold, silver, gems and other artifacts recovered from the dive site.

## Harry S Truman Little White House Museum★★

*111 Front St., in Truman Annex. Entrance on right just past the corner of Front St.* ☞Visit by guided tour only. ☎305-294-9911.

This large, unpretentious white clapboard home (1890) gives a rare glimpse into the private life of America's 33rd president, **Harry S Truman** (1884-1972)

---

## A Key to Wildlife

The Keys provide visitors an opportunity to see and interact with a variety of wildlife. For a close-up view of the dazzling kaleidoscope of vivid coral and sea creatures—parrot fish, sea fans, sponges—on the offshore reef, rent gear at one of the many dive shops on Key Largo and try snorkeling or diving at **John Pennekamp Coral Reef State Park**★★ (MM 102.5, Key Largo; ☎305-451-1202; www.pennekamp-park.com). The park also offers glass-bottom boat tours of the reef (Coral Reef Park Co.; ☎305-451-1621). Another good place for underwater exploration is at **Bahia Honda State Park** (MM 36.8, Bahia Honda Key; ☎305-872-2353), which boasts one of the chain's largest stretches of sand **beach**★★—rarely found in the Keys.

Visitors can learn about dolphin behavior, socialization and physiology, and then interact with these playful mammals in a special program offered at the **Dolphin Research Center**★ (MM 59, Grassy Key; ☎305-289-1121; www.dolphins. org). And you can spot the smallest species of North American deer, the petite **Key Deer** (Odocoileus virginianus clavium), at the **National Key Deer Refuge**★ (MM 30.5, Big Pine Key; ☎305-872-2239).

## Hemingway in Key West

One of Key West's most legendary figures, novelist **Ernest Hemingway** (1889-1961) spent his most productive years on the island. Hemingway and his second wife, Pauline, wintered here in the late 1920s, and in 1931 they purchased a home in the town Hemingway dubbed "the St. Tropez of the poor." Here in Key West, the author cultivated his macho "Papa" image, spending his days writing, fishing and drinking with a coterie of locals. Hemingway's image continues to infuse the island and is the impetus behind the annual **Hemingway Days** festival, held in conjunction with the writer's birthday *(July 21)*.

Fans can visit the **Ernest Hemingway Home & Museum**★★ *(907 Whitehead St.; ☎305-294-1136)*, the gracious yellow stucco house where "Papa" wrote such classics as *Death in the Afternoon* (1932) and *For Whom the Bell Tolls* (1940) in his **studio**★ above the carriage house. Other Hemingway landmarks include "Papa's" favorite hangout, **Sloppy Joe's Bar** *(201 Duval St.)*, and **Blue Heaven** *(729 Thomas St.)*, a former brothel (now a cafe) where Hemingway attended boxing matches.

eginning with a sojourn to Key West in 946, Truman spent his "working vacaons" over the next seven years of his rm in office at this former naval station plex, which he called his "Little White ouse." While here, he ran the country om the **desk** that still sits in a corner the living room.

## an Carlos Institute

6 Duval St. ⚒☎305-294-3887. www. banfest.com.

e roots of this 1924 Spanish Colonial ructure date back to 1871, when it erved as the hub of social and revoluonary activity for Cubans in Key West. round-floor displays focus on **José** **arti** (1853-95), organizer of the second fort for Cuban independence.

## Excursion

### Dry Tortugas National Park ★

*69mi west of Key West. Accessible only by plane (Seaplanes of Key West, Inc. ☎305-294-0709) or boat (depart from Lands' End Marina; ☎305-294-7009). ⚠ ☎305-242-7700. www.nps.gov/drto.*

Encompassing 100sq mi in the Gulf of Mexico, the park protects the small cluster of reef islands known as the Dry Tortugas. One of these, Garden Key, is the site of **Fort Jefferson**, the largest coastal stronghold built by the US in the 19C. The half- to day-long excursions to the island allow time for touring the fort, as well as diving, snorkeling and fishing in the surrounding park waters.

# PALM BEACH★★

MICHELIN MAP 584 S 15
EASTERN STANDARD TIME
POPULATION 9,852

ccupying the northern part of a 16mi-long subtropical barrier island, this strip f real estate harbors one of the highest concentrations of multimillion-dollar ansions in the world. The picture-perfect island of palm-lined thoroughfares ttracts streams of tourists—particularly in winter—who come to sample fine estaurants, stay in world-class hotels and shop along chic Worth Avenue.

- **Information:** ☎561-233-3000. www.palmbeachfl.com
- **Don't Miss:** The luxurious Breakers Hotel.
- **Organizing Your Time:** Leave plenty of time (and money) for shopping. Worth Avenue rivals Chicago's Michigan Avenue and New York's Fifth Avenue.
- **Also See:** MIAMI, ORLANDO.

# A Bit of History

Railroad magnate Henry Flagler proclaimed Palm Beach "a veritable paradise" in the late 19C when he was scouting a site for a new South Florida resort. Flagler's Royal Poinciana Hotel (now gone) opened in 1894, the same year his railroad made the town accessible from points north. Today, Flagler's indelible mark on the city is most apparent in The Breakers hotel and in Whitehall, his former home.

The growth of Palm Beach in the early 20C owes much to architect **Addison Mizner** (1872-1933), who gave the city its elegant look. Taking inspiration from Spanish colonial manor houses and Italian Renaissance villas, Mizner designed estates with pink stucco walls, red-tile roofs and breezy loggias. His Mediterranean Revival style is exemplified in many of the two-story villas along swanky **Worth Avenue**★★ (between Ocean Blvd. & Cocoanut Row), lined with pricey shops and delightful alleyways that thread off the avenue into charming courtyards graced by tilework fountains and tropical flowers. Among these, **Via Mizner**★ stands out for its labyrinthine passages and yellow, pink and aqua pastel walls.

# Sights

### The Breakers★★
1 S. County Rd. ⟜Visit by guided tour only. ⚹♿☎561-655-6611. www.thebreakers.com.
The third incarnation of Henry Flagler's famous hotel (the first two, constructed of wood, were destroyed by fire) cost $6 million and took over 1,200 craftsmen close to a year to build. The present grand hotel features belvedere towers with open arches, and a colonnaded porte cochere. The lobby runs the entire 200ft length of the center section with an 18ft-high vaulted ceiling. Behind the lobby, the **Florentine Dining Room** is adorned with a domed ceiling painted with frescoes and Italian pastoral scenes.

### Flagler Museum (Whitehall)★★
1 Whitehall Way, off Cocoanut Row. ☎561-655-2833. www.flaglermuseum.us.
Built by **Henry Morrison Flagler** (1830-1913) as a wedding gift for his third wife, Mary Lily Kenan, the mansion (1902, Carrère and Hastings) served as the Whitehall Hotel from 1925 to 1959. Now a museum, the house is fronted by a landscaped walkway leading to a two-story verandah that spans the façade. Inside the mansion, **Marble Hall**, an imitation of a Roman villa's atrium, dazzles the eye with its masterful ceiling mural by Italian artist Benvenuti. Hung with Baccarat-crystal chandeliers, the **Louis XIV Music Room** was Kenan's favorite; the ornate **Ballroom** was used to entertain society's elite. The second floor contains the Rococo-style **Master Suite** dressed in yellow watered-silk damask, and 14 guest suites.

### Norton Museum of Art★★
1451 S. Olive Ave., West Palm Beach. ⚹♿🅿 ☎561-832-5196. www.norton.org.
Founded in 1941 by steel tycoon Ralph H. Norton, this museum boasts a wonderful spectrum of some 6,500 pieces in its galleries. Permanent holdings place special emphasis on 19C-20C American (O'Keeffe, Homer, Marin, Warhol, Pollock) and European artists (Monet, Renoir, Matisse, Picasso, Klee). A renowned **Chinese collection** encompasses tomb jades, ceramics and ritual bronzes dating from as far back as 1500 BC. Ever-changing traveling exhibitions are also on display.

# SOUTHERN GULF COAST★

MICHELIN MAP 584 R 15
EASTERN STANDARD TIME

Florida's southern Gulf Coast stretches south from Sanibel and Captiva Islands to the Ten Thousand Islands that border Everglades National Park. Life runs at a calmer pace here, with smaller cities and waters that lap more gently on the shore.

- **Information:** ☎239-262-6141, www.naples-florida.com (Naples); ☎239-472-1080, www.sanibel-captiva.org (Sanibel & Captiva).
- **Don't Miss:** Alligators at the J.N. "Ding" Darling National Wildlife Refuge.
- **Warning:** This area can get hit during hurricane season.
- **Kids:** Nothing entertains kids like building a sand castle on the beach. Try Lowdermilk Parka, a perfect public beach.
- **Also See:** MOBILE.

## A Bit of History

Though Ponce de León and other 16C Spanish explorers sailed along this coast, they concentrated their attentions for the most part on Tampa Bay and left the southwest coast to the Calusa Indians. White settlement began in the mid-19C and proceeded in fits and starts until the turn of the century. The railroad finally reached Naples in 1927, opening the way for sun seekers to revel in the gulf's lovely beaches and breathtaking sunsets.

## Naples★

Basking on the gulf shore just north of the Everglades, Naples has grown from a fishing hamlet to an outpost of culture and fashion. Opportunities abound here for fine dining, upscale shopping and golfing. Naples' historic downtown, **Old Naples**★ *(5th Ave. S. & 3rd St. S.)*, offers chic shops and restaurants on palm-lined streets, as well as shaded courtyards perfect for sipping tea or taking a respite from shopping. Numerous art galleries line **Third Street South**; other upscale shops can be found along **Fifth Avenue South**. To see some of the city's most luxurious beachfront homes, take the **scenic drive**★ along **Gulf Shore Boulevard** south to Gordon Pass. Along the way you'll pass popular **Lowdermilk Park**★ with its pristine public beach. Located just west of Big Cypress National

Reserve, Naples makes a good base for excursions to the Everglades or to the **Ten Thousand Islands**, an archipelago of islets that are covered collectively with one of the largest mangrove forests in the world *(cruises depart from Everglades National Park Gulf Coast Visitor Center on Rte. 29 in Everglades City; ☎239-695-2591)*. At this chain's northern end lies the popular resort of **Marco Island** *(from Naples take US-41 South to Rte. 951 West)*.

## Sanibel and Captiva Islands★★

Spanish explorers first discovered these lovely barrier islands, which arc 20mi into the Gulf of Mexico. Now a shell collector's paradise and winter resort in close proximity to Fort Myers, Sanibel and Captiva were slow to develop until the building of a causeway in 1963 linked them to the mainland. By the 1990s, the islands had become so popular that conservationists rallied to protect the land from unchecked development. One noteworthy result of their efforts, the "Ding" Darling National Wildlife Refuge, preserves more than one-third of Sanibel's total acreage and provides a haven for native species.

### J.N. "Ding" Darling National Wildlife Refuge ★★

*1 Wildlife Dr., off Sanibel-Captiva Rd.* ☎239-472-1100. www.dingdarling.org.

Courtesy Lee Island Coast V&CVB

## Shelling: A Favored Island Pastime

Combing Sanibel and Captiva beaches for the islands' bountiful cache of shells is a popular pastime. The islands' unusual east-west orientation acts as a natural catchment for the more than 200 species of mollusks that inhabit the Gulf of Mexico's shallow continental shelf. Arrive an hour before low tide, or after a northwesterly wind for the best finds. And keep an eye out for common varieties such as calico scallops, kitten's paws, fighting conchs and tiny coquina clams *(taking live specimens is prohibited by state law).* Lovely **Bowman's Beach** *(3mi north of Ding Darling Refuge)* and **Turner Beach** *(at Blind Pass)* are popular with beginning shellers. For those wishing to venture farther afield, a number of **shelling excursions** are also available *(for information, contact the Sanibel-Captiva Islands Chamber of Commerce, 1159 Causeway Rd., Sanibel; ☎239-472-1080).*

A showcase of barrier-island wildlife abounds here in canals, bogs, inlets, mangrove swamps and upland forests. Begin at the **visitor center**, where displays and videos offer insight into the natural history of the 6,300-acre refuge. For a glimpse of alligators and a host of water birds, including roseate spoonbills, egrets and great blue herons, take the unpaved 5mi **Wildlife Drive**★★. Be sure to leave your car and meander along the 4mi of interpretive hiking trails, or paddle the 6mi of marked canoe courses. *Visitors can rent canoes and bicycles in the refuge. Guided canoe excursions and tram tours are available (call Tarpon Bay Recreation; ☎239-472-8900).*

## Excursion

### Edison and Ford Winter Estates★★

*17mi northeast of Sanibel Island in Fort Myers. Take Rte. 867 (McGregor Blvd.) to no. 2350. ↘Visit by guided tour only. ☎239-334-7419. www.efwefla.org.* This riverside complex holds the winter homes and tropical gardens of inventor **Thomas Alva Edison** (1847-1931) and auto manufacturer **Henry Ford** (1863-1947). Edison built his spacious "Seminole Lodge" with its wide verandahs in Fort Myers in 1885. The house tour includes Edison's **laboratory** and the adjacent **Edison Museum**★, chockablock with his inventions. After meeting at a conference in 1896, Edison and Ford forged a life-long friendship. In 1916 Ford bought a modest cottage on a piece of land adjacent to Edison's Florida home. The "Mangoes," as the two-story frame house was called, is furnished with reproductions in the Ford fashion.

# MILWAUKEE AREA

Milwaukee is a modern Midwestern city that bears the marks of its no-nonsense, hard-working German character—an industrial center that today prides itself on its clean streets and clean politics. The city is set on the shore of Lake Michigan in the southeastern corner of Wisconsin, 90mi north of Chicago,

Milwaukee

The state now known as Wisconsin hosted ancient mound builders who decorated the land with effigies of birds, animals and human forms between AD 700 and AD 1300. In more modern times, tribes including the Menominee, Chippewa, Fox, Sauk, Winnebago and Potawatomi wandered through this area to hunt and fish. Searching for a North-West Passage to Asia, French explorers combed Wisconsin in the 1600s, beginning with **Jean Nicolet,** who landed at Green Bay in 1634.

Ceded to Britain under the terms of the Treaty of Paris in 1763, Wisconsin was largely ignored as "Indian country," until the American government organized these lands as part of the Indiana Territory in 1800. Wisconsin became the 30th state in 1848, with Madison as its capital and Milwaukee poised to become a center for grain trading.

Today the Milwaukee area offers much beyond the cultural attractions of the city. To the north, Door County peninsula offers a waterside respite from the city; its scenic shorelines draw thousands of visitors each year. Located 77mi west of Milwaukee, Madison combines the governmental bustle of a state capital with the college-town atmosphere created by the University of Wisconsin. North of Madison you'll find the natural—and man-made—attractions of **The Dells**★ (the town of Wisconsin Dells is 52mi north of Madison via Rte. 12), dramatic layered limestone cliffs carved by glacial melt into a 7mi section of the Wisconsin River. West of Madison in Spring Green, you can tour Taliesin, Frank Lloyd Wright's famous home and studio.

© VISIT Milwaukee

*Usingers Building, Old World Third Street*

## Area Address Book

*♨ For coin ranges, see the Legend on the cover flap.*

### WHERE TO STAY

**$$$ Hotel Metro** – *411 E. Mason St., Milwaukee, WI.* ✗ ♿ 🅿 ☎414-272-1937. *www.hotelmetro.com. 64 suites.* An all-suite Art Deco landmark in east downtown that offers loft-like, pet-friendly guest quarters averaging 640sq ft. Bamboo floors, hand-woven Tibetan rugs and contemporary furnishings update the look.

**$$ The Pfister Hotel** – *424 E. Wisconsin Ave., Milwaukee, WI.* ✗ ♿ 🅿 🛒 ☎414-273-8222. www.pfister-hotel.com. 307 rooms. East downtown's oldest property (1893) remains the city's grand dame. A hand-painted mural of the azure sky, with cherubs and garlands, decorates the lobby's three-story ceiling. The world's largest hotel collection of Victorian paintings adorns the public areas. Bedrooms are done in florals, with walnut armoires and crystal lamps.

**$$ White Lace Inn** – *16 N. 5th Ave., Sturgeon Bay, WI.* ♿ 🅿 ☎920-743-1105. *www.whitelaceinn.com. 18 rooms.* Four early-20C houses connected by winding garden paths make up this romantic B&B, just two blocks from downtown Sturgeon Bay. Accommodations are whimsically designed with Laura Ashley chintz, and antique four-poster beds with lace canopies. Most rooms have whirlpools and/or fireplaces.

### WHERE TO EAT

**$$ Karl Ratzsch's Old World Restaurant** – *320 E. Mason St., Milwaukee, WI. Closed Sun.* ☎414-276-2720. **German.** Family favorites have been served here since 1904. Dark walnut panels, beamed ceilings and stag-horn chandeliers make the downtown locale feel like a hunting lodge. Beer comes to the table in traditional steins. Best-sellers include roast goose, and sauerbraten with potato dumplings and red cabbage.

**$ Elsa's on the Park** – *833 N. Jefferson St., Milwaukee, WI.* ☎414-765-0615. **American.** Milwaukee's people-watching haunt sits across from Cathedral Square. Visiting celebrities and sports pros stop in for pork-chop sandwiches and the specialty half-pound burgers with baskets of waffle fries (called „eight fries"). Choose from six exotic variations or opt for the house favorite with American, Swiss, white Cheddar and Colby cheeses. The quirky decor changes every few months.

# MILWAUKEE★★

MICHELIN MAP 583 O 7
CENTRAL STANDARD TIME
POPULATION 573,378

Defined by the Milwaukee, Menominee and Kinnickinnic rivers, the city of Milwaukee was chartered in 1846. Before the Europeans arrived, Indians lived on the natural abundance of this area, with its fish-filled waters and hardwood forests, prompting the local Chippewa to name it *Millioki*, meaning "gathering place by the waters."

- 🄸 **Information:** Greater Milwaukee Convention & Visitors Bureau. ☎414-273-7222. www.milwaukee.org.
- ▶ **Orient Yourself:** Less than two hours north of Chicago.
- ⊙ **Don't Miss:** The Pfister Hotel lobby, even if you have other accomodations.
- 🄺🄸🄳🅂 **Kids:** See sea-lion shows and take camel rides at the Milwaukee County Zoo.

## A Bit of History

Nascent Milwaukee comprised three settlements divided by the Milwaukee River. In the 1830s Montreal fur trader **Solomon Juneau** and his partner, lawyer Morgan L. Martin, laid claim to most of the land on the east side of the river

(Juneautown), while the west side (Kilbourntown) was secured by Connecticut engineer **Byron Kilbourn**. In 1849 Virginian **George Walker** purchased the land on the south side of the settlement, naming it Walker's Point. Today, **Historic Walker Point** includes a collection of late-19C landmarks on National Avenue *(between 5th & 6th Sts.)*.

Rivalry between the early east- and westside settlements proved intense. Attempting to cut each other off from municipal services, Juneau and Kilbourn laid out their streets so that they did not meet at the river, thus posing an obstacle to bridge construction.

The city's population increased between 1840 and 1860, bolstered mainly by immigrants—who made up half of Milwaukee's population by 1860. Germans became the dominant group in 19C Milwaukee, proving to be a significant political force into the 20C. German brewing traditions, supported by grain and hops from the state's central grain-growing region, made Milwaukee America's beer capital.

By the late 19C, access to rail and water transportation and the availability of cheap and abundant raw materials catapulted Milwaukee to the forefront of industry.

Milwaukee nurtures the performing arts downtown, staging ballet, symphony and Broadway shows in a variety of venues, including the restored Renaissance Revival **Pabst Theater**★ *(144 E. Wells St.; ☎414-286-3663)*, designed in 1895 by Otto Strack.

Acres of parks ring the city, and west of downtown, **Marquette University** *(Wisconsin Ave. & 11th St.)* provides an institutional anchor.

For the sports enthusiast, Milwaukee is home to the **Brewers**, a National League baseball team that plays in a retractable-roof stadium, Miller Park. The city also claims the **Bucks** NBA basketball team, and the International Hockey League's **Admirals**.

Beginning in late June each year, the city hosts the renowned 11-day music festival called **Summerfest, the world's largest music fest,** in Henry W. Maier Festival Park on the shores of Lake Michigan, where nationally known acts draw thousands of music buffs.

# Downtown

Historically the center of government and finance, the east side remains Milwaukee's business center. It is bounded on the south by the renovated warehouse lofts, design studios and antique shops of the **Historic Third Ward** (home to Milwaukee's 19C Irish immigrants) and on the north by the tony residential **Yankee Hill** and **Historic Brady Street**—a onetime Italian neighborhood that has evolved into a strip of boutiques, restaurants and coffeehouses. The 200 block of East Michigan Street reveals 19C Milwaukee in the Second Empire roofline of the **Mitchell Building** *(no. 207)* and the adjacent **Mackie Building**★ *(no. 225)*. The second floor of the Mackie Building houses the nation's first trading pit, the ornate **Grain Exchange Room**★. Farther east on Wisconsin Avenue, the 1899 **Federal Building**★ *(nos. 515-19)* is a landmark with its tall central tower and limestone façade. Atop the 1930 Art Deco **Wisconsin Gas Company Building** *(no. 626)*, the flame finial glows red for warm weather, gold for cold, and blue for no change; it flickers for rain or snow.

On the west side of the river, which is characterized by its cultural and commercial attractions, **Old World Third Street**★ *(1000 & 1100 blocks of 3rd St.)* preserves the city's German heritage (you can still select the best of the wurst at Usinger's Famous Sausage shop).

## Milwaukee Art Museum★★

*700 N. Art Museum Dr.; entrance on lake side.*
&♿ 🅿 ☎414-224-3200. www.mam.org.
This block-like concrete structure, designed by Eero Saarinen in 1957 and renovated in 2001 to add the Quadracci Pavilion, designed by Santiago Calatrava, rises above Lake Michigan. Spanning civilizations from ancient Egypt to the present, its collection shines in 19C European art and 20C American painting and sculpture. In the **Flagg galleries** you'll find a significant group of Medieval and Renaissance religious artworks. The mezzanine level displays a large collection of **Haitian art**. On the upper level, the Bradley Collection contains a prized group of **20C European and**

**American art**★; nearby, cubical **lake overlooks** set with modern sculptures are framed by the lake's horizon.

## Milwaukee Public Museum★★

*800 W. Wells St.* ⏱*Open daily 10am–5pm.* ✆*$8.* ☎*414-278-2728. www.mpm.edu.*

Now part of the Museum Center complex, the 1963 Milwaukee Public Museum has been updated with the addition of **Discovery World**, **The James Lovell Museum of Science, Economics and Technology** Kids *(500 N. Harbor Dr.* ☎ *414-765-9966;*

---

## Beer in Milwaukee

The foundation of Milwaukee's early economy, beer has played a defining role in Milwaukee's history. Though the city is no longer the official brewing capital, brewing continues to define its cultural identity. Started in 1840 by three Welshmen, the city's first brewery produced ale and porter, both English-style top-fermentation beers. Light golden lager, a bottom-fermentation beer, was introduced to the city the following year. Milwaukee's port location, combined with a profusion of local barley and hops, fostered a vibrant beer industry, dominated by such giants as Blatz (1846-1959), Pabst (since 1844), Schlitz (1849-1981) and Miller (since 1855). By the 1880s, Milwaukee boasted more than 80 breweries.

Prohibition devastated the smaller breweries, however, and postwar consolidation left **Miller Brewing Company** *(4000 W. State St.; daily tours are free;* ♿ ℗ ☎*414-931-2337)* as the one large brewer in Milwaukee. Today the nation's second-largest brewer still operates from the site its founder purchased in 1855. Tours begin in the visitor center and take in the bottling and packaging operations and the **brewhouse**, where rows of massive copper kettles boil hundreds of barrels at a time. Before leaving, visitors can sample the company's products in the 1892 Miller Inn or beer garden (seasonal).

Begun in reaction to the mass-market approach of large beer companies, the modern microbreweries revive historic brewing methods and the distinctive quality of regional beer. **Sprecher Brewery** *(701 W. Glendale Ave., Glendale;* 🚶*visit by guided tour only; reservations required;* ♿ ℗ ☎*414-964-2739)* was the bellwether in Milwaukee (since 1985). Visitors here learn how the company's single brew kettle turns out products ranging from Imperial stout to root beer—although its output is literally a drop in Miller's bucket.

*Miller Brewery*

© VISIT Milwaukee

*www.discoveryworld.org)* and the IMAX Theater. Permanent exhibits include Bugs Alive! and the Puelicher Butterfly Wing, both on the museum's first floor. The second floor, devoted to Native Americans, showcases **Crow Indian Bison** Hunt, an evocative diorama of 19C American Plains Indians.

## Additional Sights

### The Charles Allis Art Museum★

*1801 N. Prospect Ave.* ○*Open Wed-Sun 1pm–5pm.* ☜*$5.* ☏*414-278-8295.*
Housed in the 1911 Tudor-style mansion where Charles Allis, the first president of Milwaukee's Allis-Chalmers Company, once lived, this museum is best known for its collections of **Asian pottery and stoneware**, European and American painting, and decorative arts.

### Villa Terrace Decorative Arts Museum★

*2220 N. Terrace Ave.* ○*Open Wed-Sun 1pm–5pm.* ☜*$5.* ☏*414-271-3656.*
Designed by David Adler, the 1923 **mansion** was modeled after a 16C Northern Italian villa. Cypress-beamed ceilings and a lovely courtyard adorn the interior, while outside, terraces cascade down toward Lake Michigan and end in a formal garden. The collection includes paintings, furnishings and decorative arts dating from the 15C to the 18C.

### Pabst Mansion★★

*2000 W. Wisconsin Ave.* �&☏☏*414-931-0808. www.pabstmansion.com*
A remnant of Milwaukee's grand days as America's beer capital, the elegant 37-room Flemish Renaissance Revival-style mansion (1892, Ferry & Clas), with its terra-cotta ornamentation, was the home of the German-born Great Lakes steamship captain **Frederick Pabst** (1836-1904). In 1864 Pabst joined the brewery business of his father-in-law, Phillip Best, and took over the operations nine years later.
Tours begin on the east side of the house in the Neoclassical domed **beer pavilion**, a relic of the 1893 World's Columbian Exposition in Chicago where Pabst

won the blue ribbon that still characterizes the company's beer. Inside the mansion, the French Rococo **ladies' parlor** is balanced by the masculine **music room** with its heavy oak furniture.

### Mitchell Park Horticultural Conservatory★

*524 S. Layton Blvd.* ☐ ☏*414-649-9800.*
Three striking parabolic **domes** support a range of plant life, representing exotic flora from the Sonoran Desert to the Brazilian rain forest. Floral displays in the **Show Dome** change seasonally.

### Milwaukee County Zoo★★

☒*10001 W. Bluemound Rd. From downtown, follow I-94 West to US-45 North and take Exit 39/Bluemound Rd.* ○*Open daily 9am–4:30pm.* ☜*$9.* ☽&☐☏*414-771-3040. www.milwaukeezoo.org.*
In this sprawling 200-acre zoo, layered outdoor environments place predators behind prey: Jaguars lurk on bluffs behind South American alpaca; Amur tigers sun themselves on boulders beyond camels; and African lions form the backdrop for zebras.

## Excursions

### Harley Davidson Motor Company Capitol Drive Factory★★

*10mi northwest of Milwaukee in Wauwatosa, WI. Take I-94 West to US-45 North; exit at Capitol Dr. and turn left. 11700 W. Capitol Dr.* ☞*Visit by guided tour only. Children under 12 not permitted; closed-toe shoes without heels of one inch or less.* ☐☐☏*414-343-7850. www.harley-davidson.com.*
America's only remaining motorcycle maker began in a Milwaukee shed in 1903 and still assembles its distinctive "V" twin-cam engines in this 450,000sq ft facility. A tour here starts out with an introductory video, after which visitors are guided through the actual plant, viewing the machining of parts and the assembly of engines by workers, computers and even robots. The foyer exhibits historic and contemporary engines and motorcycles.

## Door County

*120mi north of Milwaukee.* **⏹** *For information, contact the Door County Visitor Bureau: P.O. Box 406, Sturgeon Bay, WI 54235, ☎920-743-4456, www.doorcounty.com.* Consisting of the tapering finger of land that separates Green Bay from Lake Michigan, Door County takes its name from early French explorers, who called the treacherous water passage at the peninsula's tip "Death's Door." Anchored by **Green Bay** at the base of the peninsula and by Washington Island 6mi off the northern tip, Door County attracts a steady stream of tourists who transform the peninsula into a midwestern Cape Cod each summer. Routes 42 and 57 outline the peninsula, merging at **Sturgeon Bay** *(38mi north of Green Bay)*, the seat and commercial center of Door County. North of Sturgeon Bay, you can explore tiny scenic fishing villages with names such as Sister Bay, Egg Harbor, Fish Creek, Ephraim and Ellison Bay. Ferries *(Island Clipper, ☎920-854-2972; and Washington Island Ferry, ☎920-847-2546; www.wisferry.com)* depart from Northport on the northern tip of the peninsula for recreational **Washington Island**, settled by Icelandic fishermen more than a century ago. The Rock Island Ferry *(departs several times daily summer–fall; ☎920-847-3322)* leaves Washington Island for secluded **Rock Island State Park** *(☎920-847-2235)*, a 912-acre nature preserve.

### Annunciation Greek Orthodox Church★★

*9400 W. Congress St. 22mi northwest of Milwaukee in Wauwatosa, WI. Take I-94 West to US-45 North and exit at Capital Dr. East; follow Capital Dr. to 92nd St. North.* **⌁** *Visit by guided tour only.* **Ⓟ** *☎414-461-9400. www.annunciationwi.com.* One of architect Frank Lloyd Wright's last works (completed in 1961, after his death), this blue dome rising above a ring of eyelid windows resembles a flying saucer. The cross-shaped structure rests on cylindrical pylons, and the arched entrance is fronted by a saucer-shaped fountain. Space Age ornamentation fills the sanctuary.

# MADISON★

MICHELIN MAP 583 N 7
CENTRAL STANDARD TIME
POPULATION 202,735

Considered one of America's most livable small cities, Madison owes its existence to Judge James Doty, who moved Wisconsin's capital to the mile-wide isthmus between lakes Mendota and Monona in 1836, thus enhancing his real-estate holdings. John Nolen Drive follows smaller Lake Monona to the south, passing the curving white façade of **Monona Terrace Community and Convention Center★** *(1 John Nolen Dr.)*. The center's Frank Lloyd Wright design was not realized until 1996, a half century after his death, by Anthony Puttnam and Taliesin Architects. Its curving terrace repeats the form of the windows while offering lovely lake **views★**. Some 40,000 students who attend the **University of Wisconsin at Madison**, which covers 932 acres on the shore of Lake Mendota west of downtown, help support a vibrant arts and entertainment scene.

**⏹ Information:** ☎608 255-2537. www.visitmadison.com
**Ⓟ Parking:** Scrap the wheels and walk the picture-perfect downtown streets.
**☺ Don't Miss:** The quirky collections of the House on the Rock.
**Kids Kids:** Learn a condiment song at the World Famous Mustard Museum

# Sights

## Wisconsin State Capitol★★

*On Capitol Square.* ♿☎608-266-0382. *www.wisconsin.gov/state/capfacts/tour_select.html.*

The capitol's towering Beaux-Arts-style white Vermont-granite dome, designed by New York architects George B. Post & Sons in 1906, is one of largest in the world by volume. Four massive temple façades with overscaled statuary characterize the capitol building, the dome of which is capped by Daniel Chester French's 15ft bronze, **Wisconsin**. Step inside for a breathtaking look at 43 types of stone, glass mosaics and the soaring rotunda. Guided tours take in the Venetian **Governor's Conference Room**, the marble **Supreme Court chamber★★**, and the **Assembly chamber★**, where the first electronic voting machine was installed in 1917.

On the west side of Capitol Square, two museums commemorate the state's history: the **Wisconsin State Historical Museum★** *(30 Carroll St.;* ☎608-264-6555) and the **Wisconsin Veterans Museum★** *(30 W. Mifflin St.;* ☎608-267-1799). Here, too, downtown's commercial heart, **State Street★** *(closed to automobile traffic)*, links the capitol to the university via an urbane mix of restaurants, shops and craft galleries.

## Unitarian Meeting House★★

*900 University Bay Dr.* 👓*Visit by guided tour only.* ♿🅿☎608-233-9774. *www.fusmadison.org.*

A triangular prow of glass slicing through a hillside on a residential street announces this late work (1951) by Frank Lloyd Wright. Metal roof overhangs ramp the entry, initiating a passage that sweeps dramatically upward into the sanctuary,, suggesting "the wings of a bird in flight."

## Chazen Museum of Art★★

*800 University Ave.* ◑*Open Tue-Fri 9am–5pm, Sat-Sun 11am-5pm.* ◑*Closed Mon.* ☎608-263-2246.

This excellent collection is attractively arranged on three floors around a central skylit court. You'll find the bulk of the permanent collection on the

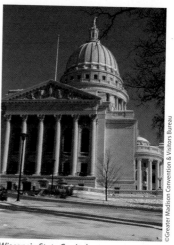
*Wisconsin State Capitol*

©Greater Madison Convention & Visitors Bureau

third floor, where holdings range from ancient Greek vases to 19C American and European paintings. The third-floor mezzanine exhibits a wonderful selection of early-20C works (Georgia O'Keeffe, Grant Wood, Alexander Calder). Contemporary art is the focus of the bright fourth floor.

# Excursions

## Circus World Museum★★

📷*40mi north of Madison in Baraboo, WI. Take I-90/94 West and exit on Rte. 33 West toward Baraboo; in Baraboo, take Rte. 113 South and follow signs.* ◑*Closed Sun.* 💲$14.95. 🍴♿🅿☎608-356-8341. *www.circusworldmuseum.com.*

Fifty acres of exhibits surround the historic winter quarters of the Ringling Brothers, whose 1884 Baraboo circus became the nation's largest circus company—the "Greatest Show on Earth." Collections in the Irvin Feld Exhibition Hall and Visitor Center convey the bombast and showmanship of these traveling extravaganzas through circus posters, costumes and reconstructed spectacles. The **Fox Wagon Restoration Center** and **Deppe Wagon Pavilion** display over 100 historic circus wagons. .

## Taliesin★★★

*35mi west of Madison. Take US-14 West to Rte. 23 South through Spring Green* and cross the Wisconsin River to County Rd. C. ⮕ Visit by guided tour only (open May-Oct); several different tours are available. $16–$80. ☒♿🅿 ☎608-588-7900. www.taliesinpreservation.org.

Renowned architect **Frank Lloyd Wright** (1867-1959), born in nearby Richland Center, returned in 1911 to build Taliesin (Welsh for "shining brow") as his home. Wright eventually began an atelier here, where prospective architects could work. The 600-acre complex still welcomes Taliesin fellows, who study their discipline in the countryside that fostered the master.

The horizontal sweep of limestone that Wright designed in 1953 as a restaurant now holds the **Frank Lloyd Wright Visitor Center**, where tours begin. His home, **Taliesin**, perches on a hill above a small waterfall across from the visitor center. Wright began his famed Fellowship here and built and rebuilt the original Prairie-style house over five decades. To the south lies Wright's 1930s **Midway Farm** and the layered wooden slats of the **Romeo and Juliet windmill** on the hill. A small road leads to the tiny stone and shingle **Unity Chapel**, designed in 1886 by Wright's first employer, J.L. Silsbee. Around the bend, the broad eaves of Wright's **Hillside Studio and Theater** (1902), the office of Taliesin Architects, rise above the road.

### The House on the Rock

Kids 5754 State Od., 23 Spring Green, WI 53533. 60mi west of Madison, in Spring Green, WI. Take US-18 West to Dodgeville and go north on Rte. 23 to no. 5754. Several different combination tours are available. 🅿 ☎608-935-3639. www. thehouseontherock.com.

This limestone house was built on a rocky outcrop as a weekend retreat by collector Alex Jordan in the 1940s. Today more than 16 buildings in the complex are filled with an eclectic collection of music machines, armor, weaponry, dolls—and the world's largest indoor carousel.

### Effigy Mounds National Monument★★

100mi west of Madison near Marquette, IA. Take US-18 West 97mi to Prairie du Chien and cross the Mississippi River to Marquette, IA. In Marquette, take US-76 North 3mi and follow signs. ♿🅿 ☎319-873-3491. www.nps.gov/efmo.

Located on a 2,526-acre bluff overlooking the west bank of the Mississippi River, the national monument contains some of the country's largest earthworks. Visible via a web of hiking trails, nearly 200 burial mounds lie within the park's borders. While most of these are conical, 29 are animal effigies—unique to the upper Mississippi River Valley. Archaeologists have dated the mounds as far back as 500 BC and as recently as AD 1300, but little is known about the prehistoric Late Woodlands culture that created them.

### The World Famous Mustard Museum

Kids 20mi southwest of Madison in Mount Horeb, WI. Take 151-S/US-18 W towards Dodgeville. ◷Open daily 10am–5pm. ☎800-438-6878. www.mustardweb.com.

This quirky museum displays more than 4,400 mustards and countless pieces of this condiment's memorabilia. The gift shop is packed with, of course, mustard of all kind. An educated staff will help you find (and sample) mustards that meet your culinary needs.

# MINNEAPOLIS/ST. PAUL AREA

Minneapolis/St. Paul, a metropolitan area of more than three million people, contains the lion's share of the state's cultural treasures—and many natural ones, too. Situated in the southeastern portion of Minnesota, less than 20mi from Wisconsin's western border, Minneapolis and St. Paul are often called the Twin Cities because of their close proximity. As siblings, they have much in common: both nurture the arts, especially music and theater; both value, and attempt to preserve, their historic architecture.

The region served as stomping grounds for Native Americans for nearly 10,000 years before the French arrived in the early 18C to build a network of fur-trading posts. In 1763, after the French and Indian War, the land was relinquished to the English, and finally to the US, which acquired it in 1803 as part of the Louisiana Purchase. Only during the latter half of the 19C did the two cities' paths diverge. Minneapolis became an industrial center, St. Paul the nexus of the area's steamship and railroad lines. Today, Minneapolis is larger and more cosmopolitan, its skyline a glittering showcase of modern architecture. St. Paul remains more of a sleepy, European enclave, home to a quiet, well-preserved downtown; and the government seat, which in 1998 claimed the first professional wrestler to become a state governor, Jesse ("the Body") Ventura.

Twin Citians like to say that the two cities complement each other: St. Paul's staid traditionalism reveals itself in its historic mansions, landmark conservatory and

century-old annual **Winter Carnival** *(Jan–Feb)*, while Minneapolis' urban progressivism can be found in its contemporary art museums, sculpture garden and funky summer arts and music festival, **Aquatennial** *(July)*.

Located 150mi north of Minneapolis, **Duluth** anchors two scenic routes: north along US-61 and east along US-2 and Route 28. Here the remote Lake Superior shoreline reveals its breathtaking natural beauty.

*Spoonbridge and Cherry (1988), Minneapolis Sculpture Garden*

© Ryan Glanzer/SXC

## Area Address Book

🪙 *For coin ranges, see the Legend on the cover flap.*

### WHERE TO STAY

**$$$ Saint Paul Hotel** – *350 Market St., St. Paul, MN.* ✗ ♿ 🅿 ☎*651-292-9292. www.stpaulhotel.com. 254 rooms.* Downtown's 1910 landmark has hosted the likes of Sophia Loren and Bill Murray. Gold-leaf columns, a 20ft-wide antique mirror and vibrant Oriental rugs highlight the ornate lobby. Guest rooms, by contrast, claim warm earth tones and simple Colonial-style furniture. The award-winning **St. Paul Grill** is known for its regional classics.

**$$ Nicollet Island Inn** – *95 Merriam St., Minneapolis, MN.* ✗ ♿ 🅿 ☎*612-331-3035. www.nicolletislandinn.com. 24 rooms.* Located on a small island 2mi from downtown Minneapolis, this elegant guest house was built of locally quarried limestone in 1893. The lobby is set up like a cozy living room with two fireplaces flanked by wing chairs. Guest rooms, in subtle colors with antique canopy or four-poster beds, boast Mississippi River views.

### WHERE TO EAT

**$$$ La Belle Vie** – *510 Groveland Ave.* ☎*612-874-6440. www.labellevie.us* **American.** An elegant decor including crystal chandeliers and mueum quality paintings and sculptures set the stage for this popular spot. Choose from prix fixe or a la carte menus in the formal dining room, or more casual but still outstanding selections in the adjacent lounge. Start with a warm goat cheese tart with tomato confit and tapenade vinaigrette, followed by grilled poussin with sauteed wild baby leeks, morel mushrooms, and cured foie gras, and finish with organic olive oil cake.

# MINNEAPOLIS ★

MAP P276
CENTRAL STANDARD TIME
POPULATION 372,811

While hosting a population of only about 372,800, making it the 45th-largest city in America, Minneapolis nurtures a wealth of diverse neighborhoods, from the warehouse district to the pristine neighborhoods that flank the verdant parkways of its 22 lakes. The city is also an urban mecca for visual and performing arts, boasting scores of theaters, a world-class symphony and several rock and pop bands (Prince; the Replacements) who have made it big in the music world. A handful of excellent museums round out the cultural scene.

🔲 **Information:** ☎612-767-8000. www.minneapolis.org
▶ **Orient Yourself:** Minneapolis hugs the southwest bank of the Mississippi River, which makes a switchback here on its journey south.
💿 **Don't Miss:** The remarkable permanent collection at the Walker Art Museum.
🪙 **Also See:** ST. PAUL.

## A Bit of History

The name Minneapolis derives from the Dakota word for water, *minne*, and the Greek word for city, *polis*—an appropriate moniker considering the huge role water has played, and continues to play, in the city's cultural and economic life. The last ice sheet retreated from present-day Minneapolis about 12,000 years ago, leaving behind a landscape covered with relatively small, but deep, craters. Glacial runoff filled the holes with water, creating today's lakes; it also carved out the Minnesota and Mississippi rivers, which connect at the southeastern corner of the city before the Mississippi jogs north through St. Paul. Initially it was at this intersection that St. Anthony Falls were located, but as water continued to wear away the limestone riverbed, the waterfall moved farther and farther up the Mississippi, leaving behind a dramatic gorge. Facilitator of the city's modern development—and the only waterfall on the entire 2,348mi-long Mississippi— **St. Anthony Falls** is now located 8mi upstream from its original location. In 1680 Franciscan missionary Father Louis Hennepin became the first white man to see the falls, which he named after his patron saint, Anthony of Padua.

In 1819 the construction of Fort Snelling marked the beginning of US rule in the region. Minneapolis was incorporated in 1872; it was the milling capital of the world. After World War II, Minneapolis began the process of converting to a white-collar, service economy. The city's success in doing so has provided an example that has been followed by cities of similar size nationwide.

# Sights

## Downtown★★

Its distinctive skyline visible for miles around, downtown Minneapolis displays some architectural gems, from late-19C sandstone piles to glittering late-20C office towers. One of America's first pedestrian thoroughfares, 1mi-long **Nicollet Mall** (Nicollet Ave. between Washington & Grant Sts.) is the site of most of the town's outdoor retail activity in the summer months, while the celebrated 5mi-long **Skyway system** links up more than 100 downtown buildings with climate-controlled corridors lined with restaurants and shops that bustle year-round. A **visitor center** is located on the ground level of the City Center mall (40 7th St. S.).

At 821 Marquette Avenue, the 32-story obelisk **Foshay Tower** (1929) is one of the city's most recognizable landmarks, if only for the 10ft-high letters spelling out FOSHAY above its 31st-floor **observation deck** (open Apr–Sept). **IDS Center** (1973, Philip Johnson), at 777 Nicollet Mall, contains Minneapolis' tallest skyscraper, the octagonal blue-glass **IDS Tower** (51 stories), as well as the Plexiglass-enclosed **Crystal Court**, one of the city's most fetching public interiors. The second-tallest building, Cesar Pelli's 1988 **Norwest Center** (Marquette Ave. & 6th St. S.), is sheathed in warm Kasota sandstone.

## Riverfront and Mill District★

Centered around St. Anthony Falls, the multi-use district contains fascinating relics of Minneapolis' earliest industry. Soldiers at Fort Snelling (◐see ST. PAUL) built the first mills on the falls in the early 19C. By the 1880s, some two dozen gargantuan flour mills lined a three-block corridor surrounding the falls, and warehouses cropped up nearby. Recent gentrification has turned some of the old brick buildings into bars, restaurants and loft apartments.

**St. Anthony Falls Heritage trail** (pedestrian and bicycle traffic only) loops for 2mi along the riverfront and passes two important landmarks: the 1881 blue limestone **Pillsbury "A" Mill** (not open to the public), the largest flour mill in the world at the time of its opening; and the 1883 **Stone Arch Bridge**. Celebrated as an engineering marvel, the curving, 2,100ft-long span is the only stone bridge to cross the Mississippi River.

## Walker Art Center★★

Vineland Pl. & Lyndale Ave. S. ※ ⅙ ℗ ◐Open Tues, Wed, Sat and Sun 11am–5pm, Thurs-Fri 11am–9pm. ◐Closed Mon and major holidays.☎612-375-7600. www.walkerart.org.

The award-winning Walker Art Center contains the most extensive—and most intelligently curated—collection of contemporary art in Minneapolis. Housed in a modern, angular building (1971, 1984, Edward Larrabee Barnes), selections from the museum's permanent collection—including works by Roy Lichtenstein, Andy Warhol, Joan Mitchell, Chuck Close and Jasper Johns—are displayed alongside thought-provoking traveling exhibits. A 2005 expansion added new galleries, educational areas, and a 385-seat theater. The Walker hosts the largest museum-based perform-

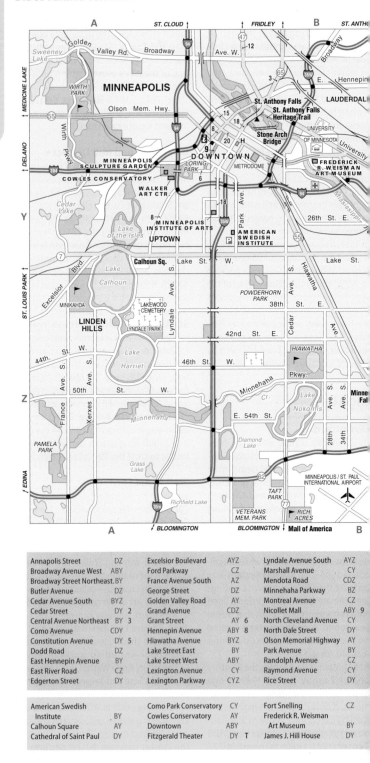

| | | | | | | | |
|---|---|---|---|---|---|---|---|
| Annapolis Street | DZ | Excelsior Boulevard | AYZ | Lyndale Avenue South | AYZ | | |
| Broadway Avenue West | ABY | Ford Parkway | CZ | Marshall Avenue | CY | | |
| Broadway Street Northeast. | BY | France Avenue South | AZ | Mendota Road | CDZ | | |
| Butler Avenue | DZ | George Street | DZ | Minnehaha Parkway | BZ | | |
| Cedar Avenue South | BYZ | Golden Valley Road | AY | Montreal Avenue | CZ | | |
| Cedar Street | DY | 2 | Grand Avenue | CDZ | Nicollet Mall | ABY | 9 |
| Central Avenue Northeast | BY | 3 | Grant Street | AY | 6 | North Cleveland Avenue | CY |
| Como Avenue | CDY | Hennepin Avenue | ABY | 8 | North Dale Street | DY | |
| Constitution Avenue | DY | 5 | Hiawatha Avenue | BYZ | Olson Memorial Highway | AY | |
| Dodd Road | DZ | Lake Street East | BY | Park Avenue | BY | | |
| East Hennepin Avenue | BY | Lake Street West | ABY | Randolph Avenue | CZ | | |
| East River Road | CZ | Lexington Avenue | CY | Raymond Avenue | CY | | |
| Edgerton Street | DY | Lexington Parkway | CYZ | Rice Street | DY | | |

| | | | | | |
|---|---|---|---|---|---|
| American Swedish | | Como Park Conservatory | CY | Fort Snelling | CZ |
| Institute | BY | Cowles Conservatory | AY | Frederick R. Weisman | |
| Calhoun Square | AY | Downtown | ABY | Art Museum | BY |
| Cathedral of Saint Paul | DY | Fitzgerald Theater | DY T | James J. Hill House | DY |

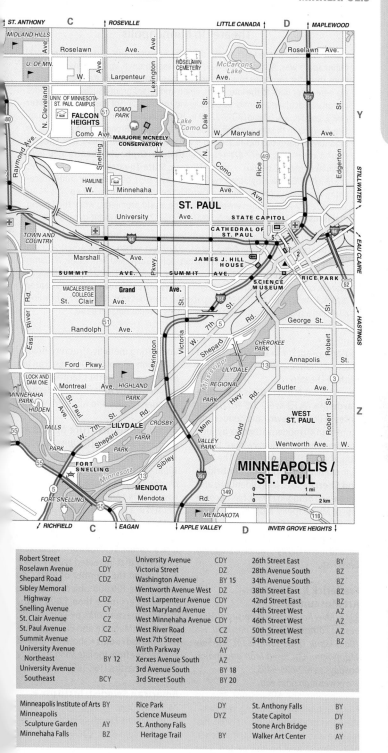

## Theater In Minneapolis

Boasting more theaters per capita than any American city outside of New York, Minneapolis was, is, and may always be a thespian town, with dozens of plays—from absurdist comedies to wrenching dramas—on stage every night. While drama here dates back to the late 1800s, when immigrant groups such as the Swedes put on vernacular plays in social clubs, it was the founding of the **Guthrie Theater** (818 S. 2nd St.; ☏612-377-2224) in 1963 that really put the city on the map. The downtown theater scene is dominated by touring Broadway crowd-pleasers mounted in gorgeous old-fashioned jewel boxes such as the **Music Box Theatre** (1407 Nicollet Mall; ☏612-871-1414), the **Historic Orpheum Theatre** (910 Hennepin Ave.; ☏612-339-7007) and the **Historic State Theatre** (805 Hennepin Ave.; ☏612-339-7007). Nearby stand two of the city's best black-box, or non-proscenium, theaters. In the Warehouse District, the intimate **Guthrie Lab** (700 N. 1st St.; ☏612-377-2224) stages envelope-pushing world premieres; while the **Loring Playhouse** (1633 Hennepin Ave. S.; ☏612-486-5757) puts on avant-garde plays.

Clustered in the artsy Calhoun Square district uptown are the well-respected **Jungle Theater** (2951 Lyndale Ave. S.; ☏612-822-7063), which stages American classics by playwrights such as David Mamet, John Guare and Tennessee Williams; the **Brave New Workshop** (2605 Hennepin Ave. S.; ☏612-332-6620), specializing in satirical comedy revues since 1958; and the **Bryant-Lake Bowl Cabaret Theater** (810 W. Lake St.; ☏612-825-8949), a space that manages to meld a diner, a bowling alley and a space for small-scale performances without missing a cue.

ing-arts program in the country and shares its building with the acclaimed Guthrie Theater.

The adjacent **Minneapolis Sculpture Garden**★★ (♿🅿 ☏612-375-7622) comprises 11 acres of lawns and hedges and more than 40 modern artworks by such acclaimed artists as Henry Moore, Isamu Noguchi and Alexander Calder. The 29ft-high aluminum sculpture **Spoonbridge and Cherry**★, by Claes Oldenburg and Coosje van Bruggen (1988), has become one of Minneapolis' most playful landmarks. In glass-paneled **Cowles Conservatory**★, tropical plants cluster around Frank Gehry's massive Standing Glass Fish.

### Frederick R. Weisman Art Museum ★

333 E. River Rd., on the University of Minnesota campus. ◷Open Tues-Wed, Fri 10am–5pm, Thurs 10am-8pm, Sat-Sun 11am–5pm. ◷Closed Mon and major holidays.☏612-625-9495. www.weisman.umn.edu.

Overlooking the Mississippi River is Frank Gehry's awe-inspiring stainless-steel and brick **building**★★ (1993). His mission was to not build "just another brick lump," and he succeeded. The

undulating metallic structure holds a collection of mostly 20C American art, including the world's largest groupings of work by **American Modernists** Marsden Hartley and Alfred Maurer.

### Minneapolis Institute of Arts ★

2400 3rd Ave. S. ♿🅿◷Open Tues-Wed 10am–5pm, Thurs 10am-9pm, Fri-Sat 10am–5pm, Sun 11am–5pm, ◷Closed Mon and major holidays. ☏612-870-3131. www.artsmia.org.

Housed in a Beaux-Arts structure (1915) by McKim, Mead, and White, the Minneapolis Institute of Arts recently undertook a 10-year, $150 million revitalization campaign that increased gallery space and tripled the number of works on display. The 100,000-object collection, which covers more than 5,000 years, includes masterworks by Rembrandt, Van Gogh, Magritte and El Greco. **Chinese period rooms**★ showcase art and architecture from the late Ming and early Ch'ing Dynasties (16C-18C).

### American Swedish Institute★

2600 Park Ave. ♿✕🅿 ◷Open Tues, Thurs, Fri-Sat 12pm–4pm, Wed 12pm-8pm, Sun 1pm-5pm. ◷Closed Mon and major holidays. ☎612-871-4907. www.americanswedishinst.org.

The 33-room French Château-style mansion (1904) that houses the American Swedish Institute was built for Swedish entrepreneur Swan Turnblad. With its raucous assemblage of turrets, balconies, pillars and gables, the gray limestone structure resembles a fairy-tale castle. In 1929 the house became the headquarters of the American Swedish Institute, created to "foster and preserve Swedish culture in America."

The interior of the house showcases intricately carved **woodwork**★★ as well as 11 rare porcelain-tile *kakelugnar* (stoves), each of a different design. Upper floors contain Scandinavian artifacts ranging from a 5C AD pre-Viking drinking vessel to a 600-piece collection of contemporary glasswork.

### Uptown and Chain of Lakes ★

Confusingly, what locals refer to as uptown is actually located southwest of downtown Minneapolis. Roughly clustered around the city's in-town lakes (which are connected by parkways and paths that are perfect for in-line skating, jogging and bicycling), these Uptown neighborhoods are where Twin Citians live, play and eat. **Calhoun Square** (*Lake St. & Hennepin Ave.*) is the epicenter of

*American Swedish Institute*

©Meet Minneapolis.com

the local Generation-X and Generation-Y scene, with thrift stores crowded alongside cafes and bars. **Linden Hills** (*44th St. S. & Upton Ave.*) is known for its quaint shopping district.

# ST. PAUL★

MAP P276
CENTRAL STANDARD TIME
POPULATION 275,150

While Minneapolis has been called the first city of the West, and a sparkling paean to commerce and wealth, St. Paul is considered the last city of the East; close to its Old World roots, protective of its architecture, and like many European burgs, difficult to navigate without a map. The area around Rice Park epitomizes St. Paul's pristine elegance, and its science and children's museums are the finest in the state. Some of the best cafe-crawling and window-shopping in the Twin Cities can be done on Grand Avenue, where boutiques crowd into old Victorian structures.

- **Information:** ☎651-265-4900. www.stpaulcvb.org.
- **Orient Yourself:** Contiguous St. Paul lies on the northeast bank of the Mississippi River.
- **Kids:** Bad weather doesn't bother little ones thanks to the convertible-dome IMAX Omnitheater.
- **Also See:** MINNEAPOLIS.

# A Bit of History

Their city centers less than 10mi apart, St. Paul and Minneapolis were both part of Sioux territory before white settlers arrived, and their modern histories can both be traced back to the 1819 construction of Fort Snelling, which was key in promoting the mill industry that fueled the subsequent growth of Minneapolis. Initially called "Pig's Eye"—the nickname of one of its first residents—St. Paul became a trading and transportation hub. The city was named the Minnesota state capital in 1849 and received its charter five years later. Today, Minnesota's palatial **State Capitol**★ *(Aurora Ave., between Cedar St. & Constitution Ave.;* ✗ ♿ 🅿 ☎*651-296-2881)*, severed from downtown by I-94, is the most famous local work of onetime St. Paul architect **Cass Gilbert** (1859-1934).

Throughout the latter half of the 19C, St. Paul thrived as the site of the Twin Cities' three main steamboat landings. After local railroad tycoon James J. Hill connected St. Paul with Washington State in 1893 via his Great Northern Railroad, the city became the most important transportation hub in the upper Midwest. Dependent on Minneapolis' lumber and flour mills to provide the goods that fueled its transport-based economy, St. Paul crashed hard during the Great Depression. New downtown construction since the 1950s has met with mixed success, yet sensitive architectural renovations—such as the acclaimed 1904 Richardsonian Romanesque **Landmark Center**—have been hailed by preservationists nationwide. One of the newer projects, **RiverCentre**, brought 46 conventions to the city in its first year.

# Sights

### Rice Park★★

Hemmed in by Fourth and Fifth Streets and Washington and Market Streets, Rice Park (1849) still holds sway as St. Paul's prettiest public space. To the north stands **Landmark Center**★, whose red-roofed, pink-granite assemblage of cop-per-topped turrets and gables features a soaring, six-story skylit **courtyard**★★ surrounded by a Scandinavian bakery and the **Minnesota Museum of American Art** *(75 W. 5th St.;* ☎*651-266-1030)*. The museum's 3,500-piece collection includes works by Grant Wood, and members of the Ash Can school.

East of Rice Park towers the 1910 **St. Paul Hotel** *(350 Market St.)*. South of the park is the ornate 1916 **James J. Hill Reference Library** *(80 W. 4th St.)*, whose two-story **Great Reading Room** features a soaring coffered ceiling and inlaid marble floors. The city's largest performing-arts venue, the **Ordway Center for the Performing Arts** *(345 Washington St., 651-224-4222)* looks like an upright tray of ice cubes, with its two-story, glass-paneled front lobby on the park's west side.

### Fitzgerald Theater

*10 East Exchange St.* ♿ 🅿
☎*651-290-1200.*
Named for onetime St. Paul resident F. Scott Fitzgerald, the 1910 Beaux-Arts Fitzgerald Theater is St. Paul's oldest. Here, Twin Cities denizen **Garrison Keillor** broadcasts his famous radio show, "The Prairie Home Companion," in front of a live audience.

### Science Museum of Minnesota★

🅺🅸🅳🆂 *120 W. Kellogg Blvd.* ✗ ♿ 🅿 🕙*Open Mon-Sat 8:30am-10pm, Sun 8:30am-7pm.* ☎*$14-24.* ☎*651-221-9444.*
Among the first-rate exhibits at this Mississippi riverfront facility are an expanded paleontology exhibit, an experiment gallery, a human-body gallery, an exhibit on the ecology and history of the Mississippi River, and a convertible-dome IMAX Omnitheater.

### Summit Avenue ★★

Sprawled across the highest ground in St. Paul, just west of downtown, this prestigious 4.5mi thoroughfare is one of the best-preserved Victorian boulevards in the country. Summit Avenue begins at the copper-domed **Cathedral of Saint Paul**★, which enjoys a commanding view over downtown from its bluff-top perch *(♿ 🅿 ☎ 651-228-1766)*. Lined with more than 300 mansions, Summit

# Mall of America

*Located a 30min drive from the Twin Cities just south of I-494 and east of Rte. 77/Cedar Ave. in Bloomington, MN. ☎952-883-8800. www.mallofamerica.com. The mall's public-transit station is located outside the first-floor entrance to East Broadway. Express buses run between the Mall of America and the Twin Cities International Airport, Nicollet Mall, and downtown St. Paul. Call ☎612-373-3333 for fares and schedules.*

If ever there was a place that epitomized the American maxim that bigger is better, this is it. The largest shopping and entertainment complex in the US, it encompasses—under a single roof—more than 520 stores, an indoor theme park, 20 restaurants, 30 fast-food joints, 14 movie screens, an aquarium, a college campus and a wedding chapel. Drawing more than 40 million visitors a year, the mall is one of the most visited tourist attractions in Minneapolis.

Completed in 1992 at a cost of $650 million, the 4.2-million-square-foot mall is shaped like a giant three-story rectangle, with four department stores (Macy's, Bloomingdale's, Nordstrom and Sears) anchoring the corners. Besides a red-neon Mall of America sign on its exterior, the structure is hardly visible from the outside, due to the web of highways and the 13,000 parking spots (all within 300ft of an entrance) that surround it. Inside, massive corridors with the height and girth of airplane hangars are lined with every store imaginable. Although the atmosphere is especially chaotic during the Christmas season, at any time of year the mall affords a fascinating glimpse into the heart of American capitalism.

Courtesy of Mall of America®

venue was the stomping grounds for the fin-de-siècle elite, and remains one of the city's toniest addresses. Author and St. Paul native **F. Scott Fitzgerald** (1896-1940) wrote *This Side of Paradise* in a third-floor apartment at 599 Summit in the summer of 1919. Running parallel to Summit one block south, **Grand Avenue** may be the most interesting shopping district in the Twin Cities. Many of its boutiques and restaurants are tucked into quirky Victorian houses centered on the eastern end of Grand at Victoria Street.

### James J. Hill House★★

*240 Summit Ave. ♿⌚Visit by guided tour only Wed-Sat 10am-3:30pm, Sun 1pm-3:30pm. ⊙$8. ☎651-297-2555. www.mnhs.org.*

This 1891 Richardsonian Romanesque manse stands as a tribute to the work of Canadian-born railroad tycoon James Hill. Its 42 rooms comprise 22 fireplaces, 13 bathrooms, the 2,000sq ft **Great Hall**★, a two-story skylit art gallery and a marvelous stained-glass window.

### Fort Snelling★

*Rtes. 55 & 5.* ☎*612-726-1171. www.mnhs. org/places/sites/hfs.*
Begun in 1819, Fort Snelling ranks as the westernmost fort built by the US government after the War of 1812. It was set on a bluff overlooking the confluence of the Minnesota and Mississippi rivers, allowing soldiers to control fur-trade routes. Soldiers at the fort helped build the first flour mills on St. Anthony Falls, while officers oversaw the "treaties" that wrested land from Native Americans. Today the re-created diamond-shaped fort encompasses a store, a hospital, a school and the original Round and Hex-agonal towers. A 20min film introduces the fort's history, and costumed guides *(May–Oct)* interpret what life was like here 170 years ago.

### Como Park Conservatory ★

*1325 Aida Pl.* ◷*Open daily 10am–4pm.* ☎*651-487-8200.*
Situated in 450-acre Como Park, one of the largest green spaces in the Twin Cities, this 1915 conservatory, made of aluminum, steel and glass, underwent a $12 million renovation in the 1990s. Six public areas within provide botanical delights for the senses.

# WESTERN LAKE SUPERIOR★

MICHELIN MAP 583 M, N 4, 5
EASTERN STANDARD TIME AND CENTRAL STANDARD TIME

Lovely coastal and forest landscapes occupy this remote corner of the US and provide a stunning setting for the jewel that is Lake Superior. On its bottom lie 350 shipwrecks, many of them victims of the lake's infamous autumnal north-easters. Ancient volcanic and glacial activity along with wind and water erosion created the "sweetwater sea," trimming its edges with basalt cliffs, soaring escarpments, fine sand beaches and dunes, and multihued sandstone.

For the Ojibwa, the region's first inhabitants, Lake Superior and its surrounding forests provided sustenance and spiritual energy. In the centuries after the Europeans arrived, commerce in furs, lumber, sandstone, copper, iron and fish brought settlers and entrepreneurs to the region. Today its rich harvest of natural beauty and historic sites supports tourism, the latest local industry. A visit here logically begins in the small city of Duluth★, Minnesota, where the north and south shores of western Lake Superior converge to form the Great Lakes' largest and busiest harbor.

▯ **Information:** ☎651-296-5029. www.exploreminnesota.com
▸ **Orient Yourself:** Covering 31,700sq mi, Lake Superior is the largest body of freshwater in the world and the deepest, cleanest, clearest and coldest of the Great Lakes.
⌒ **Don't Miss:** The views on the Brockway Mountain Drive.

## South Shore ★

Broad bays and sand beaches characterize much of Superior's southern coast, which spans Wisconsin and the Upper Peninsula of Michigan. Silent remnants of the 19C copper and iron mining booms—smokestacks, headframes and company towns—mark the landscape as well. Two scenic peninsulas are worth exploring. Route 13 leads around the Bayfield Peninsula in Wisconsin through small coastal towns, including quaint Bayfield itself. In Michigan, reminder of the copper rush linger in towns along the Keweenaw Peninsula★, where Route 26 and US-41 end in remote and beautiful Copper Harbor. East beyond the Huron Mountains lies Marquette the region's largest city.

*Western Lake Superior, Apostle Islands National Seashore*

## Apostle Islands National Lakeshore★★

*Visitor center is located in the handsome 19C Bayfield County Courthouse, Washington Ave. between 4th & 5th Sts. in Bayfield, WI.* ⛺ 🅿 ☎715-779-3397. www.nps. gov/apis.

Though trapped, hunted, logged, fished, farmed, quarried and visited for 400 years, this cluster of islands off Wisconsin's Bayfield Peninsula remains unspoiled. Today accessible by private boat and a regular schedule of cruises run by the **Apostle Islands Cruise Service** (☎715-779-3925) out of Bayfield, these 21 islands were exposed by retreating glaciers during the last Ice Age. Characterized by pink-sand beaches, dense forests, sandstone cliffs and sea caves, the Apostles offer sailing, hiking and kayaking in summer and a variety of winter pastimes for those adventurous enough to cross the ice. Six historic light stations built between 1857 and 1891 still mark the treacherous outer islands, and park staff conducts interpretive programs at several of them. The park also includes 12 mainland miles along the northwest coast of the peninsula at Little Sand Bay *(off Rte. 13 between Meyers Rd. & Little Sand Bay Rd.).*

## Porcupine Mountain Wilderness State Park★

*Boundary Rd., Ontonagon, MI. Visitor center located at S. Boundary Rd. &* *Rte. M-107.* ⛺🅿 ☎906-885-5275. Established in 1945 to preserve the last large stand of virgin hardwood between the Rockies and the Adirondacks, this lovely park includes 60,000 acres of deep wilderness and 100mi of rugged hiking and skiing trails. The "Porkies" lie astride a 500ft-deep escarpment that parallels the lakeshore. From the beach, the gentle slopes resemble the hunched backs of porcupines covered in a dense, bristly forest. Stunning scenery abounds from such viewpoints as **Escarpment Lookout★** and the **Summit Peak Observation Tower**.

## Brockway Mountain Drive★★

*Off State Rte. M-26 between Eagle & Copper Harbors.*

The highest road between the Alleghenies and the Rockies, this 9mi stretch climbs the spine of the Keweenaw through a drooping corridor of birch and hardwoods. It peaks at a windblown 1,337ft above sea level for a spectacular **view★** of Lake Superior and the forests below. The road is unplowed in winter.

## Pictured Rocks National Lakeshore★

*Off County Rd. H-58, Munising, MI. Visitor centers located at Munising (Rtes. M-28 & H-58; ☎906-387-3700); Grand Marais (E21090 County Rd. H-58; ☎ 906-494-2660); and Miners Castle (end of Miners Castle Rd., off H-58).* ⛺🅿

*Split Rock Lighthouse*

A 42mi shoreline foot trail runs the narrow length of this 72,000-acre park, which is famed for its multicolored sandstone cliffs. Paved or dirt roads access several of the park's features, including **Munising Falls; Miners Castle**, a natural rock outcrop; and **Sand Point** in the west. For the best **view** of the "pictured rock" formations on the water's edge, take one of the **boat tours** that leave from Munising *(Pictured Rocks Cruises, Inc., City Pier; ☎906-387-2379).*

# North Shore★

This rocky and rugged coast spans 150mi between Duluth and the Canadian border. Along the way, scenic **Highway 61** connects fishing villages, seven state parks, and an abundance of natural beauty. To the west lie Minnesota's iron ranges, a broad expanse of national forests, and the **Boundary Waters Canoe Area Wilderness**, which can be accessed by car along the **Gunflint Trail** out of Grand Marais. Eighteen miles

off Grand Portage lies wild **Isle Royale**, an island wilderness and national park accessible on a limited basis only by boat from May through October *(Grand Portage-Isle Royale Transportation Line; ☎715-392-2100).* Boats depart as well from Houghton and Copper Harbor, Michigan. *For information, contact park headquarters at 800 E. Lakeshore Dr., Houghton, MI, ☎906-482-0984.*

## Split Rock Lighthouse★
*3713 Split Rock Lighthouse Rd., Two Harbors, MN.* ♿🅿🕐*Open daily 10am–6pm. ☎218-226-6372.*
From its rocky perch 130ft above treacherous Lake Superior, sturdy Split Rock Lighthouse (1910) blinked its warning for nearly 60 years. Accessible only by water until 1924, the lighthouse required an elaborate system of derricks and tramways to construct and provision it, remnants of which remain today. Stop in the history center, then descend 171 steps to the beach below.

## Grand Portage National Monument★
*Off Hwy. 61, Grand Portage, MN. Closed late Oct–mid-May.* 🅿🕐*Open daily 9am–5pm.* ⊗*$3. ☎218-387-2788. www.nps.gov/grpo.*
This remote compound once bustled with activity as the largest fur-trading depot on the Great Lakes. Hardy French Canadians called *voyageurs* were hired by fur-trading companies to paddle birch-bark canoes in the late 18C and early 19C. They set out from here, carrying their canoes past the rapids of the Pigeon River over the 8.5mi Grand Portage on their way to the Canadian interior for winter trapping. Each July, hundreds of *voyageurs* returned here to trade their furs. Several buildings have been reconstructed and are manned by costumed interpreters.

# MISSISSIPPI

amed for and defined by the 2,348mi "Father of Waters"—an early Indian name
r North America's longest river—the state of Mississippi extends 47,000sq mi
om the Appalachian ridges of the northeast across to the delta (Mississippi
ver's broad alluvial plain) and then to the crumbly loess soil and pine trees
the East Gulf Coastal Plain. Along the way are some of the finest antebellum
omes and most productive farmlands in the US, juxtaposed against some of
e nation's most intractable poverty. Celebrated American writers and musi-
ans, from author William Faulkner to blues musician B.B. King, hail from the
agnolia State.

hen Hernando de Soto first viewed the
ant river near present-day Clarksdale
1541, the Chickasaw, Choctaw and
atchez tribes occupied its fertile valleys
nid ancient ceremonial mounds. The
ench settled at Natchez in 1716, and
e first Africans arrived—as slaves—in
719. As the American colonies grew
d attained independence over the
ext century, the region passed from
ench to British to Spanish control
efore becoming the 20th US state in
817. By the 1840s, vast tracts of central
d lower Mississippi were planted with
otton—tended by slaves—and these

regions claimed more millionaires than
any other part of the US except New
York City.

ngwood, Natchez

Mississippi Development Authority / Tourism Division/www.visitmississippi.org

Control of Mississippi's plantation wealth and port cities was critical for both sides in the Civil War. As a result, Mississippi's homes were burned, its imports and exports were blockaded, and thousands of acres of cotton and food crops were destroyed. The war's devastation and the struggles of impoverished former slaves haunted Mississippi for decades as cotton plantations gave way to share-cropping, with whites imposing cruel restrictions on the civil rights of blacks. By the 1950s and 60s, however, public officials were working to revitalize the economy, and civil rights leaders were breaking down centuries-old barriers to public universities, government and employment.

Without question, the Mississippi of today retains visible reminders of its pre-colonial history and plantation pa▮ as well as a genuine sense of optimis▮ about the future. Visitors who ventu▮ beyond the coastal cities of Biloxi ar▮ Gulfport (⌖ see GULF COAST) will fir▮ an intriguing mix of modernity ar▮ old-fashioned Southern ruralism—su▮ as glitzy casinos dishing up fried ok▮ cornbread and sweet iced tea. **Jackso▮** Mississippi's capital, is by far the lar▮ est city in the state today (with mo▮ than 177,000 people). Every four yea▮ it hosts the USA International Ball▮ Competition, a world-class gatherir▮ with sister events in Moscow and Varr▮ Bulgaria (the next competition is sche▮ uled for June 2010). In the smaller citi▮ of Natchez and Vicksburg, a sense of th▮ Old South pervades, despite contemp▮ rary commerce.

## Area Address Book

*⌖ For coin ranges, see the Legend on the cover flap.*

### WHERE TO STAY

**$$  Monmouth Plantation** – *36 Melrose Ave., Natchez, MS.* ✕ ♿ 🅿 ☎ *601-442-5852. www.monmouthplantation. com. 30 rooms.* Framed by towering oak trees and 26 acres of landscaped grounds, this mansion is located just .5mi from downtown. Rooms are beautifully designed, with hand-carved period antiques and the kind of rich fabrics that Scarlett O'Hara would have dressed in. Reserve ahead for the five-course Southern-style dinner *($48)* served in the opulent dining room.

**$  Cedar Grove Mansion Inn** – *2200 Oak St., Vicksburg, MS.* ✕ ♿ 🅿 ⌗ ☎ *601-636-1000. www.cedargroveinn. com. 32 rooms.* An antebellum estate, in the middle of town, surrounded by five acres of gardens with rose-covered arbors and gazebos. The Greek Revival-style inn is filled with marble fireplaces, French Empire gasoliers and gold-leaf mirrors. Posh bedrooms, named for *Gone With The Wind* characters, are furnished with canopy beds and hand-made armoires.

### WHERE TO EAT

**$$  Cedar Grove Mansion Inn** – *2200 Oak St., Vicksburg, MS. Closed Mon.* ☎ *601-636-1000.* **Southern.** Rustic brick walls, white linens and floor-to-ceiling windows create an ideal romantic setting. The chef's special blend of Creole seasonings jazzes up his New Orleans-style dishes.

# NATCHEZ★★

MICHELIN MAP 584 N 13
CENTRAL STANDARD TIME
POPULATION 16,966

The architectural splendor of the antebellum plantation is lovingly preserved in Natchez, which avoided destruction during the Civil War by promptly surrendering to invading Union troops. Many of Natchez's wealthiest citizens had friends and family in the North and in general opposed secession.

- **Information:** ☎601-446-6345. www.visitnatchez.com
- **Don't Miss:** The Oriental architecture of Longwood.
- **Organizing Your Time:** Plan your trip in the spring or fall so you can enjoy the Natchez Pilgrimage tours.
- **Also See:** NEW ORLEANS.

## A Bit of History

The oldest city on the Mississippi River, Natchez takes its name from its first known settlement, the **Grand Village of the Natchez Indians** (400 Jefferson Davis Blvd.; ◷Open Mon-Sat 9am–5pm, Sun 1:30pm–5pm. ☎601-446-6502), where ceremonial plazas and mounds date back to the mid-16C. In 1716 the French explorer and governor of Louisiana, Jean-Baptiste Le Moyne de Bienville, established Fort Rosalie on a bluff over the river.

### Mississippi Pilgrimages

A pilgrimage in Mississippi is not a religious experience; rather, it is a journey back in time. In the spring of 1932, Natchez society leader Katherine Miller, president of the Pilgrimage Garden Club, organized the first "pilgrimage," or tour, through some of the city's stately antebellum homes to fund the club's program to restore historic houses. Complemented by a pageant (a hoop-skirted musical extravaganza) presided over by the pilgrimage queen, the event attracted tourists as well as interior designers seeking a uniquely American style. Since then, many more home owners have opened their doors to visitors and pilgrimage weeks have been added in October and December.

During Natchez's month-long spring pilgrimage season (mid-Mar–mid-Apr), visitors are strongly advised to make advance reservations for lodging and home tours. Between pilgrimages, however, at least a dozen historic homes (most in public or institutional hands) are open for daily tours anytime (fees average $10 per house).

For a glimpse of how the interior-design and home-furnishings professions have adapted "the Natchez style" to contemporary American tastes, visit the decorator's showroom of the **Historic Natchez Collection** (204 State St.), where you'll see high-end, licensed reproductions of Natchez-inspired antique furniture and decorative arts.

Additional Natchez mansions open for tours include the following. The designation (B&B) indicates properties that operate as bed-and-breakfast inns.

**The Burn** (c.1834) – 712 N. Union St., ☎601-442-1344 (B&B)
**Dunleith** (c.1856) – 84 Homochitto St., ☎601-446-8500 (B&B)
**Governor Holmes House** (c. 1794) – 207 S. Wall St., ☎601-442-2366 (B&B)
**Lansdowne** (c.1853) – 17 Marshall Rd., ☎601-446-9401
**Linden** (c.1800) – 1 Linden Dr., ☎601-445-5472 (B&B)
**Monmouth Plantation** (c.1818) – 36 Melrose Avenue, ☎601-442-5852 (B&B)

The first steamboat docked in Natchez in 1811, opening new possibilities for trade and lavish lifestyles. A burgeoning plantation aristocracy, supported by far-flung cotton fields and slave labor, built elaborate "town estates" in and around Natchez, where they lived during the winter months between trips to Europe or New York. Emulating the great estates of Europe, they named their houses, landscaped their "parks," and filled their rooms with decorative arts: oil portraits and imported silver; fine French and Chinese porcelain; gold-leaf mirrors to rival Versailles; unique wallcoverings; hand-carved pediments; cornice boards with Grecian motifs; and custom-made furniture of the finest walnut, mahogany and rosewood.

In present-day Natchez, many of these vast estates are no longer in private hands, but have been rescued and restored by civic or public organizations such as local garden clubs, the city of Natchez or the National Park Service. Others operate as bed-and-breakfast inns hosting tours, overnight guests and special events. Many of these homes can be toured during the semi-annual **Natchez Pilgrimage** (*see infobox on previous page*) in the spring and fall.

For a less genteel view of Natchez, visitors have long turned to the riverfront enclave of saloons and bawdy houses known as **Natchez-under-the-Hill** (*Silver St. at Broadway*). Today Silver Street is lined with restaurants, bars and shops catering to tourists from town and from the three riverboats (*Delta Queen, Mississippi Queen* and *American Queen*) that offer weekly cruises on the Mississippi.

## Sights

### Longwood★★★
*140 Lower Woodville Rd.* Visit by guided tour only. ☎601-446-6631. From a distance, this magnificent octagonal "Oriental villa," as its architect, Samuel Sloan, described it, is an elegant shell. Only the nine-room basement floor was ever finished; work on the upper floors was halted in 1861 when the Yankee workmen fled after the Confederates fired on Fort Sumter.

Longwood's architecture is elaborate and rare. The house boasts 120 Corinthian columns on verandahs on the first and second floors, 26 fireplaces and a stunning circular fourth-floor observatory with openings for 16 floor-to-ceiling windows offering panoramas of Natchez and the Mississippi River. Atop the observatory is a reproduction of the original Byzantine-style onion dome, topped by an ornate spire.

The tour takes visitors through the below-ground rooms, where many of the original furnishings remain, and then up into the unfinished floors. As your footsteps echo in the cavernous rooms, 150-year-old woodworking tools and half-carved timbers lie abandoned in the corners as silent reminders of long-lost ambitions and skills.

### Magnolia Hall★
*215 S. Pearl St.* Visit by guided tour only. ☎601-442-6847.
Distinguished by ornately carved magnolia-motif ceiling medallions, Magnolia Hall was built in 1858 and was one of the few Natchez mansions to suffer shelling damage (from a gunboat) during the Civil War. Now owned by the Natchez Garden Club, the house includes a small costume museum, with hoop skirts, corsets, and mannequins outfitted in the antebellum garb worn by Natchez belles during the Spring Pilgrimage pageants over the past 20 years.

### Melrose Plantation/Natchez National Historical Park★★★
*1 Melrose-Montebello Pkwy.* Visit by guided tour only. ☎601-446-7970. www. nps.gov/natc.
Now owned by the National Park Service, Melrose is an authentic antebellum town estate (c.1845) complete with slave quarters and other "dependencies," including the kitchen, stables and privies. A guided tour of the house and grounds informs visitors about the lives of slave owners and the enslaved alike, including the slaves' individualized bell-summoning system and the tragedies linked to a then-innovative lead-lined cistern system.
In 1910 an heir of the former owner moved to Melrose with his bride, who restored the home and opened it for th...

## The Natchez Trace Parkway

A 444mi National Park Service parkway *(no traffic lights, no commercial traffic)* running diagonally from Natchez, Mississippi, to Nashville, Tennessee, the Natchez Trace follows an ancient path first traced by buffalo and prehistoric hunters more than 8,000 years ago. At **Bynum Mounds** *(milepost 232.4, about 25mi south of Tupelo)*, archaeologists discovered flint tools and clay cooking pots dating from 100 BC. The most impressive evidence of early cultures along the Trace can be found at **Emerald Mound** *(milepost 10.3, 10mi north of Natchez)*, an eight-acre earthen mound crowned with a broad ceremonial plaza, probably constructed around AD 1200.

Until the steamboat brought speedy two-way traffic to the Mississippi River in the mid-19C, the trail carried some 10,000 travelers a year. Most were "Kaintucks"—hardy adventurers from Kentucky and points north—who floated goods downriver to New Orleans, sold their barges for lumber, then trekked home along the Trace. Plagued by bad weather, wild animals, hostile Indians and rough terrain, they often sought overnight shelter at roadside "stands" like **Mount Locust** *(milepost 15.5)* or **French Camp** *(milepost 180.7)*, named for French trader Louis LeFleur. At **Grinder House** *(milepost 385.9)*, a traveler named **Meriwether Lewis**—the famed commander of the Lewis & Clark Expedition—died of a gunshot wound one night in 1809. Whether his death was murder or suicide remains a mystery. Lewis is memorialized here by a marker in the form of a tall, broken column.

Contemporary travelers will find no operating inns or other commercial establishments on the Natchez Trace, but plenty of wildlife, bicyclists, hikers and horse trailers heading for park-maintained riding trails. The **Natchez Trace Parkway Visitor Center** (☎662-680-4027; www.nps.gov/natr), located at milepost 266.0 just north of Tupelo, offers a film, interpretive exhibits and a bookstore.

first pilgrimage tour in 1932. Original furnishings include a set of carved Rococo Revival chairs in the drawing room, from whose rose pattern the Gorham sterling-silver flatware pattern "Melrose" was derived.

## Rosalie★★

*Canal & Orleans Sts.* ☜*Visit by guided tour only.* ♿ 🅿 ☎ 601-445-4555. www.rosaliemansion.com.

From the second-story portico of Rosalie (c.1820), visitors get a marvelous view of the broad Mississippi—a feature that also appealed to invading Union general Walter Gresham when he arrived and commandeered the house as his personal residence for three years beginning in 1863. With Gresham's consent, the Wilson family, Rosalie's owners, protected their belongings during the Union occupation by locking everything, including the 20-piece John Henry Belter rosewood parlor set, safely away in the attic and storing two huge gilt mirrors (swathed heavily in cotton) in a nearby cave. Amazingly, the mirrors

reflect Rosalie's glory as clearly today as they did in 1863.

## Stanton Hall★★

*401 High St.* ☜*Visit by guided tour only.* ✗ ♿ 🅿 ☎601-442-6288. www.stantonhall.com.

Master builder Thomas Rose completed this grand white stucco mansion, with Corinthian columns, 17ft-high ceilings and 50ft-long double parlors, for Irish-immigrant cotton broker and planter Frederick Stanton in 1857. Stanton called his home "Belfast" and planted 19 live oak trees (17 survive) on his property, which encompasses an entire block in the heart of downtown.

Unfortunately, Stanton died only nine months after moving in. Over the next 80 years, the house went through a succession of owners before being bought by the Pilgrimage Garden Club in 1938. Intricate gas-lit chandeliers (called gasoliers) in the dining room depict scenes from Natchez history, and the original Sheffield silver doorknobs miraculously remain.

# VICKSBURG★

MICHELIN MAP 584 N 12
CENTRAL STANDARD TIME
POPULATION 25,752

Sitting proudly on a 200ft bluff at a sharp bend of the mighty Mississippi River, Vicksburg was so strategically positioned that it took Union commanders Ulysses S. Grant and William T. Sherman more than a year of planning, canal-digging and fierce fighting before they were able to besiege the city and capture it in July 1863. Called "the Gibraltar of the Confederacy," Vicksburg was a key commercial, cultural and transportation center whose fall spelled a turning point in the Civil War.

🛈 **Information:** ☎601-636-9421. www.vicksburgcvb.org
🚫 **Don't Miss:** McRaven House, which survived cannonballs and more.
⏱ **Also See:** Confederate trenches at Vicksburg National Military Park.

## A Bit of History

First settled by the Spanish in 1790, Vicksburg got its name from a Methodist minister, Newit Vick, who bought 1,120 acres and laid out a town just before his death from yellow fever in 1819. The new town soon became a booming river port and railroad center, boasting 4,500 residents at the beginning of the Civil War.

As the crow flies, the heart of downtown is well within artillery range from the famous Civil War battlefield. Of the many fine houses built of antebellum prosperity, only a handful have survived, primarily by heroic eleventh-hour conversions into bed-and-breakfast inns in the face of unrelenting neighborhood decline. These include **Anchuca** (1010 First East St.), where Jefferson Davis once addressed a crowd from the balcony; the **Duff Green Mansion** (1114 First East St.), used as a Civil War hospital while its owners lived in a nearby cave; **Balfour House** (1002 Crawford St.), commandeered as Union headquarters after Vicksburg fell; the **Cedar Grove Mansion** (2200 Oak St.), with river views and four acres of antebellum gardens; and

*Vicksburg National Military Park*

## Mississippi Writers

For Southerners, "The past is never dead. It's not even past," observes a troubled resident of Yoknapatawpha County, the fictitious Mississippi setting of some 20 novels *(The Sound and the Fury; As I Lay Dying; Absalom, Absalom!)* and short-story collections by **William Faulkner** (1897-1962). Faulkner, who won the 1949 Nobel Prize for Literature, is perhaps the best known among a pantheon of Deep South writers. Born in New Albany, Mississippi, Faulkner lived in an 1840s plantation house, **Rowan Oak** *(Old Taylor Rd., in Oxford, MS; ☎662-234-3284)*, from 1930 until his death.

Serious readers the world over carry an image of the struggling 20C South—faded aristocracy, deluded hopes and lost fortunes, bitter but resilient descendants of African slaves—based on the fictional works of an extraordinary generation of Mississippi writers such as Faulkner, Jackson's **Eudora Welty** (1909-2001), Columbus' **Tennessee (Thomas Lanier) Williams** (1911-83) and Natchez native **Richard Wright** (1908-60). Contemporary movie and crime-novel fans, meanwhile, stay up late to read thrillers by former Oxford resident **John Grisham** *(The Firm)*. Still others seek out lesser-known writers such as Barry Hannah (Oxford); Civil War historian Shelby Foote, the father-and-son Hodding Carters, and Walker Percy (all from Greenville); or the newest issue of the prize-winning general-interest monthly *The Oxford American* (published in Oxford with Grisham's support).

**Pemberton House** *(1018 Crawford St.)*, Confederate Army headquarters during the siege. The **Martha Vick House** *(1300 Grove St.)* was built for a daughter of Vicksburg's founder and is open for tours.

## Vicksburg National Military Park★★

3201 Clay St, .25mi west of I-20. ♿ 🅿
☎601-636-0583. www.nps.gov/vick.
Ranging over the meadows, hills and forests of this 1,800-acre site, Confederate and Union armies clashed in a decisive 1863 Civil War battle for Vicksburg, a critical Confederate port. After a 47-day siege and incessant cannon fire, Vicksburg surrendered on July 4, 1863, thus giving the North control of the "Father of Waters" and slicing the Confederacy in two from north to south.

At the park **visitor center**, realistic displays show officers' tents, Confederate trenches and furnished caves where Vicksburg residents waited out the shelling, and a video gives a blow-by-blow account of the battle. The 16mi self-guided **driving tour** *(cassette tapes and guides available)* leads past more than

1,324 memorials marking the positions of various state regiments. Highlights include the **Illinois Memorial**, whose dome is modeled after Rome's Pantheon; the **Wisconsin Memorial** with "Old Abe," the war eagle; and a statue of General Grant on his horse. At the northern edge of the park is the raised hulk of the **USS Cairo**, an ironclad gunboat sunk by Confederates in 1862.

*Old Courthouse Museum, Vicksburg*

Mississippi Development Authority / Tourism Division/www.mississippi.org

# NASHVILLE AREA

Nashville, Tennessee's centrally located capital, anchors a sprawling state that extends almost 500mi from the Appalachian Mountains to the flat coastal plain along the Mississippi River. Between these extremes are ridge upon ridge of forests, divided by wide rivers and broad valleys supporting abundant wildlife and agriculture.

Tennessee's fertile countryside shows traces of nomadic hunters as far back as the last Ice Age. More recently, Woodland and Mississippian Indians left burial mounds and structures such as the mysterious earthen walls of 2,000-year-old **Old Stone Fort State Archaeological Park** *(732 Stone Fort Dr., Manchester; ☎931-723-5073)*. Long before the British and the French began staking claims in the 1700s, Cherokee, Chickasaw and other tribes had villages across the region.

Because of the Cherokee opposition to white settlement in the area, both Nashville (founded 1779) and Knoxville (founded 1786) began as stockaded forts. The independent-minded Tennessee settlers, cut off from the eastern colonies by the mountains, created their own early governments: the Watauga Association (1772), the Cumberland Compact (1779-80) and the State of Franklin (1784). The area was declared a US Territory in 1789 and became the 16th state in 1796. By 1838, the last Cherokee families departed for Oklahoma on the infamous "Trail of Tears."

During the Civil War, Tennessee was the last Southern state to secede from the Union and the first to rejoin it. Despite reluctance to affiliate with the plantation- and slave-owners of the Deep South, Tennessee endured some of the bloodiest battles of the war at **Fort Donelson** *(1mi west of Dover on US-79, ☎931-232-5706)* and **Stones River** *(3501 Old Nashville Hwy., Murfreesboro; ☎615-893-9501)* as Union troops advanced steadily southward.

*General Jackson Showboat*

Railroads, river traffic, roads and air waves conspired to eliminate any lingering feelings of isolation by the early 1900s, especially after listeners nationwide began tuning in to the **Grand Ole Opry** on Nashville radio station WSM. The US government also lent a hand, establishing the Tennessee Valley Authority (TVA) for electricity and flood control in 1933, and then choosing Oak Ridge, just west of Knoxville, for the huge government installation that developed materials necessary to build the first atomic bomb. More than 70 years later, the Grand Ole Opry is more popular than ever, and Nashville reigns as the world's country-music capital.

## Area Address Book

*For coin ranges, see the Legend on the cover flap.*

### WHERE TO STAY

**$$$ Blackberry Farm** – *1471 West Millers Cove Rd., Walland, TN.* ♿🅿🚮 ☎*865-984-8166. www.blackberryfarm. com. 51 rooms.* Memorable views abound at this 1,100-acre retreat *(17mi southeast of Knoxville airport)* bordering Great Smoky Mountains National Park. Overstuffed sofas in florals and plaids, English antiques, hand-painted vanities and lots of chintz create an elegant country-house look. Choose from rooms in the main house or cottage suites nestled in the trees. Hefty rates include all meals, afternoon tea, and snacks stocked in several pantries; bicycles are available for touring the grounds.

**$$$ Sheraton Music City Hotel** – *777 McGavok Pike, Nashville, TN.* ♿🅿🚮 ☎*615-885-2200. www.sheratonmusic-city.com. 412 rooms.* Though it was built in 1978, this place resembles a Georgian mansion on its 23-acre estate. Nine miles from downtown in Century City, the hotel's interior reflects both the Old and New Worlds. The cherry-paneled lobby looks out on the trellised verandah. Guest rooms have balconies facing the courtyard or garden.

**$$ The Hermitage Hotel** – *231 6th Ave. N., Nashville, TN.* ♿🅿 ☎*615-244-3121. www.hermitagehotel.com. 123 rooms.* Four blocks from the downtown historic district, this Beaux-Arts beauty opened its doors to guests in 1910. A skylight lets sunlight stream into the ornate three-story lobby, featuring plaster-molded arches and huge floral arrangements. The all-suite accommodations have separate living- and bedrooms with top-notch creature comforts. Dine on updated Southern specials at the elegant **Capitol Grille**.

### WHERE TO EAT

**$$ Bound'ry** – *911 20th Ave. S., Nashville, TN.* ☎*615-321-3043.* **Contemporary.** Music moguls come to this Hillsboro Village spot for dishes that fuse global flavors with local staples. Tennessee trout, roasted on a cedar plank, comes with corn pudding. And the smoked double pork chop, glazed with rosemary-honey tamarind sauce, is served with macaroni and cheese in addition to traditional applesauce. Abstract murals decorate the two-tiered dining room.

**$$ Restaurante Zola** – *3001 West End Ave., Nashville, TN. Closed Sun.* ☎*615-320-7778.* **Contemporary.** Gauze fabrics, potted ferns and a mural of the Moroccan desert make this dining room a West End oasis.

**$ Loveless Motel & Cafe** – *8400 Highway 100, Nashville, TN.* ☎*615-646-9700.* **Southern.** For more than 50 years, the neon sign on the Loveless Cafe has beckoned locals and country-music stars like Reba McEntire to breakfast in West Nashville. Heaping plates of country ham and eggs with red-eye gravy, piping hot biscuits and homemade preserves are the standard. Look around the small dining room for photos of celebrity regulars.

**$ Marche Artisan Foods** *1000 Main St. Nashville, TN.* ☎*615-262-1111. www. marcheartisanfoods.com* **American.** This East Nashville bistro is hipster central, where musicians dine on brioche and egg salad. is perfect for take-out service for picnics and the like. You may see a music celebrity or two here.

# NASHVILLE★★

MAPS P295 AND P297    CENTRAL STANDARD TIME
POPULATION 569,891

Set on the banks of the Cumberland River, Tennessee's capital is perhaps better known as "Music City USA." With a sports arena and restored 19C warehouses-turned-nightclubs drawing crowds to the waterfront, Nashville is a lively, upbeat tourist town with both historical and contemporary attractions.

- **Information:** Nashville Convention & Visitor Bureau. ☎615-259-4700. www.nashvillecvb.com.
- **Parking:** Public transportation is limited, but parking is usually not a problem in the Music City.
- **Don't Miss:** How all genres of music come together at the Country Music of Hall of Fame.
- **Kids:** A giant sculpture of Athena delights kids of all ages at the Parthenon.
- **Also See:** MEMPHIS.

## A Bit of History

The city's history is evoked on the waterfront in a replica of the 1780 log **Fort Nashborough** (170 1st Ave. N.), built by James Robertson and his men after a journey of 400mi on foot through the Cumberland Gap. A few months later, John Donelson brought the men's wives and children by boat, a treacherous 1,000mi journey from the other side of the mountains.

Nashville grew rapidly with the opening of the west, attracting ambitious men including Andrew Jackson and James Polk—both of whom became US presidents. After the Civil War, the city emerged as an educational, religious and cultural center, celebrating its rebirth with a Centennial Exposition in 1879. A world's only full-sized replica of **The Parthenon** (West End & 25th Aves. at Centennial Park; ☎615-862-8431), complete with a 42ft statue of Athena, was built for this exposition (its lower floor now houses an art museum). In 1916 a catastrophic fire destroyed more than 648 buildings in east Nashville. Glimpses of the historic downtown remain along **Printer's Alley** (between Union & Church Sts. at 3rd & 4th Aves. N.) and in the glass-roofed 1903 **Arcade** (between 4th & 5th Aves.), which now houses shops and restaurants.

By the 1920s, Nashville had its own radio station, WSM, and the station's live broadcasts attracted guitar-pickers, fiddlers and singers from across the South. The Grand Ole Opry required its performers to be available every Saturday night—a restriction that, in those pre-airline days, meant that hundreds of professional musicians (and those who did business with them) found themselves living in Nashville.

Today "Music City USA" is home not only to the Opry and its parent company's myriad enterprises, but also to a large segment of the multibillion-dollar US recording industry. **Music Row** (Division St. & Music Square E.) is a neighborhood of office towers harboring artists' agents; music publishing houses; offices for Arista/J Records, EMI, RCA, Sony BMG and Warner Bros.; and signature buildings for ASCAP and BMI. With world-class recording studios, specialty shops like the legendary **Gruhns Guitars** (400 Broadway), and a resident population of skilled session musicians who readily "cross over" from country to rock and roll, gospel, soul and jazz, Nashville ranks as the major recording venue for American popular music.

## Sights

### Tennessee State Capitol★

*Charlotte Ave. between 6th and 7th Avenues.* ♿🕐Open daily 9am–4pm ☎615-741-2692.

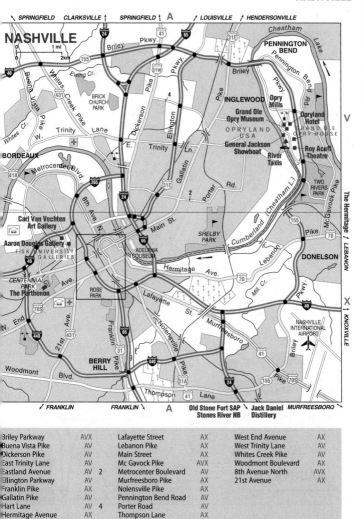

The self-professed masterpiece of architect **William Strickland** (1788-1854), this Tennessee limestone Greek Revival "temple" sits high on a hill and boasts ancient Athenian models for its Ionic porticoes and towering cupola. Inside are marble stairs, ceiling frescoes, and the restored library, where the balcony railing displays cast-iron profiles of famous figures, from Shakespeare to 1830s-era Tennessee Governor William Carroll.

## Bicentennial Capitol Mall State Park

*James Robertson Parkway ♿ 🅿 ⏰Open daily 6am–10pm. ☎615-741-5280. www. state.tn.us/environment/parks/bicentennial/.*

Built to honor the state's 200th birthday, this 19-acre outdoor park is in the shadow of the Tennessee State Capitol. Among the many interesting elements here are a granite wall with a timeline of the state's history, a granite map of

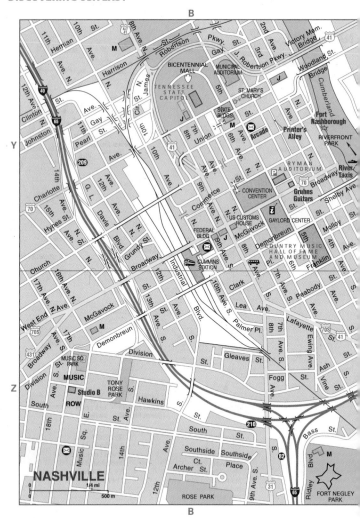

NASHVILLE

*ountry Music Hall of Fame, Nashville*

e state, a landscaped replica of the anging foliage of the state from east west and an amphitheater. A circle bells plays (what else?) the *Tennes- e Waltz* every hour. The local farmer's arket is nearby.

## ountry Music Hall of Fame d Museum★★

*2 Fifth Ave. S. ♿ 🅿 ⏱ Open daily m–5pm.☎615-416-2001. www.coun- musichalloffame.com.*

is jam-packed facility is generally con- dered the best of Nashville's numer- is "museums" of country music and stars. The maze of displays begins th the instruments and styles of untry music—including a lovely col- ction of **stringed instruments**—and ogresses to showy performers and eir costumes (Vince Gill's shiny red seball jacket, Loretta Lynn's dress); rs of the stars (Elvis' "Solid Gold" dillac); and the development of e Grand Ole Opry. The Hall of Fame

itself is a room with more than 60 plaques honoring country-music artists and executives.

Admission includes a tour of RCA's legendary **Studio B**, where Elvis Pres- ley and Patsy Cline played the 1940s Steinway grand piano and guitarist Chet Atkins perfected a recording style that the world now recognizes as "the Nashville Sound."

Nearby in downtown Nashville is the home of the honkytonk. All along Broad- way are bars where talented musicians play shows after the sun sets. Most of these bars do not have cover charges, so you'll pay nothing (except the cost of your beer) to hear these sounds. there's no reaosn not to just pop your head in and see if there's someone playing who strikes your fancy and, if not, head to the next honkytonk. Favorites include the only-in-Nashville experience of **Robert's Western World** (*416 Broadway, ⏱Open daily 11am–3am.☎615-244-9552. www. robertswesternworld.com*) where you can

## Country Music

"Country" music incorporates elements of bluegrass and Cajun and cowboy, gospel and honky-tonk, rockabilly and western swing. Names associated with this musical genre include Mary Chapin Carpenter and Willie Nelson, Garth Brooks, Reba McEntire and Vince Gill. What was branded early on as "American folk tunes" (according to *Billboard* magazine in 1948), then "country and western," then "crossover country"—is now mainstream American music.

To purists, contemporary country music may seem homogenized and predictable. But the vast majority of country-music fans appear well pleased with Nashville's steady stream of catchy three-chord tunes and heart-warming lyrics, especially when delivered by Faith Hall, Wynonna (Judd) or Tim McGraw. Nomenclature aside, modern country music remains "folk" music—accessible, easy to imitate and adapt on various stringed instruments, and derived from English, Scottish and Irish folk-music traditions that came to the Southeast with white pioneers.

For beginning performers, breaking into an entrenched multi-billion industry is much different from the early days. Back then, Roy Acuff might simply hear a nervous young singer and decide to put her on the Opry live. Yet aspiring guitar, mandolin and fiddle virtuosos, songwriters and singers inevitably head to Nashville. For visitors, this means that in any ordinary bar, the musicians before the microphone are probably superb.

The **Bluebird Cafe** *(4104 Hillsboro Rd., Nashville; ☎615-383-1461)* is a hot spot to hear up-and-coming singers and songwriters, but live music crops up all over middle Tennessee. The fiddler in any small-town club may not be as polished as those in Nashville, but the tunes probably date back to his Scotch-Irish great-grandfather and the clogging (buck dancing) will be spontaneous and very, very good.

buy cowboy boots while you drink and dance. Other options include **Tootsie's Orchid Lounge** *(422 Broadway, ☎615-726-0463. www.tootsies.net)* and **The Stage** *(412 Broadway ☎615-726-0504)*.

### Gaylord Opry Entertainment Complex★★

*2802 Opryland Dr.* ♿ 🅿 ☎615-871-6779. www.opry.com.
The world's longest-running live radio show, the **Grand Ole Opry** features the best in country, bluegrass and Cajun music. Its home is the **Grand Ole Opry House**★★ — a 4,400-seat concert hall that forms the centerpiece of this mega-entertainment complex on the Cumberland River about 9mi northeast of downtown. In 1943 the Grand Ole Opry settled into the late-19C **Ryman Auditorium**★ downtown *(116 5th Ave. N.;* ♿ 🕐 *open daily 9am;* 💲*$12.50;* ☎615-889-3060; www.ryman.com) and played to packed houses every weekend

for the next 31 years. In 1974 the natio country music stars moved to this glit. high-tech performance venue outfi ted with Hollywood-caliber lightir and television and recording capabi ties. Today the Opry continues to dra crowds for its weekend shows, as w as studio audiences for Opryland's cab television networkand **Country Mus Television** (CMT). *Advance reservatio are required for all Opry and TV shows* For a behind-the-scenes look at th Opry, take the midday backstage to which includes a chance to stand befo the microphone on the grand sta itself. Adjacent to the Opry House a the **Bell South Roy Acuff Theatre** a the colorful, exhibit-filled **Grand O Opry Museum**. The four-deck **Gener Jackson** showboat (music and dinin plies the river, and **Opryland Riv Taxis** ferry visitors to the downtow riverfront.

he hotel at the **Gaylord Opryland esort and Convention Center** (2800 pryland Dr.; ☎615-889-1000) is a spectacle in itself, with nearly 3,000 rooms ustered around nine acres of gardens, vers and waterfalls—all under glass. **pry Mills** retail and entertainment omplex includes many factory outlet ores, a movie theater and family-iendly restaurants.

## isk University Galleries★

n the Fisk University campus, 1000 17th ve. N. ♿🅿 ☎615-329-8720. www.fisk. du/gallery/index.html.

fter the death of her husband, American photographer Alfred Stieglitz, ainter Georgia O'Keeffe donated their ersonal art collection to this black institution. Today the **Carl Van Vechten Art allery** (Jackson St.) is named for the upporter of the New York-based Harm Renaissance who later chaired Fisk niversity's fine-arts commission. Holdgs include more than 100 paintings, rawings, photographs and sculptures y outstanding artists from Stieglitz nd O'Keeffe to Cézanne, Picasso nd Rivera.

he **Aaron Douglas Gallery** (on third oor of the library, across from Van echten Gallery) features work by African-American artists Aaron Douglas, omare Bearden, and Henry Tanner, mong others.

## elle Meade Plantation★★

025 Harding Rd. ⟋Visit by guided tour nly. ♿🅿 ☎615-356-0501.

ost antebellum plantation homes splay portraits of family members in lded frames, but at Belle Meade—a ud farm and breeding operation since 816—the portraits are of Thoroughred racehorses. For more than 80 years, cehorse owners worldwide came to ok for promising yearlings at Belle eade's annual sale. The 1853 Greek evival mansion boasts 26ft limestone olumns (quarried on the property), arbleized woodwork, and ornate furshings (1840-60) by John Henry Belter, uncan Phyfe and Joseph Meeks. The **arriage house and stable** (c.1890) now off 19C cabriolet carriages and uxurious horse stalls. A well-crafted film

dramatization provides an overview of the plantation's history.

## Cheekwood

1200 Forrest Park Dr. ✗♿🅿🕓Open Tues-Sat 9:30am–4:30pm, Sun 11am–4:30pm. ⊛$10. ☎615-353-6982. www.cheekwood. org.

This 55 acre-attraction is all about beauty, whether it grows in the garden or it hangs on the walls. The building itself is the former Cheek estate, and now holds a place on the National Register of Historic Places. See the boxwood gardens, artworks by Red Grooms, Andy Warhol and other artists. The collection houses more than 600 paintings and 5,000 prints, as well as photographs and works in temporary exhibitions.

## The Hermitage★★

4580 Rachel's Lane. ✗♿🅿🕓Open daily 8:30am–5pm.⊛$15.☎615-889-2941. www.thehermitage.com.

Built for Tennessee military hero and seventh US president **Andrew Jackson** (1767-1845), The Hermitage in its heyday was a prosperous 1,100-acre plantation with cotton fields, fine horses and illustrious visitors. Jackson, a controversial personality nicknamed "Old Hickory" for his steadfast loyalty to his soldiers, was elected president for two consecutive terms (1828-36). Both Andrew and his wife, Rachel, are buried in the mansion garden.

Begun as a Federal-style home in 1819, The Hermitage was expanded in 1831,

*The Hermitage*

Nashville CVB/Mike Rutherford

damaged by fire in 1834 and rebuilt in the Greek Revival style in 1836 (the period to which the house has been restored). A self-guided tour *(audio-cassette supplied)* highlights exquisite original furnishings and daily activities in the kitchen, garden and slave quarters (where archaeologists are still uncovering new details). Tours begin and end at the visitor center, which has a theater, exhibits and a restaurant.

## Excursion

### Jack Daniel's Distillery★

*75mi southeast of Nashville in Lynchburg. Take I-24 to Rte. 55, follow Rte. 55 South 30mi to distillery visitor center. Visit by guided tour only, daily 9am–4:30pm. Closed major holidays.* ☎931-759-6180. www.jackdaniels.com.

The oldest registered whiskey distillery (1866) in the US, this rustic-looking establishment is the sole production facility for Jack Daniel's "Tennessee sipping whiskey," now sold in more than 130 countries. The fascinating tour *(1hr 30min)* covers the clear Cave Spring of iron-free water, essential to making good whiskey; the rickyard where native sugar-maple trees are burned into charcoal; the giant mash vats, where a golden-colored mixture of corn, rye and barley malt ferment pungently; and the charcoal filtering rooms, where 140 proof whiskey seeps slowly through 10ft of charcoal. A walk through one of the aromatic barrelhouses, the liquid's last stop before bottling, offers a glimpse of hundreds of oak barrels aging thousands of gallons of whiskey.

# EAST TENNESSEE★

MICHELIN MAP 584 P, Q 10, 11
EASTERN STANDARD TIME

East of Nashville, Tennessee's landscape is dominated by the Great Smoky Mountains, a section of the Appalachian range that runs along the state's eastern border with North Carolina. These peaks proved a daunting barrier for early settlers, until frontiersman Daniel Boone *(see WESTERN KENTUCKY)* discovered the **Cumberland Gap** (a passageway that breaches the mountains where Tennessee, Kentucky and Virginia meet) and led the way west in 1775. The gap remained the major westward route until the 1830s when steamboats and the Erie and the Pennsylvania Main Line canals gave travelers new alternatives.

▪ **Information:** ☎423-756-8687. www.chattanoogafun.com.
▪ **Don't Miss:** The combo of manmade and natural attraction at Ruby Falls.
▪ **Kids:** The ultimate kids' attraction is the Chattanooga Choo-Choo.
▪ **Also See:** NASHVILLE, ATLANTA.

## A Bit of History

The first area of the state to be settled, East Tennessee developed a rich folk culture of handcrafts, music and dance that has passed down to the mountain people from the pioneers. Knoxville and Chattanooga, the region's largest cities, were both born in the late 18C. **Knoxville**, 100mi up the Tennessee River from Chattanooga and 40mi from Great Smoky Mountains National Park *(see*

*GREAT SMOKY MOUNTAINS NATIONAL PARK),* served as the first capital when Tennessee became a state in 1796. (The capital moved several times before being permanently established in Nashville in 1826.) Today its downtown is dominated by the 400-acre campus of the University of Tennessee and enlivened by restaurants and clubs in the restored **Old City** *(W. Jackson Ave. & Central St. S.).* A popular tourist destination since the 1920s, Chattanooga offers a first-rate aquarium, fine

*Library of Congress*

*Se-Quo-Yah (1836), Lithograph by McKenney & Hall*

## Sequoyah and his Alphabet

Scholars of the world's languages marvel over the achievement of a Cherokee silversmith named **Sequoyah** (1776–1843), who single-handedly created an alphabet for his native language and brought literacy to the Cherokee Indian nation. Born in the village of Tuskeegee (now underwater at the Tellico Reservoir near present-day Vonore), Sequoyah was the child of a Virginia fur trader and a Cherokee chieftain's daughter. At the **Sequoyah Birthplace Museum** *(576 Hwy. 360, Vonore, TN; ☎423-884-6246)*, owned and operated by the Eastern Band of Cherokee Indians, his life and accomplishments are vividly described.

arts, natural wonders and a fine selection of lodging and eateries.

## Chattanooga

Two distinct geographic features define Chattanooga: the wide bend of the Tennessee River and the hulking ridge of Lookout Mountain. Both have been pivotal in the city's history. The Cherokee splinter group called the Chickamauga settled in what is now Chattanooga around 1777, and in 1815 Cherokee chief John Ross built Ross's Landing, a trading post and ferry dock. Steamboats and railroads followed, and Chattanooga—an Indian name for **Lookout Mountain**—became a transportation hub. As such, Chattanooga was crucial to both sides during the Civil War. In 1863 the Battle for Chattanooga raged over Lookout Mountain and south to Chickamauga Creek in Georgia for nearly three months before Southern forces retreated.

Irving Berlin's 1941 song, "The Chattanooga Choo-Choo," immortalized train travel in the early 20C. Visitors to Chattanooga can relive the experience by riding trains at the **Tennessee Valley Railroad Museum** *(4119 Cromwell Rd.; 423-894-8028, www.tvrail.com)* and the restored **Chattanooga Choo-Choo Terminal Station** *(1400 Market St., ☎800-872-2529, www.choochoo. com)*, now a Holiday Inn with shops, guest rooms and restaurants in retired railroad cars.

Set high above the Tennessee River, Chattanooga's **Bluff View Art District** *(High St.)* is the site of the art museum as well as galleries and cafes. A free red-striped electric shuttle bus geared to tourists makes getting around Chattanooga a breeze.

### The Tennessee Aquarium★

*1 Broad St. ☎423-265-0695. www.tnaqua.org.*

This towering stone-and-glass structure dominates **Ross's Landing**, Chattanooga's restored riverfront, and opens onto a sunny plaza with fountains and rock-lined streams. Housing more than 12,000 fish, reptiles, amphibians, birds and mammals on four levels, the aquarium's major exhibits trace the course of the Tennessee River from its origins in the Smoky Mountains. The new Pen-

## Davy Crockett, American Pioneer

Born into the rough life of a mountain pioneer, Davy Crockett (1786-1836) grew up to become a celebrated Indian fighter, bear hunter, trail blazer and US congressman before heading off to Texas to join the ill-fated fighters at the Alamo. (All 187 Americans, including Crockett, were killed in this pivotal battle with Mexico for Texas' independence.)

Crockett's exploits and his legend are amply displayed at the visitor center at **Davy Crockett Birthplace State Park** (1245 Davy Crockett Park Rd., off Rte. 11 East near Limestone, TN; ☎423-257-2167). A reconstructed log cabin here on the Nolichucky River represents the approximate location of the Crockett family's primitive dwelling. When Davy was six, his family moved farther west, eventually settling on the Knoxville-Abingdon trail and opening their rough-hewn home to travelers. The **Crockett Tavern Museum** (2002 Morningside Dr., Morristown, TN; ☎423-587-9900) replicates the original inn.

guins' Rock exhibit chronicles two cold-climate species of this well-loved water bird, while the nearby IMAX 3D Theater offers deep-sea themed film features.

### Hunter Museum of American Art★

10 Bluff View. ♿ P ⓒ Open Mon-Tues, Fri-Sat 10am–5pm, Wed, Sun 12pm-5pm, Thurs 10am-9pm.◉$8. ☎423-267-0968. www.huntermuseum.org.

This fine collection is housed in a two-part facility—the restored 1904 Hunter mansion and an attached 1975 modern wing. Arrayed above hand-carved fireplace mantels in the mansion are major Hudson River School paintings and examples of American Impressionists (Childe Hassam). The modern wing offers contemporary sculptures and works by members of the Ashcan School (Robert Henri, George Luks, William Glackens).

### Houston Museum of Decorative Arts

201 High St. ☜Visit by guided tour only, Mon-Fri 9:30am–4pm. P ⓒ Closed major holidays. ◉$8. ☎423-267-7176. www.the houstonmuseum.com

Anna Safley Houston (1876-1951) spent her later years as an antiques dealer in Chattanooga amassing stunning **American glassware**, from Tiffany and Steuben to early Amberina. Her collection, which includes rare Mettlach beer steins, and 19C English and American pewter, is crammed into a

Victorian house a half-block from the Hunter Museum.

### Rock City Gardens★

Kids 1400 Patten Rd. (Rte. 58), Lookout Mountain, GA. ✗ P ⓒ Open daily 8:30am.◉$14.95-$38. ☎706-820-2531. www.seerockcity.com.

Anyone who has driven the rural South has seen "See Rock City" painted on barn roofs—and this kitschy 1932 tourist attraction still attracts hordes of visitors. Here a self-guided walking tour threads through a 14-acre expanse of windblown mountain vegetation amid giant boulders and cliffs, an ancient seabed carved into exotic shapes during the Ice Age. On a clear day, the **view**★★ from Lover's Leap spans seven states.

### Lookout Mountain Incline Railway★

Kids 827 East Brow Rd., Lookout Mountain. ✗ P (at lower station, 3917 St. Elmo Ave.) ☎423-821-4224.

This cable-drawn railway, constructed in 1895 and modernized since, is both a National Historic Site and a National Historic Mechanical Engineering Landmark. And yes, the track is really steep—a 72.7 percent grade near the top, so that passengers feel almost perpendicular.

### Ruby Falls at Lookout Mountain Caverns

1720 S. Scenic Hwy. ☜Visit of caverns by guided tour only. ✗ P ☎423-821-2544. www.rubyfalls.com.

## The "Secret City" of Oak Ridge

In 1942 the US military bought 59,000 acres in an isolated valley about 24mi west of Knoxville, built a "secret city" of 75,000 people almost overnight, and began producing the fissionable material necessary for atomic weapons. The "**Manhattan Project**" came to fruition on August 6, 1945, when a US-made bomb destroyed the Japanese city of Hiroshima. The bombing of Nagasaki followed on August 9, and the Japanese surrender ended World War II only five days later.

Today, Oak Ridge's three gigantic, mysteriously named facilities from the war years—K-25, Y-12 and X-10—harbor more benign research under the US Department of Energy. The former K-25 is now a technology park, while Y-12 remains a high-security plant devoted to manufacturing technology. The former X-10 is now **Oak Ridge National Laboratory** *(10mi west of Rte. 62 on Bethel Valley Rd.; ☎865-574-4163 or ☎865-574-7199)*, home to state-of-the-art research on such ventures as new energy sources and radioisotopes for medical use. Guided tours here lead to the control room and catwalk just outside the massive **Graphite Reactor**, the world's first model nuclear reactor—decommissioned in 1963.

For an in-depth view of Oak Ridge, head for the **American Museum of Science and Energy** 📷 *(300 S. Tulane Ave., in the Oak Ridge Convention and Visitor Center building; ☎865-576-3200).*

ke Rock City, Ruby Falls is an old-fashioned tourist attraction built around a enuinely interesting natural phenomon. Entering through the brooding, y-covered stone Caverns Castle, visirs descend 1,100ft inside the mountain an elevator and follow a long, narrow ail through stalactites and stalagmites 145ft **Ruby Falls**★, an underground aterfall.

## he Museum f Appalachia★★

mi north of Knoxville at I-75 Exit 122 in rris. ☎865-494-7680.

is 65-acre collection of weathered C log cabins and outbuildings (smohouse, corn crib, hog house, corn ill) sits behind split-rail fences encloig placid horses and sheep. Gobbling rkeys and clucking hens roam the ounds, and the occasional fiddler n be found sitting on a cabin porch. e provenance and estimated age of ch structure is documented, usually rough a story about its owners. Selfided tours start in the **Appalachian all of Fame**, a three-story edifice ammed with marvelous handcrafted

items, from a walnut writing desk to handmade musical instruments.

## Cumberland Gap National Historical Park★★

*60mi north of Knoxville at the border of KY, TN & VA. Take I-75 North to Rte. 63 North and follow US-25 East to the visitor center in Middlesboro.* △ ♿ 🅿 ☎606-248-2817. *www.nps.gov/cuga.*

A buffalo and Native American pathway for centuries, 800ft-high Cumberland Gap (half as high as nearby peaks) was discovered by white explorers in 1750 but became popular only after **Daniel Boone** (*see WESTERN KENTUCKY*) led the way in 1775. Authorized as a national historical park in 1940, the 20,000-acre site encompasses the long, high ridge of Cumberland Mountain, offering spectacular vistas and 70mi of hiking trails. For sweeping **views**★★ of Virginia, Tennessee and Kentucky, take the steep, hairpin-curve drive from the visitor center up to **Pinnacle Overlook** (2,440ft). By prior arrangement, visitors can hike or take a half-day trip via park shuttle bus to the abandoned **Hensley Settlement**,

*Chattanooga Choo-Choo*

a pioneer community whose last inhabitant left the mountain in 1951.

## Excursion

### Chickamauga and Chattanooga National Military Park★★

*Park visitor center is 9mi south of Chattanooga in Fort Oglethorpe, GA. From I-75, take Exit 350 West (Battlefield Pkwy.) turn left on Lafayette Rd., and go 1mi to park.* ♿ 🅿 ☎706-866-9241. www.nps.gov/chch.

The nation's oldest and largest Civil War park (8,200 acres) commemorates the hard-fought 1863 campaign for Chattanooga, a key Confederate rail center. Begin at the park visitor center on the edge of the Chickamauga battlefield to view the splendid multimedia production, **The Battle of Chickamauga**★, and wander through the **Fuller Gun Collection of American Military Arms**. A 7mi automobile tour *(cassette tape availab[le] at visitor center)* of Chickamauga lea[ds] past some 1,400 monuments and ma[rk]-ers that recall Confederate general Bra[x]-ton Bragg's humiliating defeat of th[e] Union army in September 1863.

About 5mi north on Lookout Mounta[in] is the Chattanooga section, **Point Par[k]**. Here, two months later, General Gra[nt] routed Bragg's forces at Lookout Mou[n]-tain, thus gaining control of East Te[n]-nessee. The **Point Park Visitor Cent[er]** *(off Rte. 148 on E. Brow Rd.; ☎423-82[1-] 7786)* features the mural-sized "**Batt[le] of Lookout Mountain**," painted [by] James Walker in 1874; inside the pa[rk] you'll find three batteries of canno[n,] the **New York Peace Memorial** and t[he] **Ochs Museum and Overlook**. Farth[er] down the mountain, **Cravens Hous[e]**, the Confederate headquarters durin[g] the assault, is accessible by a steep hi[k]-ing trail or by car.

# NEW ORLEANS AREA

The Gulf Coast regions of Louisiana, Mississippi and Alabama comprise a varying landscape of beach-rimmed shorelines along the Mississippi Sound and bayou-laced swamps of the Mississippi delta. Punctuated by the charming and diverse southern cities of New Orleans, Biloxi and Mobile, each area affords myriad recreational opportunities. Seekers of sun and sand gravitate to Mississippi's waterside resorts. History buffs delight in touring Mobile's stately homes or the plantations that line the Mississippi River between New Orleans and Baton Rouge. Despite the devastation from Hurricane Katrina, the moniker, "The Big Easy" still applies to New Orleans. It lives up to its reputation as a haven for pleasure-seekers; its restaurants serve up finely crafted traditional Cajun and Creole dishes redolent of seafood and spices. And the genial peculiarities of the Cajun Country around Lafayette, Louisiana, can make a visit here feel like a trip to a foreign land.

Sections of this region have changed hands numerous times since European explorers laid their claims in the 17C. France, Spain and England all grappled for control throughout the 18C, and all left their marks on regional culture before the US acquired the territories by treaty and by purchase in the early 19C. During the heyday of the slave trade, ships bearing human cargo for sale arrived here from Africa and the West Indies. On the backs of these slaves were built the massive cot-

*Ironwork in the French Quarter, New Orleans*

# Area Address Book

*For coin ranges, see the Legend on the cover flap.*

## WHERE TO STAY

**$$$$ Windsor Court Hotel** – *300 Gravier St., New Orleans, LA.* ☎*504-523-6000 or 888-596-0955. www. windsorcourthotel.com. 322 rooms.* Frequented by European royalty and celebrities, this opulent hotel on the outskirts of the French Quarter is decked out with 17C–20C furnishings and art, including works by Reynolds and Gainsborough. High tea is served each afternoon in the lobby's Le Salon lounge. The Windsor Court's **New Orleans Grill** is one of the country's top-rated restaurants thanks to chef Greg Sonnier creative international dishes.

**$$$ Madewood Plantation House** – *4250 Hwy. 308, Napoleonville, LA.* ☎*985-369-7151 or 800-375-7151. www.madewood.com. 8 rooms.* This 1846 Greek Revival mansion sits in the middle of an active sugarcane plantation 75mi from New Orleans. Period antiques, including scrolled canopy beds, add authenticity. Breakfast, evening wine and cheese in the library, and candlelit dinners around the dining room's huge oak table are part of the deal. Private dining in the Music Room can be reserved in advance.

**$$ Soniat House** – *1133 Chartres St., New Orleans, LA.* ☎*504-522-0570. www. soniathouse.com. 33 rooms.* A short walk from Cafe du Monde, this classic Creole-style town house in the residential French Quarter hasn't changed much since its beginnings in 1930. Spiral staircases lead to rooms decorated with European and Louisiana antiques and hand-carved canopy beds, leading out to flower-filled balconies. Don't miss breakfast by the lily pond in the courtyard.

**$ T'Frere's House** – *1905 School Rd., Lafayette, LA.* ☎*337-984-9347 or 800-984-9347. www.tfreres.com. 8 rooms.* You'll be immersed in Acadiana at this colonial house on the edge of town. Louisiana antiques from the 18C and 19C take you back to 1880, when it was built. But the huge Cajun breakfast is the highlight: eggs, spicy smoked sausage, and crepes topped with sugar-cane syrup.

## WHERE TO EAT

**$$$ Cafe Vermilionville** – *1304 W. Pinhook, Lafayette, LA.* ☎*337-237-0100. www.cafev.com.* **Louisiana French.** Site of the town's first inn back in the early 1800s, this cafe now houses one of Lafayette's finest restaurants. Located in the Oil Center, the cafe's unvarnished wooden beams, hanging plants and candlelight blend romance with country elegance *(jackets required)*. Jumbo shrimp in a spicy herb sauce, and pecan-crusted tilapia with crawfish tails get raves.

**$$$ Emeril's Delmonico Restaurant and Bar** – *1300 St. Charles Ave., New Orleans, LA.* ☎*504-525-4937.* **Creole.** When celebrity chef Emeril Lagasse restored the former Delmonico restaurant, he framed the 18ft windows of this century-old building in ultra suede and velvet panels, and covered the walls with neutral shades of grass cloth, linen and cotton. Located on the edge of the Garden District, Delmonico features such updated classics as crabcakes with mango butter and cucumber kimchi and a 20-ounce bone-in ribeye steak.

**$$$ Mr. B's Bistro** – *201 Royal St., New Orleans, LA.* ☎*504-523-2078.* **Creole.** A French Quarter supper club—complete with frosted-glass partitions and a piano player—known for its contemporary spin on local favorites. Mr. B's BBQ shrimp in a fiery pepper sauce and Gumbo Ya Ya (a soupy version of hearty chicken-and-andouille sausage stew) keep fans coming back. Bread pudding is the signature dessert.

**$$ Brennan's** – *417 Royal St., New Orleans, LA.* ☎*504-525-9711.* **Creole.** A New Orleans classic since 1946, Brennan's three-course prix-fixe Sunday brunch will satisfy the heartiest appetite. Starters include turtle soup and Southern baked apple with double cream. Entrée items range from Eggs Nouvelle Orléans (poached eggs atop lump crabmeat napped with brandy cream sauce) to oysters Benedict. The most requested item on the menu is Brennan's famed dessert creation, bananas Foster. *Reservations recommended.*

**$$ La Crepe Nanou** – *1410 Robert St., New Orleans, LA.* ☎*504-899-2670.* **French.** Behind the velvet maroon curtains of this uptown bistro's doorway is a rustic, casual dining room with vivid original paintings of Garden District street scenes. On the menu: typical fare with a New Orleans twist, such as peppery escargot baked in butter, crepes stuffed with crawfish, and roast lamb in cognac sauce. Reservations are not accepted, so be ready to wait in line.

**$$ Prejean's** – *3480 I-49N, Lafayette, LA.* ☎*337-896-3247.* **Cajun.** Nightly Cajun bands and award-winning cuisine make this a hot spot for residents and visiting dignitaries. Sautéed snapper topped with crawfish, crab and artichoke cream sauce and the wildgame, such as rack of elk and cajun duckling, are among the best-sellers at this northern Lafayette eatery. "Big Al," a 14ft alligator captured in nearby Grand Chenier swamp, oversees the dining room.

ton, indigo, rice and sugarcane plantations that fueled the region's economic prosperity in the 18C-19C. Life along the coast during this period was difficult at best; epidemics of mosquito-borne yellow fever and malaria regularly swept through the cities, and hurricanes threatened each summer and fall. Transportation was limited to the steamboats that plied the gulf waters between the population centers of Mobile, Biloxi and New Orleans. Today Interstate 10 links these cities.

A profusion of exotic plants flourishes in this subtropical climate, including moss-draped **live oak trees** (which maintain their green foliage year-round), fragrant magnolias, azaleas, hibiscus and bougainvillea. High temperatures and inland humidity quell tourism during the summer months, except at the breeze-cooled beachfront areas. The months from November to April are generally mild and comfortable. Lenten Mardi Gras celebrations in Lafayette, Mobile and New Orleans pack hotels and restaurants with visitors.

# NEW ORLEANS★★★

MAP P308

CENTRAL STANDARD TIME

POPULATION 1,200,000

In its topography, architecture, people and music, New Orleans resembles no other American city. Lying an average of 5ft below sea level, its naturally swampy lands—laced with secondary tributaries called bayous—are made livable by an extensive system of levees, pumping stations and drainage canals. The city's long succession of inhabitants—encompassing the Native American indigenous population, French Creole and Spanish colonists, West Indian and African slaves, and settlers from Europe and the eastern US—has created a rich mix of peoples and cultures that characterizes New Orleans today, even as its rebuilds from Hurricane Katrina. The city's distinctive architecture is the result of European ideas adapted to the subtropical climate.

- **Information:** ☎504-566-5095; 800-672-6124. www.nawlins.com.
- **Don't Miss:** The antebellum mansions of the Garden District.
- **Organizing Your Time:** Eating is a sport here; leave time to sample plenty of Cajun cooking.
- **Kids:** Imitation is the sincerist form of entertainment at the Musée Conti Wax Museum.
- **Also See:** GULF COAST, CAJUN COUNTRY.

# A Bit of History

New Orleans was founded in 1718 by French explorer **Jean-Baptiste Le Moyne**, sieur de Bienville, in an effort to solidify French claims in the New World. The site he chose, atop a naturally raised levee (or embankment) along the Mississippi, was militarily and economically important as the gateway to the Louisiana Territory, but proved inauspicious for settlement. French engineers laid out a town plan in 1721, and early colonists (forerunners of the city's non-indigenous Creole population) battled hurricanes, floods and epidemics as they maintained the trappings of French society in the muddy outpost. In 1769 the city came under Spanish rule, but was returned to France in 1803. A month

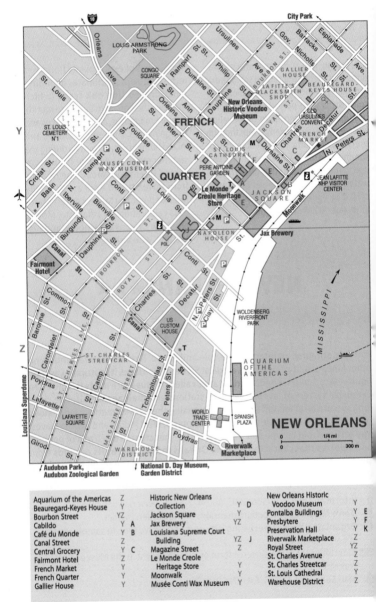

| | | | | | |
|---|---|---|---|---|---|
| Aquarium of the Americas | Z | Historic New Orleans Collection | Y D | New Orleans Historic Voodoo Museum | Y |
| Beauregard-Keyes House | Y | Jackson Square | Y | Pontalba Buildings | Y E |
| Bourbon Street | YZ | Jax Brewery | YZ | Presbytere | Y F |
| Cabildo | Y A | Louisiana Supreme Court Building | YZ J | Preservation Hall | Y K |
| Café du Monde | Y B | Magazine Street | Z | Riverwalk Marketplace | Z |
| Canal Street | Z | Le Monde Creole Heritage Store | Y | Royal Street | YZ |
| Central Grocery | Y C | Moonwalk | Y | St. Charles Avenue | Z |
| Fairmont Hotel | Y | Musée Conti Wax Museum | Y | St. Charles Streetcar | Z |
| French Market | Y | | | St. Louis Cathedral | Y |
| French Quarter | Y | | | Warehouse District | Z |
| Gallier House | Y | | | | |

ater Napoleon sold the entire Louisiana Territory including New Orleans to the US for approximately $15 million.

The decades following the **Louisiana Purchase** saw an explosion in the city's population as settlers flooded west to occupy the new American territory. New Orleans grew to be the fourth-largest city in the US by 1840, its prosperity buoyed by the river trade. Shunned by the Creoles, Anglo-American newcomers settled in suburbs upriver from the French Quarter. Staunchly Confederate on the eve of the Civil War, New Orleans capitulated to Union takeover in 1862 and was spared destruction.

The 20C saw numerous improvements to public-works systems, most importantly the development of flood-control measures that diverted river swells into shallow **Lake Pontchartrain** north of the city. The discovery of oil beneath the waters of the Gulf of Mexico brought new economic prosperity, along with continued port activities and, increasingly, tourism. Despite its ever-present socioeconomic and urban woes, the city remains one of the most popular tourist destinations in the US, a stature dampened by Hurricane Katrina, which ravaged the Gulf Coast region in 2005. Many areas are still rebuilding.

Creativity, romance, drama and fun are encouraged here. The uniquely American music form of **jazz** was born in Sunday-afternoon slave assemblages at Congo Square, and refined in the ballrooms, brothels and riverboats of the early-20C city. New Orleans' annual **Mardi Gras** celebration in February is world-renowned, capping a months-long social season of festivities.

Be sure to stroll through the **Garden District**★★★, the rectangle formed by St. Charles Avenue, Jackson Avenue, Magazine Street and Louisiana Avenue, to see an unmatched assortment of antebellum mansions (Greek Revival and Italianate styles predominate) erected mostly for Anglo-Saxon newcomers to New Orleans in the mid-19C. Built in the center of large plots of land, the homes allow space for front "gardens" where exotics such as banana, bougainvillea, magnolia, crape myrtle and oleander

still flourish. Prytania Street and the numbered streets leading from it to Magazine Street make for delightful wandering.

To explore **St. Charles Avenue**★★, a wide, beautiful thoroughfare overhung with enormous live-oak trees, hop aboard the **St. Charles Streetcar**★★ Kids line that traces the 5mi from Carondelet and Canal Streets to Lee Circle. Because the line's historic red Canal Street cars were damaged in Hurricane Katrina, service runs with equally historic green cars. Gracious antebellum and Victorian mansions line either side of the avenue.

## French Quarter★★★

Historically known as the Vieux Carré, the fabled rectangle that for many embodies the essence of New Orleans occupies roughly a hundred blocks historically bounded by **Canal Street**, Rampart Street, Esplanade Avenue and the great curve of the Mississippi River. The grid pattern laid out in 1721 survives today, but devastating fires in 1788 and 1794 wiped out most early French Colonial constructions. The distinctive architectural flavor of the French Quarter—with its stucco surfaces in bright pastel tints, intricately patterned cast-iron galleries and secluded interior courtyards—developed during the city's Spanish and early American periods. New Orleans' French Creole population remained firmly entrenched here from the city's earliest days through the Civil War and Reconstruction, but by the late 19C an influx of immigrants had moved in and the genteel quarter became a rowdy commercial and nightlife district. Today most Quarter residents live quietly behind the closed shutters of Creole cottages and town houses lining the streets on the lake side of Bourbon Street and downriver of Dumaine. But on Bourbon, Royal and Decatur Streets, on the broad pedestrian malls surrounding Jackson Square, and on the plazas near the French Market, the vibrant public life of the Quarter plays out like a daily urban musical comedy.

## Jackson Square★★

*Bounded by Chartres, St. Philip, Decatur & St. Ann Sts.*

Laid out as a military parade ground known as Place d'Armes, the fenced and landscaped square at the foot of Orleans Street was renamed in 1851 to honor **Andrew Jackson** (1767-1845), hero of the Battle of New Orleans and seventh US president. The monumental statue of Jackson astride a rearing horse was dedicated in 1856. Surrounded by elegant **St. Louis Cathedral**★ (1794), government buildings and the 1840s **Pontalba Buildings**★, the square served as the focal point of the old city; today street performers, artists and vendors set up shop on the square's flagstone perimeter. Across Decatur Street downriver from the square, **Café du Monde** serves up a quintessential New Orleans treat: café au lait and beignets (square donuts dredged in powdered sugar). Opposite looms handsome **Jax Brewery**, erected in 1891 and now renovated as a mall packed with shops. A stairway between the two leads to the **Moonwalk**, a boarded riverside promenade where visitors can watch steamships navigating the bend in the Mississippi that gave rise to New Orleans' nickname "the Crescent City."

For a view of the city from the Mississippi River, take one of the paddlewheeler and steamboat **cruises** that depart from the waterfront near Jackson Square.

## Cabildo★★

701 Chartres St. ♿☎504-568-6968.

To the left of the cathedral stands th Cabildo, erected by the Spanish gov ernment in 1799 to house offices of th town council; the papers completing th territory transfers of the Louisiana Pur chase were signed here in 1803. Toda the handsome building and the adja cent Arsenal contain excellent display of Louisiana history; on view here is on of the four original bronze death mask made of Napoleon in 1821.

Complementing the Cabildo to the righ of the cathedral is the **Presbytère**★★ (1813), built to house the bishops of Lou isiana and today containing an extensiv exhibit on the colorful history of Mard Gras in New Orleans.

## French Market★

Extending from Jackson Square to Bar racks Street, this bustling marketplac (1813) served the daily needs of New Orleans' Creole population. Shop and restaurants occupy the renovated structures today; the downriver buildin remains open to the air, as it was in th 19C. Step across Decatur Street to th old **Central Grocery** (923 Decatur St. and pick up a muffuletta, the pungen New Orleans sandwich made of Italia deli meats and cheeses layered on round bread and spiked with chopped-olive salad.

St. Louis Cathedral

*Bourbon Street*

New Orleans CVB/Richard Nowitz

## Royal Street★★

Elegant Royal Street is best-known for the many shops and galleries occupying the street-level façades of its early-19C town houses. It is a street for meandering, with frequent pauses to poke through galleries for fine contemporary art or antique furnishings and to gaze upward at intricately whorled galleries of wrought and cast iron. The massive white marble and granite **Louisiana Supreme Court Building** *(no. 400)*, completed in 1910. Selections from the wealth of holdings at the **Historic New Orleans Collection**★★ *(no. 533; by appointment only; ☎504-523-4662)* furnish excellent changing exhibits presented in the ground-floor gallery of the 1792 Merieult House *(visit by guided tour only)*. Departing from **Le Monde Creole Heritage Store** *(no. 624; ☎504-568-1801)*, an intriguing guided **walking tour**★ accesses several romantic interior courtyards while illustrating the intricacies of the city's French and West African Creole society. Also on Royal Street is the **Gallier House**★ *(nos. 1118-1132; ☎504-525-5661)*, former home of noted local architect James Gallier, Jr., who melded Creole and American style elements in his home's design.

*A horse parking post on Royal Street...the day after Mardi Gras*

© iStockphoto.com/Frank Aymami

## Bourbon Street★

Year-round but especially at Mardi Gras time in February, Bourbon Street teems with cocktail-toting revelers who come to celebrate, to drown sorrows or simply to indulge in the pleasures of this unabashedly hedonistic city. Lights flash, music booms and hawkers stand in doorways beckoning the unsuspecting to the dubious wanton pleasures within. Some of the finest traditional jazz is performed nightly just off Bourbon at **Preservation Hall**★ *(726 St. Peter St.; ☎504-522-2841)*, one of the city's best-known jazz venues.

## Aquarium of the Americas★★

Kids *1 Canal St. Tue-Sun 10am-5pm.* $17. ✗ ﴾ . ☎504-861-2537. www.audubon institute.org.

Innovative exhibits highlighting marine specimens from North, Central and South America delight visitors to this fine aquarium, distinguished by its slanted blue-green cylinder rising at the foot of Canal Street. Moray eels, silvery tarpon and other colorful creatures glide overhead as visitors navigate the walk-through tunnel of the **Caribbean Reef**. The **Mississippi River** exhibit reveals a wealth of catfish, bass, crappies and such rare specimens as an endangered paddlefish and a white alligator. Other features include a Adventure Island, an interactive play zone for kids with a 2,600-gallon pool filled with hownose rays, as well a penguin colony and an IMAX theater next door.

---

### Cities of the Dead

New Orleans' notoriously high water table necessitates the practice of burying the dead in aboveground tombs. Picturesque cemeteries filled with elaborate examples of funerary architecture dot the city. It's dangerous to visit these sites alone; plan to take a guided group tour.

**Save Our Cemeteries**
☎504-525-3377
**Historic New Orleans Walking Tours**
☎504-947-2120
**Magic Walking Tours**
☎504-588-9693

---

## Musée Conti Wax Museum★

Kids *917 Conti St. Private tours only.* ﴾ ☎504-525-2605. www.get-waxed.com.

Waxen figures, many of them exceedingly lifelike, offer a surprisingly informative walk through New Orleans history via a series of tableaux depicting key events and personages in the city's development.

## Beauregard-Keyes House★

*1113 Chartres St.* ✎ *Visit by guided tour only.* ☎504-523-7257.

During the late 1940s beloved American author **Frances Parkinson Keyes** (1885-1970) restored this gracious home, which had been the residence of Confederate general P.G.T. Beauregard for 18 months following the Civil War. Beauregard family portraits and heirlooms are on view here, as are the intriguing collections of Mrs. Keyes, who wintered here until her death.

## New Orleans Historic Voodoo Museum

*724 Dumaine St.* ☎504-680-0128.

Altars, dolls and myriad bizarre talismans offer glimpses into the world of voodoo, the occult religion that arrived in New Orleans with the slave trade, and continues to flourish today.

## Warehouse District★

In the once-bland industrial sector extending upriver from Poydras Street thrives the center of visual arts in New Orleans. Warehouses that sprang up behind riverfront docks in the early 19C are now reborn as studios and museums, while street-level storefronts along **Julia Street** house a wide variety of contemporary art galleries. **Riverwalk Marketplace** *(☎504-522-1555)*, a festival shopping mall, ranges along the area where riverfront loading docks once fringed the Mississippi *(Poydras, Canal & Julia Sts.)*.

## Confederate Memorial Hall★

*929 Camp St.* $7. ☎504-523-4522.

The dark, Romanesque-style building (1891), with its stunning cypress interior, houses a fine collection of paintings, photographs, uniforms, battle memorabilia and other artifacts of the

vil War, including personal belong-
gs of Robert E. Lee, Stonewall Jackson
nd Jefferson Davis, the Confederacy's
nly president.

### ontemporary Arts Center

*00 Camp St.* 🍴♿🅿 ☎ *504-528-3805.*
*ww.cacno.org.*

equently changing temporary exhibits
f modern visual art occupy the sleekly
enovated gallery spaces of this former
e-cream factory and tobacco ware-

house. Live performances are held in
the facility's two theater spaces.

## Additional Sights

### Audubon Park★★

*Bounded by St. Charles, Walnut & Calhoun
Sts. and the river.*

Formerly the site of a 400-acre sugar
plantation, this serene park opposite
Tulane and Loyola universities served

## Mardi Gras ★★★

New Orleans' **Mardi Gras** celebration is world-renowned as an unabashed invitation and tribute to escapism, ribaldry and decadence, a final hurrah before the spartan, sober season of Lent. The day before Ash Wednesday, Mardi Gras crowns the Carnival season, which officially begins on Twelfth Night (January 6). This season of parties, private masked balls and parades organized by exclusive social clubs known as "krewes" reaches its crescendo during the week and a half before Mardi Gras, during which time some 60 parades roll along established routes through various parts of the city. Costumed riders aboard elaborately designed floats toss strings of beads, aluminum doubloons, plastic cups, toys and other trinkets to crowds who line the streets begging for handouts. On Fat Tuesday itself, businesses and services shut down as residents and visitors alike take to the streets for a day-long citywide binge. Families dressed in costumes or in the Mardi Gras colors of purple, green and gold congregate along the St. Charles Avenue parade route to try for the prized coconuts handed out by the members of the Zulu Social Aid and Pleasure Club; or to toast Rex, King of Carnival, as he passes by with the Krewe of Rex. Diehard revelers don costumes and head for the French Quarter to pack themselves like sardines into the throngs of people on Bourbon Street. Here they gape at the outrageous creations of costume-contest participants, drink and dance, and indulge in New Orleans' quintessential celebration of escape from life's worries to focus on the pleasures of today.

*New Orleans CVB/Jeff Strout*

*Mardi Gras Parade*

# New Orleans Cuisine

Rooted in traditions more than two centuries old, New Orleans cuisine reveals the divergent influences of the varied cultures who populated the city. The origins of Cajun cooking lie in the simple foodways of agrarian France, brought to Louisiana by Acadian farmers and adapted with local ingredients. Considered more complex, Creole cuisine began in New Orleans and was influenced by the culinary traditions of the city's Spanish, African, West Indian and Native American populations.

Dependent as they are on the use of fresh local ingredients, many Cajun and Creole specialties are difficult to duplicate outside the region, making eating out, for some visitors, the raison d'être of a visit to the "Big Easy." Fish and seafood drawn from Louisiana rivers, lakes, brackish coastal wetlands and the Gulf of Mexico headline many a menu, accompanied by mellow Creole tomatoes, sweet satsuma oranges and other fruits and vegetables unique to the region's soil and climate. Complex combinations of herbs and spices spike many dishes. **Roux**, a mixture of flour and fat cooked until dark brown, forms the base of myriad sauces and soups. These include **gumbo,** a rich stew typically made with okra (a green pod vegetable brought by slaves from Africa), **andouille** (a spicy smoked pork sausage) and chicken or seafood, and thickened with **filé** (powdered sassafrass, first used by the region's Choctaw Indians). Shrimp, oysters and crawfish (a freshwater shellfish resembling a miniature lobster) appear in countless forms: **étouffée**, or "smothered," in rich, vegetable-laced sauce; simmered with rice, tomato, meats and spices in **jambalaya**; chilled and dressed with piquant **rémoulade** sauce; or dusted with cornmeal, then fried and heaped on French bread in a **po' boy** sandwich. Amberjack, redfish, pompano and trout are all fished locally and served up sautéed with almonds, napped with meunière sauce, or broiled and topped with sweet lump crabmeat. For dessert, try **bananas Foster**, a decadent preparation of bananas sautéed in butter and brown sugar then flamed with rum at table and served over ice cream.

as a Union encampment during the Civil War and as the site of the 1884 World's Cotton Centennial, which sparked residential development of uptown New Orleans. **Exposition Boulevard**, a pleasant footpath on the downtown side of the park, skirts a row of elegant residences.

On the river side of Magazine Street, **Audubon**★★ 🧒 (*6500 Magazine St.* ✗ ♿ 🅿 ☎*504-581-4629*) features state-of-the-art displays for its 1,500 specimens, which represent such rarities as white alligators and a Komodo dragon.

## Magazine Street★★

*Seven blocks south of St. Charles Ave.*
Erstwhile commercial thoroughfare of uptown New Orleans, Magazine Street today undergoes radical transformations—from upscale to downtrodden—as it proceeds from Audubon Park through the Uptown, Garden, Lower Garden and Warehouse districts to Canal

Street. Along the way you'll find a head mix of coffeehouses, eateries and trend boutiques; arts and crafts galleries of every type; commercial and residential blocks; myriad antique emporia and secondhand stores.

## City Park★

*Entrance at Esplanade Ave. & Wisner Blvd* ☎*504-482-4888*.
Fifth-largest urban park in the US, City Park encompasses 1,300 lush acres at the head of **Esplanade Avenue**★, a broad boulevard that traces an old Choctaw Indian path from the river to the head waters of Bayou St. John. (French artist **Edgar Degas** lived at 2306 Esplanade Avenue briefly in the winter of 1872-73.) Heralded by a heroic statue of Confederate general **P.G.T. Beauregard**, the park's main entrance leads along a gracious oak-lined allée to the art museum. Attractions include the **New Orleans Botanical Garden** (☎*504-483-9386*) and a **miniature train**, **Storyland** and

**Carousel Gardens** [Kids] amusement areas for the younger set.

**New Orleans Museum of Art★**
*Collins Dibboll Circle, in City Park.* ⊚$8. ☏504-658-4100.

Housed in a much-expanded Beaux-Arts-style building (1911), the collection of more than 40,000 pieces encompasses major European and American schools of painting, with significant concentrations of Louisiana and African-American artists. Holdings also include fine examples of silver and art glass, a fascinating assortment of portrait miniatures, Japanese Edo-period paintings, and creations of Russian jeweler Peter Carl Fabergé.

## Excursions

### Chalmette Battlefield★
*6mi southeast of New Orleans in Chalmette. Go east on Rte. 46 to park entrance at 8606 W. St. Bernard Hwy.* ♿ P ☏504-589-2636 ext. 1.

At this riverside battlefield on January 8, 1815, Gen. Andrew Jackson and a force of about 5,000 soldiers successfully defended New Orleans against British invasion in the final major confrontation of the War of 1812, thus securing US ownership of the Louisiana Territory. An excellent video recounts the Battle of New Orleans; afterward, visitors can drive or walk the 1.5mi road leading past key battle sites.

**Barataria Preserve** – 6588 Barataria Blvd. in Marrero, *17mi south of New Orleans near Crown Point. Take US-90 West over the Mississippi River; exit at Barataria Blvd. and go south on Rte. 45 to park.* ♿ P ☏504-589-2330.

Part of the Jean Lafitte National Historical Park and Preserve, this 20,000-acre wetland wilderness characterizes the constantly shifting terrain of the Mississippi delta region. Ranger-led hikes and guided canoe trips unlock the mysteries of this unique environment, as do exhibits in the preserve's visitor center.

One way to see the Bayou Barataria up close is to take one of the **swamp tours** that ply the dark, reptile-infested waters in pontoon boats. *For information, contact the New Orleans Convention & Visitors Bureau (☏504-566-5095 or 800-672-6124).*

# CAJUN COUNTRY★
MICHELIN MAP 584 M 13
CENTRAL STANDARD TIME

A broad landscape of sugarcane and rice fields, boggy swamps and sinuous bayous, Cajun Country offers visitors an excellent opportunity to sample the rich cultural heritage of one of the nation's best-known ethnic groups. Comprising 22 parishes (the Louisiana term for counties), the region extends north of the rugged Gulf Coast and west of the Mississippi River, encompassing the boggy Atchafalaya Basin and relatively high prairies ranging west of Lafayette to the Texas border. The oil and petrochemical refineries that support the local economy dot the riverbanks and outskirts of the region's urban centers.

**Information:** ☏225-342-8119. www.louisianatravel.com
**Don't Miss:** The beauty of Shadows-on-the-Teche.
[Kids] **Kids:** Send little ones to see Vermilionville, a restored farmstead.
**Also See:** NEW ORLEANS.

## A Bit of History

Formally nicknamed "Acadiana," the Cajun Country is inhabited principally by descendants of French colonists who were deported from Acadia (now Nova Scotia) in 1755 for refusing to swear allegiance to the British Crown. After suffering terrible hardships in the British colonies and in Europe, Acadian refugees

*A pan of spicy Cajun crawfish étouffée*

began arriving in southern Louisiana, infusing the region with the distinctive culture that flourishes today. Fun-loving, hardworking and fervently Catholic, the Cajun people (the word is derived from "Acadian") welcome visitors to join their enthusiastic pursuit of a good time. Fiddles and accordions set feet flying in myriad dance halls; headily spiced gumbos, seafood stews and boudin (rice and pork sausage) appear on local tables; and Cajun French is as prevalent as English on these sidewalkss.

## Sights

### Lafayette★

*135mi west of New Orleans via I-10. Visitor center at 1400 N.W. Evangeline Thruway. ☎800-347-1958. www.lafayettetravel. com.*

Founded in 1836 as Vermilionville and renamed in 1884, Louisiana's fifth-

*Vermilionville*

largest city is known as the "Hub City of Acadiana." Several Acadian-related sights lie within its boundaries, and i' many hotels and restaurants make it natural headquarters for exploration of the surrounding region.

### Acadian Cultural Center★★

*501 Fisher Rd. ♿ 🅿 ☎337-232-0789. www nps.gov/jela.*

This well-conceived visitor cent operated by the Jean Lafitte Nation Historical Park and Preserve is an excellent place to begin forays into the Caju Country. A series of displays focuses c various aspects of Cajun life in Louisian highlighting the ways in which Acadia traditions and methods—farming ar building techniques, clothing, languag crafts, music—were adapted to conc tions in the new land. A 40min vide presentation dramatizes the Acadia expulsion from Nova Scotia.

### Vermilionville ★

*Kids 300 Fisher Rd. ☎$8. ✗ 🅿 ☎337-23 4077. www.vermilionville.org.*

Colorfully re-created and restore buildings, including a 1790 farmstea range along tranquil Bayou Vermilic at this living-history museum devote to commemorating the Acadian way life (c.1765-1890). Costumed artisa demonstrate traditional crafts such weaving, boatbuilding and blacksmit ing, while Cajun bands perform daily a large performance hall.

*Louisiana Office of Tourism/www.louisianatravel.com*

## cadian Village★

00 Greenleaf Dr. ⬯$8. 🅿☎337-981-2364. et around a placid "bayou," this rustic e-created village offers a glimpse of life a Acadiana around the mid-19C. Most f the structures were moved here from ther locations in the region; others were onstructed on-site with period mate-als. Helpful plaques provide insights to architectural practices of the time, while displays in each building focus on cadian culture and traditions.

## hadows-on-the-Teche★★

17 E. Main St., New Iberia. ⬱⬯Visit by uided tour only. ☎318-369-6446. www. hadowsontheteche.org.

Moss-draped live oak trees create a play of light and shadow over this elegant brick Greek Revival mansion, built by sugarcane planter David Weeks in 1834. The house remained in the Weeks family for four genera-tions before being left to the National Trust for Historic Preservation. Nearly every item in the house is original, including fine Federal and Empire-style furniture from New York and Philadelphia, Staffordshire china and family portraits. Family members lie interred in a tranquil corner of the for-mally landscaped grounds fringing the slow-moving Bayou Teche.

# GULF COAST★

MICHELIN 584 O 13

CENTRAL STANDARD TIME

ong a popular resort haven, the coastline fringing the Gulf of Mexico from Mobile, labama, to New Orleans, Louisiana, boasts a wide variety of attractions for gamblers, portsmen and history buffs, as well as those seeking the pleasures of sun and sand. laimed by the French government in the late 17C, this area came under British rule 1763 following French defeat in the French and Indian War, and was ceded to pain following the American Revolution. The American flag was first raised over e territory in 1811, and resort communities sprang up.

**Information:** ☎225-342-8119. www.louisianatravel.com; ☎228-896-6699, www.gulfcoast.org (Biloxi); ☎251-208-2000, www.mobile.org (Mobile).

🅿 **Parking:** Long distances between resort towns make driving essential here. During the winter, parking lots will be full of cars with license plates from nor-thern states.

⬯ **Don't Miss:** Mardi Gras in Mobile.

👧 **Kids:** Curious kids may like exploring the gun turret of the USS Alabama, World War II battleship.

⬯ **Also See:** NEW ORLEANS.

## A Bit of History

taunchly Confederate through the Civil Var, the Gulf Coast fell to Union forces in 864. In the years following Reconstruc-on, tourism again boomed in the area. he resort communities of **Gulf Shores**, **ascagoula**, **Biloxi**, **Ocean Springs** nd **Gulfport** continue to attract visi-ors to their white-sand beaches, warm ulf waters and moderate year-round emperatures.

## Biloxi

This bustling coastal Mississippi city teems with activity from its resorts, fish-ing port, seafood canneries and boat-yards, all blessings of its waterbound location on a peninsula between Biloxi Bay and the Mississippi Sound. Founded in 1699, Biloxi was accessible only by steamboat during the antebellum period; it nevertheless became one of the most popular resorts on the Gulf Coast.

Today, enormous casinos punctuate the miles of beach along Biloxi's shorefront. Charming homes used to line the residential stretches of Beach Boulevard before Hurricane Katrina. The city welcomes thousands each May to the popular **Biloxi Shrimp Festival**.

### Ocean Springs★

*1mi east of Biloxi via US-90.*

This waterside artists' colony in Mississippi invites strolls along pleasant sidewalks lined with antique shops, potteries, art galleries and cafes. Also in town is the **William M. Colmer Visitor Center** (3500 Park Rd., off US-90; ☎228-875-0821) of the **Gulf Islands National Seashore**, a national park that preserves the Gulf Coast barrier islands.

## Mobile★

Second-largest city in Alabama, this gracious port combines the genteel atmosphere of the antebellum era with the bustle and verve of a contemporary southern metropolis. Mobile (*mow-BEEL*) served as the capital of French Louisiana from 1711 to 1719. Its prime location at the head of Mobile Bay made the city a major Confederate port during the Civil War, one of the last to fall to Union control.

Today the Port of Mobile and shipbuilding activities at the Alabama Shipyards fuel Mobile's economy. The city prides itself on its French heritage; the Mardi Gras celebration here predates the better-known festivities in New Orleans and signals the start of the dazzling annual **Azalea Trail Festival**. Local maps and information are available at the visitor center in **Fort Condé** 🧒 (150 S. Royal St.; ☎251-208-7569), a reconstructed version of the early-18C French outpost. The city's population has exploded as people have moved from New Orleans since Hurricane Katrina.

### USS Alabama Battleship Memorial Park★★

🧒2703 Battleship Pkwy., off US-90 1mi east of downtown. ☜$12. ⚒♿🅿☎251-433-2703. www.ussalabama.com.

Launched in 1942, this massive ship served in both the Atlantic and Pacific theaters of World War II, and earned nine battle stars shooting down 22 enemy planes and participating in six land bombardments. The self-guided tour offers a rare opportunity to enter a massive barbette supporting one of the ship's 16-inch gun turrets. Other attractions in the park include the World War II submarine USS *Drum*, and 23 historic aircraft.

### Museum of Mobile ★

*355 Government St.* ♿🅿
☎334-208-7569.

An extensive and varied collection of documents, portraits, Civil War artifacts, and Mardi Gras memorabilia tell the story of Mobile from colonization to the present. Be sure to see the display of fine sterling ware created by Mobile silversmith James Conning.

### Gulf Coast Exploreum Museum of Science ★

🧒 *Government St. at Water St.* ☎251-208-6873. www.exploreum.com.

Occupying a sparkling new facility in the heart of downtown Mobile, the Exploreum features a large Hands-On Hall of interactive physics displays to entertain and educate visitors.

## Excursion

### Bellingrath Home and Gardens★★

*20mi south of Mobile via I-10 to US-90. 12401 Bellingrath Rd., Theodore AL.* 🚶*Visit by guided tour only.* ⚒♿🅿☎334-973-2217. www.bellingrath. org/gardens.

Begun in 1927, some 65 acres of beautifully landscaped gardens surround a charming Mediterranean-style villa (1935) of antique brick and ironwork. Mobile soft-drink magnate Walter Bellingrath and his wife created this exquisite haven on the bank of the Fowl River as a personal retreat, decorating the house with Mrs. Bellingrath's extensive collection of European antique furniture, china and porcelain.

# RIVER ROAD★★

MICHELIN MAP 584 N 13
CENTRAL STANDARD TIME

One of the finest collections of antebellum plantation homes in the South lies along the River Road, a historic thoroughfare. Lined with more than 2,000 plantations in its early-19C heyday, the banks of the Mississippi here have unfortunately been marred in recent decades by a glut of oil and chemical plants.

- **Information:** ☎225-342-8119. www.louisianatravel.com.
- **Orient Yourself:** The River Road traces both banks of the Mississippi for approximately 120mi between New Orleans and Baton Rouge.
- **Also See:** NEW ORLEANS.

## A Bit of History

Beginning in the early 18C, Louisiana's French colonial government encouraged agricultural development of this area by granting plots of land to wealthy individuals who established plantations and contained the river with levees. Cotton, indigo, rice and especially sugarcane all thrived in the rich soil of the Mississippi River floodplain, providing planters with the means to live extravagantly.

Large homes built by slave labor formed the heart of most plantations. The principal entryway faced the river, to welcome visitors arriving by boat, and many homes incorporated a separate wing called a *garçonnière,* where the young men of the family would live when they reached the age of majority (around 15 years). After the Louisiana Purchase in 1803, Greek Revival became the popular style, and many Creole-style homes were updated with the Classical ornamentation that became popular during the antebellum period. **Madewood**★ (1846), designed by noted Louisiana architect Henry Howard, is considered among the finest examples of Greek Revival architecture in the area *(4250 Hwy. 308, 2mi south of Napoleonville; P ☎504-369-7151).*

The term "River Road" designates roadways on both sides of the river and incorporates sections of several state highways (notably Highway 18 on the west bank, and Highway 44 on the east bank). Route numbers change along the way; it's best to keep to the levees. The Hale Boggs Bridge *(I-310),* the Veterans Memorial Bridge *(Hwy. 641)* and the Sunshine Bridge *(Hwy. 70)* allow access between the east and west banks.

## East Bank

> *The following sights are organized from south to north.*

### Destrehan★★

*13034 River Rd., Destrehan.* 🚶Visit by guided tour only. ☜$10. ♿P☎985-764-9315. www.destrehanplantation.org.
Completed in 1790 as the heart of a 6,000-acre indigo (later sugarcane) plantation, this raised Creole-style manor is considered the oldest documented plantation house in the Mississippi Valley. In 1793, it was purchased by Jean Noel Destrehan who, with his brother-in-law Etienne de Boré, perfected the process of granulating sugar. The house was expanded in 1810, and Greek Revival ornamental details were added in 1839 to conform to antebellum tastes.

### San Francisco ★

*2646 Hwy. 44, Garyville.* 🚶Visit by guided tour only. P ☎985-535-2341. www.sanfranciscoplantation.org.
The eye-catching exterior style of this ebulliently decorated plantation house (1856), with its latticework, scrolled cornices and balustraded captain's walk, was dubbed "Steamboat Gothic" style for its fancied resemblance to riverboats passing on the Mississippi. The interior is restored to c.1860.

*State Capitol Complex, Baton Rouge*

### Houmas House★

*40136 Hwy. 942, Burnside.* Visit by guided tour only. $20 mansion and gardens, $10 gardens only. ☎225-473-9380. www.houmashouse.com.

A stately white plantation home gained its name from the land it was built upon, which was originally owned by the Houmas Indians. Houmas pairs a modest four-room c.1790 house with an 1840 Greek Revival mansion built for John Smith Preston, a son-in-law of Revolutionary War hero Wade Hampton.

## West Bank★★

*The following sights are organized from north to south.*

### Nottoway★

*30970 Hwy. 405, White Castle.* Visit by guided tour only. $10. ☎225-545-2730. www.nottoway.com.

Largest plantation home in the South, this ornate white mansion (1859) on the Mississippi displays a fanciful mix of Greek Revival and Italianate styles. Designed by Henry Howard for Virginia sugarcane planter John Hampden Randolph and his family, the 53,000sq ft house boasts 64 rooms sporting elegant appointments.

### Oak Alley★

*3645 Hwy. 18, Vacherie.* Visit by guided tour only. $10. ☎225-265-2151. www.oakalleyplantation.com.

Named for the gracious quarter-mile long **allée**★ of 28 live oak trees that approaches it on the river side, this stately Greek Revival mansion was completed in 1839 as the heart of a flourishing sugarcane plantation. (The trees predate the house by more than a century.) A total of 28 massive columns support the two-story gallery surrounding the house. The interior is furnished with fine period antiques.

### Laura★★

*2247 Hwy. 18, Vacherie.* Visit by guided tour only. ☎225-265-7690. www.lauraplantation.com.

The Creole culture of New Orleans and the lower Mississippi Valley are the focus of excellent guided tours of this colorfully painted raised Creole cottage (1805). Also on the site are twelve historic outbuildings, including original **slave cabins** where, in the 1870s, the African folktales of Br'er Rabbit (se ATLANTA) were first recorded.

## Baton Rouge★

Incorporated in 1817, this busy port city on the banks of the Mississippi has been Louisiana's state capital since 1849. Its colorful name comes from the "red stick" placed by local Indians to mark a hunting boundary and spotted by Pierre Le Moyne during his exploration of the area in 1699.

## Music on the Bayou

In Cajun Country, the fun begins when the day's work is done, and for many Cajuns fun means heading to local stages or dance halls to step, swing and stomp to the pulse-quickening sounds of **Cajun** and **zydeco** music. Typical Cajun bands incorporate accordions, fiddles and guitars along with bass and percussion (including washboards and tambourines), all accompanying a lead singer warbling in French about ill-fated love, family relationships and the joys of eating, drinking, dancing and living life to the fullest. In the course of its evolution from its roots in Acadian folk music, Cajun music has been much influenced by African, country and bluegrass musical traditions. Today it is enjoying a resurgence thanks to star performers such as Michael Doucet and his band BeauSoleil. Also accordion-based, zydeco music developed in the mid-20C on the prairies of southeastern Louisiana at the hands of such pioneers as Clifton Chenier and Boozoo Chavis, who applied rhythm-and-blues elements to traditional Creole music forms. Soul, disco and reggae music continue to exert an influence on zydeco, and a profusion of zydeco dance halls attests to its growing popularity.

### tate Capitol Complex★

*tate Capitol Dr. at N. 3rd St.* ✕ ♿ 🅿 ☎225-42-7317. www.legis.state.la.us.

ouisiana's **State Capitol**★★ building, n ornate 34-story Art Deco skyscraper 1932, Weiss, Dreyfous & Seiferth), is he tallest state capitol in the US. The ain level features a stunning, marble-heathed Memorial Hall, and the House nd Senate chambers; excellent displays f Louisiana folklife are displayed on the ower level. Views from the 27th-floor **bservation gallery** encompass the ver and the **Pentagon barracks**, stablished in 1819 to house a US army arrison serving the southwestern US. he **Old Arsenal** (1838) to the east con-ains a museum presenting the military istory of the capitol complex site.

### ld State Capitol★

00 North Blvd. ☎225-342-0500. ww.sec.state.la.us.

t this castle-like, Gothic Revival-style tructure (1850), with its stunning inte-ior rotunda, representatives in 1861 oted to withdraw from the Union and orm a separate nation (the republic xisted for four weeks). Today the build-g houses the Center for Political and overnmental History, with artifacts ncluding the handgun that was used o assassinate governor Huey P. Long 1935.

concrete promenade along the east ank of the river near the Old State Capitol makes for a pleasant stroll past shopping areas, riverboat casinos and the **USS Kidd** 🄺🄸🄳🅂, a decommissioned World War II destroyer (305 S. River Rd.; ☎225-342-1942). The adjacent **Nautical Historical Center** features ship models and several World War II aircraft.

### Magnolia Mound Plantation★

2161 Nicholson Dr. ☞☞Visit by guided tour only. ☞$8. ☎225-343-4955. www.brec.org.

Visitors may view an open-hearth cooking demonstration in the detached kitchen before touring the gracious house (c.1791), considered one of the finest examples of Creole-style architecture in the area.

## Excursion

### Rosedown Plantation★★

12501 Louisiana HWy., 26mi north of Baton Rouge on US-61, St. Francisville. ☎225-635-3332.

Don't miss this beautifully restored Greek Revival-style home (1835) with a 28-acre historic formal **garden**★ where owner Daniel Turnbull's wife Martha experimented with exotic plant species, successfully introducing azaleas and camellias to the southeastern US. All items in the house are original and placed exactly as they were in the antebellum period.

# NEW YORK CITY AREA

New York is arguably the most stimulating and sophisticated urban center in th
US, and its environs, north along the Hudson River Valley, among the most beau
tiful. The 320-acre city proper consists of five **boroughs**: Manhattan, Brookly
Queens, the Bronx and Staten Island. They spread over swatches of mainlan
scattered islets and a chunk of western **Long Island**. "The island" itself rank
as the biggest land mass adjoining the continental US, covering an estimate
1,723sq mi as it stretches eastward opposite the Connecticut coast almost as fa
as Rhode Island. It is hard to tell where one town ends and another begins i
the densely populated suburbs nearest New York City, but the relatively quie
forked "tail" at the eastern end of the island offers an unforgettably lovel
seaside landscape of bluffs, dunes and salt ponds.

Northward out of the city, a stunning succession of historic homes and Revolutionary War sites advances up the **Hudson River Valley** in a living catalog of American history and architecture. The riverine landscape, immortalized by the artists of the Hudson River school, easily ranks among the most spectacular in the Northeast.

New York City

The city, Long Island and the Hudson River Valley offer every imaginable diversion and recreational pastime to be found in town or country. Because of the beaches, summer is a great time to visit Long Island, but it is also the busiest. Many people favor the fall for exploring the greater New York City region. Between early October and mid-November, nature explodes in a blaze of color as Indian summer arrives. Tempe
atures often linger in the 70s, making
ideal for strolling Central Park, enjoyin
a drive on Long Island, or wandering u
the Hudson River Valley amid the turr
ing leaves.

*Ice-Skating in Central Park*

## Area Address Book

### GETTING THERE

**John F. Kennedy International Airport (JFK):** ☎718-244-4444; 15mi southeast of Midtown. Information counters in all terminals. **LaGuardia Airport (LGA):** ☎718-533-3400; 8mi northeast of Midtown. Information counter between Concourses C and D on departure level. **Newark International Aiport (EWR):** ☎973-961-6000; 16mi southwest of Midtown. Information counter in terminal B, lower level.  For further information on all three aiports, including ground transportation, contact: Port Authority of New York & New Jersey, 225 Park Ave. S., 18th floor, ☎212-435-7000 or ☎800-247-7433, www.panynj.gov/aviation/aviframe.htm. Rental car agencies are located at the airports.

**Pennsylvania Railroad Station** *(32nd St. & Seventh Ave.)* provides national and regional rail service by **Amtrak,** ☎800-872-7245, www.amtrak.com; **Long Island Railroad,** ☎718-217-5477; and **New Jersey Transit,** ☎201-762-5100. **Grand Central Railroad Terminal** *(42nd St. & Park Ave.)* provides local service by **Metro-North,** ☎212-532-4900. **Port Authority Bus Terminal** *(42nd St. & Eighth Ave.)* provides bus service by **Greyhound** *(☎800-231-2222; www.greyhound.com)* and **Peter Pan** *(☎800-343-9999).*

### GETTING AROUND

**Bus** and **subway** maps and timetables are available on buses, at subway stations and visitor information centers, or by online *(www.mta.info/nyct/maps/index.html)*. The Travel Information Center *(☎718-330-1234)* offers route and fare information. Foreign language information: ☎718-330-4847. All fares $1.50 one-way *(exact change required)*. **Taxi:** Yellow Medallion cabs, ☎212-692-8294.

### VISITOR INFORMATION

For a free visit planner, maps and information on accommodations, shopping, entertainment, festivals and recreations, contact the **New York Convention & Visitors Bureau**, 810 Seventh Ave., New York NY 10019, ☎212-484-1222, www.nycvisit.com; or **Times Square Visitor Center**, 1560 Broadway between 46th & 47th Sts., ☎212-768-1560, www.timessquarebid.org.

### WHERE TO STAY

*For coin ranges, see the Legend on the cover flap.*

**Hotel reservation services**: Accommodations Express, ☎609-391-2100, www.accommodationsexpress.com; Central Reservation Service, ☎407-740-6442. **Bed & Breakfast reservations**: Ahh! Bed & Breakfast #1, ☎212-246-4000; City Lights Bed & Breakfast, ☎212-737-7049. **Hostelling International**: ☎212-932-2300 or www.hinewyork.org.

**$$$$$ New York Palace** – *455 Madison Ave., New York City.* ✗ ♿ 🄿 *☎212-888-7000. www.newyorkpalace.com. 893 rooms.* The entrance to this 55-story skyscraper is the 19C Villard House opposite Midtown's St. Patrick's Cathedral. Just inside, you'll see the mansion's original molded ceilings before descending the grand staircase into the marble-columned lobby. Pricey oversize guest rooms are adorned with gold-brocade bedspreads. **Gilt** is right downstairs.

**$$$$ W New York** – *541 Lexington Ave., New York City.* ✗ ♿ 🄿 *☎212-755-1200. www.whotels.com. 688 rooms.* Earth, wind, fire and water are the cardinal elements that inspired this new hotel's Zen-like ambience. Soothing natural light filters through the two-story lobby. Clusters of comfortable couches and a magazine rack make it feel like

*New York City Taxis*

Brigitta L. House/MICHELIN

your best friend's living room. Relaxing earth tones, fluffy featherbeds and top amenities compensate for the small bedrooms.

**$$$$ The Castle at Tarrytown** – *400 Benedict Ave., Tarrytown, NY.* ✗ ♿ 🅿 🏊 ☎*914-631-1980. 31 rooms.* Resembling a medieval fort—with towers and arched windows—this mansion sits on a hilltop overlooking the Hudson River 25mi north of New York City. Inside, stained-glass windows, Oriental rugs and period tapestries soften beamed ceilings and stone walls. Hand-carved four-poster beds draped in goose-down comforters, and custom-made chandeliers decorate the rooms. Dinner at **Equus** is memorable.

**$$$ The Melrose Hotel** – *140 E. 63rd St., New York City.* ♿🅿🏊☎*212-838-5700. www.thebarbizon.com. 306 roooms.* Grace Kelly and Liza Minnelli called this 1927 landmark home when it was known as the Barbizon Hotel & Towers, an "exclusive residence for young women." A recent $40 million renovation has refreshed the residential appeal of its rooms with contemporary furnishings, wrought-iron headboards and shuttered windows.

**$$ Washington Square Hotel** – *103 Waverly Pl., New York City.* ✗ ☎*212-777-9515. www.wshotel.com. 170 rooms.* Across Washington Square Park in Greenwich Village, this intimate 1910 property is introduced by the small, green-and-white marble lobby, with hand-painted tile murals of wildflowers. Most rooms have Art Deco furniture.

**$$ The Ivy** – *244 N. Main St., South-hampton, NY.* 🏊 ☎*631-283-3233. 5 rooms.* This 1860 Colonial-style structure, complete with picket fence, is located right in town. Its elegant interior is filled with French and English antiques. Each guest room is decorated according to a different theme, from romantic country florals to Ralph Lauren-style equestrian.

## WHERE TO EAT

**$$$ Park Avenue Cafe** – *100 E. 63rd St., New York City.* ☎*212-644-1900.* **American.** This Upper East Side ode to Americana transforms with the seasons into a new restaurant every three months. Changes are made to everything, from the menu, and place settings to most of the decor, thanks to convertible panels, which slide into steel wall frams. The menu is heavy on fresh seafood and modern takes on American classics like burgers and chicken and waffles. Try its signature chocolate cube dessert, filled with caramel mousse.

**$$$ The Central Park Boathouse Restaurant** – *72nd St. & Park Dr. N., New York City.* ☎*212-517-2233. Dinner from April-November only.* **Contemporary.** One of the city's best-kept secrets is hidden inside Central Park. The lakeside eatery switches from its outdoor verandah in summer to a ski lodge-style interior room during colder months. Dishes reflect the city's melting-pot culture.

**$$ Gramercy Tavern** – *42 E. 20th St.* ☎*212-477-0777. New York City.* **Contemporary.** Like an old friend to many New Yorkers, this cozy Gramercy Park spot wins rave reviews for contemporary fare that's more about comfort than panache. Menu standouts include bacon-wrapped trout and stuffed meatballs.

**$ Lobster Roll** – *1980 Montauk Hwy., Amagansett, NY. Closed Nov–mid-Apr.* ☎*631-267-3740. www.lobsterroll.com.* **Seafood.** Sand dunes surround this highway shanty, midway between Amagansett and Montauk. Regulars, including Barbra Streisand and Alec Baldwin, have taken to calling it "lunch" thanks to a neon sign above the outdoor patio. Their famous lobster rolls, deep-fried Atlantic cod, and crabcake platter make it a worthy stop.

**$ Katz's Delicatessen** – *205 E. Houston St.* ☎*212-254-2246. www.katzdeli.com. New York City.* **Deli.** A Lower East Side fixture since 1888, Katz's is a part of New York City history. More recently, it was the side of Meg Ryan's famous scene in the movie, *When Harry Met Sally.* For many New Yorkers, it's the only place to go for Matzoh ball soup, chopped liver, and a good corned beef on rye.

# NEW YORK CITY ★★★

MAPS P330 AND P338
EASTERN STANDARD TIME
POPULATION 8,214,426

ew York City is a world unto itself by virtue of its dynamic economic activity,
s vibrant cultural life and the size and density of its population. The area, once
ooded and wild, was the province of Native Americans until Giovanni da Ver-
azano began the influx of Europeans in 1524. First a Dutch colony, then British
y 1664, New York blossomed as an important trading post. The city was among
e first British targets during the Revolution; British troops occupied the area
r the duration of the war.

**Information:** ☎212-484-1222. www.nycvisit.com.

**Parking:** Don't even try. Parking in NYC is expensive and difficult; save your
time and money and take the subway or hail a cab.

**Organizing Your Time:** Plan gallery hopping mid-week: most art galleries
are closed on Mondays.

**Kids:** The gold vault in the Federal Reserve Bank of New York will wow
little ones.

**Also See:** BOSTON, WASHINGTON, DC.

## A Bit of History

etween 1785 and 1790, New York
erved as US capital and hosted the
auguration of George Washington,
he first president. By 1820, the city
vas the most densely populated in the
ation, growing steadily as the flow
f European immigrants accelerated.
prosperous shipping and banking
enter, New York established itself as a
ultural mecca and home to a burgeon-
ng upper class following the success of
merica's first world's fair held in the
ity in 1853. Commercial and industrial
rowth perpetuated a rush of immigra-
ion that ebbed and flowed into the 20C.
1898, the five boroughs were bundled
nto Greater New York City, creating a
metropolis of three million people, the
argest in the world.

t the dawn of the 20C, the city grew
kyward as architects developed new
vays to construct ever-taller buildings.
heater and the arts flourished, fueled
y a large contingent of avant-garde
vriters, poets, thespians and artists who
ived in Greenwich Village and other
nclaves. In Harlem, African-American
rts, letters and music flowered. While
he trials of the stock market crash in
929, the ensuing depression, gang-

ster activity and World War II took their
toll, New York endured to solidify its
international position in industry, commerce and finance in the late 1940s. New
immigrants from Puerto Rico and Asia
contributed to the melting pot, and a
controversial group of poets—known
as "the Beats"—and modern artists
redefined New York's bohemian character. A haven for refugee intelligentsia
from post-World War II Europe, the city
emerged as the center of modern art.
**Abstract Expressionism**, America's
first radical artistic movement, rose from
the studios of New York's painters.
Racial and labor tensions beset the city
in the 1960s. The 1964 **Harlem Uprising**
marked the first major Northern black
unrest of the civil rights era. In 1975 an
economic downturn forced the city government to default on its debts. (That
year, the *New York Daily News* ran an
infamous headline "Ford to City: Drop
Dead" after President Gerald Ford
refused to help the city with its fiscal
woes.) The city's budget was balanced
by 1981, however, and later that decade,
an upswing in the world economy led to
massive expansion on Wall Street. The
events of September 11, 2001 forever
changed the landscape of downtown
Manhattan, but today New York contin-

*A street cafe*

Brigitta L. House/MICHELIN

ues to cope with urban challenges on a grand scale as it moves forward in the new century.

# MANHATTAN

This tongue-shaped island, flanked on the west by the expansive Hudson River and on the east by the Harlem and East rivers, measures 13.4mi in length and 2.3mi at its widest point, making it the smallest borough. It is, nonetheless, the best-known and synonymous with the city itself. Manhattan, whose name derives from an Algonquin word meaning "island of the hills," was acquired from those Indians by Dutch governor Peter Minuit in 1626, in exchange for trinkets valued, during that period, at a mere $24. The Dutch settlement of Nieuw Amsterdam developed on the island's southern tip. After British occupation, the town expanded northward, following a neat grid of numbered streets and avenues that eventually predominated throughout most of the island. Today, some of the most historic sections are found in the areas south of 14th Street, occupied by "Lower Manhattan" and "Downtown." Manhattan's commercial core is "Midtown," the vicinity between 34th and 59th Streets. "Uptown," or anything above 59th Street, offers a broad cross section

of cultural and educational institution fashionable residential blocks, and wel entrenched neighborhoods. For all it sophistication, Manhattan retains remarkably diverse physical and soci makeup, epitomizing the melting pe that makes New York so fascinating explore. The famous landmarks shoul not be missed, but a stroll off the beate path will also reward visitors with a tast of the "real" city, where brownstone and bodegas are as much a part of th urban fabric as skyscrapers and Sak Fifth Avenue.

## Lower Manhattan★★

Crowded onto the southernmost ti of Manhattan below Chambers Stree cathedrals of commerce, religion an government comfortably coexist i the **Financial District**★★★ and **Civi Center**★★. The first site of 17C Dutc settlement, Lower Manhattan still bear the imprint of Nieuw Amsterdam's wind ing streets. The most famous, **Wa Street**★★, so-called for a defensiv stockade built by the Dutch in 165 between the Hudson and East River to discourage attacks, symbolizes th nation's financial power. At the corner c William Street in 1792, 24 brokers met t found the forerunner of the **New Yor Stock Exchange**★, today located in 17-story building (1903) at 11 Wall Stree The visitor center has been closed to th public since 9/11. **Trinity Church**★★, striking Gothic Revival presence at th head of Wall Street at Broadway, wa the tallest building in the city in 1846 Northeast of the Financial District, Civi Center includes **Foley Square**, sur rounded by the monumental **New Yor State Supreme Court**, Cass Gilbert' 1936 **U.S. Courthouse**, and the colossa **Municipal Building**★. In the midst of shady park several blocks south alon Centre Street stands handsome **Cit Hall**★★, completed in 1811.

### World Trade Center Site★★

This site of the former World Trad Center, destroyed in the terrorist attack of September 11, 2001, the solemn plo is bounded by Liberty, Church, Bar clay and West streets. Rebuilding here has been mired in criticism and fierce debates, and it's mostly still a hole in the ground. The plan includes five towers, a memorial plaza and museum. One tower, the 52-story 7 World Trade Center (212-490-0600) (named for the building that originally stood here) is complete and open to the public. Visitors can go to the 45th floor to take pictures and see the memorial exhibit. The area surrounding the site is overrun with street vendors selling all kinds of souvenirs in the memory of 9/11.

## National Museum of the American Indian★★

*1 Bowling Green.* ○*Open year-round daily from 10am-5pm; open Thursdays until 8pm. Closed Christmas Day. Free.* ♿☎*212-414-3700.* Cass Gilbert's former Beaux-Arts **US Custom House**★ (1907) makes a splendid setting for this Smithsonian museum. Beautifully displayed collections, including masks, weapons and ceremonial garments, represent the history and culture of indigenous peoples of the Americas.

## Liberty and Ellis Islands★★★

▥ *Ferry departs from Battery Park South.* ○*Open year-round, daily from 9:15am-5pm.* ☞*Ferry fee $11.50.* ✗♿☎*212-269-5755.*

On these two tiny islands in New York Harbor stand the twin symbols of America's rich immigrant heritage. Listed on the coveted roster of UNESCO World Heritage sites, the **Statue of Liberty**★★★, her torch upraised in welcome since 1886, was a gift from the people of France. Alsatian sculptor Frédéric-Auguste Bartholdi and French engineer Alexandre Gustave Eiffel created the 225-ton, 151ft colossus. American architect Richard Morris Hunt designed the base, which contains an observation deck affording spectacular city **views**★★★.

Buildings on nearby **Ellis Island**★★ served as gateway for 12 million immigrants between 1892 and 1954. After 30 years left empty, the main structure in the 33-building complex was returned to its 1920s appearance during a massive restoration and now houses the poignant **Ellis Island Immigration Museum**★★. Ferries to both Liberty and Ellis Islands depart from **Battery Park**★, a 21-acre greensward at the water's edge. Ticket booths are located in **Castle Clinton National Monument**★, an 1811 fortification with a colorful history of adaptive reuse. Walks through the park offer splendid views across the harbor.

## South Street Seaport★★

ᴷⁱᵈˢ*Admission is free to historic district, shops, restaurants, piers and Fulton Market.* ☎*212-748-8600 (visitor's center). www.southstseaport.org.*

One of New York's leading tourist attractions, this historic district encompasses an 11-block area of South Street along the East River just south of the Brooklyn Bridge. Hub of the city's worldwide shipping activities in the early 19C, it contains the largest concentration of early commercial buildings in Manhattan. Many of the oldest have been rehabilitated for commercial use, including **Schermerhorn Row**, constructed in

*Statue of Liberty*

© PhotoDisc, Inc

*View of the Manhattan Bridge over the East River*

1811-12. The **Fulton Market Building** (1983) and the **Pier 17 Pavilion**★ offer restaurants and shops in the heart of former **Fulton Fish Market**, which relocated to a new facility in the Bronx in 2005. The **South Street Seaport Museum**★★ (☎212-748-8786) maintains a variety of historic attractions, including a fleet of **historic vessels**★ dating from 1885 to 1935. Begin in the visitor center (*12 Fulton St.*) for an introductory exhibit on seaport history.

## Brooklyn Bridge★★★

The pedestrian walkway can be reached by crossing Park Row from City Hall Park, or from the Brooklyn Bridge-City Hall subway station. A link between Manhattan and Brooklyn, this elegant 5,989ft bridge is one of the oldest suspension bridges in the United States and ranks among the great engineering triumphs of the 19C. German-born designer John Augustus Roebling began work in 1869, succumbing shortly thereafter to a gangrenous injury. His son Washington took over, but was stricken with the bends while working in the deep underwater construction caissons and had to supervise the construction from his bed until the bridge was completed in 1883. A sunset stroll across this enduring landmark offers magnificent **views**★★ of the city.

© PhotoDisc, Inc

## Downtown and the Neighborhoods★★

In the patchwork of neighborhoods below 34th Street abides much that is quintessential New York. Shaped by rich and poor, immigrants and bohemians, these districts include such enduring residential communities as Gramercy Park and Murray Hill, along with the fabled Villages and the ethnic enclaves of Chinatown and Little Italy. On the Lower East Side, once teeming with Jewish immigrants, **Orchard Street**★ still bustles with merchants and street hawkers. Trendy neighborhoods like **TriBeCa**★ (an acronym for triangle Below Canal) and **Chelsea**★ epitomize the late-20C urban flair for

adapting warehouses for residential and mercantile use. Elsewhere, 19C brownstones mark the blocks once favored by New York's elite before the more remote uptown neighborhoods became fashionable. In between, peaceful squares and small parks punctuate the built-up landscape with greenery and open space.

### Chinatown and Little Italy

These adjacent enclaves rank as the most famous (i.e., touristy) of New York's immigrant neighborhoods. While once distinct, their borders have blurred as **Chinatown**★★ expands. Throughout the entire area, narrow streets lined with colorful shops selling souvenirs at rock-bottom prices, produce stands and

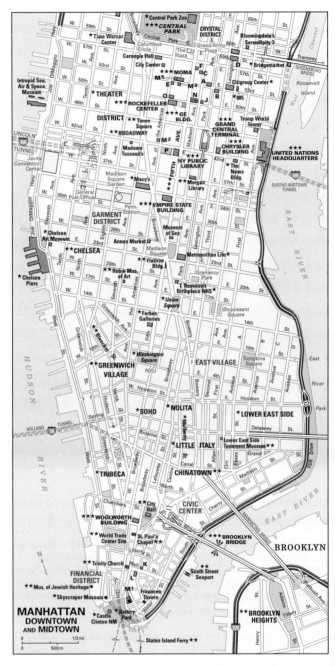

**MANHATTAN**
DOWNTOWN
AND MIDTOWN

restaurants bustle with locals and visitors, particularly on weekends.

New York's first Chinese came from the American West, where they had worked as laborers before 1880. Today the majority of Manhattan's nearly 150,000

Asians and Asian-Americans live in the area around Canal, Mott, Bayard and Pell Streets, the heart of Chinatown. The neighborhood comes alive with a bang during the **Chinese New Year** (first fu...

*soon after January 19)* with traditional parades and fireworks.

**Little Italy**★, roughly bounded by Canal, Lafayette, Houston Streets and the Bowery, was the destination for thousands of Italian immigrants between 1880 and the 1920s. Its hub lies along **Mulberry Street**★. The corridor throngs with visitors during Feast of San Gennaro in mid-September.

### East Village★

Defined by Houston and 14th Streets east of Broadway, this neighborhood may be best known as the haven of the Beat writers of the 1950s who gravitated to its low rents and romantic seediness.

Though you'll find an occasional Gap or Starbucks, the counterculture still frequents the atmospheric bars, restaurants and coffeehouses here, including an array of inexpensive ethnic eateries that line **Second Avenue**. Shopping abounds west of Avenue A, especially at St. Mark's Place *(between 2nd & 3rd Aves.)*.

### Greenwich Village★★

West of Broadway, venerable Greenwich Village wears well its reputation as New York's historic bohemia. A country village into the 19C, "the Village," as locals call it, still retains a small-town feeling in its narrow, bending streets and alleys. Rising

*Lucky Paper Lanterns, Chinatown*

©iStockphoto.com/John Chu/Terraxplorer

# Building Manhattan

American author Edith Wharton once wrote that New York would become "as much a vanished city as Atlantis or the lowest layer of Schliemann's Troy." On the crowded island of Manhattan, the architectural strata are especially deep. The oldest layers are now visible only in isolated outcroppings; the more recent define entire city blocks. From the long-gone step-gable roofs of Nieuw Amsterdam to the new skyscrapers to be built at Ground Zero, the Manhattan skyline now more than ever is a work in progress. And though much here changes, the city leads the nation in protecting thousands of buildings and historic districts that illustrate its development.

Only one 18C Dutch Colonial-style farmhouse, Dyckman House, still stands in Manhattan (4881 Broadway at 204th St. ☎212-304-7422). The English introduced the Georgian style, which emphasized the symmetry and decorum of Classical architecture, well-illustrated by the handsome **Morris-Jumel Mansion** *(W. 160th St. & Edgecomb Ave. ☎212-923-8008)* in Harlem. After the Revolution, Americans adapted Classical forms to suit the new nation, and the elegant results became known as the Federal style. New York's 1811 **City Hall**★★ *(between Centre St. & Broadway at Chambers St.)* despite the influence of its French architect, makes an exquisite example. That same year the city released the Randel Plan for Manhattan, a monotonous grid of streets that divided the city into narrow east-west blocks and provided a framework upon which Manhattan could grow. Two serious fires in 1835 and 1845 accelerated the building process, and the growth of public transportation helped ferry people north. Slums grew along with the city, and shantytowns filled the still-vacant lands in Central Park and upper Manhattan.

Throughout the 19C a flurry of Revival styles, drawing on Greek, Gothic, Italian Renaissance, Romanesque and even Egyptian design motifs, left an ever more eclectic imprint on the city. By mid-century, the vertical, rectangular façades of the Renaissance-inspired Italianate style proved ideal for the narrow lots of the booming city. It became the basis for the brownstone and the cast-iron commercial warehouse—both quintessential New York innovations. The elegant **E.V. Haughwout Building**★ *(488-92 Broadway)* boasts the oldest complete cast-iron façade in the city (1857) as well as the first safety elevator, an invention that would help push civilization skyward.

In 1893 the success of Chicago's World's Columbian Exposition created a rage for Beaux-Arts architecture, and the New York firm of **McKim, Mead and White** led the way. They modeled their incomparable Pennsylvania Station (demolished) on the ancient Baths of Caracalla. Daniel Burnham's 1902 **Flatiron Building** *(junction of Broadway & Fifth Ave.)* made the style popular for skyscrapers.

In 1916 the city passed the nation's first zoning law to ensure that adequate light and air reached the deepening street-level canyons. Zoning required buildings to set their façades back from the street as they grew higher, and soon there sprouted a profusion of ziggurat-shaped towers. The zoning laws, new technologies such as field riveting (a more efficient method of connecting steel pieces

*Chrysler Building*

on site) and the streamlined aesthetics of modern art inspired the Art Deco sky-scraper, which achieved its greatest expressions in New York. By the late 1920s and 1930s landmarks like the **Chrysler Building★★★** (1930, William Van Alen), at 405 Lexington Avenue, with its zigzag steel conical crown, and the muscular **Empire State Building★★★** *(350 Fifth Ave.)* best exemplified the modern style.

After the Depression the International style emerged. Its ultra-sleek look rejected ornament and setbacks for boxlike slabs set in open plazas. The new technology of the glass-curtain wall attained its clearest expression in the 1958 **Seagram Building★★** *(375 Park Ave.)* by Ludwig Mies van der Rohe. Before long, however, architects began another round of embellishment, applying historical elements and materials to modern steel-frame buildings. The former **AT&T Headquarters** (1982, Johnson & Burgee), in Sony Plaza, introduced this Postmodernism with its whimsical "Chippendale" roofline. In the 21C, the flash of Postmodernism will likely yield to a new range of practical possibilities. The revitalization of Times Square, a focus on neighborhoods, and waterfront development along the Hudson and East rivers all signal a renaissance for a city with its head in the clouds.

become the political, artistic and literary center for New York's intelligentsia in the early 1900s, the neighborhood still offers a diversity of lifestyles. **New York University (NYU)**, the largest private university in the US, makes **Washington Square★★** its unofficial campus. This plaza at the foot of Fifth Avenue serves as the district's hub and can be instantly identified by its emblematic arch designed by Stanford White in 1892. For another taste of the Village, stroll **Bleecker Street★**, famed for its pastry shops and coffeehouses, as well as for the small cabarets, music clubs and bars that flourished in the 1960s.

**SoHo★★**

The site of the first free black community on the island, this area was settled in 1644 by former slaves of the Dutch West India Company. Today, Soho (an acronym for South of Houston Street) mixes up a lively blend of chain emporiums, art galleries and bargain outlets, particularly along West Broadway and **Broadway★**. Here also is the largest concentration of 19C **cast-iron warehouses** in the US, a legacy of the district's history as a thriving industrial dry-goods center between 1850 and 1890. The oldest, built in 1857 and known as the **E.V. Haughwout Building★**, stands at 488-92 Broadway. **Greene Street★** boasts a rich assortment of these buildings, most converted to modern uses.

# Along the Way

## Lower East Side Tenement Museum★★

*108 Orchard St. Open year-round for visits by guided tour only. Call for seasonal schedules.* ☎212-431-0233. *www.tenement.org.*

Exhibits here capture the gritty essence of life as it was in New York's tenements and sweatshops. The museum also sponsors guided tours of a partially restored tenement building at 97 Orchard Street.

## Museum for African Art★

*1280 Fifth Ave. & 110th St.* ☎718-784-7700. *www.africanart.org.*

One of only two in the US devoted to African art (the other is part of the Smithsonian Institution in Washington, DC), this museum is scheduled to open in a new home in Harlem in late 2009. It will include 16,000sq ft of gallery space and an interactive educational center.

## Macy's★

*Bounded by Broadway, Seventh Ave., 34th & 35th Sts.* ☎212-695-4400.

The "world's largest store" was built in two parts: the 1901 classically inspired eastern section and the western wing, built in the Art Deco style in 1931.

*Times Square*

## Midtown★★★

Midtown is New York City at its most cacophonous and exciting. Situated between 34th and 59th Streets, the area is as famous for its avenues and cross-streets as for its skyscrapers and shops. Midtown's backbone, **Fifth Avenue★★★**, separates the East and West Sides. Known in the late 19C as "Millionaires' Row" (home to the Goulds, Astors and Vanderbilts), the avenue is now bordered by famous department and jewelry stores.

West one block, an imposing line of 1960s skyscrapers creates a dramatic canyon of glass and steel along the **Avenue of the Americas★** *(Sixth Ave.)*. A block east of Fifth, **Madison Avenue★**, once a choice residential address, now ranks among the city's most exclusive shopping thoroughfares. One more block east, **Park Avenue★★★** boasts some of New York's architectural gems.

New York's major crosstown thoroughfare, **42nd Street★★** features a line-up of distinguished Art Deco structures at its eastern end. Ongoing revitalization efforts aim at returning its western length to its former splendor as a byway of the **Theater District★★**. The most famous New York street, however, may be **Broadway**, which runs the leng of Manhattan and lends its name to th entertainment district between 40 and 53rd Streets. At Broadway and Se enth Avenue, **Times Square★★** mar the epicenter of that district, whe some 40 theaters cluster. The **nigh time illuminations★★★** in the squa pulse the rhythm of the city, as the have since the early 20C when the sig industry moved here.

### Empire State Building★★★

Kids *350 Fifth Ave. Consult a visibility cha before buying tickets to the observ tory.* $20. Open year-round, da from 8am-2am. Last elevator at 1:15a X &212-736-3100. www.esbnyc.com Completed in 1931, this Art Deco ma terpiece remains the most distincti feature of the Manhattan skyline. Th needle-nosed tower, rising to 1,454 was the world's tallest for four decade The top floor was intended as a moc ing platform for dirigibles until a nea catastrophic trial run in 1932. Enjoy t 80mi view from the 86th-floor **observ tory** by both day and night, or visit t glass-enclosed circular observato on the 102nd floor. From afar, noti the colors of the tower lights, whi hange to honor seasons, holidays, and pecial events.

## ockefeller Center★★★

*etween Fifth & Seventh Aves. and 47th 52nd Sts.*

his "city within a city" ranks among ne most vital and cohesive design omplexes in America. Brainchild of il magnate John D. Rockefeller, Jr., the enter's 19 buildings, which cover 22 cres, were erected between 1932 and 973. Among the first, the Art Deco **GE eneral Electric) Building**★★★ *(30 ockefeller Plaza),* formerly the RCA uilding, soars 70 stories up and houses oth the **NBC Studios**★ 🚸 *(year-round; ▸visit by guided tour only, lasting an our and ten minutes, Mon-Thu, 8:30am- :30pm, Fri-Sat 9:30am-5:30pm, and Sun :30am-4:30pm; ☎212-664-4000)* and ne legendary restaurant and ballroom, **e Rainbow Room**. **Radio City Music all**★★ was the largest theater in the orld when it was erected in 1932, seat- g 6,000 people. It remains a must-hit r throngs of tourists who come to see ne Radio City Christmas spectacular ith the Rockettes each year. Outside, vely **Channel Gardens**★★ incorporate k pools and lush seasonal flower beds. he annual lighting of the Christmas tree ere is one of the city's most beloved oliday traditions. A promenade leads the sunken plaza where the reclin- g figure of **Prometheus** (1934, Paul lanship) presides over winter skating nd summer dining.

## nited Nations★★★

*rst Ave. between E. 42nd & E. 48th Sts. ▸Visit by guided tour only; children nder 5 not admitted on tours. Tours in a nguage other than English require reser- ations (☎212-963-7539) after 9:30am the ay of the visit. ▸Tours are conducted arch-December, Mon-Fri 9:30am- :45pm, and Sat-Sun, 10am-4:30pm. urs leave every half hour and last 45 inutes to 1 hour.☞$13. ☎212-963- 440. www.un.org.*

he four buildings of the UN, designed 1946 by an international group of chitects, occupy 18 acres overlooking e East River. Here 192 member states, hose flags flutter in English alphabeti-

cal order from north to south at the buildings' front, work to resolve global problems and disputes. In the low-slung **General Assembly Building**★★, the UN's main body holds its annual three-month session, beginning in September. Constructed of white Vermont marble and glass-and-aluminum panels, the striking **Secretariat Building**★★ houses UN offices on its 39 floors. The five-story **Conference Building**⊶ connects the two and provides meeting and council chambers. Located on the southwest corner of the grounds, the **Hammar-skjold Library**⊶ is dedicated to the second secretary-general who was killed in a 1961 plane crash while on a peace mission to the Congo.

## Museum of Modern Art★★★

*11 W. 53rd St.* 🍴♿🕐*Open year-round, Wed-Thu and Sat-Mon, 10:30am-5:30pm; Friday 10:30am-8pm.* 🕐*Closed December 25th and Thanksgiving.* ☞*$20.* ☎*212-708-9400. www.moma.org.*

One of the world's pre-eminent cultural institutions, MOMA offers an unparalleled overview of all the modern visual arts. The original 1939 marble and glass building was one of the first examples of the International style in the US; it underwent extensive renovations in 2002-2004, and reopened after heavy redesign by Japanese architect Yoshio Taniguchi. The museum itself dates to 1929 when three benefactors—Abby Aldrich Rockefeller, Lillie P. Bliss and Mary Quinn Sullivan—launched a show of Postimpressionists. Since the initial 1931 bequest of 235 works, holdings have grown to encompass more than 100,000 pieces including painting, sculpture, photography; decorative, graphic and industrial art; architectural plans and models; and video and film.

# Along the Way

## New York Public Library★★

*476 Fifth Ave.* ♿☎*212-930-0080. www.nypl.org.*
Housed in a 1911 Beaux-Arts masterpiece, this facility is the second-largest research library in the US (after the Library of Congress in Washington, DC).

## New Art from New York

As Europe staggered under the overlapping tragedies of two world wars, political oppression and economic depression in the first half of the 20C, a host of her most gifted artists sought refuge in New York City. They came steeped in Surrealism and Expressionism and imported an intense interest in the new science of psychoanalysis. Many had been influenced by Picasso, whose expressionistic masterpiece *Guernica* (1937) took the city by storm upon its arrival in 1939. As émigrés like **Willem de Kooning**, **Hans Hofmann**, **Max Ernst** and **Arshile Gorky** mixed and mingled with New York artists, the avant-garde cauldron began to boil. At the end of World War II, it combusted into a full-blown movement called **Abstract Expressionism**, and New York City emerged as a cultural mecca and world leader in the production and promotion of modern art. Painters of the New York school found it impossible to reconcile traditional subjects and styles to the "moral crisis of a world in shambles," as artist Barnett Newman later described the postwar dilemma. "We actually began... from scratch... as if painting never existed." The results combined a subjectless abstraction with the expression of raw emotion. Large-scale works emphasized the picture plane and spontaneous brushwork while ignoring bounds imposed by the physical canvas. Considered by many to be the first truly influential American movement, Abstract Expressionism reflects something of the national psyche in its monumental canvases.

### Radio City Music Hall★★

*1260 Ave. of the Americas. Visit by guided tour only.* ☎212-632-4041.
Since 1932 this fabulous Art Deco music hall has hosted live musical spectaculars and the world's finest precision dance team, the **Rockettes**.

### Carnegie Hall★

*156 W. 57th St. Visit by guided tour only.* ☎212-247-7800.
Opened in 1891 and later named for its benefactor, steel magnate and philanthropist Andrew Carnegie, this majestic structure is regarded as one of the world's most prestigious music halls.

### St. Patrick's Cathedral★★

*Fifth Ave. between E. 50th & 51st Sts.* ☎212-753-2261.
Designed by renowned architect James Renwick and consecrated in 1879, St. Patrick's is the city's major Roman Catholic cathedral.

### Grand Central Terminal★★★

*Park Ave. & 42nd St.*
Opened in 1913, the sumptuous Beaux-Arts "gateway to the city" is among New York's great civic monuments and recently underwent a $196 million renovation.

### Morgan Library and Museum★

*29-33 E. 36th St.* ☎212-685-0610.
This venerable institution houses an outstanding collection of books, prints and rare manuscripts assembled by 19 industrialist J. Pierpont Morgan.

## Uptown★★

Northern Manhattan above Midtown comprises three vibrant and interesting districts. The **Upper East Side**★ covers the blocks between Central Park and the East River, from 59th Street to 97th Street. The area remained rural until the mid-19C, when high society began migrating uptown, extending **Fifth Avenue**★★ northward with lavish mansions. New York's most prestigious addresses still border the avenue along Central Park north of the **Grand Army Plaza**★★. Two blocks east, **Park Avenue**★ makes its way north, lined with dignified apartment buildings. Across Central Park, the ethnically diverse **Upper West Side**★★ extends north from Columbus Circle to 125th Street. The area has attracted an eclectic blend of residents over the years, evidenced by its mix of luxury apartment buildings, stylish row houses, artists

*The Lake at Central Park*

© Allison Simpson/MICHELIN

studios and urban renewal projects. The presence of **Columbia University**★ *(main entrance at W. 116th St.)* adds a large student population.

At the top of Manhattan, **Harlem**★ became world-famous during the 1920s Harlem Renaissance as a center for black arts and culture. The **Apollo Theatre** *(253 W. 125th St. ☎212-531-5300)*, legendary for its all-black revues of the 1930s, still offers variety shows. Still home to a predominantly black population, Harlem encompasses some outstanding architecture, several landmark historic districts and renowned churches and institutions. **Harlem Spirituals, Inc.** *(☎212-391-0900)* offers gospel and jazz tours of the neighborhood.

## Central Park★★★

Manhattan swirls around this lush 843-acre sanctuary, which provides refuge and recreation for millions of people annually. Construction began in 1857, interpreting the "picturesque" designs of Frederick Law Olmsted and Calvert Vaux; Central Park opened 19 years later as the first large-scale recreation space in America. Favorite park destinations include the **Central Park Zoo**★ Kids *(200-800 Fifth Ave. ☎212-439-6500; www.centralparkzoo.org)*, which includes creatures from penguin to red pandas in replications of their natural habitats

and the **Children's Zoo**, a petting zoo with farm animals. **Bethesda Terrace** and the lake beyond spanned by its famous **Art Deco bridge**, is perfect for people-watching on a warm, sunny day, and the **Henry Luce Nature Observatory**, which occupies two floors of fanciful **Belvidere Castle**, has microscopes and all manner of exhibits. **Strawberry Fields**, once a favorite park spot of Lennon, is now a memorial to the musician. In winter, one of the most popular park spots is **Wollman Rink**, where ice skaters take advantage of prices that are a fraction of those at Tony Rink at Rockefeller Center. In summer, the place to be is the **Delacorte Theater**, where the free, annual Shakespeare in the Park Festival usually includes big-name talent.

## The New-York Historical Society★★

*2 W. 77th St. ☎212-873-3400.*
The collections of the city's oldest museum (founded in 1804) cover three centuries of Americana. Temporary exhibits on the history of New York occupy the main galleries on the first floor. The Henry Luce Center for the Study of American Culture *(4th floor)* now houses the entire museum collection—including a superb assemblage of Hudson River school paintings, Audubon watercolors and Tiffany lamps.

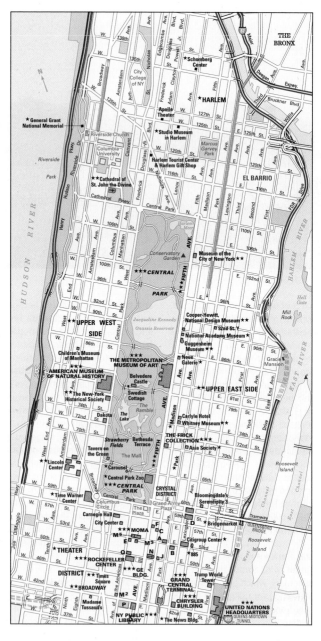

## American Museum of Natural History★★★

Central Park West, between 77th & 81st Sts. ⏰ Open daily 10am–5:45pm. ☏212-769-5100. www.amnh.org.

The holdings of this venerable institution (1869) include more than 30 million specimens related to all facets of natural history. The museum is best known for having the largest collection of fossil vertebrates in the world, and their display in six **fossil halls**★★ on the top floor represents a visual and intellectual tour de force.

| | | | | | | | |
|---|---|---|---|---|---|---|---|
| American Museum | | General Grant | | Park Avenue | DV | | |
| of Natural History | CV | National Memorial | CU | Plaza Hotel | CV | | |
| Apollo Theater | CDU | Grand Army Plaza | CDV | Radio City Music Hall | CV | | |
| Asia Society | DV L | Grolier Club | DV | Riverside Church | CU | | |
| Bethesda Terrace | CV | Guggenheim Museum | DV | Rockefeller Center | CV | | |
| Bloomingdale's | DV | Harlem | DU | St. Patrick's Cathedral | CV E | | |
| C.A. Dana Discovery Center | DU | Henry Luce | | Seagram Building | DV | | |
| Carlyle Hotel | DV | Nature Observatory | CV K | Sony Plaza | CDV | | |
| Carnegie Hall | CV | Jewish Museum, The | DU | Strawberry Fields | CV | | |
| Cathedral of | | Lake, The | CV | Studio Museum in Harlem | DU | | |
| St. John the Divine | CU | Lexington Avenue | DV | Theater District | CV | | |
| Central Park | CDUV | Lincoln Center | CV | Times Square | CV | | |
| China Institute | DV | Madison Avenue | DV | Upper East Side | DV | | |
| Columbia University | CU | Metropolitan | | Upper West Side | CUV | | |
| Conservatory Garden | DU | Museum of Art, The | CDV | Villard Houses | CV F | | |
| Cooper Hewitt National | | MOMA | CV | Whitney Museum | | | |
| Design Museum | DV | Museum of the City | | of American Art | DV | | |
| El Museo del Barrio | DU | of New York | DU | Wildlife Conservation Center | CV | | |
| Fifth Avenue | CDV | National Academy Museum | DV | 57th Street | CDV | | |
| Frick Collection, The | DV | New York Historical | | | | | |
| | | Society, The | CV | | | | |

## The Frick Collection★★★

*1 E. 70th St. Children under 10 not admitted.*  ⏰*Open year-round, Tue-Sat, 10am-6pm and Sun 11am-5pm.*👝*$15.* ☎*212-288-0700. www.frick.org.*

A Pittsburgh coke and steel industrialist, Henry Clay Frick (ⓘ*see PITTSBURGH*) commissioned this 40-room mansion in 1913 to display his outstanding collection of 18C English paintings, sculpture, drawings and decorative arts. Also of note are works by Jean-Honoré Fragonard and 16C masterpieces by Bellini and Titian.

## Metropolitan Museum of Art★★★

*1000 Fifth Ave. at E. 82nd St.* 🕐*Open year-round, Tue-Thu and Sun, 9:30am-5:30pm, Fri-Sat, 9:30am-9pm.* 👝*$20.* 🍴♿📇 ☎*212-535-7710. www.metmuseum.org.*

Founded in 1870 by members of New York's Union League Club, this great monument to world culture has occupied its present location since 1880. The building itself has grown in stages over the years, with contributions by an impressive roster of architects, including Calvert Vaux, Richard Morris Hunt and McKim, Mead and White. Its three million objects dating from prehistory to the 20C make it the largest museum in the Western hemisphere.

The Met's assemblage of **Ancient Art**★★★ encompasses four wellsprings of civilization (Egypt, Greece, Rome and the Near East); impressive installations like the magnificent Egyptian **Temple of Dendur**★ give the museum a breathtaking scale. **European Sculpture and Decorative Arts**★★★ emphasizes French and English furniture and porcelain from Germany and France. A superb assemblage of **Impressionists and Postimpressionists**★★★ takes in works by Cézanne, Manet, Monet, Renoir, Gauguin and Seurat.

The **American Wing**★★★ spans three centuries and includes 25 full-scale room interiors and the sculpture, stained glass and architectural fragments that occupy the stunning **Charles Engelhard Court** on the first floor. **Primitive art** from Africa, Oceania and the Americas include masks, clay vessels and mosaic jewelry. The **Medieval collection**★★ comprises more than 4,000 works from the early Christian, Byzantine, Romanesque and Gothic periods. Many pieces from this collection are exhibited farther uptown at **The Cloisters**★★★ *(Fort Tryon Park* 📇 ☎*212-923-3700)*, the museum's lovely re-created hilltop monastery devoted

### Yankee Stadium

Located in the Bronx, the only borough on the mainland, **Yankee Stadium**★ *(161st St. & River Ave;* ☎*718-293-6000)* was built in 1923 as the playing field for the American League baseball team beloved by many in New York and hated almost everywhere else. A bronze plaque here commemorates such Yankee greats as Babe Ruth, Joe DiMaggio and Mickey Mantle.

to the art and architecture of Medieval Europe.

## Solomon R. Guggenheim Museum★★

*1071 Fifth Ave.* ✗ ♿ ⏰*Open year-round; Sat-Wed, 10am-5:45pm and Fri 10am-7:45pm.* 👓*$18.* ☎*212-423-3500. www.guggenheim.org.*

In 1943, art patrons Solomon R. Guggenheim and his wife, Irene Rothschild, commissioned architect Frank Lloyd Wright to design a permanent home for their collection of modern art, which today numbers 6,000 works. The building is as much a work of art as the masterpieces it contains, and Wright considered it his crowning achievement. Indeed, few public spaces in New York rival the drama of the main gallery, encircled by the famous spiral ramp, more than a quarter-mile long.

## Museum of the City of New York★★

📷 *1220 Fifth Ave. at 103rd St.* ♿ ⏰*Open year-round, Tue-Sun, 10am-5pm.* 👓*$9.* ☎*212-534-1672. www.mcny.org.*

Founded in 1923 as America's first institution dedicated to the history of a city, this museum chronicles the changing face of New York through its rich collections of decorative arts, furnishings, silver, prints and paintings. Especially beguiling is the Toy Gallery with its exquisite series of **doll houses**★.

## Whitney Museum of American Art★★

*945 Madison Ave.* ✗ ♿ ⏰*Open year-round, Wed-Thu, 10am-6pm; Fri, 1-9pm; Sat-Sun 11am-6pm.* 👓*$15.* ☎*212-570-3676. www.whitney.org.*

The Whitney, which grew from the collections of Gertrude Vanderbilt Whitney in the early 1930s, is dedicated to the advancement of contemporary

artists and is known for provocative exhibits. Its outstanding collection of **20C American art** includes more than 10,000 works by such artists as Hopper, de Kooning, Nevelson and Calder. The Whitney Biennial, an exhibition of recent art mostly by young, lesser-known artists, is considered trend-setting.

# Along the Way

## The Plaza★

*Southeast corner of Central Park at Fifth Ave.*

The elegant Plaza has been a bastion of New York society since 1907. After closing in 2005 for renovations, the hotel reopened in January with both hotel rooms and private condo units.

## Asia Society and Museum★

*725 Park Ave.* ♿☎*212-288-6400. www.asiasociety.org.*

The society provides an elegant setting for Indian bronzes, Chinese and Japanese ceramics, exquisite screen paintings and other works of Asian art.

## Lincoln Center★★

*On Broadway between W. 62nd & 67th Sts.* ✗ ♿ 🅿 ☎*212-875-5350. www.lincolncenter.org.*

This 16-acre complex includes five major theater and concert buildings, with the **Metropolitan Opera House** at its center.

## Cathedral of St. John the Divine★★

*Amsterdam Ave. at W. 112th St.* ⏰*Open Mon-Sat 7am–6pm, Sun 7am–7pm.* ☎*212-316-7540. www.stjohndivine.org.*

Under construction since 1892, the seat of the Episcopal Diocese of New York is reportedly the largest Gothic-style cathedral in the world, with room for 8,000 worshipers at once.

# THE HUDSON RIVER VALLEY★★★

MICHELIN MAP 583 T 6, 7
EASTERN STANDARD TIME

Originating high in the Adirondacks, the Hudson River passes through a rich landscape of hills, highlands and history. At **Albany★**, the state capital, the river becomes navigable, connecting upstate New York to the world. Named for explorer **Henry Hudson**, the first European to navigate the river in 1609, the majestic waterway has been widely celebrated in literature and art. Honored in 1996 as a Heritage Area by the National Park Service, the valley itself is also notable for its man-made environment. A remarkable concentration of historic homes reflects the centuries-old Dutch settlement pattern that carved feudal estates from the lands flanking the river. Latter-day barons flocked to the river's edge to add their mansions to the mix. Along the East Bank, Route 9 links these historic homes with quaint villages such as **Cold Spring★** and **Garrison-on-Hudson**. West of the river, Route 9W connects a variety of sights—many related to the Revolutionary War. Beyond Kingston, the velvety blue-green **Catskill Mountains★★** loom on the western horizon. Seven bridges cross the river at convenient intervals.

- **Information:** ☎914-291-2136. www.enjoyhv.com.
- **Orient Yourself:** The Hudson River flows 315mi to the Atlantic Ocean. The following sights lie within a day's drive of New York City, and are organized traveling up the East Bank and down the West Bank.
- **Don't Miss:** The ancestral home of Franklin Delano Roosevelt.
- **Organizing Your Time:** Leave plenty of time to pull over of and take photos of this breathtaking landscape.

## Sights

### Sunnyside★

W. Sunnyside Lane, off Rte. 9, Tarrytown. Visit by guided tour only Apr-Nov, daily except Tuesdays and weekends in December, 10am-5pm. $10. P ☎914-591-8763.

Focal point of "Sleepy Hollow Country," this quaint hideaway still evokes the storybook setting cultivated by its famous owner, author **Washington**

## An American Aristocracy

It's hard to get far in New York without encountering the names J.P. **Morgan**, Cornelius **Vanderbilt**, Andrew **Carnegie**, Jay **Gould** and John D. **Rockefeller**. Members of America's first generation of self-made millionaires, these men built American industry in the boom years after the Civil War. Until then, New York's high society revolved around established and modestly wealthy Dutch and colonial families whose inheritance came from early land holdings and trade. By the 1870s, however, expanded markets, a growing labor force and laws favoring big business spawned a brash new breed of American entrepreneur.

Constructing empires around oil, railroads, banking and steel, these capitalists accrued an unprecedented bundle of personal wealth. Befitting the domestic requirements of America's new "aristocracy," Fifth Avenue between 42nd and 92nd Streets blossomed with French "châteaux" and Rhine "castles." And, lest there be any doubt of their royal aspirations, scores of young heiresses sought out European dukes and princes to marry for their titles.

*Vanderbilt Mansion*

**Irving** (1783-1859). Its fanciful architecture and lovely views embody the essence of the 19C Romantic landscape. Built around an existing farmhouse in 1835, this "snuggery" blends English, Dutch, Spanish and Scottish elements.

### Lyndhurst★

*635 S. Broadway, off Rte. 9, Tarrytown.* ꗯ*Visit by guided tour only mid-April-October, Tue-Fri, 10am-5pm and Sat-Sun 10am-3:30pm; open November-mid-April Sat-Sun, 10am-4pm.* ✖ ♿ 🅿 . ◎ *$10.* ☎*914-631-4481.*

An astonishing Gothic Revival castle, Lyndhurst was designed in 1838 by Alexander Jackson Davis, the most prolific architect of Gothic country houses in America. The manse represents one of the finest residential examples of this style, associated more often in the US with churches and universities. Tiffany stained glass and a dark-wood Gothic interior complement its picturesque exterior.

### Kykuit★★

ꗯ*Visit by guided tour only, May 12-Nov 4 daily except Tuesdays. Tours begin from Philipsburg Manor Visitor Center, Rte. 9, Sleepy Hollow. Reservations required several weeks in advance. Call for tour times and prices.* ✖ ♿ 🅿 ☎*914-631-9491.*

One of the last grand homes to be built in the Hudson River Valley, Kykuit (Dutch for "lookout;" pronounced KYE-cut) offers a glimpse into the lives of four generations of Rockefellers. Original construction was begun in 1906 by John D. Rockefeller, Jr., for his father, patriarch of Standard Oil; the present Beaux-Arts façade was added during a later redesign. Rooms date to the residency of New York State governor Nelson Rockefeller, beginning in 1963. By then the house brimmed with antique furniture, Chinese ceramics and Rockefeller's burgeoning **modern art collection**★. Spectacular **views**★ across the Hudson blend with gardens and art into painterly tableaux.

### Boscobel Restoration★★

*1601 Rte. 9D, 4mi north of the junction with Rte. 403.* ꗯ*Visit by guided tour only, April-October daily, 9:30-5pm and November-December 9:30am-4pm.* ◎*$12.* 🅿 ☎*845-265-3638.*

Fastidiously appointed and furnished, this crisply elegant restoration embodies the essence of the American Federal style. Originally built 15mi to the south in 1804, the house was rescued from destruction, moved to this site, and opened to the public in 1961. Federal architecture with its light and delicate aspect represents the "antique taste" made popular in the 18C by archaeological study of the ancient world. Indoors and out, note Boscobel's slight columns, narrow windows and dainty, shallow ornament. Restrained and slender period furniture fills the home, some of it the work of New York's virtuoso craftsman Duncan Phyfe.

## Home of Franklin D. Roosevelt National Historic Site (Springwood)★★

*On Rte. 9, Hyde Park.* 🅿 ☎*845-229-2414.* ⏰*Open year-round daily 9am-5pm.*

Ancestral home of **Franklin Delano Roosevelt** (1882-1945), Springwood offers an exceedingly personal encounter with the 32nd president of the US. Born in the house in 1882, Roosevelt took his bride, Eleanor, there in 1905 and soon launched his political career. He enlarged the house over the years, designing the present fieldstone wings. Stricken with polio in 1921, FDR convalesced here. He and Eleanor are buried side by side in the rose garden. The Roosevelt presence remains palpable in the rooms, furnished comfortably and filled with family mementos. Also on the property is the **FDR Library and Museum**, which features extensive exhibits about the family.

A short drive away on Route 9G stands the **Eleanor Roosevelt National Historic Site**★ *(visit by guided tour only;* 🅿 ☎*914-229-9422)*, a cozy complex of stone buildings known as "Val-Kill" (named for the nearby stream). In 1925, Franklin built a stone cottage as a retreat for Eleanor on the Springwood grounds. After FDR's death, she took up permanent residence and remained there until her death in 1962.

## Vanderbilt Mansion National Historic Site★★

*4097 Albany Post Rd., on Rte. 9, Hyde Park.* ⏰*Open daily 9am-5pm.* ⏰*Closed January 1, Thanksgiving, and December 25.* ⛶*$8.* 🅿 ☎*845-229-7770. www.nps.gov/vama.*

Commissioned by Frederick (grandson of Cornelius Vanderbilt) and Louise Vanderbilt in 1898 for fall and spring entertaining, this mansion epitomizes the extravagance of the Gilded Age nouveau riche. The 50-room Beaux-Arts edifice designed by McKim, Mead and White overflows with art and furniture

befitting America's self-styled "nobility" and ranging from Renaissance to Rococo in style.

## West Point★★

*On Rte. 218, Highlands.* ⏰*Open year-round daily 9am-4:45pm.* ⏰*Closed January 1, Thanksgiving, and December 25.* ⛶*Guided tours available.* ⛶⛶🅿 ☎*845-446-4724.*

Fortress West Point was established in 1778 to protect the strategically important Hudson River at its most defensible location. After the Revolution, the grounds became a repository for trophies and captured equipment. In 1802 Congress installed the US Military Academy at West Point, and it remains the nation's oldest continuously occupied military post. Today this sprawling campus can easily fill a day of walking and driving from point to point.

West Point offers layers of history to peel away at leisure, beginning at the **visitor information center**. The chapels, monuments and military **museum**★★ (☎ 845-938-3590), which presents a thorough examination of martial history, are open to the public. At mid-campus, hike or drive up to **Fort Putnam**★ (☎845-938-3590), the historic heart of West Point, for its commanding views 500ft above the river. In fall and spring, the **Parades**—troop reviews famous for their precision—are held. *(Call for schedules: ☎845-938-2638.)*

## Washington's Headquarters State Historic Site★

*Corner of Washington & Liberty Sts., Newburgh.* ⛶*Visit by guided tour only; closed in winter; tours mid-April-October, Wed-Sat 10am-5pm, Sun 1-5pm, and Mon 10am-5pm.* 🅿 ☎*845-562-1195.*

Of the many Revolutionary War "Washington's Headquarters" in the Northeast, this site is of particular importance as the one he occupied the longest. Even with peace imminent, Gen. George Washington distrusted the British and chose to watch the river from this simple Dutch farmhouse.

## Storm King Art Center ★

*Off Rte. 9 West on Old Pleasant Hill Rd., Mountainville.* ⛶⛶🅿 ⏰*Open April 1-*

*November 3, Wed-Sun 11am-5:30pm, November 4-15 Wed-Sun 11am-5pm.* $10. ☎845-534-3190.

Begin a visit to this stunning outdoor sculpture park at the Normandy-style museum building (1935). From there, set off in any direction across the rolling landscape to seek out more than 125 works by masters of modern sculpture. Founded in 1970, the art center changes with the seasons and the addition of new pieces.

## Excursion

### National Baseball Hall of Fame and Museum★★

*25 Main St., 70mi west of Albany in Cooperstown, NY. Take US-20 West to Rte. 80 South.* ♿ ⌚ *Open daily Memorial Day through Labor Day, 9am-9pm. Open th day after Labor Day until the Thursda before Memorial Day weekend, 9am 5pm. Closed January 1, Thanksgiving, an December 25.* $14.50. ☎607-547-7200 *www.baseballhalloffame.org.*

Dedicated in 1939, this shrine to base ball covers its subject with encyclope dic thoroughness. Steeped in history personalities and statistics, bright an imaginative galleries cover every aspec of the sport from the evolution of equip ment and uniforms to touch screens tha give instant access to records made an broken. At the heart of the museum' three floors, the **Hall of Fame** honor more than 200 baseball greats an inducts new members every year.

# LONG ISLAND★★

MICHELIN MAP 583 T, U 7
EASTERN STANDARD TIME

Claiming some of the finest beaches and best-protected harbors on the Atlanti seaboard, Long Island is New York State's oceanside vacationland. Along th North Shore, wealthy New Yorkers built vacation homes among the rocky neck and beaches, thick woodlands and steep bluffs that overlook Long Island Sound The picturesque town of **Oyster Bay** typifies the "Gold Coast" with its histori landmarks and quaint shops. **Cold Spring Harbor** preserves its history as a 190 whaling center at the **Whaling Museum★** Kids *(Main St.;* ☎516-367-3418*)*. The idylli rural hamlet of **Stony Brook★★** is noted for its historic planned business distric (1941) as well as for its complex of museums. Farther east, the unspoiled villag of **Cutchoque** and the hardworking port of **Greenport** occupy the North Fork which culminates at Orient Point. Beachy barrier islands, 32mi-long **Fire Island★** the most famous among them, line the scenic South Shore.

The exclusive "Hamptons" dominate the South Fork, and the charming whal ing village of **Sag Harbor★** is a living museum of Colonial and 19C architecture For peaceful biking and hiking, **Shelter Island★** lies a short ferry ride from Sag Harbor. Long Island **wineries** on both forks enjoy an ever-increasing reputatio for their Merlots and Chardonnays, and local steamer and quahog (pronounce KOE-hog) clams, oysters, scallops and lobsters are not to be missed. Visitors ca enjoy all the waterfront perquisites, along with tennis, golf, horseback riding touring and other holiday pleasures, between the din and congestion of the island's western end, and its remote eastern tip, which splits into the North and South forks.

- **Information:** ☎516-951-3440. www.licvb.com
- ▶ **Orient Yourself:** The island extends 125mi into the Atlantic, and 20mi separate the North and South shores at its widest point.
- **Don't Miss:** The popular resorts of the Hamptons.
- **Also See:** NEW YORK CITY.

*Montauk Point Lighthouse, Shelter Island*

©iStockphoto.com/Sylvana Rega

# Sights

## Planting Fields★★

*Planting Fields Rd., Oyster Bay.* &♿&🅿&🕒*Open year-round daily 9am-5pm.* 🕒*Closed December 25.* 👁*$6.50.* ☎*516-922-9200. www.plantingfields.org.*
Formerly the private estate of financier William Robertson Coe, the 409 acres of planting fields include 160 acres that have been developed as an arboretum; the remaining have been kept as a natural habitat. Rhododendrons, azaleas, ornamentals and camelias highlight the collection. In their midst stands **Coe Hall**, a fine example of the Tudor Revival style.

## Museums at Stony Brook★

Kids *1200 Rte. 25A at Main St.* ♿🅿 ☎*631-751-0066.* 🕒*Open year-round Wed-Sat 10am-5pm and Sun 12-5pm.*
This nine-acre complex comprises **history, art** and **carriage** museums as well as several period buildings, including a blacksmith shop, schoolhouse and barn. The art museum features the work of 19C artist **William Sidney Mount**, who settled in Stony Brook.

## Old Bethpage Restoration Village★★

Kids *Round Swamp Rd.* 🍴🅿 ☎*516-572-8400.*
Nestled in a 200-acre valley, this active farm community re-creates a pre-Civil War village that reflects the architectural heritage of Long Island. Blacksmiths, cobblers, tailors, farmers and other workers ply their trades among more than 25 historic buildings that have been moved to the site.

## The Hamptons★★

Beginning at **Westhampton Beach**, the Hamptons form a 35mi chain of vacation colonies. Once a seafaring community, this chic summertime retreat is now favored by rich and ffamous who escape New York City on the weekends. Dune Road, though narrow and sometimes impassable after a storm, offers a lovely drive along the beach. The largest of these villages, **Southampton**★ boasts superb estates as well as the **Parrish Art Museum** *(25 Jobs Ln., Southhampton 613-283-2118; www.parishart.org;* 🕒*open June 1-September 15, Mon-Sat 11am-5pm and Sun 1-5pm; open September 16-May 31 Mon and Thu-Sat 11am-5pm and Sun 1-5pm;* 👁*$7)*, which focuses on American art. Quaint **East Hampton** has long attracted artists and writers, and among the magnificent elms on **Main Street** stand a number of historic structures.

## Jones Beach State Park★★

*Ocean State Pkwy., Wantaugh.* ☎*516-785-1600.*
More than 6mi of sandy beaches make up this famous bathing resort, with its double exposure to ocean and bay. The park includes the well-known **Jones Beach Theater**, a nautical stadium, heated pools, sports fields and play areas. Be sure to take the beautiful **coastal drive** along Ocean State Parkway between Jones Beach and **Robert Moses State Park**★ on neighboring Fire Island.

# NORTHERN NEW ENGLAND

Composed of the states of Vermont, New Hampshire and Maine, northern New England boasts tracts of wilderness seldom associated with the densely populated eastern seaboard. Stacked on top of Massachusetts, triangular Vermont and New Hampshire fit together to form a tall rectangle. Maine extends north and east from New Hampshire toward Canada and into the Atlantic Ocean; its landmass totals that of the other five New England states combined, though its population is smaller than many of them.

Although the coast of Maine was explored as early as the 11C by the Vikings, European settlement in northern New England did not take place in earnest until the early 17C, when French and English towns started cropping up along the coast. Battles were frequent between the two colonial powers until the Treaty of Paris of 1763, which formally ended the American Revolutionary War, ceded control of the area to the British. Inland settlement proceeded slowly due to the enormity of the Appalachian ridge (the White and Green Mountains) that forms the region's backbone. Vermonter **Ethan Allen** and his **Green Mountain Boys** were typical of those farmers who did penetrate the rugged wilderness. Such free-thinkers turned out in droves

to fight the British, guerrilla-style. Later many rebelled against government encroachment of any kind—including statehood. To this day, New Hampshire's motto, "Live Free or Die," describes the

*New Hampshire Winter*

state's virulently anti-taxation stance, while Vermont continues to resist large-scale development with batteries of lawsuits and legislation.

Despite these differences, both states draw large numbers of visitors year-round: the eye-popping reds, yellows and oranges of the leaves in early October turn the forests into a brilliant wonderland, while the mountains beckon hikers, campers and cyclists during the other temperate months *(May–Sept)*. Winter is ski season, when enthusiasts frequent the snowy slopes of Vermont and New Hampshire. Maine's chief attraction is its 3,500-mile coastline, one of the most dramatic in the US. Rugged cliffs, fjords and rocky offshore islands offer stunning vistas, and cozy seaside towns provide ample opportunities to sample the state's richest delicacy, lobster.

Depending on the time of year and what your interests are—skiing, hiking, scenic drives, history, or just hanging out at the beach—you can spend a day or a week in this area. Make sure you don't miss the regional seafood specialties. There's plenty to entertain the little ones here too, from old-time amusement park fun at Old Orchard Beach in Maine to the funky art at the Shelburne Museum in Burlington, VT.

## Area Address Book

*For coin ranges, see the Legend on the cover flap.*

### WHERE TO STAY

**$$$ The Balsams Grand Resort Hotel** – *1000 Cold Spring Rd., Dixville Notch, NH.* ☎603-255-3400. *www.thebalsams.com. 203 rooms.* An all-inclusive 15,000-acre resort in the White Mountains. The original 25-room inn was built in 1866 and gradually expanded into a Spanish Renaissance-style palace with prominent red-tile rooftops. This luxe resort is perfect for families, with kids' camps, all-ages hiking and biking tours, and a small number of pet-friendly rooms.

**$$$ The Pitcher Inn** – *275 Main St., Warren, VT.* ☎802-496-6350. *www.pitcherinn.com. 11 rooms.* Located in the Green Mountains near the Sugarbush Ski Resort and Mad River Glen ski areas, this New England guest house offers Old World ambience with the comforts of a luxury hotel. A locker room providing storage for ski and hiking equipment features a ski-boot and glove warmer. Most rooms come with whirlpools and wood-burning fireplaces plus extras like wi-fi access and radiant-heat floors.

**$$ 1811 House** – *3654 Main St., Manchester Village, VT.* ☎802-362-1811. *www.1811house.com. 13 rooms.* Guests at this historic B&B are encouraged to help themselves to coffee and home-made cookies from the kitchen. Locals frequent the pub for its extensive list of single-malt whiskies.

**$$ The Captain Lord Mansion** – *6 Pleasant St., Kennebunkport, ME.* ☎207-967-3141. *www.captainlord.com. 20 rooms.* The innkeepers of this early-19C Federal mansion have handpicked everything from the four-poster beds to the dust ruffles and quilts. Bathrooms have Jacuzzi-style tubs, double vanities, and heated floor tiles. A family-style New England breakfast (buckwheat pancakes or giant waffles) is served in the country kitchen.

**$ Graycote Inn** – *40 Holland Ave., Bar Harbor, ME.* ☎207-288-3044. *www.graycoteinn.com. 12 rooms, 6 available year-round.* About a mile from Acadia National Park, this 1881 residence is just a short walk from the town center. Breakfast is served in courses on the glass-enclosed porch overlooking the flower beds in the warmer months and in the dining room next to the fireplace when it's cold.

**$$$ Portland Harbor Hotel** – *468 Fore St., Portland.* ☎207-775-9090. Located in the heart of the historic Old Port district, this hotel mixes old world charm with modern luxuries. Butter yellow rooms have his-and-hers armoires, and bathrooms feature soaking tubs, separate enclosed showeres, and sound systems.

## WHERE TO EAT

**$ The Clam Shack** – *2 Western Ave., Kenneebunkport, ME.* ☎*207-967-3321.* Don't drive through—or even past—Kennebunkport without making a pitstop at this roadside eatery next to the Kennebunkport Bridge. There's always a line for the namesake ride

clam strips and lobster rolls (made with butter or mayonaise) that have caught the attention of many food writers passing through these parts.

**Merrimach Restaurant** – *786 Elm St., Manchester, NH.* ☎*603-669-5222.* The slightly musty diner is a requisite campaign stop for presidential candidates who stop here along the primary trail. Everything from scrambled eggs to eggplant parmigiana is on the menu.

# MAINE COAST★★

MAP P349
EASTERN STANDARD TIME

Tumbling down glacier-sculpted cliffs of jagged rocks to meet the Atlantic Ocean, this is a wind-whipped landscape. Fierce storms called "northeasters" batter the shore in winter, and summer visitors are hard-pressed to find sandy beaches. Driving this rugged coast, with its tranquil harbors and lonely lighthouses, is its own reward. Here the local fare spotlights lobster right off the boat and tart delicious Maine blueberries.

- 🛈 **Information:** ☎207-439-1319. www.mainetourism.com
- ▶ **Orient Yourself:** The coast of Maine defines the eastern edge of the state, stretching 3,500mi from Kittery north to the border of New Brunswick, Canada.
- 🕭 **Also See:** NEW HAMPSHIRE, VERMONT.

## A Bit of History

In 1604 Pierre du Gua, Sieur de Monts, and Samuel de Champlain established a small colony on an island in the St. Croix River from which they set out the following year to found the Acadian territory. An English settlement, the **Popham Colony**, was established at the mouth of the Kennebec River in 1607; then in 1635 English monarch Charles I gave the region of Maine to Sir Ferdinando Gorges. From that time on, the coast was the scene of constant battles between the French and the English. In 1677 the Massachusetts Colony bought Maine from the descendants of Sir Ferdinando Gorges. Maine was granted statehood under the conditions of the Missouri Compromise in 1820.

Vestiges of the Maine coast's 19C shipbuilding heyday can be glimpsed in sights such as **Maine Maritime**

**Museum**★★ (*243 Washington St., Bath,* ⏱*open year-round daily 9:30am-5pm;* 🚸$*10;* ☎*207-443-1316; www.mainemaritimemuseum.org*) and the **Penobscot Marine Museum**★ (*5 Church St., just off Rte. 1, Searsport;* ☎*207-548-2529*). Fishing, especially lobstering, is a major industry here; more than 50 percent of the nation's lobster catch comes from Maine.

## Kittery To Portland

US-1 traces the entire length of the Maine coastline, which begins just north of Portsmouth, New Hampshire, at the town of **Kittery**. Maine's first incorporated city, Kittery is now known for its retail outlet stores (*US-1;* ☎*888-548-8379; www.thekitteryoutlets.com*).

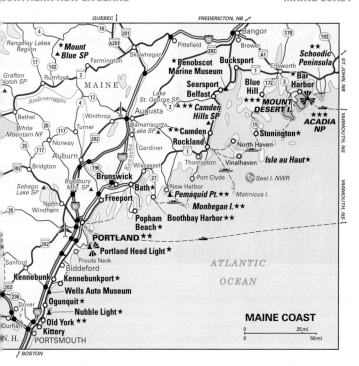

MAINE COAST

| 0 | 25mi |
| 0 | 50mi |

## Colonial York★★

*Along US-1A in York Village, just off US-1. Museum buildings are open Jun-mid-October, Mon-Sat 10am-5pm. $10. Tours are also available. Tickets available at Jefferds Tavern. ☎207-363-4974. www.oldyork.org.*

A group of 18C structures flanking the village green here recall colonial times. Across US-1A from the **Town Hall** is the **Old Burying Ground**, noteworthy for its 17C tombstones. Surrounding the cemetery you'll find cozy **Jefferds Tavern**, the 1740 **Emerson Wilcox House** and the **Old Gaol Museum**, which held prisoners from 1720 to 1860.

## Ogunquit★

*6mi north of Kittery on US-1.*

Christened Ogunquit ("beautiful place by the sea") by the local Indians, this beach town is a haven for artists and writers, as well as a large gay population. At the end of Shore Road, dozens of shops and seafood restaurants hug the man-made anchorage of **Perkins Cove**★. From the cove, stroll out along **Marginal Way**★, a coastal footpath that leads around the windswept promon-

tory called Israel's Head, providing striking **views**★.

## Kennebunkport★

*17mi northeast of Ogunquit via US-1 and Rte. 99 East.*

A seaside resort since the 19C, Kennebunkport is known as the summer home of **George Bush**, 41st president of the

*Lobster Buoys*

© PhotoDisc, Inc

*Stale Street Architecture, Portland*

US (1989-93). The Bush family estate is visible from Ocean Drive. The town's commercial center, **Dock Square**, harbors a variety of charming shops set along the tidal Kennebunk River.

Old Orchard Beach — 20 miles via Rt. 1 to Rt 98. Seven miles long, croded and noisy, Old Orchard Beach is nonetheless a popular spot for its wooden pier along the beachfront dotted with clam shacks and tourist shops, and for Palace Playland, an amusement park with an old-fashioned feel and a large, seaside ferris wheel.

## Beacons of the Maine Coast

While not all of the 60-some **lighthouses** on the coast of Maine are still active, these venerable beacons played a key role in New England's maritime history. Below is a selection of some of the more prominent Maine lighthouses. *www.lighthousegetaway.com*

**Cape Neddick "Nubble" Light★** *York Harbor. Take Nubble Rd. to the tip of Cape Neddick.* **Portland Head Light★** *10mi south of Portland in Fort Williams Park, 1000 Shore Rd.Cape Elizabeth. 1000 Shore Rd.* ☎*207-799-2661.* **Pemaquid Point Lighthouse Park★** *12mi south of Damariscotta via Rtes. 129 & 130 in Pemaquid Point.* ☎*207-677-2492.*

# Portland To Bar Harbor

Largest city in Maine, Portland sits o Casco Bay, known for its picturesqu **Calendar Islands** *(cruises depart fro Portland's Maine State Pier; Casco Ba Lines,* ☎*207-774-7871).* An importar oil and fishing port, the city is also th financial, cultural and commercial cente of northern New England.

Just 18mi north of Portland, the town c **Freeport** is a favored shopping spot alon the coast. This comely town is the hom of **L.L. Bean** *(95 Main St. at Bow St.; ope 24hrs/day year-round;* ☎*207-373-2700;ww llbean.com),* the famous sporting-goo mail-order enterprise, as well as some 1Z retail outlets *(on Main St./US-1).*

## Portland★★

Portland began as an English tradin post in 1658. Called Falmouth in its ear days, the village was shelled by the Bri ish in 1775 owing to the anti-Loyali sentiments of its residents. Followin the Revolutionary War, the few hundre colonists who remained in Falmout rebuilt the city, renaming it Portland. From 1820 to 1832 Portland served the state capital. The city prospered a shipping center until 1866, when a fir swept through the downtown area, le eling the business district. From thos ashes rose the revitalized Victorian stru tures that remain today in the **Old Po Exchange★★** *(along Exchange, Middle Fore Sts. downtown),* where art gallerie craft shops and restaurants now occup many of the 19C warehouses.

## Portland Museum of Art★

*7 Congress Square.* ○*Open year-rour Tue-Thu and Sat-Sun 10am-5pm. Mem rial Day-Columbus Day open Mon 10an 5pm. Closed Jan 1, Thanksgiving, ar December 25.* ◎*$10.* ✕ ₺☎*207-775-614 www.portlandmuseum.org.*

Maine's oldest (1882) and largest publ museum is known for its collection **19C and 20C American art**—in pa ticular the **State of Maine** paintinc by the likes of Winslow Homer, Andre Wyeth, Edward Hopper and other ar ists who drew their inspiration from th striking Maine landscape.

## Visiting Acadia National Park

### VISITOR INFORMATION

*170mi north of Portland via US-1 North & Rte. 3 South.* The park is open daily year-round, although snow and ice close most park roads in winter *(Dec–Apr).* May-October; $20 per vehicle for a seven-day pass and $5 per individual pass. The speed limit within the park is 35mph. Expect roads to be crowded during peak foliage season *(late-Sept–early Oct)* and during the summer. A free shuttle bus runs from April 15-November 30. Temperatures range from the 70s in summer to well below freezing in winter. The Hulls Cove Visitor Center, located on Rte. 3 north of Bar Harbor, ⊙April 15-November 30, and offers a free audio-visual program about the park in several languages. There are also guided tours and a bookstore. **Acadia National Park Headquarters** is located on Rte 233 west of Bar Harbor (⊙*Open year-round daily 8am–4:30pm;* △ ✕ ☎207-288-3338). For information on camping and recreational activities, contact **Acadia National Park Headquarters**, P.O. Box 177, Bar Harbor, ME 04609, ☎207-288-3338, www.nps.gov/acad. Accommodations are available in Bar Harbor,contact the **Bar Harbor Chamber of Commerce**, 1201 Bar Harbor Rd., Trenton, ME 04603., P.O. Box 177, Bar Harbor, ME 04609, ☎207-288-5103. `

### Wadsworth-Longfellow House

*39 Congress St.* ⊙*Open year-round Tue-at 10am-4pm.* ⌐*Guided tours available May-October.* ⌐*$7, includes admission Maine Historical Society Museum on site* ☎*207-774-1822. www.mainehistory.org.* The 1785 brick dwelling was the childhood home of poet **Henry Wadsworth Longfellow** (1807-82)—the first American to be memorialized in the Poet's Corner of London's Westminster Abbey.

### Farnsworth Art Museum★★

*52 Main St., Rockland (44mi north of th on US-1).* ⊙*Open year-round Tuesn 10am-5pm. Memorial Day-Columbus ay open Mon 10am-5am.* ⊙*Closed January 1, Thanksgiving, and December 25.* ⌐*$10.* ⌐ ☎*207-596-6457. www.farnsworthmuseum.org.*
The Farnsworth is a nationally acclaimed center for the study of Maine artists—notably three generations of Wyeth painters: **Newell Convers** (1882-1945), **Andrew** (b.1917) and **Jamie** (b.1946). The museum's main galleries contain works by Fitz Hugh Lane, George Inness, Thomas Eakin and Rockwell Kent. In the new adjacent 9,000sq ft **Wyeth Study Center** wing hang study drawings by the Wyeths. The white clapboard Methodist church on Union Street at Elm Street has been reborn as the **Wyeth Center★★**, showcasing hundreds of canvases by all three Wyeths. Next to the main museum on Elm Street, the 1850

**Farnsworth Homestead** was home to the family who provided seed money for the art museum.

### Camden★★

*8mi north of Rockland on US-1.*
Surveying the island-speckled waters of Penobscot Bay at the foot of the Camden Hills, Camden rates as one of the loveliest towns on the New England coast. Spend a day here exploring the shops and galleries in the village center, having a leisurely meal in a waterfront restaurant, or driving up to the top of Mt. Battie in **Camden Hills State Park★★** *(off US-1 just north of Camden;* △ ☎207-236-3109) for a spectacular **view★★★** of Camden harbor and Penobscot Bay.

## Acadia National Park★★★

Located primarily on **Mount Desert Island★★★**, with smaller sections on **Isle au Haut** *(off Deer Isle; access by boat from Stonington)* and **Schoodic Peninsula** *(across Frenchman Bay; access via US-1 North to Rte. 186 South)*, Acadia National Park welcomes some four million visitors each year. In 1916 individual landowners donated 6,000 acres to form Sieur de Monts National Monument. The land became Acadia National Park in 1929, in honor of the historic French territory of Acadia.

More than one-third of the park's 40,000 acres (33,000 of which fall on Mount Desert Island) were donated by John D. Rockefeller, Jr., who created the 45mi of carriage paths that web the eastern side of the island. Bordering the temperate and subarctic climate zones, Acadia harbors 1,100 plant species and almost 300 types of birds.

**Loop Road**★★★ *4hrs. 20mi.*
The park's main attraction, Loop Road parallels a spectacular section of open

coast with myriad scenic overlook affording vistas from sweeping sea scapes of island-studded waters t inland panoramas of pink granite moun tains. Awesome 360-degree **views**★★ from the top of **Cadillac Mountai** *(3.5mi off Loop Road)*—named for Anto ine de la Mothe Cadillac, 17C proprieto of Mount Desert Island—take in French man Bay and Mount Desert Island.

# NEW HAMPSHIRE★

MICHELIN MAP 583 T, U 5, 6
EASTERN STANDARD TIME
POPULATION 1,109,252

Known for its militant Revolutionary War-era motto, "Live Free or Die," New Hamp shire has long been a land of uncompromising extremes. Although a settlemen **Strawbery Banke**, took hold at Portsmouth as early as 1623, the dense forest and rugged mountains in the state's interior rebuked intrusion well into the 19C when the Industrial Revolution gave entrepreneurs a foothold in southern Nev Hampshire. Mills harnessing the power of the Merrimack River fueled the state burgeoning economy, which was based at the time on granite quarrying and lum bering. At the turn of the 19C, the area's natural beauty began to draw thousand of tourists to **Mount Washington**, the Northeast's highest peak.

- **Information:** ☎603-271-2665. www.visitnh.gov
- ▶ **Orient Yourself:** Northern New Hampshire is dominated by the dense forests that cover more than 80 percent of the state's land.
- **Also See:** MAINE COAST, VERMONT.

## A Bit of History

Today southern New Hampshire still contains the state's largest cities—Manchester, **Concord** (the state capital), Nashua and Keene—where politicians flock to pound the pavement every four years, vying for top ranking in the country's **presidential primaries**. Site of the biggest textile mill in the world in the 19C, **Manchester** ranks as New Hampshire's largest city. The state's only port town, Portsmouth, lies at the northern tip of New Hampshire's 18mi of shoreline. To the north the **White Mountains** rise majestically in a north-south ridge passable via U-shaped valleys called notches.
Vigorous hiking, fall-foliage driving tours and winter skiing all enjoy tre-

mendous popularity, as do quaint Nev England villages such as **Hebron**★ an **New London**★. Up near the Canadia border, more placid diversion can b found fishing or camping in the **Cor necticut Lakes** region. New Hampshir also claims one of the nation's prom nent Ivy League schools, **Dartmout College**★ *(6016 N. Main St., in Hanove ☎603-646-1100)*, which offers its 5,70 students top-quality instruction in th arts and sciences.

## Canterbury Shaker Village★★

*13.7mi north of Concord. From I-93 tak Exit 18 and follow signs (7mi) to Shaker Vi lage, 288 Shaker Rd. ◯Open May-Octob*

*Canterbury Shaker Village*

©David Shafer/The New Hampshire Division of Travel and Tourism Development

daily 10am-5pm. ⊚$15. ☞Guided and self-guided tours available. ℁ ☎603-783-9511. www.shakers.org.

Attracted by the serene countryside and the gift of a large tract of land in Canterbury, the Shakers established a community near the village of **Canterbury Center**★ in the 1780s. As in other Shaker communities, residents here made their own clothing, tools and furniture. The 24 original buildings—including the **Dwelling House**, the well-equipped **Schoolhouse**, and the 1792 **Meeting House**, which contains Shaker products—still stand on 694 acres.

## Portsmouth★★

New Hampshire's only seaport, Portsmouth lies the mouth of the Piscataqua River across from the southern border of Maine. Settlers arrived here as early as 1623, after which time Portsmouth thrived as a center for maritime commerce. Today many grand mansions remain, and the site of the original Strawbery Banke settlement has been preserved. Sightseeing **cruises** to the **Isles of Shoals**, a group of nine picturesque islands, depart in summer from Market Street dock *(reservations recommended: ☎603-431-5500).*

### Strawbery Banke Museum★★

20 Court St. ⦾Open May 1-October 26 daily, 10am-5pm. ☞Visit by guided tour only October 27-April 30 (Sat and Sun only, 10am-2pm). Open in December for holiday house tours, Mon-Fri 10am-2pm. ⦾Closed New Year's Eve, New Year's Day, Christmas Eve and Christmas Day. ⊚$15. ℁ ☎603-433-1106. www.strawberybanke.org.

This 10-acre restoration project remains a living model of the techniques used to rehabilitate an entire district. Slated for the wrecking ball in the 1950s, more than 36 buildings spanning three centuries have been preserved, showing the town's growth from a 1623 farming community to a prosperous port. Ten homes and period gardens are open to the public, ranging from the 17C timber **Sherburne House** to the elegant 1811 **Goodwin Mansion**.

### Historic Houses★★

☞Visit of houses by guided tour only, mid-Jun–Oct. ☎603-436-1118. www.portsmouthhistorichouses.org.

Sprinkled throughout the town are nine furnished dwellings illustrating the decorative and architectural styles and high-quality craftsmanship that reigned in Portsmouth in the 18C and 19C. Of note are the **Warner House**★★, a 1716 Georgian mansion *(150 Daniel St.; ☎603-436-5909)*, and the 1763 **Moffatt Ladd House**★ *(154 Market St.; ☎603-742-7745)*. Times and fees vary by house.

## White Mountains★★★

Spreading across northern New Hampshire and into Maine, the White Mountains boast the highest peaks in New England, as well as some of its most

*White Mountain National Forest*

1,200mi of hiking and cross-country skiing trails. Downhill skiing dominates the winter months at resorts including Attitash, Loon, Mt. Cranmore, Black Mountain, Wildcat Mountain and Waterville Valley *(trail conditions & information: ☎ 603-745-9396, www.skinh.com).*

### Mount Washington★★★
*Off Rte. 16. ☎603-466-3988.*

Highest point in New England, Mt. Washington experienced the strongest winds recorded on earth (231mph) in 1934. The mountaintop is accessible via the Auto Road, four strenuous hiking trails, and the **Mount Washington Cog Railway**★★ Kids *(departs from Marshfield Base Station 6mi east of Rte. 302. ◷open year-round; ⌔$59, winter rate $31; ☎603-278-5404; www.thecog.com).* Built in 1869, the railway offers passengers a thrilling 3.5mi ride to the summit. Here the view from the rooftop deck of the **Sherman Adams Summit Building** offers a 240mi **panorama**★★★ of the entire region.

spectacular scenery. Named for the snow that blankets the area during most of the year, these massifs, dominated by Mt. Washington (6,288ft) of the Presidential Range, are characterized by rounded summits and deep, U-shaped notches. Scenic roads, including the magnificent **Kancamagus Highway**★★★, pass through breathtaking notches such as **Pinkham**★★, **Crawford**★★ and **Franconia**★★★.

Much of the area is protected as the 772,000-acre **White Mountain National Forest**, renowned for its

# VERMONT★★

MICHELIN MAP 583 T 5, 6
EASTERN STANDARD TIME
POPULATION 562,758

In 1609, when the French explorer **Samuel de Champlain** first set eyes on the forested mountains extending southward from the lake that now bears his name, he reportedly exclaimed, *"Les verts monts!"* ("The green mountains!"). Vermont was the last New England colony to ratify the Constitution. Despite the presence of the granite and lumber industries, the state fostered no sizable cities, owing in part to the rugged Green Mountains, which discouraged east-west travel. The state's high taxes and fierce opposition to outside forces have earned it the tongue-in-cheek sobriquet "the Republic of Vermont."

- ▯ **Information:** ☎ 802-828-3237. www.travel-vermont.com
- ▸ **Orient Yourself:** Most of the state is a five hour drive from Boston.
- ◔ **Don't Miss:** Grandma Moses exhibitions at the Bennington Museum.
- ◔ **Also See:** MAINE COAST.

## A Bit of History

Today Vermont remains strikingly old-fashioned and picturesque. White clapboard Colonial architecture reigns in its small town centers, such as **Manchester Village**★, while larger town such as **Burlington**★, the state most populous city, have ingenious adapted old buildings for modern us

## Ben and Jerry's Ice Cream Factory

Kids *1281 Waterbury-Stowe Rd., Waterbury, VT, 15mi northwest of Montpelier via I-89 & Rte. 100.* Open year-round, daily. October 22-May 31 10am-6pm; June 1-June 30 9am-6pm; July 1-August 19 9am-9pm; August 20-October 21 9am-7pm. *Tours leave at least every 30 minutes; last tour leaves one hour before closing.* $3. *802-882-1260.* When native Vermonters Ben Cohen and Jerry Greenfield signed up for a $5 correspondence course in ice-cream-making and opened a tiny scoop shop in Burlington in the late 1970s, they didn't know that their venture would grow into a multimillion-dollar global operation. Tours of their small factory conclude with free samples.

Burlington also claims the **Ethan Allen Homestead**★ Kids *(Rte. 127, 2mi north of downtown; open seasonally; call or check websits for specific hours;* $5; *802-865-4556; www.ethanallenhomestead.org)*, believed to have been the final home of the enigmatic folk hero.

In between lie vast tracts of undeveloped wilderness and pastureland studded with tiny lakes and country inns. Along the scenic country roads, used bookstores and antique shops are more common than gas stations. Autumn is the most popular time to explore Vermont, when the leaves take on blazing hues and apples are ripe for picking. During the winter, more than 40 ski resorts draw thousands to the steep slopes *(trail conditions & information:* *802-229-0531. www.skivermont.com)*.

## Bennington★

*In the southwest corner of Vermont at the intersection of US-7 and Rte. 9.* Situated 2mi west of Bennington Center's prim boutiques and cafes, **Old Bennington**★ is a small historic district known

for its role in the Revolutionary War. In May 1775 **Ethan Allen** and the **Green Mountain Boys** gathered here before they marched north to attack Fort Ticonderoga. Two years later, in August 1777, a British plan to seize munitions from a local supply depot was thwarted by colonial troops in the **Battle of Bennington**. Today a 306ft dolomite **obelisk** *(2mi west of Bennington Center on Monument Ave.;* *802-447-0550)* commemorates the battle and offers a sweeping mountain **view**★★ from its observation deck.

### Bennington Museum★

*75 Main St. (Rte. 9). Open year-round, daily except Wednesdays 10am-5pm. Closed New Years Day, Thanksgiving, and Christmas.* $8. *802-447-1571. www.benningtonmuseum.com.* **Grandma Moses** (1860-1961), the beloved American folk artist who began to paint when she was 75, is the star attraction here. The museum contains 30 of her canvases, as well as extensive collections of Vermont-made art objects, including pressed and blown glass.

## Maple Sugaring

With an annual average yield of 500,000 gallons, Vermont is the leading producer of maple syrup in the US. From early March to mid-April, when the nighttime temperature still drops below freezing, but the days get steadily warmer, more than a million hard-rock, or sugar-maple, trees in the state are tapped with small metal spouts. Under these spouts, buckets are hung to collect the 10 to 15 gallons of sap each tree is liable to produce. The sap is then taken to a ventilated sugar house to be boiled down to the desired thickness, filtered through layers of cloth, and jarred. Each gallon of syrup is the product of some 40 gallons of sap. Some sixty outfits throughout the state invite you to witness the maple-sugaring process in early spring, and to sample their wares. Syrup comes in three grades—delicate light amber, all-purpose medium amber and robust dark amber.

*John James Audubon – Red Breasted Marganser (1830), Shelburne Museum*

## Woodstock★★

*On US-4, 10mi west of I-89 Exit 1.*
One of the most pristine villages in Vermont, Woodstock was established in 1761. Today, art galleries, restaurants and a general store occupy historic storefronts along Central and Elm Streets, and the elegant Woodstock Inn borders the oval village green.

### Marsh-Billings-Rockefeller National Historical Park★★

*Across the street from* **Billings Farm and Museum**★★ *(Rte. 12 and River Rd. &.☎802-457-2355. www.billingsfarm.org). Open daily year-round. The Billings Farm & Museum is open April 30-October 31, daily 10am-5pm. Park and museum admission $16; guided mansion tours $8. ☎802-457-3368. www. nps.gov/mabi.*
Opened in June 1998, Vermont's first national park centers on a meticulously preserved, art-filled Queen Anne-style mansion and the conservation efforts of three of its residents: 19C environmentalist George Perkins Marsh; Frederick Billings, founder of Billings Farm; and Billings' granddaughter Mary French Rockefeller.

## Shelburne Museum★★★

*12mi south of Burlington on US-7. Open late-Man-October daily 10am-5pm. $18. ☎802-985-3346. www. shelburnemuseum.org.*
"I was anxious to create something in arrangement and conception that had not been tried," wrote **Electra Havemeyer Webb** (1889-1960) of her life project, the Shelburne Museum. Indeed, this sprawling 45-acre complex, comprising 37 historic buildings, blends a formal art museum and a living-history museum into a "three-dimensional collage" whose 150,000-piece collection of art spans 300 years.
Architecturally the museum embraces a panoply of vernacular styles, ranging from the mansard-roofed **Colchester Reef Lighthouse**★ (1871) to the rare wooden **Round Barn**★★ (1901). The eye-catching **Ticonderoga**★★, a luxurious 1906 side-wheeler steamship, now sits in a scooped-out basin in the middle of the grounds.

# ORLANDO AREA

One of the most popular tourist destinations in the US, the Orlando area in central Florida attracts nearly 50 million visitors annually. Best known as the home of Walt Disney World, the region also boasts the elaborate theme parks of Universal Studios, SeaWorld and a number of major corporate headquarters. Orlando itself, the state's largest inland city, serves as the region's hub.

Central Florida experienced its first influx of settlers—largely north Florida cattlemen who were attracted to the area's lush grasslands—after the end of the Second Seminole War in 1842. Forty years later, towns mushroomed along the line of Henry Plant's **South Florida Railway**. Railroad access encouraged tourism and other economic ventures, including lumbering and the naval stores industry. After a killing frost in the 1890s, citrus farmers from northern Florida migrated south to this area, and the citrus industry burgeoned.

The ever-growing pace of tourism increased exponentially in the early 1970s with the opening of Walt Disney World, 20mi southwest of Orlando. The corridor stretching between the two, and south to **Kissimmee**, quickly sprouted a host of commercial attractions, hoping to ride on Disney's coattails.

Today Orlando and its environs rank among the fastest-growing metropolitan areas in the US. The city's centralized location provides easy access to the historic riches of St. Augustine (northeast of Orlando), to the Kennedy Space Center (east of Orlando), to the culturally diverse Tampa Bay area (southwest of Orlando) and to the sophisticated arts scene of Sarasota on the Gulf Coast.

Courtesy of The John & Mable Ringling Museum of Art, the State Art Museum of Florida.

*View of the Ca d'Zan mansion from Sarasota Bay*

⚜ *For coin ranges, see the Legend on the cover flap.*

## WHERE TO STAY

**$$$$ Disney's Grand Floridian Resort & Spa** – *4401 Floridian Way, Lake Buena Vista, FL.* ✗♿🅿🛝 ☎*407-824-3000. www.disneyworld.com. 867 rooms.* Walt Disney World's most luxurious property is a Victorian-era waterside resort set on 40 acres along the Magic Kingdom's monorail route. The five-story lobby—with an aviary, carved moldings, and an open-cage elevator—is topped by illuminated stained-glass domes and metal scrollwork. Elegant guest rooms feature late-19C-style woodwork and old-fashioned sink fittings.

**$$$$ The Peabody Orlando** – *9801 International Dr., Orlando, FL.* ✗♿🅿🛝 ☎*407-352-4000. www.peabodyorlando. com. 891 rooms.* The modern outpost of Memphis' original Peabody is in the Plaza International district. Its palm-studded atrium lobby features a two-story waterfall. In keeping with tradition, the red carpet is rolled out twice a day for the resident ducks to march to the marble fountain. Light woods and pastels extend the hotel's tropical theme to the bedrooms.

**$$$ The Colony Beach & Tennis Resort** – *1620 Gulf of Mexico Dr., Longboat Key, FL.* ✗♿🅿🛝 ☎*941-383-6464. www.colonyresort.com 208 rooms.* An idyllic island getaway, less than 5mi from Sarasota. The all-suite (one- and two-bedrooms) property combines informal attitude with luxurious amenities, including 21 tennis courts, two spas and terrific American cuisine. Fully equipped accommodations come with kitchenettes, whirlpools and balconies. The year-round children's programs rank among the country's best.

**$$ Casa Monica Hotel** – *95 Cordova St., St. Augustine, FL.* ✗♿🅿🛝 ☎*904-827-1888. www.casamonica.com. 137 rooms.* Downtown's resurrected Medieval-style fort was built in 1888 as a winter getaway for America's top-tier families. Its regal features—gilded iron tables and chairs, columns and arches—will make you think you're in Moorish Spain. Designed with plush velvets and tapestry fabrics, accommodations are fit for a modern-day king.

**$$ Rennaissance Vinoy Resort** – *501 Fifth Ave. N.E., St. Petersburg, FL.* ✗♿🅿🛝 ☎*727-894-1000. www.renaissancehotels.com. 360 rooms.* Babe Ruth was among the elite group who wintered at downtown's opulent 1925 landmark. A 2002 renovation brought the salmon color back to its exterior, and restored the lobby's quarry-tile floors and stenciled cypress beams. Bedrooms are done in contemporary blond oak furnishings and muted colors.

**$$ The Don Cesar Beach Resort & Spa** – *3400 Gulf Blvd., St. Petersburg Beach, FL.* ✗♿🅿🛝 ☎*727-360-1881. www.doncesar.com. 277 rooms.* A flamingo-pink sand castle off the St. Petersburg coast, the Don recalls its jazz-age heyday—when F. Scott Fitzgerald was a regular—with crystal chandeliers and tropical gardens. Guest rooms, designed in Florida pastels and light woods, overlook the Gulf of Mexico or the Boca Ciega Bay.

**$ The Courtyard at Lake Lucerne** – *211 N. Lucerne Circle E., Orlando, FL.* 🅿 ☎*407-648-5188. www.orlandohistoricinn.com. 30 rooms.* Four historic residences (1893-1940) center around a tropical courtyard overlooking downtown Orlando's Lake Lucerne. Each one reflects the period of its heyday, from Victorian fabrics and sleigh beds to Art Deco suites with kitchenettes. Breakfast is served on the verandah of the antebellum manor house, which includes three lavish guest rooms.

## WHERE TO EAT

**$$$ Bern's Steak House** – *1208 S. Howard Ave., Tampa, FL.* ☎*813-251-2421. www.bernssteakhouse.com.* **American.** Hyde Park's 40-year-old landmark offers meat connoisseurs six cuts of aged US prime beef, from chateaubriand to T-bone, served with garlic butter and baked potatoes. The encyclopedic **wine list** boasts more than 6,500 entries. Gilded plaster columns, red wallpaper and murals depicting French vineyards set the mood. *Reservations required.*

**$$ Harvey's Bistro** – *390 N. Orange Ave., Orlando, FL. Closed Sun.* ☎*407-246-6560.* **American.** Comfort food with a modern slant keeps residents coming back to this stylish eatery inside the

Bank of America building downtown. Hearty entrées include pot roast in rosemary-Burgundy gravy and roast duck with strawberry sauce. Dark-wood paneling, black and white marble floors and mirror-lined walls give the buzzing dining room a chic, yet casual look.

# ORLANDO ★★★

MICHELIN MAP 584 R 14
EASTERN STANDARD TIME
POPULATION 213,223

Once a sleepy orange-producing area, the sprawling metropolitan Orlando region now ranks as one of the nation's fastest-growing cities, as well as a tourist mecca. While the rapidly expanding southwestern corridor is filled with malls, hotels, restaurants and entertainment complexes, the older downtown area retains the charm of early-20C Florida in its historic architecture.

**Information:** ☎407-363-5871. www.orlandoinfo.com
**Don't Miss:** The non-Disney attractions in this city known for the mouse.
**Kids:** Universal Studios offers more than 40 rides for families.

## A Bit of History

In 1824 swampy Mosquito County stretched southward from St. Augustine and westward to Alachua County, encompassing the 2,558sq mi of land that today defines the Orlando metropolitan area. Some 700 settlers inhabited Mosquito County when the Second Seminole War broke out near Ocala in 1835. To protect the area's pioneers, the US government established several forts in the county, including **Fort Gatlin**, built in 1838. After hostilities ended in 1842, the Fort Gatlin settlement formed the nucleus of the future city of Orlando.

In the early 19C, cattle and cotton reigned as the major moneymakers in central Florida. Citrus intruded as a major crop in the 1880s when the new South Florida Railway provided access to wider markets. Despite the financial havoc wreaked by two disastrous freezes in 1894–95, Orlando rebounded into a thriving agricultural town by the early 20C. Its economy remained rooted in agriculture until 1965, when **Walt Disney**—animated-film wizard and creator of California's Disneyland—announced his plans to build a new theme park here.

Overnight, land values in the area skyrocketed. During the remainder of the 1960s, development engulfed the southwestern part of the city. Walt Disney World opened to great fanfare in 1971. SeaWorld followed two years later, and Universal Studios joined the local theme-park ranks in 1990. Since Walt Disney World's inauguration, metropolitan Orlando has tripled in population. The area currently ranks as one of the world's top commercial tourist destinations and boasts the largest concentration of hotel rooms in the US. With it burgeoning local industry, Orlando is expected to continue as one of the country's fastest-growing areas into the 21C.

## Sights

Since Orlando's incorporation in 1875, downtown has been the city's administrative hub. Revitalized in the last two decades, an eight-square-block core, designated the **Orlando Downtown**

*Entrance to Universal Orlando resort*

**Historic District**, centers on **Orange Avenue**★.

### Church Street Station and Exchange★

**Kids** *129 W. Church St.* ✗ ♿ 🅿 ☎*407-422-2434.*
Begun in the 1970s, this entertainment and shopping complex served as the rejuvenating force behind the area's redevelopment. Now downtown Orlando's main attraction, Church Street Station comprises restaurants and themed showrooms, featuring live music.

### Orlando Museum of Art★

*2416 N. Mills Ave., in Loch Haven Park.* ♿🅿 ☎*407-896-4231. www.omart.org.*
The heart of the permanent collection here is rotated in four large contemporary galleries. More than 600 works of 19C and 20C **American art** include paintings by John Singer Sargent, George Inness, Georgia O'Keeffe, Maurice Prendergast and Gene Davis. An excellent African collection features Yoruba beadwork, Asante statuary and Benin metalwork. Youngsters will enjoy the hands-on "**Art Encounter**" **Kids**.

### Orlando Science Center★

**Kids** *777 E. Princeton St., in Loch Haven Park.* ✗♿🅿 ☎*407-514-2000. www.osc.org.*
This cylindrical building with its four-story central atrium features five interactive display areas on four levels, covering subjects from Florida ecosystems to computer technology. The center's two theaters are complemented by the **Crosby Observatory**, which houses Florida's largest refractor telescope.

## Universal Orlando★★★

**Kids** ▥▥▥*1000 Universal Studios Plaza. Take I-4 to Exit 29 (Sand Lake Rd.); turn right on Sand Lake Rd. and take next right on Turkey Lake Rd. and follow signs to park entrance.* 🕐*Open daily year-round 9am–10pm; hours vary seasonally.* ☞*One day ticket for both parks; $83 (adult), $73 (child). One day ticket, one park; $71 (adult), $60 (child).* ✗♿🅿 (☞*$11*). ☎*407-363-8000. www.universalorlando.com.*
Formerly a single theme park and working movie studio, Universal Studios has expanded its focus (and its name) with an impressive new theme park, **Universal Studios Islands of Adventure** which opened in 1999. "Islands" is linked to **Universal Studios Florida** (the original park), which includes an upscale dining, entertainment and shopping complex, **Universal Studios CityWalk** This walk is designed as a two-tiered, 30 acre promenade of individually themed entertainment venues wrapped around a four-acre harbor. Highlights include jazz, rock and reggae nightclubs, and the Latin Quarter featuring the culture and cuisine of 21 Latin American countries. Several new resort hotels, including the first-ever Hard Rock Hotel, and

more studio production space have nearly tripled the size of the park.

## Universal Studios Florida★★★

The original 110-acre theme park and working studio (with nine soundstages), Universal Studios Florida ranks as the largest motion-picture and television facility outside Hollywood. Taking in all the shows and rides requires an entire day; plan to arrive 30 minutes to one hour prior to opening time. Head for thrill rides first and see shows during midday, when ride lines are longest. The VIP Studio Tour gives visitors priority entrance to leading attractions *(reservations: ☎407-363-8295)*.

Over 40 rides, shows and attractions here will keep you amused for the entire day. From activities for kids of all ages—**A Day in the Park with Barney** and **Fievel's Playland**—to live shows and 3-D action movies enhanced by multisensory special effects—**Twister! Ride It Out** and **Terminator 2: 3-D Battle Across Time**—the park guarantees fun and excitement for children and adults alike. Suspense fans will appreciate **Alfred Hitchcock: The Art of Movie Making**, set in a multimedia theater where the audience watches 3-D film clips of Hitchcock thrillers, as the master of suspense explains his methods.

The park often closes with Universal 360—A Cinesphere Spectacular, in which 360-degree, high-definition images are projected around the surfaces of huge what globes afloat in the Universal Studios Lagoon.

## Universal Studios Islands of Adventure★

Characterized by a unique and eclectic architecture representing a variety of international cultures, **Port of Entry** constitutes mainly a shopping and dining area. Island-Hopper Cruises depart from here and ferry visitors to Jurassic Park. **Seuss Landing** features the whimsical characters of the late children's writer Theodor "Dr. Seuss" Geisel. **Toon Lagoon** brings cartoon characters to life. Realistic dinosaurs stalk visitors at **Jurassic Park**,

*The Blue Man Group*

© 2006 Universal Orlando Resort

while high-tech thrill rides are the main attractions of **The Lost Continent** and **Marvel Super Hero Island.**

## Seaworld Orlando★★★

Kids ▥▥ *7007 Sea World Dr. Take I-4 to Exit 28 and follow signs to park entrance.* ◷*Open Apr–Sept daily 9am–10pm. Rest of the year, daily 9am–7pm. Extended hours during holidays.* ⊛*$64.95.* ✗⚙🅿☎*407-351-3600. www.seaworld.com.*

Enter the park through a six-acre gateway area with a 55ft lighthouse at its heart. A large lake dominates the southern half of SeaWorld's roughly elliptical maze of walkways. This 200-acre marine adventure park mixes entertainment and education in its numerous animal shows, touch pools and aquariums. Opened in 1973, the park is one of three Anheuser-Busch-owned SeaWorlds nationwide, which together support one of the world's largest collections of marine life. SeaWorld also conducts research programs and has successfully bred fifteen killer whales. Along with the park's thrill rides, Journey to Atlantis and Kraken, many of SeaWorld's most popular attractions are the marine mammal shows. Plan your visit around show times. Don't miss SeaWorld's new killer whale show, Believe, in an elaborate three-story set.

Dolphins leap 18ft above the water and execute full flips and triple twists at **Key**

*Sea World, Orlando*

**West SeaWorld.** Visitors can observe gentle **manatees** in their pool from a lower-level viewing area and walk through an acrylic archway under water inches away from sharks and other denizens in **Shark Encounter**. SeaWorld's signature attractions are the killer-whale shows starring the renowned five-ton orca, Shamu, Baby Shamu and the rest of the orca family.
On **Journey to Atlantis**, one of the park's thrill rides, a high-speed water coaster carries passengers through dark, misty passageways, and down a nearly vertical 60ft waterfall. **Wild Arctic**, the other thriller, takes passengers on a virtual-reality helicopter ride over a northern landscape above caribou, polar bears and narwhals to a mock-up of an arctic research station, featuring above- and below-water views of beluga whales, polar bears, walruses and harbor seals.

# WALT DISNEY WORLD® ★★★

MAP P365
EASTERN STANDARD TIME

Located 20mi southwest of Orlando, this immense 47sq mi complex encompasses four extensive theme parks; Magic Kingdom, Epcot, Disney's Animal Kingdom and Disney-MGM Studios. The four combine the romantic nostalgia of Disney's mid-20C vision with today's technology. In addition, 32 separate resort hotels—with nightclubs, water parks, 18-hole golf courses, a 9-hole course, and a 200-acre sports complex—enhance the world's most visited theme park.

- **Information:** ☏407-824-4321. www.disney.go.com.
- **Parking:** Shuttle buses and trains will take you from one park to another: no need to drive.
- **Don't Miss:** The movie-themed rides at MGM Studio.
- **Organizing Your Time:** Days at the theme parks are tiring, plan enough day to get everything in and take time for afternoon naps.
- **Kids:** Epcot, Animal Kingdom, it is all about kids in Walt's World.

## A Bit of History

Born in Chicago, **Walter Elias Disney** (1901-66) showed early signs of a keen imagination and an aptitude for drawing—talents that would be key to his career. Disney was operating an animation studio in Kansas City, when, a

# Address Book

## GETTING THERE

**Orlando International Airport (MCO):** ☎407-825-2001; 28mi northeast of Walt Disney World. Airport information booths located in main lobby of airport and in third-level atrium. Mears Motor Shuttle provides shuttle service to Walt Disney World *(departs from baggage-claim area; $19/one-way; ☎407-839-1570)*. Limo and taxi service is also available. Rental car agencies are located at the airport. If you are driving from Orlando airport, take the Beeline Expressway/Rte. 528 West *(toll)*, then continue on I-4 West and follow signs to individual parks.

**Amtrak train** station: 1400 Sligh St., Orlando *(24mi from park)*, ☎800-872-7245, www.amtrak.com. **Greyhound/Trailways bus** stations: 555 N. McGruder Blvd., Orlando *(26mi from park)*, and 16 N. Orlando Ave., Kissimmee *(12mi from park)*; ☎800-231-2222; www.greyhound.com.

Walt Disney World is located 20mi southwest of downtown Orlando. Take I-4 West to Exit 26B for best access to Epcot, Typhoon Lagoon, Downtown Disney, River Country and Discovery Island. To reach Disney's Animal Kingdom, Wide World of Sports, Disney-MGM Studios and Magic Kingdom, take Exit 25B (Rte. 192) West, and follow signs. Trams shuttle visitors to main gates from pick-up areas throughout the parking lots.

## GETTING AROUND

Monorail trains, buses, ferries and water taxis *(all free)* link all attractions, including hotels and resorts, throughout the complex. Buses operate approximately every 20min, from one hour prior to park opening until closing. Bus routes painted in red are direct after 4pm, with the exception of service to Magic Kingdom, Epcot and Disney-MGM Studios from Disney's Old Key West Resort and the Disney Institute, which operates on scheduled pick-up times between noon and 6pm.

## VISITOR INFORMATION

⏱ *Disney parks are open year-round daily, 9am–9pm; Animal Kingdom is open sunrise–sunset. Hours vary seasonally; call for information ☎407-824-4321.* △ ✗ ♿ 🅿. For general information and to request a free Vacation Guide, contact Walt Disney World Guest Information, P.O. Box 10040, Lake Buena Vista FL 32830-0040, ☎407-824-4321, www.disneyworld.com. For visitor services (foreign-language maps, information for guests with disabilities, baby facilities, storage lockers, banking facilities, camera centers and information about Disney character greetings), contact Guest Relations at individual parks: City Hall, Main Street, USA at Magic Kingdom; near Gift Stop at Epcot; Hollywood Boulevard at Disney-MGM Studios; and next to Creature Comfort at Animal Kingdom.

## WHERE TO STAY

Walt Disney World complex offers more than 25,000 rooms at 27 properties including resort hotels, villas, condominiums, cabins and campgrounds. Rates vary and generally are lower early Jan–mid-Feb, mid-Apr–mid-Jun and Sept–mid-Dec. For all reservations, call ☎407-934-7639; dial *88 from specially marked phones in the complex; or visit the Guest Relations booths at individual parks.

**Outside the Disney Complex** – Numerous lodging facilities, ranging from luxury to budget, lie within a 5-10min drive of main entrances. Many offer free shuttle service to Disney attractions. Make reservations 3 to 5 months in advance, especially for summer and holidays. For further information, contact the **Orlando/Orange County Convention and Visitors Bureau**, 6700 Forum Dr., Suite 100, Orlando FL 32821, ☎407-363-5872, www.go2orlando.com.

---

...ge 22, Walt and his brother Roy left to establish the Disney Brothers Studios in Hollywood, California. Their studio scored its first hit in 1928 with *Steamboat Willie*, starring a character named Mickey Mouse. In 1937, *Snow White*, Disney's first feature-length animated film, met with instant success.

More than a decade later, disillusioned with the tawdriness of existing amusement parks, Disney began planning his own in Anaheim, California. Inaugurated in July 1955, Disneyland changed the face of global amusement. Owing to its enormous popularity, Disney launched plans in 1965 to open a second park on nearly 30,000 acres of land in central Florida. Disney envisioned this property as an **Experimental Prototype Community of Tomorrow** (Epcot), a place that would function as a model for future communities and highlight the creativity behind American industry. However, as construction began, the renowned cartoonist was diagnosed with cancer and died in 1966. In deference to his brother, Roy Disney named the Florida complex Walt Disney World, preserving Walt's concept for the park. In 1971 Magic Kingdom opened, followed by Epcot in 1982, and seven years later by Disney-MGM Studios—a combination working film studio and theme park. Animal Kingdom was added in 1998. The immensely popular Disney concept has also been exported abroad. In 1983 Tokyo Disneyland was launched, followed in 1992 by Disneyland Paris.

## Magic Kingdom★★★

Kids ▥▥▥Take I-4 west to Exit 25B (US-192 West); turn right on World Dr. and follow signs to park entrance. ⬤$67.
The 100-acre Magic Kingdom includes seven areas—Main Street, U.S.A., Tomorrowland, Mickey's Toontown Fair, Fantasyland, Liberty Square, Frontierland and Adventureland—radiating out from the Central Plaza in front of Cinderella Castle. Shops, eateries, attractions and costumed "cast members" (ride attendants, shopkeepers and other staff) in each area echo the dominant theme of their "land."
Magic Kingdom is the most popular of the four parks and the most time-consuming to access. Thrill rides—Space Mountain, Splash Mountain and Big Thunder Mountain Railroad—along with the ever-popular Pirates of the Caribbean, tend to attract the greatest crowds; head for them first. Tidy Victorian storefronts holding commercial shops re-create the milieu of an early

19C town on **Main Street, U.S.A.** During the summer and Christmas holidays, the nighttime parade of lights fills the street each evening.
Disney's "fantasy future city" of **Tomorrowland** is the location of the popular thrill ride **Space Mountain**, a roller coaster that hurtles passengers through near-darkness. **Fantasyland** is the most popular area in all Walt Disney World. With its rides based on Disney's animated feature films, Fantasyland centers around the 189ft-high **Cinderella Castle**—a Gothic extravaganza ornamented with turrets, towers and gold spires.
The Old West lives on in the wooden walkways, country stores and saloon of **Frontierland**. Inside the ever-popular **Splash Mountain**, riders board dugouts and careen down the mountain to a soaking splash. The **Big Thunder Mountain Railroad** rollercoaster negotiates a terrain of hoodoos, caves and canyons. **Adventureland** features one of the most popular amusement park rides ever created, **Pirates of the Caribbean**. Here visitors board boats for a ride through a darkened swamp to a Caribbean village, where they drift past sets peopled by lifelike buccaneers, pigs, parrots and more.
Scaled to visitors under age 10, the whimsical village **Mickey's Toontown Fair** is the best place for kids to meet their favorite Disney characters.

## Epcot★★★

Kids ▥▥▥Take I-4 West to Exit 26B; go west on Epcot Center Dr. and follow signs to park entrance.
The 300-acre Epcot is divided into two distinct areas: Future World, housing pavilions devoted to technology and ingenuity, and World Showcase, where the culture and architecture of 11 nations are represented. The Future World complex celebrates American industry and serves as a "showcase for new ideas," as Disney intended. The Land and Living Seas pavilions function as working research centers as well as attractions. To maintain its innovative

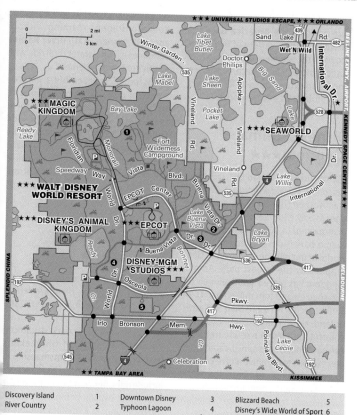

| | | | | | |
|---|---|---|---|---|---|
| Discovery Island | 1 | Downtown Disney | 3 | Blizzard Beach | 5 |
| River Country | | Typhoon Lagoon | 4 | Disney's Wide World of Sport | 6 |

character, Future World is ever updating and revamping its exhibits.

## Future World

Encircling the 180ft-high, faceted geosphere that symbolizes Epcot, nine large pavilions house rides, interactive display areas and films, all saluting humankind's ingenious technological achievements.

Spiral up 18 stories in a time machine vehicle inside Epcot's giant landmark sphere, **Spaceship Earth**, where you'll ride past animated scenes depicting the history of human communication from prehistoric tribes to present-day technology. Then go on to explore **The Seas with Nemo and Friends**, a 5.7-million-gallon aquarium, and **The Land**, an enormous working greenhouse where scientists perfect plant-growing methods and develop new hybrids. In Future World you'll also ride through the **Universe of Energy**, examine the human body inside the **Wonders of Life** dome, and journey into **Imagination! Presented by Kodak**.

## World Showcase

The 1.3mi promenade at World Showcase circles a 40-acre lagoon and passes the pavilions of 11 different countries: Mexico, Norway, China, Germany, Italy, America, Japan, Morocco, France, the United Kingdom and Canada. Each pavilion—staffed by natives of the country it represents—reflects the architecture, foods, crafts, costumes and traditions of that culture. The Norway pavilion includes **Maelstrom**, which plunges riders through treacherous northern seas; other pavilions screen films in a CircleVision 360 Theater or feature multimedia presentations.

Located in front of the American Adventure pavilion, the **America Gardens Theatre** holds a variety of live stage shows. In the evenings, World Showcase lagoon and pavilions become the setting for an extravaganza of laser lights, music, fountains and fireworks.

## Disney's Animal Kingdom★★★

Kids 🚗 *Take I-4 West to Exit 25B. Head west on US-192 and go north on World Dr., then west on Osceola Pkwy. and follow signs to park entrance.*

Inaugurated in 1998, Disney's newest theme park is devoted to the natural world: animals living and extinct. Geographically the largest park, Animal Kingdom has placed 1,500 animals (of 250 species) and four million plants (of 3,000 species) on more than 500 acres of land. Here, visitors can move from colorful parades to a re-created African savanna, from sophisticated rides and exhibits to primitive native villages. Moreover, visitors can meet with animal-behavior experts, monitor animal-care facilities and learn about the depletion of world rain forests and grasslands.

Animal Kingdom extends in four directions from its hub, the **Tree of Life**, located in the heart of **Safari Village**. Fashioned as a tropical artists' colony, **Safari Village** occupies a man-made riverine island; footbridges link it to the other segments of the park. The trunk of the 145ft-high man-made **Tree of Life** displays 325 intricately carved images of animals of all stripes.

In the **Africa** quadrant of the park you'll find Animal Kingdom's leading attraction, **Kilimanjaro Safaris**. On this ride, open-sided all-terrain trucks carry passengers down a twisting dirt road, across river fords to the grasslands of the Serengeti Plain. Here, travelers can observe rhinoceroses, elephants, lions, cheetahs, zebras and other residents of the savanna.

The **Asia** quadrant centers on a rural Asian village set amid rain-forest vegetation. Departing from here, the **Maharajah Jungle Trek** winds past decaying temple ruins and allows passengers a glimpse of Bengal tigers and Komodo dragons roaming without apparent barriers. **Kalli River Rapids** combines a white-water thrill ride with an environmental theme.

Constructed to resemble a paleontological research camp, **DinoLand U.S.A.** appeals mostly to the elementary-school set. In the popular ride **Dinosaur**, visitors journey back to late Cretaceous times along a twisting and bumpy route, where riders dodge nine different species of Audio-Animatronics® dinosaurs and narrowly escape meteoric disaster.

## Disney-MGM Studios★★★

Kids 🚗 *Take I-4 West to Exit 26B. Go west on Epcot Center Dr., then turn left on Buena Vista Dr. and follow signs to studio entrance.*

This 154-acre theme park/studio celebrates the magic of filmmaking, from animation and stuntsmanship to adventure and romance. The attractions include rides, film performances and live shows that explain behind-the-scenes moviemaking. As a working studio, Disney-MGM produces scores of television shows and Disney animated films.

The least crowded of the four parks, this one also has a more compact design that makes visiting easy. As in the other parks, thrill rides and newest attractions tend to have the longest lines. Head for Tower of Terror, Star Tours, and the new **Rock 'n' Roller Coaster Starring Aerosmith** first.

Lined with palm trees and sleek Art Deco buildings filled with commercial shops, **Hollywood Boulevard** opens onto a central plaza next to a replica of Mann's Chinese Theater in Los Angeles. In the evening, **Fantasmic!**—a 25min multimedia show—is presented in a 6,500-seat amphitheater.

Visitors to MGM can take a trip through the celluloid classics on **The Great Movie Ride**, or explore the wonders of the animation process at **The Magic of Disney Animation**. Audience volunteers take positions behind wind-blowing and door-creaking devices of

Foley stage in **Sounds Dangerous**, which provides a comical look at the way sound is added to film. The inner workings of filmmaking are revealed in the **Disney-MGM Studios Backlot Tour**, and the mysteries of movie stunts are unraveled in **Indiana Jones Epic Stunt Spectacular**.

At the end of Sunset Boulevard looms the **Hollywood Tower Hotel**, where guests travel back in time in **The Twilight Zone Tower of Terror** ride. Based on an episode from the popular 1960s television series *The Twilight Zone*, the ride culminates in a 13-story plunge in the old service elevator. The futuristic thrill ride **Star Tours** takes travelers on a simulated high-speed voyage to the Moon of Endor.

# KENNEDY SPACE CENTER★★★

MICHELIN MAP 584 S 14
EASTERN STANDARD TIME

Protruding from Florida's Atlantic coast, Merritt Island is home to the nation's space program. Every US rocket, from the one that carried the *Explorer I* satellite in 1958 to modern space shuttles, has blasted off from here or from adjoining Cape Canaveral. Opened to the public in 1966, the **Kennedy Space Center Visitor Complex**, Florida's fourth-largest tourist attraction, receives over three million visitors a year.

**Information:** ☎407-452-2121. www.kscvisitor.com
**Parking:** Leave the car in the parking lot and take one of the bus tours.
**Don't Miss:** The wonders of the Merritt Island National Wildlife Refuge.
**Kids:** Little ones love the great beyond at the Gallery of Space Flight.

## A Bit of History

The National Aeronautics and Space Administration (NASA) was founded in 1958 and charged with the mission of space exploration. In May 1961, President John F. Kennedy challenged the nation "to achieve the goal, before the decade is out, of landing a man on the moon and returning him safely to Earth." Based on Kennedy's speech, the press soon declared a "space race" between the two Cold War superpowers, and NASA began buying land on Merritt Island for its main launch facility.

Moving "Spaceman" at Kennedy Space Center Visitor Center

## Watching a Shuttle Launch

To obtain a launch schedule, write to **Florida's Space Coast Office of Tourism**, 8810 Astronaut Blvd., Cape Canaveral FL 32920, ☎407-868-1126. To request complimentary vehicle passes for viewing a launch, write three months in advance to NASA Visitor Services, Mail Code: PA-Pass, Kennedy Space Center FL 32899. Tickets for launch viewing go on sale approximately five days prior to launch date and must be purchased in person at the Kennedy Space Center Visitor Complex Ticket Pavilion. For updated information, call ☎407-867-4636.

In 1963 the US Fish and Wildlife Service gained management of the 95 percent of land not needed by NASA and created the **Merritt Island National Wildlife Refuge**★★ *(4mi east of Titusville on Rte. 402; ☎407-861-0667)* as a haven for migratory waterfowl.

Between 1961 and 1966, the Mercury and Gemini missions captured the world's attention. In 1961 Alan Shepard became the first American in space. The following year, John Glenn was the first US astronaut to orbit the earth. In 1965 Edward White walked in space, another first. Kennedy's goal was accomplished on July 20, 1969, when Neil Armstrong and Buzz Aldrin became the first humans to walk on the moon.

NASA's answer to a reduction in funding in the late 1970s was a fleet of reusable space shuttles, which have formed the centerpiece of the space program since the maiden voyage of *Columbia* in 1981. NASA's primary goal in the first part of the 21C is to establish an **International Space Station**, a combined effort with Russia, Canada, Japan and the 14 member nations of the European Space Agency. In June 1998, the first of 38 flights from the US and Russia carried into orbit parts for the construction of this permanent orbiting scientific laboratory, scheduled for completion in 2005. NASA's long-range plans call for a permanent lunar base and a manned mission to Mars.

## Visit

### Bus Tours

*Bus tours depart year-round daily every 10min, first tour at 9:30am, last tour at 3:30pm. ☞$14. Commentary and video on tour. Special operations or imminent* shuttle launches may alter tour itineraries. ☎407-452-2121. The best way to visit the facility is via the **Kennedy Space Center Tour**★★ *(2-4hrs)*. Buses first pass the 525ft-high **Vehicle Assembly Building** (VAB) where the shuttle is assembled. At **Launch Complex 39** visitors can climb an observation gantry and, with luck, see a shuttle waiting to be launched. Here, a short video provides an overview of the beginning of the space-flight era, and a second film replays the launching of *Apollo 8*, the first manned spaceship to orbit the moon.

Next, a stirring multimedia review of the Apollo series and an excellent movie about the *Apollo 11* mission culminate at the **Apollo/Saturn V Center** with a close-up inspection of a 363ft *Saturn V* moon rocket, one of three such rockets in the world. In the **International Space Station Center** visitors learn about the venture that is driving the space industry into the 21C. Exhibits include a 5min video about the station and mock-ups of its various elements.

Focusing on space-flight history, the **Cape Canaveral Tour** takes in shuttle facilities and the ships that salvage rocket boosters. A simulated launch is staged in the actual Mission Control Building used for the Mercury program. Launch site of the first US satellite, the **Air Force Space Museum** (&☎407-853-3245) offers an impressive array of rockets and historical artifacts.

### Gallery of Space Flight ★

This cornucopia of space gear highlights the 1960s and 70s. Included are the Apollo spacecraft that docked with a Soviet Soyuz in 1975, a Gemini capsule that orbited the earth in 1966, and a piece of moon rock. Full-scale mock ps of a Lunar Rover and a Soviet Soyuz spacecraft complete the exhibits. Outside the museum, the **Rocket Garden** displays eight rockets, as well as gigantic tracking antennae and the access arm through which the *Apollo 11* crew entered their space capsule before liftoff.

## IMAX 1 & 2

On screens more than five stories high, two IMAX theaters project three compelling **films**★—*The Dream Is Alive, Mission to Mir* and (in 3-D) *L5: First City in Space*—featuring stunning footage shot from space.

A gallery of space-related art includes paintings and sculptures, and the "Spinoffs from Space" exhibit demonstrates the benefits of space exploration for such fields as medicine and sports. Behind the IMAX theaters, the **Astronauts Memorial** is a moving tribute to astronauts who have made the ultimate sacrifice. Just to the right of the memorial, a full-scale replica of the **Space Shuttle Explorer** gives visitors an idea of the relative roominess of modern space vehicles.

# ST. AUGUSTINE★★★

MICHELIN MAP 584 R 13
EASTERN STANDARD TIME
POPULATION 12,263

The oldest continuously occupied European settlement in the US lies on Florida's east coast. Historic St. Augustine mingles one-story 18C structures with 19C architectural showpieces and 20C tourist attractions. Today "America's Oldest City" attracts more than two million visitors annually.

**Information:** ☎ 904-829-1711. www.visitoldcity.com.

**Don't Miss:** Castillo de San Marcos National Monument, the oldest masonry fort in the US.

**Kids:** What kid could resist the St. Augustine Alligator Farm?

## A Bit of History

In 1565 Spanish explorer **Pedro Menéndez de Avilés** made landfall near present-day St. Augustine, charged by Philip II of Spain with obtaining a Spanish foothold in Florida. A 208ft stainless-steel cross today marks the spot where Menéndez and his men came ashore. Menéndez's chaplain celebrated the event by saying Mass, thus establishing the **Mission de Nombre de Dios**★ (*27 Ocean Ave.;* ☎ *904-824-2809*), the first Catholic mission in the US. St. Augustine, the colony Menéndez built between the Matanzas and San Sebastián rivers, became the capital of Spanish Florida in 1587.

During the first half of the 17C, new French and English settlements along the coastline to the north challenged

Spain's tenuous foothold in Florida. To defend their city, the Spanish began construction on a massive coquina (stone formed from the sedimentation of seashells) fort, Castillo de San Marcos. The fort fended off Spain's enemies until 1763 when Spain relinquished possession of Florida to England in exchange for Cuba. The British ruled St. Augustine for the next 20 years; in 1783 the terms of the Treaty of Paris gave Florida back to Spain. Unable to maintain economic independence, Spain ceded Florida to the US in 1819.

But it was tourism—ushered in by New York industrialist **Henry Morrison Flagler** (1830–1913)—that finally put St. Augustine on the map. By 1889 Flagler had linked the city to the rest of the East Coast via his Florida East Coast Railway and built a triumvirate of

*Castillo de San Marcos*

hotels: the Mediterranean Revival-style **Ponce de Leon Hotel**—now **Flagler College**★★ *(74 King St.)*; the less luxurious Hotel Alcazar (now the Lightner Museum), and the Casa Monica Hotel. They attracted throngs of visitors, and St. Augustine enjoyed a brief heyday as Florida's premier resort destination. Today the city still relies on tourism as its economic mainstay, capitalizing on its history and miles of beachfront.

## Sights

Begin your visit at the **Visitors Information Center** *(10 Castillo Dr., near San Marco Ave.; ☎904-825-1000)*, where you can make reservations and purchase discount tickets to most of the city's attractions. The visitor center also sells tickets for the **sightseeing trains** that tour the city throughout the day, stopping at points of interest.

### Castillo de San Marcos National Monument★★★

*1 S. Castillo Dr. Daily, 8:45am-5:15pm. ☜$6. 🅿 ☎904-829-6506. www.nps. gov/casa.*

Defender of St. Augustine since the beginning of the 18C, the oldest masonry fort in the US stolidly overlooks Matanzas Bay at the northern boundary of the old city. The increasing threat from English and French forces, coupled with a pirate raid in 1668 that left St. Augustine a smoldering ruin, convinced Spanish officials in Madrid that the city needed a permanent stone fortification. By 1695 the four-sided coquina rock fortress was largely complete: pointed triangular bastions formed each corner of the structure's 12ft-thick outer walls. The Castillo withstood every enemy attack that beset it, including an attack by English general James Moore in 1702. In 1924 the fort was designated a national monument and today ranks among the best-preserved examples of Spanish colonial fortifications in the New World.

Ranger talks and audiovisual presentations provide an introduction to the Castillo's long history. Afterward, you can explore the fort and climb the staircase to the **gundeck** for a panoramic **view** of the Matanzas River.

Following a visit to the fortress, a slow meander down **St. George Street** offers the best exposure to St. Augustine, past and present. This city backbone retains its historic flavor despite a plethora of gift shops, craft boutiques and restaurants. In the former Avero House you'll find **St. Photios National Greek Orthodox Shrine**★ *(no. 41; ♿ ☎904-829-8205)*. At number 143 is the **Peña-Peck House**★ *(☎904-829-5064)*, erected in the 1740s.

### Spanish Quarter Village★★

*33 St. George St.* ☎*904-825-6830.*
Behind a low wall, the heart of colonial St. Augustine beats on in a living-history museum dedicated to re-creating the 18C city. Based on historical and archaeological research, eight structures have been rebuilt here. Upon entering through Florencia House, visitors can explore St. Augustine's grassy "streets." Costumed guides demonstrate spinning, carpentry, basketry and other daily activities of 18C life. Don't miss the **De Mesa-Sanchez House**★, one of the city's fine restored historic residences.

### Cathedral-Basilica of St. Augustine★★

*North side of Plaza de la Constitución.* ○*Open daily* 6am-5pm. ♿☎*904-824-2806. www.thefirstparish.org.*
The scalloped façade and tower gracing the north side of the Plaza de la Constitución mark the home of the parish of St. Augustine. Founded in 1565 at the first Mass said upon Pedro Menéndez's landing, this cathedral ranks as the nation's oldest Catholic parish. After an 1887 fire destroyed all but the walls and façade of this church, noted architect James Renwick aided in the reconstruction, enlarging the structure and adding a transept and a bell tower.

### Government House Museum★

*48 King St.* ○*Open Tue-Sat* 10am-4pm. ○*Closed Sun-Mon.* ☜*$2.50.* ♿☎*904-825-5079.*
Throughout 400 years of existence, this stately, two-story masonry edifice has retained its official purpose. Now restored to its 1764 appearance, Government House holds colorful displays that document the city's development.

### Lightner Museum★★

*75 King St.* 9am-5pm. ☜*$8.* ✗♿🅿☎*904-824-2874. www.lightnermuseum.org*
Across from Flagler College rises the former Hotel Alcazar, a poured-concrete structure completed in 1888. After closing its doors as a hotel in 1937, the building was purchased in 1946 by Chicago publisher Otto C. Lightner to house his assemblage of objects and decorative arts. Of note on the first level is a beautiful steam engine created entirely of blown glass. The second level holds Lightner's extensive collection of **art glass**★★, grouped according to type, style and manufacturer. Lightner's collection of decorative arts graces the third level.

### Ximenez-Fatio House★★

*20 Aviles St.* ○*Open Tue-Sat* 11am-4pm. ○*Closed Sun-Mon.* ☜*$5.* ☎*904-829-3575. www.ximenezfatiohouse.org.*
This two-story coquina residence was built in 1798 by Spanish merchant Andrés Ximenez as his residence and general store. It exemplifies the way early St. Augustine buildings were expanded and adapted for various uses—including incarnations as a boarding house and an inn. Today the house reflects the period from 1830 to 1850.

### González-Alvarez House (The Oldest House)★★

*14 St. Francis St.* ○*Open daily* 9am-5pm. ☜*$8.* 🅿 ☎*904-824-2872. www.staugustinehistoricalsociety.org/oldhouse.*
This National Historic Landmark is thought to be St. Augustine's oldest extant residential structure. It offers a fascinating look at the progress of St. Augustine from Spanish colony to British outpost to American city. The house was built in the early 18C for Tomás González y Hernández, a settler from the Canary Islands. The second story and balcony were added during the British period. In 1918 the St. Augustine Historical Society purchased the property and restored it to its 18C appearance.

## Excursions

### St. Augustine Alligator Farm★★

🄺🄸🄳🅂 *On A1A, 1mi south of St. Augustine on Anastasia Island.* ○*Open daily* 9am-5pm. ☜*$19.95.* ♿🅿 ☎*904-824-3337. www.alligatorfarm.com.*
Founded in 1893, the alligator farm claims some 2,500 crocodilians who reside in landscaped habitats. A special indoor exhibit, **Gomek Forever**★, pays homage to a 1,700-pound saltwater crocodile from New Guinea who was the park's star resident until his death

in 1997. Don't miss the **Land of Croco-diles**★, a rare collection of all 23 species of crocodilians that hail from every tropical area of the world.

## Fort Matanzas National Monument★★

*15mi south of St. Augustine via A1A.* ⏱*Open daily 9am-5:30pm.* 🅿 ☎*904-471-0116. www.nps.gov/foma.*
This 300-acre park preserves the site where Pedro Menéndez's forces slaugh-

tered some 250 French Huguenots in 1565. After the 1740 siege of Castillo de San Marcos, the Spanish realized the threat of British invasion and built an armed coquina fortification at this site. In the visitor center, a short film describes the turbulent history and restoration of Fort Matanzas. From a nearby landing, you can board a ferry to cross the Matanzas River to the fort itself, which includes a coquina watchtower erected in 1742 to defend Matanzas Inlet.

# TAMPA BAY AREA★★

MICHELIN MAP 584 R 14
EASTERN STANDARD TIME

Blessed with perennially fine weather, Florida's second-largest metropolitan area is known as the state's west-coast capital. Tampa Bay, the state's largest open-water estuary, opens onto the Gulf of Mexico. Its two densely populated centers—Tampa on the east side of the bay and St. Petersburg on the west—are linked by three causeway bridges. Just north, **Tarpon Springs**★ *(on the Gulf Coast 35mi north of St. Petersburg)* adds international flair, supporting a community of Greek sponge divers with a host of authentic Greek restaurants. On the Gulf Coast, just south of Bradenton, Sarasota attracts visitors to its fine museums and sparkling white-sand beaches.

🛈 **Information:** ☎813-223-2752 or www.thcva.com (Tampa); or www.visittampabay.com; (St. Petersburg); ☎941-957-1877 or www.sarasotafl.org (Sarasota)
☺ **Don't Miss:** The weird world exposed at the Salvador Dali Museum.
Kids **Kids:** The entertainment and rides at Busch Garden Tampa Bay are made for kids.
☖ **Also See:** ORLANDO

## Tampa★★

Set on the blue waters of Tampa Bay, Florida's third-largest city is both port and resort. Its subtropical climate makes Tampa a year-round recreational paradise with a host of attractions ranging from the Latin accents of Ybor City to the thrill rides of Busch Gardens.
On Good Friday, 1528, Spanish explorer Pánfilo de Narváez landed near what is now Clearwater, Florida, and marched north with his men to the site of modern Tallahassee. More than two and a half centuries later, Cuban and Spanish fishermen established the village of Spanishtown Creek west of present-day downtown.
In the 1880s railroad tycoon **Henry Bradley Plant** (1819-99) chose Tampa as

the port for a new railroad that would connect Florida with the rest of the East Coast. Plant built a multimillion-dollar transportation empire that eventually included 14 railway companies and several steamship lines. Railroad transportation and a bustling port assured Tampa's growth by attracting new businesses. One such venture, the cigar industry, flourished here in the late 19C and early 20C.
After recovering from a 1921 hurricane, Tampa hit its peak during the Roaring Twenties' real-estate boom. Unfortunately, the land boom did not last, and Tampa's economy failed even before the Great Depression. Its economy revived, the city today continues to attract new businesses, residents and visitors.

Henry B. Plant Museum

*The minarets of the Tampa Bay Hotel (Henry B. Plant Museum)*

## Bayshore Boulevard★

From the Hillsborough River to MacDill Air Force Base, this scenic drive provides some of the finest **views**★ of Hillsborough Bay and the downtown skyline. The boulevard rims the historic **Hyde Park** neighborhood *(centered on Swann Ave.)* and continues south to Ballast Point.

## Henry B. Plant Museum★

*401 W. Kennedy Blvd., on the* University *of Tampa campus.* ○*Open daily 10am-4pm.* ◉*$5.* ✗ ♿ 🅿 ☎*813-254-1891. www.plantmuseum.com.*

Facing the Hillsborough River and a clutch of downtown skyscrapers, the silver minarets atop the former **Tampa Bay Hotel**★★ have been synonymous with Tampa since the hotel's lavish opening in 1891. Built by Henry Plant to fortify his transportation empire, the red-brick, Moorish Revival-style structure with its distinctive white wood **fretwork** today preserves rooms from the original hotel; the rest of the building houses offices and classrooms for the University of Tampa.

## The Florida Aquarium★

🅚 *701 Channelside Dr. at Garrison Seaport Center.* ○*Open daily 9:30am-5pm.* ◉*$17.95.* ✗ ♿ 🅿 ☎*813-273-4000. www.flaquarium.org.*

Beneath a signature green glass dome, Tampa's aquatic-life facility harbors more than one million gallons of fresh- and saltwater and provides a home for more than 10,000 aquatic plants and animals both from Florida and across the globe. Opened in 1995, the 200,000sq ft aquarium is unique in that it focuses solely on Florida ecosystems. Viewing galleries are laid out in a self-guided tour of four aquatic habitats: **Wetlands**, **Bays and Beaches**, the **Coral Reefs**★ and **Sea Hunt**★. Marine-life videos are shown in a main-floor theater.

## Busch Gardens Tampa Bay★★

🅚 ▥▥▥*3000 E. Busch Blvd.* ○*Open daily 10am-6pm.* ◉*$57.95.* ✗ ♿ 🅿 ☎*813-987-5082. www.BuschGardens.com.*

In 1959 August A. Busch, Jr., then president and chairman of Anheuser-Busch, Inc., opened a bird sanctuary and garden on the grounds of the Busch brewery.

# Ybor City

*1.6mi northeast of downtown Tampa. The visitor center is located at 1600 E. 8th Ave.* ☎813-248-3712. Center of Tampa's 19C cigar-making industry, **Ybor City★** retains its historic heritage even as it evolves into one of the city's hippest nightspots. Off-beat galleries, chic retail shops, nightclubs and ethnic restaurants line **Seventh Avenue★**, Ybor City's main thoroughfare. On weekend evenings, the district takes on a carnival atmosphere as crowds spill onto Seventh Avenue from dozens of bars and nightclubs.

The district is named for cigar manufacturer **Vicente Martínez Ybor**, who chose Tampa as the new site for his operations when labor-union pressures in Key West forced him to relocate here in the late 19C. Ybor's cigar factory opened in 1886 and soon became the largest in the world. By the 20C, cigars fired Tampa's main industry with some 150 factories and Ybor City teemed with a lively mix of young laborers—Cubans, Spaniards, Italians and Germans. Sadly, the advent of machine-rolled cigars, the popularity of cigarettes, and the Depression caused Ybor City's cigar industry—and the community itself—to decline.

The 1990s ushered in a resurgence of interest in Ybor City, resulting in the restoration of many historic landmarks. Personnel from the **Ybor City State Museum** *(1818 9th Ave.; 9am-5pm; $3;* ☎813-247-6323*)* lead free walking tours through the historic district. Housed in the 1923 yellow brick Ferlita Bakery, the museum outlines the development of Ybor City. Guided tours take in adjacent **La Casita** (1895), an early-20C cigar-maker's cottage. Ybor City's oldest and largest hand-rolled-cigar factory, the Martínez Ybor Cigar Factory, was once housed in a three-story 1886 building in **Ybor Square**. The remodeled factory complex still contains a cigar company, as well as specialty shops and eateries.

Since then, Busch Gardens has become the queen of Tampa attractions. More than 2,000 animals roam 300 acres of tropical gardens. Rides, trams, trains and shows add to the entertainment. The park is divided into 10 sections that correspond to African countries (Morocco, The Congo, etc.). Arrive early to avoid long lines, and note that thrill rides (roller coasters, including Montu, Kumba, Python and Scorpion; and water rides Tanganyika Tidal Wave, Stanley Falls and Congo River Rapids) are the most popular attractions.

### Museum of Science & Industry (MOSI)★★

Kids *4801 E. Fowler Ave.* ◷Open daily 9am-5pm. ᴍ$49.95. ✗ ♿ P ☎813-987-6100. www.mosi.org.
One of the largest science centers in the Southeast, this quintessential hands-on science museum houses some 450 permanent exhibits that address subjects from butterflies to nuclear fusion. These are complemented by annual special exhibits and a county library on the first floor offering high-tech computer games and Internet access.

# St. Petersburg★★

Lying on the west side of Tampa Bay, sunny St. Petersburg is Tampa on holiday. A thriving mix of young professionals, retirees and sun-seeking vacationers enjoy St. Pete's relaxed lifestyle, first-rate museums and sparkling gulf beaches. Pánfilo de Narváez and Hernando de Soto landed on the Pinellas Peninsula in the early 16C in search of gold but abandoned the area after encountering hostile natives. In 1888 the peninsula caught the attention of Russian speculator **Peter Demens**, who brought his Orange Belt Railroad to the estate of **John Williams**, a retired Union general. By beating Williams in a lottery, Demens earned the right to name St. Petersburg for his hometown.
Around the early 20C, the city began attracting a large number of tourists. By the beginning of World War I, another

*The Salvador Dali Museum*

railroad connected St. Pete to Tampa and development of the beaches began. The 1920s land boom elevated St. Pete to resort status.

Today St. Petersburg ranks as Florida's fourth most populous city, with tourism as its leading industry. Downtown, handsomely landscaped waterfront parks attract visitors to the bayside, where you can stroll **The Pier**★ with its distinctive upside-down pyramid, and take in the art museums. A 30-minute drive west, **Gulf Boulevard** stretches from **St. Petersburg Beach**★ up to **Clearwater**, the most popular strand on Florida's Gulf Coast.

## Florida International Museum★

*100 2nd St. N. Open Tue-Sat 10am-5pm, Open Sun 12pm-5pm. $10. 727-341-7800. www.florida museum.org.*

Located in the heart of downtown, St. Pete's slick international cultural center hosts at least one grand-scale traveling exhibition from the world's leading art institutions each year.

## Museum of Fine Arts★★

*255 Beach Dr. N.E. Open Tue-Sat 10am-5pm, Sun 1-5pm. Closed Mon. $8. 727-896-2667. www.fine-arts.org.*

Housed in an attractive Palladian-style building, this museum presents an impressive range of masterpieces from around the world. All 20 galleries here are located on one floor. Starting from the marble-floored Great Hall, the museum features **Impressionist** treasures, a remarkable trove of early **Asian sculpture**, as well as modern American paintings. Of special note is the luminous collection of **Steuben glass**★.

## Salvador Dalí Museum★★★

*1000 3rd St. S. Open Mon-Sat 9:30am-5:30pm, Open Sun 12pm-5:30pm. $15. 727-823-3767. www. salvadordalimuseum.org.*

The world's most comprehensive collection of works by the flamboyant Spanish surrealist **Salvador Dalí** (1904–89) resides in this museum, which opened in 1982. The collection contains 2,140 pieces, including 95 oil paintings and more than 100 watercolors and drawings. Early paintings and various self-portraits demonstrate young Dalí's talent and the strong influence of painters from the 17C Flemish masters to the Impressionists and Cubists. Between 1929 and 1940, Dalí experimented with Surrealism, often attenuating figures to emphasize his obsession with time, death and sex. The main gallery contains a permanent retrospective of oil paintings arranged in chronological order, beginning with Dalí's childhood works (1914) and ending with his monumental **masterworks**★★. Painted between 1948 and 1970, each of the masterworks took more than a year to complete.

375

# Sarasota★★

Lying on Florida's Gulf Coast, Sarasota offers numerous and diverse attractions. Here you'll find the official art museum of Florida, a host of cultural and sports activities, upscale shopping districts, a variety of restaurants and a 35mi stretch of pristine white-sand beach.

The bulk of the area's pioneers began arriving in the late 1860s. In 1902 the town elected its first mayor, John Hamilton Gillespie, who built one of the country's first golf courses in Sarasota, thus introducing a sport that now is played on more than 40 area courses. Another influential city father, **John Ringling** (1866-1936), of the Ringling Bros. and Barnum & Bailey Circus, bought a house in Sarasota in 1912. Five years later he founded a local real-estate development company in the city and for a decade thereafter poured much of his time, money and energy into the area.

In 1927 Ringling moved the circus' winter headquarters to Sarasota, providing a boost to the local economy in the wake of the Florida land bust. That same year, Ringling and his wife began construction of a grand Italian Renaissance residence and museum to house their growing art collection.

Today the Ringling complex, the adjacent Florida State University Center for the Performing Arts, and the Van Wezel Performing Arts Hall present the best in art, music, dance and theater. Along Palm Avenue and Main Street lies the hub of Sarasota's **Downtown Art District**★, full of galleries, theaters and restaurants.

## John and Mable Ringling Museum of Art★★★

*5401 Bayshore Rd.* ○*Open daily 10am-5pm.* ⊛*$15.* ✗ ♿ 🅿 ☎*941-359-5700. www.ringling.org/museum_art.asp.*

Spreading over 66 landscaped acres, the museum complex comprises the art gallery, Ringling's mansion and the **Circus Museum** Kids, which contains circus artifacts from the Ringling era. The Historic Asolo Theater and Mrs. Ringling's rose garden are also included on the site.

A treasury of European culture, the museum of art stands as the artistic triumph of southwest Florida, and was designated as the official state art museum in 1946. Complemented by magnificent architecture, the Ringling concentrates on paintings of the late Renaissance and Baroque periods (1550-1750), featuring an extensive private collection of works by Baroque master **Peter Paul Rubens** (1577-1640). The museum's **Baroque Collection**★ is considered one of the finest in the US.

*Clearwater Beach*

Giovanni Lunardi/The John and Mable Ringling Museum of Art

*The Rubens Gallery of The John and Mable Ringling Museum of Art*

## Art Galleries★★★

A wing of 11 rooms, the **North Galleries** offer a broad survey of late Medieval through early Baroque art of Italy and northern Europe, with an emphasis on 16C and 17C Italian works. The **Rubens Gallery**★ consists of four huge paintings, part of a series called *The Triumph of the Eucharist*, executed around 1625. Continuing through this wing, you'll find many other Baroque masterpieces, as well as fine examples from the Middle Ages and Renaissance. The **South Galleries** present a survey of 17C-19C European art, as well as Dutch Garden Painting and Art of France. The new Ulla R. and Arthur F. Searing wing opened in 2007 to showcase special exhibitions.

## Cà d'Zan★★

A pathway leads from the museum to Ringling's extravagant Venetian-style palace (1926) overlooking Sarasota Bay. The Cà d'Zan (Venetian dialect meaning House of John") incorporates Italian and French Renaissance, Venetian Gothic, Baroque and modern architectural elements. Inside, note the 30ft-high **court room** with painted cypress beams and the stained glass in the **tap room**. The **marble terrace** offers a sweeping **view** of the bay. Ceiling panels in the **ballroom**, depicting dance costumes from various nations, were painted by Willy Pogany, set designer for the New York Ziegfeld Follies.

## Barrier Islands

Flung out north and south along Sarasota's Gulf Coast lie several idyllic barrier islands, connected to the mainland by causeways. To the northwest, **Longboat Key** offers vacation condos and a wide variety of beachside hotel accommodations. **St. Armands Key**, across the John Ringling Causeway from downtown Sarasota, boasts the area's upscale shopping district, **St. Armands Circle**★. Just west of St. Armands Key lies **Lido Key**★, site of **Mote Marine Aquarium** *(1600 Ken Thompson Pkwy.; ☎941-388-4441)* as well as several popular beaches.

# PHILADELPHIA AREA

One of America's most historic pockets is solidly anchored in the Middle Atlantic region. Philadelphia, along with neighboring Bucks County, Brandywine Valley and, farther afield, Lancaster County and Gettysburg, preserve a rich store of monuments to the past. Nearby New Jersey attracts visitors not only to try their luck at the glittering Atlantic City casinos, but to soak up the sun on the state's Atlantic Ocean beaches.

Long before any white man admired these landscapes, the Lenni Lenape Indians inhabited the area. It was from this peaceful tribe that **William Penn** (1644-1718) purchased tracts in the late 17C. Penn's city of Philadelphia gave birth to the American Revolution in 1776 when Thomas Jefferson read the Declaration of Independence here. Eleven years later the framers of the Constitution reconvened in Philadelphia to form a new government for the fledgling United States of America.

During the Revolutionary War, the region became contested ground, now famous as the site of George Washington's Valley Forge encampment and his crossing of the Delaware River. Nearly a century later, one of the most pivotal battles of the Civil War raged 124mi west of Philadelphia in Gettysburg. Here, in the summer of 1863, Robert E. Lee, commander of the Confederate Army of Northern Virginia, confronted Union forces under Maj. Gen. George Meade. The three-day battle turned out to be a pivotal but hard-won Northern victory.

Hub of the region, Philadelphia offers a rich history, myriad cultural opportunities and an ethnic diversity that guarantee the visitor a fascinating stay. Wher

*Boathouse Row at Night, Philadelphia*

ou tire of the city's bustle, bucolic ancaster County, an hour's drive west, eckons 20C travelers back to a simpler me: Amish inhabitants of the Pennsyl-ania Dutch Country eschew modern onveniences such as electricity, and avel in horse-drawn buggies as they have for decades. Just beyond Phila-delphia's southwestern boundary lies the verdant Brandywine Valley, whose beauty attracted both 19C industrialists and 20C artists. Tony Bucks County, just east of the city, is heralded for its artsy ambience.

## Area Address Book

*For coin ranges, see the Legend on the cover flap.*

### WHERE TO STAY

**$$$ The Latham Hotel** – *135 S. 17th St., Philadelphia, PA.* ⚙ 🅿 ☎*215-563-7474. www.lathamhotel.com. 139 rooms.* Doormen welcome you in English riding habits at this boutique property. One block from Rittenhouse Square, the building hasn't changed much since 1915 when it opened as a high-rise apartment. Coffee makers and hanging wire baskets filled with toiletries lend a homey touch to the guest rooms, done in period reproductions and jewel-tones.

**$$ Fairville Inn** – *506 Kennet Pike, Chadds Ford, PA.* 🅿 ☎*610-388-5900. www.fairvilleinn.com. 15 rooms.* Two miles from Longwood Gardens, the Federal-style house (c.1857) has loads of country charm. Behind the sunny yel-low façade, Chippendale reproductions, handmade pierced lampshades, and Winterthur-inspired wallpaper decorate the rooms. A tempting assortment of home-baked cookies is laid out for afternoon tea.

**$$ Penn's View Hotel** – *Front & Market Sts., Philadelphia, PA.* ✗⚙🅿 ☎*215-922-7600. www.pennsviewhotel.com. 40 rooms.* An Old City gem inside two con-necting 19C warehouses overlooking the Delaware River. Individually deco-rated accommodations—reproduction Chippendale, delicate floral wallpapers and hardwood floors—recall bedrooms at Grandma's house. Downstairs, the bar at Ristorante **Panorama** offers over 500 types of wines.

**$$ The Virginia Hotel** – *25 Jackson St., Cape May, NJ.* ✗⚙🅿 ☎*800-732-4236. www.virginiahotel.com. 24 rooms.*

Service is key at this historic downtown inn, known for the wedding-cake trelliswork on its porch and balconies. Unlike most local Victorians, the 1879 building is designed in soothing beige and green tones. Furnishings blend period reproductions with contem-porary overstuffed sofas. The hotel's acclaimed **Ebbitt Room** lures diners from near and far.

**$$ The Whitehall Inn** – *1370 Pineville Rd., New Hope, PA.* 🅿✗ ☎*215-598-7945. 5 rooms.* An elegant, late-18C B&B just 4mi from town. Horses and an impressive rose garden highlight the 13-acre estate. Most bedrooms come with fireplaces, and all are outfitted with 19C American antiques, including Victorian, Shaker and Bentwood pieces. The four-course, candlelit breakfast is an elaborate feast.

**$ The Inn & Spa at Intercourse Village** – *3542 Old Philadelphia Pike., Intercourse, PA.* 🅿 ☎*717-768-2626. www.amishcountryinns.com. 12 rooms.* Sit on the front porch of this Victorian house and watch Amish buggies trot by. Original dark woodwork is the backdrop for early-20C furnishings and lace curtains. Suites in the homestead buildings out back have a more rustic feel, with sloping beamed ceilings and handmade quilts.

### WHERE TO EAT

**$$$ Striped Bass** – *1500 Walnut St., Philadelphia, PA.* ☎*215-732-4444.* **Sea-food.** One of the city's top restaurants, three blocks from Rittenhouse Square, sits in a former brokerage house with 28ft ceilings. Muslin-draped windows and rose-colored marble columns front-ed by potted palms create a glamorous look that is offset by casual rattan chairs and cozy banquettes. Memorable dishes: yellow tin tuna tartare with Asian ginger dressing, sautéed lobster and, of course, striped bass.

**$$$ Dilworthtown Inn** – *1390 Old Wilmington Pike, West Chester, PA.* ☎*610-399-1390.* **American.** Fifteen intimate dining rooms with fireplaces, gaslit chandeliers, and handmade chestnut tables take you back to colonial days, when this tavern fed Revolutionary heroes. The menu offers everything from crabcakes with preserved kumquats to a chef's duet of filet mignon and South African lobster tail. Choose from an 800-bottle wine list.

**$$ Fork** – *306 Market St., Philadelphia, PA.* ☎*215-625-9425.* **American.** Old City's hottest bistro offers comfort food with a creative edge. The menu makes mouths water with dishes like pan-seared, citrus-crusted salmon with roasted tomato sauce and sea scallops with green papaya mango slaw. Don't miss the addictive onion mashed potatoes served as an ala carte side dish. The stylish dining room features a cast-concrete bar and handmade

silk-screened curtains. Note the antique mosaic doormat at the entrance depicting—what else?—forks.

**$$ The Meritage Restaurant at Groff's Farm** – *650 Pinkerton Rd., Mount Joy, PA.* Closed Sun & Mon. ☎*717-653-2048.* **Pennsylvania Dutch.** Meritage recently moved from downtown Lancaster to this 18th-century farmhouse on Groff's Farm Golfcourse. Contemporary American is the flavor here, with dishes such as pan-seared duck breast, hazelnut sea scallops with lemon-herb risotto, and fliet mignon with mashed sweet potatoes.

**$$ The City Tavern** – *138 S. 2nd St., Philadelphia, PA.* ☎*215-413-1443.* **Colonial.** This Old City eatery recreates the original 1773 tavern where Revolutionary War heroes, including George Washington and John Adams, dined and strategized. Waiters dressed in period costume serve Thomas Jefferson's favorites: cornmeal-coated fried oysters and clover-honey-glazed roast duckling. The house ale is brewed using Jefferson's own formula.

# PHILADELPHIA★★★

MAPS P382 AND P387
EASTERN STANDARD TIME
POPULATION 1,448,394

Cradle of US history, William Penn's "City of Brotherly Love," marks the country's earliest strides toward nationhood. The city's history has been shaped by religious freedom seekers, immigrant success stories, industrialist robber barons and the creative genius of **Benjamin Franklin**. Although skyscrapers now pierce the skyline, the spirit of industry and culture, which has been Philadelphia's legacy since Franklin walked these streets, still prevails, making Philadelphia one of America's great destinations.

- 🛈 **Information:** ☎215-599-0776 or www.gophila.com
- 🅿 **Parking:** Train service makes Philadelphia accessible without a car.
- 😊 **Don't Miss:** The sounds of freedom of at the Liberty Bell.
- 👆 **Also See:** NEW YORK CITY, WASHINGTON, DC.

## A Bit of History

Beginning in the mid-17C, Swedes, British and Dutch began settling along the banks of the Delaware River. A power struggle ensued, with each side vying

for control of the Delaware River Valley Britain prevailed, and in 1681, **William Penn** (son of British naval hero Admiral Sir William Penn) began his "hol experiment" in the New World. Escaping religious persecution in England

enn established a peaceful Quaker
olony along a stretch of land bounded
y the Delaware and Schuylkill rivers.
enn's new settlement thrived, and by
700 ranked second largest in the New
World after Boston, populated not only
y Quakers but by European immigrants
f every stripe.

s the 18C drew to a close, the inde-
endent-minded colonies were begin-
ing to chafe against British rule. As the
nost populous and wealthiest city in
he colonies in 1774, Philadelphia was
n obvious place for the First Continen-
al Congress to discuss the colonists'
trained relations with the Crown. A year
ater the Second Continental Congress
et an irrevocable course for separation
rom Great Britain.

or the last decade of the 18C, Phila-
elphia served as interim capital of the
ewly formed United States, until the
ation's capital relocated to Washington,
)C, in 1800. Fueled by the engines of
he Industrial Revolution, the economy
oomed and immigrants flocked to Phil-
delphia to keep the wheels of industry
urning. The city generally prospered
ntil the end of World War II, after which
ime Philadelphia drifted rudderless for
everal decades and finally declared
ankruptcy in the late 1980s.

he 1990s have seen the "City of Broth-
rly Love" reborn with a revitalized
enter City. Today the economy of the
ation's fifth-largest city is bolstered
y health care and service industries.
hiladelphia boasts a vibrant arts and
heater scene, a wealth of fine muse-
ms and myriad upscale restaurants.
hree major universities—University
f Pennsylvania, Drexel and Temple—
dd a lively student flavor. The former
ncludes the excellent **University of
ennsylvania Museum of Archaeol-
gy and Anthropology**★★ *(3260 South
t.;* ✕ ♿ ☎ *215-898-4000).* In addition,
ur national sports teams (the Eagles,
hillies, Flyers, and Sixers) entertain the
ty's ardent fans.

/illiam Penn still looks down on all
e has wrought from his unassailable
osition atop City Hall, as though pro-
laiming, as he once did: "And thou,
hiladelphia … what love, what care,

what service, and what travail has there
been to bring thee forth."

# Independence National Historical Park★★

Encompassing roughly twelve blocks
*(bounded by 2nd & 6th Sts. on the east
and west, and Market & Walnuts Sts. on
the north and south)*, the historic heart
of Philadelphia witnessed the turbulent birth of the United States. Now
juxtaposed against modern architecture, the historical park includes the
country's most revered icons of liberty:
Independence Hall and the Liberty Bell.
Events surrounding America's quest for
independence come alive at the modern **Visitor Center** *(3rd & Chestnut Sts.;*
♿ ☎ *215-597-8974; www.nps.gov/inde)*
through interactive computer stations
and a 30min film, *Independence.*

## Independence Hall★★★
*Chestnut St. between 5th & 6th Sts.*
One of only a handful of works of architecture on the UNESCO World Heritage
List, the steepled Georgian brick building (completed in 1756) was constructed
as the Pennsylvania State House. In May
1775, delegates of the Second Continental Congress met in the Assembly Room
here to determine the colonies' response
to increasing British hostility. In reaction
to the colonists appointment of George
Washington as commander-in-chief of
the Continental Army later that summer,
George III declared the colonists to be in
"open and avowed rebellion." The following year, the Congress adopted the
Declaration of Independence in this hall
on July 4, 1776; the Revolutionary War
had begun. The first public reading of
the Declaration of Independence took
place behind the Hall in **Independence
Square** on July 8, 1776. When independence finally seemed imminent in 1781,
Independence Hall saw the adoption of
the Articles of Confederation. Six years
later, the Constitutional Convention conceived a new government here and ratified the US Constitution on September
17, 1787. Today the building has been

PHILADELPHIA
INDEPENDENCE NHP
OLD CITY

Gloria Dei Church/Old Swedes Church \ South Philly

restored to its 18C appearance, with much of its woodwork original.

Flanking the west side of Independence Hall is **Congress Hall**★, the meeting place for the House of Representatives and Senate of the fledgling United States from 1790 to 1800. On the east side, **Old City Hall**★ housed the US Supreme Court from the building's completion in 1791 until 1800.

### Second Bank of the United States/National Portrait Gallery★★

*420 Chestnut St. ☎215-597-8974.*
This columned marble structure (1819, William Strickland) is a superb example of Greek Revival architecture. Opened in 1824, the bank was one of the world's most powerful financial institutions until Congress let the charter expire in 1836.

Since its restoration in 1974, the building has provided a permanent home for "**People of Independence**." Prominent among the paintings in this exhibit are more than 100 Charles Willson Peale portraits of delegates to the Continental Congress, signers of the Constitution and officers of the Revolutionary War.

### Liberty Bell Pavilion★★★

*Across Chestnut St. from Independence Hall (on Market St. between 5th & 6th Sts.).* ♿
The glass-fronted pavilion on Independence Mall, completed for the US Bicentennial in 1976, enshrines the revered **Liberty Bell**★★★. Crafted in London's Whitechapel Foundry in 1751, the bell developed a crack soon after its arrival in Philadelphia and had to be recast by local metalsmiths John Pass and John Stowe. Beginning in 1753, the 2,000-pound bell hung in the State House belfry for almost 100 years. The bell—bearing the inscription from Leviticus 25:10: "Proclaim Liberty throughout all the Land unto all the inhabitants thereof"—heralded the first public reading of the Declaration of Independence on July 8, 1776. In the mid-19C, abolitionists declared it the "Liberty Bell"; since that time, the bell has become the national symbol of freedom.

*Liberty Bell*

©2002 Comstock, Inc.

## Benjamin Franklin

The 15th child of an English soapmaker who immigrated to Boston in the early 18C, Benjamin Franklin (1706-90) had only two years of formal schooling before he was apprenticed to his brother James to learn the printing business in 1718. At 17 Franklin headed to Philadelphia, where he established himself as a successful printer. To engage his creative restlessness, in 1732 Franklin began publishing his popular *Poor Richard's Almanack,* homilies on such virtues as thrift and industry. Gradually he became a city leader and helped set up many Philadelphia institutions such as the Library Company of Philadelphia, Pennsylvania Hospital and the Philadelphia Academy—precursor to the University of Pennsylvania. Franklin took great delight in his scientific endeavors; his experiments with electricity earned him fame in Europe. In his fifties Franklin was elected to the Pennsylvania Assembly, and thereafter much of his life was dominated by politics and the fight for nationhood. While the nation now reveres him as a Founding Father, Philadelphians proudly claim Franklin as their own "uncommon citizen."

## Franklin Court★★

*Entrance on Market St. between 3rd and 4th Sts.*

Philadelphia's most prominent citizen, Benjamin Franklin, built a three-story brick house here for his family in the 1760s. Demolished long ago, the residence has been re-created as a steel-frame "ghost structure," as has the 1786 print shop Franklin built for his grandson. An underground **museum**★ houses an ingenious array of audiovisual presentations that celebrate Franklin's life and genius.

At the north end of Franklin Court, reproductions of the **Market Street Houses** that Franklin built as rental properties in the 1780s re-create the 18C printing office and bookbindery run by Franklin's grandson, Benjamin Franklin Bache.

## Old City★★

The core of Penn's original settlement, this once bustling Colonial waterfront just north of Independence National Historical Park has seen a revival from its mid-20C decrepitude. Hip restaurants and restored historic buildings—many housing performing arts groups, artists' studios and galleries—now punctuate the area. The strong Quaker presence in early Philadelphia is preserved in the 1783 **Free Quaker Meeting House** (5th & Arch Sts.).

On **First Fridays** (the first Friday of every month year-roound 5-9pm; ☎215-625-9200), Old City galleries, showrooms and theaters extend their hours until 9pm.

## Christ Church★★

*2nd St. north of Market St.* ☎215-922-1695.

From a small Anglican chapel erected here in 1695, Christ Church evolved into an elegant Georgian brick edifice (completed in 1754) with a tower and "Philadelphia steeple." The church's Royalist congregation changed dramatically during the Revolution, when George Washington and 15 signers of the Declaration of Independence worshiped here. The 600-year-old **baptismal font** in the back of the church first served in an Anglican church in London; the infant William Penn was baptized in it.

Four blocks west, **Christ Church Burial Ground** (N. 5th & Arch Sts.; March-December weather permitting; guided tours only; $2 adult) includes Benjamin Franklin's grave.

## Elfreth's Alley★★

*Between N. 2nd & Front Sts.*

Named for its mid-18C owner, blacksmith Jeremiah Elfreth, this charming block-long alleyway dates back to the early 18C. Several of its 32 brick row houses have stood here since 1725 and today house urbanites. The **Elfreth' Alley Museum**★ (☎215-574-0560) provides a look at daily working-class life.

## ...y Ross House★

*... Arch St. Open daily 10am–5pm.
...5-686-1252. www.betsyrosshouse.org.*
...ker seamstress Betsy Ross, who is
...ited with making the first Stars and
...es flag, lived here after her husband,
...iot John Ross, died in 1776. Her living
...rters and shop are preserved in the
...k, gable-roofed home (c.1740).

## ...nn's Landing and
## ...ciety Hill★

...along the Delaware River just east of
...ependence National Historical Park,
...area now known as **Penn's Landing**
...tered Penn's first settlers in caves
...y dug in its riverside cliffs. The water-
...nt between Vine and South Streets
... been recast as a recreational area
...n jogging paths, a skating rink, an
...phitheater and the seaport museum.
...minating its northern end, the **Ben-
...in Franklin Bridge** spans the Dela-
...e, while South Street's restaurants
... nightclubs anchor its south side.
...structed during the turbulent years
...t surrounded the nation's quest for
...ependence, 18C churches and homes
...te the **Society Hill** section that abuts
...n's Landing from Independence Hall
...ombard Street. Now restored to its
...oric glory, Society Hill contains some
...he city's most venerable churches:
...1 **St. Peter's Church** (313 Pine St.);
...3 **Old St. Mary's Church** (252 S.
... St.); and **Gloria Dei Church/Old
...edes Church★** (Columbus Blvd. &
...stian St.), the oldest church in Phila-
...phia (c.1700), founded by Swedish
...herans.

## ...lependence
## ...aport Museum★

*...211 S. Columbus Blvd.; pedestrian
...ss via Walnut St. walking bridge.
...pen daily 10am–5pm. ☐ 215-
...-8655. www.phillyseaport.org.*
...ering 100,000sq ft, this contempo-
...waterfront facility comprises several
...manent maritime exhibits, including
...me Port Philadelphia," which traces
... transatlantic crossing of early-20C
...migrants. Docked just to the muse-
...s south, two National Historic land-

### South Philly

Immigrants have long flocked to this section of Philadelphia, which takes its cue from the Italian community that has provided the dominant culture in the 20C. Today the action centers around the boisterous **Italian Market** (9th St. between Christian & Wharton Sts.; 215-551-3054), where a panoply of vegetable stalls, and meat, fish and poultry markets offer everything from dried *bakala* (salt cod) to Parmigiano-Reggiano cheese to Sicilian olives.

South Philly's signature **Mummers Museum** (1100 S. 2nd St. at Washington Ave.) holds the glittering costumes worn in the annual January 1 Mummers parade, which traces its roots to the area's Swedish settlers. Today this Philadelphia frolic taps the creativity of the area's myriad ethnic groups.

mark ships are berthed side by side: the **USS Olympia**★, Admiral Dewey's 1892 cruiser, and the **USS Becuna**, a World War II Guppy-class submarine.
Across the Delaware River from Penn's Landing, Adventure Aquarium Kids contains denizens ranging from baby sharks to frolicking seals *(1 Aquarium Dr., Camden, NJ; 856-365-3300; access via Riverlink ferry from Penn's Landing, 215-925-5465).*

### Physick House★★

*321 S. 4th St. 215-925-7866.*
Purchased in 1815 by the "father of American Surgery," Dr. Philip Syng Physick, this stately home (1786) was occupied by the Physick family until 1940, when it was willed to the Pennsylvania Hospital. In the 1960s, philanthropists Walter and Lenore Annenberg purchased the property and funded the renovation that turned the house into a Federal-period showpiece. The fine collection of furnishings reflect the Federal and Empire styles.

### South Street★★

Forming the southern border of Society Hill, trendy South Street has been a mecca for the counterculture since the 1960s. The blocks between the waterfront and 10th Street are lined with myriad shops, hip restaurants and cutting-edge clubs.

## Center City★★★

Bound on its north-south axis by Vine and South Streets, this historic area has been Philadelphia's main commercial district from the 1870s, when the current City Hall was built. Nearly 100 years later new construction began in an effort to revitalize the area from its mid-20C malaise. The first structure to exceed the height of Penn's statue atop City Hall's dome, **One Liberty Place** (1650 Market Pl.) inspired new growth. A boon to the city's finances, the **Pennsylvania Convention Center** (1101 Arch St.; ☎215-418-4700) opened in 1993 and covers 1.3 million square feet. Incorporated into its design is the Victorian-era train shed whose head house now contains the lively food bazaar of **Reading Terminal Market** (N. 12th St. & Arch St.; ☎215-922-2317). Performing-arts venues abound along South Broad Street; chief among them is the 1850s Baroque-style **Academy of Music** (1420 Locust St.), the winter quarters of the Philadelphia Orchestra. Art and commerce meet in the antique shops that line **Antique Row** (Pine St. between S. 9th & S. 12th Sts.). Respite from Center City's bustle can still be found in the eight acres of parkland in **Rittenhouse Square**, one of the public parks from Penn's original city plan.

### City Hall★★★

*Broad St. & JFK Blvd.* ✎*Interior rooms accessible by 12:30pm guided tour only.* ♿*(except tower)* ☎215-686-2840.
Centerpiece of downtown, this 700-room French Second Empire structure designed by John McArthur Jr. is the largest municipal building in the country. Upon its completion in 1901, the enormous structure with its solid masonry walls was almost obsolete, and in the early 20C there was talk of demolishing it. The very cost of demolition saved it, and City Hall still functions as Philadelphia's ceremonial "palace." Its 548ft tower is crowned by a statue of city founder William Penn. Below the statue, an **observation deck** provides panoramic views. Notable interior chambers include the **Mayor's Reception Room**, with its mahogany wainscoting, and **Conversation Hall**, with its plaster and aluminum-leaf ceiling.

### Masonic Temple★★

*1 N. Broad St., on north side of City Hall.* ✎*Visit by guided tour only.* ☎215-988-1900. www.pagrandlodge.org.
Considered one of Freemasonry's most magnificent temples, this Medieval Norman-style granite structure (1873) marked by spires and towers was conceived by Masonic brother James Windrim. Elaborate interior rooms—designed by George Herzog—are decorated in motifs reflecting the orders of Masonry: Moorish, Gothic, Ionic, Egyptian, Romanesque, Renaissance and Corinthian.

### Pennsylvania Academy of the Fine Arts★★

*Broad & Cherry Sts.* ♿☎215-972-7600. www.pafa.org.
Portraitist Charles Willson Peale founded the country's first art school and museum in 1805. Housed in an ornate brick and limestone Victorian structure (1876, Frank Furness and George Hewitt), the museum exhibits three centuries of artistic styles. Arranged in chronological order, galleries display works from the 18C "Grand Manner" tradition, 19C American sculpture, early-20C Modernism and post-World War II Abstract Expressionism.

### Rosenbach Museum and Library★

*2010 Delancey St.* ✎*Guided tour available.* ☎$8. ☎215-732-1600. www.rosenbach.org.
The museum occupies an 1865 town house that was once home to book dealers Philip and Abraham Rosenbach. A fine group of decorative arts complements the library's 30,000 books and 300,000 manuscripts; a prize among the latter is James Joyce's handwritten **Ulysses manuscript**★. Also of note

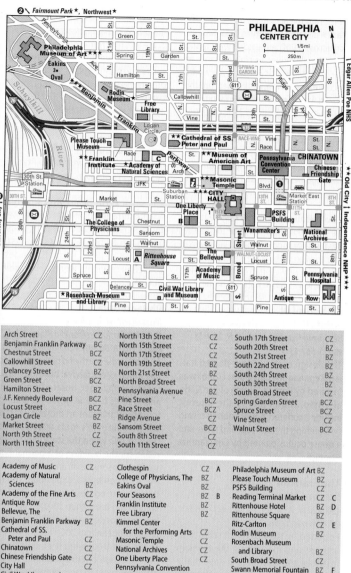

the oldest Hebrew bible in North America, which is on exhibit here.

## Benjamin Franklin Parkway★★★

Modeled after the Champs Elysées, the parkway cuts a broad swath from City Hall to the Philadelphia Museum of Art. Designed by architects Jacques Gréber and Paul Cret in 1917, this avenue encompasses Logan Circle (*southeast end*), marked by Alexander Stirling Calder's elegant **Swann Memorial Fountain**. Facing Logan Circle at 19th and Vine Streets, the **Free Library of Philadelphia** (1927, Horace Trumbauer) models the twin palaces that grace the Place de la Concorde in Paris.

Bordering the art museum, **Fairmount Park**★ became a reality in 1855. Sweeping across 8,900 acres northwest along the Schuylkill River, Fairmount ranks as one of the largest city parks in the world. Encompassed within its borders are the Beaux-Arts **Memorial Hall** (42nd St. & N. Concourse Dr.), one of 250 structures built in the park for the 1876 US Centennial Exposition; a spring-blooming **Azalea Garden** (off Kelly Dr.); and the **Horticulture Center** (N. Horticultural Dr. & Montgomery Dr.), with its serene Japanese **Pine Breeze Villa**★. One of Philadelphia's most picturesque landmarks is **Boat House Row**★ (off Kelly Dr. along the Schuylkill River north of the Azalea Garden). For more than 150 years amateur rowing clubs have headquartered in this row of Victorian cottages, which is outlined in white lights at night.

## Cathedral of Saints Peter and Paul★★

*Benjamin Franklin Pkwy. & N. 18th St.* ☎215-561-1313.
The design of this copper-domed Italian Renaissance cathedral (1846) was inspired by Rome's Church of San Carlo al Corso. Highlights of the interior include a coffered, barrel-vaulted ceiling overarching the transept and nave, and a dome oculus painted by Constantine Brumidi.

## The Franklin Institute Science Museum★★

Kids 222 N. 20th St. ✗ ♿ P ☎215-448-1200. www.fi.edu.
Founded in 1824 to teach science to artisans and mechanics, the Franklin Institute and its museum have made science entertaining. Enter the cavernous 300,000sq ft museum through the domed Benjamin Franklin National Memorial, dominated by a 122-ton likeness of a seated Franklin. Inside, three floors of exhibits treat subjects from communications and transportation to computer technology and geology.

## The Academy of Natural Sciences of Philadelphia★

Kids 1900 Benjamin Franklin Pkwy. at Logan Circle. ✗ ♿ ☎215-299-1000. www.acnatsci.org.

Dating from 1812, the Academy is one of the oldest science research institutions in the Western Hemisphere. On the first floor, the acclaimed **Discovering Dinosaurs**★ exhibit displays skeletons and details the rigors of uncovering fossils. Life-size dioramas throughout the facility showcase native animals from North America, Asia and Africa.

## Rodin Museum★

*N. 22nd St. & Benjamin Franklin Pkwy.* ♿ P ☎215-568-6026. www.rodin museum.org.
The small 1920s Beaux-Arts structure and its surrounding gardens, designed by Paul Cret and Jacques Gréber, house 124 sculptures by French artist **Auguste Rodin** (1840-1917). This is the largest collection of Rodin's works to be found outside France.

## Philadelphia Museum of Art★★★

*N. 26th & Benjamin Franklin Pkwy.* ✗ ♿ ☎215-763-8100. www.philamuseum.org
Anchoring the north end of the parkway, this stately Greek Revival building (1928, C. Clark Zantzinger, Horace Trumbauer and Charles L. Borie, Jr.) ranks among the most significant art museums in the US. The museum's roots trace back to the late 19C, when the state legislature called for the building of a permanent structure to serve as an art gallery during the 1876 Centennial Exposition. Today the museum houses a superb collection comprising more than 300,000 objects in four major departments: Asian, American, European and 20C.
In the first-floor wing is an outstanding collection of **European Art 1850-1900**★★, ranging from pieces by Courbet and Whistler to works by Cézanne (*The Large Bathers*, 1905). The adjoining section of **20C Art** houses an extensive collection of Cubist, Expressionist and Surrealist works. Noteworthy 19C Philadelphia artist Thomas Eakins figures prominently in the **American Art** wing, along with Colonial silver, Shaker furniture, and Pennsylvania-German decorative arts.
Take the **Great Stair Hall** to the second floor, which is devoted to European art. Earliest examples are found in **Euro-**

Greater Philadelphia Tourism Marketing Corporation

*Philadelphia Museum of Art*

**ean Art 1100-1500**★, housing a rare roup of architectural details from honasteries and chapels and a host of eligious paintings and sculpture. The Renaissance is represented in **European Art 1500-1850**, which includes e-created period rooms from French, nglish and Dutch homes. The **Asian Art**★★ wing exhibits exquisite Thai uddhist pieces and a stone **temple all** from India. Chinese and Japanese rt includes a 17C Chinese nobleman's **eception hall** and an early-20C **Japanese ceremonial teahouse**.

## Philadelphia Zoo★

3400 W. Girard Ave. ✕ ♿ 🅿 ☎215-43-1100. www.phillyzoo.org.
overing 42 acres, this is the oldest zoo 1859) in the country. Modeled on a Victorian pleasure garden, the grounds feature paths that ramble past more than ,700 animals from around the globe. Be ure to see the rare **snow leopards**, the rimate House, and some of the world's host endangered species in the Rare Animal Conservation Center.

## Historic Houses★

or house information or special tours, all ☎215-684-7926.
n the 18C and early 19C, well-heeled Philadelphians built rural retreats on he bluffs above the Schuylkill River.

Today the seven elegant homes open to the public provide fine examples of domestic period architecture. Among them is the oldest, 1746 **Cedar Grove**★, a fieldstone farmhouse *(off Lansdowne Dr.)*; the 18C Neoclassical gem **Lemon Hill**★ *(off Kelly Dr.)*; elegant **Mount Pleasant**★ *(off Fountain Green Dr.)* with its elaborate interior woodwork; and the 1756 late-Georgian-style **Woodford**a *(off Dauphin St.)*, noted for its fine **Colonial furnishings**.

## Excursions

### The Barnes Foundation★★

*5mi from Center City in Merion at 300 N. Latch's Lane. Advance reservations required.* ☜$10. ♿☎610-667-0290.
Doctor, businessman and art connoisseur, **Dr. Albert C. Barnes** (1872-1951) believed all people were entitled to education and an appreciation of fine arts, and to that end he established the Barnes Foundation in 1922. Several years later he commissioned architect Paul Cret to design an Italianate gallery to house his collection. Today more than 1,100 paintings are exhibited here, notably a wealth of **Impressionist and Post-impressionist works**★★, including 180 pieces by Renoir, 59 by Cézanne and 60 by Matisse.

## Valley Forge National Historical Park★★

*20mi northwest of Center City via I-76 West. Take Exit 26B and continue 1.5mi in King of Prussia, PA. &P ☎610-783-1077. www.nps.gov/vafo.*

Initiated into the national park system for the US Bicentennial, the 3,620-acre park preserves the fields and ridges where George Washington's exhausted and poorly provisioned 12,000-man Continental Army camped from December 19, 1777, to June 19, 1778. Begin at the **visitor center** to view the 18min film dramatizing the travails of Washington's men, and to see artifacts used by the encamped army. Then take the 10mi self-guided **driving tour**★ past earthworks and historic stone buildings, including **Washington's Headquarters**, where George and his wife, Martha, spent that stark winter.

## Bucks County★★

*Northeast of Philadelphia bordering the Delaware River.* Named for William Penn's birthplace of Buckinghamshire, England, Bucks County occupies 625 square acres beyond Philadelphia's northern border. With the prosperity that infused the new country after independence, the **Delaware Canal** was built in 1832, extending 60mi between Bristol and Easton. Although boats no longer "lock through," the canal, the towpath that runs along its length still attracts bikers and hikers. You can best experience the region's rural ambience by driving along lovely **River Road**★. Be sure to spend some time relaxing in the fine inns and restaurants of such towns as **Doylestown**★ and **New Hope**★, or hunting for treasures in the trove of antique shops that line Route 202.

## Washington Crossing Historic Park★★

*On Rte. 32 South between New Hope an[d] Yardley. ➤Visit building interiors b[y] guided tour only. &P ☎215-493-4076*

In two separate parcels this park pre[-] serves sites connected with Georg[e] Washington's famous crossing of th[e] Delaware River in the winter of 177[7] to launch a surprise attack on Britain['s] Hessian forces encamped across th[e] river in Trenton, New Jersey. The **Lowe[r] Park** *(7mi south of New Hope)* contain[s] the visitor center and a row of restore[d] buildings from the 18C ferry-crossin[g] town of Taylorsville. The **Upper Par[k]** *(3.5mi north of visitor center)* preserve[s] the 1702 fieldstone house, called th[e] Thompson-Neely House, that serve[d] as the Continental commander's head[-] quarters during December 1776.

## Pennsbury Manor★★

*400 Pennsbury Memorial Rd., via US-[1] or US-13 to Tyburn Rd. ☎$5. ☎215-946[-] 0400. www.pennsburymanor.com.*

The 43-acre site on the Delaware Rive[r] 26mi north of Philadelphia was th[e] personal summer estate of Pennsylva[-] nia's founder, William Penn. The statel[y] Georgian **manor house**★★ *(➤vis[it] by guided tour only)* that stands toda[y] is a re-creation of the manse. Pen[n] began building in 1683; its brick façad[e] overlooks formal English gardens an[d] the river beyond. Filled with fine 17[C] and 18C English and Dutch furnish[-] ings—including several Penn famil[y] pieces—the interior rooms illustrat[e] Penn's upper-class social status, whic[h] belied his Quaker beliefs.

# BRANDYWINE VALLEY★★

MICHELIN MAP 583 T 8
EASTERN STANDARD TIME

The narrow Brandywine Creek (locally known as the Brandywine River) creates in its wake a valley so charming that it has spurred industrialists to build elaborate mansions and artists to immortalize its verdant countryside on canvas. Situated between the metropolises of Philadelphia and Wilmington, Delaware, the Brandywine Valley retains a rural, yet tony, atmosphere.

**Information:** ☎610-719-1730. 800-228-9933. www.brandywinevalley.com.
**Orient Yourself:** The valley weaves it way through Chester County, Pennsylvania, and into Delaware.
**Don't Miss:** An American decorative arts gem at the Winterthur Museum.

## A Bit of History

In the late 17C, the Lenni Lenape Indians greeted Francis Chadsey, one of the first European settlers in this crossroads community. His son, John Chads, a farmer and ferryman, is considered the founder of the village of **Chadds Ford** in the heart of the valley, noted today for its craft shops and winery.

The area's rolling hills saw action during the Revolutionary War when General Howe outmaneuvered George Washington's Patriot forces here in September 1777. Today **Brandywine Battlefield Park** (on US-1 just east of the village of Chadds Ford; ⊜$5; ✗ ☐☐ ☎610-459-3342) preserves the battlefield and two Quaker farmhouses used during the fighting as headquarters for the Marquis de Lafayette and General Washington.

Realizing the river's potential as a source of hydroelectric power, French immigrant **Eleuthère Irénée (E.I.) du Pont** established a black-powder mill here on the banks of the Brandywine in the early 19C. Du Pont's mill community, called Hagley, became one of the world's largest manufacturers of black powder and begot a family of philanthropists who immeasurably enriched the region.

## Sights

### Longwood Gardens★★★

Located off US-1 just west of Rte. 52 in Kennett Square, PA. ✗ ☐☐ ☎610-388-1000. www.longwoodgardens.org.

**Pierre S. du Pont** (1870-1954), great-grandson of E.I. du Pont, created this world-renowned 1,050-acre horticultural masterpiece despite a demanding career as chairman of the board of both Du Pont and General Motors. After purchasing the initial 200-acre core in 1906, Du Pont added significantly to the property over the next 30 years.

As you enter the garden, follow signs for the **Peirce-du Pont House★**, the 1730 brick farmhouse built by Quakers Joshua and Samuel Peirce and later used by du Pont as a country home. A film and exhibits here explain du Pont's life and his development of the gardens. Behind

Longwood Gardens

Greater Philadelphia Tourism Marketing Corporation

the house, a path leads through the original arboretum to the **Italian Water Garden**★★. The enormous Beaux-Arts **Conservatory**★★★ to the northwest houses spectacular floral plantings that are changed seasonally. Below the conservatory is the **Main Fountain Garden**, where 380 fountainheads, colored lights and music create a **Festival of Fountains**★★ on summer evenings.

### Winterthur Museum★★★

*On Rte. 52, 5 mi south of US-1, in Winterthur, DE.* ◤*Visit of mansion by guided tour only; special-interest tours are available.* ◉*$20.* ✗ ♿ 🅿 ☎*800-448-3883. www.winterthur.org.*

A premier showcase of American decorative arts, the 1,000-acre former home of collector **Henry Francis du Pont** (1880-1969) occupies a green swale on the outskirts of Wilmington, Delaware. Built in the 1830s, the original three-story Greek Revival structure forms the core of the current mansion. The property now includes the du Pont mansion, 60 acres of **gardens**★, a research library and a gift shop.

Tours of **Winterthur** mansion take in different combinations of the 175 re-created **period rooms**★★★ that showcase du Pont's unsurpassed **decorative-arts collection**★★★. Consisting of more than 89,000 objects, the collection represents the best in American porcelain, furniture, pewter and silver, and portraiture from 1640 to 1860. A mansion addition, the **Galleries** feature the interactive exhibit "**Perspectives on the Decorative Arts in Early America**"★ *(1st floor)*, and Winterthur's **furniture study collection**★★ *(2nd floor)*. An audio iPod tour is also available.

### Brandywine River Museum★★

*On US-1, just south of intersection with Rte. 100 in Chadds Ford, PA.* ◉*$8.* ✗ ♿ 🅿 ☎*610-388-2700. www.brandywinemuseum.org.*

Set on the banks of the Brandywine River, this Civil War-era gristmill has been converted into a three-story museum. Renowned for its collections of paintings by illustrator **Newell Convers (N.C.) Wyeth** (1882-1945), his son **Andrew** (b. 1917) and Andrew's son **Jamie** (b. 1946), the museum also features work by Howard Pyle, Maxfield Parrish, Charles Dana Gibson and Rockwell Kent in the first-floor **Brandywine Heritage Galleries**★. The third floor houses the **Andrew Wyeth Gallery**★★, a collection of compelling paintings that illustrate his career beginning in 1938. Tours of **N.C. Wyeth's studio**, filled with his furniture and easels, depart from the museum.

### Hagley Museum★★

*On Rte. 141 between Rtes. 100 & US-202 in Wilmington, DE.* 🕐*Open daily 9am– 4:30pm.* ◉*$11.* ✗ 🅿 ☎*302-658-2400. www.hagley.lib.de.us.*

Tucked into the forested banks of the Brandywine River, the old granite buildings of this early-19C factory were part of a mill complex that became the largest producer of black gun powder in the world. Founded in 1802 by French immigrant and chemist **Eleuthère Irénée (E.I.) du Pont** (1771-1834), Hagley gave rise to the Du Pont Company, an industrial behemoth that still thrives today. Begin at the orientation center housed in the 1814 Henry Clay Mill. From here you can catch a tram to tour the grounds *(cars are not permitted past the orientation center)*, where the day-to-day activities of factory workers are interpreted through a host of historic mills, waterwheels and a machine shop. Crowning a hilltop upstream from the factory stands the stately Georgian **Eleutherian Mills**★, home to E.I. du Pont and his descendants resided from 1803 to 1890, when a powder explosion forced an evacuation of the premises.

# GETTYSBURG★★★

MICHELIN MAP 583 S 8
EASTERN STANDARD TIME
POPULATION 8,103

olling farmland and forest surrounding this crossroads town witnessed the vorst carnage of the Civil War in July 1863—four months later, one of the greatst oratories in the nation's history.

- **Information:** ☎717-334-1124, ext. 431; www.nps.gov/gett.
- **Don't Miss:** The permanent home of President Dwight D. and Mamie Eisenhower, which served as their second White House.
- **Also See:** PHILADELPHIA, WASHINGTON, DC

## A Bit of History

apitalizing on recent losses suffered by nion forces in the spring of 1863, **Robrt E. Lee** (1807-70), commander of the onfederate Army of Northern Virginia, nade a strategic decision to invade the lorth, hoping to capture the Pennsylvania state capital at Harrisburg. To counr Lee, Union commander Maj. Gen. Joe looker moved his Army of the Potomac orth. Neither general anticipated the mpact of the battle that began on that rizzly July 1 morning. Just before the attle caught fire, Hooker was replaced y Maj. Gen. George Meade, who would ommand the 93,000 Union troops gainst the 75,000 Confederates during the three-day conflagration.

At the end of the first day of fighting, the Confederates had the upper hand. By July 3, however, the tide of the battle had turned, and Lee realized that desperate action was necessary to regain the strategic high ground now held by the Union soldiers. That afternoon, 12,000 Confederates led by Gen. George Pickett attacked the Union center on Cemetery Ridge. As the Rebels surged across the open field, they were mowed down by Union fire. **Pickett's Charge** cost the Confederacy 6,000 men. The following day, Lee ordered his troops to retreat; it was the beginning of the end of the Southern cause.

In all, the Battle of Gettysburg claimed some 27,000 Confederate and 24,000 Union casualties and left the town and surrounding countryside in shambles.

©Photo Disc, Inc

Gettysburg National Military Park

## The Gettysburg Address

President **Abraham Lincoln** delivered the following address at the dedication of the National Cemetery in Gettysburg on November 19, 1863. Time has proved these words to be some of the most revered in American history.

"Four score and seven years ago our fathers brought forth, upon this continent, a new nation, conceived in Liberty, and dedicated to the proposition that all men are created equal.

Now we are engaged in a great civil war, testing whether that nation, or any nation so conceived, and so dedicated, can long endure. We are met here on a great battlefield of that war. We have come to dedicate a portion of it as a final resting place for those who here gave their lives that that nation might live. It is altogether fitting and proper that we should do this. But in a larger sense, we can not dedicate—we can not consecrate—we can not hallow this ground. The brave men, living and dead, who struggled here, have consecrated it far above our poor power to add or detract. The world will little note, nor long remember, what we say here, but can never forget what they did here. It is for us, the living, rather to be dedicated here to the unfinished work which they have, thus far, so nobly carried on. It is rather for us to be here dedicated to the great task remaining before us—that from these honored dead we take increased devotion to that cause for which they here gave the last full measure of devotion—that we here highly resolve that these dead shall not have died in vain; that this nation shall have a new birth of freedom; and that this government of the people, by the people, for the people, shall not perish from the earth."

Two local lawyers realized the need to preserve the battlefield and create a national cemetery to give the dead proper recognition. At the dedication on November 19, 1863, President Abraham Lincoln was invited to "add a few appropriate remarks" to Edward Everett's two-hour oration. Lincoln's two-minute speech met with weak applause at the time, but his **Gettysburg Address** (see infobox above) is considered one of the nation's most inspirational statements to this day.

## Gettysburg National Military Park★★★

Open daily 6am–7pm. 717-334-1124. www.nps.gov/gett.

Preserving the landscape where the Battle of Gettysburg erupted in 1863, this 5,900-acre park was declared a National Military Park by Congress in 1895. The visitors' center, expanded in 2008, displays portions of the Rosensteels' collection of 4,000 artifacts, including uniforms and firearms, in the **Gettysburg Museum of the Civil War**★★. Also in the visitor center, a 750sq ft Electric Map presentation traces the movement of troops during the battle.

The visitors' center also houses the circular concrete **Cyclorama Center, which** displays the 360ft-by-26ft circular **painting**★★ titled *Pickett's Charge*. Completed in 1884 by French artist Paul Philippoteaux, the painting is the focus of the **Cyclorama Program**★, a narrated sound and light show that traces the battle's action while the painting revolves.

### National Cemetery★★

*Across Taneytown Rd. from the visitor center.*

More than 3,500 Union casualties are interred in this 17-acre plot where President Lincoln delivered his famous Gettysburg Address in November 1863. Graves form concentric semicircles around the towering **Soldiers' National Monument**.

### Driving Tour★★★

*18mi; allow 2hrs. Maps available at visitor center, where tour begins.*

Trace the steps of Civil War soldiers along this self-guided driving tour, which recount the events of the three-day battle in chronological order. The first stop is McPherson Ridge, where the fighting began. Nearby the **Eternal Light Peace Memorial** (N Confederate Ave.) commemorates the Union dead. Continue past such well nown areas of action as **Big Round Top**; e **Wheatfield**, where heavy fighting ft more than 4,000 soldiers dead and ounded; and the **High Water Mark**, round held by the Union center that pulsed Pickett's men. Conclude your ur at the **East Cavalry Battlefield ite** (off US-30, 4mi northeast of visitor nter) where Lee's cavalry commander, en. "Jeb" Stuart withdrew in defeat. hroughout the battlefield stand more an 1,300 monuments memorializing oldiers from the North and the South.

## isenhower National istoric Site★★

ccess via shuttle bus from Gettysburg ational Military Park visitor center. Open daily 6am–7pm. ♿ ☎717-338-114 ext. 10. www.nps.gov/eise.

et on 690 acres of rolling pastureland, is farm was the permanent home

of President **Dwight D. Eisenhower** (1890-1969) and his wife, Mamie. When Eisenhower became the 34th president of the US in 1953, the Pennsylvania farm served as a second White House, where he and Mamie entertained such dignitaries as Nikita Khrushchev and Charles de Gaulle. After two terms as president, Eisenhower retired here until he died at the age of 78. Mamie lived at the farm until her death ten years later.

After a short orientation given by park service personnel, a self-guided tour leads visitors through the home, which is decorated exactly as it was during the Eisenhowers' tenure here. After the tour, stroll around the grounds for a look at the barns, outbuildings and reception center, where you can watch a short video about Eisenhower's career.

# PENNSYLVANIA DUTCH COUNTRY★★★

MICHELIN MAP 583 S 7, 8
EASTERN STANDARD TIME
POPULATION 422,822 (LANCASTER COUNTY)

et amid rolling farmlands, Pennsylvania Dutch Country is centered in Lancaster ounty. Claiming the world's largest population of **Mennonites** and the second-rgest community (after Holmes County, Ohio) of **Amish**, Lancaster County eckons visitors to experience a culture seemingly forgotten by the press of nodern life. Here a flourishing cottage industry of handmade quilts and crafts, s well as the friendly ambience of family-style restaurants lure motorists to ause and experience a simpler time.

**Information:** ☎717-299-8901. www.padutchcountry.com
**Parking:** Because horse-drawn buggies are the vehicle of choice, you may have to drive slower than you normally do.
**Don't Miss:** The quaint way of life of Amish country.
**Also See:** BALTIMORE, PHILADELPHIA, WASHINGTON, DC.

## A Bit of History

eginning in the early 1700s, Protestant roups, including Pietists, Quakers, rethren and Moravians, emigrated from witzerland and the Rhineland (now outhern Germany) seeking religious reedom in Pennsylvania. They found in the fertile piedmont in and around

present-day Lancaster County. Swiss Mennonites established the first permanent colony in Pennsylvania around 1700; German Mennonites followed. The sect that became known as the **Amish** began arriving in the 1720s.

The Amish and Mennonites grew out of the Anabaptist movement (whose members believe in adult baptism) that arose

*Amish School*

during the Reformation in 16C Europe. Followers of Menno Simons were called Mennonites; those who went with bishop **Jakob Amman** when he split with the Mennonites in 1693 became known as the Amish. Amman believed the Mennonites were not strict enough in their rule regarding excommunication; transgressors, he held, should be shunned in social and business interactions, as well as in religious ones.

Lancaster County is home to the oldest group of Old Order Amish in the US, numbering 16,000-18,000 people. The most conservative Amish sect, Old Order followers eschew telephones, electricity and motorized vehicles. (Yet teenagers can drive and own cars since they do not become members of the church until they join freely as adults.) All Amish embrace values that stress family and community, humility and separation from the world. Men, women and children dress simply in plain, solid-color fabrics. Women wear long dresses, black bonnets and no makeup. Men dress in trousers with suspenders and hats of straw or felt. Married men grow beards (mustaches are considered unsanitary and martial). Amish children attend school up to eighth grade; a more formal education is not considered necessary for their agrarian lifestyle. Today many Amish still speak a dialect that combines German and English; called Pennsylvania Dutch, the name evolved as a corruption of *Deutsch* ("German").

# Lancaster★★

Seat of Lancaster County, this colonial burg *(69mi west of Philadelphia on US-30)* anchors one of the richest farming area in the country. Main roads lead like spoke on a wheel into the heart of Lancaste market center for farmers and magnet fc tourists. From its modest beginnings i 1721, the town of Lancaster grew to serv as the state capital from 1777 to 1778 an again from 1799 to 1812.

Today visitors to the area enjoy its his toric heritage as well as its bucolic charm Three centuries of architecture are evi dent from the downtown's central **Pen Square** *(King & Queen Sts.):* the 1797 Ol City Hall, the 1889 Central Market and th 12-story Griest building (1924). Soarin 195ft, the Colonial tower and steeple c the 1761 **Trinity Lutheran Church★** *(3 S. Duke St.;* 717-397-2734) are visibl from all over town.

## Central Market★

*Northwest corner of Penn Square.* 717-291-4723.

Long heralded for its architecture, Cer tral Market's 1889 Romanesque-styl brick structure now houses more tha 60 vendors who ply a brisk trade i quilts, shoofly pie (filled with molasse and brown sugar), sausages, peppe cheeses and other local specialties.

## Heritage Center Museum of Lancaster County★

*Penn Square.* Open daily 9am–5pm 717-299-6440. www.lancasterheri age.com.

Completed in 1797, the Georgian-styl Old City Hall houses a collection of Penn sylvania folk arts, furniture and silve Changing exhibits celebrate the county long-standing tradition of fine craftsman

*phrata Cloister*

...hip as illustrated by needlework, quilts nd fraktur, an illuminated script.

### lans Herr House★★

*849 Hans Herr Dr.* Open daily 9am– om. Closed Sun. ☎717-464-4438. *ww.hansherr.org.*

...ed by Hans Herr, the county's first white ettlers were a group of 27 Mennonites scaping religious persecution in Ger-any in the early 18C. In 1719 Herr's son hristian built this two-story Medieval erman-style house, which ranks as the ldest in the county. Inside the restored tone house, rooms are furnished with imple pre-1750 pieces.

### andis Valley Museum★

*451 Kissel Hill Rd.* Open Mon-Sat 9am– om, Sun 12pm–5pm. ☎717-569- 401. *www.landisvalleymuseum.org.*

...his 16-acre living-history village ncludes some 20 restored or re-created uildings that accurately interpret 18C nd 19C Pennsylvania German rural life. raftspeople demonstrate trades such s shoemaking, quilting and weaving.

### Wheatland★★

*120 Marietta Ave.* $7. ☎717-392- 721. *www.wheatland.org.* Built in 1828 for Lancaster lawyer and anker William Jenkins, this Federal-style mansion was home to **James Buchanan** 1791-1868)—15th US president and the nly one from Pennsylvania—from 1848 until his death. Buchanan bought the estate while serving secretary of State under President James Polk. Furnishings reflect Buchanan's tenure as head of state,

and a number of the decorative pieces were gifts from foreign dignitaries.

## Lancaster County★★★

An hour west of Philadelphia, Lancaster County's landscape paints a pastoral tableau of market towns and patchwork fields. In the tiny burgs of Bird-in-Hand, Ephrata or Intercourse, you'll get a taste of the Amish culture and lifestyle through a variety of museums, historic villages, quilt shops and the like. Though the main roads are often clogged with traffic, par-ticularly on summer weekends, visitors who venture off the beaten path may be rewarded with rare glimpses of an Amish farmer plowing his fields with a team of six, or Amish children riding their home-made scooters along the roadside. Stop at some of the area's plentiful **farmers' markets** to sample the bountiful fresh local produce, and regional treats such as shoofly pie.

### Ephrata Cloister★★★

*632 W. Main St., Ephrata.* Visit of buildings by guided tour only. $7. ☎717-733-6600. *www.ephrat cloiser.org.* One of the oldest religious communi-ties in the country flourished in the northeast corner of the county from 1732 until 1813 under the leadership of German Pietist **Conrad Beissel** (1691-1768). Practicing Beissel's doctrine of hard work and self-denial, celibate members—known as brothers and sisters—worked 18 hours a day and slept on narrow wooden benches. The community ran one of the country's first printing presses, produced more than 1,000 hymns and made a fine art of the illuminated script called Frakturschriften. After enjoying prominence in the mid-18C, the cloister declined steadily following Beissel's death.Tours include a 15min introductory video and visits to the austere **Saal**, or meetinghouse (1741), used for worship services. Next to it, the **Saron** (1743) housed the sisters and included a kitchen, a workroom and sleeping cells on each of three floors. Low doorways forced members to stoop in humility and reminded them of the narrow way to heaven.

**Bird-in-Hand**★This village on Route 340 east of Lancaster drew its name from a local 18C tavern. For a closer look at Amish culture, take in the **Amish F/X Experience Theater**★ at the **Plain & Fancy Farm** (3121 Old Philadelphia Pike/Rte. 340; ✖ ♿ 🅿 ☎717-768-4400). The theater screens a 40 min multimedia show, *Jacob's Choice*, which dramatizes an Amish youth's struggle to stay true to his Amish ways.

### Intercourse★

This quaint village, east of Bird-in-Hand on Route 340 in the heart of Amish farmland, draws visitors to its antique and quilt shops and locals to its feed and hardware stores. On the second floor of the Old Country Store, the **Quilt Museum**★ (3510 Old Philadelphia Pike; 🅿 ☎717-768-7171) displays pre-1940 quilted works of art.

### Lititz★

*North of Lancaster at the intersection o Rtes. 501 and 722.*

This small industrial town was founded in 1756 by **Moravians**, a Protestan sect from Moravia and Bohemia (in the present-day Czech Republic), whose persecuted members escaped to southeastern Pennsylvania in 1741. Named for the barony in Bohemia where the Moravian church originated in the 15C, Lititz came under the rule of the Moravian church fo nearly a century. The town's **Main Street** is lined with specialty shops, restaurants and 18C-19C architecture, including the 1787 **Moravian Church**★, which dominates peaceful **Church Square** (Main St between Cedar & Locust Sts.).

### Strasburg★

*Southeast of Lancaster at the intersection of Rtes. 896 and 741.*

Linking York and Philadelphia since 1793, Strasburg was first settled by French Huguenots and evolved into a German immigrant community. Today the town is noted for its railroad attractions, including the **Strasburg Rail Road** (on Rte. 741, 1mi east of Rte. 896; ✖ ♿ 🅿 ☎717-687-7522), a coal-fired locomotive that powers trips through the countryside; and the **Railroad Museum of Pennsylvania**★ [Kids] (across Rte. 741 from the Strasburg Rail Road; ♿ 🅿 ☎717-687-8628), filled with a host of historic train cars, animated by depot noises and videos.

# SOUTHERN NEW JERSEY★

MICHELIN MAP 583 T 8    EASTERN STANDARD TIME

Lenni Lenape tribes introduced pottery and farming here a millennium ago, but it was Quaker **John Fenwick** who established the first permanent English-speaking settlement in the Delaware Valley in 1675. From the bright lights of coastal Atlantic City to the vegetable farms of the fertile Delaware River Valley, southern New Jersey offers a range of natural and cultural attractions.

🛈 **Information:** ☎609-777-0885 or www.state.nj.us.travel
👓 **Don't Miss:** Victorian charm in Cape May.

## A Bit of History

By the 1770s strife with England was fomenting talk of war. Southern New Jersey proved logistically critical during the Revolution and saw the action o two key battles at **Trenton**—today New Jersey's state capital—and Princeton

## Atlantic City

Founded as a resort in the 1820s by Dr. Jonathan Pitney to promote the sea's healing benefits, **Atlantic City★** has defined American recreation for over a century and a half. Hotel proprietor Jacob Keim and railroad executive Alex Boardman opened the first boardwalk to keep sand out of the hotel lobbies. By 1900 the resort had become an entertainment mecca with diversions including amusement parks, circus stunts and big band music. The first **Miss America** was crowned in Atlantic City in 1921, and the pageant is still held here each year. Entertainment remains the city's charter in the form of 11 glitzy casino resorts on or near the 4.5mi-long **Boardwalk★**. *Contact the Atlantic City Convention & Visitors Authority, 2314 Pacific Ave., Atlantic City, NJ,* ☎609-348-7100. www.atlanticcitynj.com.

itting atop a 17-trillion-gallon-aquifer, he 1.4 million acres of sandy, semi-forsted land comprising the **Pine Barens★** provided bog iron that was used the manufacture of the Revolutionary var's munitions. One of the first bogon furnaces in the Pine Barrens was onstructed at **Batsto Village★★** *(on te. 542, in Wharton State Forest;* ♿ 🅿 ☎609-561-0024)*, which today provides glimpse of an intact 19C rural industrial ettlement. The late 19C saw the advent f blueberry and cranberry farming; the atter is still a flourishing industry. Today outhern New Jersey suggests the rural harms of colonial life and early-19C setement while providing a restful retreat or city dwellers.

## ape May★★

he location of this lovely seaside town, ituated at the southern tip of New Jerey bordered by the Atlantic Ocean on he east side and the Delaware Bay on he west, is what first lured New England fishermen to its shores in the 1680s. hat same seaside location, which later urned Cape May into a popular 19C athing resort, is what continues to draw vacationers today.

series of 19C fires destroyed many early buildings, and Cape May was rebuilt on smaller scale, forsaking giant hotels for ffordable cottages. Homes built at the urn of the 20C favored the High Victoian style, in vogue at the time.

Designated a National Historic Landmark n 1976, Cape May has revived as a tourst mecca, attracting visitors with its fine Victorian architecture, sandy beaches

and a full calendar of events: the May-June **Cape May Music Festival**; April's **Spring Festival**; and **Victorian Week** in October. *For information on these and other local events, contact the Chamber of Commerce of Greater Cape May,* ☎609-884-5508, www.capemaychamber.com.

### Downtown★★

Cape May's Victorian charm is concentrated in the downtown area, between Congress and Franklin Streets and Beach Avenue and Lafayette Street, and is best explored on foot. You can find detailed information and walking-tour maps at the **Welcome Center**, housed in a restored church *(405 Lafayette St.;* ☎609-884-9562) one block north of Washington Street Mall.

For a sampling of Cape May's most noteworthy architecture, stroll along **Hughes Street★**; **Columbia Avenue★**, site of the **Chalfonte Hotel** (1876), an American Bracketed Villa and Cape May's oldest operating hotel; and colorful **Jackson Street★**. Take the time to drink in the fanciful ornamentation such as fish-scale shingles and cut-out balustrades that adorn the cottages in this historic district.

### Physick Estate★★

*1048 Washington St.* ✎ *Visit by guided tour only.* 🅿 ☎609-884-5404.
Noted Philadelphia architect **Frank Furness** designed this mansion (1878) for Dr. Emlen Physick Jr. An Academy of Fine Arts design, the interior features a square staircase in the Victorian foyer. Walls throughout the house are trimmed in reeded oak and covered with

*Victorian Architecture, Cape May*

lincrusta, a combination of paper and linseed oil.

### Cape May Lighthouse★

*3mi south of Cape May in Cape May Point State Park.* 🅿 ☎609-884-5404. *www.beachcomber.com.*

Dating from 1859, the lighthouse still guards the access to Philadelphia via the Delaware River. Climb the 199 steps to view exhibits about the lighthouse and admire the vistas from each landing.

### Historic Cold Spring Village★★

*On US-9, 3mi north of Cape May.* 🞔$8. ✗🅿 ☎609-898-2300.

This outdoor living-history museum consists of more than 25 restored 19C buildings. The 1894 **Welcome Center** provides an orientation video on 19C life. Demonstrations of period crafts are among the many planned events on this 20-acre wooded site.

## Princeton University★★

Sheltered by lush, rolling countryside, Princeton University moved to its present site in 1756. This prestigious Ivy League university was founded in 1746 by a group of Presbyterian ministers as the College of New Jersey. Since then, the student body—which claims US presidents James Madison and Woodrow Wilson as alumni—has grown to 4,500 undergraduate students.

Princeton's shady, 600-acre campus *(visitor assistance and maps available at the First Campus Center welcome desk*, ☎609-258-1766) comprises over 13 buildings in a variety of styles. Built in 1756, Neoclassical **Nassau Hall★** boasts a paneled **Faculty Room★** modeled on the House of Commons. Behind Nassau Hall, the Georgian quadrangle originally included East College (now demolished) and West College, both built in 1836. In the early 20C, noted Gothicist Ralph Adams Cram crafted a new campus plan, including his triumphant **University Chapel★** (1928), inspired by King's College in Cambridge, England.

Bordering the university to the northwest, **Nassau Street** is the main thoroughfare of the surrounding town of **Princeton★**. Here Colonial and Federal buildings dominate the modest downtown along with Tudor Revival structures.

### Princeton University Art Museum★★

*Off Nassau St. in the center of the Princeton campus. Free.* ☎609-258-3788.

Started in 1882 to collect objects for teaching, the museum now houses a collection of considerable range and diversity. Among the highlights are the **American Painting and Sculpture gallery**, including works by Augustus Saint-Gaudens and Frederic Remington; a substantial group of ancient Greek ceramics; the **Roman gallery**, with its sepulchral friezes; the **Asian galleries**, which trace four millennia of culture through bronzes, prints and calligraphy; and the European Art galleries, which feature a **Medieval room**.

# PITTSBURGH AND SOUTHERN ALLEGHENIES

Defined on the west by the Ohio border and on the east by the Allegheny Mountains, this region of Pennsylvania is a fascinating intersection of natural beauty, natural resources and historic destiny. The southern Alleghenies and their rolling western foothills, the Laurel Highlands, are lush forested hills cut by swift-running mountain streams and covered with wild mountain laurel and delicate trillium. The mountains descend gradually toward Pittsburgh, where the Allegheny and Monongahela rivers join to form the Ohio River. In 1753 a 21-year-old George Washington scouted the future site of Pittsburgh, knowing the strategic importance of this tiny triangle of land for the westward expansion of the British colonies. The French and Indian War (1754-63) secured the land for the British, and Pittsburgh became a launching pad for thousands of pioneers who had set their sights on the fertile lands to the west.

During the early 19C, this region saw Conestoga wagon trails replaced with the nation's first National Road; in 1834 the **Main Line canal** system—a series of canals linked by portage railroads to haul canal boats over the mountains—was established as a transportation route between Philadelphia and Pittsburgh. Twenty years later, this system was supplanted by the **Pennsylvania Railroad**, which cut the travel time

Pittsburgh and Southern Alleghenies

*Pittsburgh*

across Pennsylvania from 5 days to 12 hours.

By the mid-19C, the settlers began to profit from the rich local deposits of coal, oil and limestone, which formed the basis for Pittsburgh's legendary iron, steel and glass works. Supported by immigrant labor, these industries set the tone for the area's great productivity. Today, the region continues to prosper with a mix of manufacturing, high-tech industries and tourism, and its major city, Pittsburgh, has maintained its high-achiever image with a spruced-up modern skyline.

History buffs will enjoy exploring the wealth of historic sites here, while skiers and other outdoor enthusiasts will find a wide range of recreational activities. Hikers can attack Pennsylvania's highest point, 3,213ft **Mt. Davis**, and white-water rafters can pit their skills against the challenging rapids of the Youghiogheny River. Nature lovers will appreciate a drive along the mountains' scenic back roads—especially in the fall, when the foliage is stunning.

## Address Book

*For coin ranges, see the Legend on the cover flap.*

### WHERE TO STAY

**$$$ Omni William Penn** – *530 William Penn Pl., Pittsburgh, PA.* ✗ ♿ 🅿 ☎*412-281-7100. www.omniwilliampenn.com. 596 rooms.* Modeled after France's Fontainebleau, the lobby of this downtown historic landmark (1916) features ornate molded ceilings and arched doorways with brass accents. Oversized accommodations have traditional cherry furnishings and framed botanical prints. The Grand Ballroom *(2nd floor)* boasts 120-year-old crystalchandeliers made of 7,000 pieces of Baccarat crystal.

**$$ The Inn at Georgian Place** – *800 Georgian Place Dr., Somerset, PA.* ✗ 🅿 ☎*814-443-1043. www.theinnatgeorgianplace.com. 11 rooms.* You'll think you've returned to the Gilded Age as you approach the circular driveway to this 1915 mansion, 30mi north of Fallingwater. The oak paneling, marble floors and gold-leaf chandeliers are original to the house. Rooms are done in rich jewel tones and period reproductions that include brass beds and wicker depicting the Georgian period.

### WHERE TO EAT

**$$ Church Brew Works** – *3525 Liberty Ave., Pittsburgh, PA.* ☎*412-688-8200.* **American.** A restored early-20C church is the setting for the city's hottest beer hall, where scaled-down versions of the old pews serve as banquettes, and copper beer tanks stand at the former altar. The menu ranges from pierogi to buffalo-wild mushroom meatloaf with garlic mashed potatoes.

**$$ Grand Concourse** – *Station Square, Pittsburgh, PA.* ☎*412-261-1717.* **American.** Across the Smithfield Street Bridge from downtown on the South Side, the 19C Pittsburgh & Lake Erie Railroad station's former waiting room has been transformed into an elegant restaurant that seats 500 people. Barrel-vaulted ceilings with stained-glass panels and wrought-iron dragon light fixtures are highlights of the main dining room. Locals crave traditional favorites like spinach-and-crab-stuffed salmon, and garlicky broiled shrimp.

**$$ Pine Grill Restaurant** – *800 N. Center Ave., Somerset, PA.* ☎*814-445-2102.* Locals trust that specials, emerging from the glass-enclosed kitchen will be terrific. But traditional favorites, including grilled tuna steak with tomato-corn chutney, are also popular. For dessert, the "skillet cookie"—a nine-ounce chocolate-chip cookie topped with an ice-cream sundae—feeds four.

# PITTSBURGH★★

MAP P404
EASTERN STANDARD TIME
POPULATION 312,819

More than 700 bridges stitch together Pittsburgh, a hardworking city of modern skyscrapers, magnificent churches and ethnic neighborhoods, which is spread over the hills and flats of the Monongahela and Allegheny rivers. The triangle of virgin timber that George Washington first spied in 1753 changed hands several times during the French and Indian War until the British took final control in 1768. There they built the largest battlement in the New World, **Fort Pitt**, named for William Pitt, England's secretary of State and later prime minister.

**Information:** ☎412-281-7711. www.visitpittsburgh.com
**Don't Miss:** 15 minutes of fame at the Andy Warhol Museum.
**Kids:** There are plenty of things to explore at the Carnegie Science Center.
**Also See:** WASHINGTON, D.C.

## A Bit of History

Situated near the natural resources needed to produce iron and the rivers necessary to transport it, Pittsburgh claimed 46 foundries, 50 glass factories and 53 oil refineries by 1868. All this commerce provided fertile ground for great industrialists to thrive. Among the most renowned are **Andrew Carnegie** and **Henry Clay Frick**, who joined their steel-making and coal-producing enterprises to create the giant Carnegie Steel Company; the **Mellon** family with their banking and oil interests; **H.J. Heinz**, whose food-processing works revolutionized the concept of prepared foods; and **George Westinghouse**, known for his work in electrical systems.

To sate industry's appetite for labor, thousands of immigrants from Italy, Poland, Austria-Hungary, Russia and the Balkans poured into the city, bringing with them a rich assortment of ethnic customs that continue to enliven Pittsburgh's neighborhoods today. These early immigrants endured poor wages and harsh conditions: Unsanitary water led to epidemics of typhoid fever, and smoke from the mills blackened the sky to the point where day was sometimes indistinguishable from night. By the 1880s, industrial Pittsburgh had become such a dismal, polluted city that one English journalist proclaimed it: "Hell with the lid taken off."

Beginning to decline before World War II, Pittsburgh's steel industry rallied for the war effort. After the war, this worn-out city began the **Pittsburgh Renaissance** program to reinvent itself. Beginning with smoke and flood controls set in place during the 1950s, the plan encompassed two decades of new skyscraper construction tallying $500 million. The original site of Fort Pitt was freed from a tangle of industrial buildings to become **Point State Park**★ *(western end of Liberty Ave.;* ☎412-471-0235*)*, an inviting green welcome mat to the city.

Today Pittsburgh ranks among the nation's most livable cities and Pittsburgh International Airport numbers among the nation's top airports. With its low crime rate and close-knit neighborhoods, its thriving service and high-tech businesses and rich tradition in the arts, Pittsburgh is poised to prosper as never before in the 21C.

## Downtown and South Side★★

Wrapped in rivers and wedged in by the Appalachian foothills, Pittsburgh's downtown is located on a compact sector of land known as the **Golden Triangle**. Less than a mile long, the Golden Triangle is easily covered on foot. Several bridges, for motorists and pedestrians alike, link downtown to the North and

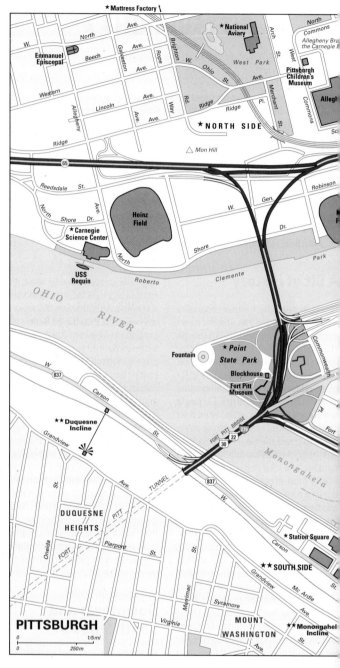

PITTSBURGH

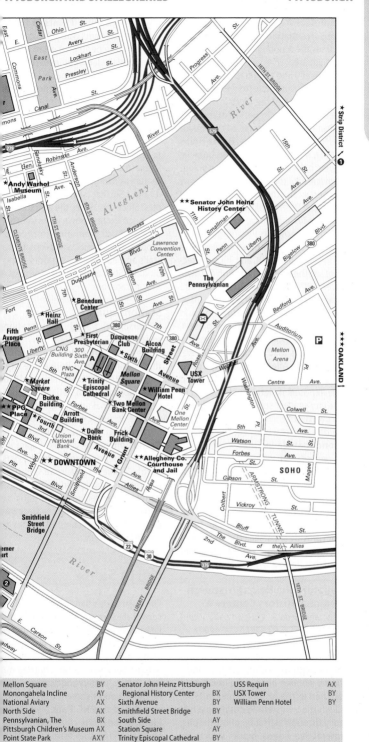

South sides. A clean, easy-to-use subway stops at central locations downtown and crosses the Monongahela River to Station Square.

Historically and topographically, Pittsburgh rolls out neatly from **Point State Park**, the site of the city's first settlements. East of the park, Pittsburgh's cultural district is home to two major performing-arts centers: **Heinz Hall**★ (6th St. & Penn Ave.), a 1926 vaudeville movie palace renovated as an opulent showcase for the Pittsburgh Symphony Orchestra; and the **Benedum Center**★ (7th St. & Penn Ave.), whose walls are gilded with aluminum.

Formerly known as Pittsburgh's "Wall Street," **Fourth Avenue**★ cradles some of the city's finest 19C and 20C architecture. At the intersection with Stanwix Street, **PPG Place**★★ (Pittsburgh Plate Glass), a Gothic tower of reflective glass, was designed by Philip Johnson and John Burgee and completed in 1984. **Grant Street**★★ boasts Henry Hobson Richardson's 1888 Romanesque Revival masterpiece, **Allegheny County Courthouse and Jail**★★ (at Forbes Ave.), and the exposed skeletal steel I-beams of the city's tallest structure, **USX Tower** (at 6th Ave.).

For the best city perspectives, ride the **Monongahela Incline**★★ (W. Carson St. opposite Station Square; ♿☎412-442-2000) or the **Duquesne Incline**★★ (W. Carson St., west of Fort Pitt Bridge; ☎412-381-1665). These two late-19C funiculars once transported factory workers up and down Pittsburgh's steep hills. Today both provide unparalleled **views**★★★ of the rivers converging at the triangle of land that holds downtown Pittsburgh.

### Senator John Heinz Pittsburgh Regional History Center★★

1212 Smallman St. ◷Open daily 10am-5pm. ⊛$8. ♿☎412-454-6000. www.pghhistory.org.

This massive renovated 1898 ice warehouse with its vaulted brick ceilings, heavy wooden beams and iron braces opened as the history center in 1996. Illustrating western Pennsylvania history through artifacts, photographs, interactive videos, model structures and live theater, the center's excellent permanent exhibit, **Points In Time**★ (2nd floor) recounts chronologically the stories of the people who settled and developed this land. Completed in 2004, the Smithsonian Wing houses temporary exhibits and the Western Pennsylvania Sports Museum.

### Strip District★

Smallman St. & Penn Ave. from 16th St. to 22nd St.

Former location of the city's turn-of-the-century iron forges, this area was named for the 1.5mi flat "strip" of land it occupies. Since the 1920s, the Strip District has been better known as a streetside smorgasbord of wholesale-produce shops, bustling outdoor markets, flower stalls and ethnic food vendors. Shopping the Strip on Saturday mornings is a local tradition.

### Station Square★

W. Carson St. ♿♿ . www.stationsquare.com

An easy walk from downtown across the Smithfield Street Bridge (the city's oldest, 1883), Station Square is a 1970s redevelopment of a 19C railroad passenger terminal and freight yard. The 52-acre complex encompasses some 60 shops and restaurants including the **Grand Concourse**, which occupies the former passenger terminal for the Pittsburgh & Lake Erie Railroad Company and retains its splendid stained-glass barrel-vaulted ceiling. Station Square is also the headquarters for the **Gateway Clipper Fleet**, which offers cruises on Pittsburgh's rivers.

## North Side★

The North Side's handful of attractions constitute some of the highlights of a Pittsburgh visit. Before it was annexed by the city in 1907, this area was known as the industrial center of Allegheny, where riverside factories churned out iron, textiles, pottery and brassware. The neighborhood's shoreline is currently dominated by **PNC Park and Heinz Field,** home of the city's professional baseball and football teams, the Pirates and the Steelers.

## Carnegie Science Center★

Kids *1 Allegheny Ave.* ◷*Open daily 10am-5pm.* ⚼*$12.* ✗♿🅿 ☎*412-237-3400.* *www.carnegiesciencecenter.org.*

Set on the north bank of the Ohio River, this slick science museum's contemporary design offers expansive views of the river and the Pittsburgh skyline. Much of the first floor is devoted to the **OMNIMAX Theater**★. On the second floor, be sure to visit the **Planetarium**★ and see the **Miniature Railroad and Village** with its 100 animated pieces. On the fourth floor you'll learn about robotics and lasers in **The Works Theater** multimedia lab. Moored in the river behind the museum is the **USS Requin**, a World War II submarine.

## The Andy Warhol Museum★★

*117 Sandusky St.* ◷*Open daily 10am-5pm.* ⚼*$12.* ✗♿☎*412-237-8300. www.warhol.org.*

Opened in 1994, this comprehensive single-artist museum sprawls over seven floors. On display at any one time are more than 500 works of art and archival artifacts, a fraction of the museum's total collection of more than 3,000 paintings, drawings, sculptures and photographs. Born of Eastern European immigrant parents, **Andy Warhol** (1928-87) grew up in Pittsburgh's Oakland neighborhood. After graduating from the Carnegie Institute of Technology's College of Fine Arts, he moved to New York and began creating the provocative persona that earned him an enduring place in the 20C art world. Start on the first floor for an introduction to Warhol's art, then take the elevator to the seventh floor and continue down through galleries that depict the diversity of Warhol's work.

## Mattress Factory★

*500 Sampsonia Way. Entrance to parking lot at 505 Jacksonia St.* ◷*Open daily 10am-5pm.* ♿🅿☎*412-231-3169. www.mattress.org.*

This late-19C warehouse is one of the few site-specific installation galleries in the US. A handful of artists is chosen each year and given carte-blanche to create their own *chefs-d'œuvre*. The results can be capricious, brilliant, or ridiculous but are never boring. An outdoor sculpture

*The Cathedral of Learning, University of Pittsburgh*

©iStockphoto.com/Robert Pernell

garden designed by Winifred Lutz recalls an archaeological dig.

## Oakland★★★

Packed onto a 700-acre plateau 3mi east of the Golden Triangle, Oakland developed as Pittsburgh's alter ego. While the city labored beneath its blast-furnace and blue-collar reputation, Oakland developed as the city's cultural and academic center. First settled as farmland, the area was well on its way to becoming another blue-collar district in 1889 when expatriate Mary Schenley gave the city 400 acres on the eastern border of Oakland for the creation of **Schenley Park**★ *(access via Schenley Dr. or Panther Hollow Rd.).* Andrew Carnegie followed suit and built his museum/library/music-hall complex, the Carnegie Institute (now known simply as The Carnegie), on the park's border.

Carnegie's philanthropy extended into education. In the early 1900s, he built the Carnegie Technical Schools, which have evolved into Carnegie-Mellon University, widely known for its computer science, engineering and drama departments. In the 1900s the **University of Pittsburgh** relocated to Oakland and built one of the district's most visible landmarks,

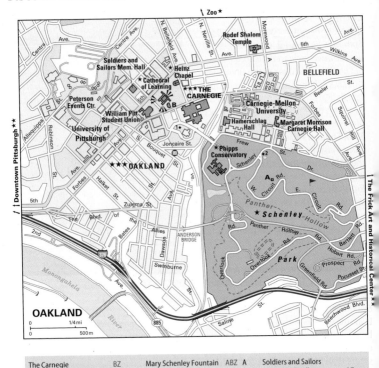

| | | | | | |
|---|---|---|---|---|---|
| The Carnegie | BZ | Mary Schenley Fountain | ABZ A | Soldiers and Sailors | |
| Cathedral of Learning | AZ | Neil Log House | BZ B | Memorial Hall | AZ |
| Hamerschlag Hall | BZ | Phipps Conservatory | BZ | Stephen Foster Memorial | AZ D |
| Heinz Memorial Chapel | ABZ | Rodef Shalom Temple | BZ | Westinghouse Memorial | BZ E |
| Margaret Morrison | | Schenley Park | BZ | William Pitt Student Union | AZ |
| Carnegie Hall | BZ | | | | |

the 42-story Gothic-style **Cathedral of Learning**★ (on the Quadrangle at Forbes Ave. & Bigelow Blvd.; ☎412-624-6000). Its 26 **Nationality Classrooms**★ reflect the cultures of Pittsburgh's many immigrant groups.

On Forbes Avenue, the **Carnegie Library of Pittsburgh** (entrance on Schenley Dr.) contains more than four million items. Adjacent to the library, **Carnegie Music Hall**★ (entrance on Forbes Ave.) is home to the Pittsburgh Chamber Music Society and the River City Brass Band. It boasts the grandest interior in the complex with green marble columns and a 45ft-high gilded ceiling.

## Carnegie Museum of Art★★

Entrance on Forbes Ave. ✗♿🅿 🕒Open daily 10am-5pm. ⊙$10. ☎412-622-3131. www.cmoa.org.
In keeping with Carnegie's wishes, the museum concentrates on European and American art from the late 19C to the present.

Based on the Mausoleum at Halicarnassus (one of the Seven Wonders of the Ancient World), the **Hall of Architecture**★ (west side of 1st floor) holds more than 140 plaster casts of architectural masterpieces. Bathed in sunlight, the adjacent **Hall of Sculpture**★ displays copies of statues from ancient Greece arrayed around the loggia. On the second floor, the **Sarah Scaife Galleries**★ are organized chronologically beginning with art from ancient Egypt to early-19C Europe. The middle of the Scaife Galleries consists of a free-flowing maze of more than 20 large rooms. Browse through the works of Tintoretto and Rubens and Impressionists such as Monet, Pissarro, van Gogh and Renoir. Contemporary art is well represented with a series of bold canvases by Pollock, de Kooning, and Rauschenberg.

*"ane" debuts at Carnegie Museum of Natural History*

## Carnegie Museum of Natural History★★

Kids *Entrance on Forbes Ave.* ⓒ*Open daily 10am-5pm.* ⊛*$10.* ✗ ♿ P ☎*412-622-3131*

Long recognized as one of the world's best dinosaur destinations, the 2007 opening of "Dinosaurs in Their Time" secures the museum's spot as a definitive place to learn about these prehistoric creatures in a replication of the environment in which they lived. Other highlights include the Hall of African Wildlifed and the Hall of Ancient Egypt, which features adult and child mummies. The Hall of American Indians displays an impressive collection of some 1,000 native artifacts.

## The Frick Art and Historical Center★★

*7227 Reynolds St. (at S. Homewood Ave.).* ✗ ♿ P ☎*412-371-0600. www.frick.org.*
This six-acre estate with its elegantly appointed 23-room Victorian mansion was the home of industrialist **Henry Clay Frick** from 1882 to 1905. Today the site includes the Frick Art Museum, a Car and Carriage Museum and a cafe serving meals and afternoon tea.

## Clayton★★

☛*Visit of house by guided tour only.*
⊛*$12.* ✗ P
Built just before the Civil War, the mansion was redesigned for the newly married Fricks in the 1890s by Pennsylvania architect Frederick Osterling. The Fricks

lived in the house until the early 1900s, when the family moved to New York City. However, Frick's daughter, Helen, maintained the residence until her own death in 1984. Tours include the small but opulent **dining room**, with its tooled-leather friezes and built-in buffet, the family bedrooms upstairs and a richly furnished **library** and **sitting room**, hung with paintings by Childe Hassam and Monet.

## Frick Art Museum★

*7277 Reynolds St.* ✗ ♿ P ⓒ*Open Tues-Sun 10am–5pm* ⓒ*Closed Mon.* ⊛*$12.* ☎*412-371-0600. www.frickart.org.*
Helen Frick built this intimate Italian Renaissance-style museum in the 1969. It houses early-16C Flemish tapestries, works by Rubens and Boucher, and a French salon adorned with early-18C decorative arts.

## Pittsburgh Zoo & PPG Aquarium★

Kids *Off Butler St. near Highland Park Bridge.* ⓒ*Open daily 9am-5pm.* ⊛*$10.* ✗ ♿ P ☎*412-665-3640.*
*www.zoo.pgh.pa.us.*
Housing thousands of animals on 77 acres, the zoo first opened in 1898. A paved trail here leads past exotic exhibits, beginning with the Asian Forest, featuring snow leopards and Siberian tigers, and continuing past the popular Tropical Forest, populated by monkeys and gorillas. **Kids Kingdom** adds interactive play. The aquarium opened in 2000 and

## Captains of Industry

Of the 86 millionaires who resided in Pittsburgh in the late 19C, Andrew **Carnegie** and Henry Clay **Frick** were among the most legendary. From humble beginnings in the railroad, coal and steel industries, Carnegie and Frick created one of the most comprehensive industrial dynasties in the country.

Poor economic conditions forced the Carnegie family to come to America from Scotland in 1848. To help support his family, 13-year-old **Andrew Carnegie** (1835-1919) found his first job in a cotton factory. It was when he started working for the Pennsylvania Railroad in 1853 that he began climbing the ladder of success. He had already amassed a small fortune in railroads and oil by 1873 when he decided on steel as his future. Fifteen years later, Carnegie was the chief owner of Homestead Steel Works, which he consolidated—along with other steel interests—into the Carnegie Steel Company in 1899.

Born into a middle-class family near Pittsburgh, **Henry Clay Frick** (1849-1919) was borrowing money by the age of 21 to start a company to produce coke—coal that is "baked" in ovens to burn out impurities—to supply to the growing steel industry. During the financial panic of 1873 Frick began buying up coal fields, and by the age of 30 he was a millionaire. In 1889 Frick teamed up with Andrew Carnegie, becoming chairman of Carnegie Steel.

As partners Carnegie and Frick controlled every aspect of the steel industry from mining coal to producing coke. They owned the barge companies that transported raw materials on Pittsburgh's rivers as well as the steel mills that devoured these resources. Together they unified their holdings and talents to create a dynasty, but their personal relationship was troubled. Both strong-willed, disciplined and opinionated men, Frick and Carnegie's relationship soured over the years. Shortly before his death, Carnegie reputedly sent a message to Frick asking for a reconciliation. "Tell Mr. Carnegie," Frick replied, "that I'll meet him in Hell." Fourteen years his junior, Frick died the same year as his former partner.

features a crawl-through stingray tunnel and a two-story shark tank.

### Phipps Conservatory and Botanical Gardens★

*1059 Shady Ave.* ○Open daily 9:30am-5pm. ∞$9. &☎412-622-6914. *www.phipps.conservatory.org.*
This 13-room Victorian glass house is a delightful refuge filled with exotic flora, an impressive bonsai collection and a hands-on children's garden.

### Heinz Memorial Chapel ★

*5th & S. Bellefield Aves.* &☎412-624-4157 *www.heinzchapel.pitt.edu.*
An elegant French Gothic memorial to H.J. Heinz from his children, this chapel's majestic, 73ft-high stained-glass windows are among the tallest in the world.

# SOUTHERN ALLEGHENIES★★

MICHELIN MAP583 R 7, 8
EASTERN STANDARD TIME

entering around 2,700ft Laurel Hill in the Allegheny Mountains, this broad swath of rolling, forested peaks, west of Pittsburgh, forms a recreational paradise. Its steep slopes challenge skiers in winter and the tumultuous currents of the Youghiogheny River attract white-water rafters when the waters run high in the spring. The area preserves its history with re-created 18C forts, monuments to the almighty railroad, and architectural masterpieces, such as Frank Lloyd Wright's Fallingwater.

- **Information:** ☎412-281-7711. www.visitpittsburgh.com
- **Orient Yourself:** These gems are nestled in southwestern Pennsylvania.
- **Don't Miss:** Frank Lloyd Wright's Fallingwater masterpiece.
- **Organizing Your Time:** Leave a day for the outdoor pleasure of river rafting.

## A Bit of History

parsely populated but alive with wildlife, this portion of the Alleghenies has supported both agriculture and industry since the 18C. From 1754 to 1763 the area was studded with forts built during the French and Indian War, including George Washington's hastily constructed Fort Necessity (1754). The **Fort Necessity National Battlefield**★ (on US-40 in Farmington, 11mi east of Uniontown; ☎724-329-5512) is the site of the only surrender Washington experienced during his military career. After the British emerged victorious, the southern Alleghenies became a gateway to the West. Bountiful supplies of lumber, oil and coal created booming steel towns such as **Johnstown**, perhaps better known for the deadly flood of 1889 that killed more than 2,000 people.

Completed in 1834, the Allegheny Portage Railroad used a series of stepped inclines and steam locomotives to physically haul canal boats over the 2,400ft Allegheny Mountain range. Today the **Allegheny Portage Railroad National Historic Site**★★ (off US-22, 10mi west of Altoona; take Gallitzin Exit and follow signs; ☎814-886-6150) pays homage to this inventive railroad-canal system that survived for some 20 years before railroads replaced it. A renowned 19C railroad-engineering feat, the 220-degree, 2,375ft curve of track at **Horseshoe Curve National Historic Landmark**★ (on Rte. 4008 in Altoona; ☎814-941-7960) ascends 2,300ft Allegheny Mountain in the tightest curve on Pennsylvania's Main Line railroad.

## Sights

### Fallingwater★★★

*9mi north of US-40 on Rte. 381; between the villages of Mill Run and Ohiopyle. Visit by guided tour only; reservations required. Closed Mon, some holidays, Jan–Feb and weekdays in Dec. Hours vary. $16. ☎724-329-8501. www.paconserve.org.*

Balancing over a 20ft waterfall, this spectacular house was built for Edgar J. Kaufmann, a Pittsburgh department-

### White-water Rafting

Leave the beaten path for a day and raft down the roiling waters of the famed Youghiogheny River. Cutting through the dramatic Youghiogheny Gorge (average depth 1,000ft), "the Yough" offers rafting opportunities for novices and experts alike. The most popular trip *(5-6 hours; minimum age 12)* leaves from scenic Ohiopyle State Park overlooking Ohiopyle Falls *(from the PA Turnpike, take Exit 9 and follow Rte. 381 South to Ohiopyle)*. Four Ohiopyle-based outfitters offer guided trips *(information and reservations: Ohiopyle State Park, ☎724-329-8591)*

*Fallingwater*

Courtesy Western Pennsylvania Conservancy

store owner who hired renowned architect **Frank Lloyd Wright** ( see *CHICAGO*) to design a weekend retreat on his rural property 75mi southeast of Pittsburgh.

From the visitor center a meandering path leads to the house, where visitors can see Wright's ideas in action. The unusual design is based on the use of cantilevers that extend out from the main structure well beyond the point of direct support. The effect is a series of terraces flowing from the natural sandstone formation upon which the home rests. The 1,800sq ft **living room**★ is Fallingwater's most spectacular space and is almost entirely enclosed by glass, allowing uninterrupted views of the woods outside. Feel the "compression and release" philosophy at work on the narrow cave-like passageways that lead to brightly lit bedrooms.

In the decades following Fallingwater's completion, Wright's ebbing career was relaunched with a host of new commissions, including nearby **Kentuck Knob**★★ *(south of Fallingwater on Chalk Hill-Ohiopyle Rd., 6mi north of US-40; visit by guided tour only; 724-329-1901)*. Fashioned of red cypress and 800 tons of sandstone, and furnished with Wright pieces, Kentuck Knob was completed in 1956. Just east of the house, the "knob"—crouched 2,000ft above sea level—affords a fabulous **view**★★★ of the Youghiogheny River Gorge.

## Johnstown Flood Museum★★

*304 Washington St., in Johnstown.* Open daily 10am-5pm. $6. 814-539-1889. *www.jaha.org*

The tragic story of the infamous 1889 flood is told inside former Carnegie Library (1891). Built in the Gothic Revival style, this library-turned-museum offers three floors of outstanding exhibits and an Academy Award-winning film, **The Johnstown Flood**. Called the worst natural disaster of the 19C, the flood was caused by a 36ft wall of water that thundered down this valley at speeds of up to 40mph from a burst dam on Lake Conemaugh, 450ft above Johnstown. On May 31, 1889, the murderous wave uprooted trees, boulders and freight cars, and claimed the lives of more than 2,200 citizens. Scandal heightened the tragedy: Several years earlier, wealthy Pittsburgh industrialists had purchased land around Lake Conemaugh to build an elite hunting club, but had failed to maintain the lake's dam.

Museum highlights include a three-dimensional wall of wreckage and an animated relief map showing the path of the floodwater. Flood victims rest among the nearly 60,000 headstones at **Grandview Cemetery** *(on Millcreek Rd.)*, including 777 unidentified bodies buried in the cemetery's centerpiece, the **Unknown Plot**.

## Johnstown Flood National Memorial★★

*Off US-219, 10mi northeast of Johnstown take St. Michael/Sidman Exit and go east on Rte. 869. Follow signs to memorial.* Open daily 9am-5pm. $4. 814-495-4643. www.nps.gov/jofl.

Overlooking what was once Lake Conemaugh, this red barn-like structure houses displays that illustrate the damage done to Johnstown with dramatic before-and-after photographs. Exhibits here also explore the question of whether the South Fork Fishing and Hunting Club's members should have been held liable for the catastrophe

# RICHMOND AND THE TIDEWATER

he first successful English settlement on the continent—Jamestown—was ounded along the shores of the James and York rivers in 1607. Wealthy 17C obacco planters later built their manor houses here; their opulent lifestyles ften supported by the invidious institution of slavery. Here again, in the 18C olonial capital of Williamsburg, Virginia's patriots decried British tyranny and rgued for independence from the Crown. With the Continental Army's victory t nearby Yorktown in 1781, that independence was won. In less than a century, he Virginia Tidewater again became a battleground, as the divided young nation ought against itself in the Civil War and the state capital of Richmond became apital of a nation—the short-lived Confederate States of America.

oday, Richmond has risen again, to ecome a commercial center of the New outh; but here and throughout Virinia's Tidewater area southeast of the apital city, the past remains a romantic verlay on the present. An endless prozession of plantation manors, antebelum houses, historical museums, batlefields and re-created colonial villages parades across this low, marsh-saturated idal land. If history has become a busiess here, it is a serious one, and such Virginia sights as Colonial Williamsburg ank among the most extensive and uthentic historic reconstructions in he world. The land itself, with its filiree of rivers, creeks, and pine and oak

Richmond and the Tidewater

forests, has preserved the same timeless promise that first attracted adventuring Europeans to its shores.

*Monument Avenue, Richmond*

Richmond Metropolitan CVB.

## Address Book

*For coin ranges, see the Legend on the cover flap.*

### WHERE TO STAY

**$$$ The Jefferson** – *Franklin & Adams Sts., Richmond, VA.* X & P ☎804-788-8000. www.jeffersonhotel.com. *262 rooms.* Despite several fires and restorations since opening in 1895, this downtown landmark remains the city's most opulent "southern belle." The palatial bi-level lobby showcases a stained-glass skylight, gold-leaf moldings and E.B. Valentine's sculpture of Thomas Jefferson. Renovated rooms feature mahogany furnishings and English country florals or deep hunt colors. Treat yourself to chef Jeff Waite's inspired Southern cuisine, accented with home-grown herbs, in **Lemaire**'s elegant dining room.

**$$$ The Williamsburg Inn** – *136 E. Francis St., Williamsburg, VA.* X & P ☎757-229-1000. www.colonialwilliamsburg.org. *62 rooms.* This elegant Neoclassical inn boasts the comfort of a private home. The living room-style lobby is outfitted with Regency-style furniture, and lush jewel-tone fabrics add a regal spark to the rich cherry and mahogany furniture in the guest rooms.

**$ Linden Row Inn** – *100 E. Franklin St., Richmond, VA.* X & P ☎804-783-7000. www.lindenrowinn.com. *70 rooms.* These six Greek Revival town houses were built on the site of Edgar Allan Poe's childhood rose gardens downtown. Traces of the past include plaster ceiling medallions and converted brass gasoliers. Rooms in the main house are furnished with Victorian antiques. Regional specialties are served in the exposed-brick dining room.

### WHERE TO EAT

**$$$ Acacia** – *3325 W. Cary St., Richmond, VA.* ☎804-354-6060. **Contemporary.** A turn-of-the-century Baptist church amid Carytown's upscale boutiques is the setting for this intimate bistro. One hundred test-tube vases with wildflowers line the walls of the contemporary room. Seafood dishes—sauteed grouper with cabage and local baby carrots and grilled salmon over cauliflower puree—are the daily menu's top choices.

**$$ King's Arms Tavern** – *Duke of Gloucester St., Williamsburg, VA.* ☎757-229-2141. **American.** This tavern was reconstructed on the site of its mid-18C predecessor. Dine by candlelight in one of eleven Colonial-style rooms, where waiters in period dress serve Old World classics including game pie filled with duck, rabbit and venison, and oyster-stuffed filet mignon wrapped in bacon. Try pecan pie or plum ice cream for dessert.

# RICHMOND★

MAP P416

EASTERN STANDARD TIME

POPULATION 192,913

Richmond offers an amalgam of antebellum nostalgia and New South vitality. Prominent colonial planter William Byrd II, who owned this land, plotted the original village in the 1730s, convinced that its location at the fall line of the James River would ensure its growth. Though it in fact grew slowly in its first decades, the city's fortunes altered dramatically and permanently in 1780 when it was chosen as the new capital of Virginia. During the next century Richmond—which was incorporated in 1782—became the industrial giant of the South. When the breakaway Confederate states formed their own union in 1861, Richmond soon replaced Montgomery, Alabama, as the Confederate capital. During the bloody and protracted Civil War, fighting swirled again and again around the beleaguered city, until April 1865, when both Richmond and the Confederacy fell.

hroughout the next half century, even as the city recovered its prosperity, it ever lost its cachet as cultural capital of the South. By the early decades of the OC, Richmond boasted elegant department stores, elaborate Art Deco theaters, museums and fine Victorian homes. As the century progressed, tobacco and industrial giants Philip Morris and Reynolds brought financial vigor to the city, which began to spread west into the upscale neighborhoods that punctuating he West End. Although founding fathers and Confederate generals are honored preserved pockets of the contemporary city, these days Virginia's capital looks more to the future than to the past—and a bright future it appears to be.

**Information:** ☎804-783-7450. www.richmondva.org
**Don't Miss:** The eclectic collection at the Virginia Museum of Fine Arts.
**Organizing Your Time:** Leave time to stroll by Richmond's stunning architectural treasures.
**Also See:** WASHINGTON, DC.

## Downtown★

nchored by the elegant Jeffersonian **Virginia State Capitol**★ (bounded by th & Governor Sts. and Bank & Broad Sts.; ☎804-698-1788), Richmond's downtown ong ranked as the most sophisticated in he American South. The downtown corridor (centered along Broad St.) has been evitalized with the addition of the 32-cre redeveloped **Riverfront** (at the foot f 5th St.). A 19C canal turning basin is the ocal point of the popular **Shockoe Slip** eighborhood (Cary St. between 12th & 5th Sts.), an area of renovated tobacco warehouses and cobbled streets that is ow one of the city's liveliest nightspots. t the west edge of downtown, the 1895 **efferson Hotel** (Franklin & Adams Sts.) emains the most elegant reminder of ichmond's gilded past.

## Museum and White House of the Confederacy★

201 E. Clay St. ⏰Open daily 10am-pm. ☜$11. ♿🅿 ☎804-649-1861. www.moc.org.

onfederate president Jefferson Davis nd his family lived in this stucco 1818 mansion during the Civil War. The ornate ictorian interior reflects the mansion's ppearance during the Davis years. In he adjacent museum is an extensive ollection of objects relating to the Confederate war effort, including the sword worn by Robert E. Lee at his surrender t Appomattox and E.B.D. Julio's monumental 1869 canvas **The Last Meeting f Lee and Jackson**★ (lower level).

## Valentine Richmond History Center★

1015 E. Clay St. ⏰Open daily 10am-5pm. ☜$10. ☎804-649-0711. www.richmondhistorycenter.com.

Noted for its comprehensive archives on the capital city, the museum uses Richmond history to explore changing social themes in the fabric of American life through its permanent and changing exhibits.

The adjacent **Wickham House**★★, considered one of the finest examples of a Federal-style interior in the US, was the home of prominent attorney John Wickham and his family from 1812 to 1854. Noted for its cantilevered, mahogany spiral **staircase**, ornate plasterwork and rare Neoclassical wall paintings, the house interprets the life of both master and slave in early-19C Richmond.

## John Marshall House★

818 E. Marshall St. ⏰Open daily 10am-4:30pm. ☜$10. ☎804-648-7998.

The Federal-era brick residence was home to the third US Supreme Court chief justice, John Marshall (1755-1835). Known as the "Great Chief Justice" for the status he brought to the court during his 34-year tenure (beginning in 1801), Marshall lived here for much of his adult life, and his family furnishings still decorate the house.

## Maggie L. Walker National Historic Site ★

600 N. 2nd St. ⏰Open daily 9am-5pm. ♿☎804-771-2017. www.nps.gov/mawa.

Located in the city's historic African-American neighborhood, Jackson Ward, this rambling brick Victorian row house was home to Maggie Walker (1867-1934), a pioneering black entrepreneur and the first American woman to found and preside over a chartered bank. Her St. Luke Penny Savings Bank opened in 1903; today it continues as the Consolidated Bank and Trust Company.

## Western Richmond★★

Fine old neighborhoods, gracious boul[e]vards, parks and historic houses chara[c]terize the area that spreads west of th[e] city center. Adjoining downtown, th[e] **Fan District** is bounded by Monume[nt] Avenue on the north, Main Street on t[he] south, Belvidere Street on the east, a[nd] Boulevard on the west. Named for [...]

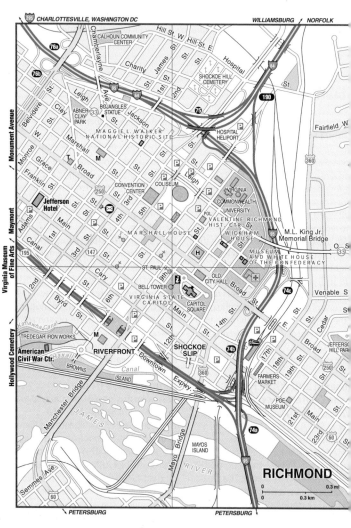

| | | | | | | | |
|---|---|---|---|---|---|---|---|
| The Carnegie | BZ | Mary Schenley Fountain | ABZ | A | Soldiers and Sailors | | |
| Cathedral of Learning | AZ | Neil Log House | BZ | B | Memorial Hall | | AZ |
| Hamerschlag Hall | BZ | Phipps Conservatory | BZ | | Stephen Foster Memorial | | AZ |
| Heinz Memorial Chapel | ABZ | Rodef Shalom Temple | BZ | | Westinghouse Memorial | | BZ |
| Margaret Morrison | | Schenley Park | BZ | | William Pitt Student Union | | AZ |
| Carnegie Hall | BZ | | | | | | |

an-like layout of streets, this lively district encompasses a wealth of restored 19C town houses, tucked-away cafes and the campus of Virginia Commonwealth University (VCU)—noted for its arts school. **Monument Avenue**★, punctuated by statues of Confederate heroes and noteworthy Virginians, links downtown with the Fan District. Confederate president Jefferson Davis and Confederate cavalry hero Jeb Stuart are buried at **Hollywood Cemetery**★ (412 Cherry St.; ☎804-648-8501), along with former US presidents James Monroe and John Tyler.

An offering of small **galleries** stretch along West Main Street, from the 1300 to the 1800 block. On the west side of the Fan, **Carytown** (Cary St. between Boulevard & Thompson St.) harbors upscale boutiques, antique shops and restaurants. In the late 19C and early 20C, Richmond's aristocracy built elaborate country estates along the bluffs above the James River in Richmond's tony **West End**.

## Virginia Historical Society★★

*428 N. Boulevard.* ⏰*Open daily 10am-5pm.* ☞*$5.* ♿🅿 ☎*804-358-4901.* www.vahistorical.org.

Built in the early 19C as the Confederate Memorial Institute, this stately structure now offers extensive historical exhibits, detailing the varied cultures and peoples involved in the making of Virginia. The permanent exhibit "**Story of Virginia: An American Experience**" chronicles the state's history through the 20C. In the Cheek Gallery, walls are lined with large murals painted in the early 20C by French artist Charles Hoffbauer and depicting the *Four Seasons of the Confederacy*.

## Virginia Museum of Fine Arts★★

*200 N. Boulevard.* ⏰*Open daily 11am-5pm.* ☞*$5 donation suggested.* 🍴♿🅿 ☎*804-340-1400.* www.vmfa.state.va.us.

An eclectic gem, the museum and its worldwide collections sprawl through four wings that reflect different periods

## Richmond and the Civil War

As capital of the Confederacy and the only city to have been under long-term siege during the Civil War, Richmond is surrounded by many significant battle sites. Pivotal conflicts of Union general George B. McClellan's 1862 campaign to control the York-James Peninsula, and the final battles culminating in the siege of nearby Petersburg in 1864-65 took place in the countryside around Richmond.

**Richmond National Battlefield Park**★ preserves nine Civil War sites (1862 and 1864) that commemorate the battles for Richmond, organized as a self-guided, 80mi driving tour. Begin at the main park visitor center, located in part of the restored **Tredegar Iron Works** (at the base of 5th St. on Tredegar St. along the downtown Riverfront), where a large percentage of the Confederate armament was forged. Also part of the park complex is the **Chimborazo Visitor Center** (3215 E. Broad St.; ♿🅿 ☎804-226-1981), a hilltop on the east side of the city that was the site of the Confederacy's largest hospital; a museum here recounts the relatively barbaric state of Civil War-era medicine.

The 10-month siege (June 1864–April 1865) of Robert E. Lee's army by Union forces under Ulysses S. Grant, who were attempting to cut railroad supply lines to Richmond, is commemorated in the 2,460-acre **Petersburg National Battlefield**. A self-guided 37mi driving tour starts at the **visitor center** (20mi south of Richmond on Rte. 36; ☎804-732-3531) and loops past elaborate earthworks erected by both armies. Grant's headquarters at City Point are also preserved.

The Civil War effectively ended 88mi west of Richmond in the tiny village of Appomattox Court House where Lee surrendered to Grant on April 9, 1865. That meeting took place in a plantation home preserved at **Appomattox Court House National Historical Park** (visitor center on Main St. in Appomattox, VA; ☎434-352-8987).

## James River Plantations

Along the banks of the James, between Richmond and Williamsburg *(a 22mi drive southeast of Richmond on Rte. 5)*, stand the great estates of Virginia's illustrious colonial gentry. Built on the tobacco wealth that cemented the colony in the 17C, these superb Georgian manor houses symbolize the grandeur of that age, when Virginia's planters lived baronial lives at the edge of a vast continental wilderness. While only a handful of these houses are open to the public, a number of others are visible along Route 5 (John Tyler Highway), also known as the **Plantation Route**. *Combination tickets are available; inquire at the plantations. Visits to all plantation houses are by guided tour only.*

The first estate you'll come to as you drive south along Route 5 is **Shirley Plantation**★★ *(Shirley Plantation Rd.;* ✗ 🅿 ☎804-829-5121). Virginia's oldest plantation has been owned by descendants of the Hill-Carter family since 1660. This Queen Anne manor (c.1720s) overlooking the James is justifiably famous for its square-rigged three-story **staircase** in the main entry hall.

Offset by towering boxwood hedges, Georgian **Berkeley Plantation**★★ *(off Rte. 5 at 12602 Harrison Landing Rd.;* ✗ 🅿 ☎804-829-6018) served as the seat of the Harrison family. This lineage of respected national figures included Benjamin Harrison IV, who built the house in 1726, and his son Benjamin Harrison V, a signer of the Declaration of Independence.

Tenth US president **John Tyler** retired to the frame house on **Sherwood Forest Plantation**★ *(14501 Rte. 5;* 🅿 ☎804-829-5377) after his tenure in office ended in 1845. Built c.1730, the house was lengthened by Tyler's wife, Julia. Only one room wide, it now measures 301ft long, making it the longest frame house in the US.

in the museum's history (built between 1936 and 1985). The collection has grown from its original 100 objects, donated in 1919 by prominent Virginia judge John Barton Payne, to more than 20,000 pieces that span 6,000 years. Arts of China and Japan, Africa, Ancient Egypt, Classical Greece and Rome are well represented, as is a fine collection of Indian, Himalayan and Islamic religious art. The strong collection of **American art**★ *(3rd floor)* spans the Colonial period through the 20C. Fourth-floor galleries feature decorative arts by Art Nouveau innovator Hector Guimard, jeweler René Lalique and Louis Comfort Tiffany. The museum's collection of Imperial Easter eggs and bibelots by Russian jeweler **Carl Fabergé** is one of the most extensive in the Western Hemisphere. Several third-floor galleries hold a comprehensive collection of **British sporting art**.

### Maymont★

🅺🅸🅳 *1700 Hampton St.* 🅿 ☎804-358-7166. *www.maymont.org.*
Topping bluffs above the James River, the former estate of late-19C railroad magnate James Dooley and his wife, Sallie May Dooley, has become a city show-

piece. The Dooleys' stone Romanesqu Revival manor house, built in the 1890 is decorated with the couple's extrava gant Gilded Age furnishings, inclu ing a Tiffany-designed table of silv and carved narwhal tusks. Maymon 100-acre grounds encompass form gardens, a children's farm and a natu center. The annual **Maymont Flower Garden Show**, held in February at t downtown Richmond Centre, is a maj mid-Atlantic horticultural event.

### Virginia House★★

*4301 Sulgrave Rd.* ☛ Visit by guid tour only, 10am-4pm. ☞$5. ♿ ☎80 353-4251.
The striking stone Tudor-style mansi was constructed from salvaged pieces the 12C Priory of St. Sepulchre that sto in Warwick, England. In 1925 Richmon born diplomat Alexander Weddell a his wife, Virginia, had the priory disa sembled and commissioned archite Henry Grant Morse to reconfigure stone façade and elaborate interi The current design is modeled in pa on Sulgrave Manor, ancestral home George Washington in Northampto shire, England. Decorated in the sty

*Dining Room, Virginia House*

Courtesy Richmond Metropolitan CVB

f an English estate, the house is decked
with European antiquities and furnish-
ngs. Acclaimed southern landscape
architect Charles Gillette laid out the
xtensive grounds with terraced hill-
ide gardens.

### gecroft Hall★★

*305 Sulgrave Rd. Visit by guided tour
nly, daily 10am-4pm. $7. ℗ ☎804-
53-4241. www.agecrofthall.com*

he half-timbered walls and leaded
windows of this home were originally
art of a Tudor and Stuart estate in Lan-
ashire, England. Dating to the late 15C,

the house was saved from demolition
by Richmond scion T.C. Williams, who
in 1926 had it dismantled and used its
pieces to build a home in the Windsor
Farms neighborhood he was develop-
ing. Today the house functions as a
museum, interpreting life in an English
manor house during the 16C and 17C.
Off the cobbled 17C-style courtyard is
a permanent exhibit detailing how the
house was dismantled, transported
to Richmond and reassembled. The
23-acre site features five separate
English-style gardens.

# COLONIAL PARKWAY★★

MICHELIN MAP 584 S 9
EASTERN STANDARD TIME

ne of the most picturesque coastal roadways in the East, the aggregate-paved
arkway sweeps past rivers and marshlands filled with birds and woodlands rich
color. Aside from its beauty, the parkway links the historic sites of Jamestown,
irthplace of the English colonies, with those of Yorktown, where the colonies
on their independence from England. The parkway was built in the 1930s by
e Works Projects Administration and the Civilian Conservation Corps, both
unded during Franklin Delano Roosevelt's tenure as president.

**Information:** ☎757-898-3400. www.nps.gov/colo.
**Orient Yourself:** This is a 22mi drive along rivers and marshlands.
**Organizing Your Time:** Most of your time here will be spent in the car; plan for
a leisurely drive.

## Pocahontas

The name of one of the most famous Native American women, Matoaka, has been changed in posterity to Pocahontas, "the playful one." A favorite daughter of the powerful Powhatan chief Wahunsenacawh (known to the English by his title, Powhatan), the young girl was apparently fascinated by the strange English colonists and befriended their leader, John Smith. According to Smith, she saved his life when her father threatened to kill him. In 1614 Pocahontas married John Rolfe, the colonist responsible for hybridizing a smokable form of tobacco, and took the Christian name Rebecca. Their marriage gave the colonists four strife-free years with the native Powhatans—years known as the Pocahontas Peace. In 1616 the Rolfes and their infant son sailed to England, where Pocahontas became the toast of the English court. However, as the couple set out on their return voyage, the young Indian woman died on her way down the Thames and was buried on English soil.

## A Bit of History

In 1607 a group of 104 British colonists, led by Captain John Smith, anchored on a small island in the James River. Here, under a charter granted by James I to the Virginia Company in London, they established the colony of Virginia with Jamestown as its capital. Disease and starvation were rampant in the early years, claiming two-thirds of the settlement's population by the end of 1610. Nonetheless, the surviving colonists persevered, enduring Indian attacks, fires and numerous other setbacks over the ensuing decades. In 1699 the colony's government was moved to Williamsburg. Although Jamestown never became the "great cittie" envisioned by John Smith, the foundations that took root here helped mold the nation that would eventually become the United States of America.

Settled in 1631, nearby **Yorktown** developed into a prosperous colonial shipping center. But the town is best remembered for its part in the American Revolution. It was here in October 1781 that British general Charles Cornwallis surrendered to Patriot George Washington. Today the village's modest Main Street preserves several historic structures.

## Sights

### Colonial National Historic Park at Jamestown★★
*West end of Colonial Pkwy.* ♿ 🅿 ☏75 *229-1733. www.nps.gov/jame.*

*The Three Ships at Jamestown Settlement*

1607 this 1,500-acre James River Island came the site of the first permanent glish-speaking colony in America. ow administered by the National Park rvice, most of the island has been turned to its natural state and 3- and ni loop drives weave across its bogs d woodlands. On the northwest corner the island, the **Jamestown Visitor nter** exhibits recovered artifacts and atures a 15min film on the founding of mes Fort. Behind the visitor center an cavated street grid outlines founda- ns of the buildings from the former lonial capital. The brick tower from a urch begun in 1639 is the only early ructure still standing. East of the tower, e brick replica **Memorial Church** was ilt in 1907 on the cobblestone founda- ns of the 1617 frame church erected the colonists.

causeway connects the island to the ainland, where the park maintains its pular **Glasshouse★** (take the first right ter park entrance). Here you'll find the ins of the original 1608 glass house as ell as a replica where costumed arti- ns demonstrate the techniques of lonial glass-making, one of Virginia's rliest industries.

## mestown Settlement★★

ar the west end of Colonial Pkwy. at Rte. . Open daily 9am-5pm. 757- 3-4838. www.historyisfun.org.

e state-run facility re-creates the life both Native Americans and English lonists in early 17C Virginia. Visits gin at the **exhibition galleries★**, here the rise of the Age of Explora- n is discussed, along with the early forts at colonization and the culture the coastal Powhatan Indians. A min documentary, **Jamestown: e Beginning**, traces one colonist's emory of the founding of the colony. palisaded reproduction of James rt surrounds the kind of simple atch-roofed structures that served the only European foothold on the ntinent for several years. Adjacent to e fort is a re-creation of a Powhatan dian village. Berthed in the river below e fort are reproductions of the three ips—the *Susan Constant, Godspeed* d *Discovery*—that brought the colo-

Visitors at Yorktown Victory Center

Courtesy WACVB

nists to Jamestown in 1607. Costumed interpreters here explain the difficult transatlantic crossing.

### Yorktown Victory Center★

*Near the east end of Colonial Pkwy. at Rte. 238.* Open daily 9am-5pm. $8.75. 757-253-4838. www.histo ryisfun.org.

Exhibits, a timeline and the 18min film *A Time of Revolution* explain the events leading up to the Revolution and the 1781 Siege of Yorktown, where the Con- tinental Army won a victory that ensured America's independence from England. On the museum grounds, a Continental Army encampment and a post-Revolu- tionary farm are re-created.

### Yorktown National Battlefield Park★

*East end of Colonial Pkwy.* $10/7-day pass 757-898-2410. www.nps. gov/colo.

Encompassing some 5,000 acres on the bluffs above the York River, this park preserves earthworks from the 1781 **Siege of Yorktown**, several homes associated with the siege, and the Yorktown National Cemetery, where Union soldiers who fell in the Civil War are buried. The park visitor center fea- tures exhibits and the 16min docudrama *Siege at Yorktown*, detailing Gen. George

Washington's crucial victory here over Lord Cornwallis in the early fall of 1781. A self-guided driving tour leads 2mi through the open battlefields to the white clapboard **Moore House**, where terms of surrender were discussed, then on to **Surrender Field**, where the British capitulated on October 19.

Rising on the river bluffs north of the visitor center, the **Yorktown Victory Monument** (1781) is an 84ft-high shaft topped by a 14ft statue of Liberty.

## Excursion

### Norfolk★
*42mi south of Yorktown via I-64.*
Occupying a broad peninsula bounded by the Chesapeake Bay, Hampton Roads and the Elizabeth River, Norfolk has been a shipping center since it was founded in 1608. Continuing its maritime traditions, the city is home to the **Norfolk Naval Station**★★ (☎visit by guided tou only; tours depart from 9079 Hampto Blvd.; ☎757-444-7955). The larg est naval base in the world (establishe 1917) sprawls across 8,000 acres edg ing the Elizabeth River and Willoughb Bay. The base is home port to 78 ship (including 5 aircraft carriers), 133 aircra and more than 70 major naval con manders. Aside from its working por Norfolk boasts the excellent **Chrysle Museum**★★ (245 Olney Rd.; ☎757-664-6200). Named for its benefac tor, automobile scion and art collecto Walter Chrysler, this art museum con tains a renowned **glass collection**★★ with pieces ranging from Roman glas c. 100 BC to works by Dale Chihuly.

Horticulturists will love the **Norfol Botanical Gardens**★ (6700 Azalea Ga den Rd.; ☎757-441-5830), whic grace 155 acres with bountiful azalea (Apr–mid-May), camellias (spring, fall winter) and rhododendrons (May).

# COLONIAL WILLIAMSBURG★★★

MICHELIN MAP 584 T 9
EASTERN STANDARD TIME

Virginia's 18C colonial capital has been painstakingly re-created on this 173 acre town site that includes 88 original shops, houses, and public building and hundreds of reconstructed colonial structures on their original sites. Th restoration project, begun in the late 1920s, continues to this day.

- **Information:** ☎757-229-1000. www.history.org.
- **Orient Yourself:** Ditch the car and plan to spend time on foot to get a sense of how folks did things in the 18C.
- **Don't Miss:** A glimpse of an era gone by wherever you look.
- **Kids:** With period costumes and hands-on exhibits, most of Williamsburg is interesting to kids.

## A Bit of History

The town's roots date to 1699, when colonial legislators decided to move their capital from Jamestown inland to Middle Plantation, where the College of William and Mary had been recently founded. The new capital, Williamsburg, named after William III, centered around mile-long, unpaved Duke of Gloucester Street, anchored on the east by the colonial capitol, on the west by the college, and in the middle by Bruton Parish Church— layout reflecting the spiritual, educationa and governmental concerns of 18C Eng lishmen. The town rapidly grew into a important commercial, governmental an cultural center. Many prominent Virginian educated at the college (Thomas Jefferso among them) became proponents of th patriotic cause, and in the 1770s the tow itself became a hotbed of Revolutionar zeal. From Virginia's House of Burgesse came some of the leading figures of th merican Revolution, such as Peyton Randolph, George Washington, Thomas Jefferson and Patrick Henry. In 1780 the Virginia capital was moved to Richmond, and the town languished until 1926, when with generous funding from John D. Rockefeller, Jr., scholars and archaeologists began reconstructing the colonial town. Today Colonial Williamsburg brings history to life with the help of well-versed costumed guides and strolling character interpreters who depict 18C citizens of Williamsburg going about their daily routines. Daily "Day in History" enactments re-create seminal events leading up to the Revolution.

## Visit

Forays to Williamsburg should begin at the **Visitor Center** (Lafayette St. near the intersection with the Colonial Pkwy. Open daily 9am–5pm. $36. 757-229-1000 or www.history.org), where you can purchase one of several different types of passes that encompass varying amounts of time and numbers of sights. Begin your visit by viewing the 35min film, Williamsburg: The Story of a Patriot, for a grounding in the town's historical significance. Historic homes are open on different days of the week; check at the visitor center when you buy your ticket. Be sure to stop in at some of the colonial taverns and shops, including the **James Geddy House and Foundry**, where smithing techniques are explained, and the **Pasteur & Galt Apothecary Shop**, where the healing techniques of "apothecary-surgeons" are detailed.

## Capitol★★★

East end of Duke of Gloucester St. Visit by guided tour only.

Originally completed in 1705, the colony's capitol was destroyed by fire in 1747, rebuilt in 1753 and destroyed again in 1832. The current reconstruction faithfully depicts the first building in its layout and distinctive rounded walls. The two-story structure's H shape symbolizes the bicameral system of British colonial government, with the elected burgesses housed on the sparely decorated east side of the building and the royal gov-

ernor and his council of 13 appointed men on the lavishly decorated west side. Here, in the impressive general court, the council sat in judgment on colonists accused of crimes. Most famous of the re-created capitol chambers is the **Hall of the House of Burgesses**, with its simple straight-backed pews. It was here in 1765 that patriotic firebrand **Patrick Henry** delivered his inflammatory lines: "Caesar...had his Brutus, Charles the First his Cromwell, and George the Third may profit by their example. If this be treason, make the most of it."

The restored **public gaol** (north of the Capitol on Nicholson St.) depicts the harsh conditions under which accused persons were held until they came to trial—leg irons, sleeping mats on the floor and only a thin blanket were the norm. In contrast, the jailkeeper and his family enjoyed pleasant living quarters.

### Raleigh Tavern★★

East end of Duke of Gloucester St., 1 block west of the capitol. Visit by guided tour only.

A reconstruction of the famous colonial tavern, the capacious building contains 18C gaming rooms, reception halls, and "above-stairs" guest chambers. In its heyday, the tavern stood at the pivot of the colonial capital's vivacious social life, welcoming such illustrious regulars as George Washington, Thomas Jefferson and Peyton Randolph. When, owing to their outspoken patriotism, Virginia's elected burgesses (representatives) were "dissolved" by the Royal Governor,

Old fashioned wagon with snacks

*The Wren building at the College of William & Mary*

they typically reconstituted themselves by meeting unofficially at the Raleigh. The original building burned in 1859; built on the old foundations, the reconstruction relies upon colonial drawings and inventories for its authenticity.

## Courthouse★

*Duke of Gloucester St., on north side of Market Square.*

Completed in 1771, the Georgian brick building, ornamented with "round-headed" windows and double doors, is topped by an octagonal cupola bearing its original weathervane. Reenactments of colonial court cases are held here daily.

## Governor's Palace★★★

*North end of Palace Green.  Visit by guided tour only.*

An elaborate reconstruction of the 1722 royal governor's palace that burned in 1781, the stately structure is deserving of its original status as the most impressive building of its era in the colonies. Elegant woodwork and period furnishings characterize its public reception rooms

and grand ballroom; an incomparab ornamental display of 18C firearm hangs in its entrance **Hall of Arm** and along the broad paneled stairwa leading to the second floor. The uppe floor private chambers feature delft-ti fireplace surrounds and finely wroug wall paneling; the **governor's offic** boasts hand-tooled Moroccan leath wallpaper. Seven royal governors an Virginia's first two independent gove nors lived here, and during the decisiv Siege of Yorktown, the palace serve as a hospital for wounded Continent soldiers. The building is surrounded b 10 acres of formal gardens, including **boxwood maze** that is as popular wit contemporary children as it was wit their colonial counterparts.

## George Wythe House★★

*West side of Palace Green.  Visit guided tour only.*

The starkly Georgian original brick hom of Virginia's most respected jurist and th College of William and Mary's first la professor was considered one of the fine structures in colonial Williamsburg. Her

George Wythe (1726-1806) mentored his students, some of whom (Thomas Jefferson and John Marshall) became the nation's founding fathers. Wythe himself was an outspoken Patriot, and many of his enlightened ideas still inform US law and government. The rich interior of the house reflects the 18C tastes of the Virginia gentry in its brightly painted paneling and wallpaper. Behind the house a row of dependencies reflect the operations necessary to sustain a well-heeled colonial household.

## College of William and Mary★

*West end of Duke of Gloucester St. The college functions independently of Colonial Williamsburg.* ☎757-221-4000.
Predating Williamsburg itself, this lovely "university college" ranks as the second-oldest institution of higher learning in the US (after Harvard University in Massachusetts). King William and Queen Mary chartered it as a theological college for gentlemen in 1693, and in 1695 the foundations for the stately U-shaped **Wren Building**★, believed to have been designed by prominent English architect Sir Christopher Wren, were laid. Today this prestigious coeducational state institution enrolls some 5,500 undergraduate students.

## DeWitt Wallace Decorative Arts Museum

*S. Henry & Francis Sts.* ☎757-220-7554.
This gallery is renowned for its collection of English and American pieces covering the period from 1600 through 1830. The gallery was named for its premier benefactor, *Reader's Digest* magazine founder DeWitt Wallace. The museum's superb **Masterworks collection**★ *(2nd-floor mezzanine)* features rare decorative arts from the Colonial period, including British silver and porcelain, and Charles Willson Peale's military portrait (1780) of the young George Washington. Highlights include an impressive collection of **"Furniture of the American South"** and an extensive silver collection. The outdoor **Lila Acheson Wallace Garden** *(2nd floor)*, designed by Sir Peter Shepheard, centers around a reflecting pool, offset with a reproduction of Augustus Saint-Gaudens' *Diana*.

---

### Williamsburg in the 21C

Aside from the pleasures of the past available in the colonial village, visitors also flock to the Williamsburg area for more contemporary attractions. Chief among them is golf. Colonial Williamsburg itself boasts three courses, including the acclaimed Golden Horseshoe. Another draw is **Busch Gardens Williamsburg** 🄺🄸🄳🅂 *(☎757-253-3350)*, a beautifully landscaped amusement park with thrill rides, games and live entertainment, all set within European-themed villages. An affiliated Busch attraction, nearby **Water Country USA** 🄺🄸🄳🅂 *(☎757-253-3350)* offers water rides, slides and entertainment in a 1950s surf-culture setting. For shoppers, a seemingly endless string of **outlet malls** lines US-60, west of the historic area.

## Excursion

### Carter's Grove★★

*8mi southeast of Colonial Williamsburg on US-60.* �🕐Open daily 9am–5pm. ⊛$10. ☎757-229-1000, ext. 2973.
Owned by Colonial Williamsburg, this imposing Georgian manor house on the James River was originally built in the 1750s for the grandson of wealthy Virginia planter Robert "King" Carter. The 1930s restoration resulted in a hybrid of Colonial furnishings in a rich, comfortable setting. Today Carter's Grove, with its paneled entrance hall and rooms overlooking the James, is decorated with antiques collected by its former owners, the McCrea family. On the estate's extensive grounds a cluster of re-created **slave quarters** depicts the living conditions and cultural traditions of enslaved African Americans in the Tidewater area during the 18C.
Also on site, the underground **Winthrop Rockefeller Archaeology Museum**★ displays artifacts recovered from **Wolstenholme Towne**, a palisaded settlement built as the administrative seat of vast Martin's Hundred plantation in 1619 and burned by Indians in 1622.

# ST. LOUIS AREA

Tucked just south of the confluence of the Mississippi and Missouri rivers, the city of St. Louis and its environs fan out over 6,400sq mi. Encompassing 12 counties, the Greater St. Louis area includes the collar counties of Franklin, St. Charles and Jefferson, as well as the Illinois communities just east across the Mississippi. From downtown, the city unfolds westward to its border with St. Louis County just beyond Forest Park. Separate entities since 1876, the city and county are often lumped together as "St. Louis," even though communities outside the city limits are identified by their location in North, West, Mid or South County. With roughly 2.5 million people, this is the 18th largest metropolitan area in the US.

From the north, the Mississippi River cuts its swath through little hills and floodplains, past farms and fields. Missouri's **Great River Road**, Route 79 between St. Louis and **Hannibal**, parallels its course and affords several spectacular vantage points where the road climbs into the oak forests that blanket the limestone bluffs. South of the city, the Mississippi rolls past the German river town of **Kimmswick** and on to **Ste. Genevieve**, Missouri's oldest permanent settlement, founded in the 1730s by French lead miners.

Ninety miles west of downtown St. Louis, the state capitol building rises grandly from the riverbank at **Jefferson City**. Completed in 1918, the handsome edifice features a comprehensive state

*St. Louis and the Gateway Arch*

museum along with a remarkable room of murals wrought by Missouri artist Thomas Hart Benton in 1936. Southwest of the capital, **Lake of the Ozarks**, the state's largest lake, sprawls over 93sq mi. Created by damming the Osage River in 1929, the lake attracts fishing enthusiasts, boaters and campers to its 90mi of shoreline, while tourists swarm the area's outlet malls, fun parks and miniature-golf courses.

# ST. LOUIS ★

MAP P430
CENTRAL TIME
POPULATION 347,181

In the 17C, some 750,000 Native Americans inhabited this landscape, embossed by the earthen mounds of their ancient ancestors. The French came next, and their influence still lingers in the architecture and atmosphere. In 1764 fur traders Pierre Laclede and René Chouteau named their riverfront trading post for Louis IX, French king and saint, and the Louisiana Purchase in 1803 established St. Louis at the edge of the frontier. Eager settlers funneled through the growing city, headed West in the wake of Lewis and Clark. As the steamboat age dawned in 1817, river traffic increased until 100 boats a day crowded the levee. The railroads arrived in 1857 bringing new waves of immigrants, many of them Germans, who built up the industrial city that would become "first in shoes, first in booze." When the first St. Louis bridge spanned the river in 1874, steamboats succumbed to railroads.

**Information:** ☎800-916-0040. www.explorestlouis.com
**Don't Miss:** The iconic Gateway Arch.
**Kids:** The open enclosures of the St. Louis Zoo.

## A Bit of History

The 1904 Louisiana Purchase Exposition, better known as the **St. Louis World's Fair**, buoyed civic spirits and gave St. Louis a new sense of culture and worldliness. Twentieth-century St. Louis shared difficult times with other industrial centers. Urban blight, suburban flight, racial tension, a declining tax base and a weakening of the manufacturing economy took their toll. Beginning in the 1960s, projects including the Jefferson National Expansion Memorial and several sports and convention venues have helped to revitalize the downtown, and a growing service sector provides jobs for upward of one-third of the labor force. Shipments of raw goods still flow through the city, which remains a major river crossing.

With a world-class symphony orchestra, Saint Louis and Washington universities, three professional sports franchises— the **Cardinals** (baseball), **Rams** (football) and **Blues** (hockey)—and some of the best **jazz and blues** music in the country, St. Louis offers the entertainment and educational variety of a much larger city. A little East, a bit of West; some North and a dash of South combine into the varietal blend of American history, custom and culture that characterizes the Gateway to the West.

## Downtown

Extending west from the riverfront for about 20 blocks, St. Louis' central business district is bounded on the north by Biddle Street and on the south by Chouteau Avenue. Defining downtown's main east-west axis, Market and Chestnut Streets border a strip of public plazas and important buildings called **Gateway Mall**. Anchored at its western end

## Address Book

ℰ*For coin ranges, see the Legend on the cover flap.*

### WHERE TO STAY

**$$$ Hyatt Regency St. Louis** – *One Union Station, St. Louis, MO.* ☎314-231-1234. www.hyattstlouis. com. *539 rooms.* Housed in one of the country's largest 19C railroad terminals, the opulent hotel lobby (formerly the station's Grand Hall) boasts six-story vaulted ceilings, stained-glass windows and bas-reliefs. Guest rooms and period furnishings reflect the Gilded Age.

**$$$ The Roberts Mayfair** – *806 St. Charles St., St. Louis, MO.* ☎314-421-2500. www. wyndham. com. *182 rooms.* This 1925 downtown landmark's elegant lobby looks as glamorous as when Cary Grant stayed here in the 1950s. Most accommodations are one-bedroom suites decorated in elegant damask wall coverings and mahogany furnishings.

**$$ Seven Gables Inn** – *26 N. Meramec Ave., St. Louis, MO.* ☎314-863-8400. www.sevengablesinn.com. *32 rooms.* Built in 1926, this Tudor Revival apartment building in tony Clayton has been revamped into a countrified guest house. Subtle rose-and-beige-backed florals set the scene for 19C hardwood armoires and brass beds in the spacious rooms. Separate seating areas with overstuffed couches complete the picture. Have breakfast in the brick courtyard.

### WHERE TO EAT

**$$$ Sidney Street Cafe** – *2000 Sidney St., St. Louis, MO. Closed Sun & Mon.* ☎314-771-5777. www.sidneystreetcafe. com. **Contemporary.** Exposed-brick walls and old-fashioned street lamps recall an outdoor courtyard, but this Benton Park restaurant is set inside a 19C storefront. Regulars dine by candlelight on updated classics like marinated filet with crispy fried onions and Jack Daniel's sauce, and applewood smoked duck breast.

**$$ Harry's Restaurant & Bar** – *2144 Market St., St. Louis, MO.* ☎314-421-6969. **Contemporary.** There are stunning views of Union Station and the Gateway Arch from almost any table at this chic downtown eatery. Vibrant multicolored walls lined with local artwork offset the somber dark wood booths edged along 20ft-tall windows.

**$ Blueberry Hill** – *6504 Delmar Blvd., St. Louis, MO.* ☎314-727-4444. **American.** Residents come to this festive U-City Loop nightclub for the best burgers in town. The block-long venue is a wall-to-wall showcase of pop-culture memorabilia, including everything from Beatles dolls to Chuck Berry's Gibson guitar.

by monumental Union Station and **Aloe Plaza**—where you'll find the frolicsome fountain *Meeting of the Waters* (1940) by Swedish sculptor Carl Milles—the strip abuts the Jefferson National Expansion Memorial to the east. Set about by convention centers and sporting arenas (Busch Stadium, Savvis Center, America's Center and Edward Jones Dome), downtown also boasts Louis Sullivan's 1891 **Wainwright Building** *(111 N. 7th St.)*, one of the earliest steel-frame skyscrapers. Another engineering wonder, **Eads Bridge**, the world's first steel-truss span (1874), crosses the Mississippi at Washington Avenue. Just north of the bridge, nine square blocks of handsome 19C commercial warehouses have been

converted into a dining and entertain ment district known as **Laclede's Land ing**. South of downtown lies the historic **Soulard** neighborhood.

### Jefferson National Expansion Memorial★

*Along the riverfront between Poplar St. & Washington Ave.* ☎314-655-1700. www. nps.gov/jeff.

This rectangular greensward occupies the historic levee once alive with waterfron commerce. In 1939, 40 square blocks o the then-decrepit area were razed to make way for a memorial to Thomas Jef ferson and his vision of westward expan sion. Within the 91-acre park the Gateway

©iStockphoto.com/Shaun Clark

*Downtown St Louis*

Arch and the Old Courthouse commemorate and document that vision.

## Gateway Arch★★

*Riverfront between Poplar & Washington Aves. ©Open daily 8am-10pm. ☎877-982-1410. www.gatewayarch.com.*
This astonishing bend of steel is, at 630ft, the tallest man-made monument in the US. An early work by architect Eero Saarinen, it was completed with much fanfare in October 1965 and has since come to symbolize St. Louis. The arch astounds for its scale, its construction and, most of all, for its shimmering skin and crisp geometry. Underground entrances at each foot access the visitor center, where the **Museum of Westward Expansion** uses historic artifacts and photographs to trace the settlement of America. In the Tucker Theater, a spine-tingling 35min film called **Monument to the Dream★** documents the precarious construction process. For those who wish to ascend the arch, small tram cars climb up inside the curve of each leg to the apex. Since by law no building in St. Louis may exceed the monument in height, small portholes at the top provide the best **view★** of the city. *To avoid crowds, purchase tickets early for timed entry to the tram and movies.*

## The Old Courthouse★

*11 N. 4th St. ©Open daily 8am-4:30pm. Free. ☎314-655-1600. www.nps.gov/jeff/arch-home.*

To the west across Memorial Drive, St. Louis' historic Greek Revival courthouse was completed in stages by the 1860s with the addition of a cast-iron dome in the Italian Renaissance style. Within these walls slaves Dred and Helen Scott won their suit for freedom in 1850; overturned by higher courts, the Dred Scott Decision hastened the Civil War. Under its elegantly restored rotunda, the Old Courthouse now houses the site's National Park Service headquarters, as well as four compact **history galleries★**.

## Basilica of St. Louis, King (The Old Cathedral)

*209 Walnut St. ☎314-231-3250.*
Completed in 1834, the cathedral served a diocese that covered half the continent. Granted basilica status by the pope in 1961 for its age and influence, the church was restored to its original appearance in 1963 and remains the seat of an active parish. The simple Neoclassical elegance of the mauve and blue **interior★** strongly reflects the church's French roots.

## Union Station★★

*Market St. between 18th & 20th Sts. ©Open daily 10am-9pm. ☎314-421-6655. www.stlouisunionstation.com.*
By every measure monumental, the Richardsonian Romanesque profile of Union Station rivals the Gateway Arch for skyline honors. Architect Theodore

*Cathedral Basilica of Saint Louis*

Link took inspiration from the walled city of Carcassonne in France to design his 1894 masterwork. Restored in 1985, the station now houses a luxury hotel, restaurants and shops. Informational panels mounted on the balustrade throughout the complex explain its history. Enter under the glass and iron porte cochere off Market Street for a breathtaking first impression of the magnificent vaulted **Grand Hall**★★. The lovely **art-glass lunette** above the entryway depicts the railroad muses of St. Louis, New York and San Francisco.

## City Museum★

Kids *701 N. 15th St.* ○*Open daily 9am.* ⊕*$12.* ✗ ♿ 🅿 ☏*314-231-2489. www.citymuseum.org.*

Mixing magic with the mundane, City Museum combines ordinary objects into a creative brew of art and ideas. The converted shoe warehouse contains three floors furnished largely with recycled materials—from conveyer belt spindles to laboratory mouse cages. Don't miss the kitschy delights in the Museum of Mirth, Mystery, and Mayhem on the third floor.

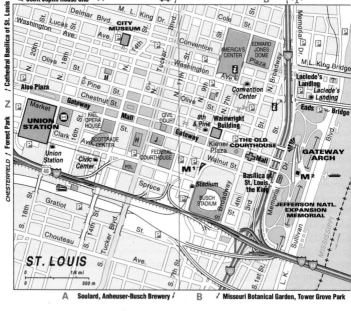

ST. LOUIS

| A | Soulard, Anheuser-Busch Brewery | | B | Missouri Botanical Garden, Tower Grove Park |

# Forest Park

St. Louis' major green space occupies nearly 1,300 acres at the city's west end. Opened in 1876, it covers more ground than New York's Central Park and is famous for having hosted the Louisiana Purchase Exposition in 1904. This pleasant park today provides the setting for several of St. Louis' major cultural institutions. A day spent here might include a stroll in nearby **Central West End**, the historic neighborhood at the park's northeast corner where elegant homes, trendy bistros and small shops share the tree-lined blocks.

## Saint Louis Art Museum★

*Fine Arts Dr.* ○*Open daily 10am. Free.* ⚓♿🅿 ☎*314-721-0072. www.stlouis.art. museum.*

Founded in 1879, the art museum took up residence here after the 1904 world's fair in the exposition's only remaining permanent building, the Beaux-Arts Palace of Fine Arts (1904, Cass Gilbert). With a collection that runs the gamut of world art from ancient to modern and eastern to Western, the museum is particularly strong in **German Expressionists**, including the largest cache of works by **Max Beckmann** anywhere.

## St. Louis Zoo★

🚌 *1 Government Dr.* ○*May–September, 10am; 9am rest of the year* 🍴♿🅿 ☎*314-781-0900.*

The impetus for this fine zoo came from the huge wire mesh "flight cage" built by the Smithsonian Institution to house the US bird exhibit at the 1904 world's fair. A pioneer in the use of open enclosures, the 90-acre zoo also includes Penguin and Puffin Coast, with an impressive collection of oceanic birds. Nearby, the **Emerson Children's Zoo** entertains young visitors with a playground and touchable animals.

## St. Louis Science Center

🚌 *5050 Oakland Ave.* ○*Open daily :30am. Free.* 🍴♿🅿 ☎*314-289-4400. www.slsc.org.*

In the mold of many modern science museums, this bustling and colorful complex offers hundreds of hands-on science and technology exhibits. A glass-enclosed bridge and an underground tunnel connect with **McDonnell Planetarium** across busy US-40/I-64, providing the perfect setting to explore high-speed roadway design.

## Cathedral Basilica of Saint Louis★★

*4431 Lindell Blvd.* ♿🅿
☎*314-373-8200. www.cathedralstl.org.*
Several blocks east of Forest Park, the handsome if reserved Romanesque exterior of this Catholic cathedral belies the breathtaking riot of color inside. From narthex to sanctuary and up to the apex of the 143ft central dome, 41.5 million pieces of glass tesserae in 8,000 colors encrust 83,000sq ft. Byzantine in style, the spectacle represents the largest mosaic collection in the world. Construction began in 1907, and the mosaics took 20 artists over 75 years to complete. A museum about the church and its mosaics occupies the lower level.

# Additional Sights

## Anheuser-Busch Brewery★

*12th & Lynch Sts.* 📷*Visit of interior by guided tour only.* 💰*$9. Free.* ♿🅿 ☎*314-577-2626. www.budweisertours.com.*
German immigrants used the cool depths of St. Louis' network of underground limestone caves to age their lager beer. On the south side, where caves were especially plentiful, Eberhard Anheuser established his brewery in 1860. Son-in-law Adolphus Busch launched the first national brand of beer with the debut of Budweiser in 1876; today Bud is the top-selling beer in the world and Anheuser-Busch is the largest brewery.
Hour-long walking tours of the 100-acre world headquarters begin at the **Tour Center** and take in the beautifully maintained brewing, aging and bottling buildings. One highlight is the pristine **stables**, built in 1885 to house the brewery's draught horses, and today occupied by one of the famous Anheuser-Busch Clydesdale teams.

## Missouri Botanical Garden★★

*4344 Shaw Blvd.* ⏰*Open daily 10am-4pm.* ⬚*$2.50.* ✗⬚🅿 ☎*314-577-9400.*

A labor of love by wealthy merchant Henry Shaw, the 79-acre Missouri Botanic Garden opened to the public in 1859. Paths wind through a variety of gardens, representing different historic styles, groupings of related plants, and theories of garden design. Highlights include **Climatron®**, housing an impressive tropical rain forest, and the **Japanese Garden**★, at 14 acres the largest of its kind in the US. **Tower Grove House**, Shaw's country estate, is the centerpiece of the Victorian Area. The **Linnean House** (1882) has exhibited camellias for over a century.

South of the garden lies the 276-acre expanse of **Tower Grove Park** (*4255 Arsenal St.;* ☎ *314-771-2679*). Also donated to the city by Henry Shaw, it survives as a rare unaltered example of Victorian park landscaping, complete with gazebos, pavilions, a bandstand and even artificial ruins.

## Scott Joplin House State Historic Site

*2658 Delmar Blvd.* ↜*Visit by guided tour only.* ♿☎*314-340-5790.*

African-American jazz musician Scott Joplin (1868-1917) composed some of his best-known ragtime works during the two years he occupied this second-floor flat.

---

### Missouri's Weinstrasse

For a fun excursion from Defiance, take Route 94 West and enjoy lunch and an afternoon of wine tasting on the **Missouri Weinstrasse**. Along the banks of the Missouri River west of St. Louis, 19C German immigrants planted vineyards and established the first American wine district. Today, Route 94, Missouri's **Wine Route**, bends along the river for 20mi from Defiance to Dutzow past wineries that date to the mid-1800s. *For maps and information, contact Missouri Department of Agriculture Grape & Wine Program,* ☎*800-392-9463.*

---

# Excursions

## St. Charles★

*22mi west of St. Louis. Take I-70 across Missouri River to the 5th St. Exit, then north to First Capitol Dr. Turn right on Main St.* ☎*636-946-7776. www.historicstcharles.com.*

Just over the Missouri River lies this historic hamlet established by French Canadian fur traders in 1769. Today St. Charles, the oldest settlement on the river, preserves its past in the **Frenchtown Historic District** (*N. 2nd St. between Decatur & Tecumseh Sts.*) and the **South Main Historic District**★ which stretches for 10 blocks south of Jefferson Street (*walking-tour brochures for both districts are available at the visitors bureau, 230 S. Main St.;* ☎*636-946-7776*). Lewis and Clark set off from here in 1804 to chart the unknown Louisiana Purchase; the small **Lewis and Clark Center** (*1050 Riverside Dr.;* ☎*636-947-3199*) recounts their journey.

## Daniel Boone Home and Boonesfield Village

*35mi west of St. Louis in Defiance, MO. Take I-40/64 West to Rte. 94 South, turn right on Hwy. F to no. 1868.* ↜*Visit by guided tour only.* ☎*636-798-2005.*

Nestled in Missouri's rolling farm country, this living-history village focuses on the limestone home of Daniel Boone (*see WESTERN KENTUCKY*), completed here in 1810. Boone spent his old age in the house and died in his second-story bedroom in 1820. Of note on the grounds is the lovely 1838 **Old Peace Chapel**★

## Cahokia Mounds State Historic Site★★

*8mi from St. Louis in Collinsville, IL. Take I-55/70 East, get off at Exit 6, go right on Hwy. 111 for .25mi. then left on Collinsville Rd. for 1.5mi. Turn right on Ramey St. to Interpretive Center.* ⏰*Open daily 9am* ⬚*Suggested $2 donation.* ♿🅿 ☎*618-346-5160. www.cahokiamounds.com.*

This 2,200-acre UNESCO World Heritage site was the largest prehistoric settlement north of Mexico, sustaining at its peak as many as 20,000 people. Begin your visit at the **Interpretive Center** with a 15min slide show and an elaborate exhibit that explores life in Cahokia between AD 700 and AD 1400. Archaeologists believe the complex and sophisticated "chiefdom" was the center of a vast trading network supported by the rich agricultural bounty of the Mississippi floodplain. Although the Cahokians mysteriously abandoned the site by the 1400s, the giant earth mounds they built for ceremony and burial remain. The largest, 100ft-high **Monk's Mound**, was a base of more than 14 acres.

### Winston Churchill Memorial and Library

*100mi west of St. Louis on the Westminster College campus in Fulton, MO. Take I-70 West to US-54 South, then turn left on Rte. F to Fulton. 501 Westminster Ave. 10am.* ↻$6. ☎573-592-5369.

A 12C English church cuts a surprising silhouette in this small Missouri college town, but St. Mary's, Aldermanbury, is indeed authentic. It marks the site where Sir Winston Churchill gave his famous "Sinews of Peace" speech on March 5, 1946—in which he immortalized the phrase "Iron Curtain." The venerable **church** was moved here in 1969. Enter through the museum, where a 12min video and exhibits will introduce you to Churchill's life and the restoration of the church.

---

## Mark Twain of Missouri

Among America's best-loved authors and humorists, Mark Twain (1835-1910) gave voice through his writings to the burgeoning culture of America's heartland. With an ear for dialect and a quick wit, Twain brought to life the people of the Mississippi River Valley and the very rhythms of the river he knew so well. Twain was born Samuel Clemens (his pen name comes from riverboat jargon for deep water) in Florida, Missouri. Today the **Mark Twain Birthplace State Historic Site** (*off Hwy. 107 East on County Rd. U in Monroe County;* ☎573-565-3449) preserves his tiny two-room home along with exhibits on the man and his work.

His father, a justice of the peace, moved the family to the Mississippi River town of Hannibal when Samuel was four. Laid out in 1819 between chunky limestone bluffs, the little town was swarming with riverboat traffic by the 1840s. River life and landscape bewitched the young boy and served, along with friends and family, as the inspiration for Twain's most famous works *The Adventures of Tom Sawyer* (1876) and *The Adventures of Huckleberry Finn* (1885).

Except that tourism now supports the town's economy, **Hannibal** (*100mi north of St. Louis via US-61*) seems little changed since Twain called it "a white town drowsing in the sunshine." Visitors can tour six historic sites with one pass from the **Mark Twain Boyhood Home and Museum** (*120 N. Main St.;* ☎573-221-9010). There are also **riverboats** to ride (*Center Street Landing;* ☎573-221-3222) and, outside of town, the **Mark Twain Cave** (*Rte. 79 South;* ☎573-221-1656), where, like Tom Sawyer, young Twain no doubt enjoyed some boyhood adventures. Twain left Hannibal in 1853 to pursue printing, riverboat piloting, journalism and, finally, writing. Ironically, he composed his Mississippi River sagas on the banks of the Chemung River in upstate New York, where he spent summers with his wife's family beginning in 1870.

© Corbis

*Tom Sawyer's House*

# UPSTATE NEW YORK

Though New York City cuts a bold silhouette on the state's landscape, much that is beautiful about New York's 47,000sq mi lies upstate. Bisected by the Mohawk River that flows between Troy and Rome, this region's varied terrain includes the ancient Appalachian Plateau south of the river and the heavily wooded Adirondack Mountains to the north. As recently as 10,000 years ago, glaciers provided the details, carving out lakes and valleys, bedecking the land with moraine deposits and melting into rushing streams and rivers.

Fertile soil, abundant wildlife and ample natural resources made the region hospitable to early humans, and there flowered the mighty **Iroquois Confederacy**. These five Indian nations, the Seneca, Mohawk, Oneida, Cayuga and Onondaga (the Tuscarora joined the confederacy in the early 18C, making it six tribes), occupied and controlled much of upstate New York from AD 1300 until the American Revolution. After siding with the British in that conflict, the confederacy faltered, only to be decimated by the Continental Army. A highly sophisticated society, the Iroquois created America's first representative democracy, which inspired Benjamin Franklin and James Madison as they crafted the bylaws of the American republic in the mid-1700s.

The Erie Canal, which linked Albany and Buffalo by 1825, and later the railroad, brought people and industry west, expedited the transport of goods and crops

east, and sealed the economic good fortune of the Empire State. A deeper and wider barge canal replaced the Erie Canal in 1918, and commercial and recreational boaters still ply the 524mi of New York's artificial waterways. Most modern upstate travelers, however, take the New York State Thruway (I-90) across the state from Albany to Buffalo through the Mohawk Valley. The crossroads of the region lies at **Syracuse**★ (where I-81 and I-90 intersect), once the central meeting

*Whiteface Mountain area, Adirondacks*

lace of the Iroquois nations. Upstate's other cities—**Albany**★, **Utica**, **Rome**, **Rochester**★ and **Buffalo**★—lie mostly along the Mohawk River-Erie Canal corridor. Near the canal's end, spectacular Niagara Falls has been awing visitors since at least 1678, when French missionary Father Louis Hennepin saw the roaring waters and proclaimed: "The Universe does not afford its Parallel." North of the Mohawk River, the wilderness of the Adirondacks prevails despite threats from logging and development. Farmlands, vineyards, historic lakeside settlements and country villages punctuate the rolling hills to the south and west. Abundant winter snow means good skiing and a range of cold-weather sports, and its incomparable fall foliage provides a stunning backdrop to hiking and camping. Summertime visitors enjoy the cool Adirondack forests and the refreshing waterfalls of the Finger Lakes.

## Area Address Book

🪙 *For coin ranges, see the Legend on the cover flap.*

### WHERE TO STAY

**$$ Geneva on the Lake** – 1001 Lochland Rd., *Geneva, NY.* ✗ ♿ 🅿 ☃ ☎315-789-7190. *www.GenevaontheLake. com. 30 rooms.* A 1910 estate, modeled after Rome's Villa Lancellotti, sits on 10 acres of labyrinthine gardens. Most guest quarters are one-bedroom suites, designed with Stickley-style oak furnishings and bright florals, that look onto Seneca Lake. The resort is located on Seneca Lake Wine Trail, near Hobart and William Smith colleges.

**$$ The Sagamore** – 11- *Sagamore Rd., Bolton Landing, NY.* ✗ ♿ 🅿 ☃ ☎518-644-9400. *www.thesagamore.com. 350 rooms.* The 70-acre private island resort on Lake George is just as luxurious as when it started out as the playground of America's millionaires in 1883. Rooms in the main house (c.1930) are done in delicate Colonial Revival pastels and ruffled draperies. Lodge rooms have a log-cabin feel, with equestrian prints and wood-burning fireplaces. They also have modern condominiums and even a six-bedroom castle for larger groups.

**$ Mirror Lake Inn** – 5 Mirror Lake Dr., *Lake Placid, NY.* ✗ ♿ 🅿 ☎518-523-2544. *www.mirrorlakeinn.com. 128 rooms.* This elegant 19C mansion has been operating as an exclusive retreat since 1925. Decked in rich mahogany, it is a cozy gathering place enhanced by stained-glass windows. Accommodations range from charming "Colonial" bedrooms to superior suites with mountain or lake views.

**$ The Red Coach Inn** – 2 Buffalo Ave., *Niagara Falls, NY.* ✗ 🅿 ☎716-282-1459. *www.redcoach.com. 18 rooms.* This charming all-suite guesthouse, just a quarter-mile from Niagara Falls is modeled after an English inn and combines the comforts of home with top service. Apartment-size accommodations, replete with cherry furnishings and chintz fabrics, have full kitchens and views of the Upper Rapids. An elaborate continental breakfast is delivered to your room every morning.

### WHERE TO EAT

**$$$ Edgar's at Belhurst Castle** – Rte. 14, *Geneva, NY.* ☎315-781-0201. www.belhurstcastle.com. **Contemporary**. This 1885 mansion/ hotel, about a mile outside town, has been everything from a casino to a speakeasy. Today all six luxurious dining rooms, featuring carved mahogany paneling and mosaic tile fireplaces, attract regulars from as far away as Rochester. On the menu: pheasant-stuffed mushroom caps and bacon in a lemon chardonnay sauce.

**$$ Anchor Bar** – 1047 Main St., *Buffalo, NY.* ☎716-886-8920. **Classic American**.

**$$Duff's** – 3651 Sheridan Dr., *Buffalo, NY.* ☎716-834-6234. **Classic American**. These two restaurants that lay claim to creating the Buffalo chicken wing have a long-standing rivalry, but not much else in common. Anchor Bar is an old downtown tavern, while Duff's is a hipper spot in a suburban area. Decide for yourself who should be king of the wing.

# THE ADIRONDACKS ★★★

MAP P 440

One of the best-protected wilderness areas in the nation, Adirondack Park com prises some six million acres (9,400sq mi) of public and private land, or one-fift of New York State's total area. It is bigger than Yellowstone, Grand Canyon an Yosemite national parks combined and encompasses more than 4,000 bodies o water; 2,000 peaks in five mountain ranges (the highest is Mt. Marcy at 5,344ft and 31,500mi of rivers, brooks and streams. More than a billion trees shelter it abundant wildlife. The park is bounded on the east by **Lake George** and Lak **Champlain** (named for the area's first European explorer), where **Fort Ticond eroga** ★★ *(Rte. 74, 1mi east of Ticonderoga; ☏ 518-585-2821)* offers views an a strong dose of history from both the French and Indian, and Revolutionar wars. About 29mi south, **Saratoga Springs** ★★★, an elite 19C vacation mecca makes an interesting gateway to the Adirondacks. To the northwest, the St Lawrence River forms the backbone of the scenic **Thousand Islands** ★ regio along the Canadian border.

- 🛈 **Information:** ☏ 518-846-8016. www.visitadirondacks.com
- 👁 **Don't Miss:** Winter pleasures at Lake Placid resort.
- 🕐 **Organizing Your Time:** Plan to spend as much time as possible in these great outdoors.
- 🕯 **Also See:** FINGER LAKES.

## A Bit of History

Long considered a "dismal wilderness," by 1850 the area's rich timber reserves had made New York the biggest logging state in the Union. To protect the water-shed, the state created a forest preserve, and in 1894 amended its constitution to ensure that all such lands, including Adirondack Park, would remain "forever wild." Since then, an often tense blend of preservation and development has succeeded in balancing pristine wilder-ness with public and private use. Today, some 10 million visitors and 130,000 permanent residents enjoy the beauty of Adirondack Park.

## Sights

### Lake Placid Village ★
*On Mirror Lake. ☏ 518-523-2445. Contact for hours. www.lakeplacid.com.*
A winter sports resort since the 1850s, this tiny village sealed its reputation as the "birthplace of winter sports in America" by hosting the 1932 and 1980 Winter Olympics. Today the village bus-tles with athletes who come to train at the state-of-the-art sports facilities an tourists who come to ski and hike in win ter and mountain bike and take sceni gondola rides in the summer. Upscal restaurants and shops line Main Street and the hulking **Olympic Center** *(263-Main St.; ☏ 518-523-1655)* offers tours You can also visit the **ski jumps** *(2m south of downtown on Rte.73; ☏ 518-523-2202)*, where jumpers practice o a special surface.

### Whiteface Mountain Veterans Memorial Highway ★★
*From Lake Placid take Rte. 86 to Rte. 431 i downtown Wilmington; continue 3mi t toll booth. Open daily, year-round, bu may be closed during inclement weathe. ☏ 518-946-2223. www.whiteface com.*
A notable exception to the 1894 "for ever wild" clause, this two-lane roa was built in 1927 as a memorial t World War I veterans. Climbing 8mi, provides the only automobile acces to a summit in the High Peaks. Park a the top and scale the final .2mi on foo from Whiteface Castle (or by elevato from the parking lot) to the summit o Whiteface Mountain (4,867ft), where th

© Gwen Cannon

aranac Lake and Whiteface Mountain

60-degree **view**★★★ extends 110mi
n a clear day.

### dirondack Museum★★★

*ntersection of Rtes. 30 & 28, Blue Moun-
ain Lake.* Open late-May-mid-October,
*aily, 10am-5pm.* $15 ✗ ♿ 🅿 ☎518-352-
*311. www.adkmuseum.org.*
ommanding a picturesque **view**★ of
lue Mountain Lake, this 32-acre com-
ound of historic buildings, galleries
nd exhibit halls explores all aspects of
he region's history. A 35min film shown
n the conference building provides a
hought-provoking historical overview.
On the grounds, explore stunning
xamples of **Adirondack architectu-
e**★, including rustic twig **Sunset Cot-
age**★ and whimsical **Bull Cottage**★.
he acclaimed exhibit on **Boats and
Boating in the Adirondacks**★★ is
ighlighted by an entire room devoted
o Adirondack **guideboats**★★—devel-
ped around 1849 to transport wilder-
ess guides and their clients. The **Road
nd Transportation Building**★ dedi-
ates 45,000sq ft of exhibit space to the
hallenge of transportation in this rug-
ed region. Vehicles of all descriptions

include an exquisitely restored 1890
**Pullman railroad car**★★.

### Great Camp Sagamore★★

*4mi south of the town of Raquette Lake,
off Rte. 28.* Visit by guided tour only.
*Memorial Day weekend-third weekend in
October.* Prices vary by tour. ✗ 🅿 ☎315-
*354-5311. www.sagamore.org.*
"Wilderness playground" of the wealthy
Vanderbilt family for more than 50 years,
Sagamore represents the passion among
America's turn-of-the-century nouveau
riche for getaways in the Adirondacks.
Built by developer William West Durant in
1897, this "great camp" was once a 1,500-
acre self-contained village, providing its
owners an "haute rustic" lifestyle. Today
the 19-acre National Historic Site incorporates the **upper camp** of servants' and
workers' quarters and other outbuildings.
In the **lower camp**, the **Wigwam**★ was
once used as a men's lodge, and the **main
lodge**★★ typifies Durant's Swiss-chalet-
meets-Adirondack-rustic aesthetic, a style
he is credited with inventing. The famous
outdoor **bowling alley**★ (1913) functions
to this day. Camps and workshops focusing on everything from sports to culture
are available to all age groups

# FINGER LAKES★★

MAP P440
EASTERN STANDARD TIME

At the heart of upstate New York hang the 11 Finger Lakes. Viewed from above the lakes appear suspended, like slender pendants on an invisible chain. Each one a jewel in its own right, these narrow lakes form the framework for landscape, leisure and life in this region. The Finger Lakes region encompasses 14 counties. Among the lakes, Cayuga is the longest at 40mi, and Seneca the deepest, reaching down more than 600ft in places. Tiny Canadice Lake, only 3mi long, is highest in elevation at 1,099ft above sea level. A happy blend of history, natural beauty and viticulture attracts millions of visitors to the Finger Lakes each year. Each lake hosts quaint communities at its north and south ends, and temperate microclimates in between make the Finger Lakes the second-largest winemaking region in the US after California's Napa Valley. Other stunning features of the area—precipitous glens and gorges and their boisterous waterfalls—are scenic by-products of ongoing water erosion, a process that began during the last Ice Age when glaciers carved up the surrounding terrain. Since 1300 the Iroquois tribes—later organized into the powerful six nations of the Iroquois Confederacy—have inhabited these lands. For more on the Iroquois, visit the living-history site **Sainte Marie Among the Iroquois★** Kids *(on Onondaga Pkwy/ Rte. 370;* ☎*315-453-6767)* just outside of Syracuse in Liverpool, which represents the first European settlement in the area. In 1825 the Erie Canal cut its swath north of the lakes bringing settlers, commerce and industry, and the **Erie Canal Museum★** *(318 Erie Blvd. E. at Montgomery St.; Mon-Sat 10am-5pm, Sun 10am-3pm; free;* ☎*315-471-0593; www.eriecanalmuseum.org)* in Syracuse explores its history.

- ℹ **Information:** . ☎315-536-7488. www.fingerlakes.org
- ▶ **Orient Yourself:** The Finger Lakes region covers 9,000 acres from Lake Ontario south to Pennsylvania, east to Syracuse and west to Rochester.
- ☺ **Don't Miss:** The views from Watkins Glen State Park.
- Kids **Kids:** Glassblowing demonstrations at the Corning Museum of Glass entertain kids of all ages.

## Sights

### Cornell University★★

*Main campus at intersection of Ithaca Rd. & Hoy Rd., Ithaca.* ♿ 🅿 ☎*607-254-4636. www.cornell.edu.*

Cornell was chartered in 1865 as New York's land-grant university to provide an education in both liberal and practical arts. Ezra Cornell, who had made his fortune in the telegraph business, donated 300 acres and a generous endowment to found the college. Today the 745-acre campus educates 19,500 students in more than 100 fields. Its lovely site above Cayuga Lake encompasses **Sage Chapel**, where Ezra Cornell is buried; and "Old Stone Row," which contains the oldest structures on campus. A good way to visit the campus is to follow one of the trails that originate at **Cornell Plantations★** *(One Plantation Rd.;* 🕐*Open daily year-round from sun-up to sunset;* 🅿 ☎*607-255-3020; www. plantations.cornell.edu),* a laboratory of local and non-native flora.

### Watkins Glen State Park★★

*Rte. 14/Franklin St., Watkins Glen.* 🕐*Open year-round, gorge trail open May-mid-November.* ⊜*$7 per vehicle* ⚠ 🅿 ☎*607-535-4511. .*

At the tip of Lake Seneca and about 25mi west of Ithaca, Watkins is perhaps the most spectacular glen in the Finger Lakes. The 1.5mi hike into the narrow gorge ascends 832 steps and 700ft in elevation alongside Glen Creek as it dances down the canyon through 19 waterfalls into crystal-clear plunge

*Taughannock Falls State Park*

pools and over well-worn rock formations. Climb Jacob's Ladder (a steep staircase) at the end and return along one of the upper trails. Then take in the view from the 85ft suspension bridge that crosses the gorge and connects the Indian and South Rim trails.

## Sonnenberg Gardens and Mansion ★

*151 Charlotte St., Canandaigua.* ○*Open the day after Memorial Day-Labor Day 9:30am-5:30pom.* ○*Open the day after Labor Day-early October 9:30am-4:30pm.* ☐ ☎*585-394-4922. www.sonnenberg.org.*
Set on 50 beautifully landscaped acres 20mi southeast of Rochester, this Queen Anne mansion was begun in 1885 for the founder of the First National Bank of New York. The gardens and the mansion's interior reflect the height of Victorian taste.

## Granger Homestead and Carriage Museum★

*295 N. Main St., Canandaigua.* ○*Visit by guided tour only, May 30-late-October, Tue-Wed 1-5pm, Thu-Fri 11am-5pm; June-September Sat and Sun 1-5pm.* ☐*$6.* ☐ ☎ *585-394-1472. www.granger homestead.org.*
Four buildings here pay homage to Canandaigua history, including an 1816 Federal-style mansion and a carriage museum showcasing more than 40 horse-drawn vehicles.

## Rose Hill Mansion★★

*3mi east of Geneva on Rte. 96A.* ○*Open May 1-October 31, Mon-Sat 10am-4pm, Sun 1-5pm.* ☐*$6.* ☎*315-789-3848.*
Find this charming 1839 Greek Revival mansion at the top of Lake Seneca, with a lovely **view** of the lake from its porch. Passed through many hands over the years, the mansion has been beautifully restored, from its temple-like exterior to the meticulously researched plasterwork, wall colors, floor coverings and furniture inside. An introductory 7min video and knowledgeable guides enhance the visit.

## Women's Rights National Historical Park Visitor Center★★

*136 Fall St., Seneca Falls.* ○*Open daily 9am-5pm.* ○*Closed major holidays.* ☐ *☎315-568-2991. www.nps.gov/wor.*
Seneca Falls, at the northern end of Lake Cayuga, is best known today as the historic center of the women's rights movement. Inspired by the movement to abolish slavery, the first Women's Rights Convention met here in 1848 in an attempt to extend equal rights to women. Today, a national historic park comprises several diverse sites important to the history of women's rights, including the home of movement leader **Elizabeth Cady Stanton**. The visitor center stands at its heart, offering detailed and thoughtful exhibits about historic and contemporary women's issues.

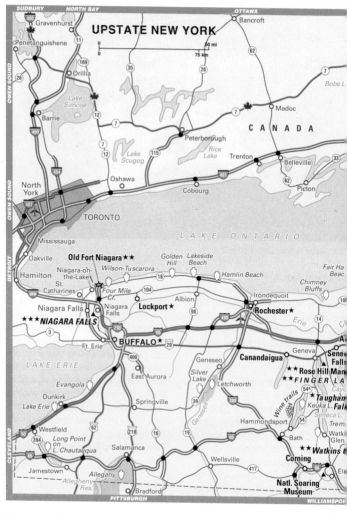

### The Seward House★★

*33 South St., Auburn. ⟶ Visit by guided tour only, February 1-June 30 and mid-October-December 30, Tue-Sat 11am-4pm. ♿☏315-252-1283. www.sewardhouse.org.*

This fine Federal-style home built in 1816 reflects the full and rich life of its gregarious 48-year occupant, statesman **William Henry Seward** (1801-72). Because five generations of the family lived here over the years, the house is remarkably appointed with personal possessions. A wonderfully thorough tour includes several rooms of artifacts relating to the attempt on Seward's life in 1865 and the Alaska Purchase, which he helped bring about.

### Corning Museum of Glass★★

*1 Museum Way, Corning. ✗♿P☏607-974-8271. ⏱Open daily Memorial Day Labor Day, 9am-5pm. Open daily the res of the year 9am-4pm. ⏱Closed majo holidays. ⟶$12.50. www.corningglas center.com.*

This huge, stunning museum contain a collection of more than 45,000 art an historical glass objects, plus hands-o exhibits about the science and technol ogy involved in glass making. There ar daily glassblowing demonstrations, a glas making program and studio offering year round courses. The museum is home to th Rakow Research Library, the largest dedi cated to the art, history, and craft of glas

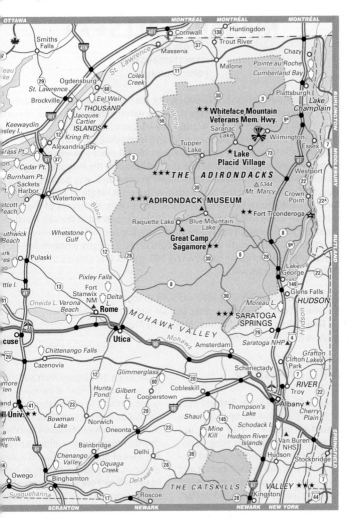

Visit the 19,000sq ft GlassMarket to peruse glass objects from all over the globe.

### The Rockwell Museum of Western Art★

111 Cedar St., Corning. ◷Open Memorial Day-Labor Day daily 9am-8pm. Open the rest of the year daily 9am-5pm. ◷Closed January 1, Thanksgiving, December 24 and 25. ☎607-937-5386. www.stny.com/rockwellmuseum

Housed in the restored 1893 Romanesque Revival City Hall, the East Coast's American western and Native American art, including works by Remington, Russell, Bierstadt and Moran amassed by local department store scion Robert F.

Rockwell, Jr. The museum holds comprehensive collections of Steuben glass.

## Along the Way

### Taughannock Falls State Park★

Rte. 89, Trumansburg. ◷Open Mon-Fri 8am-4pm; call for extended summer hours. ◷Trail closed in winter. ◷$7 per vehicle. △↻P ☎607-387-6739.

This 783-acre state park has something for everyone, including a beach on Lake Cayuga, hiking trails, picnic grounds and, of course, the breathtaking 215ft falls.

# NIAGARA FALLS★★★

MAP P 440
EASTERN STANDARD TIME
POPULATION 81,184

Near **Buffalo,** New York's second-largest city, the Niagara River suddenly plunge over a 170ft cliff, creating one of the world's greatest natural spectacles, Niagar Falls. These three sets of falls straddle the US/Canada border—American an Bridal Veil Falls on the American side, and Horseshoe Falls on the Canadia side. The falls began their evolution about 10,000 years ago when the youn Niagara River flowed out of Lake Erie and tumbled over the Niagara Escarpmen 7.5mi to the north. The river waters slowly eroded their way backward to th present-day location of the falls. Today, with a crest length of 2,200ft (1,000f flank-to-flank), Horseshoe Falls channels more than 90 percent of the wate at Niagara—some 315,000 to 675,000 gallons per second in the summertime depending on how much water is being diverted for hydroelectric power. Ameri can Falls has a crest length of about 1,100ft; Bridal Veil Falls, a ribbon-like 40f Together these two guide between 60,000 and 75,000 gallons of water ove their edges every second.

- 🏛 **Information:** ☎716-285-2400. www.nfcvb.com
- ▶ **Orient Yourself:** These majestic falls are just 20 miles from Buffalo.
- 😊 **Don't Miss:** The world-famous Maid of the Mist Boat Tour.
- 👣 **Also See:** FINGER LAKES.

## A Bit of History

Since Native Americans first laid eyes on them, the falls have been a source of wonder to all who view them, not for their height, but for their pano- ramic breadth, powerful roar and sce- nic beauty. Drawn by their tumult and spray, explorers, painters, daredevils, hucksters, honeymooners and sightse- ers have flocked to their banks. Niagara is still one of the most popular tourist destinations in the world, attracting more than 14 million visitors a year. The water's forceful flow has long been exploited as well by hydroelectric power plants, and today, upstream power projects divert half to three-quarters of the falls' water.

## Sights

### Niagara Reservation State Park★★
*Prospect St. ◌Open year-round. ◌$7 per vehicle. ✕ 👣 🅿 ☎716-278-1796.*
This strip of green—the oldest state park in the U.S. and landscaped by Frederick Law Olmsted in the 1880s—stretches

3.5mi along the Niagara River and ove the five islands located at the top of th gorge. Within it lie all the attractions o the US side. The park provides somethin of a refuge from nearby hotels and thic crowds. **Prospect Point** affords a bird's eye view of American Falls, and a glas elevator descends to its craggy bas from the **New York State Observatio Tower.** From the tower's top, walk to th outdoor deck for a panoramic view of a of Niagara Falls. A tree-lined pedestria path follows the American bank of th Niagara River to bridges that lead t tranquil **Goat Island,** which separate Horseshoe from American Falls. **Terra pin Point,** on the west end of the island affords the best view of Horseshoe Fal from the US.

### Maid of the Mist Boat Tour★★★
🆒 ⬛ *Departs from Niagara Reserva tion State Park. ◌Open April-Octobe depending on ice conditions in the rive ◌$12.50. 👣 🅿 ☎716-284-4233. www maidofthemist.com.*
Launched in 1846, the first *Maid of th Mist* was a wooden-hulled, coal-fire steamboat. Today four all-steel, diese

powered boats chug from the base of Prospect Point *(accessible via Observation Tower elevator)* past American and Bridal Veil Falls to bob at the tumultuous base of Horseshoe Falls. Visitors are given plastic hooded rain ponchos to protect them from the fantastic spray.

## Cave of the Winds★★

*Goat Island. Visit by guided tour only, daily 9am-7:30pm. $10. ☏716-278-1730.*

This tour passes within a breathtaking 25ft of roaring Bridal Veil Falls. Outfitted with heavy-duty slickers and booties, visitors descend an elevator 175ft into the Niagara Gorge and then follow a path to the base of the falls. This boardwalk culminates on the Hurricane Deck, pounded brutally with water when the wind comes from the east and lifts the mist off the falls.

## Old Fort Niagara★★

*In Fort Niagara State Park off the Robert Moses Pkwy. (Rte. 18), Youngstown. Hours change depending on season. ☏716-745-7611. www.oldfortniagara.org.*

Situated on a scenic promontory where the Niagara River feeds into Lake Ontario about 15mi north of the falls, this 22-acre complex has alternately served as a French, English and American military stronghold over the centuries. Because it controlled water access from Lake Ontario to the four other Great Lakes, the

*Observation Point, Niagara Falls*

©iStockphoto.com/Wally Stemberger

fort commanded one of the most strategic—and therefore contested—locations in western New York. Its 18C buildings have been returned to their original appearance, and each is marked with a heraldic plaque identifying the country that erected it. France, first to occupy the site in 1679, built the crown jewel of the complex, called the **French Castle**★ (1726). On clear days it affords a stupendous **view**★★ of Toronto across the lake. The British captured the fort in 1759, but surrendered it to the Americans in 1796. Except for a brief stint of British rule during the War of 1812, Fort Niagara has been maintained by the US ever since.

## Daredevils

Niagara has always posed a tempting challenge to adventurers. The first to tumble over **Horseshoe Falls**—the preferred "stunt" falls, because there are no rocks at the bottom—was an assembly of animals and birds aboard a wooden schooner pushed to certain demise in a publicity stunt in 1827. The most famous of Niagara's "rope dancers" was Jean-François Gravelet, also known as "the Great Blondin," who traversed Niagara Gorge on a tightrope for the first time in 1859. In later feats, he rode across the rope on a bicycle and made the trek carrying his manager. Another daredevil toted a small stove onto the tightrope, lit a fire, cooked two omelets, and lowered them down to passengers on the *Maid of the Mist*. Braving the falls in a barrel, though illegal, has been often attempted. In 1901 schoolteacher Annie Edson Taylor became the first to survive the ordeal by encasing herself in an oak barrel. Subsequent daredevils devised all manner of contraptions to brave the drop and survive, but most remarkable was the plunge of Roger Woodward. In 1960 the 7-year-old managed to escape serious injury when he was swept over the falls clad in only a life jacket.

# WASHINGTON, DC AREA

Conceived as a national showplace, Washington, DC, embodies the spirit of American idealism in its Neoclassical monuments, its grand museums and its sweeping vistas. Today it is a truly international city, hosting world-class performing artists, and offering fine shopping and dining. Lying 90mi inland from the mid-Atlantic seaboard, the city rises from low bottomland along the Potomac riverfront and covers 67sq mi carved out of Maryland. Though some restrictions have been put in place since the terrorist attacks of 9/11, the United States capital is remarkably accessible. The doors of Congress, the White House and other federal institutions are open to the hosts of visitors who come to witness democracy in progress.

The Washington metropolitan area fans out in densely settled suburbs reaching north toward Baltimore, Maryland; south toward Fredericksburg, Virginia; east across the broad estuarine expanse of Maryland's Eastern Shore (*see BALTIMORE*); and west toward the Blue Ridge Mountains. The rumblings that preceded the Civil War began in the mountains west of Washington in Harpers Ferry, West Virginia. Once the war exploded, some of its most noted battles were fought in the countryside within an hour's drive of the capital.

East of Washington on the Chesapeake Bay, Annapolis celebrates its 18C seafaring heritage in its bustling city marina and at the US Naval Academy. Across the Potomac from DC in Old Town Alexandria, Virginia, colonial architecture and contemporary shops stand shoulder-to-shoulder along brick-paved sidewalks. Neighboring Arlington, Virginia, is home to the **Pentagon** (*I-395 at Washington Blvd.* *visit by guided tour only* *☎703-695-1776*), the five-sided building targeted on 9/11 that houses the US Department of Defense.

With its rich history and its world-class museums, the nation's capital is truly a city for all seasons. Come in spring for the **Cherry Blossom Festival** (*early Apr*) and celebrate the riot of pink flowers bursting into bloom along the Tidal Basin; come in summer to watch

*US Capitol Building*

Brigitta L. House/MICHELIN

Fourth of July fireworks explode above the Washington Monument; come in autumn to enjoy the bright foliage (Oct) that lines the towpath along the historic C&O Canal; or come in winter to see the President light the **National Christmas Tree** on the Ellipse (early Dec).

## Area Address Book

♿For coin ranges, see the Legend on the cover flap.

### GETTING THERE

**Ronald Reagan Washington National Airport (DCA):** ☎703-417-8000, www.metwashairports.com; 4.5mi south of downtown DC. Airport information booths on the baggage-claim level of all terminals. **Dulles International Airport (DIA):** ☎703-572-2700, www.metwashairports.com; 26mi west of downtown DC. Airport information booth on lower level of Main Terminal. **Baltimore-Washington International Airport (BWI):** ☎410-261-1000, www.bwiairport.com; 28mi north of Washington. Airport information booth at entrances to piers C and D on upper level of terminal. Rental car agencies are located at the airports.

**Union Station** (Massachusetts & Delaware Aves.) provides **Amtrak** and other **rail service** to major destinations in the Northeast, Midwest and South. Reservations are recommended: ☎800-872-7245 or www.amtrak.com. **Bus** travel provided by **Greyhound** at the main bus terminal: 1005 1st St. N.E., ☎202-289-5154.

### GETTING AROUND

Washington Metropolitan Area Transit Authority (WMATA) operates **Metrorail**, Washington's rapid-transit system (runs daily until midnight; maps & tickets available at all Metro stations; ☎202-962-2733), and **Metrobus** (runs daily until midnight; ∞$1.10 base fare purchased on bus, exact change required; ☎202-637-7000). Daily and weekly passes available for Metrorail and Metrobus. For further fare information and schedules, access WMATA's Web site: www.wmata.com. **Taxi** service: DC Taxicab Commission, ☎202-645-6018.

### VISITOR INFORMATION

For a free visit planner, maps and information on accommodations, attractions, shopping, entertainment, festivals and recreation, contact **Washington, DC Convention and Visitors Association**, 1212 New York Ave. N.W., ☎202-789-7000, www.washington.org. The **Smithsonian Information Center** (1000 Jefferson Dr. S.W.; ☎202-357-2700) can help plan your visit to Smithsonian museums.

### WHERE TO STAY

**Hotel reservation services:** Accommodations Express, ☎609-391-2100, www.accomodationsexpress.com; Hotel Reservation Network, ☎214-361-7311, www.hoteldiscount.com; Washington, DC Accommodations, ☎202-289-2220, www.dcaccommodations.com; Alexandria Hotel Accommodations, ☎800-296-1000. **Bed & Breakfast reservations:** Bed and Breakfast Accommodations Ltd., ☎202-328-3510. **Washington International Youth Hostel:** ☎202-737-2333.

**$$$ The Hay-Adams Hotel** – 16th & H Sts. N.W., Washington, DC. ☒♿🅿 ☎202-662-4818. www.hayadams.com. 143 rooms. Across from the White House, this Italian Renaissance-style property has been the first choice for visiting elite since 1928. The posh lobby features walnut paneling edged with golden eagles and hand-carved fruit moldings (representing abundance) on the ceiling. Bedrooms are clad in pale, buttery colors and early-20C furnishings.

**$$$ Willard Intercontinental Washington** – 1401 Pennsylvania Ave. NW, Washington, DC ☒♿🅿🛗 ☎202-628-9100. www.washingtonintercontinental.com. 332 rooms.
Long a favorite of DC Lobbyists hashing out deals, the Willard is also an historic landmark, loved for it's Beaux Arts architecture. Rooms are decorated in

red, blue or green color schemes, in a Federal-meets-Victorian style. Many have picturesque viewes overlooking Pennsylvania Avenue.

**$$$ Inn at Perry Cabin** – *308 Watkins Lane, St. Michaels, MD.* ♿🅿️☎️*410-745-2200. www.perrycabin.com. 78 rooms.* On the banks of the Miles River, this early-19C cabin has expanded into a luxury 25-acre resort surrounded by landscaped gardens. Bedrooms are designed in chintz, florals and fruit motifs (Laura Ashley's widower, Sir Bernard, was once the owner). Some have private patios or cathedral ceilings. Furnishings range from antique armoires to simple oak pieces.

**$$ Celie's Waterfront Bed & Breakfast** – *1714 Thames St., Baltimore, MD.* ♿🅿️☎️*410-522-2323. www.celies-waterfront.com. 9 rooms.* An elegant Fell's Point inn that offers extras like whirlpools, plush down comforters and fresh flowers. Bright and tastefully decorated, accommodations have wicker furnishings and antiques, as well as harbor or courtyard views. Other in-room features include balconies, separate seating alcoves and skylights.

**$$ Morrison-Clark Inn** – *Massachusetts Ave. & 11th St. N.W., Washington, DC.* ♿🅿️☎️*202-898-1200. www.morrisonclark.com. 54 rooms.* This turn-of-the-century mansion, comprised of two townhouses, seems misplaced in the middle of downtown's business district. Past the antiques-filled parlor, with lace curtains and burgundy wall coverings, you'll find three styles of accommodations. Choose from neutral-toned Neoclassical, opulent Victorian, and country-style distressed woods and wicker. The restaurant's Southern-style specialties have made it a national favorite.

**$$$ Morrison House** – *116 S. Alfred St., Alexandria, VA.* ♿🅿️☎️*703-838-8000. www.morrisonhouse.com. 45 rooms.* There's no way of knowing that this Federal manor in Old Town was built in 1985. Butlers escort guests up the columned entrance's double staircase. The cheerful parlor is filled with framed Audubon prints, topiaries and rosy period couches. Guest rooms are fitted with early American-style four-poster beds and brass chandeliers.

## WHERE TO EAT

**$$$ Kinhead's** – *2000 Pennsylvania Ave. NW, Washington, DC.* ☎️*202-296-7700.* **Seafood.** The always crowded raw bar and dining rooms at this seafood spot manage to maintain an air of understated elegance. The influence is New England as well as Asia and Lain America; the signature dish is a pepita-crusted salmon served with a ragout of crab, shrimp, and corn. The chocolate and caramel dessert samplers is worth a visit even if you don't like seafood.

**$$$ Vidalia** – *1990 M St. N.W., Washington, DC.* ☎️*202-659-1990.* **Contemporary.** Cheerful yellow walls and antique-filled china cabinets decorate this downtown favorite. Chef Jeffrey Buben looks to the South for inspiration. Winning dishes on the seasonal menu include sautéed shrimp and grits in a sweet-onion ragu, duck breat with hot and sour baby beets and frogmore stew, made with shellfish and sweet corn. The lemon chess pie is the best-selling dessert is legendary.

**$$$ Bistro St. Michaels** – *403 S. Talbot St., St. Michaels, MD. Closed Tue & Wed.* ☎️*410-745-9111.* **Contemporary.** Set in a Victorian house on the town's main thoroughfare, this casual eatery prepares comforting modern dishes with local produce and seafood. Vintage 19C French food ads in the bi-level dining room will spark your appetite for seasonal specials such as corn and crab chowder, sautéed soft-shell crabs, and mustard-crusted chicken paillard with orange honey.

**$$ Old Ebbitt Grill** – *675 15th St. N.W., Washington, DC.* ☎️*202-347-4800. www.ebbitt.com.* **American.** This former 1856 boardinghouse has been the stomping ground of politicos since the days of Ulysses S. Grant. These days, you're just as likely to spot Washington Wizzards basketball players at one of the velvet and mahogany booths as you are lunchers from the White House, a mere two blocks away. Standard fare includes crabcakes, cheeseburgers and fried-oyster platters.

# WASHINGTON, DC★★★

MAP PP454-455

EASTERN STANDARD TIME

POPULATION 523,124

Unique among most of the world's capital cities, Washington, DC, had its beginnings not as a monarchy, but as a democracy: its broad avenues and regal monuments serve as visual paeans to the democratic ideal. Its heroes include George Washington, Thomas Jefferson, Abraham Lincoln and, more recently, John F. Kennedy and Franklin Delano Roosevelt. The city abounds with tributes to these titans of American history. In recent decades Washington has emerged from its strictly political associations with its flagship **John F. Kennedy Center for the Performing Arts★★** *(New Hampshire Ave. at Rock Creek Pkwy.; ☎202-467-4600)*, which houses four theaters and the resident National Symphony Orchestra. Culturally, the idealism of democracy is alive in the collection of outstanding museums that are open to all at no cost.

**Information:** ☎202-789-7000. www.washington.org

**Kids:** Kids will love the *To Fly* movie at the National Air and Space Museum.

**Also See:** RICHMOND.

## A Bit of History

Following the euphoria that resulted from winning independence from Britain, President **George Washington** chose a tract of land near the prosperous port of Georgetown in which to locate the seat of power for the new nation. Washington knew this area well, for his own plantation, Mount Vernon, lay just 6mi to the south along the Potomac River.

French major **Pierre Charles L'Enfant** (1754-1825) was appointed to design the new capital, a diamond-shaped federal district that measured 10mi long on each side and encompassed portions of Maryland as well as the County of Alexandria on the Potomac's west bank. L'Enfant situated the new Capitol building on Jenkins Hill, which commanded a striking view of the Potomac River. Along this east-west axis, he planned a 400ft-wide "Grand Avenue" (now the Mall) to be lined by foreign ministries and cultural institutions. The avenue would connect on a north-south axis with the "President's house," which

© Brigitta L. House/MICHELIN

*Sightseeing Tour*

would link back to the Capitol via a mile-long commercial corridor (present-day Pennsylvania Avenue).

Despite numerous setbacks—including L'Enfant's dismissal in 1792 and the loss of Alexandria back to Virginia—by the mid-19C Washington was well on its way to becoming a city. In 1871 the District of Columbia incorporated Georgetown, and improved transportation spurred the growth of suburbs in Virginia and Maryland.

Today Washington's population is 70 percent black and 30 percent white. Despite periods of racial unrest, this diversity has helped the city mature as an urban center boasting some 10 colleges and universities. Washington also owes a debt of gratitude to former First Lady "Lady-bird" Johnson, who began landscaping efforts in the 1960s that turned green spaces into showplaces bright with flowers. Today Washington's development is closely monitored to ensure that the monumental capital retains its reputation as "the City Beautiful."

## Capitol Hill★★★

Crowned by great stone buildings that house the legislative and judicial branches of the federal government, the city's high eastern ground was known as Jenkins Hill in 1791 when L'Enfant selected it as the future site of Congress. Now called Capitol Hill, the area incorporates residential neighborhoods of 19C row houses that reflect a true cross section of Washington's population.

Convenient to Congress members, the 1907 Beaux-Arts **Union Station**★ *(40 Massachusetts Ave. N.E.;* ✗ ♿ 🅿 ☎*202-371-9441)* was renovated in the 1980s to house shops, eateries and a cinema. The coffered, barrel-vaulted ceiling in its main hall was inspired by the Roman Baths of Diocletian.

### US Capitol Building★★★

▥▥*Capitol Hill, National Mall.* ✗ ♿ ☎*202-225-6827. www.aoc.gov.* ☞*Since the terrorits attacks of 9/11, the Capitol is opened to the public for guided tours only. Tours are conducted yearround,*

*Mon-Sat 9am-4:30pm.* 🕐*Closed Sun an⌐ major holidays.*

Characterized by city designer L'Enfan⌐ as "a pedestal waiting for a monument,⌐ the rising ground known as Capitol Hi⌐ is crowned by the massive Capitol build⌐ ing that has housed the US Congres⌐ since 1800. The original low-dome⌐ central section was designed by D⌐ William Thornton to resemble Rome⌐ Pantheon. Over the ensuing decade⌐ the dome was enlarged and adjoinin⌐ wings were added.

Above the **rotunda**, the ornate Capito⌐ **dome**★★—180ft high and 98ft across⌐ displays an allegorical fresco, *The Apoth⌐ eosis of Washington*, by Constantino Bru⌐ midi. Bordering the rotunda on the mai⌐ floor, semicircular half-domed **Statuar⌐ Hall** appears (unfurnished) as it did i⌐ 1857 when it served as the House Cham⌐ ber; on the other side of the rotunda ⌐ the restored **Old Senate Chamber** tha⌐ housed the Supreme Court from 1860 t⌐ 1935. The ground floor holds the **Cryp⌐** the vaulted **Old Supreme Court Cham⌐ ber**, and the intersecting **Brumidi Cor⌐ ridors**, which is embellished with th⌐ artist's murals. On the third floor (gal⌐ lery level) the **House Chamber** hold⌐ the seats of the 435-mmeber House o⌐ Representatives (Democrats to the righ⌐ of the Speaker of the House; Republican⌐ to the left). Across the hall in the **Senat⌐ Chamber** the Vice President preside⌐ before 100 Senators (two from each o⌐ the 50 states).

### Supreme Court★★

*1st & E. Capitol Sts. N.E.* ✗ ♿ ☎*202-479⌐ 3030. www.supremecourtus.gov.*

Sessions are open to the public on ⌐ first-come, first-served basis. Consult th⌐ court's Web site for the daily schedul⌐ of arguments. Visitors can also tour th⌐ court building, view exhibits relating t⌐ its history, and attend free films and lec⌐ tures about the court. Across the stree⌐ from the Capitol, the highest court i⌐ the land exercises its mandate to protec⌐ and interpret the spirit of the Constitu⌐ tion and serve as a counterbalance t⌐ the legislative and executive branche⌐ of government. The broad staircase i⌐ front of this cross-shaped marble struc⌐

*Library of Congress*

*Great Hall, Jefferson Building, Library of Congress*

ure (1935, Cass Gilbert) is flanked by two James Fraser sculptures, representing the Contemplation of Justice *(left)* and the Authority of Law *(right)*. Carved in the building's pediment are the words "Equal Justice Under Law." Within the **ourtroom,** justices sit on a raised ench ringed by massive columns. Dominating the main hall on ground level is the **statue** of John Marshall (1755-1835), the "Great Chief Justice" who held the ost from 1801 to1835.

## ibrary of Congress★★

*01 Independence Ave. S.E.* ♿ ⏱*Closed un-Mon and major holidays.* ☎*202-707-000. www.loc.gov. Buildings, research enters, exhibits and reading rooms all eep different hours.*

stablished in 1800 (and housed in the apitol) for the use of Congress, the ibrary of Congress ranks as the largest brary in existence. A richly ornamented eaux-Arts landmark, the original library uilding (1897) holds more than 16 million books, 46 million manuscripts, 4 million maps and atlases, and 8 million musical items. Noteworthy for its gold-eaf ceiling and vaulted corridors, the wo-story **Great Hall** holds a copy of he mid-15C Giant Bible of Mainz, one of the last hand-illuminated manuscript versions of the Bible. An elaborately sculpted grand staircase leads to the second-story colonnade, where a visitors gallery overlooks the **Main Reading Room**—a vast rotunda under the library's dome (160ft from floor to lantern) ringed by Corinthian columns and arched windows embellished with stained-glass state seals.

## Folger Shakespeare Library★

*201 E. Capitol St. S.E.* ♿ ⏱*Open Mon-Sat 9am–4pm.* ☎*202-544-7077. www.folger.edu.*

Established by Henry Clay Folger and his wife, Emily Jordan, in the 1930s, this library conserves 275,000 Renaissance-related books and manuscripts, including 79 of the 240 first editions of the collected works of Shakespeare known to exist. Designed by Paul Cret, the Art Deco structure's marble façade includes bas-relief underpanels featuring scenes from Shakespeare's plays. The interior features a Tudor-style **Great Hall** and an **Elizabethan theater**. The library is known for its public programs, including plays, concerts, school programs and literary readings.

*East Building, National Gallery of Art*

# The Mall★★★

Focal point for such national events as the annual **Independence Day celebration** and the summer **Smithsonian Folklife Festival**, this sweeping greensward links the country's most revered monuments and museums. The Mall was developed in the mid-19C when ground was broken for the Washington Monument and the Smithsonian Castle. Today the **Smithsonian Institution**, founded through the generosity of Englishman James Smithson in 1835, operates nine museums on the **East Mall** between Capitol Hill and 15th Street. The Smithsonian's first building, a Romanesque Revival structure known as **The Castle** (*Jefferson Dr. at 10th St. S.W.*), now serves as a visitor information center. The **West Mall** stretches from 15th Street to the Potomac River and is the site of monuments to past presidents and memorials to war veterans.

## National Air and Space Museum★★★

Kids *6th & Independence Ave. S.W.* ✕ ◷*Open daily 10am–5pm.* ☎*202-633-1000. www.nasm.edu.*
Established in 1946, Washington's most popular museum contains hundreds of authentic artifacts commemorating man's aeronautical and astronautical achievements. Gyo Obata designed the marble-faced structure that opened fo the nation's bicentennial in July 1976. Within the building's four massiv rectangles are 22 galleries displayin hundreds of aircraft and spacecraf rockets, guided missiles and satellite as well as exhibits that trace the histor of flight from its earliest days throug World War II. Topics such as the princ ples of flight and aerial photography a also addressed. In the **Milestones Flight** hall that occupies the central pa of the building hang such epoch-mak ing aircraft as Charles Lindbergh's Rya NYP *Spirit of St. Louis*, and John Glenn *Friendship 7* space capsule.

## National Gallery of Art★★★

*4th and Constitution Ave. N.W.* ✕ &◷*Ope Mon-Sat 10am–5pm, Sun 11am–6pn* ☎*202-737-4215. www.nga.gov.*
Tracing Western art from the Middl Ages to the present, the National Galle houses 3,000 paintings, 2,000 piece of sculpture, 560 pieces of decorativ art and over 47,000 works on paper. I the 1920s, financier, industrialist an statesman **Andrew Mellon** (1855 1936) funded the stately marble **Wes Building** that graces the Mall today, an started the collection with 126 pain ings and a group of fine 15C-16C Italia sculptures.
Arranged in chronological order, galle ies on the main floor of the West Build

ng progress from **13C Italian Painting** through Spanish, German and Flemish masterpieces to **19C French Painting**. Thomas Gainsborough and J.M.W. Turner are included among the collection of **British Painting**, while the portraiture of Benjamin West, Charles Willson Peale and Gilbert Stuart highlight the **American Painting** galleries. The ground floor displays sculpture and decorative arts.

In the 1970s the Mellon family again came forward to endow the museum's acclaimed **East Building**★★ (1978, I.M. Pei), which is devoted to 20C art. Considered the most impressive example of modern architecture in Washington, the East Building opens into a soaring skylit **atrium** dominated by an immense mobile by Alexander Calder. Galleries showcase the work of Pablo Picasso, Vassily Kandinsky, Mark Rothko and Georgia O'Keeffe.

The new **National Gallery of Art Sculpture Garden** (on the Mall at 7th St. & Constitution Ave. N.W.) is an urban oasis filled with 18 contemporary sculptures by the likes of Alexander Calder, Claes Oldenburg and Joan Miró. Its dramatic circular fountain becomes an ice-skating rink in winter.

## National Archives★★

Constitution Ave. between 7th & 9th Sts. N.W. ☎202-501-5000. www. archives.gov.

This Classical Revival temple (1937, John Russell Pope) safeguards the nation's official and historical records, including 5 billion paper documents, 9 million aerial photographs, 6 million still photographs, and 300,000 video, film and sound recordings. Inside the cavernous rotunda, a dais enshrines the nation's **Charters of Freedom**★★★: the **Declaration of Independence**, two pages of the **Constitution**, and the **Bill of Rights**. The National Archives also functions as a major source of historical material for both domestic and foreign researchers.

## National Museum of Natural History★★

Constitution Ave. at 10th St. N.W. ☎202-633-1000. www.mnh.si.edu.

Completed in 1911 to hold the Smithsonian's rapidly expanding collection of artifacts, this Classical Revival granite structure conserves more than 120 million specimens and provides laboratory facilities for scientists. Dominating the first-floor rotunda is a great 13ft-tall **African bush elephant**. Exhibits on the first floor encompass mammals; sea life, including a model of a 135-ton **blue whale** and a living **coral reef**★; the world's cultural regions; and dinosaurs, showcasing a 90ft **diplodocus skeleton**. The second floor displays a fabulous **gem collection**★★, which counts the Hope Diamond among its treasures; and a creepy-crawly **insect zoo**. The museum's new **Discovery Center** houses an IMAX 2D-3D theater, an atrium food court and an expanded gift shop.

## National Museum of American History★★

Constitution Ave. between 12th & 14th Sts. N.W. ☎202-633-1000. http:// americanhistory.si.edu. ○The NMAH is closed for renovation and scheduled to reopen in mid-2008. Check the Website for updates.

Repository for such national icons as a 1913 Model T Ford and various first ladies' gowns, this museum, with its 16-million-object collection, captures the essence of America's material and social development.

## Hirshhorn Museum and Sculpture Garden★★

Independence Ave. at 7th St. S.W. Open daily 10am–5:30pm. ☎202-633-1000. http://hirshorn.si.edu.

Although Gordon Bunshaft's cylindrical "doughnut" invited criticism when it was completed in 1966, the structure nonetheless houses one of the finest collections of modern art in the country. Latvian-born art collector **Joseph Hirshhorn** (1899-1981) started the ball rolling with his initial donation of 6,000 contemporary works. Today the Hirshhorn contains some 5,000 paintings, 3,000 pieces of sculpture and mixed media, and 4,000 works on paper. Small figurative works adorn the sunken **Sculpture Garden**, and the plaza on which the building stands is a showplace for monumental contemporary sculpture.

## National Museum of African Art★★

*Smithsonian Quadrangle at 950 Independence Ave. S.W.* &♿☎202-357-4600. *www.si.edu/nmafa.*

Located in the underground Smithsonian Quadrangle complex, the museum is devoted to the research, acquisition and display of traditional African arts, especially of the sub-Saharan regions. Of note in the museum's collection of more than 7,000 items is the assemblage of **Royal Benin Art** from the West African kingdom of Benin (now Nigeria).

## Arthur M. Sackler Gallery★★

*Smithsonian Quadrangle at 1050 Independence Ave. S.W.* ♿

The core of this museum's holdings was donated by New York psychiatrist and Asian art buff Arthur M. Sackler. Dedicated to the study of Asian art from the Neolithic period to the present, the facility boasts a fine group of **Chinese jades** dating from 3000 BC, and **Ancient Near Eastern gold and silver** ceremonial objects. The **Vever Collection** of 11C-19C Islamic manuscripts, miniatures and calligraphy ranks as one of the world's finest.

*Lincoln Memorial*

©2002 Comstock, Inc.

## Freer Gallery of Art★★

*Jefferson Dr. at 12th St. S.W.* ♿🕐*Ope daily 10am–5:30pm.*☎202-633-480( *www.asia.si.edu.*

These two separate galleries (whic connect underground) make up th **National Museum of Asian Art.** Th Freer Gallery is an Italian-Renaissance inspired building designed by archchitec Charles Watt. It was founded by Charle Lang Freer, a railroad car manufacture who donated his personal collection and funds for a building to house them Today it contains more than 27,00 pieces, including objects from th Ming (1368-1644) and Qing (1644-191 dynasties. The Sackler Gallery opened 1987 to showcase a collection donate by New York psychiatrist and Asian a buff Arthur M. Sackler to study Asian a from the Neolithic period to the presen The facility boasts a fine group of **Ch nese jades** dating from 3000 BC, an **Ancient Near Eastern gold and silve** ceremonial objects. The **Vever Collec tion** of 11C-19C Islamic manuscript miniatures and calligraphy ranks as on of the world's finest.

## US Holocaust Memorial Museum★★

*Just off the Mall, south of Independenc Ave. between 14th St. & Raoul Waller berg Pl. S.W.* ✗♿🕐*Open daily 10am 5:20pm.*🚫*Closed Jewish holidays.*☎20. *488-0400. www.ushmm.org.*

Conceived "to commemorate th dead and to educate the living," th museum contains a compelling pe manent exhibit that focuses on the Na extermination of millions of Jews an others during World War II. The bric and limestone building (1993, I.M. P & Partners) evokes a Postmodern pen tentiary, with its series of "watchtowers and interior of glass and exposed met beams. Exhibits present a moving arra of photographs, artifacts, archival film and voice recordings of survivors.

## The Memorials★★★

Offset by the Potomac River and th Tidal Basin, the Mall west of 15th Stree is the setting for the country's most ver erated monuments. Dedicated to firs president George Washington (1789-97

Brigitta L. House/MICHELIN

White House

The **Washington Monument** *(on the Mall at 15th St. N.W.)* is a 555ft-tall marble obelisk whose apex affords visitors one of the city's best panoramic **views**★★★. On the basin's south shore, the colonnaded **Jefferson Memorial** memorializes third president Thomas Jefferson (1801-09) with a 19ft-tall bronze statue by Rudolph Evans in its open interior. From inside the **Lincoln Memorial** *(on the Mall at 23rd St. N.W.)* Daniel Chester French's famous marble **statue**★★★ of 16th president Abraham Lincoln (1861-65) stares across the 350ft-long Reflecting Pool. The **Roosevelt Memorial** *(on the Tidal Basin, west of the Jefferson Memorial)* recounts the terms of office of the nation's 32nd president, Franklin Delano Roosevelt (1933-45). Known simply as "the Wall," the compelling black granite expanse of the **Vietnam Veterans Memorial** *(Constitution Ave. & 22nd St. N.W.)* bears the names of the 58,195 men and women killed or missing in the Vietnam War (1959-75).

## Downtown★★

Conceived by planner Pierre L'Enfant to link the White House and the Capitol, **Pennsylvania Avenue** was the city's first thoroughfare and gave rise to the commercial heart of DC. At the avenue's center sits the White House, surrounded by manicured parks and grand public structures, including the 1888 Second Empire-style **Dwight D. Eisenhower**

**Executive Office Building**★ *(17th & G Sts. N.W.)*.
Just east of the White House, Downtown is a conglomeration of retail complexes, hotels, museums, office towers and restaurants, where top-dollar lawyers and politicos take power lunches. Northwest of the White House at the intersection of Connecticut, Massachusetts and New Hampshire Avenues, **Dupont Circle**★ harbors restored mansions along with many fine boutiques, galleries and eateries.

### White House★★★

*1600 Pennsylvania Ave. N.W. &202-456-2200; www.whitehouse.gov. Self-guided tours are available to groups of 10 or more. requests must be submitted through your member of Congress up to six months in advance. Open Tues-Sat 7:30am–12:30pm. Closed major holidays.*

Designed by Irish builder James Hoban in 1792, the three-story stone Georgian manor has been the home of America's presidents and their families beginning with John Adams in 1801. Theodore Roosevelt began restoring the mansion to its original appearance during his tenure in office (1901-09), and succeeding presidents followed his lead.

Set amid 18 landscaped acres, the White House fronts Pennsylvania Avenue. Its south portico overlooks the Ellipse—an open expanse that serves as a ceremonial ground. The colonnaded north por-

**Hotels**

- Adam's Inn
1. Allen Lee Hotel
2. Beacon Hotel and Corporate Quart
3. Braxton Hotel
- Channel Inn Hote
- Doolittle Guest H
4. Fairmont Washin
5. Hay-Adams
6. Henley Park Hotel
- Hereford House
7. Hotel George
8. Hotel Helix
9. Hotel Lombardy
10. Hotel Monaco
11. Hotel Rouge
12. Hotel Tabard Inn

13. Hotel Washington
14. Jefferson Hotel
15. Jurys Washington
• Kalorama Guest House
16. Madison Hotel
17. Mandarin Oriental Hotel
• Melrose Hotel
18. Morrison-Clark Inn
19. One Washington Circle
20. Renaissance Mayflower Hotel
21. Ritz-Carlton, Washington, DC
22. St. Regis, Washington, DC
23. Washington Court Hotel
• Watergate Hotel
24. Willard InterContinental
• Woodley Park Guest House

**Restaurants**
• Ben's Chili Bowl
1. Bread Line
2. Brickskeller
3. Butterfield 9
• Café Atlantico
• Cafe Deluxe
4. Cashion's Eat Place
5. Caucus Room
6. Ceiba
• CityZen (in hotel 17)
7. DC Coast
8. District ChopHouse
• Firehook Bakery & Coffeehouse
9. Galileo
10. Georgia Brown's
11. Heritage India

12. Jaleo
13. Kinkead's
14. Lauriol Plaza
• Lebanese Taverna
15. Nooshi
16. Nora
17. Occidental Grill
• Palena
18. Pizzeria Paradiso
19. Red Sage
• Saigonnais
20. Taberna del Alabardero
21. TenPenh
22. Tony Cheng's Seafood Restaurant
23. Tortilla Coast
24. Vidalia
25. Zaytinya

• Hotel or restaurant not on the map

## Central Washington DC

★★★ Absolutely Must See
★★ Really Must See
★ Must See

Ⓜ SMITHSONIAN Metro entrance/station name

0 ____ 500m
0 ____ 1500ft

tico faces the seven-acre park named **Lafayette Square** in honor of the Marquis de Lafayette, America's ally in the Revolutionary war.

Visitors tour the mansion's first and ground floors only; upper floors are reserved for the First Family. Adorned with Bohemian cut-glass chandeliers, the **East Room** hosts White House ceremonies, concerts and dances. The **Green Room** is adorned with green watered-silk wall coverings and furnishings from the 19C workshop of Duncan Phyfe. Classical motifs in the elliptical **Blue Room** include seven of the original Bellange gilded armchairs that James Monroe ordered from Paris. Site of official dinners, the **State Dining Room** can seat 140 people.

### Corcoran Gallery of Art★★

*17th St. & New York Ave. N.W.* ✗ ♿ ◷*Open Mon, Wed-Sun 10am–5pm, Thurs 10am–9pm.* ◉*$6.* ☎*202-639-1700. www.corcoran.org.*

This private gallery was begun in 1859 by philanthropist **William Wilson Corcoran** (1798-1888), who donated a $900,000 endowment, his collection, the grounds and the original building—now the **Renwick Gallery**★ *(Pennsylvania Ave. & 17th St. N.W.* ☎*202-357-2700)*—"for the purpose of encouraging American genius." Today the Corcoran

Gallery is housed in a larger, ornate 189 Beaux-Arts building comprising an a school and fine collections of Europea and **American paintings**. its collectio of 19thC American art is considere among the best in the world; it also ha an impressive selection of contempo rary art from the likes of Andy Warho Ellsworth Kelly and Frank Stella.

### National Portrait Gallery★★

*Old Patent Office Building at 8th & F St N.W.* ✗ ♿ ◷*Open daily 11:30am–7pm* ☎*202-633-8300. www.npg.si.edu.*

The "nation's family album" conserve some 15,000 paintings, sculptures, pho tographs, engravings and drawings c "men and women who have made sig nificant contributions to the history development and culture of the peopl of the United States."

### Ford's Theatre★

*511 10th St. between E & F Sts. N.W.* ◷*Ope daily 9am–5pm.* ☎*202-426-6924. www nps.gov/foth.* Site of the assassinatio of President Abraham Lincoln on Apr 14, 1865, Ford's Theatre was opened b John Ford in 1863. After being shot b John Wilkes Booth, Lincoln was carrie across the street to **Petersen House** *(516 Tenth St.;* ☎*202-619-7225),* wher he died the following morning. Th restored Victorian theater reopened i

## Embassy Row

Embassy Row is the popular name for the 2mi portion of Massachusetts Avenue between Scott and Observatory Circles where some 50 diplomatic embassies are concentrated. Beaux-Arts architecture is a favorite here, since many of the early-20C architects retained by wealthy Washingtonians had trained in Paris. Following the Great Depression in 1929, the luxuriant Beaux-Arts mansions were sold to foreign governments seeking a diplomatic presence in the District.

The most noteworthy part of Embassy Row begins at 22nd Street and Massachusetts Avenue, where the **Embassy of Luxembourg** is ensconced in the former home of lumber magnate and politician Alexander Wilson. Continuing up the avenue past the embassies of Togo and the Sudan, Sheridan Circle is home to the grandiose **Embassy of Turkey/Everett House** *(1606 23rd St.).* The procession of embassies continues to 24th Street, ending at the sprawling **British Embassy** *(3100 Massachusetts Ave.),* designed by prominent architect Sir Edwin Lutyens to resemble an early-18C English country estate.

An annual tour that granted public access to some embassies and residences was discontinued following 9/11.

968 as a playhouse as well as a memo-
ial to Lincoln's tragic slaying.

## he Phillips Collection★★

600 21st St. N.W. ※ & ○Open Tues-Wed,
ri-Sat 10am-5pm, Thu 10am-8:30pm,
un 11am-6pm. ○Closed major holidays.
$10. ☎202-387-2151 or 877-444-6777.
www.phillipscollection.org. Reservations
recommended.

With his family's art collection, Duncan
Phillips founded the nation's oldest
museum of modern art as a memorial
o his father and brother. He and his
wife, painter Marjorie Acker, expanded
he collection; today it contains some
,500 works, including all the major
rench Impressionists, Postimpression-
sts, Cubists and 17C and 18C masters,
mong them Goya, El Greco and Char-
lin. A second-floor gallery showcases
ne museum's renowned Renoir: Lunch-
on of the Boating Party (1881). The Goh
nnex houses rotating exhibits, such as
he popular Bonnard Collection.

# Additional Sights

## Frederick Douglass
## National Historic Site★

411 W St. S.E. & P ○Open daily 9am–
pm. ○Closed major holidays. ☎202-426-
961. www.nps.gov/frdo.
Known as Cedar Hill, this quaint Victorian set above the Anacostia River was
he last residence of black statesman,
orator and abolitionist Frederick Doug-
ass (1818-95). The two-story house is
decorated with Victorian furnishings
nd Douglass family memorabilia,
ncluding a rare portrait of Douglass by
arah James Eddy.

## Washington National
## Cathedral★★

Massachusetts & Wisconsin Aves. N.W.
& P ○Open daily. $3. ☎202-537-
200. www.cathedral.org.
Dominating the skyline of northwest
Washington with its 301ft-high Gloria in Excelsis Tower, this imposing
Gothic edifice overlooks the city from
ts perch on Mount St. Alban. The final
tone of the Cathedral of St. Peter and
t. Paul—its official name—was set in

## Georgetown

A coveted Washington address,
**Georgetown**★★ is an amalgam of
popular nightspots, restaurants and
trendy boutiques concentrated along
Wisconsin Avenue and M Street N.W.
Surrounding this commercial core are
quiet residential streets lined with
restored Federal-style town houses.
Settled by Scots in the 1700s, Georgetown became a thriving port in the
late 18C owing to its location at the
head of the Potomac River's navigable
waters. In 1789 the first Catholic institution of higher learning in the country, now **Georgetown University**,
was founded at the neighborhood's
western edge. On the district's northern border, **Dumbarton Oaks**★★
(1703 32nd St. N.W.; ☎202-339-6401)
is renowned for its outstanding collections of **Byzantine**★★ and **pre-
Columbian art**★. The estate's lovely
**gardens**★★ (entrance at 31st & R Sts.
N.W.) comprise 10 acres of formal,
flowered terraces punctuated by
fountains and pools.

place in 1990, 83 years after the foundation was laid.

## Hillwood★★

4155 Linnean Ave. N.W. ※ & P ○Open
Tues-Sat 10am–5pm. ○Closed Jan and
major holidays. ⟿Visit mansion by
guided tour only. ☎202-686-8500. www.
hillwoodmuseum.org.
Above Rock Creek Park, the 25-acre
estate of Post cereals heiress and art
collector **Marjorie Merriweather Post**
(1887-1973) showcases the most extensive collection of **Russian decorative
arts**★★★ outside Russia.

## National Zoological Park★★

Kids 3001 Connecticut Ave. N.W. ※ & P
○Open Apr-Oct 6am–8pm, Nov-Mar
6am–6pm☎202-673-4800. http://nation-
alzoo.si.edu. Situated on 166 acres above
Rock Creek Park, this Smithsonian "bio-
park" (known more commonly simply as
the "National Zoo.") exhibits some 5,000
wild animals and serves as a research
institution devoted to the study, preservation and breeding of threatened
species. Most famous among them are

the giant pandas, on loan from China until 2010. The **Olmsted Walk** forms a continuous path past such exhibits such as the **Think Tank**, where you can watch trainers working with orangutans; the Byzantine-style **Reptile House**; and the **Amazonia** exhibit, a 15,000sq ft tropical forest habitat.

## Excursions

### Arlington National Cemetery★★

*3mi west of DC on the Virginia side of Arlington Memorial Bridge. ⛷ Ⓟ ⊙Open Apr-Sept daily 8am–7pm, Oct-Mar 8am–5pm.☎703-607-8000.*

This vast military cemetery holds the remains of more than 300,000 people, including presidents, astronauts, explorers, and, of course, military personnel on 612 acres of rolling hills. During the Civil War, 200 acres surrounding Confederate general Robert E. Lee's mansion **Arlington House**★ *(on the cemetery grounds; ☎703-235-1530)* were appropriated for the burial of fallen soldiers; in 1883 these lands became the official national cemetery of the US. Don't miss the eternal flame that marks the grave of assassinated president **John F. Kennedy** (1917-

63), and the **Tomb of the Unknown** *(behind Memorial Amphitheater), whe* *an elaborate changing of the guard ce emony is conducted throughout the da*

### Old Town Alexandria★★

*8mi south of DC via George Washingto Memorial Pkwy. Ramsey House Visite Center is located at 221 King St., ☎70. 838-4200.*

This area traces its beginnings to th early 1700s, when a tobacco ware house on the Potomac River spawne the prosperous seaport of Alexandri Modern Old Town is a walkable enclav of shops, restaurants, historic home and churches set on the banks of th Potomac River.

A day in Alexandria might include a stro along brick-paved **Gentry Row**★ *(20 block of Prince St.)* and cobbled **Cap tain's Row**★ *(100 block of Prince St.* where 18C town houses recall Alexa dria's early seafaring days. When you' ready for lunch, sample colonial fare a **Gadsby's Tavern Museum**★ *(134 Royal St.; ↻visit of museum by guide tour only; restaurant open to the publi ☎703-838-4242),* which dates to 177 After lunch, tour **Robert E. Lee's Bo hood Home**★ *(607 Oronoco St; ↻vis*

---

### The Civil War in Northern Virginia

The decision to move the Confederate capital from Montgomery, Alabama, to Richmond, Virginia, determined that much of the Civil War would be fought in the region between Washington, DC, and the Confederate capital of Richmond, 90mi to the south. Of the many Civil War battlefields that dot the rolling Virginia landscape, two parks today preserve the most significant Civil War sites.

Located 29mi southwest of Washington, DC, **Manassas National Battlefield Park**★ *(6511 Sudley Rd., Manassas, VA;* ⛷ Ⓟ ⊙*Open daily dawn-dusk.* ☎*703-361-1339; www.nps.gov/mana)* marks the site of the first major land battle of the war. On July 21, 1861, the 35,000-man Confederate force beat back the 32,000-man Union Army at a stream called Bull Run in Manassas, Virginia. It was during this battle that Stonewall Jackson earned his nickname. As the story goes, one officer, seeing Confederate general Thomas J. Jackson sitting tall in the saddle, shouted, "There stands Jackson like a stone wall! Rally behind the Virginians!"

**Fredericksburg and Spotsylvania National Military Park**★ *(50mi south of DC via I-95; 120 Chatham Lane, Fredericksburg, VA;* ⛷ Ⓟ *Open daily dawn-dusk.* ☎*540-371-0802; www.nps.gov/frsp),* dubbed "the bloodiest landscape in North America." commemorates four major Civil War engagements fought in and around the strategic city of Fredericksburg between December 1862 and May 1864. Occupying the midpoint between Washington and Richmond, Fredericksburg lay in the way of the Union army's attempts to capture the Confederate capital. A shrine to Stonewall Jackson is on the ground.

Mount Vernon Ladies' Assoc.

*Mount Vernon*

...y guided tour only; ☎703-548-8454), ...where the boy who would become ...famed Confederate general lived ...ntil 1825.

## Mount Vernon★★★

||||| *16mi south of DC in Alexandria, VA, ...ia George Washington Memorial Pkwy.* ...Visit of mansion by guided tour only. ...Ⓟ Ⓞ Open Apr-Aug daily 8am–5pm, ...Mar, Sept, Oct 9am-5pm, Nov-Feb 9am-...pm.* ☜ *$13.* ☎703-780-2000. www. ...mountvernon.org.

...Occupying a grassy slope overlooking ...he Potomac River south of Washing-...on is the plantation house where the ...ation's first president, **George Wash-...ington** (1732-99), enjoyed the life of a ...uccessful Virginia planter.

...he Georgian farmhouse, with its hall-...mark columned piazza facing the river, ...s set off by curving colonnades that ...onnect the flanking wings. Within, a ...arge central hall opens onto the piazza ...and four first-floor rooms. The lavishly ...ppointed **dining room** features an ...rnate marble mantel that Washington ...onsidered "too elegant and costly...for ...ny republican style of living." Upstairs, ...ive simply furnished bedrooms are ...rranged off a central hall. The **master ...edroom** contains the mahogany four-...oster bed in which Washington died.

The estate's **grounds** comprise 40 acres of forests and landscaped gardens, including 12 small dependencies; the graves of George and his wife, Martha; and a **pioneer farm** that demonstrates 18C animal husbandry and crop cultivation.

## Harpers Ferry National Historical Park★★

*55mi northwest of DC in Harpers Ferry, WV. From DC take I-270 North to Frederick, MD; then south on US-340.* ♿ Ⓟ Ⓞ *Open daily 8am–5pm.* Ⓞ *Closed major holidays.* ☜ *$6 per vehicle.* ☎304-535-6029. www. nps.gov/hafe.

Located in the northeastern corner of West Virginia at the junction of the Shenandoah and Potomac rivers, Harpers Ferry is forever connected with the name **John Brown** (1800-59). On October 16, 1859, abolitionist Brown led his 21-man "army of liberation" into town, hoping to capture weapons to wage guerrilla warfare against slavery from the nearby mountains. Although the raid failed—Brown was captured and later hanged—the incident inflamed tensions between the North and South.

Stop by the **Information Center** (*Shenandoah St.*), where exhibits outline the town's history, and pick up a copy of the *Lower Town Trail Guide* to 24 key sites clustered on Shenandoah, High and Potomac Streets. Take time to discover the heritage of this 19C manufacturing village, shop its many boutiques, and take in great **views** of the rivers as you stro Harpers Ferry's narrow, hilly streets.

# BALTIMORE★★

MICHELIN MAP 583 S 8

EASTERN STANDARD TIME

POPULATION 631,366

Maryland's largest city, Baltimore underwent a dramatic renaissance in the las quarter of the 20th century; shedding its image as a decrepit Chesapeake Ba industrial port, for that of a thriving metropolis. Gleaming skyscrapers designe by some of the nation's most noteworthy architects spike the skyline. A wide bric and asphalt sidewalk lines 5mi of the Patapsco River shoreline, linking severa well-defined nearby neighborhoods: **Little Italy**, renowned for its Old Worl restaurants; the 18C shipbuilding center of **Fells Point** (these days a charmin shopping and popular night spot); and **Federal Hill**, a great vantage point fo wonderful **views**★ of the revitalized Inner Harbor.

- **Information:** ☎410-837-4636. www.baltimore.org
- ▶ **Orient Yourself:** Oft considered a stepchild of Washington, DC, Baltimore shoul be considered a destination of its own.
- **Don't Miss:** A glimpse of Americana at the B&O Railroad Museum.
- **Kids:** Delight in the wonders of more than 10,000 creatures at the Nationa Aquarium in Baltimore.
- **Also See:** WASHINGTON, DC.

## A Bit of History

Baltimore was officially established as a town—named for Maryland's Irish proprietors, the Lords Baltimore—on the Pataspsco River in 1729. Blessed with a deepwater harbor, Baltimore thrived in its early years as a grain-shipping port and shipbuilding center (the fast schooners known as Baltimore Clippers were produced here in the late 18C and early 19C).

During the War of 1812, British troops came perilously close to capturing Baltimore. On September 13, 1814, English warships bombarded **Fort McHenry** in Baltimore's harbor for 25 hours, but failed to capture the battlement *(now a national monument; south end of Fort Ave., off Lawrence St.; ◷Open daily Jan-May 8am–5pm, June-Sept 8am–8pm. ◷Closed major holidays. ∞$7. ☎410-962-4290, www.nps.gov/fomkc).* The next day, **Francis Scott Key** (1779-1843), a young Washington lawyer who witnessed the battle, immortalized th fighting in the now-famous verses c **"The Star-Spangled Banner"**—offi cially designated as the US nationa anthem in 1931. Fragments of th original banner that Key described a "so gallantly streaming" over the fort i 1814 are displayed in the **Star-Spangle Banner Flag House**★ *(844 E. Pratt St ☎410-837-1793, www.flaghouse.org).* Baltimore's development after the wa was boosted by the establishment o the Baltimore and Ohio Railroad in 182 which eventually gave the city's grow ing number of manufacturers access t myriad new markets. In 1904 a fire rav aged the majority of the downtown 18C and 19C structures. One of the fev pre-Revolutionary buildings to surviv is **Mount Clare Museum House**, buil in 1760 *(1500 Washington Blvd. in Car roll Park; ◷Open Tue-Fri 11am–4pm, Sa Sun12pm-4pm. ☎410-837-3262).* Today the invigorated city claims suc attractions as the ever-popular Inne

*Baltimore, Inner Harbour*

Harbor, as well as the internationally known medical school of **Johns Hopkins University**. Part of the Hopkins campus is located on the grounds of the estate once owned by prominent Marylander Charles Carroll, a signer of the Declaration of Independence. Carroll's stately red-brick Georgian **Homewood House**★ dates to 1802 *(3400 N. Charles St.; ↝↝visit by guided tour only; ☎410-516-5589)*.

## The Inner Harbor

Rescued from its downtrodden state in the 1960s, Baltimore's harbor now shines as a waterfront complex of shops, restaurants, museums and hotels. Bounded by East Pratt and Light Streets, the Inner Harbor is anchored on the northeast and southwest corners by the National Aquarium and the **Maryland Science Center** Kids *(601 Light St.; ☎410-685-5225)* respectively. In between, the twin glass pavilions of **Harborplace** overlook the brick pier where the 1854 "sloop-of-war" USS *Constellation* is docked. Inside Harborplace's pavilions you'll find a festival of eateries and shops.

**Views**★ of the city and surrounding countryside are unbeatable from the 27th floor of the **World Trade Center**★ *(1978, I.M. Pei)*, making the **Top of the World**★ observation deck an excellent

place to begin a visit *(401 E. Pratt St.; ᬭ☎10-837-8439)*. A few blocks west of the waterfront, the city's beloved Orioles play in **Camden Yards** *(333 W. Camden St.; ☎410-547-6113)*, one of the nation's most beautiful baseball stadiums.

## National Aquarium in Baltimore★★

Kids IIIII *Pier Three, 501 E. Pratt St.* ✗ᬭ☎410-576-3800. www.aqua.org.
More than 10,000 creatures occupy the habitats within this 209,000sq ft aquatic museum. Housed in two imposing buildings crowned with glass pyramids, the aquarium is Baltimore's most popular attraction. Most of the exhibits are displayed in the five-story Main Aquarium. You can see the country's largest collection of rays in **Wings in the Water**, and walk down through four stories of sharks, corals and other reef denizens in the **Atlantic Coral Reef**. The fifth-floor **Amazon Rain Forest** drips with humidity, particularly when the sun shines through the glass roof. Animal Planet Australia: Wild Extremes opened in 2006 ans mimics a river running through a gorge with crocodiles, bats and even a black-headed python.

]And save time for the **dolphin show** that takes place in the Marine Mammal Pavilion's 1,300-seat amphitheater *(showtimes are written on the admission ticket)*.

## Blue Crabs

When summer settles into the Mid-Atlantic, there are few things more dear to a Marylander's heart than eating blue crabs. The small crustacean is the state's single most valuable fishery resource. Watermen harvested more than 51 million pounds of crabs in 2006.

Although found as far north as Cape Cod, the blue crab *(Callinectes sapidus)* thrives in greatest abundance in the Chesapeake Bay. In season, from June to October, you can sample this regional delicacy in several forms: by **picking crabs**, a messy but fun process of cracking the shell open and extracting the meat; as **soft shells**, a blue crab that has molted and not yet formed its new shell *(available May–Sept)*; or made into Maryland's justifiably famous **crabcakes**.

*© iStockphoto.com/2007 Ken Rygh*

*Blue Crabs*

### Baltimore Maritime Museum★

Kids *Piers 3 and 5, Inner Harbor. Ticket booth on Pier Three next to the aquarium.* ○*Open Jan-Feb, Fri-Sun 10am–5pm. Mar-Sep daily 10am-5pm. Call for extended summer hours.* ☜*$8.* ☎*410-396-3543. www.baltimoremaritimemuseum.org.*
Visitors to this partially floating museum begin their tour on the decks of the lightship *Chesapeake* (1930). Adjacent to it is the **USS Torsk** (1945), a 311ft submarine that established a naval record of 11,884 dives. Docked at Pier Five, the US Coast Guard cutter *Taney* (1936) is the last remaining survivor of the Japanese attack on Pearl Harbor. **Seven Foot Knoll Lighthouse** on Pier Five is Maryland's oldest "screwpile" building (1855), so called as it was attached to nine cast-iron pilings "screwed" into the bay floor.

## Additional Sights

### Port Discovery★

Kids *35 Market Pl.* ✗&○*Open Memorial Day-Labor Day 10am-5pm, Sun 12pm-5pm. Labor Day-Memorial Day Tue-Fri 9:30am-4:30pm, Sat 10am-5pm, Sun 12pm-5pm.* ☜*$10.75.* ☎*410-727-8120. www.portdisovery.org*

A few blocks northeast of the Inner Harbor, Baltimore's late-19C fish market has been transformed into a museum geared to children between the ages of 2 and 10. Three floors of exhibits include "**The Money Game**," a fast-paced TV game show that is produced in MPT Studio work; **Adventure Expeditions**, where "time travelers" go back to ancient Egypt to search for the tomb of a lost pharaoh; and **KidWorks**, a 57ft-high jungle gym that rises to the roof.

### American Visionary Art Museum★

*800 Key Hwy.* ✗&○*Open Tue-Sun 10am-5pm.* ○*Closed major holidays.* ☜*$1.* ☎*410-244-1900.www.avam.org.*
The "visionary folk art" of self-taught artists from around the world is displayed, and their stories told, in a modern, elliptical building across from the waterfront. Also look for large exhibits displayed in an adjacent former whiskey warehouse and a 55-ft whirligig in the outside plaza.

### Baltimore Museum of Industry★

*1415 Key Hwy.* &P ☎*410-727-4808. www.thebmi.org.*

ecognizing Baltimore's industrial her-
age is the mission of this well-kept,
pacious museum housed in an oyster
annery (c.1865) on the Patapsco River.
fter watching an informative 15min
m, visitors tour a re-created cannery,
nachine shop, garment loft and print
hop. On weekends, children can build
n early-20C auto on an assembly line.

## &O Railroad Museum★★

 *901 E. Pratt St.* ✗ ♿ ⓟ ⓒ*Open Mon-
ri 10am–4pm, Sat 10am-5pm.* ⓒ*Closed
najor holidays.* ☞*$14.*☎*410-752-2490.
ww.borail.org.*

eginning in 1830, the Baltimore and
hio Railroad provided the first regular
ail service in the US. Today more than
00 of the line's locomotives and cars
re the star attractions of this 37-acre
nuseum, located on the site of the rail-
oad's Mount Clare station. About 40
ail cars and locomotives, including a
1915 boxcar from the Paris-Lyon-Médi-
rranée line (a gift from France to the
S), are displayed in a restored brick and
ood **roundhouse** (1884). The rest of
ne collection, which features the Chesa-
eake and Ohio's "Allegheny" (1941), the
nost powerful steam locomotive ever
uilt, fills the yard outside.

## Valters Art Gallery★★

*00 N. Charles St.* ♿ ⓟ ⓒ*Open Wed-Thu,
at-Sun 11am-5pm, Fri 11am-8pm.* ☎*410-
47-9000. www.thewalters.org.*

/ith a collection numbering some
0,000 works of art spanning the years
om 300 BC to the early 20C, this gem
f an art museum—which comprises
ree buildings—is best known for its
**enaissance and Medieval art**, rare
ooks and illuminated manuscripts.
he manuscripts, as well as most of
ne ancient and Medieval pieces, are
oused in a forbidding stone building
n Centre Street. Renaissance master-
ieces by such greats as Van Dyck and
 Greco (*St. Francis Receiving the Stig-
nata*, c.1590) fill the original gallery, a
909 Italianate palazzo commissioned
y railroad magnate Henry Walters to
howcase the artwork he and his father
egan collecting in the 1870s. Here, too,
re European and American paintings
nd decorative arts from the 17C to 19C.

The museum's impressive **Asian collection** is displayed in Hackerman House
(1854), a stately brownstone attached
to the main gallery.

## Maryland Historical Society ★

*201 W. Monument St.* ♿ ⓟ ⓒ*Open Wed-
Sun 10am-5pm.* ☞*$4.*☎*410-685-3750.
www.mdhs.org.*

The society's fine 20,000-piece collection of art, furniture and other memorabilia is contained in three buildings.
In the **Heritage Wing**, which was a
Greyhound bus garage until the early
1980s, you'll find a survey of the works
of the **Peale** family, whose scion Charles
Willson Peale and sons James, Titian,
Rubens, Raphael and Rembrandt were
among America's finest early painters.
In the main building is the original draft
of Francis Scott Key's "**The Star-Span-
gled Banner,**" and distinctive **painted
furniture** made by 19C Baltimore
craftsmen.

## Washington Monument ★

*Mt. Vernon Pl. at the junction of N. Charles
& Monument Sts.* ⓒ*Open Wed-Sun 10am-
5pm. Suggested donation* ☞*$1.* ☎*410-
396-1049.*

Baltimoreans quickly point out that
the nation's first memorial to the first
president was built here, not in Washington, DC. The 178ft marble and brick
column (1829, Robert Mills) capped with
a 30-ton statue of George Washington
may be the city's best-known landmark.
Climb the narrow flight of 228 steps for
expansive **views** of the city.

## The Baltimore
## Museum of Art★★

*10 Art Museum Dr., at N. Charles & 31st
Sts.* ✗ ♿ ⓟ ⓒ *Open Wed-Sun 11am-
5pm.*ⓒ *Closed major holidays.* ☎*410-
396-7100. www.artbma.org.*

Known for its collection of 20C art
and American furnishings, this grand
Neoclassical building (1929, John Russell Pope) and its light-filled 1982 and
1994 additions house more than 85,000
objects from antiquity to the present.
The **Cone Collection**★★ is the museum's
most famous. Local collectors Etta and
Claribel Cone began buying the works
of Matisse, Picasso and other Modernists

# Maryland's Eastern Shore

Just across the Chesapeake Bay Bridge from Annapolis *(50mi east of Washington, DC)* is Maryland's Eastern Shore, a peninsula that lies between the bay and the Atlantic Ocean. Characterized by sleepy fishing villages and small farms, the low-lying coastline here is a conglomeration of quiet coves and lonely marshes. You can easily while away a couple of pleasant days exploring historic waterside villages such as **St. Michaels★** and **Chestertown**, staying in some of the fine bed-and-breakfast inns, poking through antique shops, bird-watching, and sampling the region's bountiful seafood—especially the famous **blue crabs** and oysters.

One of the shore's most unique events takes place each summer on the southern end of **Assateague Island National Seashore★** *(29mi east of Salisbury, MD, via US-50 & Rte. 611;* △&🄿☎*410-641-1441).* This part of the 37mi-long barrier island harbors several hundred **wild ponies** that roam **Chincoteague National Wildlife Refuge**. The offspring of horses brought here by 17C settlers to avoid penning and taxation laws, the ponies are rounded up annually on Assateague Island and herded across the narrow channel (at slack tide) to the town of **Chincoteague** *(across Chincoteague Bay on Rte. 175).* Here the annual **Pony Penning★**, the public round-up and sale of foals, is held on the last Wednesday and Thursday of July *(for information, call ☎757-336-6161, www.chincoteague.com).*

*Historic Waterside Village of Chestertown*

(Cézanne, Degas, Monet, van Gogh, Gauguin) in 1898. Today their collection of Matisse paintings (which includes *Large Reclining Nude*, 1935) and sculptures is one of the most comprehensive in the world. The museum has echoed the Cones' patronage of contemporary art by acquiring works by Andy Warhol, Jasper Johns, Frank Stella, Georgia O'Keeffe and Willem de Kooning.

The **American decorative arts** exhibits are displayed on all three floors of the museum. In addition to the Baltimore painted furniture (c.1800-10), Queen Anne, Federal and American Chippendale pieces are showcased in galleries and reconstructed period rooms. The Atrium Court on the main level is lined with priceless **mosaics** (5C-1C BC) from the ancient provincial Roman capital of Antioch. Don;t miss the pretty landscaped gardens.

## Evergreen House★★

*4545 N. Charles St.* Guided tour only. *410-516-0341. www.jhu.edu.* Former residence of Ambassador John Work Garrett and his wife, Evergreen (1858) is an elegant kaleidoscope of almost 100 years of trends in American architecture and interior design. The 48-room Italianate mansion includes a **Rare Book Library** that houses 8,000 volumes collected by the Garrett family. The adjoining former gymnasium was converted to a home theater in 1923 by Russian émigré set designer **Leon Bakst**, famed for the sets he created for the Ballets Russes.

## Excursions

## Hampton
## National Historic Site★★

*3mi north of Baltimore in Towson, MD. From I-695, take Exit 27B/Dulaney Valley Rd. North and turn right on Hampton Lane; park entrance is on right.* Visit mansion by guided tour only; check for renovation schedule. Open Apr-Oct Tue-Sun 12pm-5pm 9am–4:30pm. $6. *410-823-1309. www.nps.gov/hamp.* This yellow stone-and-stucco mansion crowned with a white cupola typifies Georgian architecture: The sedate three-story 1790 structure is connected to smaller wings on either side by hallways called hyphens. Part of the vast 24,000-acre estate once owned by Maryland's prominent Ridgely family, the house is largely decorated with their furnishings. Following the house tour, visitors can explore the gardens and grounds, which encompass several dependencies.

## Annapolis★

*30mi southeast of Baltimore via I-97 South and US-301 East.* Open Mon-Fri 9am–5pm. Closed major holidays. *www.msa.md.gov.* Established on the banks of the Severn River by Virginia Puritans in 1648, Annapolis became the seat of colonial government in 1694, and subsequently grew to be a busy port. The city's 1779 **State House★** *(center of State Circle; 410-974-3400)* served as the US capitol between 1783 and 1784. Today the shops and bistros crowding the blocks around **City Dock** bustle with visitors year-round. A number of historic properties, including **Hammond Harwood House★★** *(19 Maryland Ave.;* visit by guided tour only; *410-263-4683; www. hammondhardwood.org)* and **Chase-Lloyd House★** *(22 Maryland Ave.;* visit by guided tour only; *410-263-2723)*, typify the elegant Georgian-style residences built here in the 18C.

## U.S. Naval Academy★★

*Armel-Leftwich Visitor Center, 52 King George St.* Open daily 9am–5pm. *410-263-6933. www.nadn.navy. mil. Free guides tours offered most days.* Future officers in the US Navy and Marine Corps study on this peaceful, 338-acre campus established in 1850 along the Severn River and College Creek. The guided tour around "the Yard," as the academy grounds are called, includes **Bancroft Hall**, the 1906 Baroque structure in the center of campus that covers 27 acres and boasts 5mi of corridors. Few buildings in Annapolis rival the glorious copper-domed **Navy Chapel★★** *(1908, Ernest Flagg)*, modeled after the Hôtel des Invalides in Paris.

After the tour, be sure to visit the **U.S. Naval Academy Museum** in Preble Hall, where you'll find a rare collection of dockyard **ship models★★** made in England during the 17C and 18C, as well as other artifacts detailing the academy's history.

# INDEX

# INDEX

470

# INDEX

# INDEX

## WHERE TO EAT

# INDEX

# MAPS AND PLANS

## LIST OF MAPS

### THEMATIC MAPS

## COMPANION PUBLICATIONS

### MAP 583 NORTHEASTERN USA/ EASTERN CANADA
### MAP 584 SOUTHEASTERN USA

Large-format map providing detailed road systems; includes driving distances, interstate rest stops, border crossings and interchanges
– Comprehensive city and town index
– Scale 1:2,400,000
  (1 inch = approx. 38 miles)

### MAP 761 USA ROAD MAP

Covers principal US road network while also presenting shaded relief detail of overall physiography of the land.
– State flags with statistical data and state tourism office telephone numbers
– Scale: 1:3,450,000
  (1 inch = approx. 55 miles)

### NORTH AMERICA ROAD ATLAS

A geographically organized atlas with extensive detailed coverage of the USA, Canada and Mexico. Includes 246 city maps, distance chart, state and provincial driving requirements and a climate chart.
– Comprehensive city and town index
– Easy to follow "Go-to" pointers

# LEGEND

★★★ **Worth the trip**
★★ **Worth a detour**
★ **Interesting**

## Sight Symbols

| | | | |
|---|---|---|---|
| ▭●▭ | Recommended itineraries with departure point | | |
| 🏛‡⊡ | Church, chapel – Synagogue | ▭ | Building described |
| ○ | Town described | ▭ | Other building |
| **AZ B** | Map co-ordinates locating sights | ▪ | Small building, statue |
| ▪ ▲ | Other points of interest | ◉ ⁂ | Fountain – Ruins |
| ⚒ ⌒ | Mine – Cave | 🛈 | Visitor information |
| ⚚ ⚑ | Windmill – Lighthouse | ⬭ ⚓ | Ship – Shipwreck |
| ☆ ⛪ | Fort – Mission | ⁂ ⍟ | Panorama – View |

## Other Symbols

| | | | | | |
|---|---|---|---|---|---|
| 🛡 Interstate highway (USA) | | 🚌 US highway | | 180 Other route | |
| 🍁 Trans-Canada highway | | 🚍 Canadian highway | | 🛡 Mexican federal highway | |
| ═══ Highway, bridge | | | ═══ Major city thoroughfare | | |
| ═══ Toll highway, interchange | | | ═══ City street with median | | |
| ═══ Divided highway | | | ◄─ One-way street | | |
| ─── Major, minor route | | | ═══ Pedestrian Street | | |
| 15 (21) Distance in miles (kilometers) | | | ⇥⫤⇤ Tunnel | | |
| 2149/655 Pass, elevation (feet/meters) | | | ┅┅┅┅ Steps – Gate | | |
| △6288(1917) Mtn. peak, elevation (feet/meters) | | | △ 🏛 Drawbridge - Water tower | | |
| ✈ ✦ Airport – Airfield | | | 🅿 ✉ Parking – Main post office | | |
| 🚢 Ferry: Cars and passengers | | | 🖾 ✚ University – Hospital | | |
| ⛴ Ferry: Passengers only | | | 🚆 🚌 Train station – Bus station | | |
| ≺≺ Waterfall – Lock – Dam | | | ● ⬒ Subway station | | |
| ─··─··─ International boundary | | | ➊ ⌂ Digressions – Observatory | | |
| ─────── State boundary | | | ▦ ▭ Cemetery – Swamp | | |

## Recreation

| | | | |
|---|---|---|---|
| ●◦◦◦◦◦ Gondola, chairlift | | ⌇⌇ ⚑ | Stadium – Golf course |
| 🚂 Tourist or steam railway | | ⊛ ▭ ▭ | Park, garden – Wooded area |
| ⛴ ◊ Harbor, lake cruise – Marina | | 🌐 | Wildlife reserve |
| ⚓ ☑ Surfing – Windsurfing | | ◉ ⚑ | Wildlife/Safari park, zoo |
| ⚟ 🛶 Diving – Kayaking | | ───── | Walking path, trail |
| 🎿 ⛷ Ski area – Cross-country skiing | | 🚶 | Hiking trail |

Sight of special interest for children

## Abbreviations and special symbols

| | | | | | |
|---|---|---|---|---|---|
| NP | National Park | NMem | National Memorial | SP | State Park |
| NM | National Monument | NHS | National Historic Site | SF | State Forest |
| NWR | National Wildlife Refuge | NHP | National Historical Park | SR | State Reserve |
| NF | National Forest | NVM | National Volcanic Monument | SAP | State Archeological Park |
| 🛡 National Park | | 🛡 State Park | | 🛡 National Forest | 🛡 State Forest |

All maps are oriented north, unless otherwise indicated by a directional arrow.

## Michelin Apa Publications Ltd

**A joint venture between Michelin and Langenscheidt**

Suite 6, Tulip House, 70 Borough High Street, London SE1 1XF, United Kingdom

No part of this publication may be reproduced in any form
without the prior permission of the publisher.

© 2007 Michelin Apa Publications Ltd
ISBN 978-1-906261-19-1
Printed: November 2007
Printed and bound in Germany

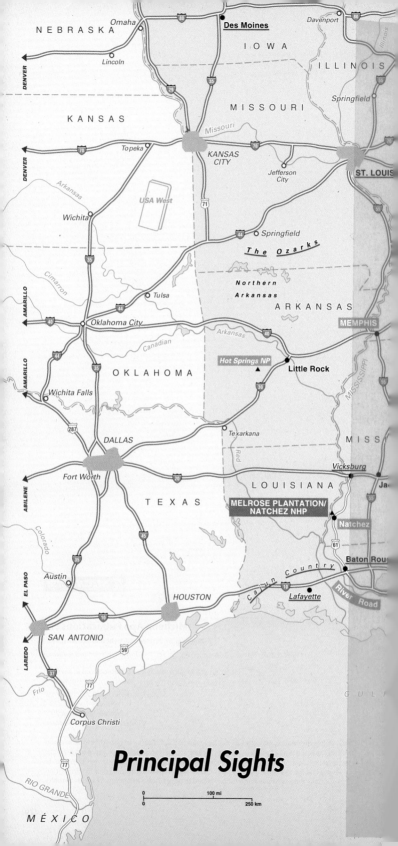

# Principal Sights